# THE CHURCH
# IN THE DARK AGES

Henri Daniel-Rops was the *nom de plume* of Henri Jules Charles Petiot. He was born in France in 1901, the grandson of peasants and the son of an artillery officer. An academic prodigy, by the age of twenty-one Petiot had earned the equivalent of three Master's degrees and became an Associate Professor of History at Neuilly a year later. He wrote more than seventy books and received a large number of distinctions and honours. In 1955 he became the youngest ever member of the *Academie Française* (eventually winning the *Grand Prix*) and went on to receive the Legion of Honour. Henri Jules Charles Petiot died in 1965.

### *A selection of works by H. Daniel-Rops*

Daily Life in Palestine at the Time of Christ (Phoenix Press)
Misted Mirror
Two Men in Me
The Poor and Ourselves
Flaming Sword
Death, Where is thy Victory?
Sacred History
Where Angels Pass
St Paul: Apostle of Nations
Jesus and His Times
Book of Books
Cathedral and Crusade
This is the Mass
What is the Bible?
The Heroes of God
The Book of Mary
Golden Legend of Young Saints
Monsieur Vincent
The Second Vatican Council

# THE CHURCH
# IN THE DARK AGES

H. Daniel-Rops

Translated from the French
by Audrey Butler

**PHOENIX
PRESS**

5 UPPER SAINT MARTIN'S LANE
LONDON
WC2H 9EA

A PHOENIX PRESS PAPERBACK

First published in Great Britain
by J.M. Dent in 1959
This paperback edition published in 2001
by Phoenix Press,
a division of The Orion Publishing Group Ltd,
Orion House, 5 Upper St Martin's Lane,
London WC2H 9EA

A CIP catalogue record for this book is available
from the British Library.

Printed and bound in Great Britain by
Clays Ltd, St Ives plc

ISBN 1 84212 465 X

# TRANSLATOR'S NOTE

I should like to express my grateful thanks to John Warrington, who completed the translation of the two final chapters of this work when illness prevented me from doing so. My thanks are also due to the publishers, without whose unfailing interest and support this translation would not have been possible.

1959                                             A. B.

# CONTENTS

# MAPS

# CHAPTER I

# THE SAINT OF THE NEW AGE

## In Besieged Hippo

SPRING, A.D. 430. Spring was always a delightful season in Rome's African provinces. But now no one had the heart to enjoy it. Throughout the length and breadth of the territories which Rome had held for centuries past there was nothing but untold misery, a chorus of weeping and wailing, refugees jamming the roads—a picture of utter hopelessness and despair. People were fleeing from one town to another, searching from east to west for the remaining places of safety, which were themselves becoming increasingly insecure. They fled with their herds, they mingled with the remnants of the retreating imperial armies. In their chance meetings with one another, the exiles would recount their frightful experiences. These, in the telling, magnified tenfold the fury of the invader. It was not simply a matter of children cleft in twain, of violated maidens, of hands severed, or of tongues torn out by the roots; human imagination was well able to improve on horrors which were, alas, only too real already. All the time people expected to see the red-haired warriors of Genseric, crazed with the lust for battle, leap up in front of them. It was like awaiting the Horsemen of the Apocalypse. Roman Africa was in the grip of a terrible panic.

It was now a year since the Vandals had crossed the straits and landed in Africa. At first it had been assumed that, like so many of the other Germanic peoples who were often seen serving under the imperial flag, they were nothing more than a pawn in the complex game—so complex that it smelt strongly of treason—that Count Boniface was playing with the emperors at Ravenna. It was soon obvious that here was something very different. These Barbarians were not at all like the Gothic tribes whom Rome had incorporated as *foederati* into her armies in the past. The advance which the Vandals had made from the sources of the Vistula to the shores of the Mediterranean, with but a brief halt in the Iberian peninsula, had been so swift that they had had no time to absorb the civilization which they had overrun. All they had acquired was a vague baptism of Arian

Christianity which had superimposed a few strange rites and new fanaticisms upon their old pagan superstitions.  When, in March 429, their king had led them beyond the Pillars of Hercules, they were still simply a horde of greedy marauders, their savage appetite redoubled by the lure of the bountiful corn-fields and fine vineyards of a fertile Africa.

By May 430 almost the whole province was at their mercy.  Nothing significant remained of the might and majesty of Rome.  A few pockets of resistance still held out here and there: the rocky fastness of Constantine, one or two isolated garrisons.  On the coast one district alone was as yet unscathed.  Tucked away beyond the Kabyle Mountains, protected in the south by the El-Kantour range, Hippo— our modern Bône—still lay basking peacefully in the sun.  There were her fine green meadows, the pink expanses of the grain-fields, the blue olive groves, still as tranquil as ever, just as if there were no enemy lurking behind the misty purple heights of the Atlas Mountains, ready to strike at her, as if there were no refugees choking the roads, as if the warning-signal had not yet sounded from the trumpets on her ramparts.  Hippo, the ancient stronghold of the Phoenicians in time of trouble, the fortress which had been rebuilt time and time again, prided herself on her massive walls, and seemed indeed impregnable.  Then, twice beaten in battle, and utterly unable to halt the barbarian torrent which many accused him of having himself unleashed, Count Boniface flung himself into Hippo with what remained of his forces.  The Vandal warriors were hard on his heels.  Out to sea the horizon was suddenly alive with a host of Vandal sails.  The siege of Hippo had begun.

The final outcome was all too obvious.  The town was over-crowded, swarming with refugees, and very soon the enemy outside the gates was being helped by enemies from within.  Famine threatened, plague was rampant, fanned by the fever-laden air of the hot African summer.  And what incentive was there to encourage this wretched mass of humanity to continue the struggle?  Only fear.  They had no hope of outside help.  Was not Italy herself being threatened by other Barbarians at this very moment?  As for Byzantium, that was so far away!  They fought on simply because they knew what would happen to them when the Vandals won; they fought on to hold off, if only for a little while, that frightful yet inevitable moment.  In besieged Hippo men had plumbed the very depths of despair.

Yet, in this beleaguered city, where defeatism appeared so complete, there was one man who was himself the incarnation of hope and courage.  He was an old man, worn with age, exhausted by the cares of a life spent in constant campaigning against one enemy or another.

He had just entered his sixty-sixth year. Though his physical strength, which had never been very great, was fast failing, his spirit had never burned more brightly, his will had never been more steadfast. During all the thirty-four years that he had lived in the people's midst, he had always been their spiritual leader; now that the hour of decision had come he continued to lead and to inspire them. Not a detail of his usual way of life did he change. He prayed, as he had always done, he prayed a great deal, he read and wrote as much as ever, he preached the Gospel, he gave generously to the groups of wretched beggars who clustered round his doorway. Every Sunday, without fail, his frail voice rang out in the Great Basilica, triumphant and confident amid the silence that gripped the stricken congregation. And, as they listened to the words of their bishop, the besieged folk of Hippo felt themselves uplifted, not by a fruitless, man-made confidence, but by a strength of purpose which stemmed direct from God.

However, as he looked about him, this old man must have felt he was watching the utter collapse of his world. What was left now of all that he had loved and fought for? As a native-born African, how could he look at the ravaged, burned-out fields of his native land without being overcome with grief? As a Christian, the proud successor of the Carthage martyrs, and the spiritual son of St Cyprian, how could he possibly reconcile himself to the fact that this flourishing Christian community was falling into the hands of Barbarians whose heresy made them even more ruthless towards the true Church? And, as a Roman citizen, how his heart must have bled at the sight of Rome so profaned, the Empire in the grip of anarchy, and universal degradation where there had once been universal order. To what could he hold fast? Events seemed to be driven along according to the ironic whim of a satanic power. What sense could a Christian make of a conflict in which the Goths, mercenary heretics hired by Christians, were struggling on the ramparts of his city against another band of heretics, the Vandal aggressors? Of a conflict in which the leader of the faithful, Count Boniface, was a man entirely without moral principles, more or less suspect to his superiors, married to an Arian wife, an individual whose personal conduct caused great scandal? In the face of so much misery and wickedness one might have expected this old man to have abandoned all hope for the future, and, in his prayers, to have confined himself to that cry of resignation which had sprung to his lips one tragic day long before: 'O Lord, give thy servant the strength to bear all the burdens which thou lettest fall upon him, or, at least, take him from the world, and call him to Thee!'

Far from it. The words which sprang to his lips now remained words of hope. He told those who believed that the world was crumbling to dust beneath their feet to look beyond the immediate future, to look beyond this earth where civilizations, like men, soon withered and died.   Not for him a barren pessimism, but a fortitude of purpose, strengthened by his awareness of the tragic future ahead, and by the only conclusion which was possible for the Christian. 'You are saying: "Miserable wretches that we are! The world is going to be destroyed!"   But listen carefully to what is written in the Gospel: "Though heaven and earth should pass away, my words will stand!"   Enough of your weeping and wailing!  Are you not yourselves responsible for this fate which is overwhelming you?   "These are difficult and dreadful times," people are saying.  But these times are part of us, are they not?  The times are what we have made them! Yes, we are all guilty, but we have been promised mercy.  Have you not been baptized in hope?  Do you not understand that God's will can be accomplished through the most frightful afflictions?  No Goth can seize what belongs to Christ!'  True riches are not things that the Vandals can steal, he went on; no Barbarian can rob you of the true life. . . .  And words such as these were far more than empty comfort. So great was this man's faith, so powerful his genius, that, from his hope, something new was created.  Faced with a situation in which civilized society was being thrown to the winds, the aged bishop appealed to another, founded on those principles which he described again and again, untiringly.  Each of his appeals was an appeal to the future.

During the third month of the siege this noble voice was suddenly silenced.   The news spread through Hippo that the bishop was on his death-bed.  He had been attacked by a high fever, caught, no doubt, from some refugee in the town.  He soon realized that his end was near at hand.  Shutting himself in his cell, he spent whole days in silence.  It was not yet a silence of exhaustion, but a silence which enabled him to re-examine the events of his life, to think, and to pray. Occasionally he thought he heard the sharp, high-pitched note of a trumpet on the walls: the signal of yet another Vandal attack.  In the street outside the bishop's monastery-palace, the crowd jostled and prayed.  The dying man begged God to forgive him his sins: he reproached himself for not having done enough for Him, declaring that he had not testified for Him sufficiently, had not done all he should to prepare for His coming again.  He ordered the Penitential Psalms to be nailed to the walls of his cell, so that he could read the verses over and over again.  This done, he repeated them aloud, fervently.

On 28th August 430 he died.   In the humility of his dying prayer little did the old bishop of Hippo suspect that his philosophy was going to illuminate the coming centuries, that his genius was to mould the world which was being born out of the travails of the present, or that his sanctity would be an everlasting example to posterity. His name? *Augustine.*[1]

## 'I Loved to Love . . .'

If ever a human soul gave the impression of being constantly 'in God's keeping,' and of being guided by Him and Him alone towards its true goal, it is surely that of this little African urchin whom the Grace of God was to fashion into a saint. He was born on 13th November 354, in central Numidia, of old country stock. His native race, to which he remained staunchly loyal all his life, gave him his shrewdness, his rapid grasp of spiritual problems, and his fiery enthusiasm, but it gave him, too, the rather extreme temperament which one sees in so many Africans. As a boy he was uncouth, undisciplined, and had little taste for serious studies. His intelligence, which was much above the average, persuaded him that it was quite pointless to make more than the minimum effort, and his hot blood would suffer no restraints. Truth to tell, no one could do anything with him, neither the schoolmasters, who thrashed him, nor his father, Patricius, a small landowner, energetic enough in his way, but more interested in his business affairs than in his sons, nor even Monica, his mother, for whom, however, Augustine always had the deepest respect.

However, the seed which would begin to grow so much later on was already planted in his heart. It had been put there by Monica. A Christian and a Catholic, born of a family which had been loyal to Christ and to the Holy Church for several generations past, this reserved, outwardly austere woman, ministering dutifully to a boorish husband, hid within her, beneath her unwavering gentleness of disposition, that all-devouring, holy flame which burns in the heart of every saint. Let Patricius remain a pagan, if he wanted, without faith and with few standards: she would find her consolation in her children, and especially in Augustine whose special potentialities she recognized. But she had to wait a very long time before her dream was realized.

Augustine's own town, Tagaste,[2] tucked away behind the mountains, among the holly-oak forests, had precious little to offer a lad who wanted to get on in the world. Augustine had the choice of becoming a country merchant or, at best, a minor civil servant. Just before he died Patricius had the sense to see that his son was worthy of better

---

[1] Hippo continued to resist for some time after Augustine's death, holding out for fourteen months altogether. The Vandals raised the siege. Boniface, who had received reinforcements from the Italian mainland, attempted to attack them, was beaten, and fled from Africa, which thereafter became a Vandal kingdom. Hippo was captured and sacked.

[2] The modern Soukh-Ahras, population 13,000, between Bône and Tebessa, near the Tunisian frontier.

things.   He dreamed of Augustine becoming a rhetorician.   This profession had made the name of several other Africans—Victorinus of Tagaste, Fronto of Cirta, even of the Emperor Pertinax.   And so Augustine embarked on his rhetorical studies—and many other experiences besides!—first at Madaura, the big city near by, where the memory of Apuleius, the poet, scholar, and magi, had served to whet youthful ambitions for the last two hundred years; and then in the capital, Carthage, the focal-point of the intellectual life of the entire African province.

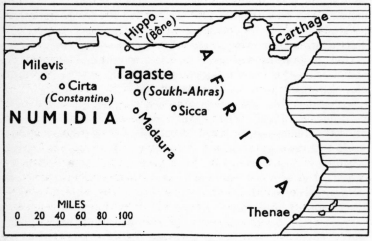

The Africa of St Augustine

It was in this opulent city, where 'the surge of shameful love seethes like boiling oil'—men called Carthage 'the city of Venus'—amid the bustle of the merchants and the rhetoricians, the harlots and the theologians, that Augustine spent three extremely formative years.   It is scarcely necessary to mention what became of his morals; without taking too literally the details which his later mood of repentance led him to list, it is nevertheless true to say that they were hardly exemplary.   Even in Africa it was not very common for a lad of eighteen to take a concubine, and to have a child by her!   More interesting, and ultimately more important, were the contacts Carthage gave him with every shade of opinion, all the philosophies, the heresies, and the schisms which his passion for dialectic led him to investigate.   His brain was still racked with all the painful, passionate tumult of the adolescent; and in his soul—or so he thought—there was nothing, save what he himself has so magnificently called 'the silence of God.'

However, by the time Augustine returned to his native town, in 374, at the age of twenty, to earn his living as a schoolmaster, that seed planted within him by Monica, long ago, had already begun to sprout. He, of course, knew nothing of this. Perhaps he never dared realize that, even at this stage, God, so far from keeping silent, had actually called him by name. Certainly he had not known how to understand that ineffable voice when, while still a child, he had thought of asking for baptism during a serious illness, but had quickly dropped the idea once he was quite recovered. Nor had he known how to find the Word of God in the Bible, which he had idly opened at Carthage, one book among many others. It had seemed a stupid book to him then, impossible to understand. Yet, even while he followed the strange paths along which his impulsive nature swept him, Augustine of Tagaste, without knowing it, was following the way of God.

God's imprint showed itself, at this point, in his restlessness, this tremor of heart and soul before the problems of the world and of his life. His words betrayed this, like his conduct. Within this rather ridiculous boy there was a deep unsatisfied urge, an urge which utterly refused to be satisfied, which was all the time seeking an answer to basic problems, and which, in secret, despaired of ever finding anything stable or permanent to which it could cling. If it is true, as Cardinal Newman said, that an untroubled soul is a soul in peril, then the obscure, pathetic soul of Augustine was indeed mysteriously protected! 'Our heart is troubled, O Lord, until it rests in Thy keeping.' At the age of twenty he was not yet capable of reaching the conclusion summed up in this great prayer of his maturer years; yet its opening words caught in his throat day after day, like the *leit-motif* of an unsatisfied existence, the promise of a hope which would one day be gratified.

And there was another way in which God's touch was obvious; in Augustine's veritable thirst for knowledge. His inquiring spirit was never still. This youthful lust for information, which takes a bite from each and every philosophy as if they are so many ripe fruits, and which experiments again and again, because there is something exciting and exhilarating in the discovery of an idea, even if it is a misleading one, has its own integral nobility, and, if the individual's intentions are worthy ones, he cannot be deceived for very long. God is truth, and he who searches for the truth will find it in the end. On the threshold of adolescence Augustine imagined that he had found the ultimate answer to everything in *Hortensius*, a philosophical tract; [1] a little later on he all but lost himself in the weird Esoteric tangles and fancies of Manichaeism; [2] God led him safely through these tortuous byways, towards the straight, true path. The illumination he imagined he had

---

[1] A work of Cicero, now lost.
[2] See the section further on: 'The Champion of Truth.'

received in his first encounter with philosophy was, in fact, but the dawn of another and greater light; and that cry of 'Truth! Truth!' which the Manichaean zealots chanted so monotonously was to rouse in him many far more profound echoes.

But, above all, it was in his urge for love that God's promise for the future was most apparent. Running all through the moving passages in which, several years later, the saint related his youthful experiences is a phrase whose richness cannot be over-emphasized, and which expresses this point exactly: 'I loved to love. . . .' This man, whose philosophical conclusions have earned him the well-deserved title of 'The Doctor of Love,' this saint, whose message posterity has summed up in the famous slogan 'Only love—and do what you will!' carried in his heart, from the moment of his birth, the consciousness of this inexhaustible power and ever-present remission, which, long ago, brought redemption to a weeping and sinful woman, and whose eternal pledge is the cross. At the age of twenty he tried hard to find the marks of this love in the physical mysteries of woman, in the material wonders of the world, and in splendid, but ephemeral, friendships. But it was another kind of love that lay in wait for him; it was ready to gather him into its safe keeping, when the time came.

But though this was the secret truth of his destiny, his outward appearance, for the next nine years, gave no hint of a future conversion. From 374 to 383, first at Tagaste, then at Carthage, Augustine seemed, in the eyes of the world, to be simply a fiery little rhetorician, who campaigned in favour of the Manichaean heresy, who published a book on aesthetics which was frankly profane, and who, living on a rich patron, wallowed in luxuries and empty admiration. Yet, though all this scandalized her completely, Monica did not despair of her son's adventurous spirit; she went on praying and weeping for him. One day, when she had gone to seek advice from a bishop whom she knew, and had given full vent to her anger, the bishop had spoken these words to her: 'Calm yourself! This son for whom you have shed so many tears cannot possibly be lost!' Many years later Augustine must have come to understand that his mother's tears had been like a first baptism for him. But Our Lord's hour had not yet sounded.

However, it was drawing near. Plagued by ambition and self-revulsion, more uncertain of himself than he cared to admit, he decided, in 383, to go to Rome.[1] But at first, instead of a setting worthy of his talents, he found only set-backs and disappointments. Sick, feverish,

---

[1] One particular incident shows how distraught and uncertain he was. He dared not tell his mother that he wanted to go to Rome. But she, with womanly intuition, suspected it. One evening, when she saw him going towards the harbour, she refused to leave him. But no! he declared. He was not thinking of embarking! He was only seeing a friend off! Let Monica go and say her prayers! And while his mother was spending the night in a chapel, her son boarded the ship and set sail. . . .

forced to scrape a living by tutoring the children of the wealthy, lodging wretchedly in one of those ramshackle hovels without the least semblance of hygiene, ignored by the public, and cheated by his pupils, he longed to return to Africa, when suddenly something so paradoxical occurred that we can see in it the hand of Divine Providence. Putting himself forward as a candidate for a chair of rhetoric at Milan, Augustine obtained it on the recommendation of some of his Manichaean friends and through the good offices of the prefect Symmachus, the head of the pagan faction, who was only too happy to place an opponent of the Church in the post. Once the matter was settled, in the spring of 384, feeling very happy (or, at least, appearing so outwardly) and probably rather proud of himself, Augustine set off for Milan, off towards what he believed would make his fortune, without realizing that at Milan, just as in the secret depths of his heart, Christ was waiting for him.

## God Answers Those Who Call to Him

In fact, Augustine's soul, when he arrived in Milan, was the soul of a deeply troubled man, fundamentally at variance with himself. He was now over thirty years old. This is the age when men seek to establish their life upon firm foundations; Augustine had none. Manichaeism, in which he had hoped to find the answers to his basic problems, had let him down utterly, and, since his wretched meeting with the chief publicist of the sect, Bishop Faustus of Milevis, he had privately cut himself off from it. The Probabilism of the *New Academy*, to which he had inclined for a few months, had not stood up very long to the scepticism of a soul which thirsted for an answer that was definite. Outwardly he was happy; he was a professor with a good following, a semi-official personage, and he had a pleasant house and a beautiful garden. Yet, deep in his heart, he knew that he was merely marking time. Since it was necessary for him to profess a faith, was it merely in order to keep his post that he decided 'to remain a catechumen in the Catholic Church, the Church of his family, until such time that a definite light came to lighten his path'? Was it simply a prudent gesture of conformity?[1] No, surely not. Unknown to him, this faith was conquering him.

At Milan one man dominated events, and seemed the very incarnation of Catholicism: Bishop Ambrose. Descended from an illustrious

---

[1] Since, in the imperial city of Milan, the imperial government could scarcely have looked very favourably on a Manichaean or Sceptic professor, at the time when Theodosius had just proclaimed Catholicism the religion of his domains. If this human argument came into play at all, one can only repeat that, in this type of crisis, God makes use of everything to achieve His ends—*etiam peccata.*

family, a former high official whom the unanimous voice of the people had called to the bishopric, Ambrose was a splendid orator, a great letter-writer, and a man whose political influence was respected by the emperor himself. He represented everything that Augustine most admired. Indeed, as soon as he arrived in Milan, he hastened to pay a visit to the great man. Much later on he admitted that this meeting had been somewhat disappointing. Ambrose received him 'in true bishop's fashion,' he said, a little maliciously. Was the bishop perhaps a little suspicious of the protégé of his old enemy, Symmachus? Or did the Roman patrician in him find the Mediterranean enthusiasm of the little African rather too much of a good thing? At any rate no spark that might have lit up a questing soul was kindled between these two men. But perhaps it was better so. For, seeing him from a distance, Augustine felt the true greatness of Ambrose. He listened to him each time he preached in the cathedral, and he read his works, and he discovered, thanks to Ambrose, the spiritual necessity of an authority distinct from reason alone; he learned, from the saint's teaching, the need to adhere to a reality which is at one and the same time both human and divine, where the individual feels himself like a brick in an enormous building, or a link in a chain.

The Scriptures, which Ambrose expounded so admirably, and the Church, which he represented so completely, these were the cornerstones of that authority whose necessity the catechumen henceforth realized. A decisive hurdle had been cleared.

From this moment onwards, as is always the case in dramas of conscience such as this, every chance happening seemed, to Augustine, to be God-ordained. His happy appetite for knowledge pushed him relentlessly forward: he read Plato, Plotinus, and the Neo-Platonic treatises, of which a friend lent him the Latin translations of his compatriot, the rhetorician Victorinus. These were an eye-opener to him. He discovered the fundamental goodness of the entire universe, and this swept away his final traces of Manichaeism. He understood that the Spirit existed, independent of all representation or material manifestation. The intelligible world of the Platonists allowed him to draw near the divine Word, and he was uplifted by the vision of a universe regulated by it and manifesting it. Of this period of his life he was to write: 'I was astonished to find myself loving Thee—loving God, an empty shadow no longer. And though I was not yet capable of possessing Thee fully, I was being carried towards Thee by beauty.'

The danger of such great enthusiasm could have been overweening intellectual pride. However, with that happy knack which enabled him to seize swiftly on a doctrine, to absorb its essential truth, and then to progress beyond it, Augustine quickly discovered the limits of Platonic metaphysics. It was impossible to 'possess' the God of the

Idealists. But was there not another God, who was the Word, and yet at the same time a living Presence, an answer to his love? And there, close at hand, was the mystery of the Incarnation. So Augustine turned at last to the Scriptures, the Scriptures that Ambrose expounded so lucidly. He read St Paul, and found there the meaning of true Wisdom, not the wisdom described by the philosophers, but the Wisdom expressed in the apparent folly of the Cross. 'Thou hast concealed these truths from the clever and the wise, and hast revealed them to children.' When Augustine read words like these his soul trembled with anticipation; he was now very near to crossing the barrier which separated intellect from faith.

Everything is not so simple as this, and it is not by intellectual feats alone that a soul gives itself to God. It was necessary to strip the old Augustine and reclothe the new man spiritually. But he had not the will to make the final break, and for a long time he argued with himself, fighting grievous temptations. The old habits 'had a physical hold' over him; he was well aware that in giving up his present way of life he was going to lose all his material comforts, and those pleasures of the flesh which he could not imagine being able to do without. When his mother, who had joined him in Milan, sensing his agitation, and wanting to push him along the right road, parted him from his concubine, under the touching delusion that he ought to marry, he simply took another mistress. No one knew better than Augustine how to describe the harrowing experience of a soul ensnared by long-standing habits, incapable of emancipating itself from sin, and at the same time ceaselessly called upon by the silent voice of God: for this experience, which is so much one of our own, he had lived right through himself.

Soon the debate between 'the two men in me' was more closely joined. Augustine knew full well the way he ought to go, but, deep within him, a power fought stubbornly against it. He compares himself with a lazy-bones who, lacking the courage to jump out of bed, quavers 'Just one minute longer!'—and then lets that moment drag on and on. What could break this mood of hesitation? Only God: the magic of His example. From now on God's call to him grew ever stronger. On one occasion the call came through a priest, whom Augustine had gone to see, and in whom he had confided his distress. The priest described to him the celebrated conversion of Victorinus—yes, that same famous neo-Platonist rhetorician, whose translations had inspired him so. On another occasion it came through Pontitian, his compatriot, who talked to him enthusiastically of the monastic ideal, citing the recluses who lived at the gates of Milan, the deserts dotted with hermits, and the two palatine officers of Trèves who, after reading the Life of St Anthony, had immediately retired from the world, and their fiancées likewise, to devote their lives solely to God.

'And let us have done with it too!' cried Augustine. But the time was not yet ripe! His emotions still fought on. 'There they were,' he was to say later, 'these old friends of mine, these wretched, wretched vanities, holding me gently by my fleshly coat, and murmuring: "Well! Are you really going to send us away? Just think! Once we are gone you will never be allowed to do this, that, and the other, never again!"' But the other voice in him said: 'What these men, women, and children could do, cannot you do too?' It was necessary for God to call him still more urgently.

And so it was in the garden of his Milan home—and how over-powering the scene still is for us to-day!—that Augustine suddenly discovered that wonderful Presence, and heard the mysterious call to his privileged soul. It was the same call which had come to Nathaniel, beneath the fig-tree, and to the troubled soul of the little Jew on the road to Damascus. Gripped by the frightful agony of a soul which is in torment, and yet which dare not free itself from its bondage, Augustine threw himself to the ground, weeping, babbling inco-herently, not really knowing if he even wanted God to hear him. 'How long, O Lord, how long?' Then, suddenly, he heard a child singing in the neighbouring garden, singing something which sounded like the jingle of a game: 'Go and read! Go and read!' In his state of agitation these words seemed like an order from heaven. He leapt to his feet and opened St Paul; the pages fell open at Chapter XIII of Paul's Epistle to the Romans: 'Let us pass our time honourably, as by the light of day, not in revelling and drunkenness, not in lust and wantonness, not in quarrels and rivalries. Rather, arm yourselves with the Lord Jesus Christ; spend no more thought on nature and nature's appetites' (Rom. xiii. 13–14). The book fell from his hands. What need had he to read further? He was at peace in his soul. At last he understood.

The incident in the garden probably occurred in the spring of 386. Its effects were not long delayed. As early as July Augustine left Milan and installed himself in a villa put at his disposal by a friend, in order to think things over and to plan his future. Here all was peace-ful and still; he was surrounded by the beauties of nature. There was the splendour of the sunsets on the Alpine horizon; the enchanted stretches of the Italian lakes were near by; the district was surrounded with fresh valleys, wooded slopes, and sparkling streams; he could smell the mint and the aniseed. In the retreat at Cassiciacum,[1] accompanied only by his mother, a few faithful friends, and by his son, the young Adeodatus, whose intelligence, he was to say, was sublime, Augustine honestly applied himself to grasping the truth about

[1] On the site of Cassiciacum and the various possible hypotheses *see* L. Bertrand, *Autour de saint Augustin.*

himself. The *Soliloquies*, which he wrote later, make one realize the violent passion of his meditations, the bitterness of that strange battle fought during the sleepless nights against the old Augustine within him who refused to die. 'Father, let me find Thee!' This cry, so like Pascal's, rings through these pages. God always replies to an appeal of such total sincerity.

Augustine was baptized by Ambrose on the evening of 24th or 25th April, along with his son, Adeodatus, and his friend, Alypius. The ceremony was neither showy nor ostentatious, as that of the rhetorician Victorinus had been. Augustine stepped forward humbly, simply one Christian sinner among the rest. Just before this ceremony he had sent the bishop an account of his past errors, together with his undertaking to renounce them for ever.

Now it merely remained for him to cope with the practical consequences of his decision. He had already resigned from his official position, since to have done otherwise might have encouraged the maintenance of misunderstanding; he had to give up the house which had been let to him as the erstwhile rhetorician friend of the Manichaeans, and return to Africa, where the burning memory of his youthful follies required exemplary reparations. All was soon settled; the will of God was so obvious! As he was about to make the sea crossing Augustine was assured of it. At Ostia Monica fell seriously ill, attacked by a deadly fever. Calm and steadfast to the end, her only thoughts, as death drew near, were of this son whom she had seen return safely from so far away, and whom her prayers had given back to God. One evening, while she was talking to him of that other life and that other light to which she was going, as they leant together by the window from which the view stretched away as far as the horizon, they both suddenly felt themselves 'borne aloft on a wave of love' towards the final clarity of truth. They 'reached their very souls, and went beyond them, attaining that inexpressibly wonderful region where God feeds one with the bread of truth, where life is merged in the divine wisdom, and, for an instant, they were a part of it.' For a blinding moment these two people escaped from the limits of human existence, and approached heaven.

Shortly after this, the Africa which, five years earlier, had said farewell to a petty rhetorician greedy for personal success, bursting with contradictory ideas and youthful ambitions, saw the return of a man utterly master of himself, who had achieved his personal synthesis, and found faith. He went back to Carthage and Tagaste. But he went back merely to sell the possessions left him by his father, to give the proceeds to the poor, and to establish himself, with a few faithful companions, in what was to be the very first Augustinian monastery.

### AN IMMORTAL MASTERPIECE: THE 'CONFESSIONS'

We are able to understand the whole drama of this soul searching for enlightenment, to know all its details and to reconstruct it with exceptional accuracy, because the man who lived through it all has drawn its outlines and marked its stages in one book of absolute sincerity. The *Confessions* of St Augustine is one of the most precious treasures of our civilization; it is one of five or six great works which will, one hopes, survive all the disasters of history in order to show future generations what sort of man Western civilization—now threatened with disappearance—could produce at its best; from the literary standpoint alone, it is a masterpiece which can be imitated, but not surpassed, and from the Christian point of view it is one of the works in which mystical enthusiasm reaches its highest peaks.

When he wrote it, round about 397-8, Augustine was well over forty, and he had been a Christian, a priest, and a bishop for a long time. His object was not the disclosure of the secrets of his past life for the satisfaction of the idle curiosity of all and sundry. Never once does he allow himself the slightest trace of that unfortunate indulgence towards his own failings in which so many personal journals revel. As Michelet so truly remarks: 'Passion, temperament, man's individuality, only appear in it in order to be offered up to Divine Grace.'[1] Moreover it was not to men that his lengthy memoirs were primarily addressed; after all, no audience was waiting for them. He wrote them for God Himself,[2] for God who had done everything for him, and whom he considered it meet and proper to thank, to praise, and to proclaim so untiringly. Whenever Augustine talks of himself, and of his sins and sorrows, it is only in order to illustrate, by concrete examples, the supreme might and mercy of God. Indeed the *Confessions* expresses this intention, time and time again; one hundred times or more the author breaks off his narrative to utter the cry of love and praise which rises in his throat; prayer is as much a part of this book as confession. The very title of *Confessions* is meant to convey much more than *confidence*, used in the sense of confiding a secret: *Confessions* is used here in the noblest sense that Christian understanding can give it, as when one says that a believer *confesses* his faith.

Nevertheless it remains true that, though attempting only to glorify God, St Augustine paved the way for a new literary style, which needed Christian soil to give it birth and nourishment. It is possible that his methods were somewhat influenced by Stoic and neo-Platonic texts; what he produced, however, was unique. Some thousand years

---

[1] In his preface to the *Mémoires de Luther*.
[2] As Papini has aptly called them, 'The Epistle to God.'

earlier, Heraclitus, the 'philosopher of darkness,' had certainly included in his one hundred and thirty-three axioms the one 'I am looking for myself,' and on the frontal arch of the classical Greek temple of Apollo at Delphi pilgrims were reminded of the following celebrated precept: 'Know thyself!' However, this demand of the Greeks had been proved impossible of fulfilment; Socrates had confessed that he was incapable of knowing himself, and Aristotle had declared that 'the perfect man never speaks of self.' But ever since Jesus had said that 'the Kingdom of God is within us,' ever since Christianity had given the individual soul, created in God's image, a unique importance, the picture had changed. Augustine understood this intuitively. 'In a miraculous way,' he writes, 'the inner man [i.e. the soul] carries, in his three faculties, the image of God engraven on his personality.' [1] From this it follows, on the one hand, that, in delving deeper into his own self, man is sure to reach the divine Presence. *Noverim me, noverim te*, if I know myself, I know Thee—and, on the other hand, it also follows that the only way of penetrating right to the heart of the human soul is to search there for the unchallengeable sign of the divine Light, a fact which our modern psycho-analysts, such as Proust and Freud, have all too completely forgotten.

So human in character, yet so enriched by Divine Grace, the *Confessions* is indeed a unique work, which reaches right into the reader's soul. Possibly only the better parts of Pascal's *Pensées* can rival Augustine for the sense of spiritual expansion which they bring their reader, and for that feeling of mysterious gratitude which texts of this kind arouse in us. One had but to open the book at random to get the full force of words and arguments in which the gift of literary expression combines with the gifts of the Holy Spirit. Most of us have already read the *inquietum cor nostrum*, which is probably the most famous of these literary jewels. But the following pathetic confession is less easily recognizable as Augustine's: 'Where I can be, I do not wish to go; where I wish to go, I cannot be: O, double affliction.' Does the reader not feel the surge within him of something more essential than life itself when he reads this call to our own personal mystery: 'Thus I turned face to face with myself, and I cried: "And thou, what art thou?" And I answered: "But a man."' There is a tale told of Petrarch, the poet of the *Canzoniere*, and of how he climbed Mount Ventoux, one clear April day in 1336. When he reached the top, having seen the gorgeous panorama spread below him, he opened his copy of the *Confessions*, from which he was rarely parted, and was overwhelmed when he chanced to stumble on the following passage: 'Men journey from afar to admire the mountain tops, yet they are content to tread only the slopes of their own souls.' How many of us

[1] Three founts: being, knowledge, and will, or even: thought, understanding, and love.

have not been through this experience, many times? In this book the man that we are, the man that two thousand years of Christianity has made us, is found in his entirety.

Yet, essential as it is for our understanding of St Augustine, it would be quite wrong to let our study of him end with this testimony. Too many biographies lay stress on the drama of his soul and the stages of his conversion, and more or less forget that this book which he wrote in his forties was to be followed by thirty busy years packed with important spiritual labours and battles on God's behalf. The *Confessions* demonstrates the birth of the saint, rather than his mature accomplishments. It is significant that after writing nine chapters which are largely autobiographical, and a tenth which is an examination of conscience, a state of mind at the time of writing, St Augustine continued his book with three entirely different chapters, feats of elevation on the sacred mysteries, as if to make the reader understand more easily where the convert of yesterday will go to-morrow. The real St Augustine was not made in the moment of baptism; he merely began to grow then. It is this new man, dead with Christ, and resurrected with Him, who, henceforth, is going forward to carry out His work, in his actions and through his books, giving both the double impress of his genius and his sanctity.

## A GENIUS AND A SAINT

The man we are going to watch for a period of more than forty years, waging the most exhausting battles in Christ's cause, writing book after book, tract after tract, carrying out to the full the functions of his episcopal office which the circumstances of the epoch made particularly burdensome, was a man of indifferent health, poorly endowed, physically, and the first obstacle that he had to overcome was the weakness of his own body.[1] But it often happens that vast enterprises are commanded by men who are physical weaklings, and the size of the tasks accomplished seems out of all proportion to their

[1] It is true, of course, that we have no portrait of St Augustine, just as we have none of Jesus or St Paul. The ancients were not curious about this kind of thing, and those of his contemporaries who have spoken of him never felt the need to give a physical description of the man. However, in 1900 a fifth- or sixth-century mosaic was found under the foundations of the chapel of Sancta Sanctorum, all that remains of the oldest palace of the Lateran. This depicts a man in a toga, with scanty hair, a short, grizzled beard, slight in build, who holds a scroll in his left hand and is sitting before a desk on which there is a book, apparently meditating. Under the figure are two Latin lines which mean: 'The different Fathers said various things; this man said everything, and it is thanks to his Roman eloquence that the mystic meaning has resounded.' One presumes that only St Augustine could merit such eulogies. But even allowing that the artist is attempting to represent him faithfully, we cannot tell to what extent he knew what Augustine really looked like, one hundred or one hundred and fifty years after the saint's death.

apparent fragility. Over-ebullient health, in encouraging one to grasp at life with too much enthusiasm, often results in a wasteful dispersal of effort; the secret knowledge of a certain personal deficiency makes one conserve one's energies for the things that really matter. After all, were not St Paul, St Bernard, St Ignatius—and even Michelangelo—all delicate in health? Without being an actual invalid, without ever losing the full use of his faculties—except in extreme old age—St Augustine, a sufferer from chronic bronchitis, asthma, and frightful insomnia, was always forced to calculate carefully the limits of his strength. But in souls of mighty faith, how great these limits are! One really wonders if they ever existed at all in Augustine's case. . . .

If the word 'genius' has any real meaning it is undoubtedly applicable to this man, with his inexhaustible richness of spirit, his unique brain, his mind so fully attuned to the demands of the present and the needs of the future. He lacked not a single one of those signs of intelligence that are capable of analysis; he possessed them all at the same time, even those which are usually thought contradictory to one another. His range of topics covered every known subject, yet his examination of each one was deep and penetrating. No abstract problem ever rebuffed or discouraged him; he applied himself as seriously to practical matters as to the most detailed points of scholarship. A model of those intuitive characters whom one recognizes immediately as outstanding geniuses, and a spirit carried instinctively towards metaphysical speculation, he is, at the same time, a redoubtable dialectician, always ready with his counter-attack in the tricky warfare of ideas. There is not a single subject that he touched on without giving it something new, marking it with his distinctive stamp, and necessitating anyone who studied it after him to examine, at least, and often to admit the validity of the Augustinian commentary on it. He si, as we have seen, one of the earliest Christian psychologists; equally he is one of the first and the most authentic of those poets which the evangelical impulse has given to literature. One stands confounded before an accumulation of such gifts, and they were admirably served by Augustine's very keen memory and prodigious capacity for work.

The most tangible way in which a genius such as Augustine impresses himself upon the observer, is in the tremendous quantity of written work which he has left behind him. Though he may be considered idle and foolish, one of the best qualities of the writer or the artist is his capacity for prolific output. When, towards the end of his life, St Augustine was drawing up a careful record of his labours, he listed no less than two hundred and thirty-two books, divided out into ninety-three major works, and this imposing total includes neither sermons nor letters, some of which are veritable treatises in themselves! It is not surprising that he seems to us to be surrounded by a massive bulwark of books, a bulwark which, it must be confessed, protects him rather too well! Though it is fairly elementary to have, at any rate, scanned through the *Confessions*, and, on a rather higher plane—these days—to have some idea of the contents of the *City of God*, only theologians (if that . . .) have studied the *De Trinitate*, only preachers the *Christian Doctrine*. Who bothers himself nowadays with works such as *Faith and the Creed*, or the *Enchiridion*, the manual of Augustinianism, rich though they are in valuable material? Only those making a detailed study of the saint. The simple enumeration of his books would fill a whole chapter of this work. In the progress towards God which is summed up in this many-sided performance, the philosopher of the *Dialogues* goes hand in hand with the theologian of the *True Religion*, *Faith*, the *Treatise on the Trinity*, and the *City of God*. In order to disseminate and diffuse the Truth, the theoretician of the *Enchiridion*, and the moralist of the tracts work alongside the propagandist of the *Christian Doctrine*, whilst in examining the foundations of the Christian faith, the exegetist who proved the *Reconciliation of the Gospels*, and the commentator on St John and St Paul, are both brought fully into play. As well as all these works we must not forget the innumerable books and leaflets which he hurled, like so many keen arrows, against the heretics of every type, whom he never stopped fighting. The experts consider that some three hundred and sixty-three sermons are certainly his, and the number may well be as high as four hundred and fifty.[1] Two hundred and sixty of Augustine's letters have come down to us, out of a total which must certainly have run into thousands. . . . A list like this gives only the most inadequate idea of this monumental spirit.

In the literary sense all this mass of material could not possibly possess equal value. It must be admitted that it is not always easy to master the tedious, ponderous character of certain of his arguments. It is even less easy to fight down the irritation we feel—especially in his oratorical works—at his misuse of witticisms, his affected antitheses, his puns and play on words which one would like to think he used simply to hold the attention of his Southern public. Extensive though the culture, which he tried to develop all his life, might be, it is clear that it always remained bounded by certain limits. They were the limits of a man who was thoroughly versed only in Cicero and Virgil, who culled his knowledge from the encyclopaedic works of Varro, who had only a smattering of Greek, who—and this is his worst failing—remained excessively attached to the grammatical and

[1] Large numbers of texts were subsequently attributed to St Augustine, and deciding the authorship of these documents, whose authenticity is very much in doubt, has frequently presented many delicate problems.

rhetorical methods taught him in his youth. One writer has described him as 'a decadent scholar.'[1] In addition, his attitude frequently strikes us as insufficiently critical, whether the point at issue be exegesis or the natural sciences, and his fantastic assertions often made the modern reader want to smile.[2] This is the weak side of his work—and what human work is without its own particular weaknesses?—the dross which the winds of time blow away. There is after all only one book in the world which is utterly faultless, precisely because it is not the work of human minds, and that book is the Gospel. But beside his faults, what extraordinary gifts Augustine possessed; and what successes he had! He has an easy knack of adapting his style to suit his purpose. It is classical in the *City of God*, romantic in the *Confessions*, incisive in the polemical works, and almost popular in character in the sermons. There are the constant flashes of genius expressed in formulae which embrace the whole field of human intelligence. And in the *City of God* this monumental architect of a man presents the entire destiny of the world in one book. Is there really anyone in the whole history of the humanities who can equal him? One is reminded of La Bruyère's famous passage, in his chapter on *Rationalists*: 'For his breadth of knowledge, for depth and penetration, for his principles of pure philosophy, and their application and development, for the accuracy of his conclusions, for dignity of expression, for the beauty of his ethics and his opinions, there is no one to compare with St Augustine, except Plato and Cicero.' In spite of its weaknesses and defects, work such as his commands respect, even from those who do not themselves possess the faith which is its guiding star.

But it commands much more than our respect alone: it captures our sympathy, for his soul reaches out to us, right across his work, touching us in a thousand different ways. What makes St Augustine so much more than just a man of letters is the absolute harmony he achieves between his own life and his books. Whatever he thinks he lives to the full; whatever he says he himself has experienced to the very core of his being. For this particular theologian God is never just an abstract concept, but that living reality which he had felt there beside him in the garden at Milan, and which, from that day on, has enveloped him with its Supreme Presence. For this propagandist and rugged champion of the faith, Christianity is never merely just a set of

[1] H. I. Marrou, in his remarkable thesis on *Saint Augustin et la fin de la culture antique*, the conclusions of which have just been published.
[2] For example, he believed in the existence of fabulous animals such as unicorns, dragons, and 'hiro-stags'; he was convinced that the eagle, which can see straight into the sun, used this test to make sure that its young were legitimate, and killed those it discovered were not; he thought that the fruit of the Sodom-tree were indeed full of ashes—that goats' blood could melt diamonds, etc.

B

positions to be held fast, nor a body of doctrine alone, but a way of life, a total engagement.  If, whenever he approaches man's greatest problems—those concerning justice, morality, and liberty, for instance —he gives the impression of never considering them in abstract terms, but of always in terms of man himself, the man of flesh and blood, of hopes and fears, this is because he spontaneously relates all these problems to his own personal experiences.  In some circumstance or another he has lived through them all.  *Vitam impendere Vero.* Then, again, he manages to breathe life into everything—even the driest discussions—such as the one on the notion of time in Book XI of the *Confessions*—because, for Augustine, the discovery of the truth is one of the aspects of Divine Wisdom, and because he believes that 'contemplation gives man a part of God's likeness.'   One can say with certainty that everything about him, his intelligence, his style, and his method, are permeated by his sensibility.   And those who can only see him as a stern doctor, a morose pessimist, and a theologian bereft of pity have understood neither his soul nor the essential truth of the message which he brought us.

It is this message which places St Augustine in the forefront of the Christian writers of all time, and higher, even, than the other Fathers of the Church, both his predecessors and his emulators.   There is within him a mighty love which shines through all his work and gives him a brilliance which is quite unique.   One frequently notices that the two words which he uses most often are *amor* and *caritas*; above all else he is indeed the Doctor of Love, the Doctor of Charity.   At the time of his wretched self-examinations, was it not love which had led him towards the light?  He never let go of it for a moment, and extreme old age, that time of men's lives when feelings, like limbs, so often harden, found him just as sensitive, just as receptive as he had been as a restless adolescent.   This love of his is all embracing; unlike most men of his epoch, he was sensitive to nature and to the beauties of the world; but it was man above all who moved him, and to man he offered a sympathy which was inexhaustible.   This great man, who is sometimes represented as a harsh pessimist, or as a sort of mouthpiece preaching damnation, though he may occasionally shock us by the severity of his theses, to which he is impelled by the rigidity of his dialectic, loved men more than anyone did, and loved them as a Christian should, in God's name, and for the sake of their immortal souls.

Such is the meaning of Augustine's charity, which is not merely human, but superhuman, a supernatural gift which embraces all the different kinds of love, drawing them all towards God and thereby transcending and at the same time fulfilling them.   Jesus said that to love God and to love men is the same thing; nothing can ever separate the two clauses of 'the greatest of all the commandments.' Augustinian charity is not philanthropy; there is no true charity without participation in the love of Christ and, inversely, the most humble charitable action takes on an immense significance from the second that it establishes the mysterious communication of love between God and man. Charity, in this sense, is therefore the golden rule of all human conduct; and the admirable slogan, 'Only love, and do what you will!' should be thus interpreted and not taken as implying some loose indulgence. If we could but love God and our neighbour perfectly, our every action would be absolutely perfect too.

So, in the final analysis, it is the love of God which dominates St Augustine. It is this which sustains him in his physical weakness, which shines out from his scholarship, and which he expresses throughout his writing. One cannot begin to understand this genius if one loses sight for a single instant of the fact that, genius though he was, he was also, and above all, a saint. Augustine was a saint not just because of those exceptional qualities of which he gave ample evidence, but because of the perfect way in which his whole life was directed towards God. The dominant force in his make-up is his spiritual enthusiasm, his power of contemplation. He possessed both the characteristics fundamental to mystical experience: the intellectual vision, which can reach things divine, and the love of God, which was his all-absorbing passion. He gives an admirable description of this mystical experience in his *Commentary on Psalm LXI*: there is no doubt at all that he fed this commentary with many most personal observations, and that God, on several occasions in his life, had made His Presence felt to Augustine.

Thus the essential factor in this inexhaustible personality is nothing less than Christ Himself. From the moment that he gave himself to Him, until his last mortal breath, Augustine never thought that his goal could be anything other than reunion with Christ. This Christ who had snatched him from his misery, this Christ whose very Presence he had been privileged to feel, this Christ whom he sensed within him 'moaning amid the afflictions of mankind until the end of time'—it was through Him alone that the 'troubled soul' had found peace. It is He whom the saint of charity saw in the faces of his fellow creatures. It is He whose existence at a certain point in time was, in his eyes, the final explanation of history. Nothing in Augustine's writing can be properly understood if we forget that, over and above all his talent and ability, he was a son of Christ and a man of God.

## An African Bishop

When Augustine withdrew to Tagaste in the autumn of 388 he had only one wish: to devote his whole life to God. Obeying the command which Christ gave to the young man with many possessions, he sold the inheritance left him by his father in order to adopt apostolic poverty. A little community gathered around him, a community composed of outstanding individuals—Alypius, Evodius, and Adeodatus, that splendid son of his who, at seventeen, was awaiting a premature death; it was not a monastery in the true sense of the term, according to the Eastern pattern, but a free association of souls, all stirred by the same desire for perfection, and dominated, albeit without title or sacramental consecration, by the personality of Augustine. What a wonderful period it was, that three years in Tagaste, teeming with new ideas and inspiration. 'There is nothing better or more exquisite, than to be able to search in the solitude of silence for the divine treasure,' declared the saint on one occasion. 'On the other hand, preaching, reproving, correcting, building—worrying about this and that—what a dreadful responsibility and effort! Who would not run from a task of this kind?' However, it was to precisely such a task that Providence was soon to call him.

At the beginning of 391 Augustine returned to Hippo, to see one of the many correspondents who was begging his advice, a government agent whom Augustine considered on the verge of conversion. He had no sooner arrived in the town than the Catholics in the district seized on him. Their bishop, Valerius, though a good man, had not really come up to the expectations of the faithful; he was Greek by origin, did not speak the Punic language, and, being very advanced in years, lacked drive in the campaign against the schismatic Donatists. In the middle of a sermon, when Valerius was piously lamenting the dearth of priests in his church, the crowd interrupted him with the shout: 'Let Augustine be our priest!' At that instant Augustine's sole desire was to be twenty leagues away, back in his precious seclusion at Tagaste. But already an enthusiastic handful of people had caught hold of him and dragged him to the foot of the bishop's throne. Valerius, delighted by this speedy capture, ordained him on the spot. Admittedly this strikes us as rather a lively way of going about things: yet at Milan had not St Ambrose also owed his election to the bishopric to circumstances very much like these? And when Augustine made his irritation fully apparent, someone burst out—with more enthusiasm than discretion!—'Nonsense! You will soon be our bishop!' Soon after this, indeed, Valerius made Augustine his coadjutor, and in 396, on the bishop's death, the former recluse from Tagaste succeeded him. Possidius, one of his pupils, and a future bishop of Guelma, notes it very calmly. 'That is how this brilliant lamp of Christianity, which was searching only for the shadows of solitude, found itself placed high on the lamp-post. . . .'

Therefore it is as a bishop, in the first place, that Augustine comes to be the embodiment of Christianity, and we should recognize that his consecration considerably widened the scope of his witness. Ever since the Church of Christ had existed, the bishop had had a fundamental position in each community. It was he who assumed, not merely in the eyes of man, but before God also, the total responsibility—material, moral, and spiritual—of the flock entrusted to his care. Everything stemmed from him, and everything flowed towards him. The bishops were indeed the foundation-stones upon which the Church rested. In this epoch almost all the men who accomplished great things in the religious sphere were bishops, men like Athanasius, Ambrose, John Chrysostom, or Martin of Tours. Something vital would have been missing from Augustine's character if he had never been bishop of Hippo, that is to say, if he had never felt the yoke of the innumerable problems and burdens, which the episcopate took for granted in that troubled age.

And these burdens were especially heavy in an African bishopric at the end of the fourth century! Rich in its saints, and overflowing with enthusiasm, the Church in Africa had always been violent in character, carried easily to extremes and constantly threatened by schisms.[1] It had needed men of exceptional vigour to keep it under control, a St Cyprian, for example, or a Tertullian, and the latter had come to a bad end. It was not very long since Optatus, a rebel 'bishop,' had travelled the country with his armed bands, attacking those faithful to Rome. In Hippo itself the Donatist bishop Faustinus was so powerful that he could forbid the bakers to make bread for the Catholics, and be well and truly obeyed! As Possidius wrote: 'It was high time for the true Church, humiliated for so long, to lift her head high once more.' But it goes without saying that an episcopal charge, in conditions like these, was far from being a sinecure!

From 396 until his death, that is to say, for thirty-four years altogether, Augustine was Bishop of Hippo, and to-day it is in this modern town of Bône, on the wooded hillside where his statue stands, in the excavated fields where the ancient colonnades of his day have been laid bare, that we like to remember him. Augustine loved Hippo. He loved the bay, the pure sweep of its curves, the circlet of mountains bounding its horizons, the tall, dark pines and the olive groves, and he has described exquisitely the ever-changing reflections

[1] On Donatus and Donatism see the following section.

of the sea throughout each hour of the day and night. But above all he loved the people of Hippo, this exacting, turbulent folk, who were convinced that their bishop should be interested in every single thing they did, who reprimanded him for the least oversight, and to whom he gave a love that was never ending.

However, realizing that the radiance of a Christian leader is exactly proportionate to the supernatural qualities which the love of God has implanted in his heart, Augustine was anxious to make certain of retaining his direct contact with Christ. He did not want it broken by the cares and labours of his official position. It was for this reason that he turned the bishop's palace into a real kind of monastery, requiring his clerks to submit to the routine of a monastic life. Without being, properly speaking, a *Rule* [1] in the sense in which one speaks much later on of the 'Rule of St Benedict,' the episcopal household led a 'regular' existence; their meals were frugal, though excessive abstinence was not practised. They ate bread and vegetables, drank a little wine, wore simple clothing, and had no luxurious furnishings. On the walls of the communal dining-hall two lines reminded each person of the duty of kindness in speech: 'You who, lacking charity, slander those who are absent, know that at this table we detest slanderers.' Women did not live in the bishop's palace, and when one came there to visit a relative, the cleric who received her was always chaperoned. Periods of manual labour alternated with periods of prayer and meditation. It was from this atmosphere of brotherly love and religious enthusiasm that Bishop Augustine drew the strength which he needed if he were not to be ground down by the weight of his responsibilities and duties.

It is hard for a modern Catholic to understand the exact scope of a bishop's functions in the year 400. However paternal in character a bishop may be, he nowadays frequently remains outside direct contact with the faithful, a deeply respected personage whom one sees on great ceremonial occasions, dressed in violet or purple, whose counsel one listens to with deference, but who is rarely found mingling with the ordinary individual members of his flock. A fifth-century bishop led a very different kind of life, particularly in Africa. Nothing which concerned his people was outside his ken. He was expected to keep his doors always open to all who wanted to discuss their affairs with

---

[2] There was subsequently much discussion, particularly in the Middle Ages, as to whether St Augustine really founded a religious order, either of regulars or hermits. It is anachronistic to talk of an *Augustinian Rule* in connection with him. The principles given by him to his followers were formulated in two sermons: life and habits of clerks (sermons 355, 356) and in the famous letter 211, written in 423 for those in religious orders (and which is in fact a complete plan of life). It is these principles as a whole, systematized even before the sixth century, which constitute what has been called *The Rule of St Augustine*, to which the founders of religious orders, such as St Norbert, had recourse.

him—and not just their spiritual problems, but their most down-to-earth ones too! In the legal sphere the bishop had possessed judicial authority ever since Constantine's time, and heaven knows that Africa had more than its fair share of disputes and litigation!

'Catholic relief' fell to him: here he discharged his duties with infinite goodness, succouring the poor, buying the freedom of prisoners, sometimes even forced to melt down a sacred vessel to parry an urgent need. The community owned the wealth: it was the bishop who administered it, and this man, who wanted for himself nothing more than self-denial, was forced to busy himself with buildings and rents. And these were not his only tasks. In an age when the most frightful menaces could threaten the people, when the State, its officials, and its exchequer were so oppressive that it was necessary to recruit 'defenders of the City,' charged with resisting—officially!—excesses of power, it was the bishop who assumed the role, though without actually bearing the title. It was not a very comfortable one when the State was represented in Africa by a military governor, a certain Gildo, who was nothing less than a greedy Moor!

On top of all these duties, and one wonders how a single individual could tackle them all adequately, Augustine had to add yet another, which was strictly obligatory according to custom, and of which, moreover, he would not have rid himself for a fortune. He was, in practice, the only preacher in the community, the man whose sermons were awaited, each Sunday, with friendly expectancy. Every single Catholic in the community would be there in the Great Basilica, still known as the Basilica of Peace. The people stood, the men on one side of the church, the women on the other. They talked and exchanged jokes. Then suddenly all was silent as Augustine began to preach. He began with the problems which preoccupied everyone, talking to them on their own level so that they could understand him better. Very soon the African congregation was uplifted. Someone called out the end of a quotation which he had just begun. Now and then there was a murmur, a grumble when he ordered the cessation of such semi-pagan practices which still existed in the community. Now and then, too, someone would applaud him, and he would reply, without illusions: 'Your praises are like the leaves on the trees; but I would like to see the fruits!' Time went by, and the orator had to excuse himself, and beg for a moment of silence, for his voice was weak and tired quickly. What an immense influence this eloquence must have had on this congregation, so close at hand, so brimful of life! Across the phrases of the sermons we still possess we can sense the strong, kindly fingers of the saint of Hippo, like a baker's, seeming to knead the dough of his Christian bread!

Did this mass of holy duties take up all Augustine's time? Far from it! Herein lies the miracle.  At the very same time that he was throwing himself so completely into his episcopal tasks, he continued to write his tremendous books, never allowing himself to be swallowed up by his administrative tasks or pastoral cares: his radiance shone far beyond the bounds of Hippo.  Duties which would have utterly worn down most men were for him only a kind of basis for living, a way of safeguarding his knowledge of people and his contact with reality.

## THE CHAMPION OF TRUTH

Moreover, even if he had wanted to confine himself to dealing with the pleasanter aspects of a bishop's life, Augustine would have been forced to abandon such an idea.  The Christian faith found itself threatened on every side.  The bishop was obliged to enter the fray simply to protect his flock against those whom he branded as 'devouring lions.'  Indeed, from the very hour when the people's voice called him to the priesthood, until he fell asleep in the Lord, not a single year passed by—and hardly a single month—without Augustine throwing himself into the breach, to face the various redoubtable forms which heresy was wont to take.

The struggle against heresies had begun almost with the dawn of Christianity itself, and it had passed through several stages in the course of the next four hundred years.  It had reached a climax in the decades immediately preceding Augustine's lifetime, when the violent waves of Arianism, Donatism, and Manichaeanism had broken against the Church simultaneously.  At the beginning of the fifth century the threat still remained serious, and was made even more so by the appearance of new enemies.  In conflicts like these, when everything was at stake, no Christian could remain neutral.  The very existence of Christianity was threatened.  Augustine saw the nature of the danger more accurately than most men, and possessed the will to parry it.

More than anyone else perhaps he possessed a complete understanding of the Church.  He has described it magnificently.  In his sermons he described time and time again the mystical bonds which bind her to God, and at the same time he glorified her mission towards men!  How wisely, and with what an accurate sense of historical demands, he set out the conditions of an ecclesiastical polity!  And with what fervour he took up the famous slogan of St Cyprian, making it one of his own: 'There is no salvation outside the Church!'  When he saw that *Ecclesia Mater* herself was being put in jeopardy by the heresies threatening her, he felt himself personally at stake.  Such was the attitude of the man who has often been called 'the Doctor of the Church.'

But when we examine the various episodes in the saint's battle against heresy, we see something more: each of the dramas in which he is engaged is, in a sense, his own personal drama. It is not simply as the Church's representative, as the official guardian of holy doctrine, that he does battle against the enemies of the true faith; on each occasion he can be said to be guided by the deepest demands of his own soul. In replying to his adversaries he answers his own queries. This fact transforms these arguments against the various heresies— which often tend to be dry as dust and tedious in the extreme—into impassioned battles, at least when St Augustine is conducting them. This too makes each of his conflicts the occasion for a step forward in his own religious experience for some new elaboration of doctrine. The struggle for truth constitutes one of the most important elements in the life's work of the saint.

From the moment that Augustine became a Christian, the denunciation of Manichaeism was, for him, much more than a formal obligation of his new state, or a task forced on him by his intellect: it was a conscientious duty. Had he not been one of the sect himself for nine years—even if, as he assures us, he was only a lukewarm catechumen, and never adhered to it completely—and, moreover, had he not placed all the resources of his talent at the service of the heresy, actually persuading some of his friends to join it? He was scarcely converted, when, in 388, he first crossed swords with his co-religionists of yesterday: the struggle was to last full twenty years.

For us, looking at it so many centuries later, the doctrine of Manes or Mani, 'the many-headed monster,' seems a misleading jumble, in which someone of considerable intelligence, but lacking any cohesive thought, has tossed together a thousand badly assimilated ingredients, Buddhism, Gnosticism, and Judaic-Christian traditions, the whole thing resting on the substratum of old Persian Dualism. The collection of myths—some pretty, others silly—gives the crazy impression of a spiritual universe in utter chaos. But to a young man searching for guidance it did not seem like this at all. Augustine himself described what had attracted him to Manichaeism: 'These men claimed to sweep aside the spectre of authority in the name of reason, they promised to snatch their disciples from error, leading them to God.' In the first place, therefore, it was his passion for truth which led Augustine's troubled soul astray. Did not Manichaeism 'explain' the most serious of problems, e.g. that of evil? In declaring the existence of two antagonistic entities, and the opposition of matter to spirit, did it not solve the enigma posed by Christianity, with its purely spiritual God? It is scarcely necessary to add that certain convenient

* B

aspects of its moral code, severe indeed for the 'perfect,' but indulgent towards the simple mass of the faithful, were possibly not exactly displeasing to a boy beset by the sins of the flesh!

To begin with, therefore, the campaign against Manichaeism was, for Augustine, a struggle within his own soul. How did he succeed in breaking away from it? His critical faculty, developing in proportion to the increase in his philosophic knowledge, led him to judge the sect's pretensions to truth at their true value. The discovery of Neo-Platonism, offering him, as it did, a deeper understanding of God, and proposing to him a solution to the problem of evil, enabled him to take a new step forward. By listening to Ambrose, and by reading the Scriptures, he discovered the value of authority, at the very moment that he became aware of the limits and pitfalls of human reason. And the victory over his own flesh finally broke the bonds.

Once he himself was freed from error he wanted to free others. His first task—and here one senses a personal need—was to denounce the false Manichaean moral doctrine and its suspicious laxities in his *De Moribus*. Then there were his first attempts to explain the bases of authority in connection with the book of Genesis. As a priest, and, later on, as a bishop, he continued the battle without thought of truce. He offered to meet the Manichaean zealots in public debates at which each side put forward its arguments. In 392 the lengthy meeting took place—forty-eight hours of discussion in all—at which he defeated Fortunatus on the problem of evil; twelve years later came the conference at which the Manichaean philosopher, Felix, confessed himself beaten, and was there and then converted to Christianity. At the same time, in a series of polemical treatises, Augustine refuted the great works of the sect, the theses of Adimantus, the *Foundations* of Mani himself, and the mighty work which Faustus of Milevis had just published against Holy Scripture and which the Bishop of Hippo attacked in no fewer than thirty-three volumes. And alongside all this, in order to make truth fight error, there were the great treatises on *Free Will* and *The Nature of Good*, which Augustine threw up like bastions against the sallies of the 'Eastern plague.'

At the end of this severe battle Manichaeism retired, exhausted. By the time Augustine died the heresy's end was near at hand, and it continued to circulate only as an undercurrent of vague superstition. For the lasting benefit of Christianity, the labours of the saint had resulted in a propounding of certain definite bases: an exact setting out of the relations between reason and authority, a definition of evil—within the great Pauline perspective—for what it really is—a deficiency, an imperfection, a lack of something, but not a reality, and an affirmation that everything created by God is essentially good. From the point of view of civilization he had contributed to the overthrow of a most menacing doctrine which threatened to destroy the foundations of collective existence, of morality, of the family, of social intercourse, and of discipline.[1]

Here we see the characteristic genius of this great man, building the foundations for the future from the lesson gained in a personal experience.

It might have been expected that Augustine would be rather less intimately involved in the campaign against what he contemptuously called 'the party of Donatus.' Even when still outside the Catholic fold, he had never had the slightest sympathy with Donatism. However, he threw himself into the struggle with a violence and a tenacity which made him—from about the year 400 until his death—the real leader of the anti-Donatist party. When, in the end, the heretical schism collapsed, Augustine can be said to have been its principal conqueror.

The enthusiasm which Augustine lent to the campaign can be explained by the extreme gravity of the situation. Donatism had originated at the beginning of the fourth century, following the Diocletian persecutions. It was suggested that certain bishops were 'traitors,' that is to say, that, having capitulated to the imperial agents, they were judged unworthy to direct the faithful and to administer the sacraments. Originating, therefore, in an excessive scrupulousness, Donatism had rapidly turned to schism, heresy, and worse besides. To schism, for it had resulted in the creation of a counter-church separated from Rome; to heresy, for the sect's theoreticians held that 'the saints' alone were a part of the church, sinners being mercilessly proscribed for ever. Implicated in a thousand personal quarrels, feuds, intrigues, and jealousies, secretly helped by senior government officials all too ready to shake off the imperial yoke, Donatism had found considerable support in the more or less separatist sentiments of numerous Africans. The movement was soon debased by a violent minority of its members, and, after eighty years, the church which called itself 'the Church of the Saints' attracted bandits and evildoers of every description, who waged a merciless war against the Catholics.

So, when he became one of the responsible Catholic leaders, Augustine was forced to confront the Donatists in a practical manner. By the year 400 the schismatic Church had probably more active members in Africa than the true Church. Well organized, and backed by their own shock troops, the *circumcelliones*,[2] these enemies of the faith

[1] This was why the Manichaeans were persecuted in such drastic fashion in their country of origin as well as in the Roman Empire. Diocletian had already condemned them to be burned, in 290. Constantine, Constantius, Valentinian I, and Theodosius revived extreme penalties against the sect.

[2] Made up of rebel peasants, bandits, slaves, and fugitives, the *circumcelliones* were, as their name suggests, 'those who attacked the isolated farms,' rather like the 'chauffeurs' in France under the Directory.

stopped at nothing. Indeed on one occasion Augustine himself only escaped one of their ambushes because, quite by chance, he took the wrong road. The pressing character of the Donatist peril did not prevent the saint from weighing up its long-term consequences. He saw the problems of the unity of the shattered Church, of a false conception corrupting her very principles of membership and property. The man who had listened to St Ambrose understood perfectly what fidelity to the true Mother implied; the former sinner could never allow his threatened brethren to remain outside salvation.

He pursued his campaign against the Donatists in every conceivable direction. All the inexhaustible resources of his talent were brought into play against the heresy. In order to circulate the idea that the opposing doctrines were false among the common people, we find this learned philosopher and theologian composing a popular song for them, a sort of repetitive jingle! To try to convince the leaders of the enemy faction of the error of their ways, he offered them, as he had offered the Manichaeans before them, public debates; being less intellectual than the Manichaeans, however, the majority of the Donatists shirked these. So then he fought them in his writing. With scrupulous honesty he set out their claims in treatise after treatise, and book after book, then demolishing them and grinding them to pieces. Even this was not enough. When at last the public authorities intervened, fearing the anarchy set in motion by the schism, it was Augustine who was the leading spirit behind the great conference held at Carthage, where two hundred and eighty-six Catholic bishops confronted two hundred and seventy-nine Donatists, and, thanks to the seer of Hippo, broke down their resistance. And when, in the end, the government ordered the suppression of Donatism by law and began persecuting its active adherents, it was Augustine again who tried to rally the crippled schismatics, in order to bring them back to the true Church. It is largely due to Augustine that the Donatist party eventually broke up, to disappear completely before A.D. 500.

Doctrinally too this struggle had great importance. Following in the footsteps of that great bishop, St Optatus of Milevis, but carrying his thesis to its logical conclusion, St Augustine sets out the doctrine which has always been that of Catholicism in such anti-Donatist books as *De Baptismo*, *Against the Letter of Parmenian*, *Against Cresconius*, etc. The Donatist schism was sectarian; it aspired boastfully to an exclusive sanctity; it was anarchical and separatist. Against this St Augustine set the true picture of the Church. She is merciful to all, even to sinners, and her dearest members are the meek in spirit; she is holy in her leader, her priests, and her sacraments; she is not confined to the jealous nationalism of a handful of provinces, but she is catholic, that is to say, universal—she shines through time and space without any limitation. Born of battle, this glorious apologia has retained its prestige, unsullied, into our own time.

The Donatist struggle was at its height when a new peril arose. Once again Augustine faced it dauntlessly. The founder of the new doctrine was a British monk who, under the name of Pelagius, became a well-known figure among Christian circles in Rome during the pontificate of Anastasius (399–401). His real name was probably 'Morgan,' and he possessed all the typical Celtic passion and obstinacy. Pelagius reopened the agitation against the various lax practices among this or that group of Catholics, and he set about denouncing the half-converted who surrounded the sanctuary, the nominal Christians whom baptism had not altered one jot. His harsh moralizing and his intransigent asceticism were extraordinarily successful, especially as his example was as good as a sermon amongst circles of devout believers. The British monk, with his spare figure, heavy jowl, and threatening expression, was looked upon as a kind of prophet.

Very gradually, something which, in the beginning, had been no more than a moral attitude, a kind of Christian stoicism, quite compatible with the principles of the Church, organized itself into a body of doctrine under the influence of two of Pelagius's followers: Celestius and Julian of Eclano, an Italian bishop. *Pelagianism* proclaimed the predominance of will; even when he does not *want* to do good and does not *do* good, man *can* do it simply by virtue of his own natural powers. It is untrue that there is an essential weakness in his nature, a secret urge which is pushing him towards evil; original sin does not exist, and Adam, created mortal and lustful, has harmed us only by his example. It follows, therefore, that baptism is not absolutely necessary, and that sanctifying grace is not indispensable to a godly life; that there is no need, since the will of man alone is concerned in the matter, for 'the divine authority to penetrate the heart.' Consequently the Redemption loses its meaning as a regeneration from death into life: at best it is an example of elevation towards God.

Such a doctrine strips religion of all its supernatural character, reducing it to pure moralism. It denies the usefulness of Christ's sacrifice, and makes prayer superfluous. Why should I pray for salvation, since I alone can save myself? Everything that is so wonderfully comforting in Christianity disappears—even the very picture of Jesus taking upon Himself the sins of men in order to rid them of their miseries and lift them up to God. But in the beginning at least this deviation from the truth was not easily recognizable, for in many ways Pelagius and his followers appeared to be remarkably good Christians; their doctrine only crystallized slowly and many of the Church's leaders did not detect the heresy. As soon as he came to hear of it, Augustine, for one, was not deceived for a single moment.

He must have felt an instinctive revulsion against this haughty naturalism, this secular and voluntarist moral philosophy. After all, personal experience had taught him only too well how feeble is the will of man, and how indispensable the help of God! 'Even before I heard of the doctrines of Pelagius, I was refuting them in my books,' he wrote. As soon as he did hear of them he had but one aim: to defend God's rights against them.

The anti-Pelagian controversy was to be a delicate and complex one. Of all the leaders of the Church, Augustine alone perhaps gives the impression of possessing a constantly clear picture of the citation and of pursuing a settled design. As early as 411, when Pelagianism reached Africa from Gaul, the Bishop of Hippo attacked it, and he had it condemned the same year at the Council of Carthage. He refuted it in treatises which have become famous—those on the *Merits of Sinners* and the *Baptism of Children*—and he set against it the true doctrine of Catholicism in his great works on *The Spirit and the Letter* and *Nature and Grace*. Then, when the Church in Palestine allowed itself to be outwitted by the heretic, and actually went as far as absolving him at the Council of Diospolis (415), Augustine refused to be discouraged. He pursued the heresy until its condemnation by Rome. The Council of Carthage of 416 prepared the way for this, and the actual condemnation was pronounced by Pope Innocent I in 417.[1] At the same time Augustine's treatises on the *Grace of Christ* and *Original Sin* diligently repeated the true doctrine, examining it in every detail. And when, at the end, with Pelagius and Celestius banished from the scene, Julian of Eclano in his turn took up the essentials of their argument, Augustine prepared to let fly the deadly dart of his second treatise, *Against Julian*; death alone stayed his hand.

Thus, in this case as in the others, Augustine's campaign against heresy simultaneously ridded Catholicism of a serious danger and resulted in actual doctrinal progress. The Church emerged from the long Pelagian conflict, not merely victorious, but better armed doctrinally. In the face of Pelagian moralism, which reduced religion from an exchange of obligations and recompenses to a system of good behaviour in which the true spiritual life was utterly lacking, St Augustine affirmed the fundamentally religious nature of Catholicism, its mystery, that is to say, its Grace. The central idea which he developed is summed up in the reproach of St Paul, the saint who had influenced him so deeply at the time of his own spiritual crisis: 'What have you that you have not received?' Grace, good works, even faith itself, only exist with divine help. When we do good it is God within

---

[1] It was on the occasion of this condemnation that St Augustine, in the course of a sermon, uttered a phrase which tradition has summed up thus: 'Rome has spoken, the matter is settled.' This phrase has acquired the status of a proverb.

us who is responsible; we are all dependent on Him. God could easily have abandoned this 'mass of perdition,' which, since the fall of Adam, constitutes humanity, to eternal damnation. In fact, His mercy, freely given, extricates certain souls from it—without any merit on their part consonant with the immensity of this gift. Such is the Augustinian doctrine of Grace, which, properly understood, is not a blow aimed at human liberty, since this liberty is all the greater when it forswears the illusions of the world and surrenders itself more wholly to the mercy and Grace of God. Pushing the logic of his ideas even further, St Augustine admits that there are some souls which are *predestined*, which are summoned by God even before their birth and led by Him towards salvation—which seems to indicate that those not so chosen are, in the same circumstances, predestined to hell. *Seems* to indicate, mark you: since, for St Augustine, in reality, the *good* which Grace necessitates and the *evil* which, considered as evil, the creature does by himself are very different. In short, he rested this concept on Christ's infinite charity; understood in too narrow a sense it was to be the origin of the violent dispute of Calvinism and Jansenism. The Catholic Church has never adhered to it. But, dismissing certain excesses, due to the very violence of the battle in the course of which the doctrine was elaborated, it must be recognized that St Augustine worked harder than anyone else to examine more deeply some of the essential mysteries of the Christian faith. The title of 'Doctor of Grace,' which is often given him, is more than amply justified.[1]

Such was the direction of all the battles fought by St Augustine. He waged them with savage energy until his dying breath,[2] but, unlike so many polemical writers, he never let himself stray to the point of confusing the details of the struggle with the essential subject at stake. Augustine saw in the heresies of his own day permanent tendencies of the human mind,[3] and he fought them by setting up a doctrinal construction which went beyond the event of the moment and rested on permanent foundations. Perhaps his genius shows most clearly

---

[1] It must be noted, however, that certain points remained to be settled, and these were the object of lively discussions among the *semi-Pelagians*. There was the question of free-will in human nature, the question of the proportion of Grace to the efforts of man, the question of the universality of salvation. Starting with Prosper of Aquitaine, a pupil of St Augustine, continuing with Pope Leo the Great, the matter was not definitely settled until the following century, as a result of the action of St Caesar of Arles at the Council of Orange, and the papal approbation which followed it.

[2] At the very end of his life he still had to face the Arian heresy, which he had come across very little in Africa until then. After the Vandal invasion he identified it with the Barbarian peril.

[3] In a slightly paradoxical fashion Giovanni Papini has noted that the tendency of which Manichaeism was the fourth-century expression is not far removed from theosophy; that Donatism, in some respects, is a forerunner of Lutheranism; and that some of Pelagius's ideas on original innocence evoke advance impressions of Jean-Jacques Rousseau.

in the way his knowledge of the present enabled him to build for the future.

## INTELLIGENCE IN THE SERVICE OF CHRIST

To put it briefly, St Augustine's historic mission was to sense the needs of the future and to prepare for them.  Alive at one of the most important turning-points in history, a clear-sighted witness of the collapse of an entire world, he stands on the threshold of the new era, like the spokesman and the guide of distressed humanity.  It might be said that four centuries of Christianity had only made such efforts and fought such battles in order to have them completed and summed up in this one powerful personality.  It is he who seeks to effect a synthesis of these still scattered results, and his philosophy is to serve as a beacon for generations yet unborn.

As the ancient world collapsed all the fundamental values of man and his civilization—intellectual as well as spiritual—were threatened with destruction.  The real problem was to find a way for them to survive, even when their political and social framework had been destroyed.  Augustine was essentially an intellectual, a giant of an intellectual, deeply stirred by ideas and acutely conscious of the role which the mind should play.  He once wrote to a disciple of his: 'Don't believe for a moment that God hates that very quality in us by which He has raised us above the animals.  God does not want us to think that He is preventing us from searching and finding out the meaning of things!  Work to understand, with all your heart!'  But this intellectual effort had to be aimed at something, had to have a definite end in view, in order to be effective.  Otherwise it resulted in a kind of sterile gratuitousness whose other name is decadence.  In the fourth century classical learning showed all the symptoms of senility: its creative impulse had dried up; everything led back to commentaries, summaries, grammatical studies, or rhetoric.  It gives the impression of running to a standstill, and all the wealth of a glorious past was petering out in colossal confusion.

But what Augustine, on account of his education, was able to understand, was that this classical scholarship of the past had a value which it was absolutely essential to preserve.  Before his time, Christian philosophers had sensed this obligation up to a point, or, more accurately, while criticizing pagan culture because of its idolatrous associations, they had realized that the intellectual methods of the classical world were a tool of which they could make good use.  In the second century St Justin was already working along these lines —rather novel ones for Christianity, which, in its early stages, included very few intellectuals in its ranks: later on the Christian school of Alexandria, led by Clement and Origen, openly supported this thesis, and Tertullian was forced to rally to it, despite his intransigence. By the third and fourth centuries, apart from some isolated centres of resistance, it was an almost general attitude. It was held by the great Cappadocians, by St John Chrysostom, St Jerome, and St Ambrose. It was an attitude which was to be of profound importance in determining future events, since it made Christianity the heir to a thousand years of intellectual effort and the trustee of a unique human treasure.

In a sense St Augustine stands in the same line as these great men. If one could speak of the *Platonism* of the Fathers of the Church, this term would be most applicable to him; like his master, Ambrose, he was brought up on Cicero and Virgil, whom he both criticizes and loves; and we must not forget the training as a rhetorician which he received in his boyhood. He is indeed an heir to classical learning; but is this all? At the beginning this is certainly the case; it is still so at Milan and Cassiciacum; but the fully mature Augustine, the Bishop of Hippo, is something far more than this. Close to his simple people, living a Christian life that was burdened with responsibilities, Augustine seemed to rise above cultural preoccupations and to put them back in their proper place, in the context of life itself. If the Barbarians came to-morrow, if everything collapsed to-morrow, would civilization be saved by the declamations of Cicero, the poems of Virgil, or even the sublime thoughts of Plato? No, true salvation lay elsewhere, in the living Word, which carried men beyond their bodily selves and gave the mind its true significance. So, while his predecessors had been more or less entangled in their classical culture, incapable of imagining any form of intellectual life other than that to which they were accustomed, Augustine's intuition led him to conceive new foundations for the human mind. Before his time the Fathers of the Church had thought of classical learning as a prop for Christianity; but Augustine understood that Christianity was the only bastion capable of protecting the wealth of the mind against the Barbarism which threatened.

Thus it is Christ, and only Christ, who must permeate our intelligence, who must be the alpha and omega of all the effort of the human mind. Intellectual life must be entirely consecrated to God, not simply as homage due to Him, but because it contributes directly to the spiritual life. Writing to a friend who had showed him some literary trifles, Augustine declared: 'What do these verses matter? In them I only see a soul and a mind which I cannot offer to God.' The treasure of intelligence which God has entrusted to us must be used for His glory alone. There are no human values which can be separated from the supernatural order of things. It is a perfectly logical attitude, the moral consequence of a faith which is absolute, and which absorbs the whole being: it was to be the attitude of the Middle Ages, and it is only necessary to describe it to make plain its decisive influence in the future.

Intelligence, put to the service of Christ. This means that the different branches of knowledge gain in value according to the extent to which they allow man to draw near to God and to know Him. The outstanding branch of knowledge is therefore *theology*, the science of God. It can be said that even though he did not conceive theology as something entirely complete in itself, but still occasionally associated it too much (superficially, at least) with scriptural commentary or with philosophy, it is St Augustine who contributed most to ensuring its primacy. There had been various attempts before him, often remarkable attempts—if somewhat hesitant ones—those of Justin or Irenaeus; above all, there had been Origen's great work, on which the Church in the East had been nurtured. St Augustine, however, is the real founder of the theological school of the West; even if the theology dates formally from the Middle Ages, it would never have existed at all without his penetrating flashes of intelligence. With Augustine, speculation on dogma, the attempt to elaborate the gift of the Revelation, assume an importance which they were never to lose henceforth. Theology, which he conceives as the science and the understanding of faith, has as its object the 'production, nourishment, defence, and affirmation of the faith of the Saviour, which leads to true happiness.' It is doubly blessed, both by virtue of its object, the revelation of truth, and by the enlightenment it derives from God's Wisdom. Thus all intellectual activity leads to it; we have seen how the campaigns against the heresies led the saint to formulate decisive theological principles. Aside from his polemical writing, one massive work dominates this side of his activity: the treatise *On the Trinity*. In this he summons all branches of learning to his aid, metaphysics and psychology, the conclusions of Plato and Aristotle, and all his scriptural knowledge, in order to bring human intelligence face to face with a mystery which surpasses human understanding. Together with the *Summa* of St Thomas, the *De Trinitate* is one of the twin bastions of Christian speculative writing.

If learning to know God constitutes the fundamental human effort, the human soul has been given a means of achieving this: a text exists which bring us the Word of God. Therefore the Bible, the sacred book, the expression of the Word (this same Bible which the young student at Carthage had spurned so contemptuously), must be studied above all other books. *Exegesis*, the science of Scripture, had been flourishing for a long time. Although his exegetic work is immense, St Augustine does not dominate this field: he does not possess the critical qualities of St Jerome (whose very principles he seems to have found difficult to understand), nor, in the interpretation of symbols, the lofty majesty of the Alexandrians. But he did make it very clear that henceforth true culture must be biblical and scriptural, and he applied to his studies the methods he had learned as a grammarian. Moreover to his study of inspired Scripture he added the study of the living Tradition through which Christ perpetuates Himself in His Church. He was the first great writer to collate the labours of his predecessors in the history of Christian philosophy: he was an enthusiastic reader of Origen, Tertullian, St Cyprian, and, above all, of St Ambrose, was fairly well acquainted with the works of the Cappadocian Fathers, Basil, Gregory of Nazianzos, and even with those of Hilary of Poitiers, and he thereby opened up an entirely new avenue of culture. The Middle Ages are more indebted to Augustine for his study of the Fathers than for his exegesis.

These branches of knowledge are strictly orientated towards the divine: did St Augustine conceive of any others? Does he admit that certain efforts of human intelligence, though not directly aimed at the fundamental goal, can still be useful in helping man to approach the truth? This is one of the most often debated questions and it turns on this formula: does a *philosophy* exist, as distinct from theology, and did Augustine conceive it as doing so? Some critics have exalted the philosophy of the convert of Milan to the point of misunderstanding the part played by faith in the progress of his thought; others, more numerous, have denied that he possessed a separate philosophic sense, and have suggested that everything in his mind was subordinate to theology. The truth lies somewhere between these two extremes. If by 'Christian philosophy' we mean an effort of thought supported by reason, in other words, an effort in which revelation and faith are not called upon for support, like elements of proof in practical demonstrations, or even if we mean a doctrine elaborated by Christians and used by them to express their faith and to aid their search for God, then undoubtedly St Augustine was a Christian philosopher in the fullest sense of the term. This does not imply that reason can attain truth through its own powers alone, nor that philosophy must be entirely separate from supernatural knowledge; but it should be separable from it, and this Augustine understood perfectly; he laid down the bases for this separation. He himself defined his fundamental attitude: 'Before faith you must understand in order to believe: after faith you must believe in order to understand.' Thus philosophy and theology ought to be distinct, yet associated.

The effort made in the East by Origen and his innumerable successors, and in the West by Tertullian, Minucius Felix, Arnobus, Lactantius, and Ambrose with varying success, was taken up anew by the philosopher of Hippo and given a new significance by him.

Undoubtedly his starting-point is not always nicely placed between the areas of reason and of faith.   This great realist, set in the midst of humanity, has none of the qualities of systematic analysis which were to be the glory of St Thomas Aquinas.   His gifts are very different; his doctrine is slanted towards life.   Nevertheless, with Augustine, Christian philosophy took a decisive step forward; it reached maturity. He relied on the bases of the Neo-Platonic system, but he crowned them with the idea of the creator-God instead of with the nebulous, immanent God of Plotinus.   He paved the way in so many directions —psychology and moral philosophy, the theory of ideas, the doctrine of knowledge.   His conception of *illumination*, an intellectual perception of fundamental truths, sustained by God, and leading to Him, has an endless richness.   Of course he does not explain everything, any more than he constructs a complete system.   But in the history of Christian philosophy he played a role analogous to that played by Plato in classical philosophy; he encouraged men to think.

That was his real role in this field.   He led those who followed him to ponder, along Christian lines, on the great eternal questions.   In mustering intelligence to Christ's service he literally saved it.   Is it necessary to add that he was to play another saving role, though on a lower plane, during one of the darkest periods in history?   This great intellectual and book-lover, for whom books were an essential part of life, from the *Hortensius* of Cicero to the *Enneads* of Plotinus, impressed a respect for and a love of books on all who came under his influence.   In a later age, when the work-rooms of the monastic copyists were the last refuge of philosophy, it was probably because the memory of St Augustine was venerated there.   The last of the great Latin writers, the connecting bond between classical antiquity and modern culture, was it not his style which served as a model for those last Latinists who survived the Dark Ages?   The Middle Ages were scarcely to know classical literature at all save from the quotations of St Augustine. . . .

Thus Augustine saved the vital weapon for the society which, much later, was to be born out of the great catastrophes; he prepared the way for the future rebirth of men's minds.   But it was not merely spiritual values that he acted to preserve, but social virtues also.

### 'THE CITY OF GOD'

At the end of August 410 a dreadful piece of news reached Africa, causing great consternation there.   Rome had just been sacked by the Barbarians!   The ancient capital, inviolate since the far-off days of the Gallic invasion, had been stormed by the followers of Alaric the

Goth, and was still shuddering from their outrages.[1] Very soon refugees began to trickle in, bringing all the frightful details of the story with them. 'Ruin upon ruin, fire and plunder, massacre and torture.' It all seemed unbelievable, such was the picture of Rome's majesty which still dominated men's minds; and yet it was true. At Bethlehem the redoubtable St Jerome wept. And at Hippo, expressing the thought of all his people, the bishop exclaimed—we can almost hear his voice breaking with emotion: 'The body of Peter is at Rome! The body of Paul is at Rome! There at Rome lie Lawrence and the bodies of the martyrs! Rome—distressed and devastated! Destruction and slaughter everywhere! Where are the memories of our saints?'

But for a man of Augustine's stamp the terrible event was much more than an occasion for lamentation. For a Christian even the most frightful catastrophes had a meaning within the unfathomable intentions of God. So Augustine's reaction to the news was what might have been expected of a man of his temperament and his faith. He reacted to it as a philosopher, a writer, and a believer, but his reaction held too the understanding of the genius. He went beyond the episode itself and built the future from it. Everyone else at the time was struck numb with horror; they could actually see a world crumbling before their eyes, sliding into the abyss, they could see nothing beyond this, and they expected to see nothing. Augustine, however, quickly collected his thoughts. The fall of Rome was not the end of *the* world, but the indication of the end of *a* world; it was one catastrophe among many others, similar to that experienced by Troy. Civilizations, like men, are mortal: this incident is not important in itself. What is important is that we should understand the meaning of this drama, its place in time and in the divine scheme. . . . Starting from a wholly Christian viewpoint Augustine arrives at the only legitimate historical conception; in life's continuous stream it is quite certain that the capture of Rome is not a halt in time, nor even a symbolic milepost, and that man's proper task is not to mourn, but to build for the morrow.

Augustine reacted, as he so often did, by making a polemic issue out of it. He had needed Pelagius, in order to clarify his doctrine of Grace; to undertake his great masterpiece and evolve his philosophy of history, he needed an adverse event. The pagans were flinging remarks such as this from mouth to mouth: 'It is in Christian times that Rome is devastated. Rome flourished, did she not, whilst men offered sacrifices to the gods? You Christians pray to your God and you have forbidden us to pray to ours: now see what has happened!'

[1] The incident is studied later in the book. See Chapter II, section: 'The Stages in the Drama.'

Did this propaganda affect the Christians themselves? It must have done, since Augustine judged it necessary to refute it. Pressed by several friends, led by Count Marcellinus, he began his task towards the end of 412. Despite all the burdens of his episcopal duties, he worked furiously at it for thirteen years. It grew month by month, spreading far beyond the boundaries of its original subject, rising to heights never before attained. When he stopped writing, towards the beginning of 426, the masterpiece comprised no less than twenty-two books: this then is his *City of God*.

It is impossible to do justice to a book which is one of the monuments of human genius in a few lines of description. It embodies a philosophy of history, a theory of the State and of social life, and a précis of the relationships between the spiritual and the temporal authorities; at the same time it is a kind of manual of the art of living in times of trouble, a book of consolation. It begins with the sack of Rome and ends with the Day of Judgment. Now wandering off into interminable detail on the customs of the Barbarians, the various philosophical systems, the wars of the Empire, the hierarchies of the angels, even the scandals of the day, now summing up an idea, and demonstrating it in definite terms, it is a massive, difficult, and inexhaustible book, like all the great masterpieces of the world. In this masterly synthesis everything finds unity, earthly phenomena and divine wishes, knowledge of the past, prescience of the future. The genius's eye takes in the entire human destiny and orders it around the Christian religion, which, if one only knows how to understand it, is 'of lasting value to the human spirit'—in other words, he goes back to the origins of human society, which it explains, and leads one forward to the end of all things. And it is all done, not by dull arguments, by dry, empty phrases, but is enlivened throughout by a reference to the eternal problems, making us understand all the time that this drama of history is our own drama, and that our destiny hangs on its result. One eminent commentator [1] has remarked: 'The *City of God* is theology brought to life in the historical framework of humanity, just as the *Confessions* is theology brought to life in the experience of one soul: in both books God is the one and only inspiration.'

The title, which was almost certainly inspired by certain Donatist works, derives from the biblical tradition of the Psalms and the Epistle to the Hebrews, which promised believers a perfect and ineffable city, a place of eternal justice. But, opposite this ideal city, was there not another, the kingdom of the Devil, the city of sin? St Ambrose had already insisted on this antithesis. It is the basis for St Augustine's book. 'Two loves have built these two cities. In the terrestrial city it is the love of self, flaunted even in defiance of God.

[1] Father Portalié.

In the celestial city it is the love of God, pushed to the very exclusion
of self . . . we can separate humanity into two types, those who live
according to the will of man, and those who live according to the will
of God.' Thus history is a drama, a drama confronting these two
human groups, and its object must be to raise the city of men as much
as possible towards its divine archetype, the ideal city. Put another
way, the effort of civilization should be to bring man nearer his divine
destination. Baudelaire summed this up in an unsurpassed phrase, the
day that he declared that true civilization was to be found neither in the
winds nor the mists but in the 'diminution of the traces of original sin.'

Reduced to a scholarly scheme, the plan of the *City of God* can be
fairly accurately summed up like this: Books I to X are a vigorous
attack on paganism, which is unqualified to ensure man's earthly prosperity, and even more unfit to prepare for their eternal happiness;
Books XI to XXII contain the exposition of the doctrine of the two
cities, their origins, developments across the centuries, and their ends.
But, viewed on a higher plane, the logic of this work is that of a five-
act Greek drama, the acts showing, one by one, man created in God's
image, man growing up in pride and falling from grace, then God
taking man, teaching him the true principles, and Christ showing him,
by His example, how it is both necessary and possible to regain God's
likeness; finally, on the last day, there is the great decision, the great
division, the separation of men according to their own choosing. It
is therefore divided in turn into the Creation, the Fall, the Revelation,
the Incarnation, and the Resurrection. The extraordinary thing is
that such a dizzy mass of metaphysical speculation should result in a
collection of concrete principles, of marvellous value.

This is the real significance of this book. Writing in a style
analogous to that of the apologist of the second century, but soaring
far above the methods of the scholars and disputants, Augustine set
down Christianity as the one undeniable fact, the one thing which can
stand the test of time. A society may crumble, but what does it
matter? Another is there ready to take its place, against which
nothing will prevail. In order to save the world it is necessary to put
Christ's principles into practice, to apply them in the city of men as
fully as possible. The heroic effort of the 'Revolution of the Cross'
results, in this great revolutionary work, in this serene declaration:
even if history must wipe out the past, all will not be lost; a bastion
exists in which the real values of man will be saved.

Thus it is this tragic book, haunted by the spectre of abysses, which,
more than the easy urbanity of a Symmachus or an Ausonius, or the
resigned scepticism of the 'last of the Romans' brings humanity the
one valuable lesson of hope. 'The world is growing old, the world
perishes, the world is about to disappear! But you, Christian, you

need fear nothing, for, like the eagle, you shall have your youth renewed!'[1]

## FOUNDATIONS FOR THE FUTURE

The idea that Christianity carried with it a renewal of the values of man and of society was as old, in essence, as Christianity itself: had not St Paul spoken of 'the new man' born of Christ? For four hundred years generations of the faithful had drawn more and more complete conclusions from these premises. By the end of the fourth century the conception was fundamental to all believers. St Ambrose had already applied it to many aspects of the social and political order. For St Augustine the starting-point is obviously the same. But whereas his predecessors had only an intuitive sense of the revolution they were in the act of carrying out, rather than a complete and systematic picture of the whole, Augustine, with penetrating logic, quickly seized on all the conclusions of the idea. For example, St Ambrose, St Hilary of Poitiers, and St John Chrysostom had perfectly understood the necessity of defending the Church against the demands of the State: but St Augustine proceeded to build up a general theory of the relationship between the spiritual and temporal authorities. His action was inspired by the conviction that, not only was Christianity the most comforting of religions for man's soul, and the most satisfying for his mind, but that it was also, in the order of things on this earth, the answer to everything. In adopting, as far as it could, the divine city for its model, the terrestrial city would rest on unshakable foundations. What sprang from this conviction was nothing less than a theory which embraced every aspect of human life, a society ordered according to the law of Christ.

One precept permeates the theory: 'Thou shalt love the Lord thy God with the love of thy whole heart, and thy whole soul, and thy whole mind, and thy whole strength, and thou shalt love thy neighbour as thyself.' Three consequences followed from this. Firstly, that the ultimate aim of human institutions is to make man's heart glow with the love of God, or, to put it another way, to work to realize the desire of the prayer: 'Thy kingdom come!' In order to do this, since to love God and to love man are one and the same thing, they must be steeped in charity. And, finally, because he is called upon to love God, because he is, as Cardinal de Bérulle has so magnificently expressed it, 'un néant capable de Dieu,' man carries within him a unique value, on condition that he never forgets his supernatural goal.

[1] Indeed, there are several weak passages in the *City of God*. Augustine often hangs his examples on the scientific knowledge of his period (he is not the only apologist and theologian to do this!). His reasoning, his analogous comparisons (the six days of the Creation set in relation to historical epochs), are often open to criticism. But these faults do not fundamentally compromise a book of such solid worth.

The priority of the spiritual factor, the necessity of the brotherhood of man, the paramount importance of the individual over all values and all needs; all St Augustine's moral philosophy, sociology, and political thought is no more than the putting into practice of 'the greatest of all the commandments.'

The moral philosophy of St Augustine is not the most original part of his work by any means. Although on several occasions he shows himself to be a shrewd and accurate moralist, he contributed nothing new to a field well covered by Christians who had gone before him. For Augustine, just as for St Ambrose or St John Chrysostom, the ancient Platonic virtues of justice, wisdom, strength, and temperance are given a new lease of life by the Christian faith and take on a different meaning. Time and time again he insists on the importance of the role which charity takes in this transmutation of virtues. It should be noted, however, that he relied far more than his predecessors on the spiritual element which must supernaturalize all human activities. Practising morality does not simply mean obeying abstract commandments, it means a reunion with the one and only model that man has. It is perfectly legitimate to pursue happiness, but the only real happiness resides in God. In several cases this insistence results in a new light being thrown on various fields of human activity. Thus, when Augustine talks of love, when he shows it to be completely permissible within the framework of marriage, he is going much further than his predecessors had. They justified marriage by bodily exigencies ('better to marry than to feel the heat of passion,' said St Paul) or on grounds of social utility, in order to bring about the 'growth and increase' of the human race. For Augustine the love of man and woman, which he related, according to the ancient biblical tradition, to the love between God and the human soul, has a real spiritual value. The communion of hearts helps the effort of elevation towards God. Here he puts before the world the great idea of 'sacramental love,' something entirely different from the love which is concerned with nothing but physical pleasure, or the love inspired by social necessity; this specifically Christian concept has played an immense part in Western civilization.[1]

---

[1] The expression 'sacramental love' is the Abbé Maurice Zundel's. The idea has been brilliantly developed by Denis Rougemont in his *L'Amour et l'Occident*. It is interesting to see that the noble Augustinian notion of the *completeness* of the marriage bond between man and woman, the complete union of flesh and spirit, of body and soul, is to-day regaining its full importance. For centuries this fruitful ideal has been lost from sight. The courtly ideal and its seventeenth-century successor dissociated sentimental love from conjugal love, the latter being judged inferior because of its physical appurtenances. Paul Renaudin, in his book, *Amour sacre, amour profane*, which is far too little known, has written penetratingly on this topic, and his pages reflect little credit on the age of Louis XIV. For far too long marriage was regarded as a second-class sacrament. The Jansenists, though disciples of St Augustine, came to believe this!

Social goods must be subordinated, even more than the personal goods of the soul, to the double precept of loving God and one's neighbour.   Augustine shows himself at his most constructive in his analysis of this subordination and its consequences.   It is significant to see that the great idea, which, much later on, was to be expanded in the majestic tomes of the *City of God*, had already been expressed in an enthusiastic page of *De Moribus* by the newly baptized Milan convert. There he showed the Church as ordering all social activities, regulating family relationships such as those between masters and their slaves, making the people obey their rulers, but teaching those rulers to be devoted to the public good, eliminating from human relationships the causes of hate and war. . . .   It is a magnificent picture, and was to be systematized in the great masterpiece of his maturity.

We cannot develop, or even enumerate, here all the sociological and political points on which St Augustine set forth the Christian ideal so firmly, and in such lasting principles, that they have never since been outdone, not even in our own age.   Suffice it to say that there is scarcely a single problem touching on any social aspect whatsoever which the prodigious genius of the saint of Hippo has not noticed, gone into, and almost always solved.   What about his consideration of man in society?   He saw clearly the degrees and limits of collective demands.   For him *the family* was the first natural grouping beyond the single individual: willed by God, it is the unit forming the basis of human society.   The *motherland* is a kind of extension of it.   St Augustine possessed a lucidity of thought which many modern thinkers have lost, and he never confused the motherland with her administrative trappings—that is to say, with the *State*.   The motherland is a living reality to him: 'a sensual passion,' as Péguy has called it, a jumble of emotional loyalties and concrete demands.   It seems much more real to him than the cumbersome Roman State, the despotic, centralizing Empire which he obviously distrusts.   It can actually be said that this man, who knew no other rule save that of the Empire, had the astonishing foresight to envisage the birth of future nation-states, which he saw as respecting one another's rights, within a sort of federation of equal members.   This wonderful picture was not to take shape until very much later on, when, at about the turn of the year 1000, the baptized peoples of France, Hungary, and Poland tended to develop into national entities.   It was only then that the idea of *Christendom* was to assert itself.   The genius of St Augustine was to mould the Future.   As understood by him, the motherland has her especial place in the hierarchy of human obligations; she can even demand great sacrifices.   But her real purpose is to give a foretaste, here on earth, of the heavenly community based on brotherly love that exists in the city of God.

As for the State, St Augustine spoke of it at great length and in great detail. It was one of his principal preoccupations. We realize that he had in front of him the example of a State whose increasing decrepitude did not prevent it from being oppressive—quite the contrary! The late Empire, the Empire in decline, was in fact a gigantic system of enslavement. And here Augustine makes a declaration of great importance: the State can never be the supreme goal; the Christian is not only and not primarily a citizen. This does not mean to say that St Augustine was unconscious of the State's natural right, and consequently of its legitimacy. An authority exists because God has willed it to do so. 'The will of the Almighty gives power to some and not to others,' he wrote, being in this respect a rigid disciple of St Paul in the Epistle to the Romans (xiii. 1-2). However, it is essential that the principles of government should be consistent with the ideal of the spiritual destiny of man. He says repeatedly that the ruler's duty is to promote the rule of justice! Charlemagne was to ponder over this precept; later on St Henry and St Louis were to put it into practice. When this ideal is betrayed the State becomes unlawful, and on this basis Augustine declares the Roman Empire to be 'unworthy of the name of State,' because it has not known real justice, the justice of Christ. Men should obey those who use their authority to promote amity among men with a view to eternal happiness. Wicked rulers should not be obeyed. . . . The political science of St Augustine is based on these two precepts.

Contrary to what he has often been understood as saying, St Augustine never wrote that the entire State was sinful and the work of the devil; he did not equate the city of man with his city of perdition. He said, on the contrary, that sin very often disorganized the State and even caused its disintegration. He saw in *wars* one of the most obvious signs of this. 'Without justice are these kingdoms anything but associations bent on brigandage?' Augustine fully recognized that there could be just wars, when a people was attacked, and rose to defend itself against the aggressor. But were not even wars like these the consequences of sin, for 'does not peace rest on eternal happiness alone'? It follows from this that Christians must do all within their power to maintain peace and to abolish war, even though they know that here on earth peace can only be a precarious ideal. They must try to eliminate the real causes of violence and hate, the vices which cling to the sinful heart.[1]

Man is, therefore, the member of a family, the faithful son of a

[1] We can find in the philosophy of St Augustine valuable principles for a real League of Nations, in which each people retains its own language, customs, and institutions, and in which a collective authority resolves disputes by arbitration. Augustine distrusted the over-controlled, over-centralized Roman Empire of his own day, and he therefore visualized a kind of federal union of peoples.

motherland, the citizen of a State. But he must never forget that he has a divine vocation, in other words, he belongs to a body superior to all these other human associations: the *Church*. How does St Augustine interpret this relationship? In the city of God the Church appears as the terrestrial incarnation of the kingdom of Heaven; but in fact she understands also those men who are not dedicated to God alone, the sinners and the wicked. She encompasses humanity in its entirety, and strains to push it heavenwards. This infinitely humane and comforting conception makes the least significance of the baptized a humble brick in the great structure built by generation upon generation, whose summit is Christ.

This tangible association of men, orientated towards their spiritual ends, finds itself, in practice, in close contact with that other human association, directed to very different ends: the State. This weighty problem of the *relations between Church and State* began to rear its head in urgent terms as soon as Constantine adhered to Christianity, a decision which, if not actually Machiavellian, was at any rate made with definite purposes in mind. Each succeeding reign aggravated it. Should the Church become the State's collaborator, which would mean, in fact, the Church's dependence on the State? We know that her leaders refused any such abdication of their authority instinctively. St Augustine built up a doctrine from this spontaneous attitude.

For him—and this is the essential point—the 'terrestrial city' and the 'celestial city' are fundamentally opposed to one another, since they are dependent on two quite contrary *spirits*. In practice Church and State can collaborate: no matter, so long as we never forget that the objects of their efforts are radically different. The Church, an organization charged with the task of assuring the salvation of the souls of the faithful, possesses special rights, which cannot be challenged. She has a *jus sacrum*, which Augustine claims for her. More than this: since the Church is the peculiar possessor and guardian of Christ's justice and charity, and since it must be remembered that the State is legitimate in so far as it serves the practical fulfilment of these virtues, it follows that the Church has supervisory powers over the State. A capital declaration. During the centuries which were to follow, the Church's capacity to defend her independence against the civil authorities—sometimes successfully, sometimes indifferently, in extremely difficult conditions—resulted from her having been permeated by this Augustinian doctrine. She was to go even further: for did not the idea of a control exercised by the spiritual power over the temporal contain a germ of the doctrine of *theocracy*—the 'Utopia,' of Maritain's, which would attempt to make the Church pass from spiritual control even to the exercise of temporal power? St Augustine never went as far as what was to be termed 'Augustinian polity';

his conception of the two cities, of the two opposing spirits, saved him from such error.

However, this is not the only field in which his remarkably well-balanced philosophy has been distorted by his successors. His doctrine of the employment of the *secular arm* furnishes another example of similar exaggeration. The necessary harmony between Church and State led him to claim from the latter help and protection for the Church. She has a special *right* to this protection, when false religions cannot claim a similar favour. How far ought this protection to go? The question came up during the Donatist episode, when the violence of the heretics led the Empire to deal severely with them. On this point St Augustine's philosophy shows itself infinitely flexible, dominated at one and the same time by the ideal of charity, and by a thorough understanding of the reality of the situation. In practice, toleration of a non-Catholic cult seems quite proper to him, since he relies more on the power of the truth to extend the dominion of Christ than on the support of Caesar. But this toleration has its limits. If the peace of the community is disturbed, if the law is brought into disrepute, stringent measures can be taken: he entirely approved of the steps taken against the Donatists, but he never asked that the Manichaeans or the Jews should be forcibly converted. Besides, the use of force had its limits: he expressly says that it must never go as far as the death penalty, at least among Christians, and that it must be preceded by a charitable exploration of the areas of agreement. 'Freedom of error is the worst death of the soul,' but violence is not meet in the sight of God. Unhappily these rich yet complex ideas were to be exploited by human passions and given meanings quite contradictory to Augustine's own. The stakes on which the heretics of the Middle Ages were to suffer were claimed to represent the Augustinian doctrine of the 'secular arm,' but Augustine himself never justified them.

Thus, in all the solutions proposed by this genius of a man for the great problems of humanity, we are struck by the profound wisdom of his attitude; he enunciates rules inspired by positive right, completing or developing them with a keen sense of the Christian contribution and of the future interests of Christianity. He is never found taking up extreme positions—they might almost be called anarchical—as is the case with some of the earlier Fathers of the Church. For instance, when faced with the most tragic problem of the classical world, that of *slavery*, he does not offer the solution which would have been that of the facile demagogue. Augustine does not condemn the institution of slavery as such; he is acutely conscious of the economic needs of the society in which he lives. Nor does he justify it by natural law, as Aristotle does. No, indeed. 'God did not create man to dominate other men,' he writes, 'but to dominate the animals!' The existence of slavery is like a kind of punishment inflicted upon sinful humanity, and this institution, abnormal in itself, has become conformable with Divine Grace. It follows that slaves do not have the right to rebel against their servitude; but their masters must never forget that their slave is not merely a man like themselves (Seneca had already expressed this admirably) but a brother in Christ. They should treat their slaves, therefore, as a father treats the members of his own family, and, whenever they could, they should give them their freedom: 'Until the day when iniquity passes away, when all human sovereignty disappears, when God becomes all in all!'

Augustine displays the same extraordinary wisdom and moderation in his handling of another delicate problem: that of *worldly wealth*. God has placed the goods of the world at man's disposal: 'They should not be condemned without reflection.' They are there to serve man, and not for men to serve them: all must lead towards God. *Wealth* does not seem to him bad in itself: in several passages he recognizes the right to worldly property. In his eyes it forms a part of those gifts 'given us by God, of which we men must make good use.' 'Let the rich build the solid foundations of the future on the treasures of charity in order to attain the true life.' Give more alms, make good as far as possible the injustice of a society wounded by sin; the forgiveness of the rich man is in the social function which he assumes. These ideas are found over and over again in the Christian doctrine of money, right up to the present day.

The Christian philosophy of *work* is set out in full by St Augustine. In contrast to a certain ancient tradition which considered that work degraded man ('One cannot make a citizen out of an artisan,' said Aristotle), the Christian doctrine that comes out of the *City of God* asserts the dignity of labour. Citing the examples of St Joseph and St Paul, St Augustine shows that human labour is compatible with sanctity, and that it is actually an important element in it. He brings out perfectly the creative value of labour, and its part in the process of atonement and spiritual purification. He grades the various types of work in accordance with these double values—human and spiritual: intellectual work he regards as superior in worth to all others. Regarding agriculture he highly commends its cosmic harmony with the work of God; of the work of the artisan he aptly says that man's tasks should not be such that they prevent him from fixing his soul on higher things—oh, how our work holds us in bondage! Finally Augustine does not expressly condemn commerce, but he is not unaware that in its pursuit justice is often disregarded,[1] and he regards it with suspicion. . . .

---

[1] He expressly condemned loans where interest was demanded. This was the customary attitude of the Fathers of the Church and is largely explained by the frightful extension of the practice of usury in the late Empire.

These few pages can only indicate the main axes of Augustine's immense philosophical construction. Admittedly, after St Augustine, many points on which more precise definition was necessary would remain, and it must be repeated that he did not make any fundamental innovations in respect of the explicit or implicit doctrines of the Christians who had gone before him. But only Augustine enumerated all the great human problems, showed where the Christian answers to them could be found, and, above all, linked the solutions to fundamental principles. In seeking simply to draw, in terms of logic, and from Christian premises, all the inferences useful to life here on earth, St Augustine laid the foundations for the future.

## The Lasting Influence of St Augustine

Could such a colossal literary output and such a radiant personality really remain enclosed within a minor African bishopric? In actual fact they completely overflowed these boundaries, and, even in his lifetime, St Augustine was what is nowadays known as a celebrity. It might have been thought that the modest nature of his episcopal seat, provincial and isolated as it was, would have cramped the saint's style; but the reverse occurred; with Augustine as its bishop, Hippo very soon became one of the most important centres of Christianity, the spiritual rendezvous of all who counted for anything in the Church, a crucible from which emerged the pure gold of fidelity.

He was unquestionably the most outstanding person in Africa. In theory traditionally subordinate, more or less, to the Bishop of Carthage, the staunch administrator, Aurelius, he compelled the latter's attention by the sheer marvel of his intelligence, and a sincere friendship united the two men in the same struggle for truth. Augustine assumed a spiritual primacy over the other African bishops, though he did not desire it. Many of them were his former pupils, for numerous churches in search of bishops asked for one from Hippo, the nursery of saints. Tagaste, Cirta, Uzalis, Sicca, Thenae, and Milevis were thus all governed by 'sons' of Augustine. And he dominated even those whom he had not known before his consecration. He had only to appear at a council or a meeting, and the decision of all yielded to his: his learning and his sanctity were undisputed.

And his influence extended far, far beyond Africa. The two hundred and sixty odd letters of his which survive show that he was in touch with people in Italy, Gaul, Spain, the Eastern Empire, Palestine, and Egypt. People sought his advice on every conceivable topic; he replied to them all and dealt with every subject. He dealt with the most varied problems, and the most unexpected. His correspondents come from all walks of life: they include not only bishops and senior government officials but also humble monks, troubled by the problem of Grace, or recluses experiencing difficulties with their superiors, or heads of families anxious to arrange good marriages for their children. There are some famous names among them: St Paulinus of Nola, for example, the poet-bishop, who, although extremely advanced in years and of very noble lineage, wrote to Augustine spontaneously to congratulate him on his writings, which he had read, and to which he gave the adjective 'divine.' There is the gruff St Jerome, with whom the discussion nearly turned sour, but who was disarmed by the meekness and absolute honesty of the saint of Hippo. Eventually a firm friendship was established between the two men.

Thus, over a period of more than thirty years, Augustine appeared to his contemporaries as he appears to us: as the conscience of the West, the beacon of the Church. As the years slipped by his influence only increased. When he felt the day he had been waiting for drawing near, the day on which he would see, face to face, Him whom he had loved so wholeheartedly, he was able, without the slightest difficulty, amid popular acclamation, to designate the man he judged worthy to succeed him in the see of Hippo, Heraclius. And one of the last acts of his long life is proof of the extraordinary authority of this sick old man; when the Vandals invaded Africa a few priests, and even one or two bishops, yielded to the general mood of panic and thought of fleeing. Augustine learned of this and straightway sent them a sublime letter, in which he charged them to remain faithful to the flocks in their care, to stand firm, witnessing to Christ where Providence had seen fit to place them. And as for himself, he barricaded himself in Hippo with his own people, and remained there until he died.

Death did not dim this great light. Some months after it, Pope Celestine II, writing to the bishops of Gaul, paid a striking tribute to 'this blessed memory, on whom not the slightest suspicion has ever been cast, and whose learning ranks with that of the most excellent masters.' This anticipated the decision of the Church, which not only canonized St Augustine but proclaimed him 'doctor,' and even gave him a special place in the leading rank of Christian witnesses: with St Ambrose, St Jerome, and St Gregory the Great he is one of the four 'great doctors' of the West. Doctor of the Church, Doctor of Grace, Doctor of Charity; it is indeed under these three headings that he influenced the history of dogma; but within the general historical framework of the world, his role was to be a much wider one, and, in a sense, much more decisive.

The influence of St Augustine endured from century to century, increasing continuously. Two figures suffice to give a practical demonstration of this: firstly, the libraries of Europe contain no fewer than five hundred manuscripts of the *City of God*, the oldest dating from the sixth century, and, secondly, after the invention of printing twenty-four different editions of his masterpiece were produced between 1467 and 1495—all in the short space of twenty-seven years!

In the period immediately following his death, the faithful who followed exactly in his footsteps were numerous indeed: his young friend Orosius applied Augustine's principles to his *General History*; Marius Mercator, Prosper of Acquitaine, Claudian Mamertus, and Fulgentius continued his theology; Paulinus of Pella and Ennodius of Pavia wrote *Confessions* after his model; Eugippius made a selection of his finest passages; St Caesar of Arles was continually quoting him as an authority. In the shadow epoch of the Invasions he was the un-rivalled master of every student of theology. In 534 Pope John II wrote unhesitatingly: 'It is from Augustine that the Roman Church follows and safeguards her doctrines.' Isidore of Seville and St Gregory the Great were to carry on his task.

It is not in the religious field alone that his influence was to be so penetrating and so effective. Unquestionably the political and social ideas of St Augustine weighed very heavily—and very fortu-nately—on certain consciences, and thereby considerably influenced events. It was not for nothing that Charlemagne was to make Augustine his bedside book: the idea of a 'Holy Roman Germanic Empire,' was the direct result of this. But, in addition, as Canon Bardy writes, 'political Augustinianism enabled the popes to save Christendom from the mortal grip of the German rulers.' And, on the intellectual plane, it can safely be said that all those who were to strive to live a life of philosophic speculation during the next eight centuries were to be indebted to the great Bishop of Hippo: an *Augustinianism* was to develop, which, as we have already indicated, was not always to be free from extraneous influences, influences actually conflicting with the original philosophy of Augustine himself. But the vigour of his ideas was to inspire every doctrine and every system of thought, especially the liveliest ones, up to those of St Bonaventure, St Thomas Acquinas, and Duns Scotus. Between them all he was to create an 'intellectual and spiritual relationship.'

It is easy to demonstrate that this Augustinian influence is still with us to-day. 'In our own time,' writes the Protestant author, Harnack, 'the inner, living piety found in Catholicism, and its expression, are essentially Augustinian.' Would a Pascal ever have existed had not Augustine trodden before him, groping his way towards God? How many philosophic systems would not be what they are but for the deep, fertile influence of the saint? The Cartesian *Cogito ergo sum*, Spinoz-ism, even, in a sense, the systems of Hegel and Schopenhauer, and, more directly, those of Malebranche, Kierkegaard, and Cardinal

C

Newman. . . . Augustinian theology represents one of the two great streams of living Catholic thought.   The other is Thomism, which it is quite wrong to set against Augustinianism, for at their bases the two doctrines meet and permeate each other.   And in the principles of action which the Church puts into practice to-day, in 'social Catholicism,' and in the encyclicals on the most pressing of our modern problems, it is not difficult to see his decisive influence at work. Indeed Pope Pius XI made this very clear in the encyclical *Ad salutem*, published on the fifteenth centenary of the saint's death.

Thus this man, who died so long ago, still seems conspicuously present among us.   Of how many people can this be said?   And he seems not merely present, but close to us.   We feel the same closeness to him that we feel for the living, for people of solid flesh and blood. Whoever takes the trouble to study his character and his work thoroughly cannot help loving the man as much as he venerates the saint.   In the problems which he set himself, in the depth of his feelings and his aspirations, in the passion which he put into everything he did, he impresses himself upon us like one of our own contemporaries.   Dare we add that even his sanctity is of the kind which most moves us?   It is such a simple kind of sanctity, which needs no miracles [1] to make us believe in it, and which springs, like a sublime flower, from the very ground ploughed by our most familiar sins. . . .

Historically St Augustine's influence on the generations which were to follow him appears to us to be that of a powerful enlightener. Let us jump eight or nine centuries, and consider Western society at the moment when it regained its equilibrium following the terrible chaos of the invasions and the era of disorganized Barbarism.   Look at the civilization of St Bernard and St Louis, of Dante and St Thomas, of the cathedrals and the Crusades!   It is strikingly clear that the Middle Ages owe their intellectual inspiration to St Augustine.   All the scholastic leaders of the Western world were disciples of Augustine and recognized their debt to him: Scotus Erigena, Abelard, Anselm of Canterbury, St Bernard, the Victorinuses, Master Eckhart, and St Thomas, the last-named being his only equal.   In the literary sphere, and grammatically, as well as spiritually, medieval scholarship depended closely on his books, notably on the *Christian Doctrine*.   And all the great political ideas on European Unity, on the rights and duties of governments, on war and its legitimacy, on the relations of Church and State—all the social concepts regarding slavery, money, labour, and many other subjects—are those of the *City of God*.

---

[1] Miracle holds scarcely any place in his life.   Possidius, his biographer, attributes the cure of a few demented people to him, and describes how, during his last illness, he restored a sick child to health.   That is all.   Later on the hagiographers were not always to observe this restraint.

This alone is enough to bring home to us Augustine's quite unique importance. Because he was, simultaneously, a traditionalist and a revolutionary, both saint and genius, Augustine took upon himself the entire past of the classical world—that past which was then awaiting the abyss; he extracted from it everything which deserved to survive, and, in propping humanity upon the wood of the Cross, he turned its troubled face, which was pondering on the dying past, towards the future. It is thanks to Augustine that the Barbarian soul was slowly expanded, and led, through Christianity, to civilization. It is thanks to him that the indispensable continuity between the classical and the medieval world was assured. And for us, viewing the event in the perspective of history, it is St Augustine's work which enables us to understand fully that the break-up of the classical world was not just the end of something, but the sign of a birth to come, the genesis of a new form of civilization.

Here we see the application of a law which knows no exceptions. At every decisive moment in history, the Church always possesses a significant personality who seems to have been placed at the turning-point of the centuries as God's own witness. What St Paul had been, in those early days when it was absolutely essential that the new-born Church should be made aware of her basic problems, so St Augustine became in the equally decisive hour when the foundations of the world were about to undergo a change. The sickly old man of Hippo, the erstwhile *enfant terrible* from Tagaste, set before Western humanity the glorious vision of a society arranged in Christian terms, of an intelligence enlightened by the Gospel. Slowly, with the feeble resources at their command, the finer spirits would strive to recapture this model. But history, which is long-suffering, and knows full well that human societies take a long time to die and a long time to be born, was about to open six centuries of conflict between the precepts laid down by Augustine's genius and Barbarism at its most unfettered.

# CHAPTER II

# THE BARBARIAN HOLOCAUST AND THE PILLARS OF THE CHURCH

## BARBARISM

ONE winter's night, when the air was misty with hoar-frost, an astounding noise set the guards at the watch-posts on the alert. A jumbled mass of people was milling about on the right bank of the Rhine; there was a sound of raucous shouting, a clatter of war chariots, the stamping of a thousand feet. Weapons gleamed in the moonlight. It was very cold. Had the hour which Rome had dreaded for so long come at last? The Roman legionaries and their Frankish allies—but a thin curtain of troops—hurried to their battle positions. The river was already choked with swimming horses and with rafts filled with men, and armed warriors were clinging to floating tree trunks. The great Barbarian onslaught began. Vandals, Alans, Suevians, and a whole conglomeration of greedy tribes had discovered the weak spot in the Roman defences, the sector of the frontier which was almost unguarded. What could the wretched defenders do? Swept from their posts, massacred where they stood, they quickly surrendered. And, when day dawned, the sleeping Empire was already in the power of the Barbarian hordes. Wave upon wave of tribesmen was rolling across its territories, and henceforth no one would be able to stop them any more.

Such is the picture, romantic, if one fancies it so, and yet strictly historical, in which the event of incalculable importance known as 'the Great Invasions' is often portrayed. It occurred on the night of 31st December 406, at the approaches to Mainz. This Barbarian tide—this 'ethnic waterspout' as Ferdinand Lot has called it—swept over the whole of northern Gaul, devastated it, and occupied it. But nothing would be more false than to reduce the Barbarian entry into the Empire to the scale of this one tragic scene. That entry had its roots in the distant past, and it developed in many different ways. The Rhine crossing was only one episode among many, and was certainly not the most important one.

The Roman world had had dealings with these formidable hordes for a long time past. From time to time their pressure forced breaches in her frontiers, but over the centuries they had always been overpowered in the end. The name by which they were known,

'Barbarians,' which had been given them by the Greeks, had a ring of scorn to it—the scorn felt by the civilization of the city and the state towards the civilization of the tribe. And, ever since the dreadful period when, about one hundred years before our era, Marius had been unable to stop the first big Germanic raids until they reached the shores of the Mediterranean, the Teutons at Aix-en-Provence (102) and the Cimbri at Verceil (101), all the politicians at Rome had never lost sight of what they well knew to be the Empire's greatest threat. Caesar had been flung into Gaul to bar the advance of the Suevian Ariovistus (57), and his genius had seen clearly that, in order to stop the pressure on the frontiers, it was necessary to carry the fight right into Barbarian territory itself, into the lands from which the hordes obtained their fighting men. Augustus had followed his uncle's example. But after the disaster of Varus, and the loss of the legions in the Hercynian forest (nine years after Caesar), Roman policy had tended to go on the defensive; the 'wisdom' of Tiberius and of Hadrian, which their contemporaries eulogized so, stupidly abandoned the project of occupying Germany, Central Europe, Caledonia, and Ireland, although such a project was still perfectly possible. Henceforth Rome relied only on powerful fortifications—as if the Great Wall of China or the Maginot Line could make good human weakness—on the *limes* and the legions in the frontier barracks to bar the way to all attacks. She accepted the sight of a swarming mass of unreliable peoples beyond her frontiers, whom only respect for her war-engines held in check.

During the third century the situation had altered. Certain changes had taken place within the complex mass of differing Barbarian tribes. Without disappearing completely, the petty groupings of Germanic peoples were absorbed into large military confederations: Franks, Vandals, Alamans, Goths, Saxons. In the same way, at the other end of the Empire, the Parthians, successors of the Persians, had their ranks closed again by the powerful Sassanid dynasty (227). From this time forward the Barbarian threat was a permanent one. There were some tragic episodes, as, for example, in 258, when the Alamans and the Franks had swept over Gaul, northern Italy, and Spain, or in 378, when the Goths had wiped out the Roman army at Adrianople and killed the Emperor Valens. However, in the main, the Barbarian peril did not seem very serious to the average Roman citizen until the time of the death of the great emperor, Theodosius (395). Of course the frontiers had to be shortened a good deal, the Decumate Fields (the future Grand Duchy of Baden) were abandoned to the Alamans, and the Dacian territories to the Goths; but after the clean sweep under the Illyrian emperors, did not people feel fairly confident? After all, these Barbarians were all so eager to come and enrol under the Roman eagle!

This was the most serious aspect of the situation; but everyone was so used to it that not the slightest attention was paid to it. For three hundred years now, slowly at first, then with increasing momentum, the Barbarians had been infiltrating into the *Imperium*. It had all started with the acceptance of individual Barbarians into the army, mainly in the auxiliary corps, or as contracted labour in the agricultural colonies. Subsequently, under the title of *foederati*—Federates—the Romans had recruited soldiers of all races, Germans, Arabs, Asians, and even Negroes, in complete racial units, in order to lighten the burdens of military service and the field duties of the decadent descendants of the soldier-labourers. The senior command of these units, which was initially confined to Romans, passed little by little into the hands of Barbarians, who were adorned with Latin titles. In this way whole tribes, still under the orders of their chiefs, and retaining their customs, language, and methods of war, were installed along the whole length of the frontiers, replacing the thinning legions and the missing farmers. And, during the civil wars which had been so frequent over the past three hundred years, the rival factions often made simultaneous appeal to the Barbarian armies in order to gain or to maintain power.[1]

This situation, serious enough in itself, was accompanied by a barbarization of the entire Roman world. One or two emperors were dimly aware of the dangers of this. In 375 Valentinian and Valens had promulgated a law forbidding marriages between Romans and Barbarians, on pain of death. All the evidence shows that very few people obeyed them: mixed marriages multiplied, even at Court! After all, what law could prevent the kind of morbid fascination which the wholesome violence of the Barbarians exercised on a senile society like the Roman?[2]    What law could alter the eternal rule of history, which ordains that those who hold authority end by wielding power? How could these Germanic generals, into whose hands the might of Rome had been allowed to fall, fail to play a decisive role in an epoch when ambition of every kind had free scope? From the end of the fourth century all the protagonists in important political affairs are Barbarians, more or less Romanized, of course, but no longer desiring to hide their origin. There is Stilicho, a Vandal who assumed the responsibilities of the Empire after the death of Theodosius with such

---

[1] When, in 394, Theodosius defeated his rival, Arbogast, at the second battle of Aquileia, his army included Goths, Alans, Iberians from the Caucasus, and even Huns, and among his generals was Stilicho the Vandal, the future defender of the Empire, and Alaric the Goth, who was to capture Rome fifteen years later. Arbogast, on his side, had an army of Franks and Alamans. How complex Roman politics had become. . . .

[2] There are innumerable proofs of this fascination: the most astonishing is the story of Honoria, the daughter of the Empress Galla Placidia, who sent a ring to Attila and a love-letter asking him to marry her! (See pp. 93–4.)

heroism; Aetius, a semi-Barbarian, the son of a Pannonian German and a Latin mother, and the future conqueror of Attila; the generals Victor, Magnentius, Sylvanus, and Sebastianus were, despite their Roman names, all Barbarians, and, among those whose names do not disguise their racial origin are Merobaud, Dagalaif, Bauto, and Ricimer. . . . Were these men faithful to Rome? The majority of them were. Stilicho and Aetius sacrificed their lives in obedience to this loyalty. But they were also tempted to play their personal hand in the imbroglios of a policy that was entirely without morality; between the general who served the emperor and the rebel who dreamt of seizing the Empire, there was often nothing but the flimsy barrier of a satisfied vanity or assuaged greed. Several of the outstanding episodes which fall under the general heading of the Invasions—the adventure of Alaric is one of these—are indeed simply the results of a reversion to ancient loyalties. And since it was hard to tell where treason began or where it ended, why prevent a Barbarian from the Empire summoning help from Barbarians beyond its frontiers, if he was in need of troops?

For, on the other side of the frontiers, the mass of invaders at the ready went on growing. A reservoir of excellent warriors existed there. New tribes were continually joining the old; all the time the pressure grew. Since the revolutions of the third century, the Barbarians, now better organized, had become more conscious of their own strength. Right from the North Sea to the Caspian it was as if a succession of wild beasts was poised, all ready to spring. The greater part of these Barbarians were Germans, a branch of the Aryans which had originated in the foggy lands around the Baltic, and which was now, after much wandering, coming together again. For the most part they were tall, strong, aggressive, greedy folk, organized nearly everywhere into highly disciplined tribal communities in which the 'principle of chieftainship' operated rigidly. About the year 400 the Barbarian map looked rather like this: the federation of the Franks stretched the whole length of the Rhine, from the North Sea to the Main, and was bounded, from the basin of the Weser as far as the Elbe, by the Saxons, and, between the Elbe and the upper Main, by the Lombards; a little farther south were the giant-like Burgundians, who had come originally from Brandenburg, and whose territory adjoined the lower reaches of the Rhine around Mainz. The Alamans, momentarily checked by the victories of the Emperor Julian in 357, were henceforth installed in the former Roman territories known as the Decumate Fields; known as prodigious raiders, they were among the most dangerous of the Barbarians. This left the Marcomans in Bohemia and the Rugians and the Herulians in the surrounding areas. These were less important. In contrast to this two stronger

Germanic federations were drawn up along the Danube.    The Vandals occupied the area extending as far as present-day Austria.    Tacitus had already described them as a vicious people, familiar with all the tricks of warfare.    Beyond them were the Goths, who had arrived in the region sixty-five years before from their original home around the Vistula.    Henceforth they were to be masters of Dacia, the ancient bastion of Trajan.    They were divided into two groups: 'the brilliant Goths' or Ostrogoths, who faced the Sea of Azov, and the 'wise Goths' or Visigoths, who faced the Empire.    And, in the rear, behind this line-up of peoples, others were waiting and pressing forward: Angles and Jutes in what is now Denmark; Skirians in Galicia, Norwegians, Geats, and Swedes in Scandinavia, and, on the Russian plains, Slavs and Wends in the north, Quads and Gepidae in the south, and Alans on the shores of the Black Sea.    Meantime, way back in the infinity of the Asiatic steppes, sprawled the Ural-Altaic tribes, shifting, intermingling with one another, getting ready for the future.    It was the thrust of these yellow-skinned folk which was to set the drama in motion.    The most famous of them were the Huns.

Such is the general picture of the Barbarian world at the moment when the drama of the fifth century was about to begin.    But in considering it in this global fashion, there is a risk of making numerous errors of interpretation.    Even if the Huns, whose case is a peculiar one, are not included among them, considerable differences existed between the different elements of which this enormous Barbarian puzzle was composed.    Physically, even, these peoples were not much alike, though they were all more or less fair-haired.    One could not mistake a 'blue-eyed Saxon, his hair shaved high off his forehead, in order to make his features appear longer' for a Sicambrian, with his enormous shock of unkempt hair falling down his back, nor the skinny Herulian, 'with bluish cheeks, pallid as seaweed,' for the ruddy complexioned Burgundians, gigantic in stature, who were over six feet tall!    Morally and psychologically, too, the dissimilarities were very great.    Whilst the Burgundians were well-meaning, cheerful brutes, free from malice, the Alamans were considered violent and avid for plunder, and the Alans had a reputation for implacable cruelty that the Vandals—whose name has become proverbial—often contested with them.    Christian writers like Salvianus recognize that they possessed certain virtues: they were loyal, well disciplined, chaste, and, in their dealings with one another, upright.    They had a civilization of a sort which we can only begin to uncover.    During their wanderings in the Russian plains they had learnt the secrets of a strange art from the Scythians and the Sarmatians, and they produced a polychrome jewellery decorated with animal designs which still fascinates us to-day.    Above all, many of them had already acquired the distinctive stamp of

Rome or Greece in varying degrees and in varying ways, sometimes up to the point of being permeated by it.

This is a fact which must never be forgotten when considering the Barbarian invasions; these peoples had at least a vague understanding of classical civilization, which was often of long-standing, and the majority of them admired it. As early as the second century the kingdoms of the Marcomans had been considerably Romanized, and perhaps Trajan and Marcus Aurelius had been mistaken in dismembering this buffer state. The Franks in the Belgian districts and the Goths on the Lower Danube had already had a good deal of intercourse with the Graeco-Roman world, with its diplomats, and, particularly, with its merchants. The Jutes' adaptation of the 'Grecian style' as a model for their decorative badges, the Scandinavian use of Roman coins, the religious conversions among the Goths are all evidence of the numerous contacts and influences. Moreover Rome's habit of bringing young Barbarian princes to Court, in order to guarantee the execution of treaties signed with their peoples, made the Barbarian nobility well acquainted with the Empire, with its civilization, and with its weaknesses. Alaric, Theodoric, and even Attila himself had been 'hostages' of this type. These Barbarian chieftains, whom we tend to group together as all of a kind, as savages in charges of savage hordes, could speak Latin, and often Greek, and knew how to appreciate the good things of civilization. This only incited them the more to steal its fruits for themselves. They were queer people, these chieftains, on the fringes of two worlds, one on its death-bed, the other in its birth pangs. In the depths of their hearts they were Barbarians, yet they were fascinated by the venerable lure of Rome. . . . So we find Alaric, the Visigoth conqueror, a scion of the 'divine' race of the Balthungs, demanding nothing more as a ransom of war, on his seizure of Athens, than the right to spend a day walking through the streets of the wonderful city, saluting Phidias' statue in the Parthenon, having the Platonic dialogue of *Timaeus* read to him, and listening to the *Persians* at the theatre; but when he marched on Rome in 410, he reverted once again to his ancestral loyalties. He threw the imperial badges denoting his rank into the Rubicon, robed himself once more in the dyed-red furs of the Gothic horseman, and put on the bronze, two-horned Gothic helmet—this was the kind of leader to whom the immediate future belonged.

Therefore, whether one is considering the decadent Romans, obsessed by the healthy violence of the Barbarians, or the Romanized Barbarians in the service of Europe, or the Barbarians who were fascinated by the splendour of Rome, even while they hated her,[1]

---

[1] There is one exception to this: Attila, King of the Huns. From this stems his exceptional role in history, which is studied further on in this chapter.

*C

there is always the same impression of ambiguity and overlap.  Suddenly the very notion of Barbarism is enlarged and freed from its historical framework of a few murderous raids and bloody intrigues. *Barbarism*: was it not the characteristic of a world where the past and the future mingled in the melting-pot?  Of a world where the old, civilized values no longer had healthy roots, but in which the new elements were not yet sufficiently assimilated to contain any humanity? In these circumstances of tragic disequilibrium, the decadence of the civilized Romans and the violence of the invaders complimented and attracted each other.  It was indeed the entire Western world which was in a state of Barbarism, a state which was to last for six hundred years, the time necessary for the painful birth pangs of a new civilization.  As for the Germanic tribes which threw themselves up on the Empire during the fifth century, they were merely the means which history used to effect an inevitable change.

## THE STAGES IN THE DRAMA

Nothing would be more erroneous than to see the Great Invasions as a gigantic and concerted attack by Barbarism as a whole against civilization as a whole.  Though alliances existed between certain Germanic peoples for the undertaking of specific operations, there was never any united plan amongst them, no unanimity of purpose, nor any deep feeling of community of race or interest.  Even the name 'German' was not used by the tribes themselves; it had been given them by the Gauls and was intended to signify simply 'neighbours.' Each of the acts in the drama was based on motives which were nearly always of an episodic nature; this does not mean, however, that there were not certain profound and decisive causes behind the phenomenon as a whole.

The actual origin of the disturbance which was to impel the tribes to assault the Empire at the beginning of the fifth century must be sought in the conditions of Barbarian life itself—in the petty divisions of the tribal system, and in the perpetual quarrelling.  Ever since the Romans had been aware of this sea of Germanic peoples, they had seen it periodically tossed by tempests, whose significance, however, eluded them.  The inborn Germanic taste for wandering, for indulging in pillaging expeditions, the custom of *vendetta* between tribes, the rivalries among individual chieftains—these were all explanations for these perennial outbursts.  Shortly after the middle of the fourth century, southern Russia, and the lands across the Danube, were the centres of a series of disturbances which were soon to burst upon the West.  The great Germanic wave which had been flowing from the Baltic towards the south for more than a century was halted by another wave of peoples advancing from the Asian steppes. They had a power such as had never been known before. They were the Huns, the same terrible Hiang-Now who had been the scourge of China for the past several hundred years. Now that they had been chased from their familiar hunting-grounds by the heroism of the Han emperors, and thrown out of their old territories as a result of the construction of the Great Wall, they were turning round and heading westwards. One by one the Sarmathians from the lower Volga, then the Alans, then the Ostrogoths, then the Visigoths, had been driven back by their cavalry squadrons. The Great Invasion at the beginning of the fifth century was no less than the direct consequence of the Mongol attack, which co-ordinated and channelled in a single purpose the unstable forces which made up the Germanic world.

The necessity of leaving their threatened lands; the pell-mell flight before a dreaded peril; the lure of the fine, rich, sunny lands of the West; the desire to be like their kinsmen already installed in agricultural colonies or as *foederati*; the burning love of war and conquest which was ingrained in the Germanic soul; and too, without question, that poetic sense of adventure, directed by splendid young heroes into a world of enchantment, of victories and catastrophes, such as that immortalized in the epic poem of the *Niebelungen*, eight centuries later —all these were causes of the Barbarian onslaught on the Empire. But parallel with these there are others too attributable not to the aggressors but to the Empire itself; Court intrigues amounting to actual treason, such as the action of Rufinus, the leading minister, in flinging the Barbarians upon Italy, or, possibly (it was generally suspected to be the case, at all events) that of Count Boniface, in throwing Africa open to Genseric's Vandals; personal rivalries among the 'Roman' generals, Barbarians themselves, with but a bare veneer of Roman civilization; the help of tribes already installed inside the imperial boundaries; more subtly, the moral connivance of a section of the civilized people themselves, and that kind of fatal invitation which utter feebleness holds out to brute force, almost begging it to reduce it, and to finish it off. Just as a human body, worn by age, attracts sicknesses, so the Empire, at the turn of the fifth century, attracted the Barbarians.

They came. They came not simply as men had been accustomed to see them come of old—as regiments of soldiers, more or less—but as whole tribes, with their womenfolk, their children, their wagons, their bundles of belongings, their reserve cavalry, their herds, and their flocks. The word 'invasion,' which brings to mind primarily the entry of an army into a specified area, is something of a misnomer here. The term which exactly describes the phenomenon is the German *Völkwanderung*, i.e. a migration of peoples. The situation which the

Mediterranean world had known several years before our era begins, when the Aryan invaders, the Greeks and the Latins, had led the assault on the ancient empires, was partially repeated at the end of the fourth century.   Not repeated exactly, however; it was just one more wave thrown up by the great Aryan sea, the last, up to the present day, that history has known—one cannot say that it is the last she will ever know.

Is it correct to date the beginning of the drama from that dreadful night of 31st December 406 ?   Unquestionably, yes.   It is true that a year before this, at the end of 405, a band of Goths, installed as federates in Pannonia (the modern Hungary), had swept down on northern Italy, under the leadership of a certain Radagase.   There they had burned and looted as they pleased.   But on 23rd August 406 the staunch imperial minister Stilicho had crushed them on the hillsides around Fiesole, and Radagase had suffered the execution he so justly deserved. This episode could still pass as a straightforward matter of internal politics, simply the rebellion of a chieftain whose ambitions had become too overweening.   The Empire had witnessed many such incidents in her time!

But when, on the last day of the same year as that in which the Goths had surrendered in Tuscany, the breach of the Rhine defences occurred, when the Alans, who had been hounded from their lands by the Huns, rushed through the newly opened gap after thirty years of wandering, sweeping the Vandals and the Suevians along with them, and pushing ahead of them a horde of Burgundians, the real invasion began.   Slowly the Barbarian wave swept on Gaul; it took a year for the Empire to react to the situation.   Then events threw up a make-shift leader, named Constantius, who at the time was more or less in revolt against the central government himself.   He took the defence in hand, temporarily contained the Burgundians by installing them as *foederati* in the country around Worms, and overtook the rest of the Barbarians near Toulouse.   But he was not able to crush them, nor to prevent them from going on to do in Spain what they had just done in Gaul.   It was not until 411 that a treaty was concluded, installing the Asding Vandals and the Suevians as federates in Galicia, the Siling Vandals near Seville, and the Alans in present-day Murcia and Valencia. This was to have tragic results!

After this informed opinion realized what was going to happen. Writing to one of his Italian friends, St Augustine remarks to him: 'Your last letter tells me nothing of what is happening in Rome. However, I would very much like to know if there is any truth in a garbled rumour which has just reached me, which says that the city is threatened.   I do not want to believe it. . . .'   The saint-bishop of Hippo's fear was to be realized two years later.   Rome was captured by Alaric—Rome the unconquerable surrendered to the marauders, and the Eternal City was shown to be mortal after all: 24th August 410 marked the first toll of the Empire's death-knell in Roman ears.

However, in its origins, Alaric's act of aggression was similar to that of Radagase, merely an affair of internal imperial politics. The Visigoth king fell short of being a really great man, but he was a cunning diplomat. He had taken advantage of Court intrigues, and especially of the hatred between the two ministers, Rufinus and Stilicho, to install himself in Illyria. A complaint about non-payment of military moneys due to him, and a host of other grievances and jealousies towards Stilicho—the Barbarian who had made good—made him decide to lead his rebel forces into Italy. On the first two occasions he failed, but he frightened the government sufficiently to make it decide to leave Rome and make its capital henceforth at Ravenna (404), which was better protected. At his third attempt, in August 410, Alaric openly discarded all pretence of being a soldier of the Empire. He marched on Rome, besieged it, and captured it during a terrible storm. The four days which followed the city's fall saw an orgy of murder, pillage, and rape, pursued in an atmosphere heady with panic. But it was a hollow victory, for, driven onward by the threat of famine, the Goth was just preparing to embark for the corn-fields of Africa when he died. His brother-in-law, Athaulf, who was somewhat wiser, then led his people towards Gaul. They settled in Aquitaine, and there, reconciled with Rome, he managed to install himself as a federate.

However, although it had certainly ended disastrously, Alaric's raid caused a tremendous stir: it showed the world, and the Barbarians, the real weakness of the Empire. And henceforth blow followed blow. From the northern frontier of Gaul the federate Franks pushed towards the interior; in 430 Clodio, one of their leaders, seized Cambrai and reached the Somme. The Burgundians, who were confined in the area around Worms, set out to emulate the Franks' example (430) and soon discovered how well violence paid; they were given Sabaudia, probably the northern part of our present-day Savoy, Switzerland as far as Neuchâtel, and the part of the Saône valley which was in the future to bear their name. The Vandals of Genseric, on being attacked in Spain by the Visigoths who were in Roman service, took advantage of the vacillations of Count Boniface and landed in Africa (429). They swept across the country with their marauding bands, brought about the fall of Hippo (430) following St Augustine's death, and occupied in practice the whole area from Morocco to Carthage, thus cutting Rome off from one of her best granaries. Everywhere the proud structure of Rome was cracking apart. Even remote Britain was invaded, once the legions were finally withdrawn (probably some time shortly before 428). The sea afforded an easy

entry for the intrepid boats of the Angles and the Jutes, against whom
the Britons offered a savage resistance in the first days of the Invasions:
but gradually they were forced to give ground, taking refuge in the
mountains or emigrating to the Continent, to the Armorican peninsula,
which was to bear their name and to become the modern Brittany.

Exactly how did these terrible events develop in practice? Here
again it is a mistake to oversimplify. The Barbarians certainly did
not storm into every province that they invaded with burning brands
in their hands and their swords wet with blood. Every shade of behaviour can be seen amid the complex jumble of the acts of this occupation, ranging from more or less obvious sympathy with the occupied
to actions that gave rise to frightful suffering. The Burgundian occupation, for example, seems to have been effected with the minimum of
violence, and that of the Franks without deliberate unpleasantness.
On the other hand, it is fairly clear that the Angles—the future English
—waged a campaign of destruction against the Celtic element in
Britain, and that in Africa the Vandals aimed to destroy everything
that was remotely Roman. Everywhere, of course, the arrival of the
Barbarians meant pillaging on a grand scale. The historian Procopius
dates the depopulation of Italy from the invasion of Alaric, and we
learn from Jordanes—a Goth by origin—that the Barbarians had the
deplorable tendency to set fire to everything as they passed on their
way. The worst atrocities seem to have been those of the Vandals in
Africa, which St Augustine has described: children were cut in two,
virgins tortured by having red-hot irons thrust on their breasts, the
local notables were impaled on stakes. . . . More often, however, the
sufferings which the invaded peoples had to bear were simply the
natural consequences, alas, of war, which they had to endure from
their allies as much as from their enemies. On several occasions, too,
there were some curious examples of Barbarian delicacy: for instance,
Alaric ordered the churches of Rome to be respected, Athaulf, who had
fallen in love with the beautiful captive Galla Placidia, the empress's
daughter, refused to force his affections upon her and waited patiently
until she married him of her own free will; Attila himself, much later
on, was to show respect to the bishops. . . .[1] In current usage the
word 'barbarian' has become synonymous with 'ferocious savage'; in
reality it is not so simple as this. In this decisive epoch, when the
world was beginning to take on a new guise, violence only played the
role that nature assigned to it; for men's societies, as well as for men
themselves, birth and death are usually accompanied by grievous
travail.

[1] Frequently, later on, the Barbarians were blamed for destruction which they never
committed. Thus the destruction of Toulouse should not be attributed to the Vandals,
as tradition claims, but to a flooding of the River Garonne.

## 'THIS WHITE-HAIRED WORLD'[1]

When we examine the rapidity of the drama which, in less than three-quarters of a century, handed the whole of western Europe over to the Barbarians, one vital question springs to mind: why did it happen? What was the reason for this collapse, this plunge into the abyss? For, in the last resort, the Empire still possessed fortresses against which these hordes could achieve nothing significant, she still retained her strategic routes, her fine traditions of military skill, and she had a diplomacy cunning enough to deceive, buy off, or divide the adversary. Though the difference in arms between the Romans and the Barbarians was not as great as that existing in our day between the white man and the Negroes of Central Africa, it remains true that the Germanic peoples lacked method and discipline, and that they were incapable of ensuring the supplying of their forces. Finally, until the Vandals' African victory, the Romans were undisputed masters of the sea. They let all these assets slip through their fingers. Why? How? There is only one possible answer: the Empire had condemned itself to death. When the Barbarians seriously attacked its structure it was already wormeaten through and through, and its strength was more apparent than real. What good were the finest arms in the world in the hands of a moribund power?

On 17th January 395 Theodosius, the last of the great emperors, died in his palace at Milan, in the midst of a huge courtly gathering. The atmosphere was charged with expectant ambitions. It was clear to anyone with the slightest knowledge of the situation that the hour of intrigues, of palace revolutions, and of civil wars was about to sound anew. All the important figures in the Empire were there, grouped round the bed of ivory and precious woods where the great man lay in his last agony, clad in his furs and his imperial purple—the dignitaries in their silken tunics, the prelates in dalmatics embroidered with black crosses, and the Barbarian heads of the army garbed like Roman generals. A great game was about to be played, in which the stake was power. The year before, Theodosius had realized that he was mortally sick, and had settled the succession, dividing the Empire between his two sons: Arcadius was to govern the East and Honorius the West. But can he really have had any illusions about these two children's actual chances? Indeed he had so little faith in either son that he had placed a stronger man at the side of each of them: behind

[1] 'This white-haired world has witnessed famine, plague, devastation, wars, and terror, and it is witnessing them yet again.' (St Eucherius, Bishop of Lyons, in his *Letter to Valerian on the Pitiable State of the World*.)

# BARBARIAN STARTING POINTS
# AND THE AXES OF THE INVASIONS

MILES

| 0 | 200 | 400 | 600 | 800 | 1000 |

Arcadius, a sickly adolescent, stood Rufinus, the son of a Pyrenean cobbler, who owed his successful advancement to his boldness and his cynicism; behind Honorius, a little booby of only eleven years, Stilicho the Vandal, whose father had commanded the squadrons of 'hairy ones.' However, these two men hated each other violently, and scarcely had Theodosius departed this life than troubles flared up which were never to cease again.

What a strange and dramatic epoch it was—these last decades of the Western Empire! Who ordered, and who obeyed? Who committed treason, and who remained loyal? He who can answer these questions is wise indeed! Men are constantly shifting from the emperor's side to that of the leading invader or rebel, and vice versa. An underlying antagonism exists between the two halves of the Roman world, both the East and the West making use of the Barbarians to score against its rival. It is an age brimful of astonishing personalities, whose actions are often ambiguous, and who are not easy to fit into a particular category. Is Stilicho, the Vandal minister, really the great servant of Roman grandeur? The ivory plaque at Monza on which he is portrayed conveys this impression quite clearly. Or is he merely the conqueror of Radagase?—the bastion which halted the first Gothic assaults? What mixed motives he must have had, when he talked with Alaric, and seemed to be preparing a throne for his son! When Honorius, though his son-in-law, had him assassinated in 408, had he put himself outside his own strictest law? And yet, at the end, Stilicho refused to defend himself against his master's emissaries, and, loyal at the last, laid bare his neck to his executioners. Should we class Constantius among the traitors, or the faithful imperial servants? It was Constantius, the Illyrian chieftain, who halted the advance of the Vandals and the Suevians into Gaul in 407, even though he was himself a rebel at the time, with a price set on his head by the government. Later on he became the second husband of Galla Placidia, the emperor's sister, adopted the name Augustus, and henceforth lived the law-abiding life of a Vice-Emperor of the Gauls at Arles. And above all, what are we to think of the unparalleled career of Galla Placidia herself, this woman who springs so vividly to the tourist's mind when he visits her mausoleum at Ravenna, where she lies beneath the green and gold mosaics there, where the light plays on the alabaster walls? Successively an imperial princess, a prisoner of the Goths, the apparently loving wife of Athaulf, and the Barbarian queen of Spain, she returned to Italy after her first widowhood and married Constantius. She proved an energetic regent of the Empire when Honorius died (423) and succeeded in imposing her two-year-old son, Valentinian III (423–455), on the armies as the new emperor. Possibly Renaissance Italy is the only other period containing such singular careers, where men gambled with power and death, triumph and assassination, as if in a game of dice.

But picturesque though it appears, in one sense, this is in fact an epoch of utter decadence. An incurable gangrene was attacking the once proud Roman organism. It is impossible to think without revulsion of those feeble masters of the world, tucked away in their capital at Ravenna, shielded by the fever-laden swamps. There they led their secret lives, a strange mixture of devoutness and luxury, surrounded by their eunuchs, their courtesans, and their Germanic bodyguards, plotting intrigues even against those who defended them, and, in the last resort, helpless, despite the shadow of ancient imperial grandeur which still clung to them, against sedition and the assassin's dagger. Those who served them inspire us with equal disgust—these important imperial officials, who, for all their power, retained the souls of slaves—a former wool-carder from a women's work-room, an ex-scullion, or actual Barbarians with but a thin gloss of Roman culture—such as these were the real masters of the Roman world. Was it astonishing that men's sense of the common good had totally disappeared, and that, in the universal confusion that existed, each man followed only the dictates of his own interests (though sometimes, by good fortune, these ambitions coincided with the general interest)?

All these fundamental causes of decline had been apparent during the fourth century. They came to a head at the beginning of the fifth. The policy of state absolutism, practised since Diocletian's time and transformed into theocratic monarchy by Constantine and his successors, tended to enclose the whole life of the Empire in an iron corset of rules and restrictions. In principle everything must depend on the State, and men must work only to increase its greatness; in fact, though this regime had taken root easily enough in the East, where it rested on ancient traditions of autocratic rule,[1] it failed totally in the West. The strengthening of the State's powers had little effect save to benefit the senior administrators, the rulers of the provinces, the counts who were in the process of converting their administrative rights into territorial possessions. The feudal system of the future was already springing from this parcelling out of authority. State despotism seemed even more intolerable when it proved itself not even capable of preserving law and order; the Barbarian menace had never been so pressing; wars between ambitious rivals ravaged the provinces; the hordes of anarchistic marauders, *Bagaudes*, toured the countryside, and too many interests protected them for them to be driven out.

Moreover the heavy yoke of the State sterilized those forces which still had some life left in them. It is scarcely necessary to catalogue the vices of the system yet again. The late Empire had no monopoly of

[1] This is why the Empire of the East was to survive.

them and they are vices which always appear whenever the State
usurps its real function and attempts to absorb everything.   There
was an enormous bureaucracy, so enormous that one contemporary
complained that there were more bureaucrats than taxpayers to pay
their salaries.   The Empire was in a state of permanent financial
crisis, which organized inflation (this had started under the Severians
with a debasement of the coinage), the usual monetary manipulations,
and all the financial ruses resorted to by governments in difficulties had
not managed to conquer.   A crushing and insane fiscal policy resulted
in widespread tax evasion, and even threats of the direct penalties could
not stop this.   The cost of living rose constantly.   Price-fixing
edicts (the first was dated 301) could not halt it, and it was accompanied
by a production crisis due to the shortage of manpower and a lowering
of the exchange rates caused by the generally anarchical conditions.
Some contemporaries grasped the moral of this harrowing tale in
pointing to where popular fury was directed.   Orosius tells us of
'Romans who preferred to live in poverty and freedom among the
Barbarians rather than submit to the crushing burdens of taxation,'
and Salvianus says almost the same thing: 'The poor, exasperated
wretches often hoped that the enemy would come; they prayed God to
send them the Barbarians.'

Upon these factors making for public decadence were superimposed
others which were even more serious—moral and spiritual in character.
Although Christianity was now established in classical society, it could
not transform it in a day.   Not only did it still contain many pagans in
its bosom, but several fairly recent converts let themselves be tainted
by the atmosphere around them.   We need only to open St Augustine,
St Jerome, or any other Father of the epoch to find proof that evangelization had not been able to halt the moral disintegration.   From the
idle upper classes who lived only for luxury—for silks from the East,
perfumes, jewelled rings on every finger—down to the ordinary idle
man in the street who spent his time gambling at dice, knucklebones,
or hopscotch, there was scarcely a free man who was willing to do an
honest day's work.   It is useless to dwell on sexual morality; divorce,
male and female prostitution, and a falling birth-rate reached scandalous proportions.   Despite imperial efforts to lessen their horror and
their number, the gory gladiatorial games continued to provide the
mob with its degrading entertainment, and St Augustine speaks sadly
of those wretches who amuse themselves with carnivals and vile
spectacles even while the enemy is at their gates slaughtering their
brethren.   And indeed, in the spiritual sphere itself, the situation was
distressing too.   Degenerate paganism was no more than a literary
loyalty, a form of conservatism among a few intellectuals and great
lords, and, among the common people, for those who still clung to it, a

hotchpotch of superstitions, astrology, and magic. From this point of view the atmosphere of the age was so full of miasmas that Christianity itself had to be constantly on its guard lest it become contaminated.

In truth, society at the beginning of the fifth century was indeed, as St Eucherius, the Bishop of Lyons, so aptly put it, 'a white-haired world.' Roman civilization had sunk to the point where no remedy in the world could save it, for its physiological wear and tear had gone so far that all aids were useless. What is so surprising is not that this world died, but that it took so long to do so. The underlying causes which determined its ruin had been there for the past two hundred years after all. But the organism was so strongly built that it had obstinately resisted destruction. In the final hour, when everything was falling apart, there were to be a few men—even if they were only ambitious careerists or semi-barbarians—who held fast and would not give in. And even among personalities as ludicrous as those of the last emperors, the sense of a kind of pride, of a last loyalty to the past, produced a few energetic gestures, such as that of Honorius, who, when trapped in the Ravenna marshes, with no army, with no means of action, obstinately refused Alaric the title of 'master of the militia' of which he judged him unworthy. . . .

It is this perhaps which encourages us to look less severely on this complex epoch, which is usually so disdainfully treated by historians. It is easy enough to regard all its elements with equal contempt—the Barbarians, these savages, and the fifth-century Romans, these incompetent decadents. But do not moments exist when the powers which determine events are stronger than human wills? The two protagonists in the drama each assumed their role with all the means of which they were capable, and in that fundamental uncertainty which is the characteristic of human destinies.

And then, although the fifth century was an epoch of chaos and degradation, it was also a time of vital preparation. From its filth and blood the future was growing. From this terrible melting-pot—much later on—was to come the civilization which is our own. The really great events of this century—the halting of Attila, for example—have had an enormous effect on the destinies of the Western world, greater by far than the Roman wars or the expeditions of Alexander. We are the descendants of this age of chaos, or, more accurately, of the order which came out of that chaos.

For an order did indeed emerge from it. It did so because, in the very bosom of this doomed society, a power remained which was capable of giving a meaning to the drama, of bringing order out of disorder, of integrating the Barbarians into civilization and of using their youthful energies to restore the world to vigour and health. This power, to which the West owes its salvation, was the Church.

## THE YOUNG CHURCH

When the Barbarian holocaust burst upon the world, the triumph of Christianity was less than a century old.   The long, tragic struggle, which had begun in Nero's reign, in which the pagan Empire had fought to crush the Revolution of the Cross, had lasted for several generations, and had only ended in 313, when, at Milan, Constantine had issued his decree: 'The Christians are henceforth entirely free to practise their religion.'   Once these initial steps had been taken, others followed almost automatically.   Now the protectors of the Church, the emperors became increasingly linked with her.   The brief attempt of Julian the Apostate to make Rome return to paganism decisively illustrated, by its very failure, the impossibility of any such reversion. The necessary train of events—this historic proof of the designs of Providence—had led on to the logical conclusion of Constantine's decision: in 380, at Thessalonica, Theodosius had ordered all his peoples to 'rally to the faith brought to the Romans by the apostle Peter.'   At the time when it felt its very existence threatened, the Empire turned for succour to the Cross.

The old enemy of Christianity was laid low; now it was the turn of paganism to be *religio illicita*.   A positive torrent of prohibitions and repressive legislation was brought to bear on the remaining pagans. From 5th August 395 Arcadius and Honorius declared that the laws against the pagans promulgated by their divine father should be enforced with redoubled vigour.   Private divination, magic, and sacrifices were all forbidden; so were the funeral banquets so dear to the heart of the ancients, and the ceremonial libations performed at the beginning of a meal!   The temple priests and the other temple servants were stripped of their remaining privileges in 396; in 408 entry into court service was forbidden all those who were 'enemies of the Emperor's faith.'   The temples were closed or else converted into churches; the statues of the old gods were either kept simply as works of art, or, more often than not, destroyed.   Pan was dead!   Naturally this uprooting of a faith which went back centuries could not be carried out without meeting some resistance.   In many areas the closure of the temples took place amid veritable riots; at Alexandria in Egypt, for example, at Gaza in Palestine, and in Syria and the Lebanon.   Whilst Augustine was Bishop of Hippo, acts of real violence were committed by the pagans in Africa against the churches and Christian communities of Carthage, Suffetula, and Guelma. Individual resistance was less obvious but more subtle in character; for how could men be prevented, in the privacy of their own homes, from pouring a libation on some secret domestic altar, or from sacrificing a sheep according to the ancient rites? When Rome was besieged by Alaric, the consul Tertullus, on taking over command, carefully studied the sacred chickens, traced circles in the sky with the augural staff, and consulted the flight of the crows. . . . But incidents like these were nothing more than the last twitches of the ancient faith in its death struggle, and very soon it could find shelter only in the undercurrents of popular superstition, or in the dilettantism of a handful of intellectuals. It no longer constituted a danger to Christianity.

In the legal sphere, not only were all the Church's rights recognized, but she was even placed above the common law. She obtained something which was tremendously valuable in an age of such crushing taxation—various precious fiscal privileges, notably the exemption of her clerks from the personal dues which all other citizens had to pay. Ever since Constantine's time she had possessed jurisdiction in civil cases, and, increasingly, people preferred her justice to that of the secular tribunals, both because it was more equitable and because it was . . . free, so much so that official steps had to be taken to curb this tendency, for fear of seeing the ordinary courts deserted! The churches replaced the temples as places of sanctuary; the only persons denied this right being proven criminals and . . . those with taxation debts. Even in penal matters the Church had the right to judge her own clerks; this is the 'clerical privilege', which was to become so important in the Middle Ages. Going even further, the State put itself at the Church's disposal by constituting itself her 'secular arm,' according to the ideas of St Augustine, and in a less gentle fashion than he had envisaged. All in all, the Church found herself in possession of a considerable collection of rights and prerogatives, and there was scarcely an emperor who, in the course of his reign, did not, like Honorius, proclaim his intention 'never to tamper with the privileges of Holy Church!'

Was this really the essential, however? The answer is, emphatically, No. Christianity's real strength did not lie in its from henceforth close alliance with the throne; on the contrary, it was the Church which sustained the imperial power. Its real strength lay in its youth, in its tremendous enthusiasm. Do our present-day Christians, all too used to seeing Christianity as a daily routine, and the Church as an established institution, think sufficiently of how overwhelming must have been the faith of their ancestors all those fifteen centuries ago, when, after so many ordeals, and so much suffering, the new doctrine triumphed at last? Can they imagine the extent of the enthusiasm, the fervour of those crowds of newly baptized folk who had just learnt that the future belonged to them? The new basilicas which sprang up all over the old Empire were truly temples of Hope and of Resurrection in those days! How heartily those awaiting their Saviour sang the 'new hymn!' They would stand for hours on end, listening fervently to the fiery preachers who spoke of heaven and earth in terms of such sublime familiarity! Of course not everything in the Church was perfect at the beginning of the fifth century.[1] She no longer had that character of a chosen minority, which she had possessed in the very early days; and yet at what epoch has the Church ever suggested that she consisted only of saints? But up to the point of her errors—in the violent actions, for example, into which certain Christians allowed themselves to be drawn,[2] and in the rather excessive ardour of the theological tussles—there was a vigour, an audacity, a will to conquer, which made her, along with the Barbarians, the only living force in this age of decay.

The expansion of Christianity, which had never ceased since Christ had ordered his disciples to 'preach the Gospel to all nations!' became much more rapid and vigorous now that it had imperial support. By the first quarter of the fifth century one could say that there was not a corner of the Empire which had not at least heard of Christ. Of course the density of the Christian population varied considerably from place to place; the great majority of the Eastern peoples had been baptized, whereas in the West (even discounting the Barbarians, pagans, and heretics) there were still large areas which Catholicism had not conquered. Though all the figures put forward are probably somewhat ambitious, it seems fairly certain that about half the population of the Empire had been converted by this date; fifty out of one hundred million. Christian propaganda influenced all strata of society; among the ruling class the conversions were perhaps rather too swift and too numerous now that it had become politically advantageous to proclaim oneself a Christian; the middle classes, the less important folk, the artisans, and the slaves made up the great bulk of the Christian population; in the countryside, despite the huge efforts made by St Vigilius of Trent, St Victrix of Rouen, and, above all, by St Martin of Tours, the great Gallic saint, the peasantry's attachment

[1] The reader can find these criticisms, such as those which St Augustine, for example, listed so unequivocally, discussed at the beginning of Chapter V.

[2] The acts of pagan resistance which we have noted explain, though they do not excuse, the all too frequent instances of violence in which newly baptized crowds in many districts, excited to the point of fanaticism, indulged. Numerous incidents, from the four corners of the Empire, show that the lesson of love preached in the Gospel was not grasped by certain converts. Faced with the iconoclastic fury which threatened to destroy temples and smash statues which, from an artistic point of view, were quite priceless, the Emperor was forced to issue edicts to ensure the protection of such treasures. Here and there there were even attacks on individuals. The most famous and most distressing of these episodes was the murder of the well-known woman philosopher, Hypatia, a leading exponent of the Neo-Platonic school, at Alexandria, in Egypt. In March 415 a band of fanatics, whipped up by a Christian lecturer, snatched her from her chariot, while she was on her way to her class, dragged her into a church, stripped her of her clothes, and tore her to pieces. Crowds can be bestial and cruel in every epoch, and even baptism itself does not suffice to free collective humanity from its worst passions.

to the old nature cults and age-old superstitions curbed the progress of
the Gospel, and this obstacle could only be overcome very slowly.
Nowhere did the Church abandon her great struggle for the conquest
of souls.   She knew no frontiers, not even those of the Empire;
Christian outposts in Armenia, Arabia, and Ethiopia made this clear,
and others were soon to swarm desertwards, and even towards India.

The triumph of Christianity must not be considered only in terms of
its territorial expansion, but in depth, in the telling influence which it
had already exercised on society for a long time, and which was
steadily increasing.   Against the absolutism of the imperial system,
which was always arbitrary and oppressive, and often bloodthirsty,
and which was sustained by the utter servility of the court, one lone
bastion of resistance stood out: the Church, in the person of her
bishops.   They alone dared raise their voices against the despots.
This privileged clergy, now become so powerful, protected public
liberties and guaranteed the people's rights.   As a true son of the
Church the Emperor might not disobey her precepts, without being
called to order publicly—as St Ambrose had dealt with Theodosius.
In general, too, the government of these Christian rulers was more
moderate and more charitable than that of their predecessors; thus the
custom of the Easter amnesty became almost an annual event.   Since
the time of Constantine the principles laid down in the Gospel had
begun to penetrate the law.   Is it necessary to recall those laws which
punished, in turn, slander, usury, and the abandonment or sale of new-
born babies?   A new delicacy, the result of the teaching of Jesus,
showed itself in the law's attitude towards women; they were exempt
from Court appearances, and actresses who became Christians were
allowed to leave the stage, notwithstanding the formal law which forbade anyone to relinquish his profession.   Public morality was
strenuously protected; though, unfortunately, the taste for gladiatorial
games was too firmly established to be broken at once, its savage
character was lessened, by forbidding human beings to fight to the
death; unnatural vice and adultery were punished in exemplary fashion.
When one thinks of this epoch as an age of decadence, particularly in
the moral field, this action of the Church should never be forgotten;
she preserved the better elements in the Empire from putrefaction; as
St Augustine sensed she would, she prepared the foundations for the
future reconstruction of civilized society.

And what of those spiritual seeds which Christianity was sowing in
the heart of society, those things which men like Ambrose and Augustine recognized as indispensable?   *Mater Ecclesiae* gave them in
sufficient strength to survive the greatest catastrophes; she preserved
them and transmitted them to future generations.   If the Roman
Catholic Church had not been an admirable temporal organization,

what would have become of those fine Gospel principles? Would they not have been broken up amid the terrible whirlpools of the invasions, and absorbed and watered down into heaven knows what kind of barbarisms? But that was precisely what Holy Church was. Thus the institutional effort made since her foundation, and which she stubbornly had pursued throughout the first four centuries of her existence, now bore fruit. Organized more and more (in the West, at least) [1] around the Pope, the Bishop of Rome, modelling her administrative boundaries on those of the old Empire, adapting herself increasingly to practical functions which the secular authority was failing to perform, [2] she represented the one stable element in a world in which everything was tottering; amid the Barbarian holocaust she was the one bastion which would never crumble. The poet Lactantius, writing in this very age, had already declared this: 'The Church, and the Church alone, conserves all and sustains all.'

## Giving the Drama a Meaning

If we want to assess the importance of the role which the Church played in this age when the fate of everything was hanging in the balance, two factors have to be taken into consideration: in the practical sphere, the position held by her supporters during the worst periods of the ordeals; in the spiritual, the decisive influence which she exercised on the actual interpretation of events. When these are assessed against one another, one asks oneself whether the latter point is not the essential one. What men most need, in order to make their earthly lives worth while, is a feeling, or at least an instinct, of the end towards which they are striving. A society which loses this sense of purpose, which understands neither the whys nor the wherefores of events, can only fluctuate between frenzy and despair. It moves in a kind of Hamlet-like anguish. The greatest service which Christianity was to render to the men of the fifth century—or, at any rate, to the more intelligent among them—was to give a meaning to their drama, and not to abandon them, lonely and distraught, on the edge of an abyss beyond which they could see no further.

What was the general reaction of contemporaries to these shattering events around them? In general, it was sadly out of focus. We are not thinking now of the masses, who, as a rule, are too occupied in the pursuit of pleasure to have time for fear. But a lucid view of the situation was rare even among the more intelligent and better educated.

---

[1] The evolution of Christianity in the East was to be entirely different. The reader will find this examined in the next chapter.

[2] The organization of the Church is studied in Chapter V.

Even those whose political concepts went beyond immediate pre-occupations believed, almost to a man, that the crisis would be short-lived. What did it matter if the West was indeed threatened? They looked to the Eastern Empire, expecting help to come from there. They were so convinced of the invulnerability of Rome and her Empire that they clung to the idea as a drowning man clings to a buoy. Was not Rome the Eternal City? Had not world domination been promised to her? In 417 the worthy Gaul, Rutilius Numatianus, filled with exuberance at the sight of the Barbarian Visigoths driving the Barbarian Vandals out of Gaul into Spain, placidly composed a poem to 'Rome the eternal, pride of a world that is filled with her power, star among stars!' A few years later Sidonius Apollinaris declared that 'Rome is for ever the summit of the world.' Men had such difficulty in emancipating themselves from a moribund past that even a man as intelligent as the Christian historian Orosius, whose opinions on the future are among the most profound, could not help devoting several pages to declaring that his epoch was not really as disagreeable as all that, taken as a whole, that it was good to be alive in it, and that perhaps it was simply its closeness that made men call it calamitous! But we must not judge this possibly deliberate ignorance too severely. . . . How many of us, in the twentieth century, accurately gauge the size of the gulf on whose brink we are stepping?

However, a few people understood the facts. There is plenty of evidence to show that those most qualified among Christ's spokesmen were well aware of what was happening. There is St Jerome, writing: 'The ship is sinking.' There is St Orentius, the Bishop of Auch, declaring: 'Why discourse on the funeral obsequies of a world which is breaking up according to the customary law, that everything mortal perishes?' There is St Augustine, noting, as a statement of fact: 'The end of the city is not yet come perhaps, but nevertheless the city soon will have an end.' Much later on, in the year 450—less brilliantly, since events had by now enlightened many people—Salvianus said, in his brutally frank way: 'The Roman Empire is already dead, or at any rate in its death agony, even where it still seems alive.'

What could the reactions of Christians be to statements such as these? Their attitude was by no means the same in every case. Some of them, those who were deeply and passionately attached to this classical world which was fast disappearing, notably the scholars who owed their personal make-up to Graeco-Roman culture, felt they had been dealt a mortal blow. From his solitude in Bethlehem St Jerome wrote: 'My voice fails me. Sobs choke my words. That great city, which once captured the whole world, has herself been seized! She is perishing from hunger as much as from the sword; she is in flames, imagine it, the august capital of the Empire herself!

To-day I wanted to devote myself to the study of Ezekiel, but as I was about to begin dictating, I thought of the catastrophe in the West, and I was forced to remain silent, knowing full well that the time for weeping had come. . . .' One cannot read such outbursts of distress without being deeply moved; but it was necessary to go beyond this heartrending agony of mind.

The Christians who were to prepare for the transformation of the world were those who never allowed themselves to be overwhelmed by the sense of inescapable doom. There were many like this. One thinks of Rufinus of Aquila, who, as a refugee in Sicily, watched the Goths setting fire to Rhegium on the far side of the narrow straits and said, with the simple sincerity of the true believer, that he would find consolation for his unhappiness by applying himself to his tasks as a writer and translator: to continue to pursue one's profession, even in the most frightful circumstances, was indeed a fine Christian example! Then there was St Augustine, who, in his famous sermon on the capture of Rome, confessed that he was grief-stricken at the news he had received, at the thought of the piles of ruins, of the killings and of the atrocities, but whose only immediate desire was to instil courage into the stunned congregation who were listening to him. Very soon after this he threw himself into his mighty work, the *City of God*, which he made the answer to his own anguish as well as to that of the world.

What the saint of Hippo was able to express better than anyone, because the resources of genius were at his disposal, was also urgently felt by other Christian thinkers, and more or less similarly stated by them. Their thesis was this: that the Church's task was to save men's hope. 'Christ is talking to you—listen to Him!' cried Augustine. 'He says to you: "Why are you so afraid? Is not all this exactly as I predicted it would be? I warned you of it so that your hope would turn, when trouble came, towards the true wealth, instead of foundering among material things."' This tremendous idea, that everything that was happening, dreadful though it might be, obeyed a divine intention and was ascribable to an infinitely beneficent logic was offered to the world by Christianity in order to bring new courage to mankind. It is this idea which the priest Paul Orosius develops throughout his *Universal History*, published about the year 417. And several years later, when Salvianus, a priest at Marseilles, was writing his numerous sermons, pamphlets, and lampoons, they all echoed the same refrain: 'Are you complaining that God is letting everything fall to pieces? But no, God rules the world. It isn't true that He isn't interested in the world: it is the object of His every care!' This is exactly what St Paulinus of Nola also said, in his bishopric where Alaric came to strike him down, and it was said too by that splendid anonymous poet from Acquitaine—somewhat tainted by Pelagianism, perhaps, but extremely moving nevertheless —when writing his *Song of Providence* in the tenth year of the Gallic invasion, that is to say, in 416.

However, if God rules the world why does He let such misfortunes loose on it? The aptest answer is that of St Jerome, who says, in his usual blunt fashion: 'The Barbarians' power is founded on our sins; our armies have been defeated by our own vices!' Similarly St Augustine, speaking a little less harshly, says that instead of appearing astonished at being chastised by God, man had better look at himself and ask whether he has not indeed deserved this chastisement. Orosius likewise declares that Alaric's capture of Rome is the city's rightful punishment for its past sins. Salvianus, in his turn, took up the same theme. He had been chased by the Vandals from his home-land and had with his own eyes seen so much devastation and suffering that he was indignant to find his contemporaries incapable of taking up a truly Christian attitude in the face of such dreadful realities. This Jeremiah of the Gauls castigated his audiences with the kind of ex-pressions of which our own Bernanos would not have disapproved.

Were all these mere preachers' phrases the usual pulpit haranguing, which over-use has made us despise so to-day? Not at all. These Christian thinkers drew from the bitter facts of the present reasons for labouring still more enthusiastically to prepare the future. They understood, and they stated, that society could not be rebuilt until man had first been spiritually remade. This call for a renewal of basic values, which St Ambrose had already recognized as indispensable, became for St Augustine and his successors the creative force which would allow civilization to be saved. And it was thus, in fact, that the Church was to save it.

## THE PILLARS OF THE CHURCH

Though this profound influence of Christianity on the evolution of events was, in the first place, the work of Christian philosophers, it was soon translated into deeds, because the Church found herself possessed, at the decisive moment, of men of action equal in calibre to her thinkers: moreover the philosopher and the man of action was often one and the same person. St Augustine was far from being the only Christian who combined philosophical gifts and practical abilities in an extraordinary number of enterprises. If the word '*élite*' has any real meaning, and if we understand by it those outstanding elements in society, conscious of their historic responsibilities and brilliantly endowed to fulfil them, it is more than certain that the Church indeed possessed a wonderful *élite*, or, to put it more accurately, that almost all the *élite* were in her ranks.

Ever since the Church's foundation, she had been able to count on some first-class leaders: *the bishops*. Assuming to the full the duties of an office which was overwhelming in the scope of its responsibilities, preachers, liturgists, orators, administrators, and fathers of the faithful at one and the same time, the bishops of those first four centuries had been the pillars upon which the great edifice of the Cross had gradually been built. *Ecclesia in episcopo*; the whole Church is in the bishop! The saying of St Cyprian, bishop and martyr, had never lost its validity. At the close of the fourth century, when the first signs of collapse became apparent, it took on an even greater significance; as the peril grew and the influence of the secular authorities progressively declined, the bishops drew themselves up to their full height: St Ambrose had been a model whom the emperor himself had admired.

Throughout the dramatic events of the fifth century, the Church had the providential good fortune to number among her bishops a veritable pleiad of mighty figures, scattered throughout the length and breadth of her territories. They were men who brought to Christ's services qualities and virtues whose richness astonishes us, until we realize that they were sustained and explained by the gifts of sanctity. These witnesses of Christ, given to penitence in their private lives, in defiance of the world, filled with humility, imbued with the spirit of justice and wisdom—these were men who almost always lived like monks, utterly devoted to God, yet who were forced at the same time to carry out all the often terrible demands of the official duties with which they were charged. They brought the Word of God to their peoples, built churches, founded monasteries, celebrated the interminable liturgies at which they alone could officiate—and at the same time administered their property, which had often become considerable: they succoured the unfortunate, the poor, and the sick, devoted themselves to redeeming captives (going so far as to sell sacred vessels for this end, as in the case of St Ambrose, St Augustine, St Hilary of Arles, and many others besides), worked relentlessly for the conversion of the pagans, for the civilization—by the Christian goodwill of their reception—of the Barbarians who occupied their lands. . . . And is this all they did? Far from it. For, in assuming their sacerdotal functions, the bishops found themselves playing a political role which they had never sought. When, as so often happened, the imperial official or the Roman officer showed himself unequal to his task, the people's representative ceased to be the bureaucrat or the soldier, and became instead the bishop. In innumerable instances it was the bishop who was the real 'defender of the city'; usually he did not bear the title, which is strictly that of a municipal magistrate, but he took over

all its duties with courage and self-sacrifice. Thus these princes of
the Church revealed themselves as astute political and military leaders.
When everything crumbled they continued to hold fast. St Augustine encouraged the defenders during the siege of Hippo; St Nicasius
sought death in his cathedral at Rheims; St Exuperius of Toulouse
offered such violent resistance to the Vandals that he was deported;
St Anianus fortified Orléans; St Lupus defended Troyes, and there
were many others who did like deeds. . . .

It would be foolish to attempt to enumerate even the principal of
these great bishops. Though two or three of them are well remembered, St Augustine in particular, or St John Chrysostom, there are
countless names which convey absolutely nothing to modern Christians, who are indeed very far from realizing what a decisive role these
pillars of the Church played in the face of the Barbarian holocausts.
Had these men not been what they were, the fate of civilization would
have been very different. We have seen the deeds done by the most
outstanding of them, Augustine, during the thirty-four years of his
Hippo episcopate (396–430)—his unlimited devotion to the cause of
Christ, his constant attention to the most diverse cares of his flock, his
inflexible courage in face of the direst perils, and, at the end, his steadfast resistance to the waves of Barbarian invaders. Many others acted
as he did, though their resources of spirit and intelligence were perhaps more modest than his; but they were equally conscious of the
responsibilities which devolved upon them!

There is *St Paulinus of Nola*, the correspondent and friend of St
Augustine. He was a native of Bordeaux, and an old pupil of
Ausonius, and his family, the *gens Anicia*, was an ancient patrician one.
Paulinus became consul and then—at the early age of twenty-five—
governor of Campania. By and by God's call came to him, and at
last he obeyed it, selling his possessions in Aquitaine and giving the
moneys to the poor. He returned to Nola and became its bishop,
henceforth utilizing his considerable experience as a former senior civil
servant in the administration of the community under his care. His
soul has a crystalline purity, full to the brim with sweetness and
gentleness, and his poetry is often charming. He is one of the last of
the Latin poets. Finally, when Alaric and his followers came fresh
from the sack of Rome to pillage Nola, Paulinus confronted them with
a tranquil courage, and died, in the following year, as a result of the
cruelties he had had to endure, and from a broken heart.

There is *Synesius of Cyrene*, a man who has not merited canonization
—and possibly this is why he seems closer to our own human frailties.
He too was a considerable figure in the literary world, and was educated in Egypt under 'the divine Hypatia.'[1] He is the poet whose

[1] See footnote 2, p. 74.

*Hymns* moved even Lamartine, the contented nobleman who (in 410) agreed to become Bishop of Ptolemaeus because of his awareness of the dangers the world was facing, thereby giving up his easy way of life, his hunting and his poetry, and devoting himself body and soul to the folk in his diocese.  Synesius undertook a multitude of exacting tasks, wrote a prophetic letter to the emperor on the subject of the Barbarian menace, stood firm in turn before Bedouin hordes, Barbarian marauders, and imperial officials—the latter being almost as much of a danger as any foreign invaders!  In 413 he died of exhaustion, having, in the very demands of his office, reached the heart of that Christian faith to which he had devoted himself, in the first place, from feelings of civic responsibility: Bossuet has dubbed him 'great.' [1]

There is *Quovultdeus*—his very name seems to predestine him to greatness—the former deacon of St Augustine, who, when the Vandal attack came, was so terrified that he badly wanted to flee.  Yet, having been made Bishop of Carthage in 437, he proved to be a fine Christian leader.  He organized opposition to the Vandal occupation of his country, put to shame those of his compatriots who tolerated the invader too easily, and encouraged resistance by filling his sermons with a thousand transparent allusions to Pharaoh, Nebuchadnezzar, Holophernes, and the other biblical tyrants whose reigns had come to a bad end.  When at last he was expelled from his bishopric, and was living in Naples as a poor refugee, having lost everything, he continued to work for the campaign of liberation, and died, declaring: 'They wage war against the Lamb, but the Lamb will surely conquer them.'

And beyond Africa and Italy?  Gaul can boast a large number of outstanding Christian leaders.  Which of us does not know the name of *St Germanus of Auxerre*, the saint so dear to Parisian hearts, the very man who, whilst travelling on the highway from Nanterre, recognized the signs of God's Grace in the face of a shepherdess, and so started Geneviève along the path of her glorious destiny?  He too was a great nobleman, and was consecrated Bishop of Auxerre in 418.  St Germanus restored his shattered diocese, and did innumerable good works with a love that was boundless; continually on the move, searching fresh grounds to convert, he twice visited Britain in order to defend the true faith against the Pelagian heresy.  On his return from the second mission, though now nearly seventy years old, he went to the help of the peoples of west Gaul, who were being attacked by both Alan horsemen and the marauding Bagaudes.  He succeeded in curbing the savagery there by the prestige of his sanctity.  When he died at Ravenna in 450, his faithful people carried his body back to Auxerre for burial.

[1] *Relation sur le quiétisme*, iii. 5.

We have already glanced at the saint-bishops who did battle with the Barbarians: the Exuperiuses, Nicasiuses, Anianuses, or Lupuses. But even those whom Providence never called to conflicts of this kind can teach us countless lessons! There is *St Hilary of Arles*, a bishop at the age of thirty (428), whose influence extended throughout southern Gaul. He it was who preached the Gospel to the pagans with the greatest success, and who opposed suspect doctrines with that greatest possession of all, true faith. There is *St Eucherius of Lyons*, a former senator and a writer of some talent. He assessed the tragedy of the age very clearly, and when he was called to the episcopate (in 434), he laboured manfully to save men's hope, defended the rights of the Church against the Burgundians, and in his own life set such an example of Christian virtue that four of his children were subsequently canonized also. At Paris there is *St Marcellus*—of whom a charming tradition has it that, as a choir-boy, whilst drawing water from the Seine in readiness for the ablutions of the mass, he saw it turn miraculously into wine as it entered his bucket.

As bishop from 405 until 436, Marcellus was the man primarily responsible for the conversion to Christianity of the Paris masses. He was also an administrator who gave the diocese of Lutetia its most outstanding position since the martyrdom of St Denis. The actions of these Gallic bishops were decisive in so many different directions. . . . We can see them at work throughout the fifth century; when, during the last three decades, the Visigoths seemed permanently settled on French soil, another great Christian leader came to the fore, *St Sidonius Apollinaris*, Bishop of Clermont-Ferrand in 471. He was a senator, a son-in-law of the Emperor Avitus, and a notable poet. He threw himself wholeheartedly into his episcopal duties, was tireless in his contacts with his people, straining every nerve to keep them faithful to the true religion and to civilization, and, from his Auvergne fastness, waged such a campaign against the occupying Barbarians that he was eventually deported by them and imprisoned at Carcassonne.

These were some of the bishops who were defenders of the city, and defenders of the faith. There are countless others whom we could mention! Yet in so many cases we lack information about them. Paulinus of Nola praises the bishops of Vienne, Bordeaux, Albi, Angoulême, Clermont, Cahors, Périgueux, declaring that their dignified stand made them the equal of St Exuperius. Throughout the entire Church there is no scarcity of outstanding figures of this kind. In Italy St Maximus of Turin, and St Peter Chrysologus of Ravenna were at one and the same time great redressers of wrongs, scourgers of heresies, and indefatigable defenders of the threatened civilization. Still more important were those bishops of Rome whose position was to extend far beyond the limits of their diocese and whose greatness

D

was to be personified in the magnificent personage of St Leo.[1]    Indeed, in the midst of this terrible agony which wracked the world, it is wonderful to note so few defections among the Christian leaders— there were only a few Spanish bishops who fled before the invading Vandals, and one or two prelates, here and there, who were too ready to collaborate with the invaders.    Taken as a whole, the entire Catholic episcopate behaved in an exemplary fashion, and its attitude was to be of supreme importance for civilization's Christian future.

Whilst paying tribute to these outstanding figures we must not forget that there is another force to which our civilization is eternally indebted.    If the bishops were the sea-walls against which the Barbarian waves hurtled in vain, there was another great Christian institution which supported and buttressed them in innumerable ways: *monasticism*.    Its role was henceforth to develop continually, until it became of prime importance.    Monasticism started in the East, in eremitical form, under the leadership of St Anthony and the Desert Fathers.    Still confined to the same region, it subsequently acquired a cenobitic character, thanks to St Pachomius, and later still was reorganized in Asia Minor by St Basil.

During the second half of the fourth century it had developed tremendously.    By about the year 400 every Christian region was familiar with these groups of men and women dedicated exclusively to God, leading a life of asceticism and prayer, according to the principles of a more or less definite rule.    Monastic communities were equally important in Rome, in the Milan suburbs, or in Africa.    In Gaul St Martin had founded Ligugé and then Marmoutier.    The latter had developed with hitherto unprecedented speed.    Cassianus had gathered round him a group of contemplative spirits in the abbey of St Victor, in Marseilles.    At Saint-Claude, St Romanus and St Lupicinus were soon to found the abbey of Condat.    But the most brilliant and most efficacious of these centres of Christian influence was *Lerins*.    Founded towards the close of the fourth century by St Honoratus, a young Gallic patrician, inspired by the example of the Eastern monks, on the island which to-day bears his name, the Lérins community quickly attracted Christians by the hundred—perhaps by the thousand.    Soon the uninhabited islands were filled with colonies of hermits and with the cells of the contemplatives—the 'seekers of God' as St Hilary of Arles, one of them himself, described them.

The monasteries fulfilled a triple role.    Firstly, they had extraordinary spiritual importance.    When we look at the power for action which the Church displayed in the Dark Ages, we must not forget that

[1] See the section devoted to him further on in this chapter, p. 97.

this capacity rested on supernatural graces, on a deep spiritual life, and a permanent contact with God. The monasteries ensured the existence of these spiritual bases. This is so much the case that the Church's men of action felt the need to have a community close to them, in the midst of which they either lived or, at all events, liked to retemper their souls: St Martin did this at Marmoutier, St Augustine at Hippo, St Paulinus at Nola, St Hilary at Arles, etc. These episcopal monasteries undoubtedly exercised a considerable influence on the bishops with whom they shared the spiritual life. St Hilary has aptly said that the monks assumed 'a kind of private episcopacy.'

Secondly, the monasteries constituted veritable nurseries of bishops —types of superior seminaries for the future leaders of Christianity. The best of the African bishops of the period came from the Augustinian community at Hippo. From Lérins the number of monks who were called to administer dioceses—albeit often reluctantly—is quite unbelievable: whilst Hilary of Arles, Eucherius of Lyons, Faustus of Riez, Lupus of Troyes, and a great many others besides carried far and wide the lessons of spiritual contemplation and action learned on the island of Saint-Honorât! And far beyond Gaul there was a former monk of Lérins, St Patrick, the apostle of Ireland, whose monks were to play such an outstanding part in the conversion of the barbaric West. Thus the influence wielded by this great monastery was immense, so much so that it eventually gave rise to a certain amount of suspicion, and some of the popes, like St Leo, resisted the invasion of the bishoprics by the monks. . . .

Finally, can we say that the monasteries assumed, from this time onward, that truly civilizing character which, according to Montalembert was to be the glory of the 'monks of the West'? Yes, indeed— it was modest enough, in these early days, but quite indisputable. In attracting Barbarian youth to their ranks the monasteries undoubtedly contributed, as Hilary of Arles said, 'to allaying the savagery,' and also, in the intellectual field, they preserved the traditions and the elements of a threatened culture. Lérins and Marseilles were intellectual centres where a goodly number of *Acts of the Martyrs* were written, where men took part in all the great doctrinal struggles of Christianity, where St Vincent of Lérins drew up that kind of first 'catechism,' the *Commonitorium*. From such a centre, too, came *Arnobus*, the Roman commentator on the Psalms, and Pelagius also, whom false pride was to turn into a heretic. . . .

If, in addition to this, we remember that in all the monasteries schools were formed, to which the prevailing fashion brought a considerable number of pupils, we can assess clearly what influence these other pillars of the Church and of civilization must have had. It was an influence which was to become still greater at the close of the following century, and subsequently, when Western monasticism was to find its master-mind in the person of St Benedict.

FACE TO FACE WITH THE BARBARIANS

The Church of Christ was now at the very height of her vitality, the only element in a disintegrating world which was firmly established, by virtue of her spiritual bases, her organization, and the qualities of her leaders.   On her was to fall the obligation of solving the gravest problem of the epoch, the problem posed by the presence of the Barbarians in the midst of Romanized Europe.   She alone could solve it, and solve it she did.

From the first moment that the Germanic peoples, for one reason or another, set foot within the Empire, relations were established between them and the people known as 'Romans' (in actual fact, a mosaic of peoples, more or less coated with a thin veneer of Latin culture, which bound them all together, up to a point), relations which were complex, contradictory, and variable according to the place, the people, and the periods concerned: we can construct a reasonably accurate picture of the situation by bearing in mind the different forms in which the phenomenon of alien occupation has reappeared in our own day and age.

Legally the position of the occupying Barbarians was easily regulated.   Had not Barbarian elements been installed within the Empire as *foederati* for a long time now?   Special legislation had been enacted fixing the conditions of their quartering; on the production of a billeting ticket each householder was bound to hand over a part of his house, which an edict of Arcadius and Honorius had fixed at a one-third share, in 398.   Moreover, when the installation was of a permanent nature, these 'guests' (this was their official name!) were allocated one-third of the revenues of the gardens, fields, forests, flocks, and even one-third of the servile labour available.   What is so extraordinary is that the Barbarians who arrived later on, as invaders, enforced this system.   Such was the prestige of Rome. . . .   Save for a few rare exceptions they considered themselves as bound as during the regime of 'hospitality.'   Here and there they demanded a little more than their due: the Burgundians went as far as claiming a two-thirds share.   But on the whole things were not too bad.   The owners of large estates—obviously the hardest hit—resigned themselves to sharing their resources with the chief of a Germanic tribe.   And this practice of hospitality, by dispersing the Barbarians throughout different areas, contributed substantially to their absorption into the Roman population, despite the precautions taken, at any rate in the early stages, to forbid intermarriage and to maintain the juridical systems and the customs relating to property and inheritance absolutely separate.[1]

Although the legal relationship might be ordered satisfactorily enough, personal relationships remained, and these were a much more complicated matter to settle. The Barbarians were in almost every nook and cranny of the Western Empire; they stayed in people's houses, one met them on the highways, and jostled against them in the towns. What did people think of them? At the very outset, at the time of the first onslaughts, the civilized folk were much impressed by these great blond warriors, who descended upon them, clothed in hides, their two-horned helmets on their heads, bows on their shoulders, spears in their hands, and a huge bag of fodder hanging from their horses' necks. As they were almost invariably followed by numerous wagons bearing their women and children, people looked upon them as a kind of irresistible tidal wave. The first shock passed, and men pulled themselves together. They became less afraid. But this hardly made personal contact with the Germanic soldiery any more pleasant! The writers of the period do not conceal the disgust they felt on meeting the Burgundians, who were 'smeared with rancid butter, roast garlic, and onion,' or those Goths, who were so hairy that they had to cut the hairs in their nostrils every day! Contempt for the Barbarians, an emotion inherited from the Greeks, was deeply ingrained in the Roman soul, and beside an Alan or a Suevian, not a single Gaul nor Iberian existed who did not consider himself a defender of civilization. Did this irritation, contempt, and disgust go any further—as far as anger and systematic hostility? During the invasion itself, amid the grief occasioned by the ruins and the atrocities, yes, from St Jerome to St Augustine, from Paulinus of Béziers to the Spanish chronicler Idatius—the eye-witnesses who have proclaimed their indignation and their fury towards the Barbarians are numerous indeed. This reaction had one excellent result, however: it gave all the peoples of Europe a sense of common destiny, a spontaneous loyalty to *Romania*—the word first makes its appearance in this epoch. But it would be an exaggeration to believe that this reaction was permanent and general (except, it must be repeated, in exceptional cases, notably in the areas occupied by the Vandals); there was no systematic 'resistance movement' against the Barbarians, considered, in principle, as enemies, but who, nevertheless, were far from considering themselves as such.

[1] The law therefore becomes *personal*, i.e. it applies to the person, and is no longer *territorial* as in the days of Roman sovereignty. The principle of juridical territoriality was not to reappear until the ninth century, when the fusion of the two ethnic groups was completed. The church, considered as a body, was to retain Roman law, although her clerks were bound by their own personal law.

It would certainly be an overstatement to say that all Barbarians admired Roman civilization up to the point of being ready to follow its teachings.  Amongst some of them the old lustful instincts, which impelled the hordes forward to seize the wealth of the fertile provinces for themselves, still prevailed; this instinct was that of the Vandals at the beginning of the Invasions; later on it was that of the Saxons, the Alamans, and the Lombards.  However, in many instances, the taste for plunder was only one amongst many other impulses.  When Alaric devastated Rome in 410, it was chiefly out of spite because he had not obtained the title he coveted from Honorius: it was like the vengeful fury of the disappointed lover.  The fact is that innumerable Barbarians thought of the Empire, as Fustel de Coulanges has said, 'not as an enemy, but as a career'; they dreamed of bearing the titles of high Roman officers.  Even amongst the tribal masses there was a somewhat confused but nevertheless sincere feeling of admiration for all that still stood for Roman organization, wealth, and tradition.  Only the Vandals professed contempt and hatred for everything civilized (at least, they were the only *Germanic* Barbarians to profess it, for there was to be Attila, the Hun, also); their king, Genseric, waged a campaign of systematic destruction against everything pertaining to *Romania* in Africa, going so far as to declare, in reply to protests that were only too well founded: 'I have sworn to annihilate your name and your race, and you dare to ask me to do otherwise!'  But possibly he was being impelled on this course mainly by religious fanaticism.  It is certainly true that a minority which has decided to dominate a people it has conquered can change its ideas profoundly; this is apparent in a later age in the work accomplished by the Turks in the Balkans, or by the Normans under William the Conqueror in England.  In the main the Germans had not this intention.

And yet they were only a minority; in other words, they knew the dread of finding themselves swallowed up by the masses they had conquered, and certain brutal reactions from time to time can be explained by this dread.  All the available figures suggest that the invaders were indeed far from numerous.  In estimating them at five per cent of the world population we are probably allowing the maximum figure; only five hundred thousand of them out of a total world population of one hundred million. . . .  At the time of their entry into Spain the Visigoths numbered less than one hundred thousand; when they crossed the Straits of Gibraltar the united tribes of Vandals and Alans numbered about eighty thousand souls, including women and children; the Burgundians never seem to have passed the twenty-five thousand mark, of which some five thousand were warriors.  In Italy, out of six or seven million people, there may have been only one hundred thousand Ostrogoths.[1] The relative insignificance of the invaders' ethnical contribution is very striking, and two facts prove this: one is the fact that the Germanic physical type is to-day scarcely ever found in Provence, Italy, or Spain; the other is the survival of Latin languages all over Roman Europe, except in the frontier regions where the Germanic concentration of population was dense, on the fringes of the Empire. And this numerical weakness explains why the famous Barbarian virtues, so dear to Salvianus, were speedily dissolved into Roman decadence, and why, from the mingling of the two elements, there emerged the rather fascinating mixture of violence, debauchery, cupidity, and cruelty which characterizes the final years of the Barbarian kingdoms and which the Merovingian era so tragically illustrates. Thus it is true to say that Europe was not Germanized but barbarized. . . .

It remains true that, to any far-sighted observer, unhampered by prejudice, conditions seemed of necessity to be preparing for a fusion between the newcomers and the old inhabitants of the West. The problem now was to know whether an area of agreement could be reached with the Barbarians, so that both elements could work together for a revival of the Roman Empire and a rejuvenation of civilization. It is in these terms that we see the problem to-day; it is wonderful indeed that, buried to the hilt as they were in the welter of uncontrolled events around them, some fifth-century men, some Christians, realized it too.

The reaction of these men appears to have been as follows. Since the cataclysm of the Invasions had not in fact marked the end of the world, the Church could not shut herself away, fruitlessly mourning the past. Her profound understanding of the drama, which we have already noticed, impelled her to adopt a different attitude. On the level of lofty speculation, where his genius ranged so happily, St Augustine had shown, in his *City of God*, that it was necessary to progress beyond the moribund Empire and to conceive a new world. Although he was himself so deeply attached to everything Roman, he sensed that it had to be replaced—Rome was 'unworthy of the name of State'—she had proved disloyal to the true justice that was Christ's. His disciple, *Orosius*, who was much younger than Augustine and had therefore concrete experience to guide him—time, in matters like this, led to a good deal of modification in men's positions—was to take for granted

---

[1] The language boundary, which has hardly changed at all during the last fifteen centuries. shows the boundary of Frankish occupation to be in north and north-east Gaul, the Alaman boundary to be in the modern Alsace and Switzerland. The 'Roman' element had lost about 55,000 sq. miles to the Germanic element out of the 375,000 sq. miles which comprised all Gaul, that is, less than one-sixth of the total. Aside from this encroachment on Roman soil, one can and one must admit that the Franks had a few settlements in Gaul itself, but these were of a 'sporadic' nature. (Ferdinand Lot, *Naissance de la France*, p. 149.)

the idea of including the Barbarians in an enlarged, transformed *Romania*, which would be a new empire. He was to develop his master's thesis and envisage a kind of confederation of Christian nations under the authority of the Pope, an idea which Otto III was to attempt to realize much later on. Twenty-five years after Orosius, *Salvianus*, in holding up the Germans to the Romans as models of virtue was not merely yielding to the declamatory inclination of the preacher and the polemicist; if he passed humbly over to the Barbarians it was in order to call on Catholic society to reject the rotten elements from the old world and to create a better state of things, a new way of life. Unquestionably it did not do to take too swift a plunge in this direction and it was wisest to take the time factor into careful consideration; for instance, Paulinus of Pella, the Bordeaux nobleman, had good cause to repent bitterly of 'collaborating' too early with the Visigoths, but what was still an extremely dangerous course in 417 was, by 460, almost the accepted state of things: in politics truth is often a matter of the moment. . . .

Thus Christian feeling towards the Barbarians evolved until it came to consider fusion desirable. Why? Firstly because the Church has always had a realistic appreciation of political exigencies, all the more so since, for her, these exigencies are not the essential, since the Kingdom of God is not here on earth. In the midst of the general disorder the Barbarians constituted a live force: why should the Church refuse to make use of it? Moreover had not the collapse of the Empire made a clean sweep of things, in wiping out the old enemy, Graeco-Roman paganism? Then again the Catholic hierarchy well knew that, as the old order disintegrated, its own role grew more important, for it now appeared as the leading force making for order: the bishops established that, in many cases, they were indispensable to the Barbarians. Finally—and this is the over-riding reason—these men whose souls were aflame with the zeal of their apostleship could not help having a passionate desire to win the souls of the invaders for Christ, which would mean, in this case, winning them for civilization too. Such were the feelings of those who held the responsibilities of the Church in their hands. This does not mean that there existed, as Ozanam has noted, with rather generous romanticism, a systematic plan for the conversion of the Barbarians: Catholicism decided to take them under her wing and to conquer them solely by virtue of that deep and radiant urge which, since her origins, had impelled her to spread the Good News through every land. And since she possessed, at one and the same time, an unparalleled spiritual power, a unique organization, and a universality which prolonged in men's eyes the old and now defunct universality of Rome, she succeeded in this most audacious of enterprises—the conquest, the conversion, of the Barbarians.

## THE UNION AGAINST THE HUNS

Towards the middle of the fifth century a dramatic event occurred which made both Romans and Germans realize that their interests could coincide; this was the invasion of the Huns. The 'yellow peril' was weighing hard upon Europe for the first time. Civilized folk and Barbarians alike found themselves in danger of falling into the power of the Mongols.

The history of this first 'Empire of the Steppes' [1] is an amazing and turbulent one. Its terrible strength fluctuated at the will of unknown forces; it shifted continually with the gallop of the thickset ponies. Only yesterday it had attacked China, to-day it hurled itself on Europe, and it was to retire to-morrow with all the suddenness of a wave, leaving behind it nothing but fury and desolation! Its history goes back to the fabulous age, more than thirty centuries previously, a time in which Chinese mythology describes the astonishing victory over the 'Hiang-Now' gained by Hoang-Ti the Tamer and his army of panthers and tigers, and, going farther back still, tells of those mysterious towns of upper Asia whose engulfment by the sands had, it was said, condemned the Huns to eternal wandering. Even in much more recent history several facts remain unexplained. Why, when halted by the steadfast force of the Han emperors and by the majesty of the 'Chinese Peace'—a Far Eastern version of the Pax Romana—did the Huns turn back some 6,000 miles to make their next efforts at conquest? Why, when they left the steppes north of the Aral Sea, about the year 370, did they cross the lower Volga in order to continue their march westwards? We scarcely know; but we have already seen that the pressure which they exerted was the decisive cause of the Germanic invasions. Having thrown the Alans and the Goths into the very heart of the Roman Empire, like a kind of vanguard, they in their turn appeared on its outskirts, and civilized folk regarded them with terror.

The famous description of the Huns by Ammian Marcellinus is so engraven in our minds that it is quite impossible for us to see these terrible nomads except in the light in which the Roman historian presents them. 'Their ferocity surpasses everything imaginable. They have squat bodies, and enormous arms and shoulders, and their heads are disproportionately large. Their cheeks are disfigured by scars, self-inflicted in order to prevent their beards from growing.

---

[1] The expression 'Empire of the Steppes' is the title of René Grousset's admirable book on the subject. In the course of history three 'Empires of the Steppes' were to succeed one another, the empires of Attila, Genghiz Khan (twelfth century), and Tamburlane (fourteenth century). The two latter showed the same surprisingly rapid growth as Attila's, and proved just as fragile.

* D

Are they men or beasts? Legend has it that they are born with the
monstrous aid of sorcerers and demons, and they pass their whole lives
on horseback. They hold their tribal meetings on horseback, do
their buying and selling on horseback, eat and drink there, and even
sleep there, resting against the necks of their steeds. They do no
ploughing, and no sowing, and they have no settled homes'; their
women and children live in the wagons which accompany the horde
on its wanderings. Then come the famous unforgettable passage:
'They do not even cook their food, but they eat raw meat which they
store under their saddles until it is bad.' For all this they are wonderful soldiers: 'No one can equal the skill with which they cast their
boneheaded arrows, sending them prodigious distances, as hard and as
murderous as iron.' Truth to tell, this description, exact enough as
far as it goes—Chinese historians confirm it—this impression of 'wild
beasts on two legs' should, to be quite accurate, have some additions
made to it. Were they really no better than savages, these men who
produced a bronze jewellery, adorned with animal motifs, that shows
considerable skill and has a peculiar charm, that is both realistic, yet
poetic? By the middle of the fifth century they had been in contact
with the civilized world for a long time. Did it not influence them a
good deal? The Greek writer, Priscos, who visited their royal camp
in the Hungarian plains, marvelled at the luxury he saw in the wood
cabins that were clustered together in circles: there were soft carpets,
stone baths, dishes of gold and silver; the wines were good, the food
exquisite, and there were even minstrels and jesters to keep the com-
pany amused. . . . Here could be seen all the contrasts of this Hun
civilization; in the primitive thatched cottages were wonderful silks,
and, pinned to ill-cut clothes, pearls or emeralds beyond price. . . .

The Huns' initial relations with the Roman Empire were very far
from being savage ones. Many of their chieftains, attracted by the
financial rewards offered, took service as auxiliaries in her armies. For
example, Stilicho engaged an entire tribe of Huns and had nothing but
praise for their loyal service. It was not at all unusual to see these
singular defenders of the West riding through the streets of Milan or
Ravenna—these men with their narrow, slanting eyes and yellow skins,
dressed in skins and furs. The legionaries would keep their distance
from them because they smelt so disgusting.

But when *Attila* arrived on the scene all this was changed. This
man, whom tradition, ever-simplifying, has tried to dismiss with the
nickname the 'Scourge of God,' is, in truth, one of the most extraordinary men of his own and possibly of all time. He belonged to
that breed of mighty conquerors who are not merely magnificent
beasts, but spirits inspired by a great design. Attila was remarkably
intelligent, though his diplomatic and political talents were greater

than his military skill.   He was adept at managing men, at winning over most, and weakening the rest by a judicious use of terror.[1]   Yet he was perfectly capable of showing mercy and generosity; he treated the bravery of others, and spiritual authority, with respect; he was intrepid, yet superstitious.   He lived extremely simply in the midst of a court where Persian silks and Chinese tapestries abounded, an ascetic for months on end, then suddenly wallowing in the luxuries of a harem from which at least sixty sons were sired by him.   Such a character as this cannot be adequately treated in a few lines.   Though he had once been a hostage at the imperial court, he had not, despite his youth, allowed the debilitating influences of this rotten *milieu* to soften him.   However, he had assessed its weakness with perfect accuracy, and had picked out the cracks in its structure; he had learnt Latin, which he spoke fluently, though with an atrocious accent. When, in 435, he inherited the throne, after the expeditious assassination of his brother, he set out to reverse the entire policy of his people. He treated the Hun chieftains who were serving in the Roman army as deserters and had them crucified; he established, between himself and the Empire, a deserted no man's land, the breadth of a three days' march—an 'iron curtain,' so that the gangrene of civilization could not contaminate his subjects in any way.   Then, when he had, either by force or guile, united all the tribes in his territories, white- or yellow-skinned, under his leadership, he made ready his gigantic enterprise. What was it?   Clearly nothing less than the establishment, in Europe, of an Asiatic Empire, replacing that of Rome, and an empire, which, without doubt, was intended to serve him as a spring-board for the conquest of the entire world. . . .   Assisted by his implacable determination, what a terrible danger this Utopian scheme held for the West!

First of all Attila nibbled at the territory on the eastern frontiers, then, having flirted gently with the armies of Theodosius II, 'the Calligrapher,' [2] he suddenly, in 450, changed the direction of his attack, for reasons which remain obscure.   Perhaps the steadfast attitude of the old warrior, Marcian, impressed him, or possibly he turned westwards because of a secret treaty with another enemy of Rome, Genseric, the Vandal.   The excuse he put forward for attacking the Western Empire is not without its amusing aspect.   Some time earlier an imperial princess, named Honoria, who was but twenty years old, had sent him a love-letter, a proposal of marriage, together

---

[1] It is quite certain that the atrocities, however limited, which he committed, were undertaken with the definite intention of annihilating possible resistance; it was his custom 'to show force in order not to have to use it.'   He liked to call himself 'the most detestable man in the world' and no one gave him greater happiness than the Gallic monk who nicknamed him the 'Scourge of God.'

[2] See Chapter III, section: 'The Theologian-Autocrats.'

with a ring.   Perhaps she was a little out of her mind, or maybe, disgusted by the decadence of the Court in which she lived, the idea of a
real savage appealed to her.   At the time Attila was wary of replying.
But in 450 he pretended to be in love with this distant princess so that
he could claim, at Ravenna, both her hand in marriage and her . . .
dowry, in other words, one-half of the Western Empire.   And when
Honoria was hurriedly married off to someone else, whilst a most diplomatic refusal was being concocted for the Hun, Attila began to harry
Gaul, and his emissaries took note of Rome's strength.   In spring
451 he attacked.

It is difficult to give an exact account of the Asiatic assault on Gaul.
Contemporaries, terrified by the appearance of the attackers, feeling
confusedly that here was a struggle infinitely more serious than that
which had just taken place with the Germans, tended to exaggerate the
ravages of the 'Scourge of God.'   Several lives of the saints make
the Huns appear in places to which they never went at all, simply
in order to bring their heroes into the story, e.g. at Trèves, Langres,
and Lyons.   One very notable fact is the extreme brevity of this
drama: it was certainly the end of March when Attila's army crossed
the Rhine in barges fashioned from the ancient oaks of the Hercynian
forests; yet, by the time summer was over, he would have vanished.
As for the estimates of the numbers of his effective forces which have
been put forward—how can they be anything but legendary?   Five
or six hundred thousand horsemen, it is said, followed by an ocean of
women and children.   The state of the roads and the impossibility of
feeding such a number makes these figures utterly unacceptable.   But
nevertheless it is true that this gigantic 'raid' by concerted Barbarian
tribes, Gepidae, Rugians, Herulians, Thuringians, and Burgundians,
all united under Hun leadership, represented a most serious threat to
the feebly defended Gallic territories.   Metz was seized on 7th April,
Easter Day, Troyes was spared, and Paris by-passed, perhaps out of
prudence or else from a desire to go south as quickly as possible, in the
direction of the Vandals of Africa.   Attila was besieging Orléans, in
order to break open the Loire crossing, when an adversary confronted
him and halted him.

This was *Aetius*: he has earned the title of 'the last of the Romans.'
He was the son of a German from Pannonia, who had been master of
the cavalry and Count of Africa, and a Latin woman of noble birth.
Aetius had a thorough knowledge of the Barbarians.   He owed this to
his enforced stays amongst them in his youth as a hostage—first with
Alaric, then with the Huns.   He had earned the highest honours in the
service of Galla Placidia and Valentinian III, and had shown them—
albeit not without occasional mental reservations—great devotion.
Aetius was very typical of the semi-Barbarians in whom the moribund

Empire found its last servants.  He was perfectly aware of Rome's decrepitude, contemptuous of the men he accepted as his masters, and yet faithful to what seemed to him a still noble ideal.  Had Aetius, who was the only opponent of Attila possessing anything like Attila's stature, a complete plan for the revival of the Empire by means of German blood?  At all events, in practice, it was to this political idea that he turned when the Hun menace attacked the West.  He arrived from Italy in May, with a few legions, and was soon joined by contingents of Arvernians, of Breoni from the Alps, of Armoricans from Brittany, of Franks under Mervig, and Burgundians under Gunther. He set about methodically organizing his reply to the Huns, and assembled around Arles a heterogeneous army, in which Saxons, Suevians, and Sarmatians jostled with Italians.  In short, he tried to create a united front of the White-skinned folk against the Yellow-skinned: his crowning triumph came when he obtained, by diplomatic negotiation, the entry of the Visigoths of Toulouse into his bloc.  He had defeated them only a short while before this, and they assessed the Mongol peril seriously enough to march alongside him.

On 23rd June, just as Orléans, at the end of her tether, had opened her gates to the Huns, Aetius arrived in front of the town, counter-attacked, and threw the marauders into a panic.  They turned back towards Champagne at the gallop.  The 'Roman army,' if we can call it that—this army, made up of all the nations of Europe—followed in hot pursuit.  And this resulted, at the end of August 451, in that terrible and decisive battle which is usually called the battle of the *Catalaunian Fields*, but which actually took place on the *Mauriacus Campus*, near Troyes.  There Europe and Asia battled with each other throughout one whole day.  The Western forces opposed the arrows and the devastating cavalry charges of the Huns with the old, well-tried legionary method of battle, that of preserving unshakable blocs of troops; then, when their assailants began to tire, they launched a counter-attack with slings and leaded darts, whose employment *Vegetius*, the military strategist, had recently advocated.  Finally there came the great tactical manœuvre, when the centre ranks of the enemy cracked, his front fell to pieces, and he retired to his camp, whither Aetius judged it more prudent not to follow him.

The next day Attila had gone.  The Hun adventure had been cut short.  Western civilization was saved.  And even if, geographically speaking, this battle of the 'Catalaunian Fields' was not a battle of the Marne, it was one in a symbolic sense, if we regard it, as we should, as an event which changed the destiny of the world, as, later on, Poitiers, Bouvines, Valmy, and the victory of Joffre in 1914 were to do again.

The decline of the Huns swiftly followed on this episode.  Though repulsed rather than defeated, Attila seems to have been not a little affected by the event.    Perhaps he wanted to remodel his army, to make it capable of confronting the legions.    Perhaps he thought of turning against the East again.    In 452 he returned to attack Italy, but allowed himself to be deflected by the promise of a tribute.    It was a stricken man, far less sure of himself than heretofore and considerably aged, who went back to his lands on the banks of the Tisza and the Koros.    Soon afterwards he died, on his wedding night, for, though nearly seventy years old, he had just carried off as a prize a German girl, a ravishing fair-haired beauty.    He was found in a fit on the nuptial bed, blood gushing from his mouth and nose.    And it was after this that Valentinian III, who had never forgiven Aetius for saving the Empire, slew him with his own hands. . . .

The swift and terrible tornado which the Hunnish hordes had let loose on the West did not make much of a permanent mark on its history.    The memory of it alone remained in the horror which the very name of 'Hun' inspired in future generations, and in certain episodes, albeit completely distorted, of the *Niebelungenlied*, where Attila appears as the dreadful Eitel.    But it had had a concrete result in producing the first collection of Western forces of many nations which halted it.    In other words, it had showed that, fragile though it still was, and permeated by suspicions on either side, union between Romans and Germans was a possibility.    In this way this incident anticipated the future.

What was the Church's part in this decisive act in Western history? There are several reasons for assuming that it was far from a minor one. It was Anianus, Bishop of Orléans, who went to Arles to bring Aetius news of the situation and to persuade him to make that march to the Loire which was to be so decisive.    It was another Christian, *Avitus*, the future emperor and bishop, who negotiated the agreement proposing the entry of the Visigoths into the anti-Hun coalition, and who succeeded in this difficult diplomatic manœuvre.    We get the distinct impression that the power of the Church is ranged behind Aetius and his incongruous army.

And this is why the anecdotes which describe Attila as being halted by the saints possess a profound historical truth.    At Troyes Bishop Lupus overawed the Hun so much that he decided not to touch the city at all; at Orléans Bishop Anianus was the soul of the defence, at the hour when the bravest faltered, and when the mercenary Alans turned traitor.    All this has symbolic value.    This symbol was made incarnate in another figure of even greater significance—Geneviève, the patron saint of Paris.    This is that same young woman whose shining faith had been recognized by St Germanus of Auxerre—the humble shepherdess, the heroic recluse who, on the threshold of the Baptistery of St John-the-Round, on the headland of the Île de la Cité, resisted the mood of the panic-stricken mob and refused to abandon Paris to the Huns. She is one of those significant figures occasionally thrown up in history, whose character can be exaggerated by popular legend without its true picture being spoilt. 'Let the men flee if they want to, if they are incapable of fighting. We women will pray so hard that God will surely hear our prayers!' And the fact is that Attila never attacked Paris. Subsequently during her long life (423–502) the recluse became the spiritual leader of Lutetia; she had a church built in memory of St Denis; and even when old she did not hesitate to go in search of food for her compatriots who were threatened with famine; at the time when Clovis made his decisive choice, she was a kind of guardian and friend to him and to Clotilda—but all this lifetime of charity fades before the light of the episode of 451. Here stands the Church, making the Barbarians recoil by the force of her prayers. This is much more than a picture; it is a historical truth. Another example also illustrates it: the life of St Leo the Great.

## LEO THE GREAT AND THE PAPACY

In August 452 Attila made his second attack on the West. After being defeated in Champagne he regrouped his forces and invaded Italy. He swept through the northern regions, causing whole populations [1] to scatter before him; he seized and destroyed the important port of Aquileia, and continued to advance, slowly and implacably. It seemed as if the yellow flood was going to cover the entire peninsula. Panic was so great that the Court fell back on Rome, considering Ravenna too close to the Mongol hordes. All hopes seemed vain. People no longer had any confidence in the general Aetius. Intrigue, jealousy, and two minor military reverses had almost ruined his reputation. The European advisers of the conqueror, the Roman Orestes and the Greek Onegeses, urged him to swoop on Rome before the autumn heat, the fevers, and the bad food exhausted the strength of his troops. Attila was just preparing to cross the Mincio when he saw a strange procession advancing towards him, shrouded in a cloud of gold-tinted dust: priests in dalmatics, monks in drugget, two patricians on horseback, and a host of deacons and choristers bearing crosses and banners, and lifting high gold monstrances which gleamed in the sunlight, were marching slowly to meet him. From the entire column the rhythmical responses of hymns and psalms rose on high, swelling into a formidable chorus. In the midst of the procession rode an old man with a white beard, praying as he rode. The Hun galloped

---

[1] It was on this occasion that the Venetians took refuge on the islands of the lagoon from which the modern Venice was to arise.

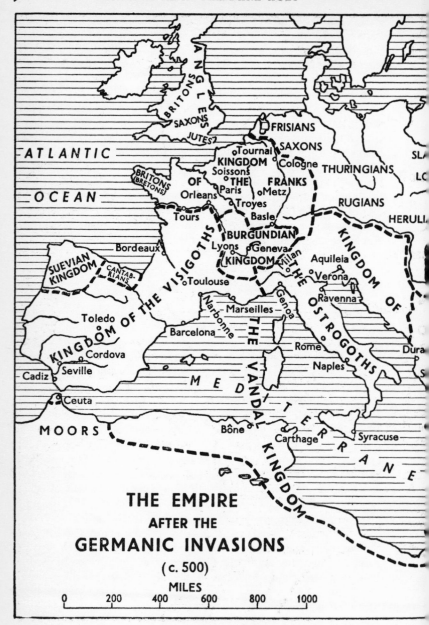

THE EMPIRE
AFTER THE
GERMANIC INVASIONS
(c. 500)

MILES

0     200     400     600     800     1000

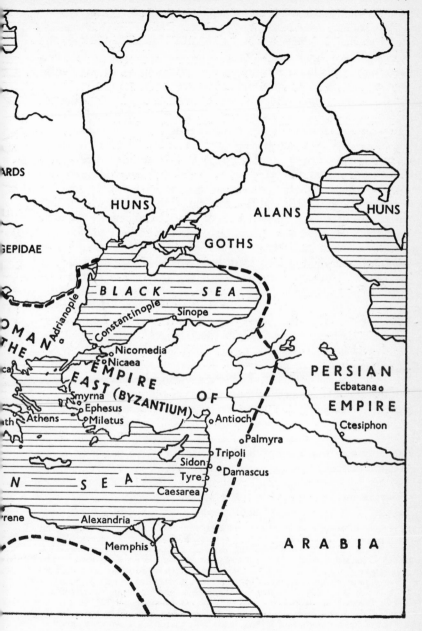

HUNS

ALANS

HUNS

GEPIDAE

GOTHS

BLACK SEA

Adrianople

Constantinople

Sinope

MAN

THE

Nicomedia

Nicaea

EMPIRE

PERSIAN

Ecbatana

EAST (BYZANTIUM)

OF

EMPIRE

Smyrna

Ephesus

Athens

Miletus

Antioch

Ctesiphon

Palmyra

Tripoli

N SEA

Sidon

Damascus

Tyre

Caesarea

rene

Alexandria

Memphis

ARABIA

towards the river, urged his horse into it, and halted on a sandy islet, within hailing distance of the strangers. 'What is your name?' Attila shouted to the old man. Came the answer: 'I am Leo, the Pope.' The singing had stopped. Attila hesitated for a moment, then, urging his horse forward into the water again, gained the far bank. And the Pope came forward to meet him. . . .

Such is the scene, well calculated to appeal to popular imagination, which sums up—albeit rather briefly—the achievement of *St Leo*, *Pope Leo I*, surnamed the *Great*. When all earthly hope had failed the Emperor Valentinian III entrusted him with the task of trying to halt the Mongol invasion. The man of God succeeded where success had seemed impossible. Attila agreed to fall back from Rome on payment of tribute. Perhaps this agreement was influenced by strategic considerations, notably the fact that the Hun army was becoming progressively weaker, coupled with its fear of advancing too far from its bases. No one knows what line of argument St Leo employed in his dealings with the superstitious Barbarian. Did he remind him of the lamentable end to which Alaric had come after plundering the city of Rome? Contemporaries remarked that the prestige of the *Lion* (Latin, *Leo*) of Rome had worked the same marvel as that worked by the *Wolf* (Latin, *Lupus*) of Troyes the previous year. No one will ever know exactly what those two men said. 'Let us give thanks to God, for He has delivered us from great danger.' This was all that Leo would say to Valentinian on returning from his mission.[1]

This episode has tremendous importance. It constituted a triumphant answer to the criticisms of the pagans who were so eager to make out that the abandonment of the ancient rites was the real cause of the imperial defeats. St Augustine had recently answered this argument in the gigantic volumes of his *City of God*; St Leo replied to it in another way, by his very action. It can be said that 'indirectly Attila probably contributed more than any other historical character to the creation of this powerful political factor: the Pope, King of Rome.' Further, by his every action St Leo was to give the Apostolic See an influence and an authority which it was never to lose.

The Church had recognized the predominant position of the Roman

[1] Legend makes much of this mystery. Men were convinced that only supernatural intervention could explain the sudden retreat of the Huns. While the Pope was talking to Attila, it was said, the latter had seen a figure robed in white, like a priest, brandishing a sword at him, standing behind Leo. According to different versions, this was said to be either an angel or St Peter, or St Paul. This story, which is passed over completely by contemporaries, appeared in the ninth or tenth century, was taken up again by Sigbert of Gembloux in the twelfth century, and, in the thirteenth, by Jacques of Voragine in *The Golden Legend*. It was he who inspired Raphael's famous picture in the Vatican. Although this is only legendary in connection with St Leo, it should be added that the erection of the famous statue of St Peter, in the Vatican Grottoes, is sometimes attributed to him. It is claimed that this was set up to commemorate the 'victory' of Mincio. In actual fact this victory occurred about one hundred years after the statue was made.

Papacy ever since the earliest times, because the most ancient of traditions traced its origins to St Peter and his primacy. As early as 106 St Ignatius of Antioch spoke of it in terms of very special veneration. This Apostolic See, increasingly conscious of its disciplinary and dogmatic prerogatives, had made Rome the capital of the Christian world —at the very moment when the prestige of being the imperial residence was being transferred to the provincial cities. What a marvellous role it was to play henceforth! [1] The history of the Papacy's progress during the first four centuries of Christianity is also a wonderful one. It made no innovations in principle, it never strayed from the path fixed for it by the Master Himself in a few decisive sentences—and several of its popes remain somewhat obscure historical figures. Yet all the while its influence tended to grow till it assumed to the full its rights and responsibilities. In the hour of peril, when civilization was sliding towards the abyss, it was vitally important that St Ambrose was able to write: 'Where Peter is there is the Church,' and that from the concluding words of one of St Augustine's sermons men could automatically cull the famous slogan: 'Rome has spoken: the matter is decided.' [2] The Church, the only force of resistance in this dying world, had her leader.

Among St Leo's immediate predecessors two had given promise of his great personality. St Anastasius I (398-491) is hardly in this category, but St Innocent I (401-17) fits it. He was the Pope who dared to defend St John Chrysostom against the despots of Byzantium,[3] who tried to bring about an understanding between Alaric and Honorius in order to prevent catastrophe and who faced the Pelagian heresy with great clarity of vision. St Zosimus (417-18) and then, following the lamentable interregnum of the antipope Eulalius, St Boniface I (419-22) are more questionable figures. But St Celestine I (422-32) showed a lofty understanding of his role. It was Celestine who solemnly confirmed the right of all the faithful to make appeal to Rome; Celestine who sent St Patrick to evangelize Ireland; Celestine who, against the wishes of the emperor of the East, Theodosius II, had the heretic Nestorius condemned. When, following the pontificate of St Sixtus III (432-40)—of whom scarcely no evidence remains save the splendid artistry of the basilica of St Maria Maggiore—the deacon Leo was chosen as Pope, the situation, as dangerous a one as could possibly be imagined, was very favourable to the expansion of apostolic authority, and this was to be the subject of the new Pope's labours.

Leo was born in Tuscany, but he came to the Eternal City when still

---

[1] The functioning of the pontifical institution is returned to later on, in Chapter V, section: 'The Organization of the Western Church.'

[2] See Chapter I, section: 'The Champion of Truth.'

[3] See Chapter III, section: 'Arcadius and the Saint.'

very young, and always spoke of it as 'my native town.' In ancestry and education he was a true Roman, a worthy representative of the race which had been so strong under the republic and during the Golden Age of the Empire.   He was admitted to the Roman clergy as a young man, and very soon acquired considerable authority on account of his personal virtues, his intelligence, and his strength of character.   While still a humble 'acolyte' he had been sent on a confidential mission to St Augustine by Sixtus, the future Pope.   In 430, as archdeacon of Rome, his influence was so immense that Cassianus, the wise monk of Marseilles, called him 'the badge of the Roman Church and of the divine ministry,' and numerous important people maintained a regular correspondence with him.   It was Leo who put the Papacy on its guard against the ideas of Julian of Eclano, the man responsible for continuing the Pelagian heresy.[1]   Next we find him advising Celestine I and Sixtus III, and on several occasions he was employed on diplomatic and religious missions.   When Pope Sixtus died he was carrying out a somewhat delicate mission in Gaul.   Leo's prestige was so immense that the Roman faithful chose him as Pope in his absence.   He was consecrated on 29th September 440, on his return.   At that time he was between forty and fifty years old.

The situation was a grave one in all its aspects.   In the West Valentinian III, a worthless adolescent of twenty, was interested only in pleasure, and left the government in the hands of his mother, Galla Placidia, in whom undoubted qualities of leadership mingled with a womanly instability of temperament.   For thirty-five years now the Barbarians had been surging across the Empire, and against them there was nought save the energy of Aetius, and he was looked down upon by the Court.   In the East Theodosius II, 'the Calligrapher,' was under the influence of his High Chamberlain, Chrysaphus, and was developing into the protector of heretics.   How vigorous Leo seems beside characters as ludicrous as these!   He had the loftiest conception of the mission which was henceforth to be his.   'The blessed Peter,' he declared, 'continues in the rocky fabric he was given; he will never abandon the government of the Church, which has been placed in his hands!'   Leo was well aware that it was the work of the Prince of Apostles which he was carrying on: he was not to fail in his task.

St Leo has all the characteristics of the born leader.   Clear-sighted, exact, and methodical, he possessed the kind of brain which instinctively analyses the most complex problems and finds the practical solution to them.   His was a firm, unflinching character; the hostile situation never had the slightest effect on him; when everything was on the verge of catastrophe he remained steadfast, and his wonderful

---

[1] On Julian, as well as on Pelagius and his heresy, see Chapter I, section: 'The Champion of Truth.'

serenity brought peace of mind to those troubled folk around him. He had, too, a generous spirit, eternally accessible, permeated with the love of Christ; though he dominated the misfortunes of his age it must not be thought that he was insensible to them. And all these qualities, of which he was fully conscious because he knew to what high purpose he dedicated them, rested on a base of true humility; his sense of mission only increased this humility. 'Do not judge the heritage by the unworthiness of the inheritor,' he once murmured, and this sentence sums him up absolutely. It epitomizes the faith and bearing of a true Christian.

It was such a man as this who was predestined to maintain the rights of the Church in this critical period. Ever since the tottering Empire had sought support in the arms of the Cross, the most far-sighted Christian leaders had felt that it would be highly dangerous to allow the Church to tie her fate to that of this threatened world. Faced with the claims of the temporal power, the finest of them had steadfastly asserted the authority of Christ's Church. This is clearly Leo's attitude. Against this Empire in the process of disintegration he set 'Rome, the sacred seat of the Blessed Peter, through whom she has become queen of the Universe.' His political influence was enormous; Galla Placidia listened to him, even the feckless Valentinian had a somewhat uneasy respect for him; but he never let himself be caught up in the unhappy shackles of the Ravenna intrigues: when men came to seek him out to beg him to negotiate with Attila, he was to hesitate, anxious not to become involved in some dubious imperial enterprise. He talked with magnificent assurance to Theodosius II; Marcian was to become his friend and to fall under the spell of his personality; but when the Emperor Leo I sinned, the Pope did not hesitate to use his sacred office and to rebuke him firmly.

In the history of the Church his role was of supreme importance. He was anxious not to let anything touching on the sacred interests in his charge to escape his attention. In Rome he was always accessible to the people, and frequently left his palace in the Lateran to attend personally to their troubles; he had ruins rebuilt, undertook excavations in the catacombs, distributed corn in time of famine. In Italy (this is proved from his correspondence) he was engaged in a thousand matters; he dealt with the conditions requiring to be fulfilled by candidates for the episcopacy, the administration of ecclesiastical property and moneys, the date when baptism should take place, and relations with the Barbarians. Even in the remotest provinces he made his influence felt: he refused to tolerate anything which compromised, however slightly, tradition, principle, or his authority. Certain bishops whom he considered a little too independent were summarily called to order: one of these was Hilary of Arles, who, being a saint, took the matter in good part, and there was also the Patriarch of Thessalonica, whose excessive zeal was moderated by the Pope; when the Patriarch of Constantinople showed signs of ambitions which might threaten the primacy of Rome, Leo resisted him strongly, even though the Patriarch had the support of a Council and of his emperor. He waged a tireless struggle against heretics of every description: Pelagianism, Manichaeism, and Priscillianism all found him equally steadfast, equally determined 'to snatch souls from the pit of error.' There was not a single question, be it great or small, concerning the Church, which he did not examine, and in which he did not try to impose a solution.[1]   By this incessant, universal activity St Leo ensured for ever the idea of the primacy of the Apostolic See; he was, according to Mgr Batiffol, the 'organizer of the historic Papacy.' 'Rome,' we read in a letter addressed by Leo on 10th August 446, to certain African bishops, 'Rome gives the solution to all cases which are submitted to her; these solutions take the form of judgments, and Rome declares the penalties for the future.'   What regal language this is!   It is the first time in the history of Christianity that we have heard anything so lofty!

An even more remarkable fact—this applies to St Leo as well as to St Augustine, whose labours Leo continued in many respects—is that this activity goes hand in hand with a considerable literary output. Less speculative than the Bishop of Hippo, more of a teacher than a theologian, St Leo helped to enlarge the field of Christian philosophy in a number of directions.   Even to-day we still find pleasure in reading—at least, in part—his sermons.   They are so worth while in content, and written on a level which we can easily understand.   His correspondence, which comprises one hundred and seventy-three letters, is filled with important details about the government of the Church and the Christian problems of his time.   His written work, though lacking philosophical and even cultural foundations (he did not know Greek), has an impact on us by virtue of its nicely defined formulae, so entirely different in character from the 'Byzantine' dissertations. Certain of his works, such as the *Volume to Flavian* play, as we shall see, are an important part in the dogmatic quarrels of the age, relating to the Person of Christ and the role of Grace.   It was probably under his influence that the first of the missals was compiled during his life-

---

[1] For instance, he intervened in the dispute which broke out again concerning the date of the Easter festival.   The Council of Nicaea had put an end to the ancient controversies by decisively condemning the *quartodecimans*, i.e. those who wished to celebrate Easter along with the Jewish festival, on the *14th Nisan*, and by fixing the festival on the Sunday which followed the March full moon.   Alexandria had been put in charge of the notification of this decision.   In the middle of the fifth century the accuracy of the Alexandrian calculations were questioned here and there.   St Leo settled in favour of the decisions taken and the calculations made at Alexandria, out of 'anxiety for the unity which it was essential to preserve above all else.'

time, the one which, in the following century, after being somewhat adapted, was to continue to be called the *Leonian Sacramentary*. And on the subjects of the Church's role, her unity, and her foundations, his teaching restated the experience of the past and helped to build a basis for the future.

This is what he was like, then, this outstanding man of God. By his single presence, by the absolute confidence in the Church's everlasting nature which he displayed in every action of his life, he was truly the incarnation of hope in an epoch when all hope was failing. Even if classical Rome must disappear (did St Leo suspect this?) the Rome of the Apostles and the Martyrs was built on the rock that no power on earth could ever destroy. It was surely this conviction which gave him, an unarmed priest, the courage to go and confront Attila as he did, and the prestige sufficient to win from the Hun the withdrawal of his troops. On one further occasion the aged Pope had to assume a similar responsibility when, in 455, the Vandals landed in Italy and seized Rome. Anarchy then was at its height; Valentinian, in his turn, had just been assassinated by the avenger of Aetius; Petronius Maximus, who had succeeded him, had been torn to pieces by the mob whom his cowardice had infuriated; Leo alone faced the enemy. By his entreaties he persuaded Genseric not to burn the city, nor to torture its citizens; but even he could not prevent fourteen days of looting. . . . In times of disaster like these no one could hope to save everything.

On 10th November 461 the great Pope died. He was buried in the atrium of the basilica of St Peter whence he would continue, as the epitaph composed by Pope Sergius I in 688 declares, 'to keep guard so that the wolf, who is always on the look-out for his opportunity, does not ravage the flock.' He has been called the Pope of the Old World, and this he indeed was, in the sense that he was the most clear-sighted witness of the drama in which a society was crumbling to dust. But above all, Leo was the Pope of salvation, whose energy and faith saved everything that was capable of being saved and prepared the Church for the effort of the morrow. Many years after the death of this great Pope of the age of defence, there would emerge another, to be the great Pope of the age of reconquest: Gregory. But a great deal more suffering and chaos had to take place before this happened!

## THE END OF THE WESTERN EMPIRE

When on 21st September 454 Valentinian III—'the palace emperor, whose pallid majesty was never seen by his armies'—personally murdered Aetius, he was, as his contemporaries observed, 'using his left hand to cut off his right.' The death of the 'last of the Romans' was the sign of the end.  For a further twenty years the Western Empire writhed in an ignoble death agony, in which the principle of assassination was the established political axiom.  Valentinian III was, in his turn, assassinated in March of the following year, and there followed an almost farcical succession of puppet princes, whose ridiculous attempts to rule were no longer taken seriously by anyone. Whilst the pretender, Petronius Maximus, collapsed in the space of a few weeks, whilst Eudoxia, the widow of Valentinian III, invited Genseric and his Vandals into Italy, later to leave the country with them together with the booty which they had just looted from Rome, a leader arose, the Suevian Ricimer, the master of the militia, who aspired to play the role of a Stilicho.  The phantom emperors did not count for very much beside a man like him!  Avitus (455–6) was fortunate indeed; he escaped, when defeated, by resigning his throne and hurriedly becoming a bishop!  Marjorian, who resisted Ricimer, was actually murdered.  Ricimer then nominated his protégés as emperors: Severius and Anthemius.  But as soon as these poor simpletons imagined themselves to be really emperors he got rid of them.  This Barbarian, we can see, was a plucky fellow, and one who did not embark on an undertaking lightly!  It must at least be said in his favour that he refused to establish other Barbarians on Italian soil, which he considered untouchable and sacred.  He drove the Vandals back to the coasts, and, during a career lasting approximately sixteen years, he maintained Roman tradition after a fashion.  When he died, in 472, to be followed to the grave shortly afterwards by the last semblance of an emperor, whom he had created out of nothing— Olybrius, whose name has taken on a symbolic meaning—the end was indeed close at hand.

The new 'master of the militia,' i.e. the generalissimo of the armies —the supreme defender of Rome—was none other than Orestes, the Roman traitor, who, as Attila's counsellor, had sent the Huns rushing into Italy!  After liquidating several new puppets, he endeavoured the master-stroke which neither Stilicho nor Aetius, nor even Ricimer himself, had dared make: he proclaimed his son, *Romulus Augustulus*, as emperor (475).  The latter's name, ironically enough, seems to sum up all the historical greatness of Rome.  Someone remarked of this pale, shadowy figure: 'He was handsome. . . .'

However, the Empire was rapidly falling to pieces.  The Angles and the Saxons were establishing themselves in Britain; in Africa the Vandals maintained power by exercising a grip of terror; the Burgundians stretched as far as Lyons and Geneva; Euric, the King of the Visigoths, seized the Auvergne, despite the resistance of its people, led by Ecdicius and his brother-in-law, St Sidonius Apollinaris; the Armorican towns proclaimed their independence; Syagrius, the son of the Aegidius who, as Aetius's lieutenant, had succeeded him in Gaul, came to Soissons (464) to do likewise; only the Salian Franks under Childeric remained faithful to their duty, as federates, but not for very much longer. . . . In front of this anarchical outburst, the Germanic mercenaries in Italy demanded to be given full ownership of land, like the Goths, the Burgundians, and the Franks in Gaul, instead of remaining confined to restricted areas. Orestes, in a final moment of pride, refused to hand holy Italy over to them. They revolted, named the Herulian, *Odoacer*, as their king, captured and killed Orestes, and imprisoned the last emperor, the wretched little Romulus Augustulus, in a villa near Naples. The Western Empire was dead. The date was 4th September 476: one thousand glorious years were drawing to a close. Very respectful of its old forms, and always dazzled by the image of this greatness which he had just destroyed, Odoacer made a neat parcel of the imperial insignia and sent it to the emperor of the East, at Constantinople, asking him, modestly enough, for the title of 'Patrician.' This Zeno was careful neither to agree nor to refuse to give him. And while Odoacer, who remained for thirteen years undisputed master of Italy, was defending it ably, and even reconquering land in Pannonia and Norica, the Barbarians managed to install themselves permanently throughout the entire Empire. When the wave of Ostrogoths under Theodoric poured into Italy in 489, the final act of the great drama, which had begun at the beginning of the century, was played. There was no longer a Western civilization, no longer one Europe, no longer a Roman unity, and a mosaic of Barbarian states had succeeded the *Imperium*.

Yet, one principle of unity remained, unchanging: the Church, Christianity, which we have seen at work all through the drama, under the leadership of St Sidonius Apollinaris, resisting the Visigoths; standing firm against the ferocious Vandals in Africa; continuing to win souls for Christ, to fashion men's minds and actions, to direct, and to administer: the Church, made incarnate in her popes, continued the work of St Leo the Great. Of the five popes who occupied the Apostolic See from the death of St Leo until the end of the century, there was certainly not one who equalled him—neither was there a single one who did not show a profound understanding of his mission. It was *St Hilary* (461–8) who applied himself to restoring the ruins left by the Vandals, and who legislated to maintain, by means of frequent provincial councils, the cohesion of Christianity, which was being threatened by the dislocation of the Roman world. *St Simplicius* (468–83) gained the respect of Odoacer, battled with the heretics in the East, and fought against the autonomist tendencies of Constantinople. Pope at the moment of the final collapse, he occupied a stronger position than ever in the West. *St Felix* (483–92), though raised to power by Odoacer and a personal friend of Zeno, Emperor of the East, never let one nor other influence him, and claimed with fearless pride 'the Church's right to act according to her own laws.'   It was *St Gelasius I* (492–6), whose intelligence and energy so impressed his contemporaries, whose unceasing charity and activity in social work, and whose protection of the poor and the weak in these savage times, was so highly praised.   It was he of whom Bossuet said: 'No one spoke more magnificently of the grandeur of the see in which the popes were enthroned.'   Did he not write to the emperor: 'Mark this well: when the see of the Blessed Peter pronounces judgment, no one is permitted to judge that judgment'?   And even *St Anastasius II* (496–8), who is sometimes accused of having been too complaisant towards the Eastern heretics (for which Dante, quite unjustly, was to allot him a place in his Hell), in fact applied himself to supporting Christian unity on the one stable element which still existed in the world, notably on Byzantium, at the moment when the decisive question was about to be posed to the Catholic West: whether she should annex the Barbarians spiritually and make them hers.

When the fifth century ended, this century which had proved such an important turning-point in history, what was the situation like? First, in the material sphere: a mosaic of Barbarian states, we have said. What can we make of them?   In Italy Theodoric, the leader of the Ostrogoths, was reigning; he had smashed Odoacer after a struggle lasting four years, and remained the sole master, not merely in the peninsula, but in Sicily, Rhaetia, Norica, Dalmatia, and part of Pannonia; he was a great ruler, with whom the emperors of Byzantium were careful to maintain relations.   In Africa, Sardinia, and Corsica the Vandals compensated for their numerical inferiority by adopting a policy of terror, and the hour of liberation there had not yet sounded. In Gaul and Spain the Visigoths of Euric (466–84) were masters of the entire area from the Loire as far south as Andalusia; they had driven the Suevians back into the north-west corner of Spain, in Galicia, and the Cantabrians into their mountain retreats; they dreamed of restoring unity to Gaul to their own advantage.   But the Burgundians occupied the south-west of the country and beyond, from Autun to the Durance, from Nîmes to the Swiss Alps, and their king, Gondebaud (474–516), easy-going and peace-loving though his peoples were, also had lofty ambitions.   In north Gaul unity had just been achieved at the expense of the last survivors of Roman authority, i.e. Syagrius, and to the benefit of the henceforth determined Franks; these too gained independence through a bold young king whose reign began in 481 and whom history was to know as *Clovis*.   In the huge peninsula which jutted out into the Atlantic itself, the Bretons, who had emigrated there from their original islands, had, since the middle of the century, set up federations of towns and tribes—the Dumnonians, the Cornouaille, the Bro Werech, 'tribe of the famous chieftain, Waroc.' These peoples were closely controlled by the clergy, consisting of ascetic monks and wandering bishops, but these, for their part, recognized no man's authority. Meanwhile, in the large island which was henceforth to be known as England, the Angles, Saxons, and Jutes, who probably came from present-day North Germany and Denmark, had established, with all the violence of their still flourishing paganism, the domination of those tribes whose memories remain in the modern names of various English counties: Essex, Sussex, etc. It was an unhappy sight for anyone harking back to the position only a century earlier, when the dying Theodosius had left behind him a still admirable Empire!

However, though the material situation of the West, consecrated to destruction as it was, appeared so tragic, spiritually all did not seem lost. One thing survived this gigantic collapse: one great picture whose prestige was not to disappear so quickly. There was no longer an emperor in the West, and, save for a brief moment in the sixth century, there was not to be another until the time of Charlemagne. However, though he had disappeared in fact, the emperor remained in existence in law. Theoretically had not Odoacer re-established the Empire in all its united majesty by sending the imperial insignia back to Byzantium? The Barbarian chieftains—save for the Vandals and the Angles—considered it an honour to bear the titles of Roman officials or Roman soldiers; Theodoric pretended to rule in the name of the emperor, and it was to be one of the proudest days of Clovis's life when he was named 'Consul' by the far-off emperor in the East. All these Germanic peoples absorbed Roman institutions, adopting Rome's governmental procedure, fiscal methods, hierarchies of officials—even the Vandals, who tried to confiscate this fine machinery for themselves rather than to destroy it. Even better, the ideal of unity which had been that of the Golden Centuries of Rome survived the collapse, this ideal which the worthy Rutilius Numatianus repeated once again in 417: 'You were a motherland for all nations, O Rome, and capital of what was once the world.' A nostalgia remained for those happy epochs of the Western Empire. . . . Thus everything tended to make the men of this age idealize the great picture: for the classical enthusiasts was it not the sign of old loyalties, and, for the Christians, the pledge for the future, when Christian Rome, changing places with moribund, pagan Rome, would assume the same unifying tasks?

Thus St Augustine's ideas on the necessary control to be exercised by the spiritual over the temporal, taken up subsequently by those continuing his work, Orosius and St Leo, were to impress themselves on the collective conscience of the future, to come to terms with the certainty, firmly anchored in the depths of every heart, that the Empire could not disappear.    It was this conviction which, four hundred years later, on the eve of Christmas, 800, impelled the Pope to place the imperial crown on Charlemagne's head, and, two hundred years after this event, towards the year 1000, convinced the Ottos and the Henrys, the emperors of the 'Holy Roman German Empire,' that they were the heirs of Constantine, Theodosius, and Justinian.[1]

Henceforth the problem posed itself in imperial terms.    Since the Empire could not disappear, since it was a 'necessary condition of the world, superior to historical accidents,'[2] it was necessary for it to integrate the newcomers, just as a graft is integrated with the actual substance of a tree.    The Church, which was henceforth the trunk of this tree, alone could accomplish this task.    But she was not able to do this until she had been freed from a serious impediment.

## GOTHIC ARIANISM, ROMAN CATHOLICISM

This impediment was a religious one.    By a deplorable mischance the majority of the Barbarians were already baptized by the time they began settling within the Empire, but not into the mighty Roman Catholic Church; they had been baptized into the Arian faith.    In the fourth century, at the very moment when Christianity was nearing its decisive victory, it was subjected to the frightful assault of the most serious heresy it had yet encountered, that of the Alexandrian priest, Arius, who denied that Jesus was God.    And just when Arianism, after being condemned by the Council of Nicaea in 325, and harried throughout the Empire (not without considerable opposition), was being eliminated from almost every part of it, it had cast a seed among the Gothic tribes camped in the Eastern Empire, and around its frontiers, and there this seed had germinated.

This conversion of the Goths to Arianism had been principally the work of one really extraordinary man, whose Grecianized name of *Ulfilas* scarcely conceals its Germanic original of 'Wolflein' (Little Wolf).    His grandparents, however, came from Cappadocia, that staunchly Christian province of the Fathers.    Born and bred a Catholic, chosen as a 'lecturer' when very young, on account of his great learning, Ulfilas was converted to Arianism during one of the visits he made to Constantinople.    There the Arianizing prelate, Eusebius, consecrated him bishop.    On returning home to the Goths, Ulfilas

---

[1] Ferdinand Lot has accurately noted that, from the point of view of constitutional law, the death certificate of the Western Roman Empire should be dated 6th August 1806, this being the date on which Francis II, after being defeated by Napoleon, renounced his title of Holy Roman Emperor of the German nation and took that of Emperor of Austria.

[2] The phrase is that of Lavisse in vol. i of *L'Histoire générale*, by Lavisse and Rambaud, p. 208.

devoted himself completely, with indisputable faith, to the conversion of his racial brethren, but it was, of course, to Arianism that he converted them.  He invented a new script, and then he translated the Bible into Gothic, thus giving his people a fundamental religious monument.  The Christian ritual was henceforth celebrated by them in this language.  The principles of doctrines were reduced to very simple formulae, excluding almost all dogmatic theology.  From the Gospel ethic something was sifted out which was, in fact, an ethical system based on strength, energy, and heroism—that is to say, on those qualities to which the rough soldiery would be most susceptible. And the liturgy acquired new aspects, all calculated to exalt the souls of the mystically minded warriors: there were masses in the middle of the night, often celebrated in the open air, where the splendid voices of the Germanic choirs soared to the heavens, mingled with the ruddy smoke from their torches.

This particular form of Christianity spread with astonishing rapidity.  When the Visigoths under Fritigern established themselves on the right bank of the Danube, in 376, after fleeing before the Hunnish attack, they had already been visited by Arian missionaries; once converted, they devoted themselves to vigorous propaganda amongst the tribes related to them.  Alaric, who occupied Illyria in 399, brought with him an entire Arian clergy.  From the Visigoths the heretical faith was to penetrate people under Hun supremacy: Ostrogoths, Gepidae, and Herulians—reaching the Vandals just as they were leaving Silesia on their way towards the Carpathians. Aside from the Franks and the Anglo-Saxons, who both remained pagan, initially all the Barbarian peoples who entered the Empire during the fifth century were Arians, right down to the late-comers, the Herulians, Skirians, and Rugians of Odoacer, and the Ostrogoths of Theodoric.

The Catholic Church counter-attacked this expansion of heresy in earnest.  St John Chrysostom sent missionaries among certain Gothic tribes, who had been baptized as Catholics, giving them authority to use the Gothic language in their prayers, so that they should not feel in an inferior position in relation to the Arians, and by the Cimmerian Bosphorus and on the Middle Danube these missionaries obtained results, since Catholic elements can be found among the Ostrogoths.  The mother of Theodoric, for example, was a Catholic. In the regions occupied by the Huns Theotimaeus of Tomi laboured to maintain charitable activity in the name of the Roman Church.  In the depths of Dacia (the modern Serbia) Nicetas of Remesiana (the author of the *Te Deum*) converted to Catholicism many Scythian, Thracian, Geat, and Dacian elements, during his long episcopate (366–415), going so far as to found some Barbarian monasteries.  The most remarkable of these Catholic advance posts was that held by the mysterious *St Severinus*, unquestionably a great Roman figure, who, towards 450, became a monk in the heart of Barbarian territory, on the Danube up-river from Vienna, founded a monastery there, and impressed himself on the entire population on account of his steadfastness and his unflagging generosity in time of trouble.   Until his death, in 482, he exercised such authority among even the Germanic Arians that he could prevent the fanatical Giro, the Rugian queen, from forcing a heretical baptism upon the Catholics in the area.   When Odoacer occupied Italy he wrote to the saint to offer him the disposal of a pardon, and this he was to grant to him on the spot.   But wonderful though these efforts were, they did not change the essential of the situation at all, namely, the fact that the great majority of the Barbarian invaders remained Arians.

This fact, however, was not entirely without happy results.   In certain cases (to which, perhaps, Catholic moralists gave a rather exaggerated importance, in order to see in the Barbarians instruments of God entrusted with punishing the sins of the wicked faithful . . .), in certain cases the Germanic chieftains considered themselves Christian enough to respect churches, sacred objects, and relics.   This attitude seems to have been that of Alaric and his followers.   Thus Orosius tells us of a Goth who, during the sack of Rome, found the precious vessels from the Basilica.   The dedicated virgin who was guarding the store told him that, assuredly, she could not prevent him from taking them, but that St Peter himself would know how to defend his own property.   The soldier was troubled at this, and when he submitted the matter to his commanders Alaric ordered that all these beautiful things should be carried, intact, to the holy place under escort.   And people therefore saw an extraordinary procession wending through the streets of Rome, a procession consisting of Roman priests, the Roman faithful, and the Barbarians, all following the sacred vases and singing together . . . !

But it must be admitted that in very many other cases the result was not so charming!   Often the religious fanaticism of these new, crude Christians, superimposed upon primitive appetites, resulted in acts of extreme violence, which were encouraged by the Arian priests in the ardour of savage proselytism.   So it was at Eleusis, where the weird chaplains of the Visigoth army belaboured the old hierophant and his assistants, like zealots dealing with idols, whilst their hardened troops nimbly looted the treasure of the sanctuary, thereby causing irreparable losses of precious works of art.

And above all, the Arian convictions of the invaders, even though they might have been initially accepted by many of them without much serious examination, became, once they were established in the

West, an element of great importance, in asserting their nationality and in distinguishing them from the Romans. The Christian Empire would have absorbed the Barbarians much more easily had there not been the obstacle of religious fanaticism between it and them. To all the problems which the occupation raised others were added—more delicate ones—the relations between Catholics and heretics. In many places the Barbarians requisitioned the churches to turn them into their own garrison churches, which were naturally Arian. To enter into contact with a Barbarian was considered as bad as degrading oneself with a supporter of the heresy; cases are quoted of priests who were excommunicated for having dined with Arians. On their side, the occupying Barbarians, in order to protect their faith, promulgated laws condemning conversions to Catholicism, even going so far as to forbid those faithful to Rome to build churches. Sidonius Apollinaris has left us a harrowing picture of the position of the Catholic communities in Visigothic Gaul, with their churches falling into disrepair and their clergy beheaded; and he never hides his own feelings towards the Goths: they are the sentiments of a true opposition, which, powerless as yet, is patiently awaiting its hour. It is essential to remember this psychological attitude of the Catholic clergy in all the areas occupied by the Barbarian Arians, in order to understand the importance of the support which the Church was to accord the pagan, Clovis.

In total what did barbaric Arianism count for, as a real force? Not very much. It relied on the arms of the Gothic, Vandal, or Burgundian chieftains, but its actual spiritual authority was scanty. The Arian clergy, cut off from classical culture as from the most ancient Christian traditions and from patristic teaching by their utter ignorance of classical tongues, were nothing but a flock of ignorant men. Nothing that the Arians had could rival the hotbeds of learning and spirituality which the Catholic monasteries were; there were no leaders among them to equal the great bishops who recognized the Roman obedience. Supported by the great mass of the indigenous inhabitants, and not by the swords of the occupiers, deeply rooted in lands of long-standing faith, the Catholic Church preserved her authority, even when physical power was in the hands of the Arian zealots. And this is why she alone found herself in a position to resolve the fundamental problem of the synthesis between the survivors of the old order and the Barbarians, agents of the new.

## Two Failures: the Vandal Solution and the Gothic Solution

Three solutions could be envisaged, which might rebuild unity in this Western world, torn asunder as it was by the Invasions, the occupation, and the religious schism.   The first, and the most radical, consisted of uprooting everything Roman, retaining only the Roman administrative machinery in the measure that it assured the domination of the conquerors, to treat the vanquished as a herd of slaves, in brief, to barbarize by means of terror.   Only one of the invading peoples attempted this plan systematically: *the Vandals, in Africa.*

Genseric (431–77), the lame dwarf in whom some historians claim to have discerned the genius of a born leader, behaved, from the moment of his installation in Africa, exactly as if the Empire no longer existed, going so far as to raze to the ground fortresses which could have been used to support imperial troops, and expelling those suspected of excessive loyalty to Rome; he soon broke officially with the usurper, Petronius Maximus, on the ironical pretext that a man like himself did not obey an assassin; he then waged a war of frightful character all along the coasts of Sicily, Calabria, and Campania; he extended his empire to Corsica, Sicily, and Sardinia, becoming so powerful that Zeno, the Emperor of the East, was forced in fact to recognize him as independent in 476.

Genseric's plan is perfectly obvious.   What did he want?   He wanted to make his one-hundred-thousand-odd Vandals into a race apart, who would exploit Africa and dominate the vanquished populations without mingling with them.   A severe law forbade marriages between Vandals and natives of the country on pain of death.   The most ordinary relationships were more than suspect, and the king's police force was extremely efficient.   On the religious plane what occurred was persecution, pure and simple.   Genseric decided that he and his followers, who were Arian, would inflict on the Catholics the same penalties which the Catholic emperors had decreed against the Arians. . . .   This Barbarian, as we can see, was not without a sinister sense of humour!   The officials received the order to round up all the sacred objects in the churches, including the liturgical linen, which the troops made into drawers; at Carthage churches which were not requisitioned by the Arians were closed by the police; at Bulla Regia Catholics who had met together to celebrate Easter were surrounded and exterminated by being shot to death with arrows.   Terror-stricken by it all, the African Catholics, who had just discovered that Genseric's name, written in Greek, gave, by totting up the letters, the number of the Beast in the Apocalypse, 666, saw themselves as well

and truly in the power of the Antichrist! Victor of Vita has recounted innumerable details concerning the Vandal persecutions, all
of them frightful: the execution and scalping of the faithful, concentration camps, the kidnapping of young Catholic girls by Barbarian
officers, the raping of women recluses. . . . The death of Genseric did
not stop the course of these cruelties; on the contrary, his successor,
Hunneric, added to them, even though he was married to the daughter
of Valentinian III.

In point of fact the results of this policy of terror were extremely
negligible. The Vandals were not numerous enough to pursue it for
long. In the early days of the occupation they 'exploited' Africa by
a methodical policy of looting, which was called requisitioning, but,
when faced with impending famine, they were forced to realize that the
labour of the native inhabitants was indispensable to them, and that,
short of putting one Vandal soldier behind every African labourer, it
was necessary to be less brutal. On the other hand, despite all their
precautions, languid, delicious Africa—'Carthage, city of Venus,' men
had referred to in St Augustine's time—acted like Capri on the rough
soldiers of Genseric; without ceasing to be cruel, in one generation,
they let themselves fall prey to all the vices of the towns in which they
lived; military occupation of countries where life was easy was never
successful with the hale and innocent Germans! Very quickly
decadence set in. Meanwhile, sustained by a clergy which was energetic almost everywhere, from which men such as Fulgentius of Ruspe
and Quovultdeus of Carthage emerged, an anti-Arian, anti-Vandal
resistance organized itself. Fulgentius coined its watchwords: 'Our
reign will return with that of the Lord!' Only the ferocity of troops
kept loyal by their pay and the weakness of Catholic power in the
West allowed the Vandal kings to retain Africa for several more
decades, but when, in 533, Justinian launched an attack against them,
the numerical inferiority of the Byzantine forces which won the victory
—a mere 15,000 men—showed well enough how fragile Barbarian
domination in Africa had become and how utterly the Vandal solution
had failed.

The second possible solution consisted of effecting the synthesis
between the Roman and Barbarian elements, with Arian Germanic
chieftains substituted for the old imperial authorities, and the maximum
consideration being shown the vanquished, thus aiming at the fusion of
these two elements. Many chieftains seem to have fancied this idea of
'collaboration.' The first was Athaulf, the brother-in-law of Alaric,
who had sought the hand of his beautiful captive, the imperial princess
Galla Placidia, and had married her at Narbonne, with full Roman
pomp and ceremony. Orosius relates how, at Bethlehem with St
Jerome, he met a former official who had been closely connected with

E

the Gothic chieftain at Narbonne, and whom he had heard report his
intentions thus: 'In the beginning Athaulf wanted to obliterate the
very name of Roman, to confer all power and all land on the Goths, so
that a *Gothicism* should replace *Romania*. He, Athaulf, would become
what Caesar Augustus had been. But eventually repeated experience
had shown him that the Goths were not capable of obeying laws,
because of their unbridled violence, and that, without respect for laws,
it was quite impossible to found a stable state. So he resolved to
declare in favour of the glory of sustaining the Roman Empire, and to
obtain from posterity the title of restorer, since, in any case, he had no
chance of acquiring that of substitute.' Death had prevented Athaulf
from attempting the realization of this plan, of this extremely interesting concept; it was to be taken up again at the end of the century, and
in more favourable conditions, since the emperor of the West had now
disappeared and the Empire was no more than a myth, by quite the
most outstanding of all the Gothic chiefs, *Theodoric*, the King of the
Ostrogoths.

Theodoric was a former hostage at the Court at Constantinople,
spoke Greek and Latin fluently,[1] and had enough of a smattering of
classical culture to grasp that civilization increased a ruler's strength.
He tried to realize this harmony between the two elements in his
territory, and to find an area of agreement between Goths and Romans,
in order that one single nation might arise from them both. The
thirty-three years of his reign (493–526) were unquestionably an epoch
of prosperity and power for Italy. Not content to rule from Hungary
to the Rhône, Theodoric was able to extend his influence far beyond
his territories, marrying his daughters to Visigoth or Burgundian
kings, his sister to the Vandal king, whilst he himself married the sister
of Clovis, King of the Franks. His influence was so enormous that, at
the end of his life, he exercised, in the name of the young Visigoth king,
Amalric, a real kind of protectorate over south Gaul and Spain. The
Byzantine emperors treated him with sincere respect, though relations
between him and them were not exempt from irritability.

His entire internal policy reveals this desire—if not of actual fusion
—since marriages between Romans and Barbarians remained, in
principle, forbidden, according to the imperial laws themselves—at
least of agreement between the two ethnic groups making up the
Ostrogoth state. Theodoric worked to rebuild the machinery of the

---

[1] The reputation for being an illiterate clung to Theodoric for a long time, but modern
scholarship has challenged it. He knew how to write, but his clumsy hand wrote badly.
For this reason, not knowing how to give the word *legi*, which he used to write at the foot
of all his decrees instead of a signature, all the elegance he wanted, he had a gold stencil
cut with which to guide his pen. He always found it difficult to learn handwriting: the
Anonymous of Valois suggests that he spent ten years trying. (Cf. Ernest Stein, *Histoire
du Bas-Empire*, Excursus D: *Théodoric savait-il écrire?*, Brussels, 1949, p. 791.)

old Empire exactly—its officials, the prefect of the Praetorium, the count of largesses, the count of privy affairs; he breathed new life into the Senate, often addressing communications in pompous style to it, full of Roman majesty. 'Our realm,' he wrote, to the Emperor Anastasius, 'is an imitation of yours.' One could not say more. In the effort at reconciliation he did indeed go a long way, since he abolished, at any rate in fact, the principle of personal law, and he wanted Romans and Goths to be judged according to the same principle of equity. There were even monuments erected for the old citizens as well as for the new, and games in the amphitheatre! The senior commands and the high administrative posts were equitably divided between Romans and Barbarians; among the latter, moreover, many forgot their Germanic tongue and judged it better to talk Low Latin. And to put the final seal on all this work, Theodoric, the heir of the Augustuses and the Caesars, followed the example they had set as good managers of the land and great builders: roads were maintained in good condition, the Pontine Marshes were partially drained, repairs were made to the imperial Palatine palace, to the theatres, aqueducts and drains in the city, whilst Ravenna, in a sumptuous imitation of Byzantium, was filled with those magnificent buildings whose mosaics still sparkle so brilliantly: the 'Spirito Santo,' the Arian Baptistery, St Apollinarius the Ninth, with its golden altar-roof, subsequently to be called St Martin's.

In this effort Theodoric found support from the Roman element, even from the most aristocratic families and from the Catholics. The most enthusiastic and also the most long-winded of his panegyrists was a bishop, St Ennodius of Pavia. And his two most eminent collaborators were both important men of ancient lineage: *Boethius*, a member of that same 'gens Anicia' which had recently included in its ranks a saint (St Paulinus of Nola), two emperors (Petronius Maximus and Olybrius), and perhaps even a pope (Felix III); and *Cassiodorus*, member of the 'gens Aurelia,' who was the grandson of a general, and the son of a diplomat. What were these men, with their cultural backgrounds and their traditional Catholic convictions thinking of, when they accepted service under the Arian Goth? Probably they saw in this well-intentioned Barbarian the only means of saving civilization, of giving *Romania* back its vigour and its faith in the future, and, as for the religious obstacle between them and these new guardians of law and order, they must have hoped that, as time went by, matters would resolve themselves.

But they did not do so. The collaborationist policy of Theodoric came up against lively opposition from both the elements which he wanted to unite in a single purpose. The Goths felt a kind of bitterness—why be masters, if not to dominate the vanquished?—and contempt towards civilization; the strength of this feeling can be seen in the following incident.   When Theodoric's daughter, Amalasontha, wished to have her child educated in the Roman fashion, the Gothic Court raised such violent objections that she was forced to abandon the scheme.   And, of course, why should the Arian clergy be prevented from winning acceptance for the Arian faith of the master, why should theological discussions and quarrels be forbidden?   On the Catholic side, in spite of the repeated assurances of Cassiodorus that no one had any need to fear for his faith, the distrust of the mass of the people, of the average bishop, even of the landed aristocracy (furious at the requisition of one-third of their possessions), was never dispelled. At the crucial moment the Ostrogoth king came up against the ill-will of a priest, the verbal intemperance of a preacher—St Ursus, who had to take refuge in the Val d'Oste—and gradually this made him mistrustful.   When Boethius, anxious to establish the foundations of civilization firmly, attempted to bring about an agreement between the Pope and Byzantium, Theodoric thought that he saw in this a Catholic plot against him.   He had Boethius arrested, condemned, and, after keeping him in prison for a year, during which time the prisoner wrote his *Consolation*, which is undoubtedly the last masterpiece of classical philosophy, he had him executed.   Henceforth the aged Gothic ruler veered to a policy of force.   Pope John I received the order to go to Byzantium in order to call for the restoration of the Arian churches there, and for the return to their ancient faith of those Goths who had been converted to Catholicism; and to punish him for not succeeding in this paradoxical mission,[1] Theodoric had him flung into a dungeon, where he died.[2]

The bridges were down.   It had been proved that the Ostrogoth solution was no more valid than the Vandal one, and the only hope which existed of rejuvenating Roman blood by new Barbarian blood, in effecting a fusion of the two races, was possessed by the Church: the means of obtaining it was called *conversion*.

But when the body of the man, who, in a sense, had well deserved his title of Theodoric the Great, was being borne into the little rotunda which can still be seen in Ravenna to-day, to rest beneath the monolithic cupola, a petty Barbarian chieftain, an idol-worshipping pagan, had already received Catholic baptism in Rheims cathedral thirty years before: it was to Clovis the Frank that the Church henceforth handed the golden key to the future.

[1] Certain reasonable demands were acceded to much later on: it appears that a limited tolerance was accorded to the heretics, and a law promulgated by Justin and Justinian in 527 safeguarded Gothic access to political offices. (Ernest Stein, *Histoire du Bas-Empire*, II, p. 261.)

[2] He was considered a martyr: at the time of his burial his vestments were torn from him.   The Church canonized him and his festival is celebrated on 27th May.

# CHAPTER III

# BYZANTIUM, EMPIRE OF THE AUTOCRATS AND THE THEOLOGIANS

## WHY BYZANTIUM WAS SAVED FROM THE BARBARIANS

A S THE century rolled by tragedy followed upon tragedy, and the Western Empire gradually fell to pieces, until finally, by about 500, it was dismembered entirely and parcelled out between the various Barbarian kingdoms. Meanwhile, in the East, the Empire stood firm. *Romania* did not merely survive there, it actually transformed itself into a new type of civilization of such vigour that it was able to face the future for another thousand years. Indeed had not the Barbarian hordes made their very first onslaught against the *pars orientalis* of the Roman world? At the end of the fourth century, at the time when the solid masses of Visigoths, Huns, and Ostrogoths had begun their decisive attack, was it not the Greek frontiers which had seemed by far the most dangerously threatened area? Later on these threats were to be never ending: more Huns came, then Bulgars, Avars, and finally the enormous Slavonic wave. . . . But none of them overwhelmed this fortress of Byzantium. Though the Barbarian tide was to lap against it, and even to flood parts of it, now and then, it never covered it completely.

What is the explanation for this mystery? There are three fairly obvious reasons for it. One is purely strategic. When Constantine the Great made Byzantium his capital in 330—the 'new Rome' of the Eastern world—was he fully aware of the military value of this site that he had been impelled to choose by the still small voice of mystical inspiration? The city of Constantine, Constantinople, was built on the rocky headland of Europe, on a promontory where the sea, the terrain, and the coastline combined to make it easily defensible, and moreover it was most carefully armed against possible aggressors. His successors were to add two other defensive systems to the ramparts thrown up by the founder himself: the 40-feet high walls of Theodosius II (built in 413) stretched from the Sea of Marmora to the Golden Horn, covering a distance of 4 miles and including ninety-six watch-towers along their lengths; subsequently the 'long walls' of Anastasius I were built (in 512). These were erected much farther out of the town, in the middle of the countryside, 15 leagues from the city, and were more than 40 miles long; this was a defensive system that equalled the Great Wall of China.   As a result of these efforts Byzantium remained indeed impregnable: although she was besieged thirty times over a period of a thousand years she was only stormed once (aside from the final assault in 1453), and that was in 1204, by the Western Crusaders; the citadel was always ready with the counterattack which would halt the Barbarian assault and hurl it back.

This fact is all the more important since, at the same time, the West was giving the world a disastrous impression of weakness.   The least circumspect Barbarian could not hesitate if he had the choice of confronting the fortifications in the East or of advancing across an ill-defended Gaul or Italy.   Thus the second cause of Byzantium's salvation lies in this disproportionate balance of forces, which, like a physical law, diverted Radagase, Alaric, and Attila on to the West, deflecting them from attacking the East.

But this strategic confidence would not have been enough on its own.   Neither the Great Wall of China nor the Rhine *limes* could save men who were no longer capable of defending their battlements. The third reason for Byzantium's continued survival is founded on the fact that the autocratic and quasi-totalitarian regime into which the Empire had evolved since the third century, ill-suited though it was to the customs and traditions of the West, could, in the East, sink its roots into a past which, through Alexander and the Persian Kings of Kings, was linked to the strict administrative rigours of the Sargonnid rulers and the Egyptian Pharaohs.   When Sassanid Persia attained her zenith, in all the fanaticism of the Zoroastrian religion, Byzantium would be able to confront her even at the same time as she faced the Germans, because, in many ways, she had borrowed her governmental methods from Asia.   Strongly controlled by her despots, the Eastern half of the Empire was to find a traditional framework in this very despotism, which was to be the means of her salvation.

These then are the explanations for the Byzantine miracle: for it is indeed a miracle, this phenomenon which the historian interprets as the sprouting of a new form of civilization, and its flowering down the centuries, this assurance expressed yet again of man's infinite richness and of his creative gifts.   Roman by tradition, increasingly Hellenic in its culture and its processes of thought, and finally, oriental not merely in its techniques of government but in a myriad details of its customs, and by virtue of numerous artistic and commercial influences, the Byzantine world achieved a highly original synthesis.   This world stretched from the Black Sea to the great Syrtis of Africa, taking in the Balkans, Greece, the Aegean Archipelago, all Asia Minor, Syria, the Lebanon, and Egypt, in other words, the entire eastern half of the Mediterranean basin; it was a vital cross-roads of the European roads leading to Asia, and those from the north leading southwards, and it was a great maritime empire as well as a colonial power. It was to serve both as a link with the Far East, rich in civilizing influences, and as a bastion against its threats. The history of Europe would have been different indeed had there not been, balancing the hotch-potch of Western barbarism, this other melting-pot, where so many subtle ideas could be blended together in the heat of Christianity.

Thus for a thousand years—and longer, until 1453—Byzantium was to survive, in other words, to undergo alternative periods of greatness and decadence, to battle both to defend and to destroy itself, to combine a thousand tragedies with the authentic elements of greatness, in short, to plough a very significant furrow indeed in the field of history. Byzantium possesses a fascination which various authors have attempted to interpret from time to time.[1] No one who has seen the imposing relics of this civilization, at Ravenna, in Sicily, and above all at Constantinople, can remain insensible to it. Byzantium brings to mind a world of prodigious wealth—quays stacked with every imaginable kind of goods, docks crammed to overflowing with grain from Egypt, meat from Thessaly, Grecian woollens, scented woods from the Lebanon, Arabian spices, and the priceless silks which the slow caravans bore across Asia, awaiting the day when someone should steal the secret of their production from China. It stands for sumptuous clothes and jewellery, purple gowns trimmed with blue serpents, flowing, vivid tunics edged with embroidery that varied according to the wearer's rank, weighty diadems sparkling with Indian diamonds, emeralds, and sapphires, and heavy necklets and massive bracelets, which the engravers fashioned from solid gold. Byzantium means, too, that unique Eastern odour which still clings, changeless, to the cities which it once possessed, with their stuffed vine-leaves, the kid-goats roasting in oil, the smell of fish and rancid fat hanging in the streets, and the sickly pastries. And Byzantium means much more than all this. It must not be forgotten that it is the privileged centre of learning, the capital whose school influenced the entire East for several centuries following the reign of Theodosius II, the metropolis of juridical studies, the mother of the Codes and the Digests. It is, too, the place where that most miraculous of architectural audacities was cast into space, and supported there, for ever indestructible, by pure geometry—the aerial mass of St Sophia's cupola.

Byzantium brings to mind all these things, together with other ideas

---

[1] A number of imaginative works have taken Byzantium as their basis. Without going back to Corneille's *Héraclius*, or to Rotrou or La Calprènede's *Bélisaire*, in which there is scarcely any regard for historical accuracy, we can cite Sardou's *Théodora*, the novels of Jean Lombard (*Byzance*), of Paul Adam (*Basile et Sophia* and *Irène et les Eunuques*), and of Alfred Rambaud, the historian (*L'Empereur de Carthage*). (*See* Louis Bréhier: *Byzance dans l'opinion et la littérature*, Révue de la Méditerranée, May–June 1946.)

and other images which strike us more strangely.  Byzantium is the realm of hierarchy and hieratism, of meticulous pomp, of an etiquette so dizzily complicated, that beside it that of Louis XIV's Versailles seems simplicity itself.  Byzantium is the promised land of the dignitaries and the officials, home of a rigorous system of precedences, of an administrative system which is quite incomprehensible to anyone who has not studied it in detail, where the excubitors and the hypogrammates, the palatine doryphores and the silentiaries, the orphanotrophes and the vestiaries—and a thousand more besides—all have their appointed task which is almost sacredly regulated.  But, at the same time, facing the autocrat who crowns the summit of this prodigious mechanism, there is also the perpetual stir of the mob, the ever possible threat of popular agitation, which, by riot or assassination, determined the limits of the almighty.  Byzantium means the *Hippodrome*, that symbol of active demagogy, the giant Circus capable of containing fifty thousand people, the place where all public life centres and comes to boiling-point, where people come to applaud the dancers, the bear exhibitors, and the jugglers, to yell for or against the charioteers galloping round the race-track, the arena where judgments, discussions, and executions take place, the hippodrome—the lists for the two enemy factions, the 'Blues' and the 'Greens.'

Thus, for an accurate picture of Byzantium, we should not stop at the externals, fixed and regulated by the great ceremonies.  Its true self is seen in its passion, in the extreme violence of its sentiments, in a kind of moral and spiritual anarchy, paradoxically linked with the rigidity of its institutions and its laws.  Nothing, therefore, gives a less accurate impression of what this world that endured a thousand years was really like than the word *Byzantinism*, which has evolved over the years into a term of contempt.  It is perfectly true that if *Byzantinism* is taken to mean a tendency to split hairs, or to argue indefinitely on the point of a needle, the Byzantines were only too guilty of this fault.  But we must not forget that, throughout these discussions, futile though they sometimes seem, passions found their full play, and often gave them a tragically moving humanity.  And in the sense in which *Byzantinism* has ended by corresponding with *insignificance*, the term is a thorough calumny.  The world which handed on to modern times the contributions of classical civilization, which did most to preserve for us Greek literature and Roman law, the world which prevented Barbarism from wiping out the second half of the Empire as it had done the first, was certainly not insignificant!

What strikes the historian who considers Byzantine civilization as a whole is not its 'Byzantinism' but its disconcerting ability—quite spontaneous withal—to live in a state of contradiction.  The Byzantine man was as far removed as it is possible to be from our habits of

'Cartesian' thinking, and he was never to think that 'Yes' or 'No' could not be said at the same time, nor that it was proven that two and two make four. Thus all contrasts were possible and admissible. We have just remarked that despotism and demagogy were intimately linked here: men might indeed fall on their knees before the emperor, but they might also call out to him 'You are a donkey!' or a mob might cut him to pieces. These despots of limitless pride were, in private, in many cases, devout men with humble hearts; yet we find these fervent Christians committing heaven knows how many crimes with a kind of innocence, a sublime lack of consciousness. Byzantium is the land of eunuchs; they swarmed over its administrative machinery and choked it; but several of these castrated men were people of admirable energy, such as Narses, the conqueror of the Ostrogoths. Contradiction thus exists everywhere in this regime and it is useless to apply our criteria to it: centralization and separatist tendencies go hand in hand here; the West is conquered even whilst the enemy is being allowed to violate its own frontiers; there is too much government, but at the same time everything is let slide. . . .

It is in this complex welter of passion, illogicality, contradiction, and violence that it is necessary to consider the development of Christianity, an integral part of this bizarre civilization, and linked to it for worse as well as for better.

## BYZANTINE CHRISTIANITY

For we must remember that the most decisive thing about this Byzantine society is that it is, above all, a religious one. If we judge it according to the usual political or economic criteria, we condemn ourselves to understanding absolutely nothing about it. Whereas for modern man collective society has as its principal end the material well-being of its members, at Byzantium its prime purpose was the realization of a spiritual ideal, and even if the practical means used in attaining this end were questionable, such an intention imbues its entire existence, colouring it, and giving it quite a different meaning. In this respect Byzantium anticipated the Middle Ages in the West, and this characteristic makes it worthy of our deepest admiration. But at the same time it constituted a formidable menace, since it meant that all opposition and all rivalry contained the makings of a religious war.

It must not be forgotten that Christianity actually originated in the Eastern Mediterranean area—in the regions which, in the fifth century, constituted the Byzantine realm. The Good News had first been spread abroad in Rome's eastern provinces. In this or that great city of hers, like Antioch and Alexandria, Christianity had first become fully aware of itself, and there it had found its first great witnesses.

* E

Greek was the generally used language of the Byzantine world, and it was in Greek that the Gospel had been spread, and in Greek that the early Fathers of the Church had written.  At the end of the fourth century the density of Christian population was still far greater in the East than in the West: in many areas the faithful made up the great majority of the population, or even its entire total.  Christianity overflowed the boundaries of the Empire a great deal, stretching beyond Egypt to Arabia and Ethiopia, beyond the Lebanon and Syria to Mesopotamia and even Persia, beyond Asia Minor into Armenia.  Perhaps this Eastern Christianity had lost something of its original characteristic of risk and high adventure which it preserved in the West, where evangelization was less advanced—or rather, it transposed this risk on to another plane, that of speculation—but, intimately associated with the everyday existence of the faithful as it was, it had lost nothing of its fervour.

We cannot speak of this Eastern Christianity without veneration. In many ways it was the origin of our own faith.  It is impossible to calculate how much Christian thought—theology, exegesis, and philosophy—owed it, what great gifts the liturgy received from the marvellous ceremonies which developed within it,[1] or how much Christian piety inherited, even without realizing it, from those admirable believers in the East.  It was the motherland of the Doctors of the Church.  Here in turn appeared the first apostolic Fathers, the first apologists, followed by the didascales of Alexandria, the rugged defenders of faith and tradition, and the great Cappadocians.  It was the motherland too of many important mystics, of St Gregory the Thaumaturgist, of Didymus the Blind, St Ephraim, and of many others.  The Christian East was a kind of granary which sent forth innumerable seeds.  From the East came St Irenaeus, bishop-martyr of Lyons in the second century; inversely it was to the East that devout souls turned in search of spiritual wealth, such as St Jerome and St Melanie, who both settled in Palestine, and St Honoratus, who wanted to learn there the methods which he was to put into practice at Lérins.  Certain Eastern prayers—the *Phos Hilaron*, for example, or the Antiphons from St Basil's liturgy—are among the most beautiful that Christianity possesses.  And it was in the East also that the cult of the Virgin Mary developed, delicately, exquisitely, like a butterfly emerging from its chrysalis.  It was to Our Lady's honour that St Ephraim the Syrian, Basil of Seleucia, and Romanos the Melodious devoted their poetic gifts.

This tradition of fervour permeates the history of Byzantium.  It is a history scattered with saintly figures, whose first desire is to serve God, in whatever human situation they find themselves placed.  They

[1] Byzantine liturgies are studied in Chapter VI.

are even around the emperor's throne. The three princesses, Pulcheria, Arcadia, and Marina, lived like nuns in the sacred palace, having
inscribed their vows of perpetual virginity on gold tablets which had
been placed in the cathedral. They actually ascended the throne.
Theodosius II, the cranky enthusiast of fine script (this was to earn
him the nickname of 'the Calligrapher') and theological fanatic was,
despite all his faults, a scrupulously ardent Christian; Anastasius I,
not withstanding his somewhat suspect orthodoxy, showed exemplary
religious devotion; Marcian, a rough soldier, had a Crusader's faith
that was so strong that the Eastern Church was to consider him a
saint. In the senior ranks of the administration too, and not merely
the episcopal administration either, but the secular, it was commonplace to see great personages—Arsenius, the tutor of the Emperor
Arcadius is an example of this—giving up their posts and their fortunes to retire into a monastery or into the desert.

Certain of these figures illuminate this epoch, which spans the period
between the deaths of Theodosius and Justinian, and in which Byzantium really becomes Byzantium. The career of *St John Chrysostom* is such a good example of this that it will be convenient to study
its stages in detail later in this chapter. Though less well known and
not so dramatic, that of *St Sabas* is also typical of the vigour of the
faith in this age. St Sabas entered a monastery when only eight years
old, and devoted himself henceforth to asceticism and prayer, founding
the monastery, the 'Great Laura,' two and a half leagues from Jerusalem, whose great walls still dominate the Cedron valley, taking part
in all the conflicts in defence of the true doctrine with unflagging
energy, travelling to Constantinople when over ninety years of age,
in order to throw the weight of his authority into the balance in favour
of orthodoxy, and dying at the age of one hundred (in 532) after giving
ninety-two years of his life wholly to God.

Eastern Christianity saw the flowering of a complete mystical
literature, of a rare quality, and of lasting influence. Here and there
it attained the heights of masterpiece. Every single region of the
Byzantine Empire witnessed the growth of schools of important
Christian meditation. We Westerners do not pay sufficient tribute
to these testimonies, but the Church in the East continues to venerate
St Cyril of Jerusalem, whose doctrines on sanctifying grace were
decisively important; Barsanuphes, who, from his hermitage in Gaza,
sent letters of spiritual guidance throughout the world; Zosimus,
leader of a Palestinian monastic community, author of *Lectures* and
*Conversations* which, in his lifetime, led to his being considered a saint;
St Nilus (who died probably *c.* 430) who sent out his treatises and
his letters with their fresh, tonic energy from his cell near Ancyra;
Diadochus of Photitia, Bishop of Old Epirus in Greece, whose *Vision*

is one of the most curious mystical texts in Christian history, and whose *Hundred Chapters on Perfection* is a complete tract on the spiritual life.   Few of these Eastern authors, who lived in the period covering the fifth and sixth centuries, have managed to clear the double obstacle of distance and time and to retain their glory in the universal Church.   The most famous of them is the mysterious forger— probably a Syrian—who concealed his identity under the pseudonym of *Denys the Areopagite*, the disciple of St Paul, on whom the Middle Ages bestowed a veneration almost equal to that given to inspired texts, and whose treatises on the *Divine Names*, the *Two Hierarchies*, and *Mystical Theology* are packed with an extremely tasty hotch-potch of Neo-Platonism and lofty mysticism.

We have already noticed that a high proportion of the exemplary figures of this age belong to monasticism.   And nothing is more characteristic of Eastern Christianity than its prodigious abundance of monks and the importance of their role in the Christian life of the community.   Monasticism had, of course, originated in the East, in the desert, where St Anthony had put his own teaching on the subject into practice.   Developed, organized, even reformed by St Pachomius and St Basil, monasticism in both its forms—eremitic and cenobitic —grew prodigiously during the fifth century.   There were monks everywhere!   There was not a desert nor a lonely mountain anywhere in the Empire which did not afford shelter to some solitary contemplative; there was not a single province which could not boast several monasteries, often occupied by 'caloyers' by the hundred.   Egypt, Palestine, the Lebanon, Syria, Armenia, even Persia, as well as Asia Minor, Constantinople, and Greece, were dotted with these holy houses, these 'streets of cells' (*laura* in Syriac means 'street'); as far away as the impenetrable Sinaitic mountains the monastery of St Catherine flourished, and we can still see it to-day.

These monks were the witnesses and the heralds of the victory of faith over the world.   Cut off from society, refusing to fight, or to pay taxes, without families or children, their sole aim was to proclaim the glory of God and the necessity of repentance; they were indeed mandatories of the absolute.   The *élite* amongst them were the *Acimites* (Akimiti: i.e. not sleeping, without sleep).   The Acimites had been founded in 405 by the monk Alexander, who had suggested the idea of perpetual prayer, of that *laus perennis* which the monks of St Maurice d'Agaune in the Valais were subsequently to borrow from them, and which was to spread throughout the West; in their monasteries, teams of monks prayed in continuous relays so that the sound of prayer should rise heavenwards without any interruption.   A little later on the Studium was founded by the patrician John Studios, in 463, thus adding a new rosette to the mystic coronet of holy Byzantium.

This was the order which was to give to the ninth century one of the purest glories of the Eastern Church, St Theodore Studites.

But these witnesses of God did not simply remain enclosed in their monasteries! Quite the contrary! They left them, impelled by what they considered to be the Holy Spirit itself. These heroic ascetics preached and propounded great lessons, and both Palladius (363–425) in his *Lausiac History* (dedicated to Lausus, chamberlain to Theodosius II) and Rufinus (345–411), in his *History of the Egyptian Monks*—'best-sellers' of the period—relate their incredible feats of prowess. They would descend on a town, tattered, frenzied, gesticulating wildly, shouting the truth to the crowds, announcing punishments for the ungodly, harrying the prostitutes and the heretics, upsetting the bishops and the theologians. And the common people made legendary heroes out of these uncontrolled ascetics, these prophets clad in wild beasts' skins, heroes who were so famous and so venerated that the authorities themselves were forced to deal gently with them.

Certain of these unkempt witnesses of God pushed their mortifications to lengths which seem very strange to us. There were, of course, the *recluses*, who had themselves walled up for a given period, sometimes even for a lifetime, in a small cell, where the bare necessities of life were handed in to them through a grille. It is much more difficult for us to visualize the life of a *Stylite*, perched on his tiny platform at the top of a column, ill-protected from the elements by only a small hut, praying, intoning the Psalms, breaking off to bless the crowd gathered around him, and living like this for fifty years or more! But when we open Theodoret's *Religious History*, we wonder whether we are not indeed delving into the pathological, with these accounts of the *Siderophores*, who spent an entire lifetime with their bodies bent beneath intolerably heavy chains, the *Stationaries*, who made a vow to remain perpetually standing upright, and, worse still, the *Browsers* who undertook to live only on grass, or a certain Sabinos who ate nothing but food that had gone bad. . . .[1]

---

[1] However, we should not generalize or exaggerate the importance of these extraordinary cases. The Stylites were an established institution of the Church in very early times, and a very legitimate one. The prayers for their installation appear in the Byzantine Rite. Their life, though indeed hard, was little different from that of the lighthouse keepers around the Mediterranean shores. We would be mistaken to hold up a few eccentricities, purposely picked out by the ancients in order to whet their readers' curiosity, just as certain pathological cases are picked out by modern authors, as being typical of the religious life of the period; they were but an infinitesimal minority. The religious life of the East was no different from our own, and it was just as edifying. Perhaps there were too many monks! But in the East, where the birth-rate was very high, there were plenty of soldiers as well as plenty of monks. In addition, there were no religious orders or institutions in the strict sense in which we understand the terms. This is a Western idea which we have transposed on the East. The Basilican orders (in the Greek rite) were only constituted in Ruthenia (Ukraine) and the Lebanon in the seventeenth and eighteenth centuries.

Even though such phenomena are very rare, they constitute a rather grave symptom; they point to one of the faults from which Eastern Christianity suffered: the tendency to rush to extremes. If it has been said that the Kingdom of Heaven belongs to the enthusiasts and that God spews forth the lukewarm adherent, it is no less true that the division between holy enthusiasm, which is virtue, and frenzy, which is the caricature of it, is not always easily attained. And though, as we have already said, the Christian faith coloured every aspect of life, in return, the ardent temperament of these fanatical peoples, carried to extremes, singularly coloured the Christian faith itself. . . .

In addition, the East had always been the area with a predilection to heresies, ever since the earliest times. Since there were scarcely any pagans left to fight by the fifth century, the taste for violence was naturally active within the Church itself, and as it went hand in hand with that endless love of argument which was congenital among the Eastern peoples, battles on points of dogma reached a quite astonishing pitch of ardour. Voltaire's well-known saying has some foundation in fact: at Byzantium people are only interested in the Hippodrome and the Hypostases. . . . Theological argument was common everywhere and among all conditions of men. 'If you go into a shop to buy bread,' reported St Gregory of Nazianzos ironically, 'the baker, instead of telling you the price of it, will set himself to prove to you that the Father is greater than the Son; if you go to the money-changer, the man will talk to you of the Begotten and the Non-Begotten, instead of giving you your money; and if you visit the baths, you can be sure that before letting you enter the water, the attendant will proceed to demonstrate to you that the Son assuredly proceeds from nothing.'

Religious motives are, as we know, the ones which make wars the most cruel; all the more so as the passion for dialectic and the fidelity to dogmas were probably not the only causes of certain opposition movements. Truth to tell, it is obvious that all these theological battles were superimposed on political, economic, or social conflicts. Between the subjects and the government, the acceptance or the refusal of a dogmatic declaration could be the sign for a submission or a rebellion; if the emperor was hated, and if he happened to profess heresy, it went without saying that the opposition would appear furiously orthodox. In certain regions separatist tendencies showed themselves, the result of temperamental idiosyncrasies, or of loyalty to national traditions; the institution of the *Patriarchates*, which takes definite shape during the fifth century and was to be laid down in concrete form in Justinian's legislation, was to hallow these tendencies on the Christian level. And, naturally enough, in their more or less straightforward rivalry to one another, in their resistance to the claims of the central government, the regional authorities called in the help of dogmatic ideas, and this led to the great battles on the heresies being, at the same time, fairly open conflicts between the patriarchates of Alexandria, Jerusalem, Antioch, and Constantinople. Even more subtly, underlying the disputes concerning Christ or the Trinity social antagonisms can be observed; in this way the rich folk in the capital supported Nestorius, and the poor were to be seen parading a savage orthodoxy; and it is sufficient to read the Syrian Christian song, known as the 'Song of Chamoun,' which is a paraphrase of Christ's condemnation of riches, to guess what truly revolutionary meaning could be given to certain acclamations addressed to Him 'who depised all the riches of the world, and at whose door the wealthy man waits in vain.' The mania for argument went so far as to mingle with the games in the Circus, since it stood to reason that if the 'Blues' supported the two natures of Christ, the 'Greens' were bound to be Monophysite!

All these reasons go to explain why the religious history of Byzantium is marked by episodes of which the least that can be said is that they are not deeds which we, posterity, find edifying. . . . Again and again, in the course of theological struggles, the monks of an entire region can be seen undergoing a proper general mobilization, arming themselves, and marching to confront the government forces, because they find themselves in disagreement with the emperor or the count of the province on this or that characteristic of the three divine Persons. We see too various frenzied crowds rushing on their bishops, and massacring them, as happened at Alexandria, on Maundy Thursday, 457. Even at Constantinople the soldiers had to enter the Church of St Sophia, not just once, but ten or twelve times in the course of a century, to re-establish order. This history does not want for comic episodes either. An example of these is the solemn entry which Acatius, the Patriarch of Constantinople, made into his church. Acatius was a schismatic and a heretic and had been condemned as such by the Pope. On his back he bore the sentence of excommunication, which a zealous and resourceful monk, risking his life to do it, had managed to pin to his cope! The most painful incident took place at Ephesus in 449, in the midst of the conflicts unleashed by the Monophysite heresy: reunited in a Council, the prelates vied at anathematizing one another, threatened to cut one another to pieces, and deposed one another. Eventually they came to blows, the police were called in and were speedily followed by all the rabble of the town, and finally the saintly Patriarch Flavian of Constantinople was manhandled so severely that he died as a result. History has named this shocking tragedy the *Brigandage of Ephesus*: the title is only too well deserved.

Thus the law of contrasts which operates throughout Byzantine civilization characterizes Byzantine Christianity in equal measure.

We can look severely on certain features of it, but we should never forget that God used it, its philosophy, its theology, the subtlety of its language, and the profound tendencies of its thought in order to clarify or to define certain delicate, vital points in our dogma, and we should not forget either its saints and its martyrs. The Eastern Church is at one and the same time the Church of apostles and of frenzied enthusiasts, of unworldly souls and of political prelates, of lofty mystics and of heretics: and above it all, impressing himself deeply upon every belief and every event, soars one incomparable figure, that of the emperor himself, the autocrat who, of course, is at the same time a theologian.

## The Theologian-Autocrats

From the very beginning the Roman Empire had never ceased evolving towards a more and more rigorous kind of absolutism, an autocracy after the Eastern pattern. Jealous though he had been of his own rights and prerogatives, Augustus, the founder of the Empire, would have been hard put to it indeed to recognize himself in his distant fifth-century successors! From dynasty to dynasty, from the last Severians to Aurelian, from Diocletian to Constantine, the regime grew more and more like the monarchies of Asia and Egypt; towards 450 the Christian Empire of Byzantium seemed the exact counterpart of the New Zoroastrian monarchy which ruled Sassanid Persia; like it, it was authoritarian, harsh, and formalist, and, like it, theocratic.

Let us have a look at the *Basileus* [1] himself, as the door-keeper throws back the curtains of the Chrysotriclinium to allow the fortunate recipient of a rarely accorded honour to enter the audience chamber. Seated on a gold throne crowned by a huge canopy, wearing the purple mantle and the slippers of the same colour which are the badges of the supreme office, motionless, laden with heavy jewels, he watches his subject advance towards him. This subject—it may be a senator, a general, or some high official—is supported by two eunuchs, as though the emotion of the occasion has hamstrung him. He drops to the floor before his emperor, and, cringing on his stomach, wriggles forward to kiss the hem of the imperial robe, or even the tip of the emperor's slipper. A few great dignitaries are in the chamber, they too clad in gowns of rigidly prescribed, almost ritual, colours; soldiers in gold armour stand guard, still as statues; the tapers burn and the

---

[1] Officially the title of *Basileus* does not appear in the imperial protocol until the time of Heraclius and his victory over the Persians in 629. But it is often found in current usage long before this date.

scented smoke from the censers fills the room.   The master raises his visitor, kissing him on the head, but as long as the interview lasts the subject will remain in a half-prostrate position, almost as if in prayer. If the emperor gives him anything, a badge perhaps or a warrant, he can only receive it with his hands covered in a corner of his cloak. What is all this—a political ceremony or a religious act?   Both. Because for the heaven-sent being, the living law, the incarnation of supernatural will which is hereafter Caesar Augustus, the divine and the human are completely intermingled.

Some forty million people looked thus to the palace, where a living idol dwelt, one man embodying within him power that far outstripped that wielded by the Persian Kings of Kings and the most authoritarian of the Pharaohs.   The common people scarcely ever saw him: they knew that he was there, in the huge palace above the Golden Horn, where the pavements were made of porphyry, where the gold and silver threads and the coloured silks of the illuminated tapestries shone on the walls, where etiquette ruled his every action, where all that was rich and beautiful was kept exclusively for him.   When he went out it was always in a sumptuous procession, to the sound of silver pipes and trumpets, the rhythmical responses of the choirs singing his acclamations.   When he died the funeral ceremonies lasted for a whole week.   Everything was done, everything was meticulously calculated to give this absolutism a character so vast that the ordinary subject, overwhelmed by its enormity, did not even think he could resist it.

And it is a fact that, on the whole, this regime obtained the desired result.   During the one hundred and seventy years that spanned the period between the death of Theodosius and that of Justinian, there were to be ups and downs, times of plenty and times of crisis, masters who were more or less qualified to govern: nevertheless the system continued to function, the decrees went on leaving the palace, absolutism held sway throughout the Empire, all nicely limited by the possibility of popular riot, from which no tyranny in the world can think itself immune.

Taken as a whole, these fifth-century emperors were not particularly outstanding until Justinian, and yet there was scarcely one of them, even the feeblest, whose reign did not witness some measures of real political value.   Was it not under *Arcadius* (395–408), a man who was virtually an imbecile, whose title and power were in the hands of eunuchs and women, that an operation of prime importance took place —the eviction of the Gothic soldiery who were holding a position of quite excessive importance in the Empire?   They were massacred, their chieftain, Gainas, being the first to be killed.   Under the amiable *Theodosius II, 'the Calligrapher'* (408–50), the emperor with the mania for fine script to which he devoted all his energy and time, three considerable achievements were made—the erection of the second defence system around the capital, the foundation of the School of Constantinople, and the drawing up of the 'Theodosian Code'—although the last-mentioned bears his name, Theodosius took care not to read it! Even in the unsettled half-century which followed, the imperial power, jeopardized though it was by struggles and brawls, held firm. An old general, *Marcian* (450–7), promoted by virtue of his seniority, was set on the throne by the will of a woman, and he was to render the Empire the signal service of cutting short the pretensions of Attila by refusing to pay him tribute. An obscure tribune, *Leo I, the Thracian*, was raised to power by the all-powerful Alan generalissimo, Aspar; he speedily got rid of his embarrassing protector and reorganized the army. Even *Zeno* (474–91), a Barbarian—his real name was Tarasicodissa, and he was an Isaurian highlander from the Taurus—grappling as he had to with incessant civil wars, found the way of getting rid of Theodoric and the Ostrogoths by directing them westwards. The two best emperors of this period were the last two: *Anastasius I* (491–518), who had the third defence line built, put the Isaurians, who had become something of a nuisance, back in their place, and even had the quite outstanding idea of modifying the fiscal system in order to make it less burdensome; and *Justin* (518–27), an old soldier who was so illiterate that he signed his name at the foot of his decrees with a stencil, was of steadfast character, nevertheless, and he prepared the succession of his nephew, Justinian.

So, all things considered, autocratic absolutism did not serve Byzantium badly on the political plane. In the midst of innumerable intrigues, of imperial conflicts against ministers or generals, of revolts, disgraces, and assassinations, the imperial authority held fast. The real danger did not lie here, but rather in the very character of this imperial power, in the confusion which it maintained between its political bases and the religious prerogatives which it increasingly tended to usurp.

The process of the emperor's divination—the creation of the heaven-sent man—had begun with the foundation of the Empire itself. It was then that the cult of 'Rome and Augustus' had been established, and then that the custom of deification had set the dead ruler amongst the gods. This, of course, had been the fundamental cause of the conflict between Christianity and the Empire. Gradually people came to worship not only the dead man and the idea of the temporal almighty; the man himself, this mortal emperor, was more or less recognized as a god even in his lifetime, actually having his own priests and *flamenses*; the efforts of certain emperors, such as Aurelian, to develop the solitary cult of the *Sol invictus* had no other object in view than to give this doctrine theological bases.

When he became a Christian the emperor had not been able to maintain such pretensions as these any longer; he had transposed them. He could not decently be god any more, but it was obvious now that he was God's lieutenant on earth.    Increasingly, ever since the conversion of Constantine, from reign to reign, the masters of the world had considered themselves invested with the heaven-ordained mission of effecting the triumph of Christianity throughout their domains. By the time of Constantius II and Theodosius, this was to be an accepted idea, and the Christian authorities themselves were in complete agreement with it.    'Whence is come the communication of a being of flesh and blood, of the imperial Might,' declared Eusebius of Caesaraea, 'if not from the Word of God, which imbues all things, and which has suggested to the mind of all men the type of magistracy modelled on that of God?'    Of course Eusebius was a courtier-bishop.    But Pope Anastasius said exactly the same thing: 'The emperor is the image of God, His representative on earth, His vicar and His figure-head.'    By the fifth century the theocratic character of the Eastern Empire was obvious.    The sovereign was officially 'the orthodox and apostolic emperor,' his court was 'the holy palace,' his possessions were designated 'the divine house,' even the taxes were called 'the divine share,' which is certainly saying a good deal!    Beginning with the accession of Marcian in 450, when the coronation was carried out in a manner which was still modest, and quietly formal, and on to the crowning of Leo I in 457, the act of coronation, with its sacramental unction and liturgical ceremony invested the emperor with an authentically sacral character.    He was the High Priest-King, like the ancient kings of Israel; at the Hippodrome, before the races started, he blessed the people from the high grand-stand; when he appeared the lawful acclamation was: 'Son of God, reign through the emperor!'

Though such behaviour seems very strange to us, it was not absolutely bound to lead to a mingling of political authority and religious prerogative.    Representing God on earth, charged with preparing the Lord's coming, the emperor could still have remained within the framework of these rights, allowing the exercise of power on the spiritual plane to remain with those who legitimately belonged to the organism which was the guardian of Christ's message and of dogmatic truth, in other words, to the Church.    This is the authentic thesis of the Roman Catholic Church; it is that of the popes; it is that which St Ambrose applied when he forced Theodosius to do penance; it is that which, as we have seen, sustained all the political doctrine in St Augustine's *City of God.*    The Church and the Empire are two powers, each having its own sphere of authority, the one spiritual, the other temporal, and they should assist one another for the greater glory of God, while understanding, of course, that the spiritual remains superior to the temporal, that when a difference arises between the two powers regarding a point of faith or morals, it is the Church which must have the last word.

But matters could not work out like this in practice. It is a fatal characteristic of authoritarian states to want to meddle in everything, and the totalitarian error does not by any means date only from our own century. Regarding themselves as defenders of the faith, the emperors were drawn to meddle in matters which were really no concern of theirs. The heretical crises of the fourth and fifth centuries gave a thousand opportunities for their encroachments on the spiritual. The Church, who had already called Constantine to help her against the schismatic Donatus, and who had incited the emperor to convene the Council of Nicaea against Arius, slid down the slope which was to end in the establishment of the Byzantine *Caesaro-Papism*. Constantine had already mingled the secular and the religious on a large scale. By the fifth century this fusion was complete. Church and State were solidly linked. To attack Christianity was to rebel against the State itself, whose laws rested on Christian doctrine. The term 'apostate' was applied both to renegades in religious matters and to political rebels. Instead of remaining separate, the spheres of authority of Church and State intermingled. And since the emperors—every single emperor without exception—and the empresses and the princesses and the ministers and the senior officials all succumbed to the taste of the epoch for theological discussion, they did not hesitate to intervene in the innumerable arguments which shook Byzantium with regard to the persons of the Trinity or the qualities of the Virgin Mary, and they used their political power in order to have the last word in all these controversies just as if they possessed a real infallibility in matters of faith.

There are endless examples of this kind of confusion. Truth to tell the Byzantine emperors meddled indiscriminately in everything that concerned the Church. They intervened, of course, in the choice of patriarchs and bishops, and did not hesitate in the least to depose those who displeased them. They even altered the ecclesiastical boundaries. They interfered in the internal life of the Church, modifying the liturgical calendar, codifying ceremonies. They claimed a disciplinary authority, formulated rules on the recruitment of monks, and on the behaviour of priests. All this, however, was nothing beside the peril into which the faith could fall because of the doctrinal convictions of this *Caesar-Pope*! It only needed the Master to adhere to a heresy for him to strive, very naturally, to lead his subjects in the same direction. Doctrinal truth was thus at the mercy of a faction of theologians who had the emperor's ear, or even (this happened several times) at the mercy of a woman's whim. The fact that religious crises in Byzantium were so grave was certainly due to this confusion of the spiritual and the temporal.

It went without saying that, from the very moment that the public power intervened in the religious sphere, the jolts of politics made themselves felt in the spiritual domain, and vice versa.   The State laid itself open to attacks, which, as we have seen, were made perilous by the very character of Byzantine despotism.   The Emperor Anastasius was to have an unpleasant experience of this danger of Caesaro-Papism; having adhered to Monophysitism, he found himself at grips with the people of Constantinople, who rebelled against him in the name of the two natures of Christ, and forced him to make due apology in the Circus.   The confusion of powers was not absolutely reliable.

Though, on the whole, the Eastern Church offered only a feeble show of resistance to this interference of the State in things pertaining to the faith, it cannot be said that the great principles were forgotten. Even in the darkest days of heresy or schism, there were always some groups of monks and clergy to call to mind the true doctrine, in other words, in so far as he was himself a Christian, the emperor remained bound by laws superior to his own will, and his authority had as its limits that of the Church.   And it is a fact that not a single Basileus succeeded in making doctrines which orthodoxy had condemned triumph in any lasting fashion.   But, in a practical sense, the confusion had very serious consequences for the Byzantine Church; it tied the fate of Christianity to that of the State (and this was to be the real reason for Islam's success in many regions which had been subject to Byzantine tyranny); it aggravated and prolonged the conflicts engendered by the heresies; it tended to make a gulf between Caesaro-Papist Byzantium and Rome, where, at the same time, the Pope was effecting his emancipation from all secular protection and was growing in importance, in proportion to the decline of the power of the State.[1]

### ARCADIUS AND THE SAINT

In conditions such as those we have just been studying, in the midst of popular passions, poised ready to break out into the open, amid court interests, budding intrigues, and the heavy-handed intervention of the Basileus himself, it was the most difficult thing in the world to follow the Christian path unfalteringly.   A dramatic and tragic

---

[1] On another plane it is obvious that the emperors' intervention in theological matters was frequently connected with variations in their policy towards the Western half of the Empire and towards the Papacy.   When the emperor wanted to assert the independence of the Eastern Church towards Rome, he tended to side with the heretics; if, on the other hand, his Western policy impelled him to be reconciled with the Pope, he displayed a faithful orthodoxy.

episode which took place at the beginning of this period well demonstrated that he who wished to preserve the principles of the Gospel and the independence of the Church risked no less than his life in doing so.

On 26th February 398 a small, slight man was enthroned as bishop of the capital in the cathedral church at Constantinople. He was of frail build, but the flame of God shone brightly in his handsome face. His name was John, and he was a priest from Antioch. In his native Syria he had acquired immense fame, due as much to his virtues, his wisdom, and his courage as to the eloquence of his sermons. For twenty years now people had crowded to listen to this marvellous voice, telling them, in language of classical perfection, real, living truths, which reached right to the heart of every listener. On one occasion, when riot shook the town, he and he alone restored peace within an hour. People nicknamed him 'John the Golden-mouthed.' [1] And it was precisely this fame which had led to his being called to the most sought-after episcopal throne in the East. In order to bring lustre to this see, after its rather drab sixteen years under the elderly Nectarus, an entire court faction had planned John's election, a faction consisting of the powerful imperial minister, the eunuch Eutropius, the empress, Eudoxia, and the wealthy bourgeoisie, all those whose underlying intention was to set the new Rome up as a rival to the old, even in the Christian sphere. John Chrysostom was literally abducted from Antioch, for it was feared that the faithful there would never let their saint leave them, on any account, and was consecrated Bishop of Constantinople without desiring it in the least. He felt more pain than happiness at this singular turn of fortune.

But those who had flattered themselves that they would make the new bishop play their game were speedily disillusioned. John Chrysostom was absolutely typical of those Christians who refuse to play anyone's game but God's. As soon as he was installed in his see, he judged at their true value the authors of the trick in which the cunning had wanted to see him play his part. There was Arcadius, the emperor, the feeble-minded son of the great Theodosius, a puny, sallow creature, with blank features, who was a docile instrument in the hands of his wife and his successive ministers; the ambitious Eudoxia, thirsting for self-glorification; Eutropius, a dubious character, entirely without moral principles and possessing a boundless vanity; and the faithful of comfortable means who had so welcomed him on his arrival, among whom there was more vainglory than morality, more self-satisfaction than true faith. With a serene intransigence, without caring whether he pleased or displeased the powerful, John acted as his conscience, and his conscience alone, demanded. First of all he reformed the bishop's household, sweeping

[1] 'Chrysostom' is the Greek for 'golden-mouthed.'

away all luxury there.   He ate alone, frugally, unlike Nectarus, who
had dined in the town or at the palace.   The clergy who had been
taking liberties with their moral rules were called to order; the monks,
who were too inclined to scatter about the town, were requested to
return to their cells at once.   From the cathedral pulpit, where the
saint preached every Sunday, truths rained down on the congregation,
equitably apportioned; anyone who deserved condemnation received
it, were it a Gothic general or an important state official, for the bishop
denounced the Arian heretics in the army as calmly as he castigated the
'whited sepulchres' at the imperial court.   And the common people,
who had at first looked coldly at the election of the bishop who had
been brought from Asia by a palace intrigue, did not long delay
becoming ardent supporters of this apostle of the poor, with his
inexhaustible charity, of this little man who told the rich exactly what
he thought of them and who stood his ground before the most
powerful.

One incident settled the positions of all the parties involved.
Eutropius, the all-powerful minister, fell into disgrace; truth to tell,
his ambition and his vanity had made him quite intolerable to everyone,
even to Eudoxia, whom he himself had first led to the emperor's bed.
In alliance with Gainas, the leader of the Gothic auxiliary troops, the
empress incited her feeble husband against the eunuch.   When he was
run to earth Eutropius took refuge in St Sophia's, invoking the right
of sanctuary—a nice touch this: this was the very right which he had
wanted to suppress in the hey-day of his power!   John Chrysostom,
without hesitating for an instant, defended him, bade him welcome,
and protected him.   He worked to save the fallen man as hard as he
had freely criticized his excesses as a minister.   In practice it was all of
no avail—except to give the world a fine example of the independence
of a Christian conscience.   Shortly afterwards, on the insistence of
Gainas, the puppet ruler Arcadius had his former favourite beheaded,
awaiting the time when Gainas, in his turn, should suffer likewise. . . .

Henceforth those who had brought John to Constantinople turned
against him; how could he be allowed to conduct himself in a Christian
fashion when they wanted him to be a political bishop?   The important clergy, whose over-easy life he had interfered with; the monks
who had broken with their monasteries; the great ladies who had heard
from the pulpit his transparent allusion on the moral excesses which
they committed alongside their ostentatious outward devotion; the
fashionable preachers, eclipsed since his arrival; the Arian Goths,
furious at the support he had given Eutropius; the bishops of Asia,
whom John had convicted of simony and had had deposed; even a few
prelates—they must certainly have been epicures!—who had found
the hospitality of their colleague in Byzantium too stingy—all these

formed a powerful coalition against the saint.    Eudoxia was a member
of it: had not various worthy souls told her that a certain sermon,
dealing with Jezebel, had been clearly aimed at her?    And Arcadius,
his mind easily changed for him by his *entourage*, was persuaded that
John was plotting against him.

In order to put the great bishop into a difficult position, one of those
confused dogmatic affairs, such as were cropping up all the time in the
East, was put in his way.    This was the problem of *Origenism*, i.e.
the theories which the extreme disciples and overbold successors of the
great Alexandrian thinker had taken from his books, not without distorting and exaggerating his philosophy.    Did not those professed
heretics, the Arians, quote the famous Egyptian didascale as an authority?    One hundred and fifty years later people took it into their heads
that Origenism constituted a danger to the Church—which was partly
true—and under the pretext of doctrinal purity serious conflicts shook
Syria and Egypt.    A genuine saint, Epiphanius, who, truth to tell, had
more virtue than sense of proportion, specialized in anti-Origenism.
St Jerome also cut the heresy to shreds on his more angry days.    And
above all, the arrogant Bishop of Alexandria, Theophilus, who had
been embittered by John's election because he had hoped to place one
of his own creatures in the see, monopolized the matter, and created
from it a machine of war against the Byzantine bishop.

Henceforth this was a permanent source of trouble to John Chrysostom.    When he supported the Egyptian monks, who had been
unjustly accused of Origenism by their bishop, he was, of course, himself accused of having Origenist sympathies.    Despite his ninety
years, Epiphanius rushed to the capital to denounce the suspected
bishop, and only left again when the worthy townsfolk, who were
passionately devoted to John, threatened to kill the intruder.    Theophilus arrived in Constantinople too, but, being more cunning, he
attached himself to the Court party of malcontents; with the support of
the empress, he convened a kind of council, 'the secret council of the
Oak'—from the name of the villa where this evil deed was perpetrated
—at which thirty-six bishops, who wished John ill, deposed him.
Arcadius, told what he must do once again, ordered John to go into
exile.    This was no easy matter, for the people refused to hear of it,
and wanted to defend their bishop against the police.    John Chrysostom himself had to intervene, to set their minds at rest, and to give
himself up to the guards who put him on board a ship bound for the
coast of Bithynia.

His first exile was not to last long.    The mob showed its fury at the
deed, and hooted down the heralds charged with reading out the sentence against John.    The Court was anxious and hesitant.    Theophilus of Alexandria made himself hated by everyone.    And then the

heavens themselves actually took a hand in events.   An earthquake
occurred, and the terrified Eudoxia thereupon persuaded her husband
to recall the saint.   His return had all the character of a triumph, of a
political demonstration.   A procession of thousands of people, and of
thirty bishops, brought John back to his church, where he preached:
'Pharaoh wished to seize me,' he cried, 'as of old he seized Sarah: [1] but
Sarah still remained faithful; and my Church has remained faithful to
me!   The adulterer is discomfited.'   Obviously the Pharaoh here
was the Egyptian prelate: he understood the allusion and speedily took
himself off.

But John's enemies were not disarmed.   They had only to wait.
They could be quite sure that, with his usual uncompromising character, he would sooner or later lay himself open to another attack.
And they were right.   Only a few months had gone by, when the
noisy inauguration of a statue of the empress, a massive silver statue
on a porphyry column, on the very threshold of St Sophia's itself, an
inauguration accompanied by a regular popular bacchanalia, provoked
the bishop's wrath.   He preached, and he inveighed against it.   Did
he actually refer to the unchaste Herodias?   Eudoxia affected to feel
personally insulted.   Once again she organized her husband; she
persuaded him that John was engulfed in heresy; she managed to make
him sign a very harsh letter against him.   Theophilus returned to the
scene, brandishing a new weapon: did not a canon of the Church condemn in advance any bishop who continued to occupy his see after
having been deposed by a council?   And this exactly fitted John
Chrysostom's case—assuming that the council of the Oak was valid!

And the ruse succeeded.   The saint was condemned a second time.
A new order of exile was signed against him.   The bishop was
speedily replaced by an aged octogenarian prelate, whom a chronicler
describes as 'dumb as a fish and mute as a frog,' but this piece of
human flotsam had understood the significance of the manœuvre, for
he opened his mouth at least once to say to the emperor: 'God has not
subjected you to us, but us to you, and you can do whatever you
wish. . . .'   And whilst the people, bursting with fury, rose in rebellion, whilst the fires crept around the palace, whilst the supporters of
John were struck down and his old enemies put in their places, he himself was on his way towards his exile in Asia.

For three years he was kept under close supervision, ill, growing old
—he was more than seventy—subjected to distressing vexations.   But,
far away in exile though he was, he remained a worry and a reproach to
the Court.   Did he not continue to lead an apostolic life, converting
the Isaurian highlanders, and even sending missionaries among the

---

[1] This is an allusion to the abduction of Sarah by Pharaoh during Abraham's stay in
Egypt.

Goths? And then, his influence amongst the political exiles living in Asia was definitely too great. And then again, when a report of the affair reached Rome, Pope Innocent did not hide his disapproval, but quashed the decisions of the false council of the Oak and wrote personally to John. . . .

It was necessary to put an end to this. And this was indeed to be the very end of it all. It was both atrocious and sublime. In spring 407 an order arrived from Arcadius: the aged bishop was to be taken as far away as possible, to the frontiers of the Empire, to a tiny village in the Caucasus! The guards grasped exactly what was intended. The old man was led along the most difficult mountain tracks, on foot, under the beating rain or the blazing sun, and good care was taken that he did not stop in a single town where he might have found rest and friends. For three months he was dragged in this way from one end of Asia Minor to the other. On 13th September the tragic little procession arrived at Comania, a town in Pontus. John could go no farther; but he was not allowed to stop in the city. His escort made him stay in a chapel consecrated to Basiliscus, a local martyr. During the night the saint had a vision in which the martyr appeared to this other martyr. 'Have courage, John,' he said, 'for to-morrow we shall be together.' In the morning, when his guards wanted to start him on his journey again, the bishop collapsed. They took him hurriedly back to the little chapel. He asked for white vestments and for the holy Eucharist, and then he died, murmuring a last prayer: 'Glory be to God in all things!'

### The Great Debates on the Natures in Christ

The same motives as those which had determined the drama of John Chrysostom recur throughout the doctrinal struggles which fill fifth-century Byzantium, overflow into the sixth century, and spring up again even in the centuries that are to follow: religious fanaticism and political passion are linked in a complexity of events, in which simple logic scarcely comes into consideration, any more than the Gospel precept of forgiveness and charity. It would be an intolerable task to recall these debates in all their details; the number of tendencies, shades of differences, sects, and schools discourages in advance any such enumeration.

It is absolutely essential, however, to be quite clear on this point: our Western reaction, that is, the reaction of twentieth-century Christians who are not expert theologians, is to see these dogmatic tussles as 'Byzantine' disputes in the worst sense of the word. The ecclesiastical historian cannot share this summary opinion at all. These struggles were of very great importance and there is even something moving in this great stir of ideas, in which, according to a pendulous rhythm, having touched the extremes, the Church, in her wisdom, established her balance. We must not forget that this—the period which spans the years between the Council of Nicaea (325) and the Council of Chalcedon (451)—is the period in which the authentic formulae of the great dogmas which have defined the faith of Catholic Christianity until our own day, were settled. And it was to be Byzantium's glory to have sought the truth in this field, painfully, through much disruption, certainly, but sacrificing her life's blood in the attempt.

By the beginning of the fourth century, though the *Arians*, who denied the divinity of the Word, had been almost completely overcome—save among the Germanic elements installed as federates within the Empire—there still remained the semi-Arians, or similar sects, such as the *Pneumatomacians*, who held that the Holy Spirit was not God. We have seen how the *Origenist* doctrines, notably those on the final fate of man and the temporary character of the pains of hell, troubled various churches. Despite official penalties against them, there were, of course, *Manichaeans* in the East. We have seen them in Africa in the years when the young St Augustine was growing to manhood, and the dualist doctrine of Good and Evil remained a subject of violent argument. And although the *Pelagians*, the heretics who denied Grace, the supporters of the all-powerful character of human will in the task of salvation, were not to spread so extensively in the East as in the West, in Palestine, notwithstanding, their doctrine caused stir enough to make two Councils condemn it.[1]

But in the fifth century the greatest conflicts, the most tragic quarrels, and the most impassioned discussions had, as their subject, the question which is really the mainstay of Christian doctrine: the natures in Christ. Following the defence of His *divinity*, the divinity which Arius had denied, it was His total *humanity* which was to be defended, and the word alone is sufficient to indicate the importance and the magnitude of the dispute.

In order to understand the essential point of these discussions and to see through their prodigious complexity, it is necessary to take them altogether, without isolating their doctrines, since, in fact, they all formulate themselves in one unbroken sequence of actions and re-actions. What was the substance of it all? Against the Arians, who saw Him as nothing but a deified man, the Council of Nicaea had declared that there are two elements in Christ, each as real as the other: divinity and humanity; moreover it had proclaimed that in Jesus, born of the Father and made man in Mary's womb, these two elements are

---

[1] On Manichaeism and Pelagianism *see* further under Chapter I, section: 'The Champion of Truth.'

united. How then can we reconcile this unity and this duality? Such is the problem. Now this mystery of faith can be approached in two ways.[1] Either in the way in which the famous prologue to the fourth Gospel invites us to do it, starting from the divine Word which resides for all eternity in the bosom of the Father, and which becomes man at a certain moment in time, for the salvation of the world; this thesis was repeated by the Alexandrian School. Or, starting from the wonderful figure that we see in the Gospels, considering all the moving characteristics which bring Him close to us, we find the proof of His divinity in His behaviour, notably in His miracles, and this was to be the thesis preferred by the theologians of the School of Antioch. The complete truth is that Christ is all these things at the same time: the Word and the perfect Man, the Son of God and the Man who is God. But according as one insists on one of the two aspects of this doctrine to the exclusion of the other, so one slips into one or other of the great heretical currents which were about to fall on the East.

Let us go back a little farther, to about 360. The important matter is still the struggle against the Arian heresy, which, though condemned at Nicaea, continued to exist and to spread in bastard forms. To resist it all the more, to show that the Word really was God, the theologians of Antioch, precursors of Diodorus of Tarsus and Theodore of Mopsuestia, emphasized the distinction between the two natures of Christ so much that the ultimate result was to compromise His unity. This reaction was especially serious as it produced to combat it a very learned, virtuous man, the friend and brother-in-arms of St Athanasius and the Cappadocian Fathers in the struggle against Arianism, who had become famous through his scholarly exegetical works and through a pamphlet attacking the Emperor Julian the Apostate: his name was *Apollinarius*, and he was the anti-Arian Bishop of Laodicea, in Syria. His aim was clear: to safeguard the unity of Christ along with His divinity. He reasoned thus: in order that the Redemption be accomplished, it cannot be accepted that there are two natures in Jesus so separate that each has its independent existence. It must really be the Son of God incarnate who suffered and died for us. So far this is perfectly sound doctrine. But Apollinarius added: how can two elements complete in themselves unite? The two halves of a fruit can be joined together again to make one fruit, but two fruits cannot make one fruit only. And, as he had read the philosophers, he went on, according to the best Aristotelian principles, that one complete nature is in actual fact one person. Conclusion: if the Word is made man, His humanity cannot be complete. From man He has

[1] This has been clearly set out in Canon Draguet's book, *L'Histoire du dogme catholique.*

taken only the body and the animal senses, but He had replaced the spiritual soul by His divinity.   Christ is thus not a complete man, but one half of a man on to which is welded the divinity of the Word. This is the stuff of pure Monophysitism.

In order to arrive at this theory Apollinarius had to disregard everything in the Scriptures which shows Jesus to be so wonderfully close to us: His emotions, His friendships, His tears, His sufferings, even His just outbursts of anger!   The psychology of Christ, the intellectual and moral life of the carpenter's son, all this counts for nothing. What does the Redemption become in these circumstances?   For this is no longer a man like us who is suffering on the cross—it is a peculiar, questionable human shell, a God clothed in our flesh, and for whom, consequently, the flesh is merely an unimportant garment. One by one the synods held at Rome (377–82), at Alexandria (378), and at Antioch (379) denounced the ideas of Apollinarius, and the second Oecumenical Council of Constantinople condemned him decisively.   But his disciples, the *Apollinarists*, continued to exist in the East and to spread their doctrines there; we shall come across their influence again when the movement of the pendulum has caused Nestorian dualism to be condemned, and cast men's minds back towards the position of the one nature: this was to be Monophysitism.

But, first of all, the pendulum swung in the opposite direction. Diodorus and Theodore were about to have a disciple and an inheritor.   In 428 a brilliant theologian from Antioch, who had formerly been a monk in one of the monasteries near the town, was called to the see of Constantinople.   His name was *Nestorius*, and he was a highly intelligent man, though brusque in character.   At the beginning of his episcopate he dealt very vigorously with the heretics, but, like almost all the theologians from Antioch, he was attached to the dualist conception of Christ, although he blurred its propositions.   In Christ, said the Nestorians, there are two complete natures, divine nature and human nature, that is to say, two persons, the divine person and the human person—indeed two hypostases.   It is necessary to distinguish clearly the man and the God that are both present in the Saviour.   Can we then attribute to the divine nature, to the Word, the properties, actions, and passions of the human nature, and vice versa?   We see the consequences of statements like these at once: on the cross it is the man alone who died; we have no right to write that 'the Son of God suffered for us' or that 'God died for us'; the essential of the Redemption, the voluntary sacrifice of God in order to redeem the world, is thus rendered void.   Of course the most skilful theologians of this school, including Nestorius himself, talked of a 'moral union' between the two persons, of the reciprocal love which they bore each other, of a liaison, a bond between them, of 'the housing of the

Word in the temple which is Man.' This 'moral union' retained the essential of the thesis.

The scandal burst out into the open through one of Nestorius's disciples, a priest called Anastasius, who, when preaching from the pulpit about the Virgin Mary, declared that men had no right to call her the 'mother of God' but only 'the mother of Jesus,' that is to say, mother of the man who was Jesus. 'Can an ordinary mortal beget God?' he cried. The cult of the Virgin Mary had not yet developed as much as it was subsequently to do (and precisely as a reaction against assertions like these); but already the custom of calling her the 'Mother of God' was dear to pious Christians, and the term *theotokos* was customary. This was a fine assertion, to be sure! Nestorius was called upon to repudiate his assistant. He did nothing of the kind. 'Mary,' he repeated, 'only begot the man in whom the Word is made incarnate.' In an attempt to palliate the scandal he added: 'However, Jesus is nevertheless a God for me, since He contains God in Him. I adore the vase because of its contents, the garment because of what it covers.'

The storm broke. The faithful actually protested in church. On one occasion a bishop who was present interrupted the patriarch. On another, Eusebius of Dorylea denounced him in writing as a heretic. The monks who supported the divine Motherhood rose in revolt. At Rome, whither the Nestorian theses were sent, Pope Celestine showed his disapproval. At the palace the princesses who governed in the name of Theodosius II regarded the affair anxiously, torn between the people, who were deeply devoted to Mary, and the high state officials, who advised them not to do anything to inflame feeling in the Syrian provinces where the doctrines of the Antioch School had considerable influence.

Suddenly a personality of extraordinary vigour intervened in the dispute—*St Cyril, Bishop of Alexandria*. It is notable that every time that a heresy threatened the Church she found in her bosom a man capable of defending the true faith. Against the Nestorian error St Cyril assumed the role which St Athanasius had assumed a century earlier, against the Arian one. Cyril was a mighty theologian, plain-spoken, enterprising, and pugnacious, and he was a nephew of that same Theophilus who had been the tool in the plot against St John Chrysostom. Sincerely scandalized to the core by the doctrines of Nestorius, Cyril, in so far as he was an Alexandrian, was also not sorry to attack both his rivals in the School of Antioch and the Bishop of Constantinople. Moreover he has been accused—wrongly, however —of having had some responsibility for various incidents which disturbed the peace of Alexandria: the descent on the town of a band of monks who all but massacred the prefect, and the horrible assassination, by Christian fanatics, of the famous Hypatia, the leader of the school of

Neo-Platonic philosophy. In taking on the task of crushing Nestorius, Cyril escaped from all these rumours, and acted according to his faith and his temperament. His tactics were extremely clever. He began by admonishing Nestorius in some moving letters, in which he spoke quite admirably of the Mother of God. The Bishop of Byzantium not only replied in a contemptuous fashion but actually sheltered the Egyptian monks who were in conflict with their bishop. Then Cyril wrote two letters, one to the Pope and the other to the princesses Eudocia and Pulcheria, the wife and sister of the emperor. Although he received no reply from the palace save a surly missive in which Cyril was more or less accused of keeping the troubles within the Church alight, a Council summoned by the Pope at Rome in 430 condemned the theses of Nestorius and ordered the bishop to retract them. The arrogant prelate jibbed at this. In vain his friend John of Antioch warned him of the peril in which he was placing himself. Then Cyril sent messengers to Constantinople bearing a letter in which he anathematized the Nestorian errors; the bishop replied with words of extreme violence, and, believing himself certain of victory, persuaded the emperor to convene a Council to settle the dispute.

This was the *Council of Ephesus* (431). Cyril attended it; by virtue of authority which he had received from the Pope he presided over it and conducted the affair in rousing fashion. In the town the mob demonstrated against the opponents of the Mother of God, but they carried Cyril, the Pope's legate, and the supporters of the traditional faith in triumphant torchlight processions. After three months of arguments during which the emperor intervened several times, going so far as to have both Cyril and Nestorius imprisoned at the same time, the Council ended by condemning the heretic absolutely and deposing him. Shortly afterwards he was exiled to Petra, in Arabia, then to the Great Oasis of Egypt, where he lived for a further twenty years, obstinately clinging to his theses, and propagating them under false names. In order to restore peace, John of Antioch, the friend of Nestorius, and St Cyril searched and found some conciliatory formulae which both the theologians of Antioch and Alexandria could support. The *Theotokos* was accepted.[1] But already by this time the pendulum had swung back again, and soon the opponents of the 'two natures' were to have their revenge.

In 444, when St Cyril died, an ambitious and violent man succeeded to the see of Alexandria. His name was Dioscorus. The new prelate

---

[1] 'When we study the history of the cult of the Virgin Mary, we see that not a single Christian church was dedicated to her before the Council of Ephesus (431) . . . which condemned Nestorius and decided that the Virgin should be called *Theotokos*, mother of God, and not *Christotokos*, mother of Christ.' (Émile Mâle, *La Fin du paganisme en Gaule*, Paris, 1950, p. 226.)

had nothing more urgent to do than to assert the pre-eminence of Alexandria over Antioch and Constantinople—we are for ever coming across these regional rivalries, these ulterior political motives! Moreover he suggested that, in his desire for reconciliation, St Cyril had been too complaisant, and that the decisions of Ephesus had not pulverized the Nestorians sufficiently, and he heaped vexations on the former friends of Nestorius, Theodoret of Cyr and Ibas of Edessa, by stating that their submission to the decrees of the Council was sham. On the dogmatic plane he and his supporters aimed so hard at asserting the personal union of the two natures of Christ, that they speedily ended up by confusing them, by making them equivalent. And thus the doctrines held of old by Apollinarius were restated once more, but the conviction of having triumphed over their adversary gave them a new impetus. This doctrine that now evolves is Monophysitism, the doctrine of the 'one nature,' or, more accurately, Monophysitisms, since this theory multiplied into an unbelievable number of variations and sects.

The reasons and emotions which led up to this thesis were not entirely base, however. Though we can always discern the rivalry between the theologians of Alexandria and Antioch in the background, we can also detect an undeniable ardour of faith, a desire to present Christ not as a Being clothed in our own miserable humanity, but as a marvellous, radiant figure, a sublime shadow, an idea, but still a shadow. . . . This desire was especially marked among the ascetics and the monks in the monasteries. The supporters of Monophysitism claimed to be defending the true faith against the last surviving henchmen of Nestorianism. They brandished texts allegedly signed by illustrious names, such as St Athanasius and St Gregory the Thaumaturgist, and which were, in point of fact, the works of Apollinarius. . . . Furthermore even within the Monophysite party there was no agreement on the manner in which the divine nature in Christ eliminated the human. . . .

There is something almost comical in the rapid multiplication of doctrines which resulted from this disagreement, and this really is one case in which we can accurately talk of 'Byzantinism!' There is *strict Monophysitism*, which states that in Christ there is a *unity of nature*, but there is also *modified Monophysitism*, which thinks this, but does not say it, shielding behind the deliberate confusion of formulae. Among the strict Monophysites we can pick out no fewer than four tendencies: those who teach the absorption of humanity by divinity 'as a drop of honey dissolves in the sea'; those who say that the Word has 'vanished into flesh' or even that it is 'condensed into flesh'; those who believe in the mingling of divinity and humanity in another indefinable nature; finally, the true descendants of Apollinarius, the supporters of the 'mixing' of a man of flesh and of God in Christ. Is this all? Far from it! And to give some idea of the limits to which extravagance in such matters can go, we should mention the *Actistetes*, for whom the body of Christ is 'uncreated,' the *Phantasiates*, who declare him impassive and incorruptible, the *Niobites* who modestly confess to being unable to distinguish the divine from the human. . . . One might stop here were it not for the *Acephalites*, whose name is not intended to imply that they have lost their heads, but that, rebelling against all doctrines, orthodox or heretical, they no longer recognize any leader.

Matters really came to a head at Constantinople. Towards 446 the leader of the Monophysite party there was a certain *Eutyches*, archimandrite of a monastery in the area, a dull-witted man, with no theological learning, a convert to the theses of Dioscorus. This man possessed great influence, because his god-son, the eunuch Chrysaphus, had become all powerful at the palace, especially with the Empress Eudocia, the wife of Theodosius II. Under pretext of attacking Nestorianism Eutyches won the imperial household and the Court over to Monophysitism, with the exception of the Princess Pulcheria, who remained orthodox, all the more faithful since she was furious to see her sister-in-law dominating her weak-willed brother more and more.

Thus the affair had obvious political repercussions from the start. It was taken up by the bishop Eusebius of Dorylea, the same man who had been one of the first to attack Nestorius. He denounced Eutyches at a local Council in 448, at which the monk refused to recant, saying that if he did so he would be betraying St Athanasius and St Cyril! The theological brawl immediately degenerated into a struggle of the people against the palace, and of Alexandria against Constantinople. When excommunicated Eutyches had the effrontery to appeal to the Pope, to Dioscorus, to various saints of the period, and, of course, to the emperor. Dioscorus hastened to declare him innocent, and Eudocia persuaded her husband to call a revisionary Council.

But in the Pope the new heresy was going to find its real adversary. The Pope at this period was none other than *St Leo*, the greatest pope of the age, and one of the greatest in the whole history of the Church.[1] The man who was soon to confront Attila was not the type of man to let himself be impressed by a heretic, and his sound Latin mind was little inclined to become ensnared in the quibbles of Byzantinism. Informed of it all by Flavian, the Bishop of Constantinople, who had remained faithful to orthodox doctrine, the Pope did not trouble to refute every detail in the tangle of Monophysitism. He confined himself to writing one text, which remains famous under the title of the *Volume to Flavian* (or the Dogmatic Epistle), in which he makes clear

[1] See the section devoted to him in the preceding chapter.

F

the true Catholic doctrine on Christ: in Jesus there is one *person* alone, but, in this unique *hypostasis*, two natures, the divine and the human, each retaining its qualities and its own faculties. This magnificent, lucid declaration, promulgated with the authority of a pontiff who was considered a saint, made an enormous impression.

Nevertheless truth did not triumph over error immediately. At the revisionary Council called by the emperor the events known as the *Brigandage of Ephesus* occurred. We have dealt with them in previous pages—with the intervention of the mob and the police and the fearful attack on the orthodox by the monks who were fanatical supporters of Monophysitism. The legates had a miraculous escape, and they straightway carried to the Pope the indignant protests of the defenders of the faith, and above all of Eusebius of Dorylea and of Flavian, the hapless patriarch, who died from the maltreatment he had received. Not for a second did St Leo hesitate. He condemned the 'Brigandage' and ordered the convening of a new Council. This Council would certainly have come to nothing had not Theodosius chanced to die whilst all this was going on, and had not his sister, Pulcheria, held power alongside her husband, Marcian, who succeeded him. At once all the ambitious and wicked men felt their faith in the single nature weaken. . . .

Convened at Chalcedon, in 451, under the presidency of the papal legates, the Council—an enormous Council, comprising six hundred delegates—formally condemned the Monophysite doctrines. St Leo's Epistle was acclaimed and a Creed was drawn up containing the fundamental assertions: 'We believe in the one and the same Christ Jesus, the only Son, in whom we recognize two natures, there being neither confusion, transformation, division nor separation between them. The difference between the two natures is in no way suppressed by their union; on the contrary, the attributes of each nature are preserved and exist in one person only.' Christian truth was thus proclaimed, a truth as far removed from Eutyches as from Nestorius.[1]

Was peace now to be allowed to reign in Christendom? Alas, no!

---

[1] In order to throw some light on these controversies it is very useful to set them face to face with the evolution of the liturgy which actually occurred in the regions which bore the brunt of these disputes. It is in the East that the devotion to Christ's humanity was born.

Unbelievable though it seems to us, there is nothing in Christian Antiquity, aside from a few quite exceptional cases, that foreshadows the emotion of St Bernard or St Francis towards the Crib or the Cross. Piety is directed towards the Father.

It is in the East that we see the stages in the life of Christ commemorated for the first time: the Good Friday ceremonies were celebrated at Jerusalem long before they were celebrated in Rome and this liturgy spread first of all throughout the Greek Church.

Likewise the influence of the East seems to have been preponderant in the origins of the use of the crucifix, as one of the most ancient examples of altar crosses that we know of comes from a Nestorian monastery in the sixth century.

(See E. Dumontet, *Le Christ selon la chair et la vie liturgique au moyen âge*, Paris, 1932, p. 13.)

The passions which had been unleashed remained too heated, and political motives, which we have just seen mingling throughout the whole of this affair, were to cause trouble to break out anew. The separatist tendencies which undermined Eastern Christianity used the resistance to these ideas for their own ends. The Churches of Egypt and Syria, those in the region around Edessa, in Mesopotamia and Armenia, even those in the Persian Empire, seceded from the true Mother, some faithful to Nestorianism,[1] others attached to the concept of the single nature. This secession was to be the origin of those churches which remain separated from *Mater Ecclesiae* up to our own time, rigidly exclusive, steadily declining in numbers as the centuries passed by, but which were to derive from their debased but nevertheless lively Christian faith the strength to stand up to Islam: the Nestorian Chaldaean Church, the Monophysite Church of Syria, known as the 'Jacobite' Church, after its principal organizer, James Baradai, the Egyptian (or Coptic) Church, and the Abyssinian Church. As far away as the shores of India the Syriac-Malabar Church was to be successively Nestorian, then Catholic, and then partially Monophysite in the seventeenth century.

These were serious rents indeed in the Seamless Robe! But there were to be others still more so. For, as they continued, these theological disputes were to provide motives of endless conflicts for another antagonism which was already more than a century old, the antagonism between the old Rome and the new, the Rome of St Peter and that of the Basileus.

## CONSTANTINOPLE OR ROME

Ever since the year 330, when Constantine the Great had inaugurated the new capital amid imperial rejoicings, a problem had been there to all intents and purposes. It was inevitable that rivalry should spring up between this second Rome, rising in all its youthful glory on the shores of the Bosphorus, and the old Rome, the Rome of Romulus and Augustus. Constantine had done everything in his power to see that Constantinople possessed all the prerogatives of the Eternal City; on the political plane, from his reign onwards, equality between the two cities was complete; later on, as the West grew progressively more feeble, a lack of balance had been bound to occur, weighted in favour of the impregnable Rome of the East. But given what we know of the inclinations of these masters of Byzantium, of this Caesaro-Papism which was so eager to venture into the realm of faith, it was equally inevitable that a similar rivalry should arise on the religious plane also.

[1] Christianity was to penetrate Central Asia, as far as China, in its Nestorian form. See further on in this book, Chapter VI, final section.

Must not the Basileus, who considered himself a spiritual as well as a temporal leader, be quite naturally inclined to regard the authentic spiritual leader of the Church, the Pope of Rome, as a kind of competitor with him?

Consequently from reign to reign numerous incidents occurred, which revealed the premonitory signs of this antagonism. The episcopal see of Constantinople had very quickly freed itself from the authority of the metropolitan of Heraclea, to which it was canonically subject. At the Oecumenical Council of 381, that same Council which had hallowed the victory of Nicene orthodoxy, the primacy of the Bishop of Constantinople immediately following that of the Bishop of Rome had been proclaimed, 'this city being the new Rome.' This honourable primacy soon went hand in hand with an administrative authority over the neighbouring religious dioceses. By the fifth century Byzantium was the seat of the State Church; intimately linked with the vicissitudes of the Empire's religious policy, its bishop strove to develop his position, and, without expressly desiring it—at least at the beginning—he was to change imperceptibly from the leader of one division of the universal Church into the head of a national Greek church. Meanwhile the popes, who were fully conscious of the danger, laid claim to their rights on several occasions, asserting their primacy and their dogmatic and disciplinary authority with majestic dignity, and they intervened as much as they could, according to their prerogatives.

The details of this incessant struggle are too numerous for us to notice them all. For example, during the drama of St John Chrysostom the saint appealed to St Innocent to help him against the tyranny of Arcadius, and the Pope intervened resolutely to re-establish the truth; later on, even though the Nestorian heresy was in fact limited to the Eastern Empire, the world saw Pope St Celestine receive the appeal of the heretical prelate and condemn him at Rome; double proof of the express will of the pontiffs to have their universal rights recognized at all times. Inversely the bishops of Constantinople frequently made use of an occasion to enlarge the scope of their authority, and to encroach on papal preserves on the doctrinal plane, and to obtain the submission of new dioceses. We have already seen the part that they played in the Christological conflicts. About the year 435, one of them, named Proclus, attempted to bring all the bishops of Illyria into his sphere of influence, and was only just prevented from doing so by Pope Sixtus III.[1] In 451 the first serious

---

[1] The reparation of a great injustice must be put to the credit of this Bishop Proclus. He obtained permission from the emperor to bring the body of St John Chrysostom back to Constantinople. The precious relics arrived in the capital on 21st January 438—and thousands of boats lit with torches covered the Bosphorus, going to meet them; and Theodosius II himself presided at their deposition in the basilica of the Blessed Apostles, the resting-place of the kings.

incident occurred, the first one which really gave some indication of the rifts that were to take place in the future.

The Council of Chalcedon was drawing to its close.   It had been, as we have seen, a triumph for the great Pope St Leo, whose Dogmatic Epistle had finally settled the issue between orthodoxy and the Monophysite heresy, and who had been acclaimed by one of his legates as 'the archbishop of all the Churches.'   But the Eastern prelates had renounced neither their ambitions nor their desire to encroach on what belonged to Rome.   Profiting from the fact that the Council was concluding the settlement of various points of discipline which were of secondary importance, and that the papal legates were absent, they had carried through a capital document—surreptitiously—according to a method dear to modern parliamentary assembles.   This was Canon 28.   Therein it was stated that as 'rights had been justly bestowed on the see of the old Rome, because that city was the imperial city,' for the same reason 'the same privileges had been bestowed on that of the new Rome, honoured as it is by the presence of the emperor and the senate.'   The stage was set ready for the deception: not a word was said of the real reasons on which the primacy of the city of St Peter was founded; this primacy was recognized only as the primacy of a political capital, in order that it could be awarded also to the other capital. And, at the same time, Constantinople was raised to the dignity of a metropolitan see, with jurisdiction over Pontus, Asia, and Thrace; in other words, Byzantium was made into a real patriarchate.   In vain the legates attempted to oppose this manœuvre: but it was too late! They could only register their protest on the official record.   As for St Leo, he was furious.   As soon as he knew what had happened he wrote a vehement letter to the imperial couple, Marcian and Pulcheria, in which he spoke of 'these impudent endeavours, contrary to Christian unity and the peace of the Church.'   But he never received any reply.[1]

Shortly after this an infinitely more serious matter was to occur. In 471 *Acatius* was elevated to the patriarchal throne of Constantinople. He was an ambitious, dictatorial man, but a skilful tactician.   Although a vigorous defender of the doctrines of Chalcedon during the reign of the Emperor Leo I, who accepted them, this prelate shifted his position as soon as the new emperor, Zeno, adopted a different attitude.   Zeno was seriously preoccupied by Gothic threats and by the plots which were incessantly being hatched against him, and he conceived the unquestionably politic idea of reconciling all his subjects—both orthodox and Monophysite—in order to eliminate all the causes of friction in his territories.   Acatius, for his part, bore Rome a grudge for her

---

[1] It was then that St Leo set up a permanent legation at Constantinople, which he entrusted to Bishop Julian of Cos: this was the first Nunciature.

continued refusal to recognize Canon 28 (this refusal was to last until the thirteenth century . . .), and he cherished the dream of being a kind of Byzantine pope ruling over all the Christians in the Eastern Empire. He therefore entered into negotiations with Peter Mongius, the Monophysite bishop of Alexandria, and a large area of agreement was reached. Consequently, in 482, the imperial decree known as the *Henotic Edict*—the 'unifying' edict—was published. In this both Nestorius and Eutyches were anathematized yet once more, and once again the humanity and the divinity of Christ were asserted, but it was all done in such vague terms, such care being taken to evade categorical formulae, and with such a truly Byzantine knack of reconciling opposites, that no one could mistake the real meaning of the document: it was the abandonment of the decisions of Chalcedon. Acatius and Peter Mongius countersigned the edict at once, and all the bishops who refused to accept it were hounded from their sees. But then Rome protested. Pope St Simplicius (468–83) and his successor, St Felix III (483–92), acted with determination. Although the papal legates had been intimidated by violence and corrupted with gifts, Felix did not allow himself to be deceived. He issued a sentence of deposition and excommunication against Acatius. (It was this sentence which Acatius bore so involuntarily on his backside when he entered his church. . . .) [1] Supported by the monks, and in large measure by the people of the capital, who detested Zeno, orthodoxy confronted the usurper vigorously. Encouraged by the emperor, Acatius then plunged into open revolt. He struck the Pope's name from the marble tables which perpetuated the memory of the head of the Church at the holy sacrifice of the mass. And thus the *first Greek schism*, the *Schism of Acatius*, broke out: it was to last for thirty-five years (483–518); that is to say, long after the death (489) of the man who had set it in motion.

This crisis shook the Church and the Empire severely, not only in the East, where opposition was so violent that the Emperor Anastasius, accused in turn of Manichaeism, Arianism, and Monophysitism, all but lost his throne, but at Rome itself, where, on the death of Pope St Anastasius II, a party favourable to a reconciliation with Byzantium raised an antipope named Laurence to the Pontificate, actually forcing the real Pope, St Symmachus, to barricade himself in St Peter's. This conflict only just missed being settled by the arbitration of Theodoric, the Arian king! The schism had great consequences in the West: for it was largely due to it that the Gallo-Roman episcopate, that of St Remigius, of St Avitus, which had until then been very attached to the imperial ideal, detached itself from this Byzantine Empire which had

---

[1] The monk responsible for this was executed.

become unfaithful to Rome, and turned instead to the Barbarian kings, and especially to Clovis, whose baptism is exactly contemporaneous with this episode (498-9).

But one fact during this painful period must be emphasized. This is the serenity and courage with which the popes claimed their rights in defending true tradition. One pope only, St Anastasius II, possibly contemplated making some concessions in order to put an end to the schism;[1] all the others faced it resolutely. Pope St Gelasius asserted before the emperor the superiority of sacerdotal over laical authority. Pope Symmachus was barely rid of the antipope, when he wrote to the same Byzantine autocrat: 'Compare, O Emperor, your dignity and that of the head of the Church. Take a look at the long line of those who have persecuted the Church. They have perished, but the Church sees her power grow with every persecution that she suffers.' And when Anastasius broke off negotiations, ill-treated the papal legates, and wrote an unacceptable letter to Pope St Hormisdas, the latter sent him this admirable reply: 'You may abuse me, and regard me as nothing; but you will never see me accept your orders.'

The drama ended in 518, when the honest soldier, Justin, ascended the Byzantine throne. Justin was a convinced Catholic; moreover two political reasons impelled him to take a fresh course: the desire to render harmless a certain Vitalian who was disturbing the provinces under the pretext of championing orthodoxy, and the underlying motives of his nephew, Justinian, who was already dreaming of reconquering the West from the Barbarians, and who wanted to be reconciled with Rome first. Pope Hormisdas, whom Justin had respectfully informed of his accession, sent him, as the emperor desired, legates to end the schism. These envoys showed themselves as forceful as they were skilful. When the patriarch announced that he would willingly discuss matters with them, they replied resolutely: 'We have not come here for purposes of discussion, but to present a formula which anyone wanting to be reconciled with the Apostolic See must accept!' Language like this carried the day. The Monophysite bishops were deposed, the patriarch, whether he liked it or not, had to sign a declaration of orthodoxy, which repudiated the Henotic Edict. The names of all the heresiarchs, including the emperors Zeno and Anastasius, were struck from the marble tables. And the the entire Eastern episcopate had to accept the famous *Formula of Hormisdas* (518), which asserted the inviolate privileges of the see of Rome, and the obligation incumbent upon anyone who wished to call himself Catholic, of remaining united to the Pope and of following his instructions.

[1] This is what made Dante place him in hell, quite unjustly. (Canto XI. 6, 10.)

Thus the successor of St Peter triumphed.[1]  He triumphed because
the bonds between the two sectors of Christianity were still too strong
to be broken just yet; even at the height of the split the emperors had
not dared push matters to the extreme conclusion, and a pope like St
Gelasius declared: 'Keep your respect for the Emperor, in so far as he
is a Roman citizen.'  He triumphed because the Apostolic See had
been filled throughout the conflict by men of energetic character.  He
triumphed too, it must be confessed, because the political climate
became favourable to him.  But the fundamental causes of friction
between the two Romes had by no means disappeared, for all this, and
it is this underlying antagonism which is to throw a painful shadow
over the great reign which began on the death of Justin, in 527.

## JUSTINIAN AND THEODORA

Justinian and Theodora!  The two names alone seem to sum up all
the glory of Byzantium, its pomp, and its vaguely mysterious glamour;
and for the historian it is certainly true that this illustrious couple
forms the most significant example of what the theocratic imperial
system could produce both at its most admirable and at its most disturbing.  We must go to the church of St Vitalis at Ravenna to see
them, in the pearly light that hangs in the apse, caressing the rosy
marble and the Egyptian breccia of the pillars, and shattering into gold
dust as it reflects on the thousand facets of the mosaics.  High up, on
the curve of the triumphal arch which leads up to the choir, Christ and
the apostles meditate in glory; but the visitor quickly has eyes only
for these two fabulous processions which face each other on opposite
walls of the church, solemnly advancing in all the glitter of the artists'
enamels and precious stones—Justinian and his dignitaries, and
Theodora and her ladies-in-waiting.

He bears a halo, like a saint, and is wearing the purple dalmatic, its
folds falling to the jewels on his slippers.  His crown is a high, two-
tiered diadem, his right shoulder is surmounted with a rosette of
diamonds, and he holds in his hand the ritual offerings, which, in a
moment, he will place devoutly on the altar.  In front of him the

---

[1] Consequently, when in 525 the Ostrogoth king, Theodoric, forced Pope St John I to
go to Constantinople (see final section of the preceding chapter) in order to claim various
rights for the Gothic Arians there, the Sovereign Pontiff was received with extraordinary
respect.  Justin went so far as to beg him to crown him for a second time, during the
Easter festival of 526, even though he had already been crowned by the Patriarch of Constantinople.  With regard to the mission with which the Goths had charged him, he
acquitted himself—deliberately, it is certain—in such a way that Theodoric had several
reasons for being furious at the result.  It was absurd to expect a pope to plead the cause
of heresy.  After being arrested, as we know, John died in prison.  (Cf. Chapter II:
final section.)

prelates are walking to the church.  There is the bishop Maximian, in stole and liturgical cope, carrying a cross in his hand; and two clerics, the one bearing the censer and the other the Holy Books, their emblazoned bindings aglitter with sapphires.  Behind him there is an entire official retinue, summed up in six persons: two ministers, a general—Belisarius perhaps—and the palace guards, in gold coats of mail, their swords in their hands, their shields, stamped with the Chrisma, resting on the ground—a retinue which conjures up the audacious political and strategic actions connected with the triumph of the Master, which have just been hallowed by military victory, and by the reconquest of Ravenna from the Goths.

She seems so slight and fragile, almost crushed by the enormous crown, the double pendants, the cloak interwoven with emeralds and rubies, by all this heavy burden of priceless jewels, and, who knows, crushed also perhaps by the large gold circlet which endows her with an official sanctity.  She too is off to the ceremony, escorted by her exquisitely beautiful young waiting-women, hieratically attired in their gowns of lamé and brocade.  Here comes a servant to lift the arras: for how can the Basilissa possibly be absent in the moment of the emperor's glory—this woman who has taken part in all his labours and shared all his risks?  She is scarcely visible beneath the straight folds of her royal cloak—along the bottom of it a wide band of embroidery depicts the Magi adoring the Infant Jesus—how is it that she gives such an impression of calm and resolute strength?  This portrait confirms and transfigures all that history tells us of her; in the charm of her heart-shaped face, and the sparkle of her expressive eyes, we can see this superior kind of serenity, just a little forced, perhaps, which this former dancing-girl had known how to attain, and in the unyielding watchfulness which is painted on her delicate features we can detect this really exceptional courage with which she faced all that life had to offer her.

Yes, it is in front of these two mosaic panels, in all the glitter of their gold and the perfect harmony of their colouring, contrasting yet blending into one magnificent whole, that we must capture the glory of Byzantium—in these, its two most complete representatives. Everything has been done here to express this glory, in a majesty which forces itself upon our souls, and yet we have only to look closely at these serious but not stereotyped faces, in which the sure skill of the craftsmen has known how to make allowance for a discreet realism, to guess that human passions worked behind these crowned brows, and within the breasts hidden beneath the imperial purple, and that love, hate, ambition, and fear influenced their actions as much as they do our own.

It is this very fact which makes this reign so moving—this reign, which is so remarkable in several respects that it seems to reduce all its

* F

predecessors of the past one hundred years to a mere preamble. Made admirable by the objects at which this man and this woman aimed, it is at the same time marked by the sign of human weakness; it admits the limits which the conditions of history—these manifestations of Providence—impose on mortal ambitions. Justinian and Theodora certainly had an exact understanding of the task thrust upon them; but in the last resort they were but an ordinary man and an ordinary woman, obedient to the traditions, to the habits of thought, to the perilous ups and downs of this Eastern world which was subject to them. They were, like it, greedy and violent, like it, quarrelsome and complex, full of contradictions and contrasts, and utterly incapable, despite the sparkle of genius which sometimes touched them, of breaking the circle of their fates.

They assumed the imperial purple together in 527, in the basilica of St Sophia, the old basilica built by Constantine, according to the minutely ordered, interminable ritual of Byzantine coronations. One after the other they knelt before the Emperor Justin, allowing themselves to be ceremonially robed, having the slippers of scarlet silk laced on their feet and their brows encircled with the diadem, whilst the generals and the dignitaries and the ladies of the Court prostrated themselves on the ground, whilst the crowd roared out its rhythmical acclamations, and whilst the silver trumpets sounded the note to the sacred choirs intoning the thanksgiving psalms. This was the way the rough old soldier-emperor had wanted it. He had only one tender feeling in the world and that was for his nephew, and he had wanted him to receive a perfect education in kingship. So he had made him successively patrician and consul, had generously forgiven him his scandalous marriage, and had finally made him co-emperor beside him some months before his death.

Justinian was at that time a man in the prime of life, having just passed his fortieth year, and his character had already been moulded by ten years of court life, high commands, and official responsibilities. Not too tall, not too short, not too thin, not too fat, neither handsome nor ugly, he certainly did not look anything other than an ordinary average man, and that is exactly how the mosaic on the wall of St Vitalis portrays him. His calm, florid face hardly seems to crackle with intelligence. What is the real truth about him? We do not know what to take as silver from the dross out of which Procopius claims to fashion his portrait.[1]  When a historian writes of a ruler

---

[1] Procopius has left us two versions of the reign of Justinian, each diametrically opposed to the other.  On the one hand, in *The History of the Wars* and the *Treatise on Edifices* he exalts its glory; on the other, in *The Secret History*, he relates its seamy side with a taste for despicable detail which is more fitted to a disloyal servant than to a serious historian.  It is unfortunate, that owing to their racy and even pornographic character, it is the anecdotes from the last-named work which are most often published.

'He was a liar and a double-dealer, violent in his hatreds, yet skilful at concealing them, weeping hot tears if his interest required him to do so —a faithless friend, an unscrupulous enemy, greedy for blood and money—utterly unprincipled, his nature vitiated with folly and spite,' we cannot help thinking that such a brave accumulation of epithets must be somewhat slanderous, and that the hack pamphleteers of every age have nearly always dealt with their enemies in like terms.   And when we read from the same pen that Justinian 'was not a man, but a devil in human form,' we are quite sure of it.   The truth is that this Thracian highlander, with his dull face and insignificant appearance, bore within him an eminent sense of responsibility of the duties of his office, a thoroughly respectable capacity for hard work, faculties of political judgment which were far from commonplace, and a quite exceptional understanding of the meaning of greatness, all curiously cut short by odd defects of character, by sudden weaknesses, as if the possibly excessive tension in which his crushing responsibilities held him fast suddenly snapped.

However, at his side, fate had placed a being whose steadfastness remained unshakable, a woman with a soul of tempered steel.   It is quite clear that history would have had a very different story to tell of the reign of Justinian had not Theodora been there, working alongside him; as long as she lived, she was his secret counsellor, his living conscience, and she played her part so skilfully that their very differences of temperament, tastes, and religious convictions could be put to the service of their common policy; then, when she died, in 548, the old man continued to live and to act for seventeen more years with a touching loyalty, as if he had the shadow of her invisible presence beside him.   This is the important side of Theodora's life, not the romantic tale with its ambiguous episodes, which the sequel of the *Secret History* scrutinizes with such pleasure.   It was a strange fate which made this bear-keeper's daughter, this dancer from the Hippodrome, this 'amusing and witty' table companion at many an intimate nocturnal supper party, into the wife of the heir to the throne, and then into the Basilissa herself.   All we need remember of this is the indomitable energy displayed by this woman, who, starting from such mean beginnings, succeeded both in reaching and in maintaining such an exalted position, and the moral excellence—and why not?— the spiritual worth that this sinner showed in restoring her chastity, and, too, the experience of men so tragically acquired by the adventuress, from which the empress derived her exceptional political understanding.[1]

---

[1] It is of far greater interest to relate her origins to those political measures concerning women—which are very modern in some respects—which she inspired Justinian to carry out.   She was an 'abolitionist' and suggested to the Basileus strict measures against the

Together then they reigned, according to those same customs which had been observed in Byzantium for more than a century now, according to the same etiquette and the same Asiatic absolutism. These characteristics of Eastern autocracy actually increased during their reign. The flattering courtly adulation was accentuated still further, and the old school of Byzantine courtiers did not fail to murmur a little when the Basilissa herself compelled all her visitors—even senators—to observe the formality of kissing her foot. Was this empty vainglory? A rather laughable show of arrogance? No. Every regime has its own needs, and just as democracies, almost inevitably, slip downhill if they remain rigidly faithful to their principles, so authoritarian regimes cannot maintain themselves if they stick just within their existing limits and crystallize there. At the beginning of their reign, with the encouragement of the great prefect of the Praetorium, John of Cappadocia, Justinian and Theodora had cherished the dream of bringing the peoples of their Empire back into civic life, of lightening the burdens of state tyranny, that is to say, of continuing the policy attempted by their predecessor, Anastasius, twenty years earlier. They had soon to realize, that, given the moral decadence of their subjects, this dream was madness; a terrible incident forced them to open their eyes to the realities of the situation.

During the first few years of this reign, on account of this policy, and also because the war against the Persians detained the army far from the capital, they let their people have rather too much rein. The only result was that insubordination grew, that the 'Blues' and the 'Greens' insulted each other the more violently, and that the disorder reached menacing proportions, probably secretly fomented by the great landowners, whose feudalist tendencies were becoming a real danger to the Crown, and one which John of Cappadocia had resisted. Naturally the theological disputes on the nature of Christ were used more than ever as a pretext for all these rivalries which were actually based on self-interest, and for the various class antagonisms. In 532, when peace was restored and the army had returned to Constantinople, Justinian and Theodora wished to react against this situation, and the jurist Tribonian and John of Cappadocia were given the task of tightening matters up, with particular regard to the police and to the taxes. The political temperature rose.

proprietors of brothels, and she campaigned against the trade in women that was carried on for the purposes of prostitution. And she did not confine herself to giving advice, however much it might be backed by the weight of her imperial authority; she gave money, too, thus providing the sinews of this war against vice. She spent a great deal in her fight against prostitution, buying the freedom of prostitutes, and founding a house for reformed women. (The *Histoire de Bas-Empire*, by the late Ernest Stein, 1949, gives this point its full due, vol. ii, p. 239.)

One January day the crowd, which was assembled in the Hippodrome as usual, displayed a very ugly mood.   A rumble of anger ran
round the tiered amphitheatre; shouts rang out which had nothing to
do with the drivers who were galloping into the arena in their chariots.
Instead of resorting to severe measures, Justinian tried three times to
argue with the crowd from his dais high above them, in the ridiculous
hope of calming the confusion.   From her latticed box, perched on
the side of the church of St Stephen, Theodora watched it all anxiously.
Suddenly a mistake on the part of the prefect, John of Cappadocia, set
the drama in motion.   Out of patience with hearing the mob demanding his head, he took several hostages at random from the party of
'Greens' who were leading the agitation.   Alas! among these
presumed ringleaders was one 'Blue'; he was well and truly hanged.

The result was a riot.   The 'Blues' and the 'Greens' were now
united, and so the whole town was in revolt.   The troops were hastily
confined to barracks; the imperial couple and the entire Court barricaded themselves in the Sacred Palace.   For three days the revolution
seemed to be mistress of the capital.   St Sophia was set on fire, and,
with it, palaces, churches, and the houses of the rich, whilst the scum
from the prisons indulged in looting on a gigantic scale.   'Victory!
Victory!' cried the rebels.   *'Nika!   Nika!'*   And in history this
drama has remained 'the Nika insurrection.'   Already men were
talking of crowning one of the nephews of the former Emperor
Anastasius to replace Justinian.

In the palace all was uncertainty and confusion.   Justinian himself,
abashed by the speed of events, collapsed completely.   He paced up
and down, hesitated, equivocated, and finally talked of leaving the
town, of embarking on a warship. . . .   But then Theodora stood up.
She faced him, quivering with energy.   'Perhaps it is not seemly for a
woman to talk in front of men, and to bid cowards have courage!
But I am convinced that in circumstances like these flight would not
mean safety.   He who has once borne the sovereignty ought not to
live any longer once he is stripped of it.   As for me, I shall never
renounce my imperial title.   You can flee if you wish, Caesar; you
have the money, the ships, and the sea is clear.   But let me tell you
this, if you leave this palace you will lose everything, even your life.
As for me, I stand by the old maxim: the purple is the finest winding-
sheet!'

These words stung the men into action at once.   The generals recovered their self-possession; the politicians sent agents to undermine
the factions, to separate the 'Blues' and the 'Greens' by a judicious dis-
tribution of silver.   The latter, drunk with rage and loot, committed
the extreme madness of assembling in the amphitheatre to acclaim
their puppet-emperor.   This sealed their doom.   It was necessary to

do no more than surround them and set the Alan federates and the mercenary Goths loose on them.  How many corpses were there on the seats and the sand of the Hippodrome when the evening of the fourth day fell?  Thirty, forty thousand?  We do not know.  But Justinian and Theodora never forgot the lesson so bitterly learned: that one cannot be only half an autocrat.

## A Great Reign's Leading Titles to Fame

Its solid achievements are here to prove that during this reign the Empire underwent an expansion unparalleled since the time of Constantine.  Building and conquest have always been the two most prominent ways in which the masters of men proclaim their greatness to mankind, and though we may query the benefits which the subjects actually derive from these costly displays of power, it is nevertheless true—the example of Louis XIV is a good illustration of this—that they are only possible if the nation itself is sound, well balanced, prosperous, and strongly governed.  Justinian and Theodora were great conquerors and great builders.  They have left their mark on history in their victories and their monuments; the very extent of these undertakings makes it clear that their power rested on solid foundations.

The internal disorder, which had made things only too easy for factional conflicts and rebellions by pretenders to the throne, ceased.  A great effort was made to maintain order on the imperial highways, and, on the high seas, the campaign against piracy and the conquest of the African kingdom of the Vandals, had the most happy results.  A flexible economic policy, which availed itself in turn of controls and *laissez-faire* methods, stimulated production and trade; for example, when the war against Persia led to a serious crisis in the important silk-weaving industry, Justinian converted it into a State monopoly in order to save it from extinction.  Soon afterwards, however, in 552, when he had succeeded in stealing some silkworm cocoons from China, together with the secret of their breeding, he ordered the planting of mulberries and the building of cocooneries throughout his domains.  He then restored the liberties of the privately owned silk industry, and saw it develop with prodigious speed, at Beirut as well as at Thebes, at Alexandria, just as at Byzantium.  It is absolutely certain that, during the third of a century spanned by this reign, the trade in fabrics, spices, perfumes, raw materials, and food-stuffs deposited a regular gold-mine on the quays of the Golden Horn.

This expansion of Byzantine civilization was equally marked in the field of learning.  Constantinople, mistress of the Mediterranean, emporium of the world, attracted too the finest minds of the age.

Her university saw a tremendous development—which the closure, in 529, of the School of Athens, which had been moribund for a long time now, encouraged still further. A brilliant culture radiated from this new Rome, not a Latin culture—since Latin was being more and more reduced to the status of a provincial tongue—but a Hellenic one, which claimed to be the successor of that of the great Greek teachers, although it was in large measure more theological than literary. The *Histories* of Procopius were read everywhere, and throughout the Empire men sang the hymns of Romanos the Melodious; at the palace itself the emperor had pretensions to being a poet. And it is to this intellectual expansion that Justinian owed the two most lasting feathers in his cap: his judicial masterpiece and the church of St Sophia; it is significant that both are marked with the stamp of Christianity.

Some months after his accession Justinian ordered the drafting of a Code, which was to bear his name, thus reviving the idea of his predecessor, Theodosius II, a century before. The concept he had formed of his powers and his responsibilities encouraged him to appear in the role of legislator; was he not the living incarnation of the law? Tribonian and Theophilus were commanded to collect and reconcile all the imperial laws promulgated since the time of Hadrian, and to make one cogent and lasting whole from the enormous mass of legislation which Rome had produced; in fourteen months the task was accomplished and the *Justinian Code* was born. Then between 530 and 533 the outstanding passages from the books of the thirty-nine most famous jurists were collated: this was the *Digest* or *Pandectae*, in which, it was said, so much material was condensed that the original source books represented the burden of several camels![1] After that the principles of law were summed up in a manual to be used by students: the *Institutes*. Out of loyalty to the past this gigantic work was drafted in Latin, but the *Novellae* were written in Greek. These were the ordinances made by Justinian himself in which all these principles were applied.

---

[1] The spread of the use of the word 'digest' contemporaneously came about through the Anglo-Saxon medium. But it is only a medium, and the source is Roman. *Digesta* —things tabulated, that is to say, classified, and restyled in the intellectual sense to a logical pattern—this is the idea which governed the drawing up of the collection. We are very far away here from the literary tabloids which have popularized the word in our own day. The *Digest* is not a *résumé*; it is more of a legal index book. When Boileau wrote his line 'Let us open the labyrinth of the *Digest* and the *Code*,' he showed that he never had opened it, for the *Digest* is by definition quite the opposite of a labyrinth. It is often said that jurisprudence is found in the *Digest*. This is not so; at least, if we take the word in its strict sense—in which we shall be alone to-day (alas)—of 'legal precedent.' We find in it, considerably retouched and altered however, works of doctrine, among them the 'replies of the prudent,' that is to say, the opinions given by the official legal advisers of the emperor (the replies of ministers to the written questions of deputies, etc.). It is the presence of this element, which, by reason of its verbal connection of the term, has led people to say that there is 'jurisprudence' in it.

THE BYZANTINE EMPIRE
AT THE DEATH OF JUSTINIAN

——— Boundaries of the Empire
- - - Boundaries of the Imperial
        Dioceses

MILES
0        200        400        600

This prodigious work has stood the test of time, and even in our own day there is not a single law student who has not a nodding acquaintance with it.   It has often been strongly criticized; it has been judged slapdash, and is alleged to have been compiled carelessly and uncritically.   In its compilation the earlier labours of the Roman jurists Ulpian and Papinian, the two great Lebanese legal scholars who had earned the title of 'legum nutrix' at Beirut, were more or less destroyed.   But, just as it is, this *Corpus juris civilis* is a work of supreme historical importance.   Roman law, released from the archaic impedimenta which had encumbered it, became a body of standard doctrines.   It was to preserve those ideas of the State, those principles of social organization, and those methods of justice, as they had been developed by the legal genius of Rome over a period of a thousand years, in order that the West might learn them again when it emerged from Barbarism on the threshold of the Middle Ages.   Some new tendencies came to the fore, tendencies which are nowadays labelled 'social' and 'humanitarian'; the notion of the common good crept in, for example, in the articles in which the rate of interest was limited, even if the parties concerned were perfectly agreeable, in the name of a superior principle.   For the first time in legal history, what we call 'the abuse of law' was watched and curbed: here the influence of Christianity can be seen.   It was very marked in all these texts.   Not only was the *Corpus juris* produced 'in the Name of Our Lord Jesus Christ,' but the code expressly laid down the Catholic faith as the basis of law, in other words, as the basis of civilization.   The new attitude which is so marked in it was a really Christian one.   Justinian's predecessors, ever since their conversion to Christianity, that is to say, ever since the time of Constantine, had been pledged in this direction, and had allowed the Gospel spirit to penetrate certain of their decisions. This tendency was still clearer in the legal monument of the sixth century.   To the glorious credit of Justinian, his Code and its append-ages made it their legal basis.[1]

But this is even more marked in the case of Justinian's other great monument!   It has kept its glory intact up to our own time, summing up in itself alone all the power and proud wealth of Byzantium, as well as the rather ostentatious fervour of its faith.   This is the monument which draws every traveller's eye towards it, as, approaching Con-stantinople from the sea, in a rosy haze, he sees its gigantic mass dominating the city, or, to put it more accurately, floating above it, the one distinct shape against the horizon, soaring above the grey jumble of the other buildings around it.   *The church of St Sophia!*

---

[1] To find out in what measure the law of responsibility, which is in process of absorb-ing all law, is indebted to Justinian, the reader is referred to the arguments of the authoritative *Traité de la Responsabilité Civile*, by the brothers Mazeaud, vol. i, p. 33.

An Eastern and Christian replica of that tawny perfection which the Greeks of old had also dedicated to Wisdom,[1] it is entirely different in spirit from that slender and austere masterpiece, and yet at the same time it is the direct heir of the serene audacity and sure technique, which, a thousand years before, had brought the Parthenon into being.

St Sophia was the ancient basilica of Constantine, the one which he had built in 325, in the brilliant moment of his victory.   His son, Constantius, and Theodosius II had added to it in turn, but revered though it was because of its glorious past and on account of all the memories that clung to its walls, it seemed none the less inadequate for the pageantry of the sixth-century Court, inadequate, for example, for the enactment of the majestic coronation ceremonies.   When the old church was damaged by fire and looting during the Nika insurrection in 532, Justinian saw the heaven-sent chance to build a new church, right in the very heart of the town, quite close to the Hippodrome and not far from the palace, a church which would eclipse every other building in the world and which would be worthy of the glory of God—and of himself.

The orders were given immediately and the builders' yards opened. Two architects from Asia, Isidore of Miletus and Anthemius of Tralles, were entrusted with carrying out the work.   Ten thousand workmen and one hundred foremen were put at their disposal. Precious materials were collected from every corner of the Empire— marble, pillars, and sculpture from the most famous pagan temples; for instance, the temple of Diana at Ephesus provided eight monoliths of green Egyptian breccia, and the 'Sol invicta' at Baalbek eight more of white marble.   Everything flowed in profusion, from gold to human sweat, and more besides perhaps, for was it not asserted that the Basileus had received the plan of the building and the necessary money for its construction from an angel, and even that celestial armies worked on its building each night?   In five years all was finished; on 27th December 537 the emperor and the patriarch attended the solemn consecration.   As he crossed the porphyry threshold of his masterpiece Justinian cried: 'I have beaten you, Solomon!'

In front of the basilica stretched an enormous atrium, surrounded by porticoes.   Five doors led into the narthexes; from these, nine doors, of which the principal one, in the middle, was reserved for the sovereign alone, opened into the church proper.   There the visitor halted, overwhelmed by its vast size.   Almost square in plan, two hundred and twenty-five by two hundred and forty feet, its centre occupied by

---

[1] Is it necessary to remind ourselves that St Sophia is not consecrated to a saint of this name but to the divine Wisdom, which is extolled in one of the books of the Bible, and which is one of the most essential attributes of the Almighty?   And that the Parthenon was dedicated to Athene, goddess of Wisdom?

the four gigantic piers which supported the cupola, it gave a strange
and confusing impression of tamed space, of a mass suspended in it in
defiance of physical laws, of an almost plant-like luxuriance, controlled
by the human mind.    The eye travelled from the mysteriously empty
place in the centre, bounded by the piers, to the complex perspectives
of the one hundred and seven pillars—the mystic number of Wisdom
—to be finally drawn, halted, and fascinated by the luminous mysteries
of the cupola, made to appear like an earthly heaven by a golden haze
that hung in the air of the building.

In this lay the ultimate secret of the masterpiece.    Instead of being
roofed in with a solid framework, as the old Constantinian basilicas
had been, St Sophia was vaulted into a cupola.    This meant erecting
a half-sphere, one hundred feet in diameter, and which rose more than
one hundred and fifty feet from the ground, in the middle of the nave,
upon a square whose sides measured one hundred feet.    In order to do
this four arcs, resting equally on the four giant piers, had been inscribed
over the four corners of the square, and to support the base of the
cupola spherical triangles—the pendentives—had been constructed,
resting on these arcs, their upper side fitting easily against the first circle
of the cupola.    This technique had been understood thousands of years
before in Chaldaea, Assyria, and Persia, but no architect had ever
before dared apply it to dimensions such as these.    The lightest
possible materials were used, spongy bricks from Rhodes, five times
lighter than ordinary bricks.    The architects imagined that the weight
of this central cupola could be supported by two half-cupolas.    Nevertheless it collapsed, twenty years after its completion, on 5th May 558;
the two architects were dead by this time; it was a nephew of Isidore
who took up the task again, and, in raising the cupola thirty feet higher
still, his calculations were so accurate that to-day it is still standing,
so daring and so delicate that, according to Procopius, it 'hardly seems
to rest on masonry, but rather to hang in the sky from a gold chain.'

This prodigious technical masterpiece was given a *décor* worthy of
its plan and its grandeur.    It called for the Persian style, for the poly-
chromy of marble and porphyry, for the light and shade of mosaics,
for the lavish use of gold and silks.    Throughout the whole church,
on the walls of the apse, on the great triumphal arches, on the pendentives, and in the cupola, there was an endless iconography, running into
hundreds of scenes—haloed saints, princes and angels, symbolic
figures, Christs in majesty, Virgins in prayer, the Holy Ghost descending to the earth—a really dazzling *mêlée* which the puritan whitewash
of the Turks was to preserve, thus enabling us to admire it so many
centuries later.    A gigantic curtain hung behind the altar, whose
central subject was Jesus and the Apostles—Jesus in gold and purple,
the disciples in white—whilst along its edges the Gospel miracles were

vividly depicted, all embroidered in gold and silver thread and brilliant silks on the heaviest of Eastern brocade.   It was a fantasy of colour, a feast of visual harmony: during the day forty windows set in the base of the cupola caught the rays of the sun one by one, and at night six thousand candelabra gave forth a light so intense that it flashed far out into the bays, so that to the traveller making for the town 'it seemed as if a magnificent fire' proclaimed the city's position.

Thus, in the realization of the masterpiece, there were united not only the will of the autocrats and the genius of the artists, but the profound ideas which made Byzantium such an original flower, springing from the fertile soil of history.   Christianity, Hellenism, and the East combined in so perfect a fashion that humanity was given an entirely new kind of beautiful creation.   It was incapable of being equalled, and no other Byzantine building was ever to reach its sublime heights.[1]   St Sophia was to remain the summit of Byzantine art up to our own time, and even now, by the perfect balance of its proportions, so perfect that it seems carved straight out of space, and by the splendour of its restored mosaics and its marble, still intact, it impresses on our souls, as a thousand years of history can never do, the tangible certainty of the glory of Byzantium.   And a Christian cannot study this monument of faith and hope without being deeply moved, for it was to make its influence felt in every land and every age, it was to call into being the cupolas of Venice, as well as those of Périgueux, and even—yes, indeed—those of the Sacré-Cœur of Montmartre. Though the intentions of its builder were strongly tinged with personal vainglory, St Sophia has nevertheless exalted, for fifteen centuries, the Wisdom of Him who directs the world and mankind. St Sophia, Justinian's greatest title to fame, remains a concrete proof of the strength of Christian conviction.   But why was it that while Byzantium could realize this perfect synthesis between East and West in the field of art, it was incapable of achieving it on the plane where it was far more vital: that of faith?

### The Grand Design of Justinian: His Victories and His Weaknesses

It was this same twofold desire to work for God and to display his own glory which pushed Justinian into what was the 'grand design' of

---

[1] Though St Sophia is much the most important item of Justinian's work as a 'builder' it is far from being the only one.   Procopius's book on *Edifices* is a veritable catalogue of churches, public baths, porticoes, hospitals, and reservoirs which the imperial couple (for Theodora played a direct part in these enterprises, particularly where hospitals were concerned) had built, not only in Constantinople but throughout the whole Empire.   Thus Antioch, which had been destroyed by the Persians, was largely rebuilt by them, achieving a magnificence it had never before known.   Likewise, at Ravenna, in celebration of their Italian victory, they built the churches which we still admire.

his reign, in the sense in which we talk of the 'grand design' of Charlemagne, Henry IV of France, or Napoleon. He aimed to rebuild the Roman Empire! To regroup beneath his sceptre that Roman world whose western half had been torn to shreds by the Barbarian invasions during the course of the fifth century! To realize that dream of unity which existed in the minds of all civilized folk! A thrilling ambition. . . . Moreover did not the economic restoration of the Eastern Empire which he was carrying out demand the destruction of the maritime power of the Vandals? Besides, how could a loyal Christian accept the domination of the Catholic populations of Africa, Spain, and even Italy by petty Arian kings? The restoration of the Empire demanded religious unity also, in other words, the conquest of the Arians. The enterprise did not appear to present insuperable difficulties, for the Germanic dynasties were being undermined by internecine strife, and constantly opposed to them, more or less, were the Roman and Catholic populations which they had forced into subjection. Justinian flung himself into the task.

His first blow was aimed at Africa, partly because the Vandals were the most savage of all the Germanic occupiers, and because the African people and their bishops never ceased appealing to the emperor for aid, partly because it was imperative to smash their naval power, and finally because they were now the weakest of the Barbarians. We know that ever since their arrival in North Africa under Genseric, the Vandals had shown themselves almost consistently odious. A campaign of persecution, continuous for a long time, then intermittent, was waged against the Roman Catholics and many, many acts of unspeakable cruelty took place. In this crisis a proper resistance movement had been organized against Arian oppression, its real leaders being the bishops, Quovultdeus, Fulgentius of Ruspe, and Victor of Vita. At the same time, gentle, pleasure-loving Africa had singularly sapped the energies of this weak minority of occupiers. Where, after a century of occupation, were the courage and savage discipline of the original conquerors? Aware of the dangers of the situation, a new king, Hilderic, whose mother had been a Roman princess,[1] tried a different policy; he sought an agreement with the Catholic clergy and envisaged the assimilation of the Vandals with the Romans. But in 530 a nationalist Germanic party was formed behind the heir to the throne, Gelimer. Hilderic was overthrown and the former policy of persecution was revived. This fact impelled Justinian to take action.

[1] This was Eudocia, the second daughter of Valerian III, emperor of the West, and of the Empress Eudoxia, who had been carried off with her mother by Genseric at the time of the Vandal sack of Rome in 455. (See the preceding chapter, section: 'The End of the Western Empire.') Forcibly married to Hunneric, she never accepted either her subjection or the sight of the Arian persecutions, and after sixteen years of marriage she fled and took refuge in Jerusalem, in 472.

This was not the first time that Byzantium had thought of attacking Africa. Back in 468 the Emperor Leo I had already attempted a two-pronged attack against the Vandal kingdom, by sea and through Tripolitania, but the *Armada* of the admiral Basiliscus had been burned by enemy fireships off the African coast. So, when Justinian talked of taking up the offensive again, his advisers and his general staff appeared rather unenthusiastic. Nevertheless he insisted on going through with it, probably informed of the real weakness of Gelimer by the priests and the wealthy African citizens who had fled persecution, and, it was subsequently to be asserted, summoned to victory by the shade of the great martyr of Carthage, St Cyprian, himself.

In actual fact the operation succeeded with a speed and ease which were truly astounding. In June 533 a fleet of five hundred vessels sailed for Africa and landed a little army of ten thousand infantry and five thousand cavalry between Susa and Sfax, commanded by the most outstanding strategist of the age, *Belisarius*, already famous for his exploits against the Persians. The best of the Vandal troops were in Sardinia quelling a revolt there. Belisarius marched on Carthage, bundled Gelimer out of Decimum (near the modern Tunis), seized the capital on 15th September, shattered a Germanic counter-offensive on 15th December, and took the Vandal king captive. Vandal Africa was gone for ever. Belisarius was able to return to Constantinople, where he celebrated his triumph in the classical fashion, and Justinian conferred the titles of *Vandalicus* and *Africanus* upon himself.

Fortune had helped him, fortune, and the active support of the Roman population of Africa, who regarded the Byzantines as their liberators. Belisarius had very skilfully worded his proclamations to this end, had severely forbidden any looting or any requisitioning without payment, had armed bands of African guerrillas against the Vandals, and had even instigated actual acts of sabotage, such as that of the postmaster who turned all the horses in his service over to the invaders, thus paralysing the Vandal communications. Such a result was encouraging to say the least. Justinian now turned his eyes on another part of the old Empire which was at present subject to the Barbarians: Italy, occupied by the Ostrogoths.

The situation in the peninsula at this particular moment somewhat recalled that which had touched off Justinian's intervention in Africa. The policy of reconciliation and of friendly collaboration with the occupied, which had been Theodoric's great idea, had, as we have seen, run up against the hostility of a large section of the population and of the clergy; moderate though the rule of the Arian king had been, it had not been accepted. Towards the end of his reign, Theodoric himself had renounced the principle of moderation.[1] Since his death, in 526,

---

[1] See the final section of the preceding chapter.

Ostrogoth Italy had been divided into two factions: the 'Roman' party, grouped around Amalasontha, the daughter of Theodoric, who ruled as regent in the name of her small son, Athalaric, and who, on the whole, favoured a policy of assimilation; and the Germanic nationalists, led by a nephew of Theodoric, Theodatus, who were hostile to all agreement with the Romans and to everything pertaining to classical civilization. In 533 Amalasontha had helped Belisarius in his campaign against the Vandals, an act of which the Germanic nationalists had strongly disapproved. When the young Athalaric died in the autumn of 534, a *coup d'état* overthrew the regent, and she was dispatched to an island in Lake Bolsena; before being strangled there she had time to send a message to Justinian, appealing for his aid.

At first Providence seemed to be on the side of the Byzantine armies in Italy, just as it had been in Africa. A double offensive, launched simultaneously through Dalmatia and Sicily, was a success. Naples was seized by Belisarius in the spring of 536, the north of the peninsula was occupied, Theodatus was deposed by his own troops, and Rome was liberated on 10th December; everything seemed to be going exactly as Justinian had wished it. In reality the situation was far less clear cut and favourable than it had been in Africa. In Italy there were a fair number of elements whose convictions and interests linked them to the Ostrogoths. The great protagonist of collaboration with the Goths, Cassiodorus, the Roman Catholic, had only just resigned his ministerial offices, in order to shut himself away from the world in the silence of his Calabrian monastery; [1] several elements distrusted the Byzantines, notably among the clergy, who suspected them of the Monophysite heresy; and, moreover, Belisarius's troops, who were not so warmly welcomed here as they had been in Africa, behaved in a far less friendly and less disciplined fashion.

It was soon necessary to bow to the obvious: the lightning campaign would not in itself be sufficient to achieve victory. To deal with the Ostrogoth resistance, which was proving infinitely more steadfast than that of the Vandals had been, reinforcements had to be sent to Italy, and a slow, patient march undertaken on Ravenna. In the autumn of 539 Belisarius managed to surround the capital, but he only gained possession of it by an ignoble trick, after persuading the Barbarian leaders, so it was said, that he was ready to betray the imperial cause and to assume the Gothic crown himself! No matter! Was the time now ripe for Justinian to style himself *Italicus* and *Ostrogothicus*? At all events he talked, with unfeigned satisfaction, of *his* city of Rome, of *his* city of Ravenna, exactly as Theodosius and Constantine had done. . . .

---

[1] On Cassiodorus see the final section of the preceding chapter, and also, in Chapter V the section on 'St Benedict.'

But it was a little too soon for this! The Goths did not disarm. Henceforth they had as their leader a young king, who, although he is passed over by most historians, was unquestionably an extraordinary man: his name was Totila. A daring innovator, he gave the slaves on the large estates their freedom, and released the tenant farmers from the dues and the obligatory duties which they owed to the great lords, thus creating a community of interest between the Goths and the Italian proletariat. The whole peninsula was already weary of the crushing Byzantine taxation, and of the blunders of the Easterners. Totila took up the struggle again. He proved himself an outstanding strategist, a kind of Gothic Napoleon. With but five thousand men he defeated a first imperial army in Emilia, a second to the north of Florence (542), and swept across Umbria, and then the Abruzzi; his ranks swelled by freed slaves and Italian peasants, he invested Naples and swooped on Rome, which he took in December 546, when it was at starvation point. And Belisarius could do nothing to stop him! It was to take no less than eight years to conquer this savage hero. Rome, captured and recaptured in turn by the two adversaries, emerged as little more than a field of ruins. All the provinces of the peninsula panted and wept in their agony. The aged Belisarius was sacrificed; his replacement, the elderly eunuch, *Narses*, whose nomination had been the occasion of much ribald mirth, then discovered the strategy of reconquest. He nibbled at the Ostrogoth territories little by little, relied for support on the Italian population which was increasingly tired of the fighting, finally surrounded Totila in the plain of Umbria, killed him (552), and, in the following year, crushed the remaining Gothic resistance at the battle of Vesuvius (553). The task was accomplished! The Pragmatic Sanction of 554 introduced the Justinian Code into Italy, eliminated the last traces of Ostrogoth rule, swept away the reforms of Totila, set the great landowners back in their place, and reserved a leading position in the new organization for the Pope and the bishops, in order that they might counter the oligarchic ambitions of the great officials. The motherland of Rome was Roman once more! But what a dreadful state it was in!

Was this all? Was Justinian's ambition now satisfied? No, for two areas remained Barbarian: Gaul and Spain. In Gaul the situation was a complex one, for the Frankish domination rested on sound foundations and the Catholic episcopate supported it: so the matter was shelved, agreement was actually reached with the Franks, Provence was abandoned to them, and Justinian confined himself to repulsing the raids which their over-enterprising chieftains launched across the Italian plains from time to time. But in Spain there was complete anarchy; the Visigothic dynasty floundered amid intrigues and assassinations. A violent reaction, Germanic and Arian in character, had just begun, and against the occupiers was ranged a large part of the population. Masters of the Balearic Islands since the end of the Vandal kingdom, the Byzantines landed in Spain, under the command of Liberius, defeated the Visigothic king, killed him, and occupied the whole of the south-east coast. They did not penetrate much farther. By this time, 555, Justinian was over seventy years old, and had lost his old enthusiasm. This gigantic accumulation of victories was enough for him.

When we examine the map Justinian's military achievement seems enormous. It was a genuine reconquest of the West from the Barbarians, analogous to the campaign waged by Ferdinand and Isabella much later on against the Moors in Spain, or even, to use a phrase of still more recent origin, a true 'liberation' of the West from Germanic domination. To the six dioceses [1] of the East (Thrace, Pontus, Asia, the Orient, Illyricum, and Egypt) were added the four Western ones (Dalmatia, Italy, Africa, and Spain). Of all the regions bordering the Mediterranean only Provence remained in the hands of the Franks, and they, moreover, were now friendly to Byzantium. How marvellous it all looks! We can well understand how, until the closing days of his life, Justinian could sincerely make himself believe that he had re-established the unity of the Empire for all time, and had restored Rome to her ancient grandeur.

In actual fact only the semblance of reunity was achieved. The law of contradictions which influenced and always would influence the history of Byzantium worked against this ambitious policy and sterilized it before it began. These conquests were fragile things in reality. In Spain they only amounted to a narrow settlement clinging to the edge of the peninsula, which itself remained largely Barbarian. In Africa Byzantine authority was so tenuous that from 544 until 548 the Berbers were in open revolt, during which time they sacked Carthage and massacred the government officials, making necessary a new expedition in order to reduce them to submission. In Italy the situation was an appalling one. Rome had been abandoned by its inhabitants and reduced to the status of a large village for centuries to come; there was a general atmosphere of anguish and wrath. The total destruction of the Ostrogoth administrative machinery, and the incapacity of the Byzantine exarchs to make their influence felt and to govern efficiently, caused such a vacuum and such disorder that the Lombards, who had been called into Italy as federates by the Byzantines themselves, were to behave as its masters, and to establish a sound kingdom there which would endure for two hundred and fifty years.

But there was an even more serious side to the matter. For, in throwing all the energies of the Empire into the West, Justinian's

[1] It should be remembered that the 'diocese' was an administrative area.

'grand design' had swung it out of balance.   Lines of fortresses had indeed been built along its eastern boundaries; from the Danube to the Euphrates a double *limes* was guarded by permanent garrisons.   But it was all in vain!   The Persians, whom Justinian thought he had neutralized by a solemn peace in 532, entered into in order that he might have both hands free to turn westwards, were now commanded by *Chosroes I the Great*.   When Justinian ran into difficulties in Italy they seized their opportunity to make a lightning attack along the Euphrates (540), captured Antioch, devastated it and burned it. Belisarius was hurriedly sent to the East, and, with some difficulty, he contained the enemy, but in the end Justinian only shook himself free of the Persians by paying them tribute.   And at the same time the savage Bulgars hurled themselves on Greece, reached Corinth, and were to plunder as far as the outskirts of Constantinople; in 558 they were to repeat this exploit.   And the endless waves of Slavs were there behind them. . . .

'Grand designs' are always costly.   At the end of his reign Justinian saw his wealth melting away; he had to reduce his armies.   Public opinion, cowed though it was, rebelled against the increase in taxes. Endless frictions occurred in the provinces, especially in Syria and Egypt, where the religious conflicts encouraged separatism.   There was a severe economic crisis.   Judged not by its appearances but by its actual results, the 'grand design' of Justinian was stricken with a mortal weakness.   And the worst feature of this weakness was this: this vast undertaking, not merely Roman but Christian in concept, and conducted by an emperor who was a sincere believer, which aimed at reconquering the West from the Arian heretics, could never really have succeeded in achieving the unity of the Empire, and there was no hope of its ever succeeding in doing so; the uncertainties of Justinian and Theodora's religious policy stood in the way of its success.

## THE RELIGIOUS COMPLEXES OF JUSTINIAN AND THEODORA

The imperial couple to whom we are indebted for these three great deeds of Christian history, the Christianization of the laws, the building of St Sophia, and the defeat of the Arian Barbarians, were both unquestionably devout believers.   Throughout the whole of his life Justinian gives us the impression of being a faithful Christian, of sound convictions and sincere piety, a man who gave his subjects a truly Christian example in his own private life, who prayed and fasted regularly, and who constantly and wholeheartedly desired the welfare of the Church: nothing would be more false than to suggest that his religious policy was dictated solely by reasons of state.   Theodora, who was a more complex character, seems to have been beset by metaphysical problems, deeply impressed, even in the luxury of the imperial purple, by sanctity and asceticism, at the same time being careful—more careful than her husband—not to let religious matters run counter to the political interests of the throne.  This entirely genuine Christianity, which they both professed, was a perfect example of Christianity after the Byzantine pattern, which we have already studied, that is to say, a Christianity which was violent and which rushed to extremes, too inclined to confuse that which belonged by rights to Caesar with that which belonged by rights to God, and, like that of their contemporaries, riddled with this mania for theological argument.  In matters of dogma, spirituality, ecclesiastical discipline, and the liturgy, Justinian possessed an astounding scholarship, of which he was exceedingly proud, and he brought to these obscure topics all the subtlety of a learned professor, while as for Theodora, it was not for nothing that she had been restored to the bosom of the Church through the efforts of those masters of theological discussion, the Alexandrian monks!

Moreover the unimaginable confusion which affected Christianity throughout the whole of their Empire at the time of their accession— everywhere the faith was shaken by the great disputes on the Person (were there one or two?) of Christ, and pulled this way and that by the Monophysitists and the Nestorians, the Origenists and the surviving Arians, not to mention the Manichaeans and some twenty other types of heretics—this confusion had its counterpart in the actual household of Justinian and Theodora themselves.  Justinian, a decent lad from the Illyrian mountains, a region where the soundest Catholic doctrines had always been maintained, took after his uncle and adoptive father, Justin, and appeared perfectly orthodox in beliefs from his adolescence onwards.  He was a vigorous upholder of the Council of Chalcedon, at which the Monophysite sects had been condemned, and was full of deference for the Pope of Rome.  Theodora, who had certainly been little bothered by religious scruples when, at the age of sixteen, she was the leading lady in the spectacles at the Hippodrome, had made a really moving conversion, in Egypt, when she was from twenty to twenty-three years old.  This happened at a time when her reckless way of life had plunged her into darkest despair, and as it chanced that the good folk who had brought her to repentance believed in the Monophysite heresy, she became a Monophysite and Monophysite she remained as long as she lived.  Thus the imperial couple suffered from a singular complex in their religious foundations.  However, this seems to have caused scarcely any disagreement between them, so little indeed that Procopius, who is always a scandalmonger, insinuates that 'the difference in their convictions was but illusory' and that they used it as a subtle instrument of government. . . .

But the devout Justinian also suffered from a more serious complex
—probably almost without realizing it.   On the one hand, he venerated the Bishop of Rome; he recognized his effective primacy.   He
had inserted into his Code the formula of Pope Hormisdas, who had
proclaimed this primacy on ending the schism of Acatius.   He wrote
to the same Pope: 'The unity of all the Holy Churches depends on the
instruction and the authority of the Apostolic Church.'   We also read,
in his *Novellae*, 'that no one can doubt that the sublimity of the
sovereign pontificate is at Rome.'   But, on the other hand, the very
concept which he had of his own authority, mingled with his passion
for dogmatizing in religious matters, inevitably led him to behave as
his predecessors had done, namely, as a real religious leader, and to
encroach continuously on the rights of the Church.   Oh, his intentions were excellent, of course, and it was all done because his mission
on earth was 'to preserve inviolate the purity of the Christian faith and
to defend the Holy Catholic and Apostolic Church against all dangers!'
From this sprang his repeated interventions in the nomination or
deposition of bishops; his dictatorial orders addressed to the Councils
which he convened, presided over, or dissolved as he pleased; his
edicts, with their air of encyclicals, which laid down decisions on
the most important matters of faith. . . .   Between the popes and the
most theologically minded autocrat of the age opposition was the
essential order of things; several ambitions encouraged its growth,
among them those of the patriarch of Constantinople, of course, whom
Justinian called 'head of all the churches in the East,' and whom he
tended to place on the same level as the Bishop of Rome, just as if there
were five patriarchs of equal importance, those of Alexandria, Antioch,
Jerusalem, Constantinople, and Rome!   Much later on, after the reconquest of Italy, the ambition of the Bishop of Ravenna was to
become obvious too.   Ravenna became an imperial capital once
again, and its bishop was to be raised to archbishop in 565, pending
the establishment of the patriarchate a little later on.[1]   When purely

---

[1] It should be added that, from 555, the date when Italy was incorporated into the
Eastern Empire, the popes were forced to ask Byzantium to ratify their election.   Until
this ratification, for which it was necessary to pay a charge (!), reached Rome, the popes
were forbidden to proceed with their consecration.   This obligation rapidly caused such
great inconvenience, since it meant that the papal throne was left vacant for months on
end, that the emperors eventually delegated the right of ratifying the election to their
representative in Italy, the exarch of Ravenna.   Thus Byzantine policy obtained an
important means of exerting pressure on the decisions of Rome, even on dogmatic questions.   It is true that, in exchange, the 'Pragmatic Sanction' of 554 confirmed and increased the temporal power of the Papacy.   The Sovereign Pontiff henceforth had a say
in the nomination of the provincial governors, and could audit their accounts and summon
them for embezzlement before his own tribunal.   At Rome itself he had official control of
municipal affairs, including the 'supervision of bridges and defences' and even 'of
markets and baths.'   He thus assumed the role of 'defender of the city' without bearing
the actual title.   The danger of this confusion of the spiritual and the temporal remained
no less great on this account.

doctrinal matters came to be superimposed on those deriving from this
political antagonism, opposition turned to conflict, and men witnessed
the scandalous spectacle of an emperor who was a very respectful son
of the Catholic Church doing violence to the Pope!

The most painful religious affair of the reign broke out in connection
with questions of heresy.   At his accession Justinian had announced
that he would harry the heretics and 'administer a just punishment to
them'; he had issued a great many edicts against the various anti-
Chalcedonian sects, the Manichaeans, the Jews, and the pagans; he had
forbidden education to those suspected of belonging to these sects; he
had ordered the closure of the Arian churches, and of the Jewish and
Samaritan synagogues.   When Monophysitism continued to trouble
the churches he sat down himself to write a number of documents,
condemning them violently, notably a *Treatise* drawn up in the correct
manner, a real dogmatic epistle firmly resting on Scripture, the Fathers,
and the Councils, in which the theologian-autocrat cleft the Christological heresies in twain.   These were indeed excellent intentions, but
they were singularly weakened in their practical effects by the fact that
at the imperial palace itself Theodora gave asylum to some of the
choicest heretics, such as the deposed patriarch, Severus of Antioch;
patronized Anthimus, the Bishop of Constantinople, whom Pope St
Agapetus had just excommunicated; and—under pretext that it was
vital at all costs to avoid pushing Syria and Egypt, areas very inclined
to the doctrines of the single nature, towards separatism—secretly
supported James Baradai, the heretical Bishop of Edessa, who established the dissident hierarchy so firmly that the Monophysite Syrian
Church has been known as the Jacobite Church from then right up to
the present day.   It was really incredible!

On top of all this a new incident occurred.   Various eminent
personages, such as the venerable St Sabas, persuaded Justinian to take
strong measures against the Palestinian Origenists, who, as we know,
quoted as their authority the doctrines of the great Alexandrian scholar,
although they distorted them enormously, and the emperor could not
possibly miss such a fine chance of yielding to his passion for theological argument.   In a *Treatise Against Origen* he disposed of the
Alexandrian philosopher and of those who had followed in his footsteps in a most summary and unjust fashion.   But the Origenists,
were they confessed or secret, lacked neither Court influence nor guile.
They astutely deflected the storm on to others and persuaded Justinian,
with the obvious support of the empress, that he would better fulfil
his role as the servant of God if he managed to reconcile all the Christians in his Empire with one another, and especially if he could win the
Monophysites back to the Church.   And Justinian rushed headlong
down the path taken by his predecessors, who had pursued the same

design, though in a different way, and who had drawn from it nothing but troubles of the worst order.

The method employed was that which was to be used against the Jansenists in the France of Louis XIV, namely, to extract certain well-chosen elements from a doctrine, in order to condemn the whole all the better. In fighting the Monophysite heresy, much reliance had been placed upon three learned doctors: Theodore of Mopsuestia, Theodoret of Cyr, and Ibas of Edessa. They were clearly the *bêtes noires* of the Monophysites. It was observed to Justinian that the doctrines of these three masters were not as orthodox as all that, that if he studied them carefully he could easily find traces of heresy in them, or, at all events, theses from which heresy had been able to sprout, and that, if their enemies were condemned, the Monophysites would be much more inclined to return to the fold of the Church. Justinian busied himself in this direction. From the works of the 'suspects' he had three sections selected, or, as they were dubbed, *Three Chapters*. He had these condemned by the Synod (531–4), and after that he anathematized them himself in an actual edict, prompted by theological motives; the Eastern episcopate countersigned this without enthusiasm, and Justinian then turned to the Pope.

At the beginning of this affair the Pope of the period was a saintly man, St Silverius (536–7), elderly in years but resolute in spirit. Although pressed to go back on the condemnation which his predecessor, St Agapetus, had delivered against the patriarch of Constantinople, Anthimus, who was suspected of Monophysitism, he refused to do so. So—very probably on the secret orders of Theodora—when Belisarius seized Rome, the unfortunate Pope was involved in an incredible trial, on a charge of high treason, was 'convicted' of having treated with the Goths, and sent into exile in Pontus, where he died. The Catholic ruler, Justinian, had made a martyr of a pope! A cunning intrigue—or what was thought of as such—organized by the empress and the general, then brought to the pontifical throne a prelate who was supposed to have been more or less party to the plot against Silverius: *Vigilius* (538–55). But, whether it was the sanctifying Grace of the pontifical consecration which had enlightened this man, or whether the difficulties stirred up in Italy by Totila the Goth had also contributed to opening his eyes to the realities of the situation, Vigilius behaved as independently as he could, instead of being a docile instrument of imperial policy. At first he refused to condemn the *Three Chapters*. When summoned to Byzantium by the emperor he yielded; but on returning to Rome he went back on his condemnation, just when Justinian was clinging even more tenaciously to his ideas. A Council convened at Constantinople under the 'protection' of Byzantine troops was preparing to ratify the imperial doctrines, always in the quite illusory hope of bringing the Monophysites back into the Church—when Vigilius intervened in opposition to them once again. And then the world saw a pope being forced out of the church in which he had taken refuge by the imperial troops, dragged by the feet, the hair, and the beard (so violently that the altar to which he was clinging collapsed!), forced to flee, to take refuge at Chalcedon, hard pressed by emissaries of the Master, demanding his submission. Eventually it was to see him, sick and at the end of his tether, being badgered into confirming the decision of the Council which had been held without him and in spite of him. . . . It was a tragic affair, and it left its mark on the history of the Church, for several bishops refused to accept the decisions of this singular Council, and various local schisms resulted from it, which lasted a long time. Meanwhile the Monophysites, ironically enough, declared that the concessions made to them were insufficient, and they behaved with such arrogance that the exasperated Justinian launched a whole-hearted persecution against them! Such was the chaos which resulted from Byzantine Caesaro-Papism.

When Justinian died, in 565, he was over eighty years old, and utterly worn out—exhausted by all these conflicts, but not a whit tired of theology! [1]   Nor had he realized that the real cause of the set-backs was in himself, in the fundamental error which vitiated the whole of his religious policy, and he was almost inclined to think that Providence had been very unjust in rewarding his loyal efforts to serve the faith so badly. As for his peoples, they were even more exhausted than he was, and, as in the case of almost all the 'great reigns' of history—e.g. those of Louis XIV and Napoleon—his subjects sighed with relief when the great reign of Justinian ended.

It had been a great reign, there is no doubt of that. For a period of more than thirty years men had witnessed a remarkable phenomenon: in every field of human activity—politics, economics, arts, letters, and the law—the imperial philosophy had regained possession of the world. Justinian was the last of the great *Roman* emperors. But this success was exceptional and paradoxical. It depended on the action of a few vigorous personalities, and on the skilful utilization of various favourable circumstances. It could not, and it was not to be, lasting. Justinian's Empire crumbled away with astonishing speed after his death. Autocratic, hieratical, and bureaucratic, Byzantium was not in fact capable of regaining control of the West and of undertaking its restoration. It did not slow up its decline into Barbarism:

---

[1] Always obsessed by theological problems, at the end of his life he fell more or less prey to the heresy of the *Aphthartodocetes*, who asserted that the body of Jesus remained impassive on the Cross, and one of his last acts was to exile the patriarch Eutychios, who refused to follow him in this direction.

in one sense it speeded it up, by completely destroying the tentative assimilation achieved by the Ostrogoths. Compared with some of the Goths—Totila, for example—it showed itself to be a force of the past, extremely poor in new ideas. Moreover it was incapable—Justinian's example proved this—of rising above its Eastern methods, its Byzantine complexes, all those contradictory influences which were made incarnate for Justinian in the person of the mysterious and subtle Theodora.

What this half of the sixth century showed very clearly—and it was indeed to be achieved for eight more centuries yet—was that it was Byzantium's destiny to save the East from the Barbarian onslaught, but not to save *Romania*. Its Church was surreptitiously undermined by Caesaro-Papism, by dogmatic confusion, and by the tendency to schism. Blessed though it was by virtue of its noblest representatives, in its latent disaffection to Rome it made plain the first signs of that great rift which was to take place subsequently between East and West. Mankind could not rely on Byzantium to reconstruct the world, and Holy Church knew it.

G

# CHAPTER IV

# THE CHURCH CONVERTS
# THE BARBARIANS

## CLOVIS AND THE GALLIC BISHOPS

THE SCENE is evoked for us in the rugged sentences of St Gregory of Tours; it is enshrined among our childhood memories and we can never forget it. There is the young king, making his way through the gaily decked streets of the town,[1] amid the cheers of an entire people. He is thirty years old, and he has just been victorious in battle. The church [2] is decorated with white hangings and is fragrant with incense; there are so many candles that, although it is a grey wintry day, the spectator imagines himself in the full brightness of an August sun. 'Is paradise here already?' the Barbarians exclaim. Waiting in the choir there is quite a gathering of ecclesiastics, clad in dalmatics of white, richly embroidered with gold, surrounding Remigius, the living saint, the man who is said to have brought a dead man back to life. The king's followers enter the church behind their leader: the handsome Frankish officers, wearing green, fur-trimmed cloaks, tunics of crimson silk, high fawn boots next to the bare skin; the Germanic soldiery, their long hair hanging over the shaven napes of their necks, brandishing in their right hands the Frankish battle-axe; and the Franks' Gallic allies, in breastplate and helmet, like the legionaries of old. Clovis is the first to disrobe; he goes down into the baptismal trough where he is to be cleansed of the long-standing leprosy of his sins. 'Bow your head, Sicambrian,' cries the bishop. 'Worship what you have burned, and burn the things which once you worshipped!' Behind him, in groups of three hundred, three thousand of his followers receive the sacrament of baptism likewise. And many years later men were to relate how, at the moment when St Remigius wished to proceed to the ritual unction of the Chrism, a dove was seen, descending from the highest heavens, holding in its beak the phial filled with holy oil.

Though this famous scene of the baptism of Clovis is wreathed in

---

[1] Probably Rheims; tradition has it so, and St Remigius, who had converted Clovis to the Catholic faith, was bishop of this town.

[2] Certain historians allow that this church was the cathedral, the old basilica which had been destroyed by the Vandals in 406 and then restored. Others think it more likely to have been the church of St Martin, then outside the city boundary; this place would have been more suitable, if, as is possible, the baptism took place in the open air, in the great troughs into which some of the waters of the Vesle would have been diverted.

imagery and legend, it is true, nevertheless, that it marks a decisive moment in history; [1] along with the vision of Constantine and the crowning of Charlemagne it is one of the three deeds which opened up the political destinies of the Christian West.  But many questions arise with regard to it.  If it is true that the fundamental problem, ever since the Barbarian invasions, had been the realization of a synthesis between the Germanic Barbarians and the erstwhile Roman society which they had conquered, why was it Gaul which was the vital centre of this evolution?  And, in Gaul, why was it this obscure group of Nordic tribes, still barely touched by civilization, which assumed the initiative for this indispensable operation?  We can find the answers to these questions by turning back a little, by considering the situation around the year 481, the year in which Clovis was 'raised on the shield.'

The West had slowly succumbed before seventy-five years of intermittent Germanic onslaught.  Five years before our date the Empire had collapsed; the last descendant of Romulus and Augustus had been swept aside; the Herulian Odoacer, the master of the militia, had taken his place, ruling all Italy, awaiting the day when, seven years later, he himself would be faced with a new wave of invasion, that of Theodoric and his Ostrogoths.  Christian Africa groaned under the heavy heel of the Vandals.  The Visigoths stretched right across Spain, and as far into modern France as the outskirts of Bourges.  The Burgundians had settled in the country around the Rhône and the Saône, and farther north, in Alsace and Lorraine, there were the Alamans.  Of the former territories of the sons of the She-Wolf only a kind of islet remained, between the Seine and the Loire, a little remnant of a state which still called itself Latin, and which was held by a representative of one of the great Gallo-Roman families, Syagrius, son of that same Aegidius who had been one of the conquerors of Attila.  But his authority rested on his own force alone, his ascendancy was secure only over those cities which were willing to accept it.

On whom could men count to restore an order and a semblance of unity into this Western world, divided as it was into its various Barbarian fragments?  Not on the East, at all events!  At this epoch the Emperor Zeno was ruling there amidst innumerable difficulties, locked in constant struggle with his rivals; and above all, the Eastern passion for theological dispute now rekindled that great quarrel about the two natures of Christ which men had believed extinguished thirty years earlier, at the Council of Chalcedon.  The year after our date, in 482, Zeno was to sign his famous *decree of union*, or *Henotic Edict*, in the

[1] Nevertheless the exact date of the baptism is uncertain.  Historians place it somewhere between 496 and 502.  On the other hand, we can be fairly certain that the ceremony was held on Christmas Day.  In this epoch baptisms only took place on great feast days.  On the chronology of Clovis, the latest work is Levison's *Aus rheinischer und fränkischer Frühzeit*, Düsseldorf, 1948, pp. 202–28.

fallacious hope of restoring tranquillity.   Its only result was to un-
leash a conflict with the Pope and to cause the schism of Acatius.
Severed from Byzantium, and with Rome in the hands of the Barbarians, the West had only itself on whom it could rely to try to bring
about its revival.

And how well they knew this, these men who had been the only
bastions capable of resisting the Barbarian holocaust: the bishops!

Gaul on the Accession of Clovis

The bishops holding office at the end of the fifth century were worthy
heirs of those great Christian leaders, who, in the moment of attack,
had proved themselves true 'defenders of the city'—of St Nicasius, St
Anianus, St Lupus, St Sidonius Apollinaris, and St Germanus of
Auxerre.   They felt henceforth that it was their role to bring about
the fusion of the races within the framework of Catholicism.   But
they came up against the enormous obstacle of Arianism, and they
pondered how they could overcome it.   It is essential to remember
this: the fact that the very great majority of the Germanic invaders had
been baptized according to the rites of this low-price Christianity

which the Goth, Ulfilas, had adapted to suit their fundamental instincts has an importance which is not simply theological.  Historically the newcomers' denial of the divinity of Christ would not perhaps
have been so serious, had this simplifying doctrine not been linked,
in their still primitive minds, with an intransigent nationalism, which
military success only increased.  As Arian Christians, the Barbarians
felt themselves set apart from the populations they had just beaten: for
them Catholicism was the religion of the defeated, the religion of the
occupied.  In practice, their attitude to it could vary a good deal: the
Burgundians were easy-going about it, the Visigoths fussy and stick-
lers for regulations, whilst the Vandals indulged in frightful campaigns
of anti-Catholic persecution; basically, opposition existed everywhere.
Even when a few Barbarian chieftains clearly grasped the problem
presented to them, and tried to set their states in order by attempting
to establish cordial relations between the original inhabitants and the
occupiers, they too came up against this insurmountable obstacle;
Theodoric was to have experience of it when he became master of
Italy.  Between the Western Catholics and the Arian Barbarians the
antagonism already caused by the difference in race was doubled by
this fact of heresy; nothing—neither the systematic persecutions of
the Vandals, nor the subtle policy of the Ostrogoths—could put an
end to a resistance which, open or concealed, and led by the bishops,
was sustained against the invader by a whole population.

It was in these circumstances that the Catholics of Gaul turned to
the Franks.  About the year 480 it is quite obvious that a 'franco-
phile' party existed in all the states which to-day form part of France.
Why?  For the Franks were, after all, Germanic Barbarians like
the rest, just a fragment of those wandering tribes who had come
from the plains in the East and joined in the assault on *Romania* in the
fourth century.  And Augustin Thierry is quite right to remind us in
his *Lettres sur l'histoire de France* how exaggerated it is to make the
history of the ancient 'French' people begin amid the misty barbarisms
of these wandering folk.

Who were they exactly?  Precisely where did they come from?
Whence did they derive the name by which we know them?  Was it
from *wrang*, 'wandering,' or from *frak*, 'brave'?  Did they give
their name to their arms, the *francae*, as the Romans called them, or
vice versa?  We do not know.  In the tenth century, in the *Liber
Historiae*, which was compiled by Suger's monks, the first historians
of Capetian France were to go so far as to link them with the
Trojans, through the intermediary of an alleged descendant of Aeneas,
Pharamund!

Truth to tell, all that we know with certainty of the origins of the
Franks is that they were one of the numerous Germanic peoples who

had seen 'a career' in the Empire.   After being beaten by the Emperor Aurelian, they became, more or less, 'federates,' in the fourth century, settling between the lower Rhine and the Main.   One of their divisions, the Ripuarians, had Cologne as its centre; another, which seemed more active, the Salians, had taken advantage of the great attack of 406 to establish itself in Belgium and along the Somme.   The first of the Frankish tribal chieftains who is an authentic historic character is *Clodio*, who, in 430, installed himself along the Somme; in the same year he received the title of legate from the Western emperor, Valentinian III, and he had his son, *Merovaeus* (*Merwig*), educated at the Court at Ravenna, half a page, half a hostage, according to the custom of the period.   The latter succeeded to the chieftainship in his turn, and took part in the struggle against the Huns in 451, and his son, *Childeric*, helped the Gallo-Roman forces to save Angers from the Saxon pirates.   Although the Frankish rule over the territory which they occupied was fairly harsh in the beginning—they burned and pillaged like all the other invaders—towards the end of the century they sobered down somewhat, and the peace-loving Gallo-Romans did not complain overmuch of their behaviour.   But this does not explain the obvious preference which the episcopate was to show them.

In order to understand the psychology of the bishops we should remember what all our modern missionaries, who carry the Gospel message among the Africans, tell us: they are unanimous in declaring that it is infinitely easier to bring to Christ Negroes who are still idolaters than those who have already been converted to the Moslem religion.   Now the Franks were still pagans.   Why?   We do not know the reason for this any more than we know the exact history of their origins: the two mysteries are doubtlessly linked.   Savage, extremely independent, and very far from possessing that idea of Germanic solidarity which was so strong among the Goths, they had never allowed themselves to be converted to the Arian Christianity of their neighbours.   Consequently, for Catholicism, they constituted virgin soil; they offered her a chance of emerging from the heretical impasse.   The bishops were quick to grasp this.

The chance was all the greater because, ever since his accession, one of the Frankish chieftains, for his part, seemed to have guessed that the Catholic Church was secretly waiting for him, and to have measured accurately the support which his skilful policy might obtain from her. His name was *Chlodovechus*—the first *Louis* of the French dynasties— a name which a custom as pedantic as it is inveterate has turned into *Clovis*.   He was the son of Childeric and of Basina, a Thuringian princess.   In 481 he was fifteen years old, barely the age when men attained their majority, according to the Frankish custom, but already he had the reputation of a splendid warrior.   It must certainly have been at Tournai (where the tomb of his father has been found, together with all those beautiful enamel jewels, set in gold) that he was freely acclaimed as chieftain, not indeed by all the Salians, but by the most important group among them.   So began a reign which was to be great indeed.

It was at this point that the Church revealed her secret intention. Remigius, who was Bishop of Rheims—in other words, his see was right in the middle of Syagrius's 'kingdom'—wrote a long and splendid letter to the young ruler.   He wrote not only to congratulate him on his accession; the congratulations appear to have been but pretexts; he wrote not only to lavish on him much most excellent advice on the principles which ought to guide him in the practical exercise of his duties; but, above all, clearly, yet without arrogance, he wrote in order to compare the episcopal power with the royal power, as if he wanted to persuade Clovis that the glory of his reign depended on collaboration between the two.   'Show deference towards your bishops; always turn to them for advice.   And, if you are in harmony with them, your land will prosper.'   This letter was obviously trying to say that the Catholic Church, seeing in the Franks and in this young king the force of the future, had decided to build on them—with this implied corollary, that she did not recognize the authority of Syagrius as any greater than that of Clovis himself.

What was the Frank's reply to this invitation?   It is famous.   It is contained in the episode of the Soissons vase.[1]   After Clovis had

---

[1] Here is how St Gregory of Tours relates the incident.   It is an interesting account, not only as regards the light it throws on the relations between Clovis and the bishops, but also on those between the king and his warriors.

'The enemy had taken a splendid vase, of marvellous beauty, from a church, together with all the other vessels used in the sacred office.   The bishop of this church sent messengers to the king, begging him at least to return this particular vase, even if he could not manage to recover the rest of the sacred vessels.   In reply to the envoy's appeals the king declared: "Follow us to Soissons, for there all the spoils are to be divided; and if this vase falls to my share, I will do as the bishop asks."   When he reached Soissons the king had the load of booty set in the midst of the warriors, and then he said to them: "My brave men, I beg you to let me have this vase here, quite aside from my share" (and he showed them the vase of which we have spoken).   At this the most judicious among them answered: "Most glorious king, all that we see here is yours, and we ourselves are subject to you; let it be according to your will, for no one can resist your power."   When they had spoken thus, one of the warriors, a foolish, jealous, hot-headed man, raised his voice, and, brandishing his battle-axe, he smashed the vase in two, saying: "You shall have nothing save what is given you by lot."   Everyone stood still, struck dumb with astonishment.   The king let the outrage pass, displaying only a patient sweetness, and when the vase was allotted to him, he handed it to the bishop's envoy, keeping his anger hidden in his heart.   A year later his army was assembled on the Champ de Mars, where each man was required to show that his weapons were in good order.   As Clovis made ready to tour the ranks, he came to the man who had struck the vase, and he said to him: "No one's weapons are in such bad condition as yours: your spear, your sword, and your battle-axe are all in a sorry state!"   And seizing the man's axe, he threw it to the ground.   The warrior bent to pick it up; then the king, lifting his own axe in both hands, buried it in his skull, with the remark: "This is what you did to the vase of Soissons."

attacked the 'king of the Romans' and beaten him, and had become master of the whole of the northern half of Gaul, that is to say, when he had proved himself the most energetic of all the chieftains and the most powerful of the Barbarians, it is significant that, in the incident of the vase, he displayed such courteous conduct with regard to the important Catholic clergy.    Here we can see proof that the episcopate of Champagne had favoured the Franks throughout the campaign.    Perhaps Clovis had already given them certain promises, but above all he had understood perfectly the meaning of the policy which had been proposed to him.    And henceforth the entire episcopate of Gaul was to consider him as heaven-sent.

It is difficult for us to understand what such support was to mean for the fortunes of the Frankish leader.    In a world where the collapse of the administrative framework had really left no authority but his intact, in a society where the Christian faith was still young and almost primitive in character, the authority of the bishop bore no comparison with that of either the bishop or the senior official of our modern age. Simultaneously pontiff and prefect, the bishop was order incarnate, the living conscience of his people; when he also possessed a reputation for miracle-working, as in the case of *St Remigius*, it was more than respect that was given him, it was veneration.    Moreover, almost always, he came from a great Gallo-Roman family, solidly established in the country, and, through his relations, was closely linked with everyone who counted : this too was true of St Remigius, a scion of the Aemilii, who were Gallic aristocrats.    Finally, it was almost always a fact that the bishop had brothers, nephews, and close relatives highly placed in the ecclesiastical hierarchy, making 'mitred families' whose influence was manifold; this again was the case with St Remigius, whose immediate family was to include no fewer than five saints.    If our modern electoral expression can be applied to this epoch, we can say unhesitatingly that these bishops 'had the country in their pockets.'

It was not only in the regions conquered by the Franks that the ascendancy of the bishops was to help Clovis.    The example of *St Avitus*, Bishop of Vienne on the Rhône, proves this.    His see was in the middle of Burgundian territory, where his authority was enormous; he too was the scion of ancient Gallo-Roman stock, he too belonged to a 'mitred family,' and he was a great scholar, a shrewd politician, and a saintly man with a profound understanding of the path which the Church must follow.    Avitus was to look to this young chieftain of North Gaul, and, at the time of his baptism, was to write him a really prophetic letter.    And though not all the bishops were to side officially with Clovis—the great *St Caesar of Arles* is one of these— the simple fact that they were opposed to the Arian kings in the sphere of faith was enough to create between them and the Frank a real moral complicity, which was to become increasingly effective once the baptismal water had made the amicably disposed pagan, Clovis, into one of their brethren in Christ.

## CLOTILDA AND THE BAPTISM

*Clotilda*, the woman on whom the historic task of converting Clovis, and thereby bringing about the Church's triumph in Gaul, was about to fall was a Burgundian princess, whose wisdom and beauty have been extolled by Gregory of Tours.   At this period—about ten years after Clovis's accession—*Burgundia* was divided into two kingdoms: Gondebaud ruled at Vienne, Godegisel at Geneva; a third brother, Chilperic, had disappeared in circumstances which have given rise to some controversy among historians.   According to St Gregory, Chilperic was murdered by Gondebaud, but it has also been maintained that he died a perfectly natural death.   The level-headed character of the King of Vienne and the estimation which St Avitus afforded him makes the criminal hypothesis appear somewhat unlikely.[1] Chilperic's widow, Caretena, went to live at Geneva, at the court of her brother-in-law, with her two daughters, Soedeleube and Clotilda. All three were Catholics: in Burgundy, although the majority of the people and the kings professed Arianism, the Catholic faith also had a fair number of adherents.   And these three women were far more than average Catholics, they were models of piety, religious fervour, and saintly behaviour.   Was not Soedeleube—under the name of Chrona, which she adopted as a religious—to found the famous abbey of St Victor at Geneva?

There is little doubt that the marriage of Clovis and Clotilda was episcopally inspired, being probably an idea of St Avitus (consecrated to the see of Vienne in 490), and it was brought to fruition by St Remigius.   The idea of placing a young woman of impeccable faith and wisdom beside this young, twenty-four-year-old monarch, a king who was indeed rich in goodwill, but who was also a man of violence, was a logical conclusion of the Church's policy.   The time was ripe for action.   Clovis, in the heat of passion, had already had a child by some concubine or other, but this was not an over-serious matter; also —and this was more serious—he had just given his sister, Aldofleda, in marriage to Theodoric the Ostrogoth, whose advance into Italy went parallel with that of the Franks in Gaul, and who was beginning to emerge as the most intelligent representative of an Arian policy of race fusion.   As for Clotilda, did she at first hesitate to marry a pagan?

---

[1] It was probably fabricated during the next century, when the Franks put an end to Burgundy's independence.   Methods of political propaganda such as this are known to us even to-day!

*G

Did she only give in on the urgent entreaties of the bishops? It is difficult to sift the actual truth from the edifying tracts that have come down to us, in which traditional mannerisms are written over her real character. At all events the marriage took place, probably in 491 or 492, and almost certainly at Soissons.

What is absolutely certain is that, from the very moment of her marriage, Clotilda worked for the conversion of her husband. She had no immediate success whatsoever. For five or six more years Clovis remained a pagan, and this obstinacy augured well for the sincerity of his future adhesion to the faith. He allowed the first child born to himself and Clotilda to be baptized, but when the baby died he declared: 'My gods would have cured him, but yours has not saved him!' A second son was born, was baptized, and also fell ill; but, so the worthy Gregory of Tours asserts, 'Clotilda prayed so fervently for the infant's recovery that God granted her desire.' The chronicler also assures us that Clotilda never stopped telling Clovis of the Christian God. Who are we to say that she was unsuccessful? Who can tell the fate of those seeds which love and faith cast into the secret depths of an erring soul, leaving the task of making them germinate to God?

The hour of Christ was about to sound for Clovis. The scene of his conversion is well known—the vow made on the battle-field, followed by the victory which no one had dared to hope for. . . . Clovis was faced with the threat of annihilation from the Alamans, the most German of all the Germanic tribes, who had just been united by their king, Wibald. Did he realize that the whole destiny of the future France and Germany was tied to the fortune of his arms? At any rate he knew intuitively that if this new wave of barbarism was allowed to break out beyond East Gaul the work which he had begun would be shattered. Already the Alamans had penetrated as far as Lyons and the Seine; they had reached Besançon and Langres. Already the Ripuarian Franks around Cologne had had to repulse their attacks at the battle of Tolbiac.[1] About 496-7 the battle was joined between Clovis and Wibald, and it was in this decisive battle that, feeling his troops wavering and almost in despair,[2] Clovis sought the help of

---

[1] The name which is often given, albeit erroneously, to the decisive battle fought by Clovis.

[2] Gregory of Tours describes him as weeping, and lifting his eyes to the heavens, and attributes the following prayer to him: 'O Jesus Christ, whom Clotilda declares to be the Son of the living God, You who desire to aid those who falter, and to give them victory, if only they believe in You, I devoutly beg Your glorious aid. If You deign to grant me victory over my enemies, and if I experience this power of which those who bear Your name assert that You have given many proofs, I will believe in You and will be baptized in Your name. I have called on my own gods and have had no help from them, etc." Gregory adds: 'And at this very moment the Alamans turned and took flight. Seeing that their king was slain they surrendered to Clovis, saying, "Have mercy, we are yours." Thus the war ended. Returning in peace to his palace Clovis related to the queen how he had gained the victory by invoking the name of Christ.'

Clotilda's God, and undertook to be baptized if victory was granted him. This episode has been the subject of much controversy, and critical historians have attempted to dismiss it as purely apocryphal, even though it seems perfectly in keeping with the character of the Barbarian in question, who, like all his kind, expected, above all else, that the invisible powers should be efficacious and should favour him personally. Was it just a political calculation, as some have alleged, and nothing more? In a human soul, however, the workings of Divine Grace are almost always complex, and it is never beyond the bounds of possibility that God, in order to win a man to Him, should make use of the worst means as well as of the best to take him for His own.

One fact remains certain, and it is the only one which really counts: after conquering the Alamans Clovis asked for baptism. What paths did he travel in his passage from paganism to the Christian faith? It would be hazardous to attempt to answer this. What do we know of the psychology of this man, whose action was to be so decisive? Almost nothing. . . . Guizot, in a famous passage in his *Essais sur l'histoire de France*, has seen him 'as a predestined force, which walks the earth, extends its territories, conquers, and subjugates, in order to assuage its natural desires, and to fulfil a mission which it does not understand.' But there is no proof that it is necessary to reduce the psychology of Clovis to this kind of instinctive impulse, and though he obviously could not evaluate the boundless consequences of his act, it really seems, nevertheless, that he had at least a presentiment of its significance, and herein lies his genius. Was his baptism simply a political gesture? How incongruous this interpretation appears, when it is applied to this epoch, in which the supernatural permeated every aspect of life, and to these Barbarians who were so ready to believe in the obscure forces which directed the world! The picture of Clovis which the chroniclers were to hand down to us, the picture of Clovis, going seriously and faithfully to his baptism, is certainly a more reasonable one: Clovis being instructed in Christian principles by the hermit St Vaast, the future Bishop of Arras; Clovis, who, on hearing the account of the Passion, cried impetuously: 'Oh, if only I had been there with my Franks!'; Clovis, who, before making up his mind, took the advice of his officers; Clovis, who for an instant hesitated, in a spiritual debate between the Arianism which his sister held out to him and the Catholicism of Clotilda; and Clovis, who, at the moment of the supreme choice, went—or may have gone, since the incident has been much debated—to meditate at Tours, at the tomb of the greatest of all Gallic saints, St Martin. This Clovis is just as likely to be the real representation as the cunning, calculating politician with whom too many historians are content. It is much more accurate to say that the politician and the believer co-existed in his personality.

What is quite certain is that, on this Christmas Day, when the king of the Franks went down into the baptismal trough, the Church won a decisive victory. There is no doubt at all that, with the admirable prescience which she has always had of the great events of history, she understood this. Pope Hormisdas, writing shortly afterwards to St Remigius, to nominate him his universal legate in Gaul, appreciated perfectly the enormity of the step which had just been taken. 'You have,' he wrote to him, 'converted these peoples by miracles comparable to those of the apostles.' It was in fact the future of the West which had just been decided.

## 'YOUR FAITH IS OUR VICTORY'

We recall the rhythmical sentences in which the *Génie du christianisme* conjures up the scene as 'halted on the plains of Lens or Fontenoy, in the midst of the thunderbolts and the reeking blood, to the fanfares of the bugles and the trumpets, a French army, raddled by the fires of war, bends the knee and prays to the God of battles. . . .' It is no exaggeration to say that Chateaubriand's splendid picture takes on its historic meaning from the moment when Clovis and his followers emerge from the baptismal waters. What has often, since Lacordaire, been called 'the Christian vocation of France' has its origin here.[1]

One man understood it so and expressed his thoughts in a text which radiates an extraordinary prescience of the future: *St Avitus*. Although several Gallic bishops expressed satisfaction at the sight of Clovis adopting the true faith (e.g. St Melanius of Rennes, who converted the pagans of Armorica), the Bishop of Vienne—and Vienne, it must be stressed, was in Burgundy!—said so in prophetic terms. His praise for Clovis knows no bounds: 'Thanks to you this corner of the world shines with a great brilliance, and the light of a new star glitters in the West!' He foresees that this deed is going to change

---

[1] In return it can be argued whether or not the ceremony that took place on this particular Christmas Day was an anointing as well as a baptism, in other words, whether it was the origin of the anointing of the kings of France. In the primitive Church an unction of holy oil was applied to the forehead of the baptized person immediately after the baptism proper, and in 326 Pope St Sylvester had made this kind of 'confirmation' obligatory (and it is curious to note how several of the contemporary text which describe the baptism of Clovis allude to Pope St Sylvester). Clovis therefore received an unction as a baptized person but not necessarily as a king. It was only much later on, probably in the Carolingian epoch, that royal unction was distinguished from baptismal unction, when the idea of 'anointing,' properly speaking, which comes from the Old Testament and which was imitated by the Byzantine emperors, was established. In the Capetian epoch the legendary tradition of the holy ampulla kept at Rheims, and identified with that used at the baptism of Clovis, succeeded in maintaining the confusion. For this see Jean de Pange, *Le Roi très chrétien*, Paris, 1949.

the destiny of the whole of Gaul: 'In choosing for yourself you choose for all.   Your faith is our victory!'   Speaking more precisely, he conjures up visions of 'all those peoples who will come under your sway, for the benefit of the authority which religion must exercise,' and, having read his St Augustine and his Orosius well, he pictures the future empire of Clovis as an association of nations, each 'keeping its own specific character,' but united by the double tie of a common faith and subjection to the same king.   The first herald of the *Gesta Dei per Francos*—'I am a sentinel!' he declared.   'It is I who bear the clarion!' —St Avitus foresaw not only the Empire of Charlemagne, but the France of the Middle Ages, the witness of Christ, the torch-bearer of Catholicism, the France of St Bernard and St Louis—and all this because of the action of one bold little Sicambrian chieftain.

The enthusiasm shown by the bishops had enormous significance in political events of a more immediate nature.   'Your faith is our victory. . . .'   A promise was implied in these words.   The Protestant Gibbon has suggested that the French monarchy owed its establishment to its alliance with a hundred or so prelates who controlled the independent or rebel cities of Gaul.   Taken literally, this statement is trying to say that from the moment of Clovis's baptism, the Christian leaders in Arian territory all adopted an attitude hostile to their own kings and favourable to the Frank, in other words, that they all 'had dealings with the enemy,' for the good of the cause.   Things were not really so simple as this.   St Avitus retained an attitude of loyalty and even of sincere friendship towards Gondebaud, his king; St Caesar of Arles told his flock to behave in docile fashion towards their Visigoth rulers, whose heretical errors he condemned without any mincing of words, and to 'obey them in all that is meet.'   Consequently it is necessary to qualify the idea of 'moral complicity' which has been alluded to earlier in this chapter; it did not manifest itself in the form of actual treason.   However, by virtue of the simple fact that a Catholic Barbarian leader now existed, and that everyone knew that this chief was a friend of the bishops, opposition to the Arian kings gathered strength and crystallized around these bishops.   Agitation grew.   At Albi, where Bishop Eugene of Carthage, an illustrious victim of the Arians, lived in exile, the crowd demonstrated as he lay dying in an odour of sanctity.   When the Visigoth king had the bell-tower of the Catholic cathedral at Narbonne demolished, in order to have a finer view from his palace, a riot broke out.   The Arian authorities reacted harshly, and, as always happens in this type of operation, succeeded in making the bishops into symbols of resistance: two bishops of Tours, Volusian and Verus, were deported; St Caesar of Arles and Ruricius of Limoges, both outstanding men of their age, were once again exiled to Bordeaux.   But these repressive measures were all in vain!   Ranged behind the prelates who were struck down was almost the entire population, and it was about to acclaim Clovis as its liberator.

As for Clovis himself, he possessed a really inspired feeling for utilizing the combination of historic circumstances. As soon as he was ready to begin his great work—the reunification of Gaul under his authority—he knew exactly how to establish himself in the position in which all the fervent expectancy of the occupied Catholic populations would become his most valuable ally in the venture. According to Gregory of Tours, he was to declare: 'I can no longer allow the Arians to occupy part of Gaul: therefore let us march against them, with God's help, and if our enemies are beaten we shall hold sway over the whole country.' Was this merely skilful propaganda? Or sincere conviction? Whichever it was, the prediction of St Avitus was about to be realized.

We know what happened next . . . at least, we know the facts as outlined in the somewhat over-simplified account of the Tours chronicler. In 500, after intervening in a war between the brother monarchs of Burgundy which had split that kingdom in two, Clovis defeated Gondebaud at Fleury-sur-Ouche, near Dijon. Gondebaud subsequently became his ally, and perhaps his tributary.[1] Six years later, in alliance with the Burgundians, and probably encouraged by Byzantine diplomacy, which was preparing the future destruction of the Goths, he marched against Alaric II, the king of the Visigoths; the heavens visibly favoured him; had not his ambassador, who had been sent to the tomb of St Martin to seek some portent of the divine will, actually entered the basilica at the very moment when the priest was intoning the anthem: 'You have girded me with Your might, O Lord, ready for the battle . . .'? When he arrived in front of Poitiers had not Clovis himself seen a column of fire rising from the basilica of St Hilary, and bending towards him? And, at the crossing of the Vienne, did not a miraculous hind show him a means of fording the river? In 501 he defeated and killed Alaric II at *Vouillé*, and seized all the land between the Loire and the Pyrénées, but he was forced to give up chasing the Visigoths from France when faced with the threatening intervention of Theodoric, who saved the Central Massif for them and occupied Provence for himself. There was not enough

---

[1] Like so many of the deeds of Clovis's reign this victory has been questioned. It has been maintained that Gondebaud was not really beaten, but that this was in fact one of those murderous battles in which both contestants emerge, exhausted; that Gondebaud afterwards defeated and killed his brother Godegisel, and united Burgundy to his own advantage; and that, finally, there was a reconciliation on terms of equality between Burgundians and Franks, the result of a diplomatic manoeuvre inspired by Byzantium which was anxious thereby to obtain the isolation of the Ostrogoths. At all events, Franco-Burgundian agreement did come into being after the year 500, before the Visigoth war began; it was accompanied by a deterioration in relations between Theodoric and Clovis.

time for Clovis to finish his work, and it was to be continued by his sons: he had at least prepared definite starting-points for them, and had shown them the direction in which to go.

On the morrow of Vouillé, even if the Gallic hexagon had not been completely freed from Arian domination, the majority of the Catholic populations had been liberated.   From Belgium to the Pyrenees, from the Atlantic to the Limousin, the Roman Church was triumphant; in Burgundy Frankish influence was used to ensure tolerance for the Church there, and very soon the Vienne dynasty itself was to be converted.   Three things in Clovis's life demonstrate the profound significance of the results achieved, in other words, they show how the victory of the Frankish monarch established the bases of a subsequent restoration of the West, under the aegis of the Church.   The first is his installation in Paris, chosen by him as his capital—*cathedram regni sui*, as Gregory of Tours describes it—even though Lutetia was still nothing but a very small city, somewhat dangerously exposed from a strategic point of view.   However, Clovis chose it nevertheless because it had been an imperial residence, the delight of the Emperor Julian. The second is his acceptance—made joyfully and gratefully—of a splendid honorary title, which Anastasius, the Byzantine emperor, sent him following his Poitevin victory, the insignia of *honorary consul*,[1] with which he was magnificently invested in the basilica of St Martin at Tours: in the eyes of the Gallo-Roman population he could henceforth claim to be the accredited agent of the imperial power, the representative of *Romania*.   Finally, and most important of all, the third significant deed in which the future is outlined is the national Council of Orleans, held in 511, attended by thirty-two bishops.   Although the king did not himself preside over this (Bishop Cyprian of Bordeaux was president of the Council, and the spirit animating its proceedings was that of St Melanius), he at least exerted a constant influence on it, proposing subjects for discussion, and appearing so humble, and such a faithful 'son of the Church' that in their final motion the bishops praised his 'truly sacerdotal soul.'   Perhaps this was saying rather a lot!

Although it was less spectacular than these, another considerable fact was also to result from Clovis's victories: this was the fusion of the

---

[1] A title which the worthy Gregory of Tours, and the majority of historians who came after him, have confused with that of 'eponymous' consul, a title borne by the most important people in the Empire.   The chronicler goes so far as to say that henceforth Clovis was called 'Augustus,' something which would have made him one of the emperor's colleagues. . . .   Legal historians, who frequently have something valuable to add to the subject of general history, and especially to the history of the Church, note that Clovis never desired to have any compilations of Roman law, analogous to the *Breviary of Alaric*, made for his Roman subjects.   To him we owe the drafting of the *Salic Law*, which was based on Germanic custom.   Justinian's legislation was not to penetrate into Frankish Gaul.

Germanic and the Gallo-Roman elements into what was to become the
French nation.   It is quite certain that Clovis himself desired this
fusion, for he forbade, as far as he was able, acts of violence against the
Gallo-Roman populations, he killed those found plundering with his
own hands, and he set free the men and the women, and in particular
the priests, whom the Visigoths had reduced to slavery.   This fusion

The Kingdom of Clovis and his Sons
1. Thierry; 2. Clodomir; 3. Childebert; 4. Clotaire

was made easier by the fact that the Franks were certainly few in
number, so that they had no need to demand the sharing out of Gallic
lands, confining themselves instead to confiscating those of the wealthy
Visigoths; and it was hallowed by the bond of one common religious
faith.   It took place with a speed, an ease, and a harmony which had
no parallel elsewhere, and the Byzantine historian Procopius confessed
himself dumbfounded by it.   The problem which neither the brutal
Vandals nor the wily Ostrogoths had been able to settle, the problem
of indispensable synthesis, was solved satisfactorily by Clovis's Franks.
   Clovis died in Paris on 27th November 511, in the prime of life, at

the age of forty-five. He died too soon to be able to join in the great slaughter of the Goths which Justinian's attack on Italy was to make possible for his sons. But it was certain that the descendants of the man baptized by St Remigius would henceforth never halt along the road which he had indicated. Although it was divided between his four sons—the bastard Thierry, and Clotaire, Clodomir, and Childebert, his three sons by Clotilda—under the perilous custom of territorial division, the Frankish monarchy was to continue the work of the man who can be said to have been the real founder of the 'Merovingians,' France's first royal dynasty. Burgundy, ill defended by Sigismund, the son of Gondebaud, was annexed by the Franks in 534, after some ten victorious campaigns against her. Provence had been seized two years before this, without much difficulty, for the Ostrogoths were now at grips with Byzantium. And even beyond their own frontiers the Franks intervened on all sorts of occasions—interventions undertaken in the same mixed spirit of high crusade and political ambition which Clovis himself had possessed: in Spain, against a Visigoth king, who, it was alleged, was persecuting the Catholic Clotilda, daughter of Clovis; in Italy, against the Ostrogoths, in alliance with the Byzantines; above all, in Germany, where Franconia, Swabia, and Bavaria came within the Merovingian sphere of influence, and where Saxony paid them tribute. . . . 'Your faith is our victory!' This policy had an enormous influence on the destinies of Christianity; the prophetic sentence of St Avitus was to retain its meaning down the centuries. Right up to the time of Charlemagne, Frankish arms were to be, in their victories, the bearers of Catholic truth. And, whatever we may think of this association between the message of Love and military violence, it is very obvious that, in these Dark Ages which we are studying here, this alliance alone could found the new order. It is to Clovis's glory that he understood this.

## GLIMPSES AT THE RELIGIOUS PSYCHOLOGY OF THE BARBARIANS

The baptism of Clovis marks a decisive step forward in the history of Western Christianity; however, it would be an exaggeration to say that all depended on him alone. The picture which represents all the Barbarians as following the example of the Frankish leader, and making their way to the baptismal troughs after him, is a far too simple one. A period of at least four hundred years was to elapse between the moment when Clovis received the baptismal unction and that at which it could be said that virtually the whole of the peoples of western Europe had been baptized. This evangelization was still to demand much suffering, devotion, and sacrifice; [1] it meant a constant effort at adaptation to varying surroundings, to the different races, and to the changing political climate; but we know that, right from the beginning, Christian propaganda's most striking characteristic has always been its ability to show itself as flexible and realistic in its approach as it is resolute in the affirmation of its ideas.

Although the lands where the messengers of Christ were to spread the Good News were very different from one another—for instance, the Celts were not to be won over by the same methods as the Angles or the Bavarians—we can nevertheless pick out certain characteristics in the realm of religious psychology which were common to all the Barbarians.   What were the thoughts and emotions of these people when they were asked by a bishop or a monk to forsake the faith of their fathers in order to adopt one which was entirely new to them? What objections might they have?   What line of thought, or what instinctive impulse, enabled them to make their decision?   Here is one of the most fascinating aspects of this great history, analogous in interest to the studies made by our modern missionaries in Africa on the Negro's understanding of the Divine and of the steps which can lead him to Christ.

It is utterly unjust to represent these Germanic conversions as acts determined solely by self-interest or superstition.   Many of the Barbarians possessed a profound and sensitive feeling for the divine mystery, which was bound up with some unknown ancestral experience, and which we find expressed over and over again in most moving terms.   So, when the missionaries sent by Pope St Gregory the Great arrived in the Anglian kingdom of Northumbria, and King Edwin— the husband of the Catholic Ethelburga—after consenting to baptism himself, courteously invited them to talk with his council (a gathering of 'friends, princes, and counsellors'), one of his noblemen expressed his opinion in the following terms: 'O King, when the winter tempest rages outside, when the rain and the snow lash at the walls, when you sit at your table with your companions, close to the hearth, in the

---

[1] Does not Fustel de Coulanges go too far in his assertion that the conversion of the Franks was almost general immediately?   He quotes a law of Childebert I which forbids men to keep idols in their houses, but he writes: 'It is very mistaken to regard this text as an indication of paganism.'   (*La Monarchie franque*, p. 508.)   However, such an interpretation is corroborated by other indications which together form a most convincing pile of evidence.   The *Lives* of the saints who exercised their apostleship in Frankish territory long after the baptism at Rheims are full of episodes which prove that they frequently encountered pagans, and laboured to convert them, just as St Martin had done before the Invasions.   For example, St Amandus's apostleship in Belgium was a continuous struggle against idolatry, and this actually took place in the seventh century.   (Cf. R. P. de Moreau, *Histoire de l'Église en Belgique*, vol. i, p. 74.)   The Abbé Vacandard has written 'a brilliant study whose title alone gives the lie to the over-optimistic thesis of Fustel (*L'Idolâtrie en Gaule au VI<sup>e</sup> et VII<sup>e</sup> siècles*).   This subject will be discussed further in Chapter V.

warm, comfortable hall, perchance a sparrow flies quickly across the room.    It flies in by one window and out again through another at the far end of the hall.    During its brief moment indoors the wind and the cold cannot touch it, but scarcely has it disappeared from your sight when it is once again swallowed up in the murky winter night.    Are not men's lives like this?    We are equally ignorant of what goes before them and of what comes afterwards.    If the new doctrine gives us a certain answer to these mysteries, we should adopt it.'    Who among us does not feel the eternal truth of these candid sentences? All the mystery that it confesses is our own mystery also; and do we exaggerate when we recognize the last sentence as a sincere and moving desire to possess the truth?

Of course, uplifted though these sentiments are, they were based nevertheless on instincts which the study of the psychology of primitive peoples brings out very clearly.    This feeling of mystery, of which Edwin's nobleman gave such poetic witness, was frequently something very much more mundane, an elementary fear of death and of what comes after it.    As they began to grasp the first inklings of the Christian religion it was often their fear of hell which incited these pagans to conversion.    On a more material plane the Barbarians were extraordinarily receptive to the miracles which rumour attributed to Christian saints, and, even more so, to those performed by the Christians whom they knew: consequently all the great missionaries performed miracles: St Remigius and St Boniface, St Augustine of Canterbury and St Columbanus.[1]    The miracle proved that the Christian God was the strongest God, and herein, as far as they were concerned, lay the essential, the *ultima ratio*.

The objections which were raised to Christianity always came back to this idea.    Loyalty to the past, invoked by several Barbarians, is summed up in this typical query: 'Our gods have protected us; if we abandon them, will not they abandon us also?'    St Gregory of Tours relates how, during the theological discussions which he had with St Remigius or St Vaast before his baptism, Clovis's two major objections to Christianity were that Christ, in allowing Himself to be crucified, had shown that He did not possess divine power, and that, furthermore, 'He did not belong to the race of the gods,' in other words, He was not descended from either Wotan or Thor!    So one of the Christian missionaries' decisive arguments was to demonstrate the uselessness of the pagan gods, compared with the efficacy of the God of whom they taught.

Surely this is how we should understand the 'vow of Clovis.'    If

[1] It is said that one Jutish king (Ethelbert of Kent) was so afraid of the 'witchcraft' of the Christian missionaries that he insisted on receiving them outside his palace, in the open air  where spells were less efficacious. . . .

Clotilda's God gave him victory, i.e. if He proved His might, then he, Clovis, would declare himself convinced.[1] When he wrote to his disciple, Boniface, who was busy evangelizing the Hessian territories, the prudent Bishop Daniel of Winchester gave him this advice: 'Talk to the pagans like this: if your gods are all powerful they ought to reward those who worship them, and punish those who scorn them. But in this case why is it that they do not harm the Christians who destroy the idols? Why do they allow the Christians to occupy good, fertile soil, overflowing with wine and oils, whilst they only give you miserable land, made barren by the bitter cold?' Peremptory arguments these, and it must be admitted that they betray a quite terrifying debasement of Christian standards. . . . But, after all, does not the Bible describe how the prophet Elijah had recourse to the selfsame argument in his defiance of the priests of Baal? It is a fact that it succeeded. Likewise, in England, we shall see a pagan priest abandoning his gods, after a 'trial' in which he had had no success, with this declaration: 'If they had had any power, they would surely have supported me, their zealous follower!' Likewise, too, St Colombanus, St Amandus, and St Boniface carried the axe in their own inspired hands into the sacred groves of Germany, defying the pagan gods to punish them for it, if they existed! [2]

It is against this kind of background that we must study Clovis's action and assess its importance. It was to have considerable repercussions, on both pagans and Arians, because it went from success to success. The victory at Vouillé contributed a vindicatory argument, all the more striking since the Frankish leader had all but been killed in the battle, but had then miraculously escaped death, whereas his adversary had perished. A pagan no longer had a reason for refusing Christian baptism, since it had now been proved that the Christian God was more efficacious than the old Germanic gods; he no longer had any reason to incline towards Arianism either, since Clovis, the conqueror,

---

[1] Gregory of Tours puts these words into his mouth, during the battle against the Alamans: 'I have called on my own gods, and have had no help from them. Since they do not aid those who serve them, it is clear that they possess no power. O God of Clotilda, I therefore call on You, on You in whom I want to believe. I beg You, see to it that I am delivered from my enemies!'

[2] We do not learn much about the Germans' religion from Gregory of Tours. It was a naturist religion. The Germans worshipped gods who 'ruled over the forests, the waters, and the wild beasts.' On the other hand, they also had their idols, and these gave the missionaries a good deal of trouble. Some authorities claim to see in them crude adaptations of the Roman divinities. The German gods are never represented as powers who govern the world, nor as judges who reward the endeavours of mortals. Over and above the gods is always Fate. However, 'what the Germans appreciate most in a god is his efficacy' (Tonnelat). The life beyond the grave was one of their principal preoccupations, and there is no doubt that this preoccupation provided a means for Christianity to enter their souls. (Cf. E. Tonnelat, 'La Réligion des Germains,' in Mana, Paris, 1948, and Georges Dumezil, Mythes et dieux des Germains, Paris, 1949.)

was a Catholic. Among the Arians the argument shaded into this variation: since a Catholic was now the master, Catholicism was no longer merely the religion of the defeated, the religion of the occupied; the inferiority complex associated with it was removed, and we know well how sensitive people are to arguments like this—even if they are not Barbarians! Finally, it goes without saying that this vindication through success and through might could be tied up with purely political considerations, especially in areas where Arian dynasties were still reigning: since the Catholic Church had proved such a powerful aid to Clovis might it not be politic to win its alliance? Consequently, on the eve of Vouillé, Alaric II, the Visigoth, reversed his whole policy, tried to effect a reconciliation with the bishops, and authorized the convening of a Catholic council in his states: it was too late, but his intention is significant.

Such were the psychological ideas which were to condition the Church's new efforts for the conversion of the rest of the Barbarians, and which, in large measure, explain her results.[1]

### THE ARIANS RETURN TO THE BOSOM OF THE CHURCH

To what method did the Church resort in order to effect this conversion? Nearly always she adopted the one which had succeeded so admirably in the case of Clovis: she worked to win the king over; for then the subjects would follow. Here again we can detect a characteristic typical of Barbarian psychology: the Barbarians marched to baptism as to a battle, behind their chieftain. St Avitus says so explicitly, in a letter to Gondebaud. Of course our modern attitude of mind, which views faith as an exclusively personal affair, is loath to approve of these mass-conversions—whose danger is only too obvious —and they do make us look back regretfully to the Church's earlier days, when God won over men's souls one by one, when the effort of conversion and of the meditation leading up to it were quite individual. But there is no reason to suppose that single conversions, conversions of individual, obscure folk, did not take place at the same time as these

---

[1] In a famous passage of his, Fustel de Coulanges has said some very fine things about the total absence of racial prejudice in the Church; this fortunate situation must have made fusion much easier.

Nevertheless fusion could not proceed without some jolts and hitches. Witness the following little incident, which is most revealing. If we can believe what John the Deacon says, the thunderously loud singing which came from the rough throats of the Franks quite ruined the melodies sung at religious services; this bawling infuriated the Gallo-Romans, who told the Franks exactly what they thought about it. The scene and its consequences can be imagined.... (Quoted by Gérold, *Histoire de la musique au moyen âge*, Paris, 1936, p. 159.)

mass-baptisms; we have examples of some.[1]   And, finally, it must be readily confessed that the method of 'general' conversion was perforce a necessity of the age.

After the Franks, the first Barbarian people whom the Church inscribed upon her roll were the Arian Burgundians.   Truth to tell, their Arianism had never been very ardent.   They had already been Catholics once, whilst they were still dwelling in the Hercynian Forest, and it was only subsequently that they yielded to the attraction of heresy, that is to say, even though they detested them, to the influence of those other mighty invaders, the Goths.   But we have noticed that they continued to include amongst them a not insignificant element which remained faithful to Rome, such as the saintly women in Clotilda's family.   King Gondebaud, who had political flair, a certain understanding of moral and spiritual issues, and even some theological learning, seems to have toyed with the idea of conversion. St Avitus, whose relations with the king were extremely cordial, never missed a chance of showing him the superiority of the orthodox faith, and the happy consequences which his conversion would have for his state.   The Burgundian ruler was held back by the fear of arousing the discontent of his subjects; he wanted to be reconciled with the Church in secret, but this the bishop refused to sanction.   Had Gondebaud had Clovis's breadth of vision and the Frank's decisive nature, the Burgundians would almost certainly have played the role which the Franks assumed. . . .

But, though he failed with his father, Avitus converted the son: this was *Sigismund*, who became a Catholic shortly after Clovis, probably in the year 500, and to him the saint-bishop of Vienne was guide, philosopher, and friend.   It was a difficult role, for this royal model of piety sometimes broke out and committed deeds of appalling violence, and indulged in various crimes for which St Avitus had to make him do penance and make reparation!   At all events, this sincere conversion, followed by that of thousands of leading Burgundians, and the underlying guidance of the Church, was to have an enormous influence on the future of the whole Burgundian people.   St Avitus very prudently forbade all reprisals against the Arians, and he was totally opposed to the use of force to hasten conversions—he had read his St Augustine well, and, following in the steps of his master exactly, he wrote that 'to resort to force is unworthy of the Dove.'   He persuaded the king to sign an edict which bears some similarities to the Edict of Nantes, so many centuries later.   This laid down equality between established

---

[1] For example, in the life of St Benedict, there is the case of a worthy Ostrogoth who was converted to Catholicism and became a monk.   This case was certainly not an isolated one.   One suspects that the history of Lérins contained several like it.   Inversely, it is reasonable to suppose that a number of individuals or families remained faithful to the gods of their ancestors, despite the mass-conversion of the general body of the population.

and newly converted Catholics, and the latter could even become bishops.

As in Frankish territory, the fusion of the two races quickly went ahead, and marriages between Gallo-Romans and Germanic Burgundians were authorized. The Gombette Law, reserved for the Germanic subjects, and the *Roman Law of the Burgundians*, which existed for the rest, worked similarly in practice, although their actual texts differed. Two hundred years later no trace of the former conquerors remained in Burgundy, save a few place-names and certain traits of character—the innate optimism, the bantering kindness, and that love of life and wine that we can still see in their descendants.

A little later on another conversion was to recall that of the Burgundians: this was the conversion of the Suevians, the people who had been flung into the north-west of the Iberian peninsula by Euric, and had there succeeded in holding their own against the Visigoths. On the whole they too had wavered between Catholicism and Arianism. About 450 their king, Richiar, had been received into the Roman Church; his successor, however, was led astray by an apostate and became an Arian. But the Suevian kings were not given to religious persecution, and they maintained excellent relations with the local Catholic clergy. Around 560 an outstanding man became the leader of this clergy. This was the Pannonian *St Martin of Braga*, who was a brilliant scholar; he was also a most saintly man, who, even when he became archbishop, retained—like his compatriot and namesake, the great Gallic apostle—the strict monastic habits acquired during a pilgrimage in the East. The good Gregory of Tours, who is always inclined to push his precursor's glory to the fore, declares that when the Suevian king Theodemir fell ill, he sent an envoy to the tomb of St Martin of Tours to bring back a relic to restore him to health, swearing that he would then be converted to Catholicism. It is more likely that it was Theodemir's successor, Miro, who took the decisive step, and that it was St Martin of Braga who brought him to it.

Although the conversion of the Burgundians and the Suevians took place so easily and peacefully, that of the Visigoths was an entirely different matter. It was indeed the occasion of a moving drama, of an actual religious war, in which a father fought his own son and put him to death. The Visigoths, like all the Goths, were Arians, and they had a fanatical attachment to their religion, of a kind which was generally unknown among their Italian Ostrogoth cousins, and which was only a little less violent than that of the Vandals in Africa. *Euric* (466–84) had pursued an overbearing, spoliatory policy which had weighed very heavily on the Catholic Church in his domains, stretching as they did from Spain to the Loire, and, following the example set by St Sidonius Apollinaris, the Catholic bishops had never ceased their opposition to it. Not that the Visigothic kings lacked ideas which might have resulted in a really constructive policy. Was it not one of their princes, Athaulf,[1] who had been the first to visualize a fusion between the Goths and the peoples of the lands they had conquered? And when Alaric II saw himself threatened by the coalition made up of Clovis's Franks and the Burgundians, have we not seen him attempting a policy of pacification, actually allowing the bishops to hold a Council, in response to the call of St Caesar of Arles? Did he not promulgate a new law, which the Middle Ages were to call 'The Breviary of Alaric,' which was in fact an effort to bring about a certain equality between the two ethnic groups? But Arian fanaticism triumphed over wisdom, and the Visigoth dynasty remained attached to the heresy.

At the beginning of the sixth century Catholicism had almost managed to impose itself on the whole Visigothic kingdom by force of arms. On the first occasion, when Alaric fell at Vouillé and the Franks swarmed as far as the Pyrenees in one fell swoop, who knows whether even the mountains would have been enough to halt Clovis's attack had not Theodoric and his Ostrogoths come to the Visigoths' rescue? At all events Provence and Septimania had been liberated and restored to Catholicism. On the second occasion, in 530, under the pretext (fully justified, however) that Amalric was ill-treating his wife, the Catholic Clotilda, Childebert, the 'King of Paris,' rushed to his sister's aid, marched on Barcelona, defeated the Visigoth near Narbonne, and had him killed by a Frankish officer. The glorious 'divine' race of the Balthungs, the race from which the great Alaric had sprung, was wiped out.

After this Spain suffered nearly forty years of troubles and violent disturbances, from 530 until 567. Restored under a new dynasty—although the boundaries of its kingdom had in fact been pushed back behind the Pyrénées—the Visigothic monarchy floundered amid frightful crises. The Frankish attacks were continuous, and Saragossa was actually besieged by them. In 554 Justinian's Byzantines were called into the country by a rebel, and they landed in the south-east of the peninsula and established themselves there. The native Spaniards made violent reply to the continuing religious persecution of the occupiers. There were uprisings almost everywhere, around Tarragona, in Cantabria, and, later on, in Lusitania, and, in the south, in Betica, where the royal armies smarted under some severe reverses. Sacrifices had to be made, an understanding had to be reached with the Franks (it was at this point that the two princesses, Galswintha and Brunhilda, married the Franks, Chilperic and Sigbert, and so began the

---

[1] See the last section of Chapter II: 'Two Failures: the Vandal Solution and the Gothic Solution.'

story which Augustin Thierry has described so movingly in his *Récit des Temps Mérovingiens*); probably it was even necessary to consider effecting a reconciliation with the Catholics.

At this moment (567), for the first time for many years, an outstanding man ascended the throne at Toledo. His name was *Leovigild*. He possessed all the old Germanic energy coupled with a certain political acumen. He defeated the rebellious Basques, chased the Franks from the Narbonnaise, annexed the Suevian kingdom, and seemed destined to take up Euric's task of conquest once again, all the more so since the Merovingians were paralysed by a severe internal crisis, and, at Byzantium, Justinian had just died. This, moreover, was a king with a love of ostentatious display, who dressed in the Byzantine fashion, who behaved like the Basileus, who struck gold coins as he did. But, in religious matters, he remained fanatically Arian, and his second wife, a Gothic woman named Goswintha, an unbridled scold, was even more fanatical than he was. In 580 Leovigild rather naïvely suggested that his Catholic subjects should become Arians, and his suggestion was accompanied by so many inducements and such weighty promises that a few people fell for it, even Bishop Vincent of Saragossa. But this policy ran up against the clear-sighted opposition of an illustrious monk, *St Leander*, the future Archbishop of Seville—a marvellous man, with a vigour equal to the king's: he denounced the manœuvre, and raged and declaimed against it, and it was then that the drama of a religious war broke out.

The hero of this war was *St Hermenegild*, who has sometimes been called the Spanish Clovis, a Clovis who sealed his fidelity to the faith with his own blood. Hermenegild was actually the king's own son by his first wife, a Greek Catholic. He had married an admirable woman, the worthy descendant of St Clotilda, the Frankish Ingund, daughter of Sigbert and Brunhilda. Influenced by his wife and by St Leander, Hermenegild had abjured Arianism, and this made the young couple targets for acts of incredible violence on the part of the king and the fanatical Goswintha. But quite a formidable party immediately formed around Hermenegild, consisting of all the Catholics who were weary of Arian persecution, above all, the bishops and Leander. Soon a proper coalition joined against Leovigild; the Suevian followers of the dethroned king Miro, the Basques, the Hispano-Romans, and the Byzantines from the south. The king ordered his son to return to the Arian faith. When Hermenegild refused, war broke out. The young Catholic leader took refuge in Andalusia, and held out there, and St Leander sailed for the East in order to obtain help from the emperor. But Hermenegild, conscious of the justice of his cause though he was, could not bear to fight his own father. He accepted his brother Recared's invitation to come and take part in peace negotiations.   Leovigild kissed him and declared him forgiven: was this a trick or a sudden change of front? Suddenly, on a signal from the king, the guards seized the young prince, stripped him of his royal robes, and threw him into a dungeon.   Thus began a 'passion' worthy of that of the martyrs of an earlier age.   In vain Arian bishops and theologians were sent to the hero in order to persuade him to return to his father's faith.   He did not yield.   For many months he languished in captivity, suffering much ill-treatment, even being deprived of the Holy Eucharist.   Finally, mad with rage, Leovigild gave an order, and Duke Sisbert went to behead Hermenegild in his prison.   It was the eve of Easter, 585: a fine time for a martyr to die.

But this is indeed an occasion when the famous phrase of Tertullian was put into practice: 'Christians spring from the blood of the martyrs.'   Easter Saturday, 585, proved to be the bloody dawn of Catholicism in Spain.   One year later, in May 586, Leovigild died in his palace at Toledo and his son *Recared* succeeded him.

Was Recared guided simply by a clear appreciation of his own interests?   Or was it the marvellous number of miracles which were taking place at his brother's tomb that impressed him most?   The new king immediately reversed the entire royal policy.   Duke Sisbert was executed; the Catholic bishops recalled from exile; St Leander, who had become Archbishop of Seville, was most respectfully commanded to come to Court.   In order to save his own face Recared devised a religious debate, to be held in public, at which the superiority of Catholicism would be explained to him; this took place at Toledo in 589—the first Council of Toledo.   The king, the queen, and several Arian bishops were reconciled to Rome.   The Catholic history of Spain had begun.

As everywhere else, the conversion of the Barbarian rulers to Catholicism resulted in various decisive consequences in Spain. Henceforth the fusion of the races went ahead there, and it was so total that by the seventh century the Hispano-Roman aristocracy was to claim descent from the Goths, and a Spanish patriotism was born, clearly seen in the works of St Isidore of Seville.   Interracial marriages were permitted.   After 654, under Recesswinth, one law sufficed for both elements in the population.   The *national councils of Toledo*, which were theoretically ecclesiastical assemblies, but were in fact as political as religious in content, were held very regularly.   They were to become the fundamental institution of the Visigothic State, a kind of senate, ensuring the lasting stability of an elective monarchy. The Spanish Church was to be illuminated by various outstanding intellectual figures, such as *St Isidore of Seville* (566-636), who worked doggedly to safeguard culture, and whose encyclopaedic works were to make him worthy of veneration as a Doctor of the Church.   Baptized in the blood of the martyr Hermenegild, the Spanish kings were henceforth (and at a time when Merovingian Gaul was in a state of eclipse) champions of the Christian faith. They continued to champion it with honour down the centuries; it was the coronation of one of their kings, *Wamba*, in 672, which provided the first occasion when a written document makes clear mention of royal unction, as distinct from baptismal unction; and the visitor to the Cluny Museum can still meditate before the magnificent bejewelled gold crown which Recesswinth had hung in Toledo cathedral, as a pledge of his fidelity, like a votive offering. . . .

## THE PART PLAYED IN THE CONVERSIONS BY THE SAINTLY QUEENS AND THE MONKS

Throughout the events we have just witnessed, whether it be the baptism of the Franks or the return to Catholicism of the Arians, one fact stands out: this is the considerable part which women and monks played in these operations. The single name of Clotilda is enough to bring to the fore the long line of saintly queens whom history sees by the side of these Barbarian kings. And almost every one of the clergy whose action was so decisive, St Remigius and St Vaast, St Martin of Braga and St Leander, were or had been monks, and, truth to tell, they remained monks even when they occupied the most dazzling offices in the ecclesiastical hierarchy. This fact must be put to the credit of the Dark Ages: that woman, the incarnation of modesty and love, was able to act so effectively in these times of violence; that the monk, the living witness of the Holy Spirit, was frequently able to exert a paramount influence over events. Here is proof that a certain scale of values existed on which civilization could one day be rebuilt.

Thus, close to several of the Germanic kings, whose natural brutality is quite terrifying, we see these moving women, whom posterity was to venerate, around whom the halo would make the legends multiply, but who were indeed witnesses, often heroic witnesses, of the Catholic faith. Women had not the same reasons as men for clinging to this religion that exalted force—which is what the Arianism of Ulfilas had become; and, in the same way, the spiritual barrenness of the heresy, and its inability to support the mystical impulse, were contrary to the fundamental gifts of the feminine soul. These young princesses, who had been baptized into the Catholic faith and who were married into the Germanic dynasties to suit political exigencies, claimed the freedom to practise their own religion, and a Catholic chaplain went with them to their husband's palace. Beside their husband they became apostles whose power was all the greater because, since they were always near them, they could take advantage of every occasion, of all those moments of discouragement and uncertainty when the most self-confident of men confesses himself a weakling, and because they could use those most human ties created by the marriage bond to bring their menfolk to Christ. Even if they did not succeed in converting their husbands, their children at least would follow their example, being baptized at their insistence, and brought up by them. As St Paul had said: 'The unbelieving husband has shared in his wife's consecration' (1 Corinthians vii. 14). This was never truer than in the Dark Ages.

*Clotilda*, the wife of the young, violent, pagan Clovis, held in her keeping not only the Catholic faith, but charity and civilization too. What a splendid picture we have of this cultivated, demure woman, standing on the threshold of France's history! We can but glimpse at her, meditating in the lovely gardens of her palace, bringing up her large family, and visiting the poor, but in the decisive episodes of the reign, how perfectly timed and how forceful her actions were! There was strength behind her outward gentleness of manner; she is the same woman who, when she became a widow, shut herself from the world in a Tours convent, there to spend twenty more years performing wonderful penances; the same woman who, to the murderers of her son, Clodomir, who came to her, proposing either to kill or to 'have shorn' (i.e. depose) her grandchildren, was to give the proud reply: 'They are better dead than shorn of their royalty!' Moreover another influence was added to her own, doubling its efficacy: that of the aged religious who lived on the top of the hill of which the royal palace occupied the slope facing the Seine, the famous octogenarian who was the conscience of the capital. . . . This was *Geneviève*, whom Clovis venerated as the living representation of sanctity, and beside whom he was to sleep his last sleep, in the church built by him at the request of his venerable friend.[1] From the stock of the first Queen of France, who was a saint, came other queens. They too were to be saintly witnesses, and almost martyrs, for their faith. Can we imagine the strength of purpose which her daughter, the second *Clotilda*, the wife of Amalric the Visigoth, must have had in order to stand up to this violent man, who hurled filth at her or struck her in the face when she made her way to the Catholic church? And was not *Ingund* almost as much of a martyr—at least in intention—as her husband Hermenegild, made by her into one of Christ's heroes—Ingund, the great-grand-daughter of the great Clotilda, who, when ordered to apostatize by her terrible mother-in-law, Goswintha, and to submit to a second and Arian baptism, answered: 'I have acknowledged the Holy Trinity, equal in one single God. I believe in it with all my heart; I

---

[1] The church of the Blessed Apostles: it was on the top of what is to-day called 'La Montagne Sainte-Geneviève,' behind the modern Panthéon, where the Rue Clovis is now which separates the Lycée Henri IV from the church of St Étienne-du-Mont.

will never renounce my faith!' Though she did not have to pay for her courage with her life, she was thrown to the ground, trampled on by the shrewish Goswintha, beaten till the blood ran, and flung into an icy pool.

We find equally wonderful women in many other chapters of the Gospel's conquest of the Barbarians! They are not always so dramatically exposed to the physical fury of the unbelievers, but they are always resolute in their faith and capable in their action. In England it was *Bertha*, a Parisian princess, another great-grand-daughter of Clotilda, the daughter of Caribert and wife of Ethelbert, King of Kent, who was to bring with her to England a Frankish bishop, to consecrate a chapel to the Gallic saint, Martin, and to give an enthusiastic welcome to Augustine, the Pope's missionary, per-suading her husband to allow him to preach before him. She too was to found a family of saintly queens, for her daughter, *Ethelburga*, was to play the selfsame role beside her husband, Edwin, and to open up the Northumbrian kingdom to Christ. Among the terrible Lom-bards, in whom we are to see some ferocious enemies of the Church and the Holy See, it was the Bavarian Catholic *Theodelinda* who was to be the Clotilda of Germanic Italy. And she would do even more than Clotilda had done, for her political role was indeed considerable. She was an affectionate link between her husband and Pope St Gregory the Great, a bearer of peace in the midst of a frightful war; by having her children baptized as Catholics she prepared for the future, and the church at Monza rightly still remembers her name. Her daughter, *Gundeberg*, twice married to Arian kings, twice cast into prison for her faith, and her nephew, whom she brought up, were to continue her work, whilst at the same time, in the duchy of Benevento, *Theodorata*, a Latin woman, the wife of the duke there, succeeded in reconciling her people to Rome.

If we can make so bold as to borrow a phrase from modern physics in order to make our comparison, these heroic women were like the 'catalytic agents' who induced the actual crystallization. As for the fundamental groundwork, the tedious preparation, the spiritual per-meation of the Barbarian peoples, this was essentially done by the monks. It is quite clear that, ever since monasticism had spread from the East and taken root in the countries of the West, everything that was most ardent and most vital in Catholicism had been drawn towards the monasteries. The still very modest little communities which had sprung up at Trèves, Verceil, and Rome itself during the fourth century, had very quickly given way to monasteries which often contained very large numbers of religious, such as that at Marmoutier, where St Martin of Tours had dwelt. We have already noted the expansion of *Lérins*, the famous foundation of St Honoratus, at the beginning of the fifth century,[1] as well as that of his Marseilles rivals, who based their Rule on the ideas of Cassian.  We know that St Caesar of Arles laid down a Rule, and that straightway large numbers of women's communities adopted it body and soul; and the frightful austerities with which St Colombanus seasoned his did not prevent thousands of monks from accepting it joyfully.  Around 520–30 St Benedict was to promulgate his Rule [2] in the majestic monastery of Monte Cassino, where he had just begun carrying out his great work, a Rule based on such firm foundations, so humanly conceived, and so nobly slanted towards the divine ideal that it immediately superseded all others, and soon the history of Western monasticism became completely identified with that of Benedictinism.

But it is essential that we understand that there is something extraordinary and almost paradoxical in the fact that it is, henceforth, the monks who are to be the most effective of Christ's propagandists. What is a monk?  Hermit, anchorite, and cenobite, he is by definition a man who has retired from a world in which it seems impossible to find peace of mind and the means of spiritual salvation.  Ever since Paul, the first solitary, had buried himself in the Egyptian desert, this had been the essential of the monastic vocation.  To meditate and to pray, be it in strict isolation, or within a fraternal community of like-minded souls, the monk's life seemed restricted to this double obligation, and his use to society and to the Church seemed to lie in the action which his prayers exerted on the mysterious intentions of Providence.  It must be admitted that this picture is very far removed from that of the life of the missionary monks—winning people to the faith, clearing forests, and creating towns, for this is how history shows them to us. How was the transition achieved from one to the other, from the *school for the service of God*, as St Benedict called it, to the mission?

Quite simply.  The most secluded hermit, the monk most resolutely attached to solitude and silence, could not prevent souls in torment from coming to seek his advice.  Had not St Anthony, when in the desert, already had to flee from the enthusiasm of his penitents on two occasions?  St Benedict was besieged in his retreat in just the same way, and was finally forced to leave it.  And if a monk's reputation became so considerable that Christian folk saw him as their leader, how could the man of God ignore their pleas?  And so we have already seen Lérins, the nursery of bishops, providing innumerable regions of France and even Ireland with pastors, and St Remigius— and many others—torn from their meditations in order to occupy an episcopal see.  The demand of Christian people was too strong to be

---

[1] See Chapter II, section: 'The Pillars of the Church.'
[2] In his role as the founder of a religious order and as a legislator, St Benedict will be studied in the next chapter, under the section which bears his name.

resisted. Among the Celts, the monastic communities actually assumed the entire ministry of their people. At Arles, around St Caesar, the monastic life and the episcopal function were inseparable, just as they had been at Tours around St Martin, and at Hippo around St Augustine. 'Go and preach the Gospel to all nations!' The monks were far too saintly to disregard the command of Christ: and so the life of meditation in God gave place to the active life for God, to the 'peregrination for God,' as St Colombanus was to call it.

## THE IRISH MIRACLE AND THE MISSIONARY MONKS

The first Western examples of this living paradox of a monk, who was a stay-at-home and a recluse by vocation, leaving his monastery to traverse the wide world in order to spread the Good News far and wide, was given by the Christians of 'Britain' and Ireland, that is to say, by the Celts.[1] The history of these Celtic Christians is an astounding and picturesque one, wreathed in poetry and mystery, tossed by gales and sea spray, emanating from lands where the northern mists rise from the cold seas, and where legend grows with the ease and speed of a dream. But from this history emerge several strange but perfectly authentic characters, whose lives are full of interest and charm.

Britain had been affected by the third-century spread of Christianity within the Empire (there had been three 'British' bishops at the Council of Arles in 314), and possibly by Eastern Christian influences also, coming from the countries bordering Persia, through soldiers or merchants who followed the trail blazed by the legions. Christians were probably fairly numerous in Britain by the time the Roman legions withdrew, some time in the first half of the fifth century, leaving the Celtic churches to face the Anglo-Saxon invasion alone— the horrors of which St Gildas, the author of a stormy chronicle, has related in the style of a jeremiad. However, these harried, persecuted Christians resisted and survived the onslaught: their courageous struggles were to provide the inspiration for the legendary cycle of *King Arthur*, so dear to the medieval *chanson de geste*, and which is even to be found depicted on cathedral walls, but which has a factual historical basis dating from this period of the invasions. These Christian communities sought refuge in the mountains and grouped themselves

---

[1] They were only the first *Western* examples, we must remember, for in the East Alexander, the founder of the Acimites, had been a convinced missionary, and his disciples had followed his lead in this direction. Also, is it necessary to remind ourselves that the term 'Britain' was exclusively applied to the modern 'Great Britain' until the fifth century? It was only after the establishment of some of the Britons on the Continent that the Armorican peninsula gradually acquired a similar name.

TRANSLATOR'S NOTE: Although in English two separate words exist, i.e. 'Britain' and 'Brittany,' the French 'Bretagne' is used for both.

around their monasteries, notably around the dozen or so religious houses which *St David* (died probably *c.* 601) founded, or helped to found, in Wales. Life was far from easy for the British Catholics of this age, and very often a monastery was so poor that its monks had to draw their own plough! But their faith was vivid and even impassioned—indeed just as impassioned as it had been in the days when the Briton Pelagius was putting forward his disastrous views on Grace, his supporters forming such a hard core of resistance in Britain that it was necessary to send St Lupus, Bishop of Troyes, a former monk of Lérins, to the island, to fight these ideas, and, on two occasions, St Germanus of Auxerre also.

Shortly after this (*c.* 430), Ireland, which was still 'a barbarous island' according to the chronicler, Prosper of Aquitaine, was the object of Pope St Celestine's attentions.[1] He sent Palladius, a missionary bishop, to work among the Irish. But the great work of converting Ireland, the building of this bastion of Catholicism which has endured into our own age, was the work of *St Patrick*, and this great missionary has rightly remained Ireland's national hero and patron saint. Patrick was a Romano-Briton, born about 385 at a place which he himself called Bannavem Taberniae. It has never been identified, but was probably somewhere on or near the south-west coast of Britain. A raiding party of Irish pirates, who had crossed 'the sea dedicated to sea-sickness,' as a contemporary called it, seized a group of captives on the British coast and took them back to Ireland, where manual labour was probably scarce. Among them was a young lad of sixteen: Patricius or Patrick. This is the first special characteristic of the Irish miracle: it was the Irish themselves who went to find their apostle! After six years Patrick managed to escape, and, going to the Continent, became, like so many other famous evangelists, a monk at the abbey of Lérins. But he always retained his affection for the worthy pagans whom he had known during his days as a slave. 'I hear the voices of children, as yet unborn, calling me from Ireland,' he often said. In 432 he was revealing to St Germanus (who had just returned from his first mission to Britain) his desire to go and evangelize the island, when news came of Palladius's death; St Germanus con-

---

[1] Ireland had remained outside the *Orbis romanus*: the legions had never sullied its soil, had never planted their eagles there. The ancients knew very little about the island. Avienus, one of their geographers, writing in the fourth century, calls it 'the Sacred Isle,' a name which probably denotes ignorance rather than admiration. St Jerome talks of its inhabitants in most unflattering terms: he relates a ridiculous story of cannibalism, ridiculous because it is a cannibalism limited to those parts of the female anatomy which usually arouse a rather different kind of gluttony than that of the stomach. There is one accurate feature running through all the ancients' accounts: they had already observed—second hand, no doubt—the verdant charms of the island, which to-day still make it worthy of its title of 'the Emerald Isle.' The same Avienus tells us that 'its green fields are spread in the bosom of the waves.' Quite a pretty verse this, for in these happy times geographers wrote their treatises in poetic form. . . .

secrated him forthwith, and St Patrick set off for Ireland at once. For thirty years, until his death about 461, he carried on a gigantic mission-ary endeavour there, and we do not know which aspect of it to admire most—its perseverance, its courage, or its success. Fighting the sorcery of the Druids with his miracles, discussing poetry and mysti-cism with the *Filid*, or school of Bards, whose influence was very powerful, winning the souls of the royal princesses for Christ (here we see the importance of women's influence once again), Patrick suc-ceeded in the wonderful feat of converting Ireland smoothly and with-out violence of any sort—there were no martyrs in Ireland—as it were, substituting Christianity for Druidism, through the action of free com-petition and by the manifestation of a power that was spiritually and miraculously superior to its rival; it was a deed of capital importance, not only for the future of the island alone, but for Christianity as a whole, which, in this instance, showed in resounding fashion, that, though cradled within the framework of Graeco-Roman culture, it could adapt itself to all other forms of culture and give them a new vitality. The second important aspect of the Irish miracle was this planting of the cross in a land where Roman rule had not first paved the way for it. The episcopal see of *Armagh*, which was to become the primatial see of Ireland, was founded in 444. And, by the time Patrick died, Ireland contained so many active Christians and so many monasteries that she could legitimately be called 'the Isle of Saints.'

Isle of Saints—where, along its sunken roads, one still comes across these moving memories of her most ancient history: the *menhirs*, the standing stones clumsily chiselled with the Christian Chrisma ... Isle of Saints—our liturgical calendar is inscribed with the sonorous names of so many of her countrymen, all too often largely forgotten to-day: Comgall, Brendan, Mochta, Kilian, Benen, Fiacre, Columba, Finian ... Isle of Saints—where monasteries swarmed literally everywhere,[1] nurseries of intense spiritual life and culture;

---

[1] No sooner was it founded by St Patrick than the Church in Ireland evolved so rapidly towards monastic institutions that one scarcely finds any secular element in it at all. Historians have pondered the reasons for this phenomenon, which is certainly a miracle— the use of the word here is not at all far-fetched—but which is extraordinary neverthe-less. Alexandre Bertrand decided that Irish monasticism traced its descent directly from the Druid communities: the monks were nothing more than converted Druids, and so, like the Druids, they lived in communities. This remains to be proved conclusively, for it is only a hypothesis, like the whole of Bertrand's reasoning. Equally hypothetical, and no more founded on fact, is the suggestion which seeks to connect Irish monasticism with Egyptian monasticism. Let us not try to find an explanation for it, but be content to acknowledge the fact. At this period the Irish saw everything from the monastic angle, so that for them the Pope was 'the abbot of Rome' and Christ 'the abbot of the Heavenly City.' Their monasteries were veritable towns, sometimes containing as many as three thousand monks. Each monk had his own hut: the whole monastery could have passed for a military camp. Dom Leclercq, who remains mischievous and malicious despite his scholarship, compares these monasteries to molehills: but those who lived in them were not sedentary beings like the moles; they were more like migratory birds.

H

Kilkenny (the oldest), Clonard, Clonmacnois, and Bangor were the most illustrious, and the monks dwelling in them ran into thousands. In no other Western country during this epoch did religious idealism burst out so powerfully as in Ireland; the asceticism of these Irish monks may appear rather excessive to us (e.g. reciting the Psalter immersed in icy water, or spending so long in prayer, arms outstretched, that the birds had time to make their nest on the praying man's head!), but their mystical yearning is no less sublime for all this. The centre of a whole clan's prayer and liturgy, and also the real seat of ecclesiastical administration, each of these monastery-bishoprics maintained around it a quite extraordinary surge of fervour. And whilst the sun of culture was setting in the West each of these centres was lighting a torch. . . .

But the most striking characteristic of these Celtic monks was surely their delight in travelling, in making their 'peregrination' for Christ. The Celtic wanderlust is well known; it reached tremendous proportions when stimulated by the desire to evangelize! In unbelievable numbers the missionaries were to set out, from the British communities buttressed against the Germanic invaders, from the young churches arising from the path trodden by St Patrick.[1] The chronicle is to be filled to overflowing with their prodigious adventures—tales of monks who vowed never to return to their native land, in order to travel the world all their lives, bearing the Gospel, of boats setting out to sea without oars, so that their occupants might submit themselves to the will of God all the more completely, even of stone troughs miraculously turning into seaworthy ships that bore the saints where Providence willed they should go. The west coast of Great Britain was to see the rise of monasteries from which the Gospel message would shine out to the whole world: Bangor, in North Wales, is said to have been founded by St Comgall, who certainly founded the Irish Bangor; and Whithorn (Candida Casa) was founded by St Ninian in 397, Ninian being a Romano-Briton who had been educated in Rome and had returned to Britain to evangelize Galloway. Farther, farther went the Irish, always farther, on towards the most unknown and the most formidable countries, doing their work for Christ! Not content with founding the abbeys of Durrow and Londonderry in northern Ireland, *St Columba*, a monk from Clonard, set sail from

---

[1] 'The original thing about Ireland,' writes Georges Goyau, 'is that behind the starting-point of the evangelistic spirit there, we can see something far greater and finer than the vocation of a few individuals; this spirit was created and sustained by a collective impulse, stemming from the whole Irish soul. The monasteries founded by St Patrick were mission stations. Immediately they sprang up they gave shelter to a spiritual *élite*, spurred by the Christian *Credo*; no sooner was a man baptized, than he wanted to become a monk, and this in order to preach, to create other baptized folk and therefore other monks.' (Georges Goyau, *L'Église en marche*, 2e série.)

Ireland with twelve companions [1] about 563, converted the wild Picts, and, on a tiny island, in a remote corner of Scotland, founded the monastery of *Iona*, which was to be a nursery of bishops, a real Scottish metropolitan see, from where the Gospel would go out to the Orkneys, the Shetlands, and the Faroes, the *Ultima Thule* of the ancients, and even, it is said, to Iceland. We can read of the kind of perils and adventures—some comical—that the monks experienced on their voyages in the delightful legends of *St Brendan the Voyager*, which are still told as fireside tales to-day. They abound with amusing or terrifying anecdotes, tales of masses being said on the back of a whale, which the saint mistook for an island, and of the fire of the polar volcanoes, like a kind of Gates of Hell amid the ice. It is not all legend, for when the Vikings discovered Iceland, in the seventh century, they declared that the 'fathers' from Ireland were there already, and that every island in the North Sea possessed its colony of ascetics.

Other groups went a different way. They made for the 'new Britain'—Armorica, to which the Anglo-Saxon invasions had forced many of the Celts to flee about 450–550, giving impetus to a migration that had already begun, for reasons unconnected with the invasions. There the Celtic race was to take root so vigorously that it literally transformed the population. Between the Celts of Great Britain and Ireland and those of Armorica an immediate, continuous, and brotherly contact existed despite the distance that separated them. Truth to tell —and this situation held good for centuries—one single people lived on each side of the grey sea, possessing one single Christianity with identical characteristics, particularist in its practices, grouped around its monastery-bishoprics, both mystical and poetic, both with the same passion for voyaging.

Here we should remember the Armorican epic of the Celtic monks who came from over the sea, the army of saints so dear to the hearts of our French Bretons, this special colonization which has left its mark in the place-names of Brittany, and which continues to nourish its folklore: St Corentinus (or Cury), who is said to have been the first Bishop of Quimper; St Samson, founder of Dol, for long the most important see in Britanny; St Paul Aurelian, who founded monasteries wherever he went—in Ouessant, on the island of Batz, and in the Leon district which now bears his name (St Pol-de-Leon); St Malo, disciple of St Brendan

---

[1] Here is evidence of the predilection of Christians of this epoch for the number *twelve*, obviously derived from the twelve apostles. Palladius was certainly sent to Ireland with twelve companions; Patrick had twenty-four; Mochta took a dozen to Armorica; the great St Colombanus had the same number when he set off for Gaul, and so on. We have seen how St David founded twelve monasteries in Wales. In the great abbey of Fulda twelve privileged monks were set apart, by reason of their sanctity and their learning. The same symbolism reappears several times in the life of St Benedict. The number of cathedral canons was also set at twelve by St Gregory the Great.

the Voyager; St Brieuc, St Tudwal, St Cadoc, St Guenhael, and so many others! There is not a town in Brittany that does not claim its own saint from amongst them! Perhaps the most famous of them all is *St Gildas*, the son of a British king, according to one tradition, who studied first in Gaul, then straightway became a monk in Ireland, wrote the chronicle of his people, and later returned to Brittany, landed— miraculously—on the island of Rhuys, and, although involved in the doings of the Bro-Werech, succeeded in living a life of contemplation, despite all the action taking place around him. It is true that everything we read in these splendid hagiographies cannot claim to be genuine history; but through the many legendary elements the great characteristics of these beginnings of Armorican Christianity can be clearly discerned: the first stage, one of installation, after which the monks took control of the whole country, helped by the fact that until this time the population there had been very small and drifting, without any organization of its own; then a progressive extension, extraordinarily rapid, with the Celtic Christian communities of the British Isles providing reserves of men for this conquest. Over two hundred years the Celtic monks really created Britanny,[1] and it has never lost the stamp of its rugged, ardent founders, even up to modern times.[2]

Every one of these wanderers of Christ lived extraordinary lives. But the most extraordinary man of them all, the one who was to make the most profound impression on the world, was a certain monk from Bangor who landed at the little cove of Guimoraie, between Saint-Malo and Mont-Saint-Michel, one day probably about 580, with a dozen companions—a stone cross still commemorates the event—and who, instead of settling in Armorica, set off towards the forests in the East. His name was *Columbanus*. He was born in Ireland about 546, and grew into such a comely youth that he was troubled by the glances of the women who were continually attracted by his handsome appearance. 'Flight is your only means of salvation, young man!' an old recluse told him. Flee he did. He went to Bangor, and after he had spent a few years applying himself to the prodigious mortifications which

---

[1] And not just Brittany! Péronne became the centre of a Celtic colony which was so important that for a long time it was called Perona Scottorum; quite near Paris, La Brie owes much to Irish monks. The founder of La Brie, St Fiacre, was himself one. The first historian who provides some details about La Brie in his writings is the Venerable Bede. (Cf. Jean Hubert, 'Les Origines historiques de la Brie' in the *Bulletin de la Société littéraire et historique de la Brie*, Meaux, 1938, p. 9.) In 1639 Nicolas Vermulaens, a professor at Louvain, published a little book on the propagation of the Christian faith in Belgium by the Irish: he gives the names of forty-two saints, three of them women, who came from Ireland to evangelize Belgium, though some scholars consider his list rather too long! And the Vosges, Alsace, Franche-Comté, and Switzerland also owe the Irish monks a great deal.

[2] Many Breton place-names are connected with this Celtic missionary conquest: the *lann* are the hermitages; the *plon*, the parishes (from the Latin *plebs* or the Gaelic *plywr*); the *tré*, the chapels of ease, etc.

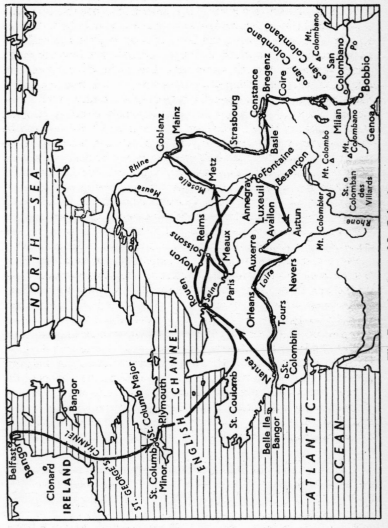

The Peregrinations of St Columbanus

were the rule there, and to which he voluntarily added others, it was very soon impossible to recognize the fresh pink and blond adolescent of yesterday in this bearded, gnarled giant, with muscles of steel, who could fell a tree with one blow of his axe, and dig the soil for fifteen hours on end without showing any signs of fatigue. Yes, it was a rugged man indeed who landed at Guimoraie! A kind of Israelite prophet, walking the sixth-century earth, as plain-spoken as Isaiah or Jeremiah, on whose face, so his biographer assures us, 'the might of God was clearly visible,' a great walker and preacher, a tireless pioneer, a healer and almost a soothsayer, and yet a man whose Irish ancestry had left him his sense of poetry and mystery, his love of nature and of day-dreaming.

Crossing Gaul from west to east, Colombanus wandered about the country for several years, clearly without any set plan—this wandering where Providence chanced to take him is characteristic of his whole attitude to life—until one day, when he reached the Vosges country, the Burgundian king offered him a site where he could establish a community, in a place where the land and the people were equally untamed. This was Annegray, the first Columbanian foundation: its fame soon spread thoughout the whole country, and it was beset by tens of thousands of sick folk, attracted by the miraculous powers of the saint-healer. Soon it was too small for the large numbers of monks who crowded to join its ranks. In 590, on the site of a little Gallic village burned down by Attila, Colombanus founded *Luxeuil*, which for several centuries to come was to be one of the most important centres of the Holy Spirit in the West, a kind of French Monte Cassino.

It is hard to imagine what enormous prestige this monk exercised during the last twenty-five years of his life.[1] People came from far and wide to seek his advice; kings venerated or feared him; the Gallo-Roman or Frankish bishops regarded him with uneasy respect. We must wait until St Bernard before we find any saint exercising a comparable ascendancy in France. Whenever he left his monastery and visited a province, vocations sprang up wherever he went; for example, those of the two brothers, Adonus and Ouen, who founded Jouarre and Rebais (Ouen is the St Ouen of the Parisians); and of Burgundo-fara, a young woman of very noble birth, who, despite her family's protests, adopted the harsh Columbanian Rule and founded Fare-moutiers. Nothing could stop this man, neither fear of punishment nor respect for the temporal power. For speaking his mind to King Thierry, a wicked man, of most vicious habits, and for vigorously

[1] The work of St Columbanus, which is treated here only in its missionary aspect, covered many other fields besides. These include his Rule, his influence on certain customs of the Church (e.g. personal, private confession, instead of public confession), and, above all, his role in the efforts to reform the morals of the age. This will be dealt with in the next chapter, in the section on 'The Church's Principle of Reform.'

refusing to bless his bastards, Columbanus, who had thought for a
moment that he was going to be put to death, was finally chased from
Luxeuil and expelled from the kingdom, being able to return there
only in secret. What did it matter? Tragic though the break with
his spiritual children at Luxeuil was, were there not still many other
souls to save and win for the Lord? And it was the lands along the
Rhine which were the next to see Columbanus, areas where the path of
the Invasions had left the people in a really barbarous state—Coblenz,
Mainz, and Basle, where his disciple Ursicinus founded a community,
Arbon on Lake Constance, and Bregenz at the foot of the Arlberg,
where Columbanus established a second Luxeuil. Then, because
King Thierry threatened to pursue him even there, the saint crossed
the lake; in the south his disciple, *St Gall*, fell ill, stopped, and thereupon founded the famous abbey at Steinach which bears his name.
Dropping down into Italy Columbanus had just founded yet another
monastery on the Trebbio, at Bobbio, when death at last allowed him
to rest from his labours (615). His wonderful life, entirely orientated
to the sole desire of spreading the Word of God, and supporting it with
the solid bastions of his monasteries, is characteristic of the great
history of the Irish missions.

The influence of the Irish monk was to last for a long time. Many
saints were to come forth from his abbeys, such as St Philibert, founder
of Jumièges and Noirmoutier, St Mummelinus of Noyon, St Omer, and
St Bertinus. The peculiar stamp with which he impressed the Christian soul is found again in several of his pupils, such as St Wandrille,
the founder of Fontenelle; it has been estimated that two hundred
abbeys sprang into being as the result of his influence. And throughout the Western world dozens of places were to bear his name, or
variations of it.[1]

For several hundred years, through the agencies of all those religious
houses founded by them and which in turn propagated others, like so
many plants, Christian Europe realized how much she owed to the
Celtic monks from the islands, and to their tireless action. But does
she still realize it? Is she to-day sufficiently aware of the importance
of what we have called 'the Irish miracle'? For, to put it briefly, the
real Irish miracle was indeed this 'second starting-point' of Christianity, this miracle of a land which had only just itself been baptized,
showing itself at once so marvellously faithful to the evangelistic

[1] It can even be said that he had an influence *a contrario*, for it was largely in order to
compete with the Columbanian influence of Luxeuil that other abbeys were founded, and,
for example, that St Eligius and Dagobert founded Saint-Denis. And it is interesting to
note that to-day the 'missionaries of St Columbanus' continue to play a considerable role.
From Navan, near Dublin, they leave in large numbers to go all over the world: in the
U.S.A. several great missionary centres still bear the saint's name (e.g. in Nebraska and
New York); it is found in China, Korea, Burma, Australia, the Philippines, etc.

spirit. In those dark days of the West, Ireland was like a second Palestine, a second cradle of the faith. This all too little known history provides us with a wealth of themes on which to meditate. A missionized land, capable of becoming, on the very morrow of conversion, a nursery for missionaries. . . . Fénelon, in a prophetic sermon, delivered before some departing missionaries, was to envisage what he called 'the transference of Christianity.' Who knows if a role analogous to that of the Celtic monks may not be promised to the present-day indigenous Christian communities growing up in Africa and Asia? The role of bringing the Gospel back to a West which has forgotten it. . . .

### The Lombards and the Dismemberment of Italy

The influence of Rome and of her bishop has scarcely been apparent in any of this propaganda on behalf of Christianity so far. We have merely seen Pope Celestine giving a first stimulus to the conversion of the Irish, and we can guess at St Leo's support for St Patrick. But we should not allow ourselves to be deceived by this seeming silence. The popes may have been too occupied with Eastern affairs to do very much in the West; they may have been hampered by the troubles in Italy; nevertheless the baptizing bishops, and the missionaries of Christ, knew quite well that the best of their work was bound up with the important spiritual power of the successive popes at Rome. 'If we once begin to doubt the authority of the Pope of Rome,' declared St Avitus, 'it is not just a single bishop who totters, it is the whole episcopate!' On the morrow of the king's baptism, St Remigius asked Clovis to offer the Pope a present of a gold crown: this was a tangible link and a visible mark of homage. And even the awesome St Columbanus, though he was not a whit averse to lecturing the Pope, whenever he imagined him to be erring doctrinally, wrote of him none the less: 'We are all the disciples of Sts Peter and Paul. We Irish, at the world's end, are especially attached to the apostolic see, and whatever greatness and glory Rome possesses, in our eyes she is great only because of the said see!' The time was drawing near when the task of converting the Barbarians would be taken up, carried through, and organized by a great pope, at the very moment when the eclipse of Rome seemed at its worst, and when the see of St Peter appeared threatened with becoming just an ordinary bishopric in a new Germanic kingdom, that of the *Lombards*.

Who were these unknown Barbarians, whose role was, quite involuntarily, to have such a decisive influence on the future of Christendom? Just one more group of those Germanic hordes, who, since the beginning of the fifth century, had hardly ever stopped exerting pressure on the West. Aryans from Scandinavia, they had been moving steadily southwards for some four hundred years, and, after some brief halts around the mouths of the Elbe, and then in Moravia, had arrived on the Danube about the year 480. Whence did they derive their name? They were 'those whose beards have never been submitted to the indignity of the razor,' according to their chronicler, Paul the Deacon. 'Warriors with the long spears' is another suggestion. Or is the word a fusion of 'Langons' and 'Bardi'? No one really knows. Tall and blond, they were considered extremely ferocious: though theoretically baptized Arians, they were in fact as little Christian as it was possible to be. . . .

As always, it was the weakness of the Romans themselves which laid the Empire open to them. The Lombards' settlements on the middle Danube were threatened by Gepidae attacks—the latter being attacked by the Avars, who were in turn being pushed forward by the Turks . . . and about 550 they were looking for an escape route southwards. Byzantine diplomacy gave them one. Under pretext of balancing his enemies and playing one off against the other, Justinian provided these formidable Germans with arms. When he plunged into the reconquest of Italy, Lombard contingents commanded by Audoin fought alongside his armies against the Ostrogoths: they enjoyed this so much that henceforth their sole desire was to return to the delightful peninsula with their tribes.

Now the situation in Italy was extremely favourable for an invasion. The amazing adventure of 'reconquest,' which Justinian had seen as his crowning glory, had in fact been a catastrophe for Italy.[1] She had been ruined by a war that had been far too long drawn out. From the Alps to Vesuvius there was not a single province which had not been bled white in the struggle. The skilful administration and the conciliatory and moderate government of Theodoric, which had permitted the 'renaissance' at the beginning of the century, in which Boethius and Cassiodorus had been the leading figures, was shattered for ever. The Byzantines, bureaucratic, formalist, more or less decadent, and very unpopular, were quite incapable of restoring order to the country. This position was aggravated because relations between the emperor's civil representatives (the prefect of the Praetorium residing at Ravenna, his two deputies in Rome and Genoa) and the military leaders (the exarch in the capital, the dukes and counts under his command in the provinces) were often stormy. In fact, these local commanders, following a course which we have already observed taking place in the East over the past century, tended to become petty potentates, as tyrannical as they were undisciplined, but completely incapable of resisting any serious attack.

[1] See the end of the preceding chapter.

* H

The Lombards had been settled in present-day Croatia since about 500, in other words, they were at the very gates of the Empire. They had learned many things whilst fighting the Ostrogoths. For example, Alboin, Audoin's son, knew very well that the Byzantine fortresses lacked garrisons, that the Italian people hated the Easterners, that Narses, furious at having been disgraced by Justin II, was awaiting his hour at Naples, and that his successor, cooped up in Ravenna, possessed hardly any soldiers. He drew the obvious conclusions, and on 2nd April 568 the Lombard people began to move towards Italy. They comprised about six hundred thousand people, of whom perhaps one hundred thousand were warriors. They went through Emona (German Laibach, now Ljubljana), along the valley of the Sava, through the passes of the Julian Alps and Friuli, to reach Aquileia, which had been abandoned by its leaders, then on to Treviso, Vincenza, and Verona, which all opened their gates voluntarily to them. The onlooker might have thought himself back at the beginning of the fifth century, when Radagase, Alaric, and Attila made their saucy raids on Italy. The following year it was the turn of Brescia, Bergamo, Trento, and Milan, all of which fell without a blow being struck, and although Pavia, Theodoric's former capital, held out for three years, Alboin succeeded in conquering the whole of northern Italy as far as Parma and Bologna, while the Lombard chieftains, judging the game an easy one, began operations on their own account, and were soon to make themselves dukes of Spoleto and Benevento. In 572 Alboin was solemnly installed in Theodoric's palace at Pavia: the Lombard state had come into being.

Was Italy actually 'Lombardized'? No. The Lombards affected it no more than Roman unity, Gothic administration, or Byzantine systematization. Alboin, founder of the Lombard state, was barely dead when the monarchy, which was elective, fell to pieces during ten years of continuous crisis, and the kingdom was divided into a mosaic of duchies and countships—about thirty of them altogether—which were all practically independent, in other words, forming a kind of military feudalism which foreshadowed that of the Middle Ages. Moreover the newcomers never succeeded in occupying the whole peninsula: the Byzantines retained an incredible tangle of very numerous territories, including most of the coastline and the islands, the Lombards holding the interior, but the Exarchate of Ravenna almost completely separated the kingdom of Pavia from the duchies of Florence and Spoleto. The piecemeal division of Italy, which was such an important factor in Western history until the nineteenth century, was thus established.

Distressing though this situation appeared to anyone who held the memories of Italy's ancient glories dear, it was to help the Papacy enormously. Already the measures taken by Justinian in the Pragmatic Sanction of 554 had, after a fashion, given official recognition to the spontaneous political authority which the Church had acquired, in her role of 'defender of the City,' by giving the bishops and the Pope real control over the civil officials. Over the twenty years during which the Lombards were devouring the country, while the Franks, called in and paid by the Byzantines, were increasing their raids on Italy,[1] the Papacy came to appear more and more like an island of liberty, a bastion of the Holy Spirit, and the Pope, this unarmed priest, as the only effective adversary of these unscrupulous Barbarians. Had Italy become totally Lombard it would have been forced to try to reduce the Bishop of Rome to the position of Primate of Lombardy, just as Byzantine autocracy, in its heyday, had done its best to make him subject to it, controlling his election and putting pressure on his decisions. But an Italy pulled this way and that by the different warring forces could only throw up one important figure from this prodigious jumble. The throne of St Peter had but to be occupied by a man of quite outstanding character, and the control of history would pass into his hands.

## POPE ST GREGORY THE GREAT

Admittedly, during the one hundred and thirty years which elapsed between the death of the great Pope St Leo (461) and the accession of another great Pope, St Gregory (590), the see of St Peter had scarcely a single occupant who was really equal to the events of the age. Not that any of them showed themselves unworthy of the office; out of a total of eighteen popes, eleven were canonized, and even those who acquired the supreme title in dubious circumstances—e.g. Vigilius and Pelagius—showed themselves quite reliable once they were invested with their responsibility to the Church of Christ. There were pious and charitable popes, popes who were great builders, and popes who were fine administrators. We see nearly every one of them defending the primacy of the Apostolic See against the Byzantine

---

[1] The Lombards and the Byzantines never exchanged blows with one another. Relations existed between them, influences made themselves felt. This can be proved by a visit to the famous treasure at Monza (9 miles north-east of Milan), where one can see the marvels of an art which is both fundamentally barbaric and yet supremely sophisticated, and in which Eastern influence is clearly apparent. Certain items in the collection are famous, such as the 'hen with her chicks' in gilded silver, which belonged to Queen Theodelinda, and, especially, the famous 'iron crown of the Lombard kings,' made of gold plates enamelled with green, decorated with enormous flowers in multicoloured settings, all mounted on a circlet of iron, forged, it is said, from a nail from the True Cross. It was this crown that Charlemagne put on in 774, Charles V in 1530, and Napoleon I in 1805.

**ITALY IN THE
AGE OF
SAINT GREGORY**

///// Byzantine
Territories

..... Duchy of Rome

autocrats, often with the magnificent resolution of a St Gelasius or a St Hormisdas.   However, the day had certainly not yet dawned when the Papacy would recognize for its own what we to-day can see was the task demanded by the age—the reconstruction of the world by the Church after all the terrible destruction of the fifth century, that task which the great St Leo had foreseen.   The Papacy could not yet break free of the notion of the *imperium romanum*, which dominated almost everyone, that is to say, it could not prevent itself from concentrating its entire gaze continually towards Byzantium, where the Empire still survived, and from whence could come commands, threats, support, or dire troubles.   To dominate this epoch and to understand its real needs, in other words to go beyond it in order to build for the future, and, without losing sight of the East, to turn to face the West, where a new world was coming into being; for this nothing less than a genius was needed.   And that is exactly what he was—this man who was to be known to history as *Gregory the Great*.

When the enthusiastic voice of the people called him to the pontificate in 590 the situation seemed black indeed; although, looking back across the perspective of history, we have noted how great the Papacy's chances were potentially, to those who were living these events tragedies and dangers loomed on every side.   Encircled by the Lombards, in the north by the Duke of Spoleto, in the south by the Duke of Benevento—and the latter, Ariulf, was particularly bellicose—abandoned by the exarch, who was 'more depraved than the Lombards,' and by Byzantium, where chaos had regained the upper hand since Justinian's death, the new Pope surveyed a spectacle of utter desolation.   Italy was in the grip of pillage, torn by a savage violence which was practised not only by the Lombards: each year more towns went up in flames; the highways were unsafe for travellers; the bands of prisoners reduced to slavery walked the streets, 'ropes round their necks as if they were teams of dogs.'   In the north the Archbishop of Aquileia, under pretext that Rome had been too indulgent towards the Monophysite heretics, refused to be in communion with the Pope, and his schism resulted in many distressing incidents within the Church. The Eternal City itself was three-quarters empty, a tragic sight indeed for those who remembered its past glories, and it was said that Providence had a grudge against this corpse of a capital, for ever since November 589 there had been catastrophe upon catastrophe—the Tiber had risen in flood, and the destruction of the granaries had resulted in famine; the dead animals thrown up by the flood-waters bred evil germs, and terrible plague broke out, one of its first victims being Pope Pelagius.   In one pathetic page St Gregory himself calls to mind these dreadful days.   Alluding to chapter xxiv of Ezekiel, he writes: 'Is not this the town of which it was justly prophesied: "The meat is broiled and the bones therein also"? Where is the senate now? Where are the people? All is destroyed, bones and flesh alike, all the glories and lawful institutions of the world. What is left to the few who still survive? Sword blows rain down on them daily, afflictions without number pile upon them. . . .' Before such desolation it is quite understandable that even this man of steel sometimes confessed that he 'felt his soul sinking beneath its burdens and drowning in a sweat of blood.'

But for some men, those who are truly great, the fundamental understanding of an apparently hopeless situation, so far from making them discouraged, spurs them on to action. Gregory turned to face these tragic conditions resolutely, sustained by a marvellous vigour, and by the loftiest conception of his spiritual mission. And his pontificate, which was not a very long one (590–604) was certainly the most outstanding in the whole period covering the centuries between the Invasions and the Middle Ages; it was the pontificate in which the Papacy assumed its leading position, its position without parallel in any field, its position which it was to maintain throughout the centuries that followed.

To enable him to undertake the immense task, whose difficulties were all too obvious to him, Gregory had the good fortune to embody within him at one and the same time two types of men, who, in different ways, were able to conceive how threatened humanity could be saved: the Roman, backed by great classical traditions, and the monk—the one drawing from the past those things which still retained their value, the other exclusively devoted to the only spiritual force capable of rejuvenating the world, Christianity. Scion of a great patrician family—if one tradition can be believed he was descended from the famous Anicii, who had included two emperors and the well-known philosopher Boethius among their number—Gregory received a good education, the best that was possible in this age of scholarly decadence (he never wrote as well as St Leo). Praetor and prefect of Rome, he belonged, like St Ambrose before him, to the class of important state officials, for whom the sense of duty still counted above all else. As 'prefect of police' and a judge of criminal cases, he showed a keen sense of discipline and of the needs of the state, throughout his years as an administrator. But this kind of life left him dissatisfied. For far too long (he himself confessed this) he put off replying 'to that inner call which he heard.' However, his own family was not lacking in examples of Christian piety; without even mentioning the Pope from whom Gregory was descended,[1] Sylvia, his mother, and his two aunts, the nuns Tarsilla and Aemiliana, were to be canonized by the

---

[1] Pope St Felix III (483–92) had lost his wife while he was still a deacon. Therefore by the time he became pope he had had children.

Church.    Finally, the call of God became too strong for him to resist it any longer, and on the death of his father Gregory obeyed it.

A monk he became, and a monk he fundamentally remained throughout the rest of his life.    He turned his own house into a monastery—it was in Rome itself, on the Coelian Hill, where the church of San Gregorio stands to-day—at the head of which he placed an abbot, himself wishing to be nothing more than a humble brother.

Was the Rule which this monastery of St Andrew followed that of St Benedict or not?    We do not know for certain; but at all events the patriarch of Monte Cassino certainly influenced it enormously, since St Gregory himself was to write the saint's biography much later on.

At every stage of his life Gregory was to surround himself with monks; he used monks in all his great enterprises; he spent his entire and considerable patrimony in founding abbeys; and, when he became pope, he retained his nostalgia for his beloved monastic existence of silence, prayer, and 'reading in God.'    For this peaceful life was not to last for very long.    Gregory very quickly distinguished himself, of course, and soon the former high government official received Pope Pelagius II's order to devote himself to one of the seven divisions of the city, as a 'regionary deacon.'    After this he left Italy to fill the most difficult post of all, that of nuncio (in those days he was called 'apocrisiniarius') at Byzantium (where his influence became so considerable that the Emperor Maurice had him baptize his son, but where he also learned to know the real weakness of the Empire); finally, he returned to Rome to administer the Papal Secretariat.    When, on 15th January 590, Pelagius II died of the plague, the terror-stricken Romans, who believed that the arrows of divine wrath were raining down upon them, rushed to put their unanimous confidence in Gregory, and, despite his protests, despite even his attempted flight, the monk of St Andrew was obliged to consent to consecration.

Was there any pontificate which was fuller than this one?    Although delicate in health (he was ashamed not to be able to obey the rules of fasting, lest he swooned), Gregory was one of those men who, by rigorous self-discipline, are able to obtain more from a sickly body than most of us obtain from a healthy one.    Ambitiously bold in his ideas, resolute in their application, following through every task which he undertook to the last detail, he was a worthy son of those great administrators whose endeavours had created the Empire.    Gregory was a hot-tempered man, somewhat inclined to intransigence, but he radiated such boundless generosity of spirit that, without trying to please, he made people love him.    His intellect matched his character: it was lucid, penetrating, quick to assess men or to judge situations; there was no danger of him confusing weakness for charity, illusion for hope; the art of government came to him naturally, and it had been further matured by his long official employment. He was a tireless worker, always busy dictating letters (we still possess nearly nine hundred of them, dealing with the most varied topics), receiving visitors, and vastly increasing the scope of a pope's duties. Yet he still found time for a considerable literary output of his own—commentaries on the Gospels and on Ezekiel, *Moralia*, the *Regula Pastoralis* on the duties of a priest, *Dialogues*, which sparkle with the genius of this marvellous Christian, and from which the Middle Ages were to derive such pleasure, and all those great liturgical treatises which were to have such a profound mark on our Christian customs. The *Gregorian Chant*, this wonder of the Church, without which our ecclesiastical ceremonies would lose so much of their mysterious charm, still links his name to-day with the great development of plain-song and with the permanent organization of the *Schola cantorum*. And all this outstandingly effective human activity rested on a profound inner life, and was supported by a wonderful spiritual experience—for Gregory possessed a truly mystical and contemplative soul, permeated by the desire 'to free itself from the limits of the flesh,' his every action, however small, conforming faithfully to his principles. He knew of no better title for himself than that of *servus servorum dei*.

This was the great pope who decisively re-established the authority of the see of St Peter in the hour when it seemed most threatened. His concept of the role of Christianity and himself was not a new one; it had been held by St Augustine; Gregory used to read the works of the genius of Hippo a great deal, and admired him deeply. To a prefect in Africa who sought his advice he replied: 'Study the writings of the blessed Augustine, your compatriot, and when you have tasted his pure flour you will not crave our chaff.' All the great Augustinian principles, particularly those of the *City of God*, are found again in Gregory's work, not merely on the spiritual plane, where he can be said to have been a faithful 'reflection' of his master, but in the field of action too: to work for the terrestrial city, with the heavenly city always in his mind, to serve humanity because of the eternal promises which it bears within it, to mould history in order to make the hour of God's reign draw nearer—such were the foundations of an action which, though applied so effectively to political and social problems, was never guided by anything save concern with spiritual interests alone.

This action was literally endless. As Bishop of Rome Gregory devoted a good deal of time to the people of his diocese, preaching to them every Sunday, but also organizing food supplies, arousing the zeal of the civil officials, supervising their work, controlling the administration of justice and the police, having new basilicas built, or restoring and beautifying existing ones; and folk in the Eternal City were always to cherish the memory of the campaign in which the plague was beaten, of those seven processions leaving the seven regions of the city to converge on Santa Maria Maggiore and beg remission from the heavens.   As the representative of Christ's charity he made repeated distributions of clothes and food to the poor, turning this 'Catholic relief' into a highly organized affair, as only he knew how, with a complex administration, regulations, and registers, but all applied so generously that an eye-witness could write that in his time 'the Church was like a great open granary.'   Force of circumstances made him into a political leader, at this time when the disintegration of all authority in Italy was abandoning the country to anarchy: he faced the Lombards, and negotiated with them, over the feeble head of the exarch, and he argued with the emperor, finding his diplomatic labours so all absorbing that he declared, with weary irony: 'In this epoch I wonder if to be pope is to be a spiritual leader or a temporal king!' And yet pope he was, with the fullest understanding of his mission, claiming for the Apostolic See the right of intervention anywhere in Christendom, corresponding with the bishops of Gaul and Spain (where St Leander was his friend), nominating pontifical representatives at Arles and Carthage, regaining control over upper Italy, over the schismatics of Aquileia, making the whole world listen to the voice which, for more than a century now, men had become used to finding so feeble.   And he made it heard not only in the West, but in the East too, where he indignantly tried to prevent the Bishop of Constantinople from assuming the title of 'oecumenical patriarch.'   His predecessors had known how to defend this primacy, which St Leo had already made manifest so energetically.   It is to St Gregory's merit that, while remaining humble to the point of refusing the title of *universal bishop*, he gave the primacy back to the world as a living reality, making it an integral part of his contemporaries' lives.

The historical consequences of this pontificate were enormous. They can be summed up under two headings.   Firstly, *now that imperial Rome was dead, the Rome of the popes was going to take her place*.   The senate, an archaic, fossilized institution, met for the last time in the year 603.   The Byzantine officials, who were more and more discredited, ceased to exercise any real influence.   The successor of St Peter, in practice independent within the duchy of Rome, made himself the heir to the imperial authority, and the temporal territory of the Pope was about to become a historical fact, not because of any political ambition on his part, but in order to guarantee the full spiritual liberty of the pontiff.   All this was the work of the man whose epitaph aptly calls him 'God's Consul.'

And the other great result of the work of Gregory was this: in assessing the weakness of the Byzantine Empire realistically, and realizing that the future of the West was in the hands of the Germanic masses, he understood also that the work of their evangelization could not be achieved without the control of the Papacy.  Instead of being achieved locally, as had been the case until this time, according to the initiative of individual bishops or monks, *the conversion of the Barbarians was henceforth to be the work of the whole Church*, in other words, it was to result, not in several more or less divergent Christian communities (which was the danger of the existing method), but in an international organization and in one common culture—the Christian Western European culture.  As we have seen, St Leo the Great had been the Pope who resisted the Barbarians in the fifth century, the man who had tried to save what could be saved; in the sixth St Gregory the Great was the Pope of the decisive reconquest: civilized Europe owes a very great deal to both these men.

## The First Pontifical Missions:
### the Conversion of England

The Barbarians against whom St Gregory directed his first efforts at conversion were, naturally enough, the Lombards, his terrible neighbours.  It is wonderful to see how this man of God, who lived under constant threat from these savage and hardened warriors, refused to despair of their souls, never uttered a single word of hatred against them, and declined to join in an enterprise which entailed the systematic destruction of their settlements.  However, there were some painful moments, e.g. in the summer of 592, when Duke Ariulf marched on Rome, 'slaughtering and executing,' and when the Exarch of Ravenna failed to give any help.  The Pope had perforce to set himself up as a diplomat, and negotiate the withdrawal of the aggressors—in a scene which his biographers compare with that in which St Leo halted Attila—an action which, however, made the Byzantines accuse him of treason!  No matter.  Gregory saw these enemies of civilization simply as souls to be won for Christ, and, difficult though the task might be, he applied himself to it diligently.

It was then that he found an ally in *Theodelinda*, a Bavarian Catholic princess, who became so popular among the Lombards on account of her goodness, that, according to the chronicler Paul the Deacon, when her first husband died (590) she was invited by the people to choose a new spouse who should then become king: this was Agilulf, Duke of Turin.  This reign was certainly not to be so decisive in securing the conversion of the Lombards as that of Clovis and Clotilda had been for the Franks: nevertheless the first stakes were firmly planted.  The royal children were baptized as Catholics; the queen had several

Catholic churches built, notably the one at Monza, which preserves her memory; she kept up a regular correspondence with Gregory and received from him ampullae filled with an oil used to light the lamps at the martyrs' tombs; thanks to her, St Columbanus was later able to found his last monastery in Italy.   Probably St Gregory wanted to do in Italy what had already been done in Gaul, namely, to promote a Lombardo-Catholic kingdom.   He died before this project was realized, but he had at least done enough to ensure its practical fulfil-ment in the future.   After his death (in 604) the crown of Pavia passed to Arian and Catholic princes in turn.   But the seventh century, the golden age of the Lombards, when their monarchy set itself in order and subjugated the dukes, was also the century of their conver-sion.   First of all in 653, under Aripert, the nephew of Theodelinda, and then, conclusively, under Bertarid (671–88), the Lombard people returned to the bosom of the Church, and Italy was soon covered with basilicas and monasteries; Cunibert (688–700), the patron of literature and the arts, modified the structure of his state in order to weld occupiers and occupied into one single people; in the eighth century the policy of St Gregory was to be applied exactly in the reign which marked the zenith of Lombard power, that of Liutprand (712–44). The corn sown by the great Pope and by Theodelinda was to grow full tall.

Whether they were near at hand or far away all the Barbarians were the object of papal attention.   Thus, with regard to the Franks, torn asunder by the frightful quarrels of Fredegund and Brunhilda, St Gregory maintained an active correspondence with Childebert II, Brunhilda's son, encouraging him to push the work of Christian pene-tration farther—and his influence was certainly one cause of the some-what naïve effort to revive Roman culture in Austrasia.   In Spain, where the conversion of Recared (589) had occurred just before his accession, St Gregory demonstrated clearly his intention to make the presence of the Holy See known there; his friend, St Leander of Seville, helped him to do this; legates, letters, and presents were sent; the Pope multiplied his good offices to ease the situation between the Visigoths and the Byzantines established on the Spanish coast; and the juridical work accomplished under Recared in preparation for racial unification showed that the profound influence of the Church was indeed begin-ning to make itself strongly felt.

But the great missionary endeavour with which St Gregory's name was to be linked, the one which best demonstrates his intentions and his genius, was that of the *Conversion of England*; in the history of Christianity its influence was to be very considerable.   'The Rome of St Peter,' writes Ernest Lavisse, 'began her conquests where the Rome of Augustus had left off: with Britain and Germany.'   The origin of it all lies in a charming episode which gives a touch of delicacy and poetry to our picture of the great Pope.   While he was still a monk on the Coelian Hill, Gregory wandered through one of the Roman markets where the traders exhibited the slaves they wished to sell.   Among the human merchandise there, for the most part Eastern in origin, swarthy and puny in appearance, he noticed three handsome boys, flaxen-haired, blue-eyed, and with fair pink-and-white complexions, three perfect specimens of young English manhood.   'Where do they come from?' the monk asked the dealer.—'From Britain.'—'Are they Christian or pagan?'—'Pagan.'—'What a pity that these figures of light should be in the power of the prince of darkness!   And what is their race?'—'They are Angles.'—'Angles?   Not Angles, surely, but Angels! [Latin, *Angli, Angeli*].   And heirs to the kingdom of Heaven, like the angels!   Where exactly do you say they come from?'— 'From Deira.'—'Ah yes, for they shall be called from the wrath of Hell (*de ira*) by the mercy of Christ.   And who is their king?'— 'Aella.'—'Better and better: so they shall sing Alleluia. . . .'   True or false, this anecdote, which is told to us by the saint's biographer, John the Deacon, announces a great intention, even in its prophetic puns. Having welcomed the three Angles among his monks on the Coelian Hill, Gregory decided that the brethren of his protégés should be given to the angels also.   And no sooner had he been chosen pope than he threw himself into this task.

What was the situation like in the large island that we now call Britain, towards the end of the sixth century?   The Germanic invaders, who had arrived by sea during the fifth century—Jutes, Angles, and Saxons—had formed themselves into small racial islets throughout the eastern half of the country, tiny realms whose history is extremely complex.   After some fifty to one hundred years these groupings had been reduced to seven in number: from north to south, Bernicia and Deira (these two later formed Northumbria), Mercia, East Anglia, Essex, Wessex, and Sussex, the *Heptarchy*.   They governed themselves according to ancient Germanic customs: the grouping of families was the basis of society (from this some authorities have traced the origin of the *hundred*), the monarch exercised control with the help of counsellors (from which the Witenagemot of later times presumably derived).   At first their occupation had been savage, and the Celtic Church had been the object of their campaign of extermination which the chronicle of St Gildas brings to life with such frightful vividness.   However, it survived, although in a precarious fashion, but retaining its bishops, its priests, and its monks, and always ready to be revived.   Gradually the persecution slackened, and amongst a few noblemen and Barbarian kings we even find traces of curiosity about Christianity.   But in order to win the Germanic occupiers over to

Christ, it was clearly no use counting on the vanquished inhabitants of the country, their hearts so full of bitterness against their conquerors, not even on those Celts who had sought refuge in Cornwall, Wales, or Armorica.    The most devout Celtic missionary revolted at the idea of going to convert the Angles.

Consequently it was necessary to send to 'England,' the country of the Angles, missionaries who had no connection whatsoever with the Christians already in the country, and, so that they should not be lost amid a foreign and perhaps hostile people, to send not merely a few isolated missionaries, but important groups, who would form a community on the spot, and who would show the pagans the splendour of Christian spirituality.    St Gregory had these groups of men there beside him, already organized and ready to bear witness to the purest in Christianity: the monks; so it was monks that he sent to England.

In 596 *Augustine*, prior of the Coelian monastery, received the Pope's order to leave for mysterious England with a strong contingent of brethren.    He left.    Not without the gravest misgivings, however. Having heard tell that the Angles ate their enemies' hearts, that they spoke an unintelligible language, and that their country was actually nothing but the abode of the dead, whence the corpses from Armorica departed on funeral barges to suffer all the pains of hell, the missionaries felt their loins melt at the command, and it needed nothing less than the formal orders and the holy encouragements of the Pope himself to persuade them to quit Provence and to set sail for the baleful mists of the Anglian land.

In fact things went infinitely better than anyone could have hoped. This may well have been thanks to a woman, *Bertha*, the Parisian princess, who, beside her husband Ethelbert, possibly played the part of a second Clotilda.    The meeting of the saint and the king was a wonderful one; sitting under a tree, surrounded by his warriors, Ethelbert watched the forty Roman monks coming towards him in slow procession, bearing a great silver cross and the figure of Christ painted on wood, singing Gregorian hymns.    Referring to this scene Bossuet wrote: 'The history of the Church contains nothing finer.' The frank discussion which then took place, Augustine's evocation of the God made man to save men, and the discreet influence of the saintly Queen Bertha—this was all that was needed.    Augustine was permitted to preach his religion and to establish himself not far from the royal palace, and the sons of the sea-rovers, the cold-eyed Angles and Jutes, who were much given to contemplation and mystery, were fascinated by the new faith, and soon began to surrender themselves to it.    On 1st June 597, at Whitsuntide, Ethelbert was baptized, and a great number of his warriors with him.

It seemed as if the entire island was now opened up to the Church.

Augustine, his head full of immense schemes, already visualized the conversion of the whole Heptarchy.   In November 597, with the approval of the Holy Father, he went to Gaul and was there conse- crated archbishop of the English Church at Arles, by the 'bishops of the Germanies.'   On Christmas Day he baptized ten thousand English altogether: it needed nothing less than a river to hold them all. Filled with enthusiasm, Ethelbert is said to have presented the new archbishop with his own palace, at *Canterbury*, and thereby was founded the oldest episcopal seat in England.   Monasteries began springing up in large numbers, of course.   And although only a small part of the Heptarchy was so far Christian, the great Pope, overjoyed with the results of the mission, on conferring the pallium, the insignia of an archbishop, on Augustine, announced his intention of marking out in advance the future ecclesiastical boundaries of the country, dividing it between two metropolitan sees, London and York, each controlling twelve bishops!

Geniuses are judged by the dimensions of their concepts.   St Gregory foresaw nothing less than an England entirely Christian. He was a born administrator and a subtle psychologist, and, from the sick-bed that he was scarcely ever to leave again, he sent Augustine instructions on the means that must be adopted in order to secure his goal, a method so intelligent, so resolute, and so reasonable that it reads indeed as the *résumé* of the Church's tactics in the matter of con- version.   'Do not destroy the pagan temples, but instead sprinkle them with holy water, set up altars in them, and place relics there.   In the places where it has been the pagan custom to offer sacrifices to their diabolical idols allow them to celebrate Christian festivals instead, in another form, on the same date.   For example, on the festival of the blessed Martyrs, have the faithful make bowers of branches, and organize love feasts there.   In permitting the converted these external pleasures, the joys of the soul will be more easily acquired.   We can- not wipe the whole past from these savage souls all at once.   A man does not climb a mountain in great bounds, but by taking slow, steady steps!'   This wise way of going about things was the one of which the Church was to make use everywhere—we are soon to see it being applied with outstanding success by the English monks in Germany. Such is the reason that lies behind this substitution, discernible in so many places, and which touches so many of our secret loyalties, of Christian customs, and Christian festivals, for the age-old feasts and customs of the pagan past.

And yet, despite these magnificent appearances, Christianity was to suffer many long and severe ordeals before establishing itself con- clusively in England.   The work to which St Gregory had given the first stimulus was far from complete when he died, on 12th March 604, his body being borne into the basilica of St Peter; before this, St Augustine, who was very soon to follow him to the grave, had been able to give him some account of the difficulties which his work was likely to encounter in the future. These fell into two categories. Within the Anglo-Saxon Heptarchy rivalries were constant and wars endemic; let one king from the seven kingdoms become Christian, and the odds were that his neighbour would immediately declare himself more ardently pagan than ever. Secondly, how could these two kinds of Christianity—the Celtic and the Anglo-Saxon—live side by side without Rome urging them to a brotherly reconciliation? But the ingrained bitterness of the Celts stood in the way of this. When St Augustine exhorted him to show charity towards the Angles the abbot of Bangor replied: 'We will never, never preach the faith to this cruel race of foreigners who have so treacherously robbed us of our native soil!' Moreover the usages and customs of the Celtic Church were so particularist, even in the minutest details, that a united Christianity, covering the whole island, seemed an impossibility.

Consequently, the battle for the faith was to last for almost one hundred years. It was to be a curious jumble of successive darkness and light, of set-backs and successes, of saintly and violent figures. A number of realms were opened up to Christ: there was Essex, where London became the metropolitan see, with St Mellitus as its first bishop, and where the abbey of *Westminster* was founded in 610; and Northumbria, where the monk Paulinus of York was the hero of the splendid anecdote in which King Edwin, persuaded by Ethelburga, his wife, and a wise pagan who had been violently attracted by Christianity, consented to baptism. In 627 the first cathedral was consecrated at York. It was a little wooden church dedicated to St Peter. Eight years later, St Aidan, the first Celt who realized where his real path of duty lay—he was monk-bishop of Lindisfarne—undertook the reconversion of Northumbria, and there King Oswiu proved himself a true champion of Christ. But against these happy results what tragic dramas there were too! It was only necessary for a ruler hostile to Christianity to ascend a Christian throne for the pagan persecution of the faith to begin all over again. This was to occur at least twice in a most formidable way; Essex was to revert to paganism for a period of thirty years. In the wars between the rival Germanic kings it seemed that the fate of Christianity was at stake: Edwin of Northumbria waged a veritable holy war against the pagans, and he fell in battle against them in 632, like a Crusader. The Britons, taking advantage of the divisions in the Heptarchy, intervened and hurled themselves on Northumbria in a most bloody onslaught. Baptized Celtic Christians though they were, they behaved more savagely than their heathen allies. Amid all this confusion certain saintly figures stand out clearly: such as St Aidan, the Celtic monk who dared to go beyond the racial antagonism and dedicate himself generously and whole-heartedly, in agreement with King Oswald, to the rebuilding of the Anglian Church which had been destroyed by the tragedy of 632. There is the picturesque St Wilfrid, the epitome of the stubborn Englishman, coldly passionate, indomitable, the man who made his bishopric at York a real bastion of a truly English Christianity, and who, with his friend, St Benedict Biscop, founded Benedictine monasteries throughout the north of the island. There is the cowherd-saint, Caedmon, who, while tending his herds, was inspired by the Holy Spirit to compose hymns of such beauty that all England was to sing them; and that other shepherd, St Cuthbert, who knew so well how to understand the things that we cannot see, and who was to make famous the foundations of Melrose, Ripon, and Durham.

By the end of the seventh century, after so many jolts and set-backs, the situation of the Church in England was stabilized. The Papacy, which continued to keep a close watch on the evolution of these communities which had been so dear to the heart of Gregory, had just sent (668) a new contingent of missionaries there, under the leadership of St Theodore, an Easterner, born at Tarsus, whose advanced age did not in any way hinder his apostolic zeal. Certain turbulent spirits were restrained, notably St Wilfrid. The relations between Britons and Angles eventually became easier, and the Celtic Church agreed to submit to Rome, even in those of her customs which were peculiar and dear to her (663). Ecclesiastical England received her organization. Monasteries developed there on a vast scale, notably at Croyland, on the borders of Mercia and East Anglia, at Whitby, Ely, and Wimborne, and at Wearmouth, on the coast to the south of Lindisfarne, which was founded by St Benedict Biscop. And it was there, within the confines of this last-named abbey, that the first great witness of Christian culture was to live his life of work and scholarship—the *Venerable Bede*.

Thus the work which St Gregory had undertaken was in the end successful. It was to have an enormous historical importance. Latin penetrated into England alongside Christianity, together with elements of Roman law, and the episcopal and monastic schools—in other words, Christianity brought civilization to the country. Christopher Dawson is not exaggerating when he writes that the appearance of a new Anglo-Saxon culture was perhaps the most important event that occurred between the epochs of Justinian and Charlemagne: these Anglo-Saxon monasteries were indeed in large measure reservoirs from which the values of the spirit and the mind would later spread to the continent of Europe. Thus, in winning over a people radically alien to the whole Latin system, Roman Catholicism spread its authority beyond the ancient boundaries of Europe. In these new countries it exercised an authority which owed nothing to that of the emperor, the Pope appearing as the veritable suzerain. Freed from entanglements with the temporal powers, a foundation of the Papacy itself, the English Church was to lead an existence far freer than that of the Churches on the Continent. She was to remain passionately devoted to the see of St Peter—right up to the dark days of the Reformation—and it was the pontifical principles of Gregory which she was to put into practice again when she sent the most outstanding of her sons to bear the Good News to his brethren in Germany.

### St Boniface, the Father of German Christianity

However, the rapid success of the Papacy's initiative in England must not encourage the reader to conclude that from the seventh century onwards—the century of St Gregory the Great—it alone had supreme control over all the missions. Other apostolates were being carried on too, stemming from other streams, such as those of the Celts and St Columbanus, and yet others, depending on the initiative of solitary individuals. But, as it happened, at the beginning of the eighth century the experience of the evangelization efforts in Germany was to prove that, in order to be lasting, a work of such size must rest on more solid foundations, and that only the Papacy could offer these.

The opaque Germanic world had already been lightly touched by the Gospel light, for at least one hundred and fifty years now. Without going back quite as far as the days when the Burgundians, then still living in the area around Worms, were Catholics, we know that certain bold missionaries had already scattered the first seeds of Christianity in these lands—St Severinus on the upper Danube, and, much later on, St Columbanus along the length of the Rhine. Bishoprics existed at Basle, Strasbourg, Constance, Mainz, Cologne, and Maastricht. But, to tell the truth, paganism still remained extremely vigorous there; the 'sacred groves' were still venerated, and one day St Columbanus fell upon an assembled mob in which pagans and baptized Christians together were sacrificing to Wotan. Yet, despite all the difficulties, Christ's spokesmen never stopped making their way to these perilous regions, where their patience and their courage were so severely tested.

Thus, from Bregenz, where his master St Columbanus had left him, and later at Steinach, where he eventually settled (and which was to bear his name), St Gall continued the battle against the Alaman idols (c. 615–20). Another monk, St Fridolin, who may have been an Irishman, founded the abbey of Säckingen and influenced the whole of Baden. One of the strangest missionaries of this type, who also lived in the seventh century, was a monk from Aquitaine, St Amandus (c. 589–676). He was more of a pioneer than an actual builder!

Brimming over with all the enthusiasm of his native race, but, above all, on fire with the love of God, he had grown to spiritual maturity firstly in a monastery on the island of Yeu, then in a recluse's cell, and finally, before the tomb of St Martin of Tours, where he had made a vow to devote himself entirely to the 'peregrination for Christ.'     He kept his word.     As a bishop without any fixed see he wandered from country to country, just as the Irish monks did: in Belgium, where the abbey of St Bavo, at Ghent, owes its foundation to him; on the banks of the Danube; among the Slavs in Carinthia (with a small evangelizing raid on the Basques in between); then, among the pagan Franks for a second time, in the flat country around the Scheldt and the Meuse; next, on to Strasbourg, and after this he actually fixed his bishopric at Maastricht for a little while.     Not for very long, however!     Soon he rushed to Anvers to effect conversions there, returning to Beauvais to chop down a sacred oak—'a champion runner, racing for the love of God,' as he has most aptly been called.[1]     Belgium recognizes him as her principal evangelizer.     Much earlier, at the end of the fifth century, St Firminus had worked in Alsace; in Bavaria, where many elements in the population were Catholic from the sixth century onwards (e.g. the Bavarian Theodelinda, the Queen of the Lombards), new missionary efforts were fairly successful, notably that of St Rupert, the apostle of Salzburg, although in Thuringia similar efforts only obtained mediocre results: the Irish monk, St Kilian, was to be martyred there.

All these attempts are undeniably heroic, but they give an impression of disorder, and of a serious lack of co-ordination.     The method of St Columbanus and his followers was always like this, as vigorous as it was haphazard.     St Amandus, however, had shown the Pope great deference and had begged his advice: yet none of these evangelizing efforts was related to the infinitely sounder and deeper intentions which St Gregory the Great had made the basis of the missionary policy of the Holy See.     Moreover if Christianity really wanted to penetrate Germany it was necessary to take an essential political reality into account: the Frankish designs on these regions.     It should be remembered that the mere halting of the Germanic thrust westwards, as marked by the victory of Clovis over the Alamans, had given place, under Clovis's successors, to a policy of aggression towards the Germanic peoples.     Started by his sons, then momentarily interrupted (e.g. during the Lombard attacks), taken up again by Dagobert, continued in the time of the *rois fainéants* by the mayors of the palace and the first Carolingians—it can safely be said that the policy of penetrating Germany, to which Charlemagne was to give an incomparable lustre, was the great ambition of the Frankish leaders for over

---

[1] Canon Du Mesnil in his book on *Les Missions*, Paris, 1948.     See also E. de Moreau: *Saint Amand, le principal évangélisateur de la Belgique*, Brussels, 1942.

three hundred years.  Could the Church ignore it?  This policy placed her in a most awkward position.  On the one hand the Franks maintained Catholic missionaries whenever they occupied a Germanic territory; but, on the other, if Roman Christianity appeared to be linked to Frankish arms, it would convert only the opportunists, and would be detested by the masses (St Amandus had been sorely tried by this problem).[1]  Consequently it was necessary to send missionaries to Germany who, though on good terms with the Franks, were not of their race; and from this fact stems the importance of the Anglo-Saxon missions.  It is beyond all doubt that this high intelligent policy bears the impress of papal influence.

The first Anglo-Saxons who rushed to the Continent met with only a qualified success.  It is true that they chose, because it lay exactly opposite the English coast, quite the most difficult area in the whole Germanic world: Friesland, the northern extremity of our modern Netherlands, beyond the Zuider Zee, where paganism was particularly savage and virulent.  Having shaken off Frankish suzerainty after the death of Dagobert, the Frisians rebuffed the conversion attempts of the two Franks, St Amandus and St Eligius, and they gave scarcely any better welcome to the first English who came, the great St Wilfrid of York first of all, and then the monk St Wigbert.  Then the courageous patience of *St Willibrord*, a Northumbrian monk, the founder of Echternach in Luxemburg, succeeded, thanks to a peace between the Franks and the Frisians, in establishing various nuclei of Christians in this difficult country, in reviving the bishopric of Utrecht, and in maintaining his spiritual authority for more than twenty years (*c.* 690–714)—so much so that he was even able to attempt a mission among the Danes in which he all but perished.  But it only needed the death of Pepin, in 714, and the Franks to be swept from the Low Countries, for a Frisian king to destroy the young Christianity, to burn the churches and set up the idols again.  This was a striking example of the difficulties which Christianity was to encounter in these still barbarous areas; but, far from being discouraged, the missionaries of Christ redoubled their efforts, spurred on by the example of a most extraordinary man, perhaps the greatest that the eighth century produced, *St Boniface*.

It is impossible to talk unsympathetically of this shining personality, of this profoundly human soul, whose brilliance the centuries have not tarnished, and whose irresistible attraction we still seem to feel, reaching out to us across the lines of the *Acta Sanctorum*—an

---

[1] Historians have gone so far as to say that the missionaries of this period were primarily 'royal messengers' and 'delegates of the State,' who 'did not so much preach as officially organize.'   From the scantiness of the churches built by them it has been deduced—all too swiftly—that they cared little for the masses.   This tendentious view is authoritatively refuted by Father de Moreau in his *Histoire de l'Église Belgique*, vol. i, p. 111.

attraction combining simplicity and nobility of character, gentleness
and steadfastness of nature, the same attraction which, during his lifetime, gathered such a cluster of youthful vocations around him.    Perhaps there is no other saint who touches us more closely through those
aspects of his character in which sanctity and human weaknesses
mingle, as through those in which the miseries which are our own are
dissipated in the love of Christ.   He had a restless, unsteady, complex
nature, dangerously wracked by the black humours of despair, and he
was extremely self-effacing and timid; although St Boniface accomplished an immense work, it was done almost reluctantly and without
his ever having had the slightest desire to push himself to the forefront
of events.   The superior interests of the Church alone guided him, but
when they were in play this timid man was carried away by his enthusiasm, and his boldness knew no bounds; he hewed down the
sacred oaks, hunted the heretics, had unworthy bishops deposed, and
went so far as to make observations to the Pope.   A magnificent type
of missionary, both prudent and enterprising, an organizer as well as
an apostle, he was not just a great pioneer like St Columbanus or St
Amandus: he was a creator, a man who founded a Church and whose
work was to be lasting.   Above all, he was a wonderfully priestly
man, penetrated to the core by the living water of the Church, unreservedly faithful to the Holy See, and a man in whom Christ's
charity was so great that it could overcome all his scruples and make him
able to find a brother in the most ferocious of the Barbarians, as well as
in the most fallen of the Christians.

The man whom history venerates as Boniface was baptized *Winfrid*;
he was an Englishman from Wessex, born about 680 in the village of
Crediton, and, like so many young folk of his time, he had been drawn
very early to the monastic way of life.   From the age of seven he was
a small Benedictine 'oblate' at Exeter Abbey, becoming well known for
his gifts of spirit and intellect.   Later, in the monastery at Nutshulling,
near Winchester, he turned from a brilliant pupil into an outstanding
teacher and head of a school.   At the age of thirty he seemed destined
to a fruitful scholastic career, of the kind pursued by his contemporary,
the great Bede, when the call of God echoed in his heart, the voice that
claimed him too for the 'peregrination for Christ.'   When a first
missionary attempt in Friesland only produced poor results he was not
a whit discouraged.   He knew that it was at Rome that the light of
Christ burned, so it was to Rome that he must journey to ask his orders
of him who, it was said, held the keys of the Father's house in his hands.
During the winter of 718–19 Boniface lived in the city of St Peter; all
his action was to stem from this stay.

The Pope of the day was *Gregory II* (715–32).   He was an outstanding man, highly cultured, extremely well aware of the problems

of the epoch and acutely conscious of the needs of his time; it was not for nothing that, on his accession, he had chosen to rule in the name of the great seventh-century Pope.[1]    In the period between the two Gregorys, the popes, though not exactly disinterested in the missionary effort in the West, did, at all events (perhaps because several of them were Graeco-Syrians), allow themselves to be excessively absorbed by the anxieties which the crises in the East caused them, for trouble had broken out there once again, and was now to be virtually continuous.[2] Gregory II was a great enough man to be able to throw himself whole-heartedly into the task of standing up to Leo III, the Iconoclast emperor, while at the same time being actively engaged in the conversion of the Germans.    The meeting between Winfrid and the Pope was a decisive one.    The marvellous brilliance emanating from the English saint impressed the pontiff so forcibly that he straightway gave him a confidence which he never withdrew until the day of his death. The privilege of being the pontifical missionary to Germany, for which Winfrid was asking, was granted him with a kindness in which we can detect a flash of inspiration.    'You shall not be called Winfrid any more, but Boniface, meaning, he who performs good works!'    When he set out again for those mysterious lands where the heathen souls were waiting for him, Boniface was the Pope's representative, a wandering bishop, without any fixed see, just as Augustine had at first been in England, a kind of direct spokesman for St Peter.    All his life the great missionary remained loyal to the oath of allegiance sworn on the tomb of the apostle, asking the Pope for orders and directions on every conceivable occasion, and exchanging letters with him which we still read to-day, as splendid in content as those written by the first Gregory to St Augustine.    And when Gregory III (732–41) succeeded Gregory II, the new Pope's first act was to send Boniface the arch-bishop's pallium, whilst the missionary's first thought was to beg papal guidance on the creation of some new German bishops.

Added to this profoundly Roman character which St Boniface brought to all his undertakings and which allowed him both to organize the areas he pioneered and to remedy the abuses which he saw in the Church of his day, there was something more—something which, as we have already seen, was absolutely indispensable if this operation was to be successful.    Sure enough, St Boniface assessed perfectly the importance of the support of Frankish arms to his apostolate.    'Without the patronage of the Frankish ruler,' he wrote to his friend, Bishop Daniel of Winchester, 'I could neither govern the faithful nor defend

---

[1] Ever since the election of John II, in 532, the popes had adopted the custom of changing their name at their accession, the choice of name being clearly related to a precise intention with regard to the manner in which they meant to exercise their pontificate.
[2] See Chapter VI.

the priests; without the order which he maintains and the fear he inspires I could not even prevent pagan practices and German idolatry.' Consequently, right from the beginning of his missionary career, Boniface maintained constant, close relations with Charles Martel, then, later on, with Pepin and Carloman, establishing a real kind of collaboration between them and him, careful nevertheless not to let himself be caught up in the toils of political intrigue and the affairs of the court, whose morals, moreover, deeply scandalized him.

Boniface returned to Germany in the spring of 719 and began by spending four years putting the Church in the Low Countries into some semblance of order again.    Then he went straight to the principal redoubt of German paganism, Hesse and Thuringia, where idolatry was still extremely vigorous.    His resolute gentleness succeeded where the somewhat wild enthusiasm of the first missionaries had failed. 'To let the heathens set out the principles of their religion, to make them understand, quite dispassionately, the contradictions in it, and finally to present them with Christianity in all its great aspects, persuading them of their errors without exaggerating them'—such was the method which he employed, as he himself expounded it in a letter to his friend Daniel.    Always on the road, escorted by monks as devoted to Christ's service as he was, first of all by Englishmen like Lullus, Denehard, and Burchard, but soon by Germans too, suffering such extreme poverty that he had often not the means with which to buy his clothes, accepting every constant risk joyfully, living like this year after year—for thirty years at least—all the time he continued preaching the Good News.    At the same time as he made his way forward, he worked to stabilize his conquests, above all, by founding great monasteries which were to be like citadels of the Gospel: in this way Fritzlar sprang up, and Hildesheim and Kitzingen, and *Fulda*, the most famous one of them all, the German Monte Cassino, for which he obtained the *exemption*, i.e. the direct link with the Holy See, in order to preserve it from the encroachments of the secular power.    Throughout the Middle Ages Fulda was to fulfil the role of a spiritual bastion in Europe.

One of the most moving characteristics of this apostolate is the bond which St Boniface wanted to maintain with his English motherland. Nostalgia for his beloved island remained strong in his heart all his life; he always felt, very sincerely, that in leaving her for ever he had made a real sacrifice to God.    He carried on a constant correspondence with the Bishop of Winchester, and with Edburga, an abbess with an intellect equal to that of any of her male counterparts, and in his letters he told his friends all his doubts and fears; he relied on their prayers, whilst from them he received material and moral support.    Even better, into this Germany, yet barely snatched from the shadows of idolatry, he conceived the idea of bringing English nuns, in order that their example might influence this new land and their supplications to Heaven sustain his work. And the picture of this man of action is given a fine touch of gentleness and delicacy by the addition of the pure and exalted spiritual friendship which linked him to one of these nuns, his kinswoman, *St Lioba*, whom he made abbess of Bischoffsheim.[1]

By 753 Boniface was Archbishop of Mainz (since 747) and, firmly established in this town, he devoted himself, in complete harmony with the Holy See, to organizing the areas which he had permanently conquered for Christ; they now stretched from Hesse and Thuringia to Franconia and Bavaria. His glory was at its height. The sacred tree of Wotan, which had been felled by his own hand at Geismar, was never again to spring forth in the Germanic forests. Four popes had succeeded one another on the throne of St Peter, and to the last two, Zacharias and Stephen II, as to the first two, Boniface repeated: 'I am the disciple of the Roman Church; I have always lived in the service of the Apostolic See,' and all had demonstrated their friendship for him. But for a true creator, what really mattered was not what had been done; it was what there remained still to do. Down there, among the flats where the Rhine flowed slowly out to the sea, there were still so many pagans who were awaiting the Gospel light! The Church was still so frail in Friesland! Boniface was now nearly eighty years old, but the blessed 'folly of the cross' was still as strong in his heart as in the days of his youth. He set off once more, with fifty monks, down the Rhine, baptizing large numbers of heathens. In the region around the Zuider Zee he stopped in order to confirm some of his new flocks, when a band of ruffians fell on him in a murderous assault: one after another the missionaries fell. It was 5th June 754. And at Fulda we can still see the book of devotions which the saint was reading when he was attacked. He instinctively shielded his head with it when he was struck down, and the gashes made by his murderers' sacrilegious swords are still clearly visible.

But, with his blood, Boniface had bought the conversion of the Germanic lands. Through him Germany was finally opened up to Christ. And not to Christ alone, but to civilization also; for each of his foundations was to be the nucleus of a town, each of his monasteries one of the crucibles where, as happened in England, the development of an autonomous culture, of a new genius, was to be

[1] In his article 'Boniface,' in the *Dictionnaire d'histoire ecclésiastique* (vol. ix), Father de Morceau has developed the *modernity* of the missionary methods of St Boniface.
  He allotted a large part of the work of his apostolate to women; it was he who created the first missionary nuns. It was but a short-lived success however. We have to wait until the seventeenth century before another appeal is made for women in the missions. (On the missions of St Boniface see also F. Flaskamp, *Die Missionsmethode des heil. Bonifatius*, Hildesheim, 1929.)

prepared. Henceforth Christian Germany took shape; and soon Carolingian Europe was to be born. And fifty years later the work of St Boniface was to be completed by the arms of the son of the Pepin whom he had anointed king in 751: Charlemagne.

## RESULTS AND PROBLEMS

Two hundred years elapsed between the baptism of Clovis and the death of St Boniface. Within this space of time—so brief in the eyes of history—enormous results were accomplished. To assess these exactly, we need only compare the state of the West at the end of the fifth century with the situation in the middle of the eighth. About 490 there was simply a mosaic of Barbarian kingdoms, mostly Arian in faith; a Church drawn in on herself, clearly certain of victory one day, but at present the target of persecution from several quarters; and, within the very boundaries of what still passed for the Empire, a hotch-potch of barbarisms, paganisms, and frightful lusts. About 750 Western Europe was completely converted to Catholicism; two mighty forces were in process of escaping from the chaos of yesterday, the one spiritual—the Church, respected everywhere—the other temporal—the Frankish power; Barbarism was henceforth kept at a distance by the conversion of the British Isles and Middle Germany. All this, it must be stressed, had been essentially the work of the Church, the result of her patient, undespairing, and often heroic efforts.

Two other results had been achieved also, even more profound though less obvious at first sight, results which were to have a decisive effect on the future of the West. The first was the fusion of the ethnic elements, which was conspicuous in Gaul and Spain, and which was to take place throughout Rome's former territories, as soon as the religious obstacle had been overcome. From this fusion emerged a population which was healthier and more vigorous than that of the age of imperial decadence, more rural than urban in character, in short, the population which was to be that of the medieval world. And the other was the coming into being (albeit still confused but full of promise) of new forms of culture—slips grafted while still young on to the old Roman trunk, or seedlings ready for grafting which were to form the foundations of the culture of the Middle Ages.

For the Church these results were of prime importance. They compensated her for the terrible amputations which she was now suffering and from which she might not have recovered without these new extensions to her authority. For, at this very moment, some grave events were taking place around the shores of the Mediterranean. While St Gregory the Great was sitting on the throne of St Peter, a young, twenty-five-year-old Arabian caravaneer was dreaming of re-forming the religious life of his people, in order to call it to a great destiny: his name was *Mohammed*, and, twenty years later, his dream was to become a reality.    Just when the monasteries were springing up all over the Christian West, when the Lombards were being converted, Syria, Persia, and Egypt were falling into the hands of Islam.    And while Gregory II was sending St Boniface to sow the seeds of Christi-anity in the forests of Germany, Christian North Africa and Christian Spain were crumbling beneath the blows of the champions of Allah.

We can see the hand of Providence at work in this simultaneous replacement.    On a strictly historical plane, the consequences were to be immense.    Western Christianity, Catholicism, would not have evolved in the way it did, if, instead of, as it were, finding its axis in what had formerly been the Barbarian world, it had rested on a Medi-terranean world that remained entirely faithful to it.    In a way, there-fore, the Church was led to opt for the West, to face up against the East, to recognize 'the light of a new star,' as St Avitus had known how to do so well.    And since, at the same time, Byzantium, borne along by her fates, was both giving way territorially in the West and drifting slowly apart from the Roman Church, the leaders of Christianity, in the silence of the cloisters and the secret of their episcopal meditations, were slowly to bring to fruition the great idea which was to become dominant by the end of the eighth century and from which sprang the first renaissance of civilization since the onset of the Dark Ages—the idea of rebuilding the Empire in favour of a German, as was proposed by Alcuin, abbot of the monastery of St Martin, at Tours, in 799.

But although these considerable results had been achieved, it was still true that at the time when the great Carolingian adventure began several problems confronted the Christian West, some of which were extremely difficult of solution.    They were essentially material ones. The Arabian tide had flowed irresistibly forward throughout the seventh century.    Was it going to submerge all Europe?    And was the civilization of the Gospels to give place to that of the Koran? Were these attacks from the south the only ones to be feared?    Were there not other Germanic peoples still teeming in the misty lands to the east, longing hungrily and greedily for the fine, sunny lands of the west?    And which of the former Barbarians—those who had now been baptized—was to take the lead in the reconstruction of Europe; in other words, on which of them was the Church, the possessor of spiritual authority, to let her choice fall: on the Lombards or on the Franks?

Other problems posed themselves in less clear-cut terms, but they were just as serious for all that.    The first can be defined thus: we have already seen how the Barbarians formed blocs living alongside one

I

another but without any common existence: once baptized, were they to continue to live so individualistically that they would bring about their own destruction? Were these Christian nations to form states hostile to one another? The Church, the universal Mother, could not accept this idea, and, faithful to the lessons of St Augustine, she was to do all in her power to maintain unity and brotherhood among the nations: we have seen her working thus among the Britons and the Angles. But it must be confessed that she ran up against an extremely strong current flowing directly counter to her efforts—for the competition of nationalism and Christianity was not born only yesterday! The opening words of the Salic Law declared: 'Long live Christ, who loves the Franks, guards their kingdom, protects their army! . . .'; St Isidore of Seville exalted the patriotism of his people and congratulated the 'flourishing Gothic nation' for having defeated the Byzantines; and in England, the extremely sagacious Bede was equally enthusiastic in his efforts to encourage his fellow countrymen to be proud of being different from other nations. The future divisions of Europe were already there potentially, when her day dawned: it was against these forces, making as they did for division, that the Church was to set her great idea, of which she slowly gained full consciousness, but which was not fully formulated until about the year 1000—the idea of *Christendom*.

A more immediate problem was that of the relationships between Christianity and the temporal powers. The Church had made use of Barbarian might—of that of some of the Barbarians, at all events—in order to bring about the triumph of her cause, but would she be able to retain control of these instruments? The danger here was enormous. It was the same danger, although manifested in a different way, as that threatening faith in the East, under the Byzantine autocracy. Of course, the Barbarian kings were to recognize the spiritual primacy of the Church, and the ceremony of regal anointing, which is found among both Franks and Visigoths, Celts and English, shows the proud Barbarian leaders kneeling before a bishop to receive the unction. But, once crowned, would not these Christian kings intervene in ecclesiastical affairs, under pretext that the Church possessed no better friends than them? It is quite frightening to hear Clovis say, quite calmly, at the first Frankish Council, called in 511, that it had been convened 'by his order,' and although it studied matters relating to the Catholic faith, they were all those which the king had submitted to it! St Isidore of Seville was to secure the passing of a canon at the fourth Council of Toledo declaring that 'he who touches the king, the Lord's anointed, makes an attempt on God Himself.' This is admissible enough if it is taken into account that all authority is derived from God, but one sees all too clearly where this can lead when the prince himself takes advantage of such principles to rule despotically! The dispute on the primacy of powers has begun, in the West as at Byzantium, in a sense which increasingly fails to recognize the Augustinian principles relating to the two orders of the two cities. And this dispute was to be a tragic one.

Finally, there was an even more serious problem confronting what we should really call the dark period of the early Middle Ages, the basic problem of civilization. Although the eighth-century Church contained a considerable number of baptized people, this is not to say that she contained the same number of Christians. It goes without saying that staunch converts did not necessarily result from these collective baptisms in which ten thousand soldiers followed their leader into the waters of forgiveness. The truth is that what happened in the West was not so much a phenomenon of *Germanization*, for, not being very numerous ethnically speaking, the Germans were quickly absorbed by the existing populations (with some striking exceptions: e.g. England), but a phenomenon of *Barbarization*. There was moral Barbarization, which made brutality and superstition into general principles. There was intellectual Barbarization, which showed itself in every field of the mind, in languages, scholastic pursuits, and the arts. But the Church fought this appalling phenomenon most stubbornly, and her efforts to overcome Barbarism on this plane were no less wonderful than those which she employed in the work of conversion.

These were difficult, complex problems, which it was to take history many centuries to solve: the Carolingian dynasty from the middle of the eighth century onwards was gifted with the ability to grasp at these problems, and it was to the glory of the greatest of her members that he tried to find them acceptable solutions—ephemeral though they were destined to be.

# CHAPTER V

# CHRISTIANS OF THE TWILIGHT

## SINKING INTO THE NIGHT OF BARBARISM

THE historical period which begins around the year 400 and which is to last for roughly six hundred years, broken only by a splendid interval of some fifty years, is certainly one of the most painful that Christianity has ever known, even up to modern times. The traditional names for it are all extremely apt: the barbaric period, the black epoch, the dark ages; to it and to it alone is applied the famous phrase 'the night before the Middle Ages.' It was a night pierced by light and crossed by hope, as we shall see, but it was a terrible night for all that, the second half of it being worse than the first. It was a night in which humanity seemed to be groping blindly amid the bloody confusion of to-day and the anguish of the morrow. Only the Church, guided by a transcendant ambition, pursued her course unwaveringly, and in working to her own supernatural ends she became the most effective means of ensuring the salvation of civilization. Considered in the mass, the Christians of the time, who were like us, just ordinary, humble wretches, were very far from giving this impression of shining righteousness; on the contrary, we see them, reeling beneath the blows fate deals them, and sinking ever deeper into the darkness.

Truth to tell, the baptized society, which about 400 was fast approaching the great ordeal, no longer possessed the vigour and the purity of that of the heroic period of the persecutions. Long-standing habit, that evil force making for disintegration, had already considerably eaten away its faith and relaxed its morals. As Christianity penetrated deeper into pagan society it became more and more hard put to it to preserve itself from contamination by that society. The *Indiculus superstitionum et pagianarum*, a Vatican manuscript, states this quite candidly, and the Fathers of the period, who never mince their words, often point an avenging finger at those baptized Christians who live in an entirely pagan fashion. According to St Augustine they held drinking orgies and committed debaucheries under pretext of doing honour to the festival of a martyr; according to St John Chrysostom they left the churches empty on the days of the games in order to rush to watch the bloody spectacles in the arena; and the vehement St Jerome even refers to a number of dandified prelates—

'whom one would take for gallants rather than priests.' Did not St Augustine himself confess that in his reckless youth he had used the mass as a social occasion on which to meet his paramours? And did not St John Chrysostom say that the barrier which separated the men from the women in church was not always high enough? This moral decadence, which eventually brought about the disintegration of the Empire, had not left the adherents of the new faith unscathed. 'I have heard tell from our fathers,' Chrysostom goes on to say, 'that there were indeed real Christians once upon a time—during the persecutions!'

The principal facts of the faith were surely beyond dispute, but various singular pagan infiltrations were obvious within it.[1] How many families still preserved pagan statues carefully hidden away? At Carthage Bishop Aurelius was to remind his flock that they could not worship the 'Syrian goddess' and Christ at the same time. A Spanish Council went to the trouble of forbidding Christians to receive the 'taurobola'—the bloody Mithraic baptism—and even in the middle of the fifth century St Leo the Great was horrified to see the faithful saluting the 'sol invictus'—the Sun God—with the old ritual gesture, before entering St Peter's basilica. Were there not many pagan deities who were still fêted beneath the cloak of Christianity? Thus at Hippo was it really St Leontius who was being venerated on 4th May, or was it the ancient goddess Laetitia? Men would open the Bible at random, just as they had been wont to do in days gone by with the Sybilline Books, and would pick out a sentence and read the future from it. Churches were built on funeral mounds, similar to the pagan tumuli. Lucky charms continued to be as fashionable as ever: at best they were given a vaguely Christian meaning. Unscrupulous profiteers already knew how to exploit popular credulity: tours were organized to Job's dunghill or Noah's Ark!

Finally—and in a sense this was even more serious—Christian society had been caught up in the irresistible current of intellectual decadence which dominated the final centuries of the Roman Empire. Of course the last classical writers of any note were Christians, Fathers of the Church, a St Ambrose or a St Augustine: but it must be freely admitted that their culture is clearly inferior by comparison with that of the masters of the Golden Age of Latin literature. They knew only one or two of the classical writers thoroughly: St Ambrose, for example, knew his Cicero and his Virgil, and that was all. St Augustine probably knew no Greek, and his knowledge of the philosophers contains serious gaps. The teaching methods in use at the time give the impression of being stereotyped and lifeless, and 'rhetoric' was richer in conceits than in real culture. The last representatives of the classical genius, Boethius and Cassiodorus, writing in the sixth century,

[1] See Chapter II, section: 'The Young Church.'

were quite clearly to conceive themselves as battling on ruins, as defending a past which was already over and done with.

Thus three serious dangers threatened Roman society about 400. It was a society which was largely baptized, but baptism had clearly been unable to deliver it either from its human miseries or from its historic fates.  The three dangers were: moral decadence, contamination of the faith, and the decline of culture—three characteristics of a phenomenon which the Invasions were to render still more obvious.  Here we should remember that the state of 'Barbarism' is by no means simply the lot of the hordes who were awaiting their hour to attack a 'civilized' world.  Between the two authors of the drama there was a kind of necessary relationship, a mysterious bond.  By the fourth century the Roman world, including the majority of the baptized, was ready to let itself be swiftly barbarized.  It is therefore not surprising that Western Europe presented the tragic sight that it did, even such a short time after the storm.

Barbarization was accelerated by the same conditions which brought about the establishment of the Germanic tribes within Roman territory.  Perhaps it would have been less swift had the invaders continued to remain savage occupiers, holding themselves aloof from the vanquished.  But as we have already noted, this never happened. Even in areas like Vandal Africa, where an attempt at enforcing nonfraternization was made—and an extremely brutal attempt at that!— it proved quite useless.  In not one single new Germanic realm was complete success achieved respecting the prohibition of interracial marriages.  From the middle of the sixth century onwards the fusion between victors and vanquished was taking place everywhere.  And it is as well to underline this paradoxical fact: conversion helped to accelerate the process, a conversion which was often rapid and superficial, as we have seen, obtained *grosso modo* by means which were political rather than religious and which could not transform men's souls outright.  Later on, and very gradually, the Church was to be the great medium which history used in order to civilize the Barbarians; but for the time being, in decisively breaking down the barriers between the two ethnic elements, her influence actually contributed to barbarization.

The principal fact which impresses itself upon the historian considering the West after the Invasions is, therefore, the appalling decline in everything which really constitutes civilization.  A great gulf separates the Roman world of Theodosius—already wormeaten, certainly, and marked with the characteristic stigmata of decadence, but still so solid, so harmonious, so truly civilized—and the tangled mass of bloody chaos which is sixth-century Western Europe.  It might be said that an opaque cloud has fallen upon the human race.

How did this drift into the darkness take place? There are many elements which merit consideration. Obviously there was the direct influence of the Germans who—without being simple savages as they are all too often imagined, and though, as we have already seen, subject to many Roman influences—were nevertheless far behind the state of civilization in the West in all respects; their victory marked a retreat for the civilization based on the city in favour of that based on the tribe; this direct influence is particularly obvious in the changes which took place in the law.

It was, however, certainly not so serious as what we must call the indirect influence of the Invasions. Materially, near and far, the Germanic or Hun incursions into the West disorganized the provinces of the Empire, made the highways unsafe, paralysed production and commerce, and started the decline of the towns. From generation to generation men lived in distress and in fear of the morrow; as in all epochs of great historic upheaval, violence and cruelty fed on the situation, and social disorder resulted in an increase in crime. Naturally, the abandonment of intellectual discipline went hand in hand with this disintegration; without being generally hostile to culture the crude Germanic warriors were entirely ignorant of it. But there was something else, too, perhaps even more serious: the intermingling of the two ethnic elements resulted in an appalling lowering of moral standards. Salvianus, the Christian polemist whose temperament tends to carry him to oratorical extremes, assures us that amongst themselves the Germans possessed high moral qualities: they were chaste, they respected marriage, they proved themselves men of honour, faithful to their word . . . but though they may possibly have possessed all these virtues when they were still living on the Elbe or in the Hercynian Forest, it is quite certain that they speedily lost them. In mingling with a population which was more refined than their own but extremely corrupt, the newcomers could only borrow its worst features: barbarians and civilized folk exchanged vices with one another! [1]

The men of the time were perfectly aware that civilization was collapsing. They saw society falling apart before their eyes, like the imposing Roman aqueducts which they could watch crumbling to pieces, arch upon arch, through lack of maintenance, till only the upright columns remained, silhouetted against the sky, like so many protests. There is not a single one of these witnesses, whose texts we can still read, from Cassiodorus to Gregory of Tours, from Salvianus to St Columbanus and St Boniface, who does not protest against this

[1] We have already noted the particularly striking example of the Vandals, who, despite all their leaders' efforts to prevent contacts between their followers and the defeated population, were, within a century, literally rotted to pieces by voluptuous Africa.

shocking debasement of moral values. They were equally aware of the intellectual decline of their age: 'Woe to our epoch!' declares Gregory of Tours, 'for the study of the humanities is dead!' The best spirits of this twilight age suffered acutely from this situation, and though they worked most usefully to promote a brighter future—like St Gregory the Great or St Boniface—they pursued their heroic labours amid anguish and often despite terrible discouragements. One cannot over-emphasize the truth of Christopher Dawson's statement: Europe was founded on suffering, a suffering which it is almost impossible for us to understand to-day, even after all the disasters of recent years.

Europe was founded . . . for it was indeed from these twilight times that Europe emerged, after centuries of slow change, of organic development, of advances and set-backs, of bounds towards the light, and of leaps backward into the darkness again. Nothing would be more misleading than to represent the centuries which followed the Great Invasions as all identical with one another, identically steeped in profound stagnation. The men of this epoch who tried, with all the means at their disposal, to labour to emerge from the darkness, were numerous indeed, and the vast majority of these pioneers of the future belonged to the Church. If the faith of Christ and the knowledge of His sublime message were not enough—they never are enough—to prevent the baptized from sliding down the slippery slopes of human misconduct, at least they gave them principles without which no moral recovery would have been possible. It was from this wretched humanity—this unhappy, barbarized humanity—that the Church was to bring into being, by her long-suffering patience, firstly the Carolingian world, this first attempt at civilization by Western society, and then, much later on, the civilization of the Middle Ages. However, during the three centuries of gigantic turmoil, its action seemed almost superficial and its grip upon men's souls extremely feeble. But because her monks were praying, because her bishops were working, because her saints were living their model lives, the Church remained the only civilizing force of the age, the only hope which the light still possessed of vanquishing the darkness in the far-distant future.

## THE AGE OF DARKNESS

Several historians have drawn us pictures of Barbarian Europe. As schoolchildren some of us have read at least a few pages from the *Récit des temps mérovingiens*, in which Augustin Thierry has so wonderfully brought to life, in quite striking style, the touching and the odious figures of the protagonists of these tragedies. Certain scenes—the death of Galswintha, for example—have left a permanent impression upon our emotions. But, accurate though it is in its major outlines, this romanticized picture is not absolutely complete: in particular, by insisting as much as it does on the violence of the epoch, it does not make nearly clear enough the profound part played by Christianity. Its action was apparently so modest, but actually so decisive, opening up as it did the perspective of a future beyond this bloody chaos.

*St Gregory of Tours*, the ancient chronicler to whom we owe most of our knowledge of this epoch, teaches us far more of this. Of course he is extremely naïve and credulous; he is never so happy as when he is relating some splendid and quite unbelievable marvel, in which the wicked man is punished and the just miraculously saved; monsters, demons, and the most extraordinary calamities are a part of his familiar surroundings. But his evidence, even though it is sometimes twisted by prejudices or political opinions, is accurate as to facts. This Gallo-Roman, born at Clermont in the Auvergne (probably in 538), educated by an uncle who was a bishop, being as well taught as it was possible to be in this epoch, and whose election, in 573, to the most famous of the episcopal sees in France, gave him the perfect opportunity to accumulate material, over the best part of twenty years, about all the highest personages in the land as well as on the thousands of pilgrims who came to visit the tomb of St Martin, was an intelligent, shrewd man, with the soul of a saint. Consequently the ten volumes of his *Histoire de France* are, in the main, a most trustworthy source, and the very tenderness that he bears the Church, and the respect which he has vowed his sovereigns, give an authenticity to the list of crimes which he attributes to various bishops and to several kings. But at the same time, radiating through page after blood-stained page, is the old chronicler's insistence that this outburst of violence is not an end in itself, but that divine intentions, though apparently incomprehensible, are impressed upon it, and that since he believes in Divine Providence the Christian has no right to despair.[1]

The dominant impression which the reader obtains from all the documents of this epoch—from the Invasions to the accession of the first Carolingians—is certainly one of untold horror. There is

[1] Aside from Gregory of Tours, we possess very little contemporary material on this period: merely some lives of saints, whose details are often suspect, and which were frequently compiled much later on (cf. Baedorf, *Study on the Lives of the Saints of West Normandy* (in German), Bonn, 1913), and a few poems, letters, and official documents. The *Histoire de France* was compiled in the seventh century, and then continued by a team of Burgundian chroniclers to whom a clerical error has assigned the single, imaginary but traditional name of *Fredegarius*. The Chronicle of Fredegarius is not nearly so valuable as that of the Bishop of Tours; it is written in an excruciating style and is full of platitudes. The other Germanic peoples also all possessed their chroniclers: Cassiodorus described the early years of the Ostrogoths; Paul the Deacon, the great Lombard adventure; Isidore, that of the Visigoths in Spain; and from Bede we know the history of the Angles and the Saxons.

*I

violence everywhere: it is ready to break out at any moment.   Nothing
holds it in check, neither family affections nor the most elementary
loyalties, nor even the Christian faith itself: a devout ruler will murder
his brother, his wife, or his sons without a moment's hesitation!
Examples of this are so numerous that we can find them simply by
turning the pages at random.   Let us pass over the crimes which are
often attributed to Clovis, for many people maintain that the anecdotes
upon the prompt methods by which he rid himself of embarrassing kins-
folk are but popular fables; it is very significant all the same, that in
order to exalt the reputation of a king the common people should strive
to show him as a treacherous liar and a murderer!   But as we know,
his descendants provided the world with a spectacle of horror over a
period of five generations, a spectacle continually renewed by more
unspeakable crimes.   From 511 until 613 the Frankish lands were
really nothing more than lists where brothers and cousins slaughtered
one another, the unity re-established by Clotaire I (558–61) not
enduring above thirty months, and after the age of relative renaissance
under Clotaire II (613–28) and Dagobert (628–38), anarchy broke out
again, the cruel and abject anarchy of the *rois fainéants*.   Certain
scenes from these countless tragedies are engraven on our minds with
strokes of blood; e.g. that in which Clotaire, the son of Clovis,
murdered two of his nephews with his own hands—children of
seven and ten years of age, who were begging him for mercy, under
the very eyes of their grandmother, Clotilda!   The feud between
Fredegunda and Brunhilda has become symbolic, as embodying all the
horror of the Merovingian period.   Nothing is absent from it,
neither the most dastardly treachery nor amorous intrigues, nor the
most unspeakable cruelties, all leading up to the ghastly finale, in
which Brunhilda, by this time eighty years old, after being delivered
into the power of her enemy's son, is bound by her hair, one arm, and
one leg to the tail of a wild horse, which is then urged into a mad
gallop, thus tearing her to pieces on the stones along the highway.   A
few of these evil episodes are spiced with a kind of savage humour:
such as that of the death of Queen Austrechilda, who, before giving up
the ghost, made her husband swear to kill all her doctors in order to
punish them for not having cured her, an oath which the worthy king
Gontran promptly carried out.   Yet he was a man who was also a
great builder of churches, and who was even, at one time, venerated
like a saint!   The Frankish kings did not have the monopoly of these
atrocities.   Similar deeds were perpetrated in every stratum of society.
Gregory of Tours even tells the rather comic though gruesome anecdote of a family, who, while actually in church attending the funeral
service of their father, began to argue about his inheritance and even
went so far as to kill one another there and then!   And it was exactly

the same in other countries: in Burgundy, where the pious Sigismund, who was to be canonized, was nevertheless the murderer of his own son; in Visigothic Spain, where the story of the martyr St Hermenegild, who was executed by his father, is no less characteristic; [1] in Britain, where the rivalries between the petty Saxon rulers and the struggles between Celts and Angles were a tangle of abominable horrors.

If only these horrors could be blamed upon human weakness alone! But it is even more serious to note that the juridical principles, the foundations of collective morality, made use of methods which share in the same state of mind. The phenomenon of the barbarization of the law, is, in a way, even more disturbing than the criminal acts of individuals: it was to take Christian Europe a very long time to free itself of this. The Roman custom of torture was retained by the new masters with this aggravating modification, that it was henceforth applied, not by the public executioner, but by the plaintiff himself. The Germanic customs of *trial by ordeal, the judgment of God*, and *the judicial combat*, although violently resisted by the Church at first, were finally imposed upon society: it was just as if they could be given a kind of consecration, by the addition of a few prayers. Some bishops declared themselves in favour of these practices. For example, in order to discover a man's guilt he was forced to plunge his hand into a cauldron of boiling water, and if, on examination three days later, the burn was found to be beginning to heal, he was declared innocent. God had spoken! To find out which of two legal adversaries was in the right, they were invited to fight each other physically; obviously the victor had heaven on his side! Even the idea that one law and one moral principle was applicable to all fell into abeyance; it was replaced by the idea of *private vengeance*, i.e. by the vendetta; thus the adulterous wife was handed over to her husband to be dealt with as he thought fit . . . or (which must have been much worse!) to the wife of her lover; the seducer of a virgin to the parents of the girl; for a crime committed against one member of a family, the whole family sought to gain reparation in blood. The ruling classes, aware of the troubles which could arise from practices such as these, made really energetic efforts to replace them by more regular procedures. It must be confessed, however, that the means to which they almost always resorted was not, morally speaking, much better: this was the process of *compensation*, based on the *wer-gild*. If you killed a man of forty you had to pay his family three hundred gold pennies, but only seventy were payable for a child of three; if you 'struck someone in the stomach, with a blow penetrating to the bowels,' you had to give the wounded man thirty pennies, and five more for medical expenses; if you cut off

[1] See the preceding chapter, section: 'The Arians Return to the Bosom of the Church.'

an arm or a nose, the compensation amounted to one hundred gold pennies, reduced to sixty-three if the injured flesh still remained attached to the body, however loosely!

The general outbreak of brutality was accompanied by an almost unbelievable sexual licence. It is in this field above all that the Barbarians acquired all the vices of Roman decadence, and even added to them! The *crimes passionnels* of the reigning families fill the history of the period: when Chilperic married the Spanish Galswintha, Fredegunda, his mistress, forced him to have her strangled; when Deuteria, the wife of King Theodebert, who ruled at Verdun, saw her own daughter reaching womanhood, she had her thrown into a river from the top of a bridge because she was afraid of being supplanted by her in her husband's affections! Certain kings maintained regular harems, with their legal wives' full knowledge. Caribert had two servant girls who were his mistresses, one of whom was a religious, and he married both of them. Dagobert, the wise and pious Dagobert, the friend and confidant of saints, had no fewer than three queens, without mentioning his dozen or so concubines; the moral turpitudes of his son, Clotaire II, do not bear repetition. By the time they were fifteen years old, all the last Merovingian rulers had had two or three children by various servants. And this immorality was rife everywhere, in all classes of society. St Caesar of Arles speaks in one of his sermons of the repulsive braggarts who boast in the taverns of the number of mistresses with whom they are involved, and, if one believes what this brave and accurate preacher says, take singular liberties with the marriage sacrament itself. Here again the decadence of juridical practice is complete; divorce by mutual consent or repudiation, with no other motive save caprice, of the wife by the husband, was so common that the bishops hardly had the courage to register any protest against it.

Another characteristic feature of these barbarized societies is the frighteningly important place held in them by what is loosely called *superstition*. Here it is necessary to distinguish between the survival of heathen ideas, the legacy of the preceding epoch, and the manifestation of the credulity of primitive peoples. The remnants of Graeco-Roman polytheism, and new elements stemming from the Germanic pagan tradition, intermingled with one another. How could these simple souls be torn from the old ancestral cults which were still celebrated amid the mystery of the forests? Was there really any difference between Wotan and God? The chroniclers relate numerous episodes which show that idolatry was clearly still very much alive, and many temples still existed in districts which were a little off the beaten track. In 626 the Council of Clichy was to condemn 'the pagans who offer sacrifices,' likewise at Rome the popes were to battle against the more or less black-magic celebration of the Lupercalia. One hundred and fifty years after the baptism of Clovis a Frankish army was to make a human sacrifice of women and children in order to propitiate the battle spirits. And it was to need royal edicts to prevent the consumption of horse meat, an ineradicable souvenir of the old pagan ritual manducation. Very often Christianity was but a veneer, thinly covering the animism or totemism of yesterday.

Needless to say, this overwhelming barbarization was translated into the intellectual field as well, manifesting itself in a swift decline in standards. Already we have been impressed by the decadence of the culture of the dying Empire; but compared with that of the Dark Ages it seems like a golden age. The intellectual debasement first showed itself in the disintegration of language; the invaders picked up Latin and began to speak it, but what dreadful Latin it was! It was the Low Latin of the common people, having little connection with classical Latin, which by the sixth century was spoken only by a few aristocratic families. A vulgar tongue emerged which simplified the vocabulary, replacing proper words with popular slang expressions, eliminating the classical adverbs and substituting others formed by adding the ending 'ment' to the adjective, using *de* and *ad* instead of case endings, and turning syntax topsyturvy (this is the epoch when the word *quod*, ancestor of the modern French *que*, is grossly overused). By elisions, schematizations, and incorrect usages the old Latin pronunciation was transformed from top to toe, the alterations differing in different regions. Our modern Romance languages eventually resulted from these crude beginnings, but, during the sixth and seventh centuries they were still little better than jargon. The worthy Gregory of Tours was well aware of this. He himself apologizes most charmingly for his own mistakes of syntax and confesses that he can hardly distinguish an accusative from an ablative!

Naturally the tools of intellectual labour became increasingly poor. The schools, which were exclusively ecclesiastical, almost always confined themselves to teaching Latin and Scripture and to making their pupils learn various sacred texts off by heart. The workrooms of the copyists were almost solely devoted to the Fathers of the Church, and if now and then someone did still transcribe a classical work, a pagan text was very rarely accorded the honour of indestructible parchment. And something worse happened: the old literary texts were obliterated and religious ones substituted. These pious intentions resulted in heavy losses for literature. One detail that we know of gives some idea of this decline: at the end of the seventh century, the episcopal library of Toledo, capital of Spain, contained only one classical author —Cicero!

Is it astonishing that, under such conditions, intellectual decline was constant and regular, passing progressively from stage to stage, from the fifth to the sixth centuries, from the sixth to the seventh? [1]    The truth of this can be verified by running through the literature of the epoch.    When Gregory of Tours declared that the humanities were in the act of dying in his lifetime in Gaul, and that he himself was considerably inferior to his predecessors, his confession, full of humility though it is, is an honest statement of fact.    And it is a very grave fact, this intellectual decline, not only for civilization but for Christianity itself.    Ever since the Canon of the Scriptures had been fixed Christianity had had a *book* as its basis; if the faithful were unable to read it was there not the danger that the dogmatic content would soon be altered?

This society of the Dark Ages thus presents a most painful spectacle. It was violent, superstitious, and ignorant.    However, was there no hope for it at all?    The brutality of a primitive has perhaps more moral resources than that of a standardized robot; mingled with Barbarian superstition there remained, as we have seen, [2] a taste for the supernatural, which was admittedly only of mediocre value, but which was nevertheless indisputable; these simple souls knew nothing of the heresy which separates modern man from God: the denial of the divine.    And this was why the Church did not despair of them, and why she worked stubbornly to enlighten them.

### A Long and Patient Endeavour

Stubbornly: this is indeed the word which characterizes the patient efforts by *Ecclesia Mater* to instil Christian principles into this barbarized humanity of which, at first sight, it would have been natural to despair.

'The Church has all eternity before her'; the proverbial phrase has never been truer than when applied to these centuries, where moral and intellectual progress seemed so slow and so tenuous, where the evangelical ideal seemed always about to be swept away by waves welling up from the depths of men's vilest passions.    On the whole it was to take six or seven hundred years for Christianity to modify the foundations of the society born of the Invasions (for the famous 'Carolingian renaissance' was but a brief, bright interlude, and besides, its brilliance is open to dispute).    Christian penetration is

---

[1] However, it should be observed here that this phenomenon of intellectual decadence contained some exceptions.    At times, an effort to enlightenment was made.    See the section further on, 'Chinks of Light,' which deals with these 'renaissance' periods, marked by the names of St Gregory the Great, Dagobert, St Isidore of Seville, and the Venerable Bede.

[2] Chapter IV, section: 'Glimpses at the Religious Psychology of the Barbarians.'

even more worthy of admiration than the great events of Christian expansions, the deeds which the most profane histories cannot ignore: the baptism of the Franks, the return of the Arians to the bosom of the Church, the evangelization of the British Isles and Germany. The true conversion of the barbaric West, this history of souls, was the fruit of this long-suffering endeavour.

The Invasions had caused severe breaches in the Christian edifice which had been built up, stone by stone, for three centuries past—if not everywhere, at least in several regions. The episcopal lists, documents which are extremely valuable to the early history of Christianity, are most revealing in this respect. They had been compiled with great care, and were religiously preserved. As deceased bishops were remembered in the mass, their list was incorporated into the liturgy, and this explains how it has come down to us. (Even nowadays do we not quote a small part of the list of the popes in the mass: St Linus, St Anicletus, etc., incorporated in the Canon?) Now, in various quarters there is a noticeable interruption in these episcopal lists, which corresponds exactly to the time of the Barbarian onslaught. Among the bishoprics which disappeared in this way, following the Invasions, we can name Horbourg, near Colmar, in Alsace,[1] Augst, Port-sur-Saône, and Yverdun. In the former Roman Helvetia it is clear that the bishops of Avenches betook themselves first to Windisch, then later to Lausanne. There is a blank in the episcopal lists at Trèves and Cologne, lists which are very carefully filled during the period preceding the Invasions. When we see the work which St Columbanus had to do along the Rhine valley we get the distinct impression that the Church in these regions, though flourishing at the end of the fourth century, must have suffered terribly from the repeated passage of the Germanic hordes. The stories of St Willibrord, St Amandus, and St Boniface lead one to assume that it was the same in the Low Countries. And we remember too the districts in the south-west, where St Sidonius Apollinaris has vividly described the dreadful plight of the Gallo-Roman Church after the establishment of the Visigoths there. It is obviously no exaggeration to conclude that, although they did not mark a general break in the development of Christianity, the Invasions caused considerable backsliding in localized areas and that a second evangelization was necessary in many places. Naturally these breaches were plugged; the second effort at evangelization was pursued with the same courage, the same relentless eagerness as the first; no area was ever considered lost; the old ground was reconquered at the same time as the gigantic task of lifting to God the souls of the newcomers was being undertaken.

What was the means which the Church used for this work? The

[1] See the reference by M. Himly, *Revue d'Alsace*, 1947, p. 129.

essential weapon was *preaching*.   We still possess a fair number of the sermons delivered in this epoch by St Caesar of Arles (clearly the model for all the rest), St Peter Chrysologus, St Maximus of Turin, St Leo the Great, and later on by St Eligius (Eloi), St Columbanus, St Gregory, and St Boniface; and in every case we are struck by their directness, their simplicity, and their brusque candour.   The time is still far distant when the humblest preacher is to feel himself disgraced if he does not use a loftily metaphysical language, quite incomprehensible to his audience, and if he does not imitate the majestic periods of Bossuet and Lacordaire!   St Caesar of Arles once stated that, in addressing himself to his entire flock and in desiring to make himself understood even to the most humble he was asking the more learned of his listeners to condescend to listen to an utterly simple, united language. . . .   Likewise St Germanus of Paris advised his priests to refrain above all from 'bombastic pathos.'   Perfectly adapted to their congregations, devoid of all theological pretensions, desirous simply of reaching men's souls, and making them quiver or tremble, these great preachers of the Dark Ages were following exactly in the footsteps of St Augustine, who had talked in the selfsame way to the folk of Hippo.   The results obtained proved beyond all doubt that the method was good.

What did these preachers say?   They were essentially concerned with fighting the great vices of the day, lust and superstition: violence they dealt with much less often, and this is a sign of the times. . . . They certainly did not mince their words when preaching against the immorality that existed everywhere!   Our contemporaries would hide their faces in horror if a present-day preacher took it into his head to read pages such as those of St Caesar of Arles on chastity in marriage or on the sin of adultery from the pulpit![1]   For the lewd and the lecherous these preachers predicted all the pains of hell: hell played an enormous part in the sermons of the time!   To those who lived in sin, maintaining servant-girls as mistresses, they declared that they would refuse them their blessing when they wanted to marry.   It is beyond any doubt that these sensible words, spiced as they were with definite threats, were to carry much weight with these unsophisticated consciences and unsettle them considerably!

The other adversary which Christian preaching fought was the idolatrous superstition which as we have seen was still a considerable menace to Christianity.   The areas where the struggle was most fierce appear to have been those occupied by the Franks.   Certain saints made it their special occupation to hunt down hidden temples and

[1] Let us simply quote here this picturesque little passage: 'I would like the man who uses his wife incontinently to tell me what sort of harvest he would be able to gather in if he thought of working or sowing his field as often in the year as he lusts after his wife.'

idols: St Amandus in Flanders, St Bavo in the basin of the Scheldt, St Lambert in that of the Meuse, St Valerius in the valley of the Bresle, Sts Romanus, Ouen, and Wandrille in the Caux district. St Gaugerigus carried out a thorough re-evangelization in the diocese of Arras and Cambrai, and St Eligius did the same in that of Noyon. The biographer of St Gall describes him as destroying a *fanum*, a kind of heathen chapel, in the neighbourhood of Cologne, for which he barely escaped the wrath of the inhabitants; and there is the well-known story of St Radegund, then still the wife of Clotaire I, who, while on her way to dine with a friend near Athis-sur-Somme, learned of the existence of a pagan sanctuary in the district and straightway went and set fire to it. Thus the queens helped the preachers whenever the opportunity occurred; and the kings did likewise, for their edicts ordered landowners to allow Christian priests to enter their domains to remove pagan statues, and forbade dances and ritual feasts in the old style. Councils such as that at Tours in 567 relate expressly to the traces of paganism which still existed in a quite lively form, especially the secret cults devoted to springs, trees, and rocks.

Although it is fairly easy to demolish a temple or to remove an idolatrous statue, it is much less simple to pluck from the human soul the dark memories which still stagnate there, mingled with elementary instincts. In many cases the Church, being well aware that this or that custom or practice was specially dear to the popular mind, did not try to extirpate it but sought rather to 'Christianize' it. As we have seen this was the method recommended by St Gregory the Great to the missionaries whom he sent to England; he advised them to 'sprinkle the temples with holy water,' and to set up altars there and place relics in them, and whenever possible to make Christian ceremonies coincide with the old pagan festivals. This method (which the great Pope had in fact borrowed from his third-century namesake, St Gregory the Thaumaturgist, Bishop of Neocaesarea, in Asia Minor) was employed a great deal, and much evidence of it still exists to-day. For example, the word *Easter*, which signifies the Resurrection festival among English-speaking Christians, was, according to the Venerable Bede, borrowed from the Anglo-Saxon pagan goddess of Spring, Eostra, whose festival fell at about the same time; likewise the Great Litanies and the procession of 25th April seem to have been instituted in Italy in order to suppress the pagan *rubigalia*, and the festival of *Collect*, or *oblatio*, to replace that of the initiation of the young worshippers of Apollo. It is absolutely certain that the *Ember Days*, whose magnificent liturgies are full of allusions to the year's work on the land, are a Christian transfiguration of the old nature worship. Anyone who is acquainted with the countries of western Europe and North America is aware of the results of this great effort.

Gaston Roupnel has paid a magnificent tribute to it in his *Histoire de la campagne français*:

'Our countrysides have fully realized their human value and fully expanded their particular spirit only under the influence of the Christian faith and its practices. It is Christianity which has given them a total understanding of the grandeurs of human life, and which has invested them with a complete humanity and a never-ending duty.'

But although this 'sprinkling with holy water' was to have the happiest results in the future, at the time it is highly probable that it led to confusion and ambiguity. One has the impression that it took the missionaries of Christ several centuries to lessen—without supplanting them completely—these pagan survivals, which held an extremely important place in the popular mind. Was not the sign of the cross very often just another kind of magic gesture, analogous to those which had been drawn in the air during the nocturnal ceremonies of the old Germanic religion? In the 'spells,' the ancient formulae which were believed to ward off sickness, Christ and the saints were substituted for the Valkyries, but the formulae did not change in meaning or in intention. Likewise, whereas in olden times men had placed a morsel of food between the lips of the dead, so henceforth they placed the Holy Eucharist there instead; similar practices were universal, for we see them denounced in Spain by St Martin of Braga as well as in Flanders by the Council of Leptinnes (743); in Brittanny they abounded. There was not a single preacher who did not condemn them, and we can still read the picturesque sermons in which St Caesar of Arles fought them, notably attacking the taking of nocturnal baths—'very bad for the health'—and the wearing of lucky charms. The repetition of priestly invectives proves how deep-seated the evil was.

*The creation of rural parishes* [1] is related closely to this endeavour of gradual penetration into the general mass of Barbarian society. Born a religion of the cities, Christianity had begun by taking firm root in the towns, which were, indeed, the basis of the Roman Empire. Up to the middle of the fourth century, when St Martin had begun a serious effort to evangelize the Gallic countryside, it had retained this exclusively urban character almost everywhere. After the Invasions the

---

[1] The word *parish* comes from the Greek *paroikia*, which the Romans translated into *parochia*. At the time it meant: *a temporary resting-place in a strange land*; for was not the Christian but a traveller on this earth? This mystical meaning rapidly changed. In the fourth century the word was almost synonymous with *diocese*, and meant an area subject to the control of a bishop, the church being established in the capital of the *civitas*; it was applied for the first time to what can be called a rural parish by Pope Zosimus, in 417, in a letter concerning the church at Arles. (*Mon. Germ. Hist. Epist.*, vol. iii, p. 6.) This new meaning did not prevail generally until the sixth century, by which time the majority of Christian writers use it in the sense in which we understand it to-day. Even to-day, *abrashiya*, in Arabic, which comes from the Greek *paroikia*, refers in the Lebanon to a *diocese*.

situation remained the same; outside the capitals of the *civitates*, where the bishop resided, permanently established clergy were scarcely ever found, save in a few fortified towns. As the leader of his city-diocese the bishop would from time to time send a priest into the countryside around to celebrate divine service there, but that was all. The situation changed during the fifth century and, above all, in the following centuries: rural parishes were formed. How? Until recently (this is the thesis of Imbert de la Tour, in his book, *Rural Parishes from the Fourth to the Ninth Centuries*, which was the standard work on the subject for a long time) it was thought that the parishes were exclusively founded by great landowners, on the land of their *villae*. These foundations indeed existed in large numbers, and it is from them that the 'right of patronage' derived, which existed in France right through the Middle Ages until the revolution, a right which allowed the lord the choice of a great many parish priests, of all those who were placed in charge of the churches founded by his ancestors. But recent scholarship, conducted principally in Belgium, Alsace, and Lorraine, has revealed that the parish had several other origins too. For example, the monks and the hermits attracted groups around them, thus constituting other religious centres outside the city walls. The presence of the tomb of a saint played a similar role. There were churches founded by communities of the faithful also, even by Germanic tribes, in the 'marches' of Alsace. These 'march' churches were often built on high ground in the neighbourhood, and usually in the place where justice was meted out and where the markets were held. At first they served several villages, just as the only church of the *civitas* was at first divided into district churches and then into communal (village) churches. These district churches played the part of mother-churches vis-à-vis the village churches: this dependence is seen in the obligation, which persisted for a long time, for the inhabitants of a village to hear mass at the mother-church on the apostles' feast-days.

In Lorraine there is the example of Saint-Elophe, which remains the parish church of four villages to this day: Saint-Elophe, Soulosse, Fruze, and Brancourt. The little town of Gérardmer had no church of its own until 1542 for the same reason. In Alsace the old parishes are very often recognizable by the word *kirch* (church) which is incorporated in their place-names, e.g. *Altkirch*.[1] Thus, very gradually, as time went by, the dissemination of places of worship became a general phenomenon, corresponding to the penetration of the faith into the baptized countrysides. Although at first they were strictly subject to the bishop, or to the priest in charge of the district

[1] See the *Histoire de Lorraine*, prepared at Nancy in 1939, under Gain's editorship; and the works of L. Pfleger on the Alsatian parish.

church, these rural parishes slowly succeeded in establishing a relative independence: they had their own priests and very soon they had their own patrimony; outside the towns, and later on outside the feudal castles, they became the only groups capable of assuring men a certain collective consciousness.    The foundation of rural parishes is therefore a fact of great historical importance, and one which goes far beyond the bounds of religious history alone.    As Ferdinand Lot has noticed in his book, *Naissance de la France*, which is crammed with interesting viewpoints, the parishes were to be the basic cells of the nation until the revolution: the signatures of the States-General were to be those of the parishes first and foremost.    Those who see our French village churches as something more than quaint rural scenes, those who see these village communities as represented first and foremost by the belfry and the churchyard, which tell of man's fidelity to the earth and his aspirations to heaven, must pause a long time before this fact.    What would our villages be if they were not parishes too into the bargain?—remote places, miserable slums, lost in the midst of the countryside, bodies without souls.    For the folk who lived on the land the foundation of the rural parishes was an event as important as the emancipation of the communes was for the folk in the towns.    In the towns themselves—Pierre Champion has described how it happened in Paris—it was the parishes which created the 'quartiers,' each with its own distinctive character.    We Western Christians owe a great deal to the men who created these centres of worship.

## The Influence of the Church made Incarnate in the Bishop

The fact that the Church was able to act as she did upon the new peoples emerging from the great turmoil of the Invasions is indisputable proof of the influence which she enjoyed amongst them.    Here is a fact which, as cannot be too often repeated, was decisive for the future; truth to tell, the chances of a subsequent renaissance of civilization depended on it.    There are several reasons for this influence.    Some are psychological; in the majority of cases it is quite obvious that the Christian leaders inspired the respect of the Barbarians; the splendid pictures of St Anianus or of Pope St Leo, standing up to the invaders and obtaining their respect, have a symbolic value.    It seems clear that, for these primitive peoples, the religious qualities of a priest, of a bishop, were spontaneous motives for veneration.    Perhaps there was also the fear that, as trustees of supernatural powers, the men of the Church might do something hostile to them.    At all events, in the main (i.e. aside from exceptions due to the violence of the age) these sentiments were to endure throughout the early Middle Ages; the privileges and prerogatives of the Church were never to be called into question—quite the contrary—and the reverence which men bore her assured her ascendancy.

Other more material causes also played their part in this ascendancy. Whenever the Barbarian chieftains were faced with the task of administering a whole state they were overwhelmed by it. They were more used to fighting on the battle-field than to sitting at a desk. They also lacked administrative personnel. The Church, however, possessed such personnel. For a century past these men had been accustomed to performing actual administrative tasks in the State: they had become adept at substituting themselves for the decadent civil administrators. Even though she was herself more or less entangled in the general decline in society's standards, the Church nevertheless remained the highest element in society; her own discipline saved her from the universal anarchy. In spite of everything she continued to celebrate services, to alleviate suffering, and to maintain her buildings. And while she existed she was bound to maintain a minimum of culture amongst her personnel; in order to say mass it was at least necessary to be able to read Latin. It is highly significant that the word which describes the man who knows how to write, the scribe, is also that which describes the man of the Church: *clerc* in French, *clerk* in English, *klerk* in Flemish and High German, and *diaca* in Russian.[1] And—and this is equally important—when Charlemagne wanted to reconstitute an administrative personnel in his state, we shall see that he turned to the clergy for help. The influence of the Church, therefore, resided not only in her religious character but also in her intellectual authority in the eyes of an ignorant, illiterate laity, and in the fact that she was a quite indispensable aid to the civil power.

This influence was made incarnate in one group of men: *the bishops.* Always the bishops! We have already seen the vital place which they held in the Church, the part which they had played ever since a Christian society existed, and which they maintained at the time of the great breakdown of civilization during the Invasions. The Dark Ages confirmed this place, and perhaps even increased its emphasis. Once

---

[1] It is worth remembering that the Greek χλῆρος means *chosen*. The clerk is the chosen man of God. Fustel de Coulanges makes some interesting but questionable remarks in connection with this etymology. He contrasts the word χλῆρος with the word πρεσβύτεροι which was at first used to describe priests and which, to the ancients, meant 'the oldest.'

He suggests that the clergy might first of all have been completely composed of the oldest members of the community; eventually they would form a body separated from the rest of the faithful, a kind of aristocracy, a 'chosen' *élite*. This is a tempting idea, but to be acceptable it would be necessary to prove that the usage of πρεσβύτεροι was earlier than χλῆρος.

The same author remarks, almost on the same page, that 'almost all the terms of ecclesiastical organization are of Greek origin, whilst the organization itself is entirely Roman.' (*La Monarchie franque*, pp. 512 and 513.)

again we must quote the phrase of St Cyprian: *Ecclesia in episcopo*, the whole Church is in the bishop; the Church is the bishop himself; without the bishop there can be no Church.   In the prelude to the Middle Ages it might be added also: and no civil society either.   In the days of persecution the bishop had been, spiritually as well as materially, the leader who took his followers into battle for God; later on, after the triumph of the revolution of the Cross, he had been the key to future reconstruction, the witness of a world which was waiting to be born; during the fifth century, faced with the Barbarians, we have seen him as the bastion of the Church, trying to quell the waves whipped up by the tempest, and to save what was capable of being saved.   In the new society, born of the Invasions, the bishop—let us think of St Remigius, for example, the man who baptized Clovis—was, in the majority of cases, the instigator of Christian reconquest, the effective agent of conversion; and when this conversion had become an accomplished fact it was natural that he should possess an absolute preponderance to which several tributes have been paid by the most 'secular' of historians.

As the representative of God on earth, in an age when religion was the only moral authority, the delegate of the king, whose chancellery had signed the document which acknowledged his position, often chosen by the people, and in all cases accepted by them,[1] the bishop of the Dark Ages combined within himself all three possible founts of authority.   Very often—indeed, almost always—he added to them the personal attribute of noble birth.   For a long time past the bishops had been chosen from members of ancient local families—Gallo-Romans, Italo-Romans, Hispano-Romans—thus forming a real kind of episcopal aristocracy, linked by ties of blood;[2] later on, from the sixth century onwards, when Barbarian elements began to reach the episcopate,[3] they were recruited from the king's entourage, from the 'palace,' from among the important Germanic families, and if the king's influence in these appointments often appears indiscreet, we

---

[1] 'No bishop should be given to a people against its will.'   This had been decided by Pope Celestine I, and St Leo had likewise declared: 'He who is over all should be chosen by all.'   Thus the principle is quite a categorical one.   The metropolitan and the bishops under him must consult the faithful before appointing a new bishop.   The kings themselves, when they intervened in nominations, were to take into consideration the good or bad will of the future flocks of their candidates, whenever they wanted to avoid anxieties and troubles.

[2] These episcopal families (to which allusion has already been made earlier in this book, in reference to St Remigius, in Chapter IV) were quite numerous and powerful.   St Avitus succeeded his father Hesychius in the see of Vienne, whilst his brother Apollinaris became Bishop of Valence.   Of the two sons of Eucherius of Lyons, Salonius became Bishop of Geneva, and Veranus Bishop of Vence.   Gregory himself notes that, save for about five exceptions, all the bishops of Tours were related to him.

[3] At Paris the first Frankish bishop was the extremely obscure Saffarac, elected in 511. He was deposed by a Council.   But he was followed by several Gallo-Roman bishops, notably by St Eusebius and St Germanus, his immediate successors.

shall see that it did not always act adversely, and that really detestable choices were the exception rather than the rule. The great majority of the bishops showed themselves fully equal to the crushing tasks which devolved upon them.

Morally, in the majority of cases at least, they were worthy of their sacred calling. Living in public as they did, under the watchful eyes of the faithful, the bishop had to possess impeccable morals or swiftly lose his authority; if he was married he separated from his wife as soon as he was elected, and henceforth lived as a celibate. His house was open to all; he was continually surrounded by people, besieging him with requests, and begging his help. He was an extremely important landowner, he managed immense estates, and hundreds, nay thousands of labourers were answerable to him: this wealth increased his influence. Moreover there is one detail which enables us to assess this influence exactly: the blood-price, the *wer-gild* for the murder of a bishop was nine times more than that of a free man, whilst that of a royal official was only three times more!

What did the bishop do in those days? Almost everything. First of all of course he preached the Word of God; he had to preach in his cathedral on Sundays and on feast-days, and Councils reminded him of this duty (e.g. that of Saint-Jean-de-Losne, in 673–5). He directed his clergy, supervised its instruction and its enthusiasm, and he really was the spiritual father of his faithful people, and the shepherd of souls. But this entirely religious role was only the crowning point of a prodigious collection of diverse functions. He was asked to make good the deficiencies of the civil administration, to be the leading organizer, to control the ruler, even to intervene in matters in which it may seem strange to find him involved: food supplies and communications! All the social work which the Church assumed devolved in practice upon the bishop: he was responsible for hospitals, schools, and prisons! Countless beggars depended upon his charity, and a special fund was provided for them out of the episcopal income! Did not St Gregory the Great name St Melanius of Rennes 'the father and the fatherland of all unfortunates'? He was also the guardian of orphans, especially of wealthy orphans, whom he protected from the rapacity of their adult relations. It was natural enough that he should be recognized as a builder of churches, but it is much more surprising to see him raising dikes at his own expense like the bishops of the Loire or the Rhine, or trying his hand at water-supplying like St Felix of Nantes, or even being hired to have fortifications built like St Desiderius at Cahors, St Leodegarius at Autun, or a certain St Rigobert at Rheims who, in order to make quite certain that the town was properly guarded, slept near the ramparts and had the keys of the gates handed to him each evening. If we add that (especially from 614) the bishop was also the principal judge, judging not only clerks but all cases in which clerks were concerned; that he was even a kind of fiscal adviser, ready to protect his flock from the excessive demands of the royal tax-collectors; and that finally, on account of his personal authority and his sacrosanct position (he could only be condemned by the decision of a Council), he was the only person, who, as we shall see, could stand up to the kings: [1] then the veneration which surrounded him is more than understandable.    During his lifetime he was inundated with tokens of affection and with generous gifts; when he died his people canonized him and raised a spontaneous cult to him which took little heed of the Church's cautionary attitude.    Is it astonishing that, alive or dead, miracles were expected of him, and that they did in fact spring up over his tomb?    The admiration of the bishop reached idolatrous proportions.    A tale is told of a certain worthy Parisian who, having managed to procure a piece of parchment on which his bishop, St Germanus, had written a couple of lines, had it boiled and actually kept the resulting infusion as a sovereign remedy to cure all ills!

The preponderance of the bishop is consequently the great social fact of the Dark Ages.    ('It is the episcopate which has served human societies most strikingly,' writes Camille Jullian.)    This preponderance is found everywhere—in France, Spain, and Italy just as in Egypt and the Byzantine East.    To quote even the principal of these men would be an almost impossible task: the calendar is full of the saint-bishops of the sixth to eighth centuries, their personalities haloed by a thousand astounding miracles.    In France their numbers were five times greater in Merovingian than in Carolingian times.    Truth to tell, a good deal of their story is not very well known.    The dates are often missing, and sometimes we scarcely know their names.    But it is significant indeed that the fact that is remembered about these saints first and foremost is that they were bishops.    However, a few of them are better known.    What region of Europe does not remember some of their number?    In Spain there is St Isidore of Seville, in the Rhineland the courageous St Nicetius of Trèves, in the Low Countries St Lambert of Maastricht. . . .    In France, is there a single diocese which does not keep the memory of one of these bishops of the Dark Ages at least fairly bright?    It would be tedious indeed to list them all.

[1] From the seventh century the bishops were actually centres of organized resistance to the excesses of royal power: this will be noticed in the drama of St Leodegarius.    At the end of the Merovingian epoch some of them, such as Savarius of Auxerre and Eucherius of Orleans, carved out real principalities for themselves, and their political power became so excessive that Charles Martel was forced to fight them.    This is a foretaste of the count-bishops of Capetian times.    There is an excellent reappraisal of this question, demonstrating the steps in the evolution which led to the absorption of the *Comitatus* by the *Episcopatus* in the authoritative work of F. Vercauteren, *Études sur les Civitates de la Belgique seconde*, Brussels, 1934.

Let us pause for a moment over three names, at least, all borne by outstanding men, whom Paris still honours in the names of her churches, her suburbs, and her streets. There is *St Germanus of Paris* (who should not be confused with St Germanus 'of Auxerre,' his equal in sanctity in the preceding century, nor with St Germanus the Scot, either, the godchild of Germanus of Auxerre), this splendid and holy priest in whose hands the miracle was a natural thing; this marvellously charitable soul, never indifferent to the slightest human suffering, who gave the poor the gifts which kings had presented to him; this tireless evangelist, always on horseback, touring a diocese which at that time included all Seine-et-Oise and Seine-et-Marne; this highly courageous man who knew exactly how to influence the difficult Childebert: he was Bishop of Paris from 565 to 576, and the church of St Germain-des-Prés preserves his memory to this day.[1]

*St Ouen* was a brilliant Frankish courtier, who had met the great Irish missionary, St Columbanus, when he was still very young, and had henceforth turned his soul resolutely towards God; he was brought up at the royal palace, and was for some time a minister of Dagobert, yet amid his worldly honours he continued to lead a saintly life, wearing a hair shirt beneath his silk robe, a true monk without a monk's habit, whom the king eventually made Bishop of Rouen. He died at the age of seventy-four, on his return from a peace mission to the two enemy sister states of Neustria and Austrasia, in 683, not far from the town which to-day is the Paris suburb which bears his name.

And then there is *St Eligius*, the 'great Saint Eligius,' whose wisdom is rightly praised in the hunting ditty about him, but who was really very different from the waggish and rather incongruous person who is portrayed in its twenty-four couplets. Born in 588 near Limoges, the son of a humble craftsman, he became an outstanding apprentice in the workshops of the royal mint, and was soon famous as a skilful goldsmith. Clotaire summoned him to court to engrave him a golden throne, and from there he went on to make a brilliant political career for himself as minister of finance and as an intimate adviser first of Dagobert, then of Clovis II; at the same time, like his friend St Ouen, he gave generously to charity, founding monasteries to which he loved to retire. In the end St Eligius obeyed the call of God and became a priest. He was consecrated Bishop of Noyon, and there he led the life of apostleship and prayer of which he had long dreamed, and there, in 660, he died.

Guides of kings, great administrators, and at the same time souls filled to the brim with the love of God. Such men make quite clear

---

[1] 'Des Prés' (i.e. 'in the fields'), for until the seventeenth century, the abbey of which this church was a part was still in the heart of the countryside.

the enormous influence which the bishops exerted on the events of their age—an age when all society was being basically remodelled, and when only the Christian bases could provide the necessary reconstruction.

One famous phrase expresses the importance of the episcopate: 'The bishops built France, just as the bees build their hive.' It is so often quoted that the identity of its author has become confused, and it has been attributed in turn to all the historians of the first half of the nineteenth century. In fact, it is a phrase of Joseph de Maistre's. It is profoundly true: with this reservation, however: that it must be remembered that the monks and abbots of the time played an almost equally important role too.

## St Benedict

The episcopate was not the only Christian institution which served to frame society in the Dark Ages. Alongside the bishops (and very often intimately linked with them by a common origin, many of the bishops coming from the monasteries and all having a more or less monastic background) the monks were to carry out an equally considerable task, though of quite a different nature.

We have already studied the place which monasticism had held ever since its appearance in the Church: not merely as a spiritual institution to which souls came to seek the means of living a Christianity which was purer and more elevated, because it was freed of the burdens of the world, but also, paradoxically enough, as an instrument of positive action, which was used in the propagation of Christianity. Thus the great page of Christian history which deals with the conversion of the Barbarians was in large measure written by the monks. This same effective action is to be observed in many fields throughout the Dark Ages and even beyond them, throughout the Middle Ages also: for, as Montalembert so admirably demonstrated a century ago, in a famous book of his, the West would not have been what it was without the profoundly fruitful work done by the monastic institutions.

Truth to tell, the development of monasticism in the West had come about in a somewhat anarchical fashion, without any overall plan, according to the whim of circumstances and individuals. All the men who had been promoters of the movement since the middle of the fourth century shared one common principal intention: that of living the Christian faith more deeply, and of making it possible for others to do the same, but in their realizations of this aim the differences had been enormous. The Gallic monasteries with the oldest traditions, those which were descended from St Martin and his first foundations,

Ligugé and Marmoutier, or those of the Mediterranean school, after the style of Lérins or in the spirit of Cassian, considered themselves to be primarily spiritual reservoirs, places of meditation and asceticism, from which men could eventually emerge, specially armed for all the battles of Christ. For *Cassiodorus*, on the contrary, the great Roman nobleman who had received the highest honours in the service of the Ostrogoth monarchy, and who had tried to realize a policy of collaboration between the conquering Germans and the vanquished, the monastery of *Vivarium* in Calabria, which he founded in 540, after the collapse of his dreams, had been a real haven of refuge for culture and thought, a kind of fortunate isle where, under God's watchful eye, the monks devoted themselves to preserving the fruits of the spirit at the very moment when classical culture seemed most dangerously threatened. Almost at the same time the institutions associated with St Caesar of Arles (convents of women, especially) appeared primarily as centres of penitence, something after the style of our modern Poor Clares, Carmelites, and contemplative Benedictine nuns. Then, a little later on, St Columbanus set up his monasteries like veritable advance posts in enemy territory, bristling with frightful mortifications, and where, as was advisable, the discipline was almost military in character. Borrowing ideas from this rule and from that, composite forms of monasticism multiplied almost everywhere, right into the seventh century—there were the monks of St John of Reomay, of St Richarius, of St Philibert, and of many others besides. This variety of rules and customs brought a number of inconveniences in its train, notably that of the existence of *perpetually wandering monks*, who were for ever changing monasteries as the mood took them, and causing an unstable situation fraught with trouble. A time came when the need was felt for a fixed, single rule which, by combining completely spiritual as well as human qualities, would compel recognition from all who wished to follow the way of God. A time came too when the synthesis had to be made between the different kinds of monasteries, the spiritual reservoirs, the centres of prayer and asceticism, the nurseries of missionaries and bishops, and the advance posts of Christian conquest. To one man fell the glory of understanding both the need for unification and of offering valid solutions to it: and this man was *St Benedict*.

*Benedict of Nursia*, the man from whom innumerable spiritual descendants were to spring over the centuries, the man whom monks of many colours and many observances still venerate to-day as the Father who pointed them the road to heaven, is almost an enigma for the historian, or, at all events, one of those brilliant figures whose very radiance prevents his individual features from showing through very clearly. It must be admitted that Pope St Gregory the Great, who tried to evoke his memory fifty years after his death,[1] has not our modern concept of biographical accuracy; because he was convinced that the miracle was the true touchstone of sanctity, he takes care not to omit a single one of the prodigious deeds which embellished his hero's life—unexpected cures, mind-reading, predictions of the future, the exorcising of satanic spirits, even episodes more calculated to astonish than to persuade, such as the one about the iron blade from a pickaxe, which fell into a lake and rose to the surface and joined itself to its handle again on a single command from the saint!   A few dates and genealogies, some indications of durations and of places would interest us much more, but even the most outstanding brains of an epoch find it hard to escape from the intellectual habits of their own age.

However, the main outlines of St Benedict's life-story can be redrawn something like this.   He was born, probably about 480, at Nursia, in the heart of the Sabine country, whose people were said by Cicero to be *severissimi homines*; the *nursina durities* was proverbial at Rome. Consequently austerity and energy were a part of his racial inheritance, as were an obvious tendency to conservatism and a keen feeling of family loyalty.   But of his family we know nothing, save the gentle figure of his sister Scholastica, who, like him, devoted her life to God, with whom his relations were touchingly close all his life, and whom he had interred in the very tomb which he had reserved for himself at Cassino.   We know very little about his early youth either: one presumes that it was filled with study and was closely supervised, for this was still the custom among those old Italian families where, despite the general decadence of society, the classical virtues of integrity and moral probity remained as firm as ever.

It is only when he goes to Rome as a young man to continue his studies that Benedict's character is revealed to us in his decisive reaction to the society he found there.   Rome at this time—towards the end of the fifth century—was Rome no longer; since 476 the Empire had ceased to exist; the Barbarian Odoacer was ruling over Italy.   To all clear-thinking people it seemed that an epoch was over, and that men must make every effort now to tear themselves away from the catastrophe.   Benedict was exactly contemporary with Boethius and Cassiodorus, and before this collapse of a world, his feelings were analogous to theirs, but alone of the three he knew how to react from them, by building for the future.

The divine voice which called to him by name in the silence of his soul seemed at first to be beckoning him to a life of solitude.   After a

---

[1] According to the information furnished by the brothers of his order, and especially by the monks of Monte Cassino who took refuge in Rome after the seizure of their monastery by the Lombards, no one had studied St Benedict before St Gregory, at least so far as we know to-day.

brief stay in the Sabine mountains with a priest of Affile, he shut himself away in a grotto near Subiaco, near a pile of ruins which had once been one of Nero's palaces, as if his penance was motivated by the desire to redeem the rottenness of the age. For three whole years he endured this life of absolute solitude, which so many anchorites have admitted to be outstandingly hard: it was in this period especially that the Devil joined battle with him most violently, and he was forced, sometimes, to roll himself among the thorns in order to humble his flesh. But although he longed to be cut off from the world, his renown soon spread far beyond his grotto. Some monks from a neighbouring little monastery at Vicovaro sought him out in his cave and asked him to be their abbot. This attempt at leadership proved a complete failure however. Perhaps it was too premature. Exasperated by their young abbot's attempts to restore monastic discipline amongst them, the monks soon had but one aim—to get rid of him. (At all events, this is what St Gregory says: one hopes that this projected murder is but a fiction, intended to reflect the greater glory of the saint who escaped it miraculously. . . .) In any case, warned of the plot, Benedict returned to his grotto.

The years passed by once more. Souls in search of God gathered around the saint's cave. A proper monastic community grew up there, then a second followed, until there were a dozen altogether. Although nothing had been formally set down, all twelve regarded Benedict as their Father. This little republic of anchorites and cenobites soon began to grow famous. Great Roman families came to ask the communities of saints to undertake the education of their sons. It was from these pupils that Benedict recruited some of his best disciples, such as St Maurus and St Placid. But once again human wickedness was to put itself involuntarily at the service of God's incomprehensible intentions. Jealous of these successes, a priest in the neighbourhood set out to pick a quarrel with Benedict and, worse still, to threaten his life (or so St Gregory says). Once more the saint saw a sign of Providence in the acts of the wicked, and leaving Subiaco he set off to look elsewhere for a place where he could establish his monastery permanently.

Half-way along the road between Rome and Naples the traveller spied the small fortified town of Cassino, dominating the valley which the *via Latina* followed. It was protected by a citadel some thirty metres farther up the mountainside. The top of the hill formed a kind of small plateau on which there stood a temple, dedicated to Jupiter. There, in 529, on the very spot where men had been wont to worship the idol, Benedict established himself with his monks: there the Benedictine Order was to be born, in this monastery of *Monte Cassino* whose name and buildings have become tragically familiar to the whole

world because of the battles there in 1944.   Based on the powerful
mountain mass of the Apennines, which protected it to the north
and east, dominating the plain, which stretched westward as far as
its fine orchards and villages, and whose fields rolled gently southwards as far as the 'delicious' hills of Capua, the strongpoint of
Cassino was a site which could only be compared with the most
important in the world, with the fortress-site of the temple at
Jerusalem, with the Acropolis at Athens, or with those hill-tops bearing basilicas consecrated more or less in imitation of it, such as Saint-
Odile or Vézelay.   Here it was then that, strengthened by the experiences of an already mature life, and having studied the monastic
attempts made elsewhere, and the advantages and disadvantages of
other rules, but possessing a greater knowledge of men and of the
needs of the age than any of his predecessors, St Benedict founded what
was to be the capital of Western monasticism, the gigantic monastery
from which so much was to be born.   Here it was that he drew up the
Rule which has governed those who claim descent from him right up
to our own time.   It was from here, through his writing, his words,
and, above all, his example, that he exerted the influence to which
several anecdotes bear witness.[1]   And it was here that he died,
probably on 21st March 547, his destiny richly fulfilled.[2]

When it is reduced to a coherent plan in this way, the life of St
Benedict seems clearly directed by divine intentions towards the
actual realization of what was expected of him.   In the case of these
great figures who bring profoundly fruitful ideas into the spiritual
field, the life-story is less important than the actual work accomplished;
the traits of character are really interesting only in so far as they shine
through the ideas expressed.   The whole of St Benedict is in his Rule,
in this little booklet of one hundred odd pages, where every paragraph,
every word, carries astonishing weight, and whose influence, from the
very moment that the text came into general use, was to be inexhaustible.   So, when we want to try to portray the character of the
saint we must pick out its features from his Rule, and perhaps the best

---

[1] One of these anecdotes is rather strange.   The Ostrogoth king, Totila (see above,
Chapter III, section: 'The Grand Design of Justinian'), who was fighting the Byzantines
at the time, had heard the sanctity of Benedict highly praised, and was curious to go and
see him.   But in order to satisfy himself that the famous abbot was indeed a saint, he sent
an equerry ahead of him dressed in the royal purple, who was to present himself as the
sovereign.   As soon as he saw him coming afar off, Benedict cried: 'Take off those
clothes, for they are not yours.'   The equerry hastened to tell his master the result of his
trickery.   Totila, overwhelmed, went to throw himself at the feet of the abbot, who told
him: 'You have already done many evil things, and you will do many more.   Put an
end to your wickedness!   I say unto you, you will enter Rome, you will cross the sea,
and you will reign for nine more years, but in the tenth year you will die.'   And everything happened exactly as he had foretold.
[2] The 'traditional' date of 543 for the saint's death is no longer considered possible.
(Cf. the article by Dom Schmitz in *Revue liturgique et monastique*, 1929, p. 123.)

picture which has ever been drawn of him is to be found in a page of purely doctrinal content, stripped of all individual detail, in the picture of the perfect abbot given by the saint who was to do most to propagate the Benedictine ideal, St Gregory the Great: 'The thoughts of the abbot should be pure; his actions should serve as an example; he should know when to keep silent and when to talk to good purpose; he should be filled with compassion for his brethren; he should devote himself to meditation; to the upright he should be a humble companion, but he should act as a resolute ruler in the battle to vanquish vice and sin; in him the care of exterior affairs should not be carried so far as to militate against the spiritual impulse, nor should the care of the inner life make him neglect the necessities of his charge. . . .' It is clear that when he drew this picture, the great Pope must have been thinking of the kindly founder and perfect model of Benedictinism himself.

The Rule of St Benedict is not, properly speaking, original. Benedict himself refers to St Augustine, Cassian, St Basil, and the *Lives of the Fathers*. Almost all its directives appear in earlier monastic rules, and it is even maintained that he may have used a *Rule of the Master* which was already current in the West as his basis.[1] The merit of St Benedict does not therefore lie in a formal originality, and this has been admirably pointed out by Pope Pius XII in the *Encyclical* of 1947 which commemorated the fourteenth centenary of St Benedict's death: his divinely ordained role was 'not to produce the ideal of monastic life but to harmonize it and successfully adapt it to the temperament, needs, and habits of the peoples of the West.' What strikes anyone who reads the *Regula* is its profoundly humane character, in the double sense that it both demonstrates a wonderful knowledge of human nature and also shows itself both merciful and resolute, generous and prudent towards the frailties of mankind. There is no excess of mysticism here: the Rule hardly mentions contemplation, and when it does so it mentions it as a spiritual height reserved for a few alone. Penitential extremes after the tradition of Cassian and above all of the Celtic monks and St Columbanus are entirely absent. Nor is there any sign of the almost exclusive preference which Cassiodorus accorded to study and intellectual pursuits. The essential of the Rule of St Benedict lies in its moderation, its balance, and what St Gregory the Great called its *discretion*. This balance and moderation showed themselves in the equitable division of the day into periods of prayer, work, and rest, and in the healthy alliance between manual and intellectual labour. It is a guide to life equal to man's capabilities, and

---

[1] It is true that it has also been maintained that this *Rule of the Master* was a first edition of the Rule of St Benedict. The material on the antecedents of the Benedictine rule is enormous and rather bewildering.

one which could be offered to anyone who wished to follow the way of
God without forcing his nature artificially in doing so.

Consequently, from the precepts of the Rule the finished product
of monasticism is to emerge—we can almost call it the 'complete
monk'—a man who is at the same time a man of prayer and of asceticism, of meditation and of culture, of action and efficacy. The Benedictine spirit was to call unceasingly to all those who sought through it to
live the two great principles of all Christian effort: that we are in the
world and must act in the impure conditions of our nature, but that
everything we do must be done with heaven as our example and our
goal. A supreme masterpiece of the Roman mind, and a lofty expression of Christian genius, the Rule of St Benedict was to become one
of the essential foundations of the work of salvation and organization
which the Church was called upon to undertake after the great turmoil
of the Invasions. It is impossible to understand the effort accomplished by Christianity in preparing the renaissance of civilization without doing homage to him who has often been called 'the patriarch of
Western monasticism.'

## MONASTIC EXPANSION

The history of monasticism in the Barbarian West has two important
characteristics: firstly, the prodigious growth of monastic institutions,
monasteries, and convents undergoing wave upon wave of multiplication and expansion, and secondly the almost exclusive preponderance
of Benedictinism in these institutions. The two phenomena are
linked however: it is largely because the principles of the Rule of
Monte Cassino gradually supplanted the older traditions that
monasticism expanded as it did.

The reasons which caused Benedictinism to take a preponderant
place stemmed in the main from the excellence and wisdom of its Rule.
St Benedict demanded three vows from his monks: poverty, obedience,
and stability. The first was not original, for all the cenobites practised
the virtue of indifference to worldly wealth; but in demanding absolute
obedience, above all in compelling the monks to remain permanently
in the religious house which they had first chosen to join, he put an end
to the licence of the *perpetual wanderers* and to the troubles which these
haphazard habits brought with them. Though extremely strict in
his essential principles, St Benedict permitted a really remarkable
amount of liberty to the various monasteries on points of detail, in
other words, he allowed their abbots to modify the details according
to the needs of local conditions, e.g. with regard to clothing and
food; in this way there was enormous scope for adaptation which
would have been prevented by an over-excessive rigidity of regulation.

The organization of the Order, which gave great liberty to each community (the Father Abbot of Monte Cassino was a spiritual superior, above all, who watched over the conduct and faith of his brethren with affectionate care, but who did not intervene in the administration of the community in any way), was also very favourable to its early growth, although later on its extreme interpretation was to cause anarchy. Finally, when set against the other rules such as that of St Columbanus, that of St Benedict was so infinitely more humane, more moderate, and less excessive, that favourable comparisons swiftly resulted, and it attracted large numbers of postulants.

Benedictine influence consequently showed itself in two ways. Firstly, the new Order's foundations multiplied rapidly; during St Benedict's own lifetime his Rule was observed in only three monasteries: Monte Cassino, Subiaco, and Terracina. The catastrophe which all but destroyed it in 589, the seizure of Cassino by a Lombard duke, gave the Order the opportunity of fresh expansion, by bringing the Benedictines to Rome: one hundred years later more than one hundred communities claimed St Benedict as their authority. For another phenomenon occurred: recognized as superior to all the other rules, propagated by Pope St Gregory the Great, by the missionaries in Britain and by St Isidore of Seville in Spain, Benedict's system competed with the older rules even in the monasteries where they were in use, and soon supplanted them. The ideas of the wise Roman Benedict were far preferable to those of Bangor, of the Irish, of the awesome Columbanus; here was less severity of discipline but more order, and prayers rather than penance. In France the substitution of rules took place conclusively during the first quarter of the eighth century. It is quite possible that Justinian had heard of Benedictinism even in the East, and that the drafting of some of his *Novellae* was inspired by it.

Another feature of the new monasticism should be underlined here: previously the monks had been laymen and each community had had usually only one priest, a kind of chaplain; this was the case in the Breton monasteries. Since the monastic life turned on penitence and mortification, it was not particularly necessary for the monk to receive the sacrament of ordination. In the first Benedictine monastery the situation was still like this: there were but one or two priests to serve the whole community. But in orientating monastic life more towards prayer and the divine office, St Benedict, without saying so expressly, was encouraging priesthood in the monasteries, since the loftiest prayer and the most perfect service is the celebration of the mass. When, under the impulse of Pope St Gregory, the monks became engaged in apostleship, it became essential to ordain the missionaries in order that they might celebrate the Holy Sacrifice themselves. This

K

was a change of perspective which was of capital importance.   A new clergy was formed, a *regular* clergy, subject to a rule, contrasting with the ordinary, the *secular* clergy, who lived in the world, and, because by its form and by its stricter methods of discipline, this new clergy was better qualified to embody the Christian ideal, life tended to recede from the secular to the benefit of the regular: it was the monasteries that attracted the Christian *élite*.

In this way the best in Christianity tended to take refuge in the monastery, whence it later emerged to make new conquests and undertake new decisive enterprises.   The fantastically large numbers of religious houses which sprang up everywhere is the great achievement of the Church in the Dark Ages: from the sixth century onwards and for several generations, kings and bishops, the influential and the wealthy, were to vie with one another in their zeal to found religious houses.   For those wishing to assure the salvation of their souls, was not the best way to ensure the foundation of a group of monks who would pray for them after death?   Monasteries sprang up in every Western land, firstly modelled on Lérins, later looking to the Columbanian principles, and later still ordered according to the Benedictine Rule.   They were no longer simply in the Mediterranean south, which in the fifth century had possessed almost the monopoly of them. Thus Clovis founded the abbey of Sts Peter and Paul, which later became St Geneviève; Sigismund, the Burgundian king, built St Maurice of Agaune in the Valais, and at the gates of Paris Childebert built Holy Cross, and St Vincent, the modern St Germain-des-Prés; Dagobert's name is linked with the beginnings of the glorious abbey of St Denis.   At the same time St Calais sprang up in Maine, St Wandrille (then Fontenelle) and Jumiège along the lower reaches of the Seine, St Riquier in the Somme valley, and St Bertin in the north. The queens did not lag behind in this pious rivalry; thus Holy Cross at Poitiers owed its foundation to Radegund, and Chelles to Bathildis. And this monastic growth was to continue for centuries to come!

Moreover it was not only buildings which sprang up everywhere. Vocations abounded.   The religious houses of the Dark Ages drew amazing numbers of souls to them.   Communities of two hundred monks were commonplace; we know of some monasteries which contained one thousand monks.   Souls in search of God came from all classes of society, finding in the religious houses an escape from the universal spectacle of violence in the world outside.   The royal families themselves provided recruits.   Among the Anglo-Saxons an actual king, Centwin, renounced his crown and took the habit in a monastery which he founded; among the Franks the last of Clodomir's children, Clodoaldus, the sole survivor of the massacre perpetrated by their uncle Clotaire, became the St Cloud of the monastery which he established. The most famous of these royal vocations is that of St Radegund. On her famous statue her moving features still seem radiant with the mystical life: she was a Thuringian captive, who was brought to the court of the brutish Clotaire. He married and loved her and betrayed her a thousand times. At last, overcome with grief by his assassination of her own brother, she took the veil and founded the Poitevin abbey which she made into a model of its kind.

For, in this pious emulation, women were the equal of men. Abbeys of nuns also multiplied at this time, although they were slightly less numerous than male foundations.[1] The nuns were strictly enclosed, according to the precept which was laid down by St Caesar, and which was adopted almost everywhere, and they devoted themselves primarily to prayer and to weaving and embroidery. These feminine communities brought a note of delicate piety and charity to every Christian country. In England, in particular, they underwent an exceptional development from 650 onwards, under important figures such as St Hilda, St Etheldreda, and the charming St Lioba, who was the spiritual friend of St Boniface; their influence was enormous, certain of their abbesses, such as St Bridget (in Ireland, c. 450–525) and St Hilda, actually having jurisdiction over *double monasteries*, made up of both male and a female community, and being obeyed absolutely by both sexes.[2]

The development of monasticism during the Dark Ages is thus a very important historical fact. What influence was it to have? This can be considered under three headings. From a specifically Christian point of view the religious houses, following exactly the idea of the first founders of the monastic institution, were always centres of a more pure and more intense spiritual life, and because of this kinds of strongholds where faith and morals could be better protected from the contaminations of the world. The real function of all the communities, to whatever rule they were subject, was always the celebration of the Divine Office and the sanctification of souls. The Benedictine Rule

---

[1] In his excellent *Histoire de l'Église en Belgique* (vol. i, 2nd edition, 1946, p. 176), which contains so much fine material, and not only concerning Belgium, Father de Moreau notes that during the Merovingian epoch women's abbeys were less numerous than those of men and that women appeared little interested in 'spiritual matters.'

In Britain, however, women's convents (apparently always being a part of 'double oundations' at the beginning) were very numerous in this epoch. But in the continental diocese of Coutance, there are none before 677, date of the foundation of the 'Parthenon of Ham' (near Valognes) by the bishop St Fromundis. (Cf. Dom Laporte, 'Les Origines de monachisme dans la province de Rouen' in *Revue Mabillon*, 1941, p. 25.)

It will be observed that the appearance of the first religious houses for women is almost contemporary with the disappearance of the deaconesses who had played a certain part in the Church in the first centuries. (Cf. *Dictionnaire d'archéologie*, by Dom Cabrel, vol. iv, column 730.)

[2] The position of St Bridget was so important that legend suggested that she had received episcopal investiture!

put the office first, that of St Columbanus, penitence, but the means only were changed, not the intention. These monasteries were, therefore, centres of prayer above all else: in many of them the *laus perennis* was practised, the perpetual intonation of prayers begun in Byzantium by the Acimite monks, and which had spread throughout the whole Church. The repetition of the psalms held a very important place in the monasteries: though St Benedict wisely limited the number that must be sung at matins to a dozen, St Columbanus was to go so far as to recite seventy-five one after another on certain Sundays! The day was completely staked out with these pious stopping-points, which we still have in our monasteries to-day: Matins, Prime, Tierce, Sext, Nones, and so on until nightfall, when the office of Compline completed the process of sanctification.

But this purely spiritual action of the monasteries was very far from being their only function. No one can ignore the picture, which is so often quoted, of the monasteries as the havens of intellectual life, at the very moment when the black waves of Barbarism were raging around their walls. 'The monasteries,' writes Chateaubriand, 'became kinds of fortresses where civilization sheltered beneath the banner of a saint: in them all that was noblest in learning and in culture was preserved.' How far is this picture really true? It is beyond dispute that, during the twilight time the monks were to take far greater care, not only than the laity, but than the secular clergy too, to safeguard the things of the mind. At Vivarium Cassiodorus urged his disciples along the path of intellectual study and was exceedingly proud of his fine library; St Caesar laid down two and a half hours reading each day for his nuns; even the gruff Columbanus did not want his monks to be 'ignoramuses'; and it has been calculated that a Benedictine monk had 1,265 hours in each year at his disposal for his intellectual studies, which, in a monastic life of fifty years, would enable him to get through some eight thousand volumes (which is all the more remarkable since even the library of a very wealthy monastery did not contain more than a few hundred books)! Under the influence of St Maurus, the beloved disciple of the saint of Cassino, the Benedictines devoted themselves increasingly to the defence and more detailed study of the culture of the mind (and this is why in 1618 the Benedictine congregation which was to be that most devoted to intellectual pursuits was to adopt the name of *Maurists*). The copying of manuscripts occupied a very important place in monastic labours, especially in Ireland and in Britain, and later on on the Continent in the Benedictine monasteries. Finally, it is also true that the only serious education of any kind corresponding to our modern 'secondary' and 'higher' education was given in the monasteries. Having said all this we must be careful not to exaggerate these merits. All the monasteries should not be represented as kinds of pillars of scholarship and culture, nor all the monks as learned men. Judging from the poor quality of many of the literary productions issuing from these communities it must be concluded that the learning in them was not always of the highest order, and that numerous men became monks whose knowledge never went much beyond the rudiments of reading and writing, plus a smattering of a few sacred books— the profane authors continuing to be neglected. The intellectual effort in the monasteries did not become general until much later on, until the beginning of the Carolingian renaissance, and it was only then that they aimed at producing an authentic culture; but long before this, in the darkest epochs the taste and the means for it had indeed been saved for the rest by some communities.

The real human merit of the monks of the Dark Ages was of a quite different order: it lay in the fact that they pioneered various countries and thus gave them to civilization. In this respect they cannot be too highly praised. The very conditions of monastic life encouraged this action: manual work was imposed by the various rules as an extremely sensible way of balancing the truly spiritual effort of the monks. Moreover, in their search for silence and meditation, the monks left the towns, where the insecurity of the age kept most of the women's convents and often established themselves in out-of-the-way places far from the cities which were now too small to house them all, often right in the country in the middle of a forest. Consequently clearing the scrub, felling trees, and draining marshes were inescapable necessities for the monks, and thus new lands were conquered or fields that had been left abandoned since the Invasions were reclaimed. The Vosges, Flanders, and the inhabited areas of Champagne were all occupied by Columbanian monks in this way. (Valfroy, the only Stylite known in the West, actually lived in the Ardennes.) The spiritual sons of St Benedict always continued this work wherever they settled. The villages and townships of western Europe which owe their origins to the pioneer monks are literally countless; there are certainly tens of thousands of them, and it is not just rural settlements which are thus indebted to the monasteries. Certain cities have their origin in the abbey too; this is true in the case of Caen and in the case of Saint-Omer, which sprang from an abbey founded in 649, and there are many others besides.

Thus populations grouped themselves under the protection of the abbey, their stay and refuge in times of peril, populations whose attitude to their monks was one of veneration as much as of gratitude. Under the monks' hands they had seen swamps become meadows and scrub turn into corn-fields; at Pontigny, Yonne, for example, as Roupnel has pointed out, the whole aspect of the village changed when

the monks took it in hand.   When St Theodolphus, the abbot of
Saint-Thierry, died, the peasants hung the plough, which he had used
constantly throughout his life, in the church as a kind of relic.   So, in
establishing themselves firmly far and wide the monks completed the
conquest begun by the missionaries: it is thanks to them that Christianity took root and endured.

## The Organization of the Church in the West

When we consider the outward appearance of Western Europe from
the fifth to the eighth centuries, it seems to be covered by a vast network of men and institutions which alone still retained almost all its
essentials.   This network, its strands supple yet firm, tended to expand
and to strengthen itself from decade to decade.   If it was torn apart
momentarily in one place, it would stubbornly mend itself and finally
emerged as stronger than any of its assailants.   This was the Church.
Without her, without these bonds which she alone knew how to
establish, from the popes and the bishops down to the monks and even
the most humble village clergy, anarchy would have been irresistible;
when one considers what these Dark Ages were like, even despite the
presence of the Church, one wonders into what frightful chaos Europe
would have fallen if the Church had not continued to exist.

The survival of the Church's organization through all the torment
of the Invasions is therefore a fact of capital importance.   Her
hierarchy remained intact; intact too (or easily reconstructed) was her
ecclesiastical geography.   Established on the foundations of the
ancient 'cities,' which corresponded to what men were beginning to
call 'dioceses,' over which was the 'province,' or, in ecclesiastical par-
lance, the see of the 'metropolitan'—our modern 'archbishop'—she
faithfully reproduced and carried on the old Roman administrative
system: here we can see how very right the Church had been, when,
with inspired prescience, in her earliest days, she had moulded her
offices and institutions on those of the Roman administration.   It was
thanks to this that she was able to take its place.[1]

---

[1] This observation retains its validity even when we take into account the restrictions
which modern criticism has placed on the principle which gives the diocese the same
territorial basis as the *civitas*.   It is quite wrong to ignore the pertinent remarks of Canon
Chaume (*Recherches d'histoire chrétien*, Dijon, 1949, pp. 66–84), which prove that the
equation Diocese = Civitas is not always accurate, but these are only a question of
exceptions, which, although they do not of course confirm the rule in accordance with the
accepted formula, only contradict it occasionally.

Nevertheless we must not transpose into these times a map of ecclesiastical boundaries
similar to our own, so many centuries later.   The first dioceses were comparable to the
apostolic prefectures which the Holy See establishes in mission country: their boundaries
were very fluid at first and only became fixed when Christianity had become stable: the
first bishops were *regional bishops*, who moved the boundaries of their dioceses back as
they extended the scope of their apostleship.

Below the bishop the organization was still very rudimentary, but it gradually tended to form its own hierarchy. The diocese came to be divided up into *archdeaconries*: in several dioceses (e.g. in Coutances and Meaux), the archdeaconry in which the episcopal town was situated bore the curious name of *Christianity*, a relic, it is thought, of the epoch when there had been Christians nowhere but there. This was going back to the time when the Church in the capital of the diocese was indeed the only church there was there; as—as we have seen—the places of worship increased in number, as the rural parishes were created, the clergy organized itself into the pattern with which we are familiar: at the head of the parish was the rector or vicar with his assistants, and, exercising a rather indeterminate control which varied from region to region, was the archdeacon, archpriest or dean, who was a kind of district rector. At first there was only one arch-deacon to each diocese, and he was termed *oculus epicopi*: in relation to the bishop he was a kind of disciplinary official who sometimes played the role of a mayor of the palace and occasionally came into conflict with the bishop who stood in awe of him. But his power declined when he ceased to be the only archdeacon in the diocese. By the end of the tenth century the dioceses had been split up into numerous areas and at the head of each of these areas, which all bore the name of archdeaconries, there was an archdeacon.

Over and above the level of the bishop, and even of the metropolitan, there was a clear tendency for certain sees to claim superiority over the rest. The reasons for these claims varied: they might be based on historical importance; on the influence of some outstanding individual, or on the significance of the town in which the see was situated, whether it was political or economic; it was often a *primacy* of prestige and influence rather than a properly hierarchical authority. Some-times the Papacy recognized and preserved this primacy. Thus in France the primacy had first belonged to the see of Vienne, the civil and religious capital of southern Gaul; at the beginning of the sixth century it was the see of Arles which held first place, both because of the influence which St Caesar, proclaimed as 'Vicar of the Church' by the Pope, gave it, and because it possessed among its archives funda-mental and unique works, collected together by St Caesar himself, which were used by all the Gallic councils of the time; later on, from the beginning of the seventh century, Arles declined, to the advantage

---

Likewise this is the explanation of the vacillation which is so obvious here and there, a vacillation which finds expression in the 'double bishoprics.' In Gaul there were various unions of cities under one single bishop: Rheims and Soissons, Tournai and Noyon, Cambrai and Arras, Boulogne and Therouanne were united in pairs, and some of these associations lasted for several centuries. Noyon and Tournai were to remain united until 1146, Arras and Cambrai until 1094. (Cf. Jean Lestocquoy, 'L'Origine des évêchés de la Belgique seconde' in *Revue de l'Église de France*, January 1946.)

of the Bishop of Lyons, who claimed the title of 'Primate of the Gauls' and even that of patriarch; it should be noted that Paris, although the royal capital, took no part in this competition, and remained a diocese suffragan to Sens until the seventeenth century.    In Spain, on the other hand, it was Toledo, the seat of the Visigoth kings, which, after the effacement of the ancient and venerable see of Seville, held the preponderant position, and the *de facto* primacy of its bishop even went so far as to secure for him (in 681) the right of appointing successors to dead bishops, in any province whatsoever.    In Italy the sees of Ravenna, Aquileia, and Milan, of which the last-named at one time hoped to rival Rome, saw their prestige decline as that of the Papacy grew greater.

Ecclesiastical leaders tended to emerge in this way in every country in Europe.    The tendency was balanced by another institution, which played a leading role in this epoch: the *national Councils*.    The holding of regular meetings of Christian leaders, in order to discuss the interests of the whole Church, was a very ancient custom, dating from the earliest times (there was the Council of Jerusalem in 49), and it was one which a canon of the Council of Nicaea had made obligatory.    As a rule the bishops and their metropolitan were to assemble twice a year in each province; these provincial councils, which fell into abeyance during the hurly-burly of the Invasions, started up again towards the middle of the sixth century.    The national Councils, comprising all the leading clergy of one country, and taking decisions on the most weighty problems touching on faith, morals, and even politics, the majority of which have been preserved for us to read, were even more important. It can be said that it was these Councils which traced the path which the Church was to follow.    In Gaul there were more than fifty such Councils between the Council of Agde in 506 and that of Auxerre in 695.    They were almost invariably convened by royal command, or at least with the king's agreement; some, like the Council of Orange in 529, set down, in decrees which were confirmed by the Pope, the Catholic doctrine as against certain heretical tendencies, particularly those of the Semi-Pelagians.[1]    In Spain, starting with the famous Council of Toledo (589), which hallowed the conversion of the Visigothic kings to Catholicism, episcopal assemblies were held annually as a rule, and really played the role of a Senate and Court of Appeal. There were also Councils in the Irish Church, the Anglo-Saxon Church, and the Italian Church.    In the last-named the Roman Councils met annually on the anniversary of the Pope's election.    It should be noted, however, that this extremely useful institution suffered a decline

---

[1] Descendants of the heretics of Grace, stemming from Pelagius, who has been dealt with in Chapter I, section: 'The Champion of Truth'; the semi-Pelagians somewhat toned down the errors of the original Pelagians however.

during the seventh century, especially in France, where no Councils at all were held between 695 and 742, an eclipse which coincided both with the growth of the Pope's authority and with the crumbling away of royal power under the Merovingian *rois fainéants*.

Such are the chief characteristics of the Church in the West at this period; but if the general ideas were almost identical everywhere, in the spiritual climate, customs and rites varied greatly from region to region. The Church in Gaul, with its bishops who were also royal counsellors, its 'Gallican' rite, its particular way of celebrating mass, its special feast-days, such as that of St Martin on 11th November, which marked the beginning of the Advent fast, was not at all like the Church in England, which was mystical and loyally Roman in every detail; nor like that in Spain, which was enthusiastic and particularist; nor like the Italian Church, which was torn at this time between Lombard and Byzantine influences. In Spain baptism by one immersion alone was practised, although the Roman custom specified three. In the Celtic parts of Britain and in Ireland the bishops were almost independent of one another,[1] and their churches clung so tenaciously to some of their customs, notably to their own particular methods of calculating the date of Easter, that this was one of the factors which retarded their union with the Anglo-Saxon Church founded by St Augustine and the missionaries from Rome. However, it should be emphasized that if, in the last resort, these particularist tendencies resulted in giving rise to what must perforce be called antagonism, such cases were very exceptional. On the contrary these differences of emphasis did not prevent any Church from being truly Catholic, that is to say, universal. In the darkest days of the Invasions, or during the vicious wars which tore the West to shreds—Gaul in particular—it is most striking to see that the missionaries of God still went everywhere and travelled from place to place with astounding freedom and ease: we have only to think of the peregrinations of St Columbanus! In those days it was accepted as a matter of course that foreigners should come to lecture Christians on matters of faith and morals: were not the two great reforms in the Frankish Church carried out by an Irishman, St Columbanus, and an Englishman, St Boniface? Here is one of the most important features of the Church in the Dark Ages: she knew how to safeguard the principle of universalism, at a time when the direst difficulties threatened to shut the peoples in on themselves, and hers was a universalism even greater than that of the *imperium romanum*, since all the Germanic peoples were henceforth included in it.

---

[1] The characteristic feature of the Irish Church was the abbey-bishopric: the diocese was centred on an abbey, not on an episcopal city. This was also the case as regards Dol, in Brittany. (Cf. Dom Gougaud, *Les Chrétientés celtiques*.)

The universalist principle of the Church is for us to-day made incarnate in a man who is the living representation of Catholicity: *the Pope*. The question which raises itself is whether he possessed such pre-eminence during the Dark Ages. It is necessary here to distinguish between two aspects of the question. It is beyond dispute that, so far as spiritual prestige and moral ascendancy were concerned, the Pope, in his dual capacity as successor of St Peter and as Bishop of Rome, a town which retained considerable fame, was deeply respected in the West; in the Christian West we find no trace of those anti-Roman, anti-pontifical tendencies which are so clearly visible in the Byzantine East. Witnesses to this fact are innumerable—in Gaul, where the Council of Tours declared: 'What bishop would dare to act against the decrees of the Apostolic See?'; in Spain, where St Isidore of Seville dubbed the Pope 'leader of the ministry of bishops,' and stated that 'the see of Rome has all the churches in its care'; and in England, where the episcopate lived in extremely close harmony with Rome, and where many of the faithful, the priests, and even the kings themselves came to end their days near the tombs of the apostles, as voluntary penitents.

But if the Pope's spiritual ascendancy was undisputed, his practical authority did not go hand in hand with it at the beginning. Forced to struggle against the emperors at Byzantium—which he did with admirable energy, as we have seen—hindered in his action firstly by the chaos into which Italy was plunged, and then by the embarrassing presence of the Byzantines in the peninsula, the Pope did not impose his authority upon Barbarian Europe in one fell swoop. It was done in stages, the first important stage being reached by St Leo the Great (440–61)—the Pope who asserted the supremacy of Rome in such lofty terms at the time of the Council of Chalcedon in 451—who strove to control the direction of all ecclesiastical affairs, whether they were in Italy, Gaul, Spain, or Africa. The chaos of the period often put the results obtained in jeopardy, but, during the sixth and seventh centuries there were numerous popes who reminded the clergy of every country that they were subject to them: and numerous popes too who intervened in difficult questions everywhere. The picture of a Church which was centralized, and, despite political divisions, grouped around the Pontiff of Rome, made steady progress. At the turn of the sixth and seventh centuries (590–604), the powerful personality of St Gregory the Great, his tireless activity, and his missionary endeavours turned this picture into a living reality and made everyone recognize it as a fact.

In the seventh century, therefore, it can be said that the Pope was clearly recognized as a leader in the eyes of the West. Although he was chosen by the bishops and prelates from the province of Rome, with the more or less tumultuous assent of the people, no one dreamed of confusing him with an ordinary bishop. One detail of his accession emphasized his extraordinary character: ever since the time of John II, in 532, the new Pope had been accustomed to change his name on being elected, and he always adopted that of an apostle, or a saint, or of one of his more famous predecessors, a fact which marked in symbolic fashion his historic affiliation and his influence. Moreover his patrimony, the *Patrimony of St Peter*, as it was called, had grown enormously since the Edict of Milan, owing to the generosity of the emperors and various great families. It was now an immense realm which included territories scattered throughout Italy, and also some in Dalmatia, Sicily, Gaul, and Africa. These estates were managed by 'rectors of the patrimony'; broadly speaking, they contributed to the Papacy's material needs, and, it should be added, they contributed considerably to its prestige. The pontifical authority was to stand up increasingly to these Barbarian kings who, when they became Catholics, had only too obvious a tendency not to allow the Church in their kingdom to escape their despotism, until the day when this antagonism would wither away in the fruitful collaboration established between pope and monarch by Charlemagne.

## FAITH IN THE MIDST OF DARKNESS

In appearance, therefore, the Barbarian West was now Christian, or was in the act of becoming so.[1] The Church controlled it. But if we try to penetrate within the souls of the men of the period, is the picture which we find there so satisfactory? It is exceedingly difficult to deal fairly with the Christians of the Dark Ages, for their psychology was so different from our own. The moral mediocrity which has been

---

[1] The progress of Christianity in Europe is marked out by the foundation of churches. One of the great preoccupations of modern scholarship is to attempt to place the sites of the first churches. Archaeology and the study of place-names help us to satisfy our curiosity: in this connection one speaks nowadays of religious topography. The name-dedications of churches are precious guides for those undertaking this research; it has been noticed that in the diocese of Strasbourg the majority of the earliest churches were dedicated to St Peter (Saint-Pierre-le-Vieux, Dompeter). Their situation is also a starting-point from which numerous deductions can be made. It has been verified that in the towns the first churches were often built outside the Castellum (this is so in the case of Saint-Pierre-le-Vieux at Strasbourg). It is presumed that they date from an epoch when the garrison was still heathen. The churches built inside the Castellum were subsequent to its conversion. Excavations, and the examination of objects found in the ground which are engraved with Christian inscriptions or patterns, provide valuable guides to which our knowledge of the Christian past of this epoch owes its continuous and perceptible progress.

The continental authority on religious topography is M. Jean Hubert, who has published a fine study of the subject in the *Bulletin de l'Académie des Inscriptions* (issue of 20th June 1945).

described earlier in this chapter leaves the reader with one quite over-whelming impression: that Christianity certainly did not seem to have much hold on this bloodthirsty and lustful mass of humanity. The most abominable aspect of it all was that crime was so commonplace that men ended by taking it for granted, that public opinion scarcely reacted against it, that the very sense of justice and moral rectitude became blunted: but is it not true that an epoch which touches us far more closely presents a remarkably similar character?

Except for a handful of superior souls, it must be recognized that men's faith at this time rested principally on ignorance and terror. The folk of this age lived in perpetual uncertainty, and in constant fear of baleful forces beyond their control or comprehension. Their *credo* can be virtually reduced to a belief in God's omnipotence, and a terror of His fearful arm. 'Even the most daring of men,' writes Fustel de Coulanges, 'if they are confronted with relics, and if their conscience is not absolutely clear, become flustered, grovel on their knees, make all kinds of confessions, and sometimes actually fall to the ground and die!' From this attitude stemmed the importance which was accorded to the great punishments inflicted by the Church in the most serious cases, *excommunication* and *interdict*. To be turned out of the Christian community, kept from the eucharistic Banquet, from the protection of the Supreme Master; to be, at the same time, completely cut off from society, to be scorned by all the faithful and rejected like a leper—this was a ghastly punishment which no one faced lightly; did not the gloomy ceremonial of excommunication signify that the con-demned man was now considered dead, although still breathing? And when a village found itself put under interdict because one of its members had committed a crime in the church, or because the parish was in revolt against authority, the suppression of all religious services would rapidly dismay the faithful so much that they would hasten to show proper repentance. So these sentiments of fear perhaps had their better side.

But they had a far worse one too. The old pagan fears were still there, seeping up in the popular mind; St Eligius protested 'against those senseless creatures who implore favours from the trees, bearing burning brands in their hands, or who, in order to cure their sick cows, make the animals pass through the cracks which age has opened up in the hollow tree-trunks—those hollow trunks that no one dares to burn!' These wretched folk could scarcely tell the difference between what belonged to the province of religion and what fell under the heading of magic, any more than they could distinguish between the priests of 'Christ the Lord' and the sorcerers and witches who swarmed everywhere. (Even good kings like Gontran lived surrounded by a cohort of sorcerers, although he had some of them burned alive from time to time.) Everything which seemed to penetrate the secrets of the unknown and to work upon the occult also found ready believers. Because of this, the men of these twilight times were the obvious prey of impostors and alleged miracle-makers. Quite a diverting book could be written about the adventurers who agitated this or that Christian country between the sixth and tenth centuries. At Bourges, about 600, one man pretended to be Christ; he wandered all over France with his sister, whom he had called Mary, and even duped some of the priests: whenever he drew near a village he sent emissaries on ahead to announce that the Lord's time had come and that everyone must now dance naked in the village square like Adam and Eve in paradise! In the eighth century a more modest visionary was content to proclaim himself a saint and an apostle: he consecrated churches in his own name of Aldebert, and exhibited a 'letter from Heaven,' which he said the angels had sent him, and which was guaranteed effective against all evils; he found a way of getting himself ordained by the bishops, and then proceeded to pardon sins in a most expeditious and agreeable fashion, telling his faithful that since he could read the secrets of their souls he had no need to hear their confessions! There were impostors of this type everywhere, in Germany and Ireland, as in Italy and Spain.

This primitive religious psychology also led to the emergence of 'superstitious' practices—in the most banal meaning of the word, for these are practices that modern man still clings to in his heart even though he is loth to admit it but which are legion nevertheless. The wearing of lucky charms—which were henceforth blessed of course! —the making of certain gestures in order to stave off destiny; the pronunciation or refusal to pronounce certain words—these were all universal customs. The most primitive fetishness was transferred to the Christian plane. Here and there the menhirs were christianized, but they continued to be the objects of superstitious fears. The almost unbelievable customs which accompanied the cult of the saints can be similarly explained. In the Dark Ages admiration and reverence towards the martyrs, formerly a proof of one's loyalty to the loftiest human examples of Christianity, acquired the character of a real cult, of a new religion; since God was so awesome it was necessary to use human mediators to reach and to move Him; the saints, who were His friends and His chosen ones, were certainly ideal for this purpose. These naïve souls needed a supernatural presence that they could touch and feel, and one which was clearly visible in their fellow men. For reasons which we often find unintelligible certain saints enjoyed tremendous popularity: it is understandable enough that St Martin should be so highly thought of that seven hundred parishes were dedicated to him, but why this exceptional devotion to St Genesius, St Julian of Auvergne, St Privatus of Gevaudan, St Ferreolus of

Vienne, and so many others? Canon Cristiani has compiled a list of French saints up to the year 752, the dawn of the Carolingian age. It comprises 1,300 names, and it is only an approximate list, which other scholars have questioned a good deal. Each saint had his legend, which grew from generation to generation, and sprouted new miracles. Men asked these patrons to be not merely intercessors with the Almighty, but to perform far more concrete services for them: these ranged from arranging the satisfactory watering of their fields to procuring happy endings to difficult confinements! And woe betide the saint who tried to shirk his duty in this direction! When the church of St Columba in Paris was broken into and robbed, the worthy St Eligius rushed into the sanctuary and spoke aloud to the saint in language like this: 'Listen well to what I have to say to you, O mighty St Columba! If you do not arrange for all the stolen goods to be returned, I shall block the door of your church with piles of thorns and then you will no longer have a cult!' Needless to say, being sensitive to arguments like this, the saint had the objects duly returned. . . .

The efficacy of the saints obviously resided in the objects which had belonged to them, and, better still, in bits of their flesh and bone. The cult of relics, which had begun in the third century, underwent enormous expansion and acquired a character, which, it must be admitted, made it almost a fetishism. Men quarrelled over possession of the robes which a saint had worn, over the hairs from his head, and even over his nail clippings. (At Tours it was constantly necessary to replace the ropes in the belfry, for the pilgrims cut them up and removed them as relics!) On the tombs of the blessed men placed pebbles of lead and fragments of rag, which were then held to have acquired their saintly qualities. The oil from the lamps which burned in their sanctuary, the wax from their candles, even the dust which was swept from the floor there—all these made good material for relics; the trade in them was a booming one. It must be confessed that these religious customs were strange indeed! The crowning-point was assuredly reached by certain men who were custodians of saints' corpses. These managed, as was done in Syria, to fix a funnel at the top and a tap at the bottom of the shrine, so that oil could be poured in, which, after being well impregnated with the 'virtues' of the dead man, was drawn off again. It sold wonderfully well!

In the fifth and sixth centuries the West Europeans were loath to touch the saints' actual bodies. In this way they were quite different from the Easterners, who literally dismembered them, and St Gregory the Great declared the removal of a saint's body from its tomb to be sacrilege. But from the seventh century onwards the Eastern custom gained ground in the West: people began wrangling over the tibia of St Genesius, the head of St Ferreolus, and other precious bones.

Passing by Bordeaux one day an important Merovingian personage learned that a Syrian there possessed the relics of St Sergius: he fell on the merchant's house, besieged it, and forced the Syrian to let him cut a finger from the wonderful skeleton. 'I do not believe that the saint was very pleased at this,' comments St Gregory of Tours philosophically at the end of his anecdote.

All these incidents are characteristic of a thorough primitivism which it would be folly to deny. Must we confine ourselves to them? Is it advisable to measure the level of spiritual life from these disappointing appearances? Without falling into the excesses of some apologists, who see in these very superstitions evidence of the 'sense of the divine' which the men of this age may have had, is it not essential to balance these rather sombre features with some brighter ones?

To the credit of these often nominal Christians must be set, first of all, and above all, a true humility. Certainly they knew what human vanity was, but they were completely devoid of overweening intellectual pride, that satanic pleasure of bragging against God. The heroes and heroines of the tales of Gregory of Tours are as turbulent, lustful, and wicked as it is possible to be: they remain Christians— great sinners, but Christians all the same. When they are excommunicated by the Church they have but one desire and that is to be absolved. From this fact stem certain reversals of character that are truly astounding, and certain conversions which are almost miraculous. The most astonishing example is that of Fredegunda, a wicked woman if ever there was one, who, when threatened with the loss of her children, declared her penitence in these moving words: 'I know all too well that my sons' death is being brought about by the tears of the widows and the orphans for whom I am responsible.' Several similar examples of reversals of character such as this one can be quoted during these centuries.

A deep understanding of the wretchedness of man and of his need for forgiveness—this is certainly the most striking characteristic of these Christians; it should never be underestimated. Consequently the sacrament of Penance held a considerable place in the religious life of the period. It was in this epoch that it acquired those aspects with which we are familiar. Public confession, followed by a *reconciliation*, bestowed through a bishop, which from early Christian times had only been concerned with the most serious sins, those which caused public scandal, was gradually transformed; the custom of confessing all one's sins, even those which existed only in the secret depths of one's own heart, in order to obtain remission for them, was established in the monasteries. St Benedict advised his monks to confess their secret errors to their superior. The Irish, and above all St Columbanus, popularized and systematized this practice which became current among the laity; *auricular confession*, i.e. private confession made to a priest, was substituted for public confession.    In the Celtic Christian communities, under the influence of the Irish monks, *Penitential Books* were drawn up for the guidance of these confessors.    These were veritable manuals of spiritual guidance, containing catalogues of sins with all their corresponding penances: if this automatism of punishment seems to neglect the state of mind of the guilty person and the circumstances of the sin, it remains true that the habit of private confession, when often repeated, tended to improve the Christian character and to give an important role to the confessors: although mediocre these Penitential Books had the merit of defining precisely the sins to avoid, and of stating clearly the evangelical ideal at which Christians should aim.

The fact that these Barbarian Christians were willing to submit to penitential discipline should therefore be assessed at its true value. All the more so, since these penances were far from being light ones. They had absolutely nothing in common with saying the rosary ten times over, which usually satisfies the modern confessor!    And this is true, even leaving out the rule of St Columbanus, which made liberal use of the birch-rod; six strokes for the monk who had forgotten to say 'Amen,' ten for the one who notched the table with his knife, six for the one that sang out of tune, and so on, up to two hundred strokes for the most serious offences!    In ordinary life, fasting, corporal punishment, and financial amends were commonplace.    Certain folk even added to their penance, e.g. the Irish saint who is said to have sung all the Psalms in the Bible with his body immersed in icy water.    We have already referred to the kings and princes who entered monasteries, or who went to end their days in Rome in literally apostolic poverty.    There were also the *recluses* who had themselves walled up in a cell, enclosed for a long period, even for a lifetime, in a cramped prison where food was passed into them through a small aperture!

The development of the sacrament of Extreme Unction, recommended by the Venerable Bede, and the custom of *pilgrimages* (which is of course also linked with devotion to the saints) are both connected with this ideal of penitence.    Pilgrimages had begun to be frequent during the third and fourth centuries, especially after the 'finding' of the True Cross by St Helena.    They became general from the sixth century onwards; countless Christians went at least once in their lives to pray at the tomb of St Martin at Tours—the most famous place of pilgrimage in Gaul—or to venerate the memory of St Maurice and his companions at Agaune in the Valais; the wealthiest and the bravest went as far as Rome, bearing letters of recommendation from their bishops which enabled them to lodge at the hostels built for them all along the roads. Pilgrims who went to Jerusalem were regarded almost as saints, and on their return they would retell their adventures over and over again, and describe the buildings which they had seen—the rotunda of the Holy Sepulchre, the basilicas of Jerusalem; whilst at Ephesus had they not visited too the cave of the Seven Sleepers, the cell of St Thecla at Chalcedon, and at Melitene the basilica lined with gold, which housed the bones of St Polyeuctus? Moreover these long and pious journeys were not without their hardships and dangers, for bandits lay in wait for the pilgrims all along the mountain passes, especially in the Alps. It is true that one obtained certain worldly pleasures from these stupendous efforts, aside from the spiritual rewards, or so the decision of a Council of Chalcedon implies. This reminded men vehemently that a pilgrimage was not an occasion for revelry!

The penitential effort of the Christians of the Dark Ages is not the only religious sphere in which a true spiritual value can be recognized. Is there not a genuine piety which shines through the superstitions which encumbered faith all too much? Can we not detect a hint of sentiments and actions something like those which we to-day consider essential to all religious experience? Is this not the epoch when the custom of votive masses was established, and the confraternities also? As for these saints, whose temporal intervention men demanded so readily, there were some Christians all the same who felt that the essential lay in their example alone, and that it was this example which had to be considered first and foremost. It is not at all unusual to see a king or a great vicious lord being converted, and begging forgiveness for his past sins, on finding himself in the presence of a genuine saint. And it is really remarkable to observe that right in the middle of the Dark Ages the devotion to *Our Lady* begins in the West (and in the East also, at the same time, it must be remembered), finally achieving that glorious radiance which we know so well. Is it not indeed wonderful to see the gentlest figure in all Christianity beginning to impress herself upon the souls of men in this most brutal of epochs? Let us but reread the Marian poetry of this period—the hymn of Andrew the Orator, written at the blackest moment in the collapse of the ancient world, towards the end of the fifth century, or, in the sixth, the *O Gloriosa Domina* of St Venantius Fortunatus, the poet of Poitou and friend of St Radegund, or, again, the hymn which Paul the Deacon wrote about 750—and we hear once more the sound of words which still move us to-day. Is this not also the time when, from 431 onwards, emulating the example of St Maria Maggiore, men built churches dedicated to her? At this period too the festivals of the Blessed Virgin began to appear in the calendar, not only that of the Purification, which was already very old, but the Annunciation, the Nativity of Mary, and, above all, the Dormition, which was fixed at the 15th August. Men who were capable of feeling the nobility of soul expressed in devotion to the Virgin cannot have been wholly superstitious brutes and nothing else besides.

Then again we find among these Christians what can be called a definite *feeling for the Church*, a feeling which modern Christians have allowed to become far too feeble. They had a profound feeling of all belonging to the same family, they believed that they were collectively responsible for everything that happened to it, whether it be good or bad. A crime committed by one of them seemed bound to draw divine wrath down on them all: this is the aspect of the idea which is sometimes exaggerated and superstitious; but it also had its good sides. 'The affairs of the Church are not the concern of the priests alone,' declared St Avitus, 'but of the whole Christian community.' Can we not detect an appeal to the laity of our own time in these words? [1] In fact, the faithful participated in all the Church's activities: the attendance at church services was enormous, the mass drew such huge crowds, especially on the major feast-days, that it was sometimes necessary to make a rule (such as that laid down by the Council of Auxerre in 585) in order to prevent the faithful from arriving the evening before and sleeping in the church. Ceremonies which were bound up with the year's work on the land gave rise to enormous demonstrations of piety, notably the *Rogation Days*, three days of processions just before Whitsuntide, instituted in 475 by St Mamertus, Bishop of Vienne, to implore God's protection for human labours, and those of the *Great Litanies* which St Gregory the Great founded at the end of the sixth century, with similar intentions, namely, in order to 'baptize' the old pagan festival of the Rubaglia. During the mass people were used to listening to sermons of a length which would seem quite overpowering to-day, they were interested in them . . . they even joined in with their own comments!

Here again an important fact can be noted: it was during these Barbarian centuries that the *liturgy* underwent the development which made it what we know it as to-day; the liturgy, that is to say the very means by which the faithful participate in the divine Sacrifice. The use of liturgical vestments, which was imported from the East, became customary in the West. The liturgical customs varied a good deal according to the country concerned: there was a Gaulish or Gallican liturgy, a Mozarabic or Spanish one, a Celtic liturgy, and above all a

---

[1] There is a curious demonstration of this state of mind in the 'right of spoliation' (*Jus spolii*), by which, on the death of a bishop, Christian folk were authorized to ransack his chattels, which were considered to belong or to have returned to the Christian community. It is obviously wrong to judge the customs of this age in relation to our own. (Cf. F. de Saint-Palais d'Aussac, *Le Droit de dépouillé*, Paris, 1930.)

Roman liturgy, and the last-named tended to supplant the rest.[1]   At this time too the *Kyrie eleison* and the *Gloria in excelsis*, both originating in the East, were added to the primitive elements of the mass, and also the Easter *Alleluia*, ordered by Pope St Gregory the Great, and the *Agnus dei*, which was introduced by Pope Sergius I (687–701).   And we should remember also that this was the period in which the liturgical chant in the admirable Gregorian tradition, that sublime chant to which we have returned so many centuries later, was first released into the air, to beat against the vaults of our churches until our own time.

## THE CHURCH'S PRINCIPLE OF REFORM

The great danger for the Church was that she might allow herself to be contaminated by the very society which she was trying to transform. This danger was not of recent origin: it had sprung into being when Christianity itself was born and it will last as long as it does; but it shows itself in different ways according to the country or the period concerned.   The Church is not *of* the world, but she is *in* the world; she is divine, and yet she is composed of men, in other words of sinners: a tragic contradiction!

In the Dark Ages there was the danger that Christianity might succumb to the general 'barbarization,' that instead of elevating the newly baptized it might slip into violence and vice along with them. This danger was all the greater because the laity all too often exercised a disastrous influence upon Church affairs, especially in the nominations of bishops.   Behaving like real 'bishops outside the Church' after the style of Constantine, the vast majority of the sovereigns of this epoch considered the clergy as a body of civil servants in their own employ.   In 614 Sigbert forbade St Desiderius to go to the Council of his province in language that is reminiscent of certain letters of Louis XIV.   However, in judging this attitude it is essential not to lose sight of the fact that the ecclesiastical provinces were often cut in two by the changing boundaries of the Frankish kingdoms: a bishop who went to his Council was sometimes going into enemy territory. From 511 until 650 a dozen Councils declared that the king had convened or authorized them.   A subject of the king was not allowed to become a clerk without his sovereign's permission.   The ordination of a free man deprived the king of a warrior: and this is why such a large

---

[1] We know a great deal about the Roman liturgy from the fifth to seventh centuries from the *Sacramentaries*, books containing the details of the mass and the services connected with various sacraments.   The three principal ones are called the Leonine (after Pope St Leo, 440–61), the Gelasian (after Pope Gelasius, 492–6), and the Gregorian (after Pope Gregory II, 715–31, or Pope Gregory III, 731–41).

number of former slaves were raised to the priesthood. Even more important: a clerk could not become a bishop without the consent of his king. In theory the bishop was chosen by the clergy of his diocese and consecrated by the metropolitan, but the matter really lay with the canons who fixed the election! In fact, it was the king who ordered the metropolitan to consecrate the man of his choice, likewise it was he who put pressure on the clergy with all the means in his power. At the beginning (until about 580) the Councils contented themselves with recognizing that the king's assent was indispensable to a bishop's election; but in 614 Clotaire II promulgated an edict in which he reserved to himself the right of naming those of his noblemen whom he pleased as bishops, and the Church dared say nothing against this. A considerable number of bishops came from the 'schola palatii,' the school of cadets where the sons of important families were prepared for the king's service under the Master's eye. It was to result in bishoprics—highly profitable prebends—being wrangled over, being acquired through influence, and even bought with gold. Simony, the sin named after Simon the Magician (Acts viii. 20), rotted the clergy in every Barbarian kingdom. And these detestable practices were taken for granted so completely that even the saints themselves scarcely reacted against the principle of illicit royal action; e.g. St Boniface clearly states in a letter to Pepin that the king has every right to nominate bishops.[1]

It is all the more astonishing, therefore, that customs such as these did not always end in catastrophe, and that in the main, as we have seen, the bishops of the Dark Ages were actually of high quality and were often even saints! On the other hand it is not in the least surprising that certain of these prelates were unworthy of their sacred calling, nor that, in view of the bad example set in the highest circles, loose morals penetrated a section of the clergy. Is it necessary to quote examples? The worthy St Gregory of Tours does not conceal these melancholy and unpleasant facts, and when one reads the lives of genuine saints, those of St Columbanus and St Boniface, for example, one sees how disgusted these men of God were to see the bishops of the royal entourages as their colleagues, men who were often immoral, coarse, and ignorant. Some of these bad shepherds have left their names behind them, because of the very enormity of their vices: there

---

[1] In fact, however, it should be made clear that most of the time the bishops valued the men whom the king esteemed. For example, Dagobert, influenced by an entourage of saints who included St Eligius among them, made excellent choices of bishops. But whenever the king was a hardened warrior, the men whom he placed in episcopal sees were bound to resemble him in their habits.

It must be noted that, in all fairness, contrary to the 'bishops outside the Church' that the Christian emperors had been, the *rois fainéants* were not interested in dogma nor in the internal organization of the Church. (Cf. Chénon, *Histoire du droit*, vol. i, p. 33.)

is Cautinus of Clermont, for example, who would become so drunk during a banquet that it needed four men to carry him from the table; it was he who, when annoyed with a priest who refused to hand his holding over to him, had him shut in a coffin along with a corpse, whence the wretched man had the good fortune to escape. Or there are Salonius of Embrun and Sagittarius of Gap, whose unbelievable day-to-day lives are recounted for us by Gregory of Tours. They spent their days in feasting and debauchery, and employed armed ruffians to hold their colleagues in the neighbouring bishoprics to ransom! It should be added that these evil habits were not confined to bishops alone. The history of certain monasteries shows analogous flaws there. Even the women were guilty! There is the story of a revolt by the nuns of the very abbey of Holy Cross, which had been founded by the gentle St Radegund, against their abbess, which is full of vile incidents in which severed noses and ears are the least of the horrors mentioned. These evil moral habits were to continue for a long time to come: on the threshold of the Carolingian epoch a certain Gewiliob, who was Bishop of Mainz, committed so many secret murders and open massacres that St Boniface was to call him an assassin to his face!

It is when we consider these extremely painful matters, over which we would dearly like to be able to throw a veil, that we can really assess the heroism and tenacity which Holy Church needed to fight such evil ways. The instrument which she used in her efforts was essentially the *Council*, the assembly of bishops, be it national or provincial, which we have already noticed meeting frequently in all the countries of the Christian West. There the abuses which crept into the Church were studied and condemned, and attempts were made to suppress them. The most detailed aspects of the moral and religious life of the people were dealt with in these Councils. Very often simony was denounced with vigour. The cases of antagonism between clerks or between priests and laymen which the Councils settled are too numerous to count. Schnürer states: 'The civilizing influence of these assemblies of bishops, composed of the most cultivated men, and of the highest moral authorities in a country, can never be rated highly enough, especially when the circumstances of the epoch are taken into consideration.'

An excellent manual on the moral and spiritual life of the clergy of the period could be compiled by collecting the principal articles of the conciliar decisions of the sixth and seventh centuries. And whenever we are tempted to pass severe judgment on the clerical morals of the age, with reference to the shocking examples which we have just noted, it behoves us to think too of these extremely wise and fruitful deliberations where the Word of God was indeed no dead letter. The principal effort of these Councils turned essentially on the moral control of the clergy.    In order to palliate the serious inconveniences of nominations of bishops by the king as much as possible, a kind of novitiate was imposed on the newly elected, consisting of a delay of between one year and eighteen months.    No man could be consecrated bishop unless he had been a priest for at least one year.    An attempt was made (without much success) to insist upon bishops always living in their sees.    On several occasions the higher clergy were reminded of their sacred calling, of the need for a certain simplicity of life, and those who possessed hounds and falcons or who bore arms were censured.    On a lower level attempts were likewise made to impose a standard moral and intellectual code on the priests and deacons.    A certain delay between their conversion and ordination was insisted upon, the tonsure was refused to the illiterate, and a minimum age was stipulated (thirty for a priest).    The celibacy of the clergy was not yet obligatory, but (in theory) carnal relations, and even cohabitation, were prohibited between a priest and his wife.    Although these directives were only irregularly observed in practice it was nevertheless remarkable that the Church knew how to show herself so resolute in the matter of principles.

Was this resolution enough?    In order to be really effective it was necessary for the best principles to be asserted by men who really knew how to make their voices heard, who dared to proclaim the will of God whatever the cost.    This had been the role taken by the prophets in Israel.    For human nature is made like this; habit weighs on it so heavily that it needs frequent chastisement to give the soul back the vigour which routine tends to dissipate.    It is characteristic of the Church's wisdom and of her profound knowledge of mankind that she understands this perfectly.    Thus, on the personal plane, she counsels 'retreats,' where the individual conscience can come to terms with itself and be rehabilitated; on the parochial plane the 'mission' plays the same reviving role.    On the higher plane of the Church herself, during the most sombre moments of the Dark Ages, there appears the great idea which is to be fundamental throughout her whole history, the idea of *reform*.    Throughout the Middle Ages, whenever the truth of the evangelical spirit was in danger of being obliterated by infamy and mediocrity, there were always some men there to arise and remind Christians of the divine commandment: this is the task which is to be assumed in turn by the monks of Cluny in the tenth century, Pope Gregory VII in the eleventh, St Bernard in the twelfth, and Innocent III and the Mendicant Orders in the thirteenth.    In the heart of the Dark Ages the spirit of reform, or, to phrase it differently, the idea of 'perpetual revolution'—for we should remember that Christianity is, in essential, the Revolution of the Cross—was made incarnate in two mighty individuals. These were St Columbanus, at the end of the sixth century, and St Boniface, in the eighth.

There is no better way of describing the action of St Columbanus, this mighty athlete of Christ, than in stressing, once again, his resemblance to the prophets of Israel. Eli, Isaiah, and John the Baptist preaching on the banks of the Jordan—he resembles them all. This great gnarled giant, who was said to be able to kill a bear with his own hands alone, would suddenly appear in a country with his team of Irish monks, as fanatical for the truth as himself, and, like him, tonsured in the Celtic style, namely, with their hair falling behind on to their shoulders, but shaven in front in a semicircle. They brandished the long staff of the pilgrim; from the bundles that they carried they drew out their liturgical books and their reliquaries and began to preach. No human glory impressed them in the least, kings no more than bishops—not even Councils before which, when invited, they scorned to appear. They stressed the necessity for penitence: they loudly denounced crimes and sin. The influence of St Columbanus rocked the conscience of Europe for nearly half a century around the turn of the year 600: wherever he went there were veritable outbreaks of sanctity. A new spirit breathed upon the clergy, and the episcopate was visibly improved by him. His own foundation, Luxeuil, became a real nursery of bishops, and his distinctive stamp was impressed on many other communities, such as those of St Wandrille at Fontenelle and St Philibert at Jumièges. Through him, the custom of auricular confession, with private, fixed penances, was imposed on the whole of Western Europe. As a contemporary aptly wrote, he 'hurled the fire of Christ wheresoever he could, without concerning himself with the blaze it caused.'

In the middle of the eighth century the task of reform was taken up again by St Boniface in quite a different way: the calm, moderate, almost timid Englishman did not possess the Irishman's meteoric brilliance of manner, but he had a tenacity which Columbanus had lacked, and above all, leaning upon Rome as he did, his action closely linked with the will of the Pope, whose influence had increased considerably since the time of Columbanus, he could conceive and undertake a much more sweeping reform. It had become absolutely essential! For seventy years—the figure is Boniface's own—the Christian communities in the West had been in a state of crisis. This was especially true of Gaul and Germany, where the sordid wars in which the last Merovingians indulged were causing complete anarchy. Under the presidency of the great missionary, who was armed with special powers in his capacity as legate of the Holy See and personal representative of the Pope, a series of Councils was held in Germany, Flanders, and Neustrian France between 742 and 747. The campaign against abuses was taken up again with extreme vigour.    Spurious priests, fornicating deacons, and bad bishops were all removed.    The calibre of the clergy was better controlled by insisting that future priests take an examination in the Holy Scriptures.    The bishops were ordered to supervise their dioceses more closely: from these Councils dates the bishop's obligation to make rounds of his diocese in order to administer confirmation.    It can be stated that, thanks to these important Councils of the middle of the eighth century, and especially to the 'Germanic Council' of 742 (the place at which it was held is not known), to that of Leptinnes or Estinne in 743, and to those of Soissons in 744 and 745, there emerged, from out of the Merovingian ruins, a new Church.    Of course the results were not all that St Boniface had dreamed of; in particular he did not succeed in establishing an absolutely strict hierarchy which, from the Pope to the metropolitans, from them to the bishops, and from the bishops to the ordinary priests, would have maintained an absolute unity of purpose and government throughout the whole Church.    This great idea of unity was premature, like that of *Christendom*, of which it would later be the corollary.    But it was very important that a step had been taken in this direction, and although the reformers of the eighth century could do nothing to prevent the excesses of royal intervention, by coming to an understanding with the first Carolingians, notably with Charles Martel, they prepared the way for new conditions of agreement between the Church and the temporal power, which, under Charlemagne, would determine such a splendid Christian expansion.[1]

## THE BATTLE FOR CHRIST

The Church's effort to resist the degrading influences of Barbarian society was in actual fact but one aspect of the general action which she waged unceasingly against the evil tendencies and vices of this society. We have already been forced to note a certain complicity with the worst forces of the period amongst the Christians of the Dark Ages; but this distressing part of the picture should not make us forget its glorious aspects, in other words, the patient and often heroic work, apparently but modestly fruitful at the time, but in reality of vital importance for the future, which it produced, or at any rate sketched out in embryonic form.

In contrast to the unworthy bishops whose morals caused such scandal, it is essential to look at those who, by the purity of their

---

[1] Once again the Church's feeling for the future, in opting for the Carolingians, the force of the morrow, as against the Merovingian *rois fainéants*, who represented decadence, must be emphasized.    Later on we shall see that the part played by St Boniface in this substitution of one dynasty for another was considerable.    (See Chapter VIII.)

personal life, the nobility of their religious ideal, often by their courage, were sometimes up to the point of actual martyrdom, true witnesses of Christ. The men in the first category were but shocking exceptions; the others were legion. There were many who knew how to face their kings, on whom they were largely dependent, and to repeat the lesson of the Gospel as loudly as the prophets of Israel had repeated the law of God to their wicked sovereigns. There were many who, in one form or another, pronounced words as admirable as those uttered by St Isidore of Seville: 'You will be king when you act justly, and when you do not act justly you will not be king!' There were many too who, in the midst of the dangers into which their steadfastness placed them, were to repeat the words of St Nicetius of Trèves: 'I will joyfully die in the cause of what is right!' Countless anecdotes describe these saint-bishops battling for morality, justice, and charity with an audacity which often leaves us breathless. Not only St Columbanus, whose temperament was naturally aggressive, and whose quarrels with various princes have a really epic quality,[1] but moderate, prudent men also—St Germanus of Paris, for example—who reminded Sigisbert and Chilperic of their duty with vehemence and resolution, when they were on the point of hurling themselves on one another in a fratricidal war. Then there were saints like St Caesar of Arles and St Nicetius of Trèves, who thought nothing of stopping a church service and refusing to continue it because they had just seen a prince or king of scandalous moral conduct entering the church. Some of these heroes of Christ paid for their courage with their lives. One of these was *St Praetextatus of Rouen*, whose whole episcopate was one sequence of constant bravery; having reproached the terrible Fredegunda for her vile crimes, he was first of all arrested, and then released upon the protests of the other bishops, notably those of St Gregory of Tours. He at once began to repeat his condemnations, and was threatened with exile—to which he calmly replied to the queen: 'In exile or not, I am bishop and always will be: but as for you, are you sure that you will always be queen?' Finally, when assassinated by a secret agent of Fredegunda's, he died with the name of his real murderess on his lips. St Desiderius of Vienne died in similar circumstances, for having rebuked his king, Thierry, for his infamous moral conduct. So too died the most famous of these martyr-bishops, *St Leodegarius of Autun*. He was arrested (*c.* 680), partly for having preached the

---

[1] Here is an example of the sort of relations that existed between this gruff prophet and the Frankish kings. He arrived one day at the camp of Thierry II of Neustria, whose private life was extremely scandalous, with the intention of rebuking him for it. On his arrival, Brunhilda, the grandmother of Thierry, asked him to baptize some of her grandchildren, all of whom were bastards and the result of illicit unions. 'These children are products of the brothels!' cried the saint. 'May not one of them live! May not one of them reign! I shall call the wrath of Heaven down upon them!'

need for morality overmuch to the high and mighty, and partly for having stood up to the despotic excesses of Ebroin, the dreaded Mayor of the Palace. His eyes were put out, and then, after a pretence at a trial, he was degraded and finally beheaded; the last words uttered by this witness of Christ were: 'May God keep the heart of faithful Christians free from all hatred!' [1]

In general, the Church's effort can be summed up in a few words: she tried to make the Barbarians less barbarous. The influence that she exerted, or tried to exert, was a civilizing one.[2]    On the theoretical plane this influence was as yet very feeble; *the law* remained firmly Germanized and the Church could do little to stop the Barbarian customs of private vengeance and of the *wer-gild* or composition: rather regrettably, some of her number too often accepted and even justified the ordeals and the judgment of God in the name of an extremely questionable religious concept. But she protested against the excessive use of torture on many occasions. And, as her influence grew greater, law evolved in a perceptibly more Christian direction: thus the new Alemannian Code, drawn up about 717, formulated regulations which marked definite progress in this direction, stipulating the prohibition of all servile labour on Sundays, the punishment of perjury, the legal recognition of the right of sanctuary, and even the desire that the judges should always be 'just and God-fearing men.'

But the Church did not make her principal effort on the theoretical, legislative plane: instead, taking society just as it was, its men for what they were, with their often appalling failings, she tried, in a practical way, to limit the worst of their violence and to force them to respect certain human principles. The most striking example of her effort in this field was the real battle which she waged in defence of the *right of sanctuary*. The character of this right, which had been inherited from Graeco-Roman paganism and transferred to the Christian

---

[1] The tragedy of St Leodegarius (French, *Saint Léger*) moved his contemporaries so much that large numbers of villages were named after him. It has sometimes been suggested that he was not put to death because he was a witness of God but because he was a leader of the aristocracy, which was then battling against the centralizing policy of Ebroin. But all the bishops had a political role to fulfil, and it is quite impossible to separate what is specifically Christian in their action from what can be considered as primarily political.
[2] The bishops were not the only agents through whom this influence worked. Women had a great part in it too, and just as—as we have seen—women had played a leading role in the work of conversion, so they also very often had the most happy effect on their *entourages*. Some of these gentle characters are famous: *St Ottilia*, the saint from Alsace, whose biography is more or less interwoven with legend, but from which it is clear that she battled with all the forces at her youthful command against the brutality of her own father (apparently one of the murderers of St Leodegarius); *St Radegund*, who resisted the savagery and immorality of her husband, Clotaire II, as much as she could, before leaving him in disgust, and taking refuge in a convent; *St Bathildis*, a young English captive, whom Clovis II married on account of her marvellous beauty, and whose charm and piety made Paris and the whole kingdom (of which she was regent) radiant, until she retired to the convent she had founded, at Chelles.

churches during the fourth century, is well known. Under it the guilty—debtors or criminals—who succeeded in taking refuge at the foot of the altars, could not be arrested while they remained there. This did not mean that the Church wished to ensure that their crimes went unpunished, but rather she wanted to allow the anger of the moment to cool, and use her own intervention to make the principles of justice respected. The refugees could not be handed over to the secular authority until an oath sworn on the Gospel had guaranteed that they would not suffer torture, mutilation, or death. The difficulties which this right encountered can well be imagined! The kings who saw an enemy escaping them used all the means at their command to try to have him handed over to them. Moreover the refugees themselves often behaved in a quite revolting manner, drinking and feasting in the church, and even, like a certain Evroul who took refuge in the atrium of the basilica of St Martin of Tours, going so far as to strike a clerk who, noticing that he was drunk, refused to give him any more to drink, and actually insulting St Gregory in the middle of a service! It is really wonderful that, caught between these two evils, the Church yet succeeded in safeguarding the principle of charity. It is true that God often took a hand in the matter, and that, as the chroniclers tell us on many occasions, violators of the right of sanctuary were almost always miraculously punished!

In this way a number of Christian ideas percolated into this hardened, brutal society, in so far as it was possible for them to do so. Charitable work, the task of social relief, which was totally unknown to the governments of the time, was assumed by the Church and by the Church alone. For her the fight against suffering, the alleviation of the distress of the poor and of those who were unable to work, was an absolute obligation, and one of which she was reminded by the Councils on several occasions. Around the cathedral lived the 'blessed poor,' still called the 'registered,' who figured on the registers of the bishop's assistance funds. The 'foundations of help,' to which the faithful were invited to contribute what they could, existed almost everywhere. It should be underlined, in passing, that this philanthropy had none of the anonymous administrative character that we are familiar with to-day.

The bishops and the priests loved these poor people, for they knew them well, they saw them all around them; [1] the remarks of St Gregory of Tours about the poor little orphans in whom he interested himself are worthy of St Vincent de Paul. There were also hostelries for

[1] A canon of the Council of Mâcon in 585 gives an amusing illustration of their tenderness for the poor: 'Episcopal residences should never possess dogs, lest the poor who come to shelter there be bitten by them.'

travellers and hospitals, all maintained by the Church, many of them owing their existence to the Irish and Celtic monks, who were great promoters of pilgrimages, and who had built them for their pilgrims. Soon, when contacts with the East brought the scourge of leprosy to Europe, the 'lazar-houses' or leper colonies would arise, again at the Church's instigation.

Everyone who was weak and threatened was, as a rule, under the powerful protection of the Church: the widows and orphans to whom, as we have seen, the bishop was a real guardian, and the debtors too, for the Church forbade creditors to abuse their rights and take advantage of those in their debt.    Clerks were forbidden to engage in usury, and the Councils made numerous decisions in which it was condemned on the ground that it exploited the poor.

In more general terms it can be said also that the influence of the Church contributed substantially towards raising the status of women, whose weakness often left them defenceless in face of men's brutality. The change in the attitude towards women which had resulted from the victory of Christianity was absolutely conclusive: never again could women in a Christian community be treated with the contempt which had been shown towards them in classical times.[1]    The immense popularity of women's religious orders proves how greatly feminine purity was admired.    Young unmarried girls and widows were specially protected against the covetousness of their suitors.    The seducer of a young girl was not allowed to marry her, and was heavily punished.    The repudiation of a wife at the simple caprice of her husband was condemned by the Councils on several occasions.    In certain dioceses the Church went so far as to excommunicate judges who were guilty of treating women unjustly.[2]

Finally, the most wretched creatures in society, the *slaves*, also benefited from this tremendous protection which the Church sought to spread over all its weakest elements.    On this subject the Christian

---

[1] Consequently nothing is more absurd than the stubborn legend—it still exists—according to which the Church was said to have declared that 'woman does not possess a soul.'    The origin of this fable is, however, rather curious.    At that same Council of Mâcon, to which we have already referred several times, which took place in 585, one bishop who considered himself something of a purist raised a point of grammar.    He maintained that the word *homo* could not correctly be applied to a woman.    This point is a debatable one, since though *vir* and *mulier* are complete opposites, *homo* can, in general, be used to describe a 'human creature,' either a man or a woman.    From this argument on a point of style, related to us by St Gregory of Tours, it has been deduced that the Church had said 'that a woman could not be called a human creature.'    (Cf. Vacandard, *Études de critique et d'histoire religieuse*, 2nd series, p. 171.)

[2] This tenderness towards the weak is even shown towards animals to a certain extent. There are conciliar decisions which, in short, forbid the ill-treatment of animals.    Episodes in the lives of some of the saints, such as that of St Hubert, who was stopped in the midst of his bloodthirsty hunting exploits by a miraculous stag, or of St Giles, the hermit of Gard, who had a tame doe to live with him, also indicate the same tendency.

attitude must be clearly defined. On the one hand, ever since the
Good News had been given to the world, there was no longer, as St
Paul had made clear, in essential 'either free man or slave'; all men were
equal in the sight of God. From this fact stemmed the real revolution
of brotherhood which had occurred in the early days of the Church,
masters and slaves being linked in the same religious community, a
revolution whose full importance was obvious when Callixtus, a
former slave, actually became pope! But on the other hand the
Church did not condemn slavery as a principle; in the economic circumstances of the age the suppression of this institution was as unthinkable as that of proletarian labour appears to-day to a middle-class
capitalist. To the Church slavery was one of the consequences of the
state of sin in which humanity had floundered ever since its original
fall, and she went so far as to recognize that a guilty man (the ravisher
of a virgin) should be enslaved by those whom he had wronged. The
Church's attitude towards slavery is explained by these two principles,
which she applied simultaneously.

Consequently she strove with all her might to improve the slave's
lot; this was actually one of her most constant preoccupations, judging
from the enormous number of Councils which devoted canons to the
subject. The slave trade was controlled: e.g. the sale of a Christian
or Jewish slave beyond his native frontiers was prohibited. Marriages
between slaves were recognized as legal and had the Church's blessing.
A man who took a slave-girl as his concubine had to marry her
(in theory . . .); at all events, the difference in status was not an
impediment to marriage. The Councils of Orange (441), Arles
(452), Agde (506), Orleans (541), Mâcon (585), Paris (615), several
Councils of Toledo, notably that of 633, and those of Rheims (625)
and Châlon-sur-Saône (650), all promulgated directives of this type:
numerous others granted special privileges to slaves living on estates
belonging to the Church.

This evolution towards an amelioration of the slave's condition was,
moreover, helped by the fundamental transformation which society
was undergoing at this time. The decline of the towns resulted in the
disappearance of those enormous gangs of slaves that had surrounded
the great folk of the classical world; the division of the land into
smaller lots gave the peasant-slave a relative independence, or at least
a greater stability on the land which he cultivated. The transition
from *slave* to *serf*, which definitely occurred between the fifth and
eighth centuries, paved the way for the slave's future freedom.

The Church encouraged the granting of this freedom, although she
did not lay it down as a general principle. In the third and fourth
centuries many wealthy Christians had already freed their slaves. The
bishops and the monasteries of the Dark Ages followed their example

again and again: St Remigius at Rheims, St Bertrand at Le Mans, and St Eligius at Noyon all set slaves free on many important occasions, especially at the Easter festival. A Burgundian Council advised Christians who owned larged numbers of slaves to offer 'the tithe of God' from amongst this number each year.

Lacking machinery as it did, the economic organization of society would allow little more than this to be accomplished at this period: at least an indication had been made of the direction in which the Church was to apply herself whole-heartedly in the tenth century.

## Chinks of Light

What the Church accomplished on the moral plane she accomplished in the intellectual sphere also; in other words, in the midst of the abysmal darkness, she kept a few lanterns alight there too, which were capable of indicating the path for the future. Of course we must not expect to see masterpieces springing forth in this age, and it is only too obvious that the whole Barbarian epoch reveals a frightful abasement in literary and artistic standards. But even here, more important than the results achieved at the time, was the fact that the essential values were afforded the means of preservation, that efforts, fumbling though they were, were made to recapture an intellectual life, namely, that in the darkest days of all we can discern chinks of light which promise great things for the future.

The important fact which dominates this epoch as far as literature and the arts are concerned, as it is to dominate the whole of the Middle Ages, is that all this intellectual activity depends exclusively on the Church. During the centuries between 500 and 1200, everything that has any significance depends on her. In the sphere of what can be called literary activity (we shall see how essential it is to apply this term in a restricted sense at this time) there is not a single name of any importance which is not that of an ecclesiastic, be it bishop, priest, or monk. The last 'lay' writer—he is also the last Roman writer—was *Boethius*, the minister of Theodoric, who, while lying in the prison where his Ostrogoth master held him for a long time before having him put to death (*c.* 525), reconsidered classical philosophy in his famous treatise, *On the Consolation*; but, neo-Platonic and Aristotelian though he seems, this writer, who only uses the name of Christ once in the whole of his book, is nevertheless completely steeped in Christian theology, and his work was to have a profound influence upon medieval scholasticism. All his contemporaries, all his immediate predecessors, and all his successors were clerics: his colleague in the Ostrogoth ministry, *Cassiodorus*, the last great scholar of the age, who ended his days in his monastery of Vivarium, among his beloved books;

the charming saint from Bordeaux, *Paulinus of Nola*, who lived a century earlier, and who, in his bishopric-monastery in Campania composed poems, several of which are written on the walls of churches, which are reminiscent of those of La Fontaine; or at the end of the fifth century, the great scholar-aristocrat from the Auvergne, *St Sidonius Apollinaris*, a fine letter-writer whose poetry was often exquisite, and whose election to the see of Clermont flung him right into the thick of the struggle on behalf of Christianity. Another writer of the epoch, who was a priest and later a bishop, and who can be described as the first of the troubadours, was *St Venantius Fortunatus* (530–600), whose wonderful hymn, *Vexilla regis*, is still sung to-day, and who maintained a most poetic and blessed friendship with St Radegund, the queen who became a nun. The vehement *Salvianus* was a monk of Lérins, a priest and a 'teacher of bishops.' Even in the darkest moment of the Barbarian holocaust he continued to shout his fanatical reminders fearlessly to the world. The last rhetorician-bishop was *St Ennodius of Pavia*; *St Avitus* was a very great bishop of Vienne in Dauphiné, and composed an epic on the creation of the world; *Corripius the African* was a priest who was the author of another epic dealing with the reconquest of Africa by Justinian. And this list could be expanded far beyond this point.

It must be emphasized that the fact that all the men capable of writing belonged to the Church resulted in a radical transformation of the actual attitude towards literary activity. To-day we are quite familiar with writers who are doctors or engineers without subordinating their art to the superior interests of medicine or applied science. In the Dark Ages, on the contrary—and later on in the Middle Ages—the creative activity of the mind was strictly subordinated to the interests of Christianity, to the apostolic design. For example, St Gregory the Great reproached St Desiderius of Vienne for teaching grammar and for 'singing what is not even advisable for pious laymen.' This exclusivism is understandable (at least in the heroic epoch at the beginning, for it was not to last): the Church had a treasure to preserve herself, and a fundamental task to accomplish, the conversion of the world. She could not allow her forces to be dispersed when the effort needed was so colossal. Thus culture came to seek refuge within sacred learning, notably in the Holy Scriptures and in theology. When he wrote his famous Rule, *St Benedict* had certainly only one purpose in mind, namely to give the monks a set of effective directions; nevertheless he created a masterpiece from it. In the same way *St Prosper of Aquitaine*, the greatest of St Augustine's immediate disciples, in studying and commenting on the theology of the genius of Hippo, produced a fine work of which parts still exist; and *St Caesar of Arles*, who was solely interested in guiding the souls in his charge, has left us a collection of instructions which has real literary merit.   This is even truer of *St Gregory the Great*, whose literary output—homilies, *Moralia*, the *Regula Pastoralis*, Dialogues—is exclusively linked with his apostolic and pontifical action and which nevertheless contains all the qualities which a true writer of his epoch was still able to possess.

For there is no disguising the fact that as the period advanced, the truly literary value of the work produced fell irresistibly.[1]   The most famous writer who lived at the end of the sixth century, *St Gregory of Tours*, author of the *History of France*, of which we have spoken a great deal, and which is invaluable to us for our knowledge of the deeds and men of the period, is a mediocre writer, with a clumsy style and a limited vocabulary, who only just knows how to make a bald list of his interminable details, without exercising any care for composition. His successor, the pseudo-Fredegarius, whose Latin is barbarously comical, was far worse.   The scholar at the beginning of the seventh century, who actually bears the name of Virgil, Vergilius Maro, and who was nicknamed 'Grammaticus' to distinguish him from the author of the *Aeneid*, was a mere compiler of dictionaries who padded his Latin with Hebrew, Greek, and Celtic words, and even with scraps of Toulouse patois, in order to show how well educated he was.   The absence of genuine learning and the abandonment of dialectic resulted in the collapse of speculative thought; consequently theology itself declined.   When the arguments provoked by Faustus of Riez in the fifth century on the 'Semi-Pelagian' doctrines had been extinguished, no further attempt at theological progress was made.   Instead men merely sought to follow faithfully the lessons of the Fathers—but they forgot that the most fundamental of these lessons had been the very need for a constant reappraisal of ideas, for an ever deeper study of the heritage of Christ.

However, through what must indeed be termed this progressive decline into darkness, a chink of light would appear from time to time, here and there.   It was not a very strong light, and it did not last long, but it was enough to show that the oil that fed the flame was not entirely exhausted and that one day the true daylight would be able to return.   Thus one of the aspects of the immense work accomplished

---

[1] And its scientific value fell just as much.   Historians like St Gregory of Tours scarcely possess any critical faculty at all; geographers show an ignorance of even the most elementary knowledge—e.g. the map known as St Alban's map, produced at the end of the seventh century, reduced the world to the shape of a large horse-shoe, with the Mediterranean occupying the middle of it; even the best of the jurists, such as the Roman monk Denys the Little, who laid the foundations of Canon Law in the sixth century, contributed nothing original, but were strictly dependent on Byzantine codes. It was Denys the Little who had the immortal idea of making the birth of Christ the start of a new era, but he made a mistake in his calculations, so that Jesus was really born between four and seven years before 'the Christian era.'

by the great Pope *St Gregory* was the temporary revival of theological studies. This theology was unquestionably less speculative than that of the ancient Fathers, it was more rigid in its articles of faith, which had to be believed absolutely and not examined too closely, but at least it brought back men's appetite for meditating on the things pertaining to God. Likewise we must pay tribute, ephemeral though the results of their efforts were, to those saints who, in the middle of the seventh century, surrounded King Dagobert, St Eligius, and St Ouen, who tried to revive the taste for learning in Frankish territory, and above all to their contemporary, *St Isidore of Seville*, who undertook the same task in Spain. St Isidore was personally but an encyclopaedist after the style of Pliny, an intelligent man with a lucid, brisk style, but he did at least ensure the transmission to future generations of all that he had derived from the classics and the Fathers. And above all we must remember with gratitude the name of the *Venerable Bede* (673–737), the great doctor of the English Church, the scholar-monk, whose labours were enormous, who was in turn the historian of his people, and an exegetist and a moralist as well, who not only introduced the Anglo-Saxons to the wealth of the Patristic Christian tradition but directly influenced the whole of eighth-century Western Christianity. Bede, as Christopher Dawson has said, represents the highest point reached by intellectual culture in the West during the period between the fall of the Empire and the ninth century. It is thanks to signposts such as these that the path of learning did not disappear into the night for ever.[1]

Among the promises of the light to come there is one particularly memorable one. This promise is expressed in the development of Christian singing, right in the very heart of the Barbarian epoch. Music has always been the consolation of those in sorrow and of periods of anarchy, and it is extremely moving to realize that the melodious voice of the Church rose into the night in the very darkest moment of the twilight age, as if she wanted thereby to strengthen men's souls to withstand the horrors surrounding them. The name of Gregory the Great is gloriously linked with this expansion of Christian music. Had music been non-existent in the Church before his time? On the contrary, from the earliest days of the Church religious services had included singing, the psalms providing the words for this, and the music deriving from the Jewish *cantilenas* or from various Graeco-Roman themes, with occasional vocalization, punctuated by the acclamations, the alleluias, the *responses* of the people: this

[1] Finally, it should not be forgotten that we must go right back to these far-off epochs to find the origins of French poetry. And it so happens that the part played by the Church is preponderant in this field too. The poetry which gave full scope later on to the poetic genius of Racine and Baudelaire 'was created by the Church.' Georges Lote demonstrates this in his posthumous book, *Histoire du vers français*, 1949.

L

was called *responsorial psalmody*.    A little later on men in the East
conceived the idea of using two choirs to sing alternately, and this was
the *antiphonic psalmody*, which St Ambrose introduced into the West.
Finally, in the fifth century, another form of singing was added to
these.    This was the *hymn*, 'the song of praise to God,' based on
words which were no longer taken from Holy Scripture but were
composed instead by Christian poets; these hymns deteriorated into a
series of verses in which the same tune was used for all.

The work of St Gregory the Great consisted, in essential, of the
orderly collation of all these elements, of their harmonization, of the
adaptation of the ancient elements, which dated from the fourth
century and earlier, with more recent ideas.    He unquestionably made
various additions, in response to the new needs of the reforms which
he had introduced, and above all he impressed on the whole structure
of ecclesiastical music the stamp of restrained dignity, of naturalness,
and of simplicity which was the characteristic genius of this great Pope
himself.    The *Gregorian chant* or *plain-song* was to span the centuries.
The *Schola cantorum*, also developed by him, in its standard institutions,
was like the conservatoire of plain-song.    Soon, during the seventh
century, *the organ*—a Greek invention—spread to the West, to Rome
during the pontificate of Vitalian, and then to Gaul and England,
where it was in use in 680.    The splendid and moving musical
atmosphere which the Catholic Church possesses to-day (in its best
elements at least) was already largely in existence thirteen hundred
years ago.

Finally, there was another field in which the Church made her
characteristic mark and assumed the same preponderant role.    Because
it had been necessary—indeed it was the sole necessity—to meditate
on God, theology had preserved intellectual activity.    Because it was
meet and fitting to praise God, the Church's singing had kept music
alive.    Likewise, because it was essential to house and to protect the
worship of God, architecture and the visual arts retained a vitality
which never quite disappeared, even despite the greatest difficulties.
The building of churches was one of the principal preoccupations of
the men of the age.    Christian monarchs, following the example set
by Constantine in olden times, gloried in being great builders of sacred
edifices.    Clovis, Dagobert, the Burgundian and Visigoth kings after
their conversion, and the English rulers, all tried to make their names
immortal in pious buildings.    The bishops had the same anxiety,
those aristocratic bishops, who, from their ancestors, the Gallo-Roman
nobility, had preserved traditions of magnificence: Leontius of
Bordeaux was famed in his own time for his generosity as a builder
for God.    The popes, the most important of all the bishops, were
great builders too.    Countless ecclesiastical edifices were certainly

erected during the sixth century. In their own day they held just as important a position as that held by the churches in the heyday of the Gothic style.

We do not know a great deal about the architecture of the Dark Ages: only a few specimens survive. For a long time it was considered clumsy and hesitant, both decadent and childish, but the recent works of Émile Mâle have demonstrated the injustice of this opinion. We can get some idea of what these great basilicas must have been like at the beginning of the period by studying buildings like the two churches of St Apollinaris at Ravenna, and of those of St Maria Maggiore, St Sabina, and St Paul-without-the-Walls in Rome. These are all imposing, although they are rather cold in appearance. Later on this style developed further; to the traditional Roman basilicas, Eastern influences, deriving from the pilgrimages or from the monks taking refuge in the West after the Arab invasions and the Iconoclastic Dispute, added the galleried churches of which the 'Martyrium' at Jerusalem is the most magnificent example, and the round churches inspired by the rotunda of the Holy Sepulchre. Composite churches sprang up, consisting of two churches, side by side, dedicated to two saints, and one baptistery, the whole forming one cathedral (there were some like this in Paris). Beginning with the Merovingian period, many interesting attempts were made to provide a substitute for the ordinary flat timber roofs—the vaulted arch, the inspired Etruscan invention used so often by the Romans, and the cupola, the ancient Assyrian discovery which Byzantium was reviving so gloriously at this time: there were vaults at Cahors, Glanfeuil, and St Victor's at Marseilles, and cupolas at Nantes, Clermont, and probably at St Martin's at Tours also. Certainly none of this was very skilful as yet; the fragments of Merovingian architecture which we still possess, e.g. the 'crypt' of St Lawrence's at Grenoble, or that of Jouarre, the baptistery of St John's at Poitiers, or, contemporary with these, the remnants in Italy such as the church at Ancona, or those in Spain such as St Eulalia at Toledo or St John at Banos, give an impression of a primitivism, clumsiness, and rusticity which nevertheless has the power to move us. With its colonnades, ill-adapted from the classical style, its squat exteriors, and its clumsy vaulting, this architecture is clearly still searching for its real self: but its resolute boldness and its balanced lines show that the Romanesque style is already powerfully present within it.

What impressed contemporaries most was the decoration of these churches. Their exteriors were very plain: they had nothing in common with the fantastic richness that is associated with Gothic façades, but the interiors had to be sumptuous. No expense was spared in order to decorate the house of God fittingly, and the inborn taste of the Barbarians led them quite naturally to these fantastic displays of wealth.

Sculpture did not hold a very important place here: although, in the fifth century, e.g. in the famous doors of St Sabina in Rome, it still maintained the great Roman tradition, it later became clearly decadent: at St Lawrence's at Grenoble the capitals, inspired by Byzantine art, show collections of animals, birds pecking at grapes, and foliage in vases that are truly Barbarian in type.   It was not sculpture which inspired the artists of this period.   It was the art of mosaics, which the pilgrims had admired so much in the East, and which they reproduced, rather clumsily, for example, in the Chrysophrys at Toulouse.   It was mural painting, those great scenes from the lives of the saints, which entranced the visitors to St Martin's at Tours, or ornamental decoration, showing strong Asiatic influence, intermingled with scrolls on which one could read little religious poems, written in gold lettering.   It was the art of working marble, and great indeed was the sorrow when the Arab invasion put a stop to the exploitation of the Pyrenean quarries.   It was the tapestries which hung behind the choir and between the colonnades, embroidered with peacocks drinking from the sacred vase, with tamed lions, and with eagles—glorious memories of the old dreams of Asia.   And it was the lights, those gold and silver candelabra, so numerous that, as a visitor to Nantes Cathedral remarked: 'You thought when you saw them that the earth too had its stars.'   A foretaste of heaven—that was how this beauty appeared to the faithful of the Dark Ages.   'It is therefore quite wrong,' writes Émile Mâle, 'to talk of decadence in relation to the Merovingian basilicas.   They represent a complete, finished art-form, just as Gothic art was to do later on.'

An astonishing art-form it was, composed of very different elements: memories of Roman antiquity, numerous ideas inspired by Byzantium, and, up to a point, vague reminiscences of the far-off and confused ancestral traditions of the invaders.   Even in painted or sculptured decoration, the 'swastika' or gammadion cross, the borders of entwined 'Ss,' and the use of the wheel, form traces of an immemorial art-form, right in the middle of Romanesque or Gothic art, a form which the Germanic peoples had acquired during their wanderings in the regions of the Urals or the Caucasus, originating perhaps in India, Persia, or China.   This influence is even more pronounced in an ornamental art, which was perhaps the favourite of the folk of the Dark Ages: *metal-work*.   The pieces we still retain, e.g. the famous votive crowns of the Visigoth kings which are in the Cluny Museum, or the golden Gourdon chalice which can be seen at the Bibliothèque Nationale in Paris, continue to astonish us to-day with their mysterious and modern beauty.   We should pay tribute to this art of the Dark Ages, which is so little appreciated, and which has been so long neglected, for it is an art which, beneath its incongruous appearance, at once primitive and decadent, is actually in process of giving birth to a new kind of beauty.[1]

Such in short is the most accurate impression which should be retained of this Christian society of the Dark Ages. Decadent in many aspects, primitive in many others, it is in fact full of unborn hopes, of dark and violent tumult, of promises for the future. These promises were to be slow of fulfilment: after a moment of brightness, when it seemed that civilization had found its feet again at last, the night would fall once more and the darkness would become even more complete. The impression which Western Europe gives us on the morrow of the Invasions will be valid for a long time to come: it is that of a world which, through blood and suffering, is searching for the right road. But the guide whom it had been given is He who never errs, and who leads us all to the true light that lies beyond our darkness.

[1] The miniatures and calligraphy of the manuscripts, which also form a very fine part of the Christian art of the Dark Ages, reveal the same jarring jumble of elements: the classical tradition is there in a fairly decadent form; Byzantium has given it the impress of her conventional style, her rich and formal decoration; the truly Barbarian touch shows in the exuberance of tracery, in the skill in ornamental design, which has the same accuracy as is found in Barbarian metal-work, and in the use of certain semi-plant, semi-animal forms which derive from Scythian art. The English manuscripts are very typical from this point of view. Some carved ivories dating from the fifth to seventh centuries have also been found, which were used as bookbindings; those of Saulieu and Saint-Lupicin, in the Bibliothèque Nationale, are the best known. Émile Mâle has shown that imported works were concerned here, and that these were made in a workshop in Alexandria, in Egypt.

# CHAPTER VI

# TRAGEDIES AND DIVISIONS IN THE CHRISTIAN EAST

## HERACLIUS, 'THE FIRST CRUSADER'

IN THE spring of 614, when the West was groping to find its balance between the Barbarian anarchy and the new order which, since the time of Gregory the Great, had been made incarnate in the Papacy, a terrible blow shook the East. The news of an appalling disaster ran through every province in Byzantium: Jerusalem had been captured! The soldiers of King Chosroes, pursuing the offensives which they had been directing against every Eastern frontier over the past ten years, had once more violated the Palestinian borders. After enduring a twenty-day siege the Holy City had been unable to resist the blows of the Persian battering-rams; once the outer defences had been forced a most frightful onslaught took place, in which religious hatred had exacerbated men's vilest passions. Several churches had been set on fire, among them the oldest one of all, the Church of the Resurrection, which had been built by Constantine. It was said that the dead numbered sixty thousand, and that thirty-seven thousand Christians had been taken into slavery, amongst them the patriarch himself. The Persians had respected nothing, save the basilica of the Nativity, at Bethlehem, and this they had preserved, it was said, because of its mosaic of 'the Adoration of the Magi,' in which the invaders had recognized their national costumes. Countless monasteries had been destroyed, and their monks and nuns scattered. Sacred treasures, rare fabrics, vessels of gold and silver had all been dispatched to the Persian capitals. Finally—oh, unspeakable horror!—the Holy Cross had been torn from the Holy Sepulchre and borne off to Ctesiphon as a battle trophy! For Palestine this was a catastrophe from which she was never to recover. For the whole of Christendom it was an unprecedented disgrace and an unimaginable tragedy. When, shortly afterwards, two relics, the Sacred Spear and the Passion Sponge, which the prefect of Egypt had been able to save, arrived at Constantinople, the people knelt weeping on the quaysides to receive them.

This dramatic episode marked the conclusion of one of those periods, of which Byzantine history knew many, in which the curve of destiny steadily declined from a glorious summit, as if it were being

drawn inevitably towards collapse, anarchy, and ruin.   In the half-
century that followed Justinian's death the Empire had had but indifferent leaders: Justin II (565–78) had had the sound enough desire
to reorganize the army and to put the finances in order again; Tiberius
Constantine (578–82) had boldly faced his enemies beyond the Empire,
and had sought to win the people's affections; Maurice (582–602) had
also shown himself to be a courageous general, a good diplomat, and
a wise administrator; of the four emperors of this period only the last,
Phocas (602–10), the former centurion, had proved as incapable as he
was cruel.   However, to maintain the vast Empire in the outstanding
position in which it had been placed by Theodora and her husband, to
keep control over such very diverse populations, and to compel
respect from all classes of the people, none of whom had the slightest
sense of civic responsibility, supermen would have been needed.   The
grandiose despotism of Justinian had given such a powerful impulse
to the ship of state that it continued on its course, somehow or other,
but no solution could be found for any of its fundamental problems.
The regime lacked solid foundations; this was very obvious on two
occasions: when the Emperor Maurice was executed after having
seen his five sons beheaded before his own eyes, and when the tyrannical Phocas was literally torn to shreds by the mob which had risen in
revolt against him, the least edifying portions of his body being
paraded on the head of a pike.   And, above all, none of these rulers
was capable of taking a clear decision on the grave problem which the
inordinate ambitions of Justinian had left with Byzantium; not a single
one of them was able to choose between the dream of one single
empire, now apparently revived but in fact ungovernable, and the
reality of defending the East against the Barbarians.

The choice was about to be forced upon Byzantium: the situation
grew worse from year to year.   On Justinian's death the Barbarians,
who until then had been contained, prepared a new attack.   The
sudden appearance, about 550, of a new empire in Central Asia, that
of the Turks, whose 'khan,' established in Tien-Shan, ruled in ostentatious pomp, seated upon a throne supported by four solid gold
peacocks, and the continual expansion of this new power, had once
more caused an immense stirring among the tribes that stretched from
China to the Urals.   Its rebound flung the Lombards upon Italy in
568; [1] the Avars, Mongolians who were hostile to the Turks, settled in
southern Russia, and later on the lower Danube.   The Avar horsemen were as threatening as their cousins, the Huns, had been of old,
and the endless waves of Slavs made common cause with them.   They
too were fearless and savage, 'burning their prisoners or battering

[1] On the Lombards see Chapter IV, section: 'The Lombards and the Dismemberment
of Italy.'

their brains out with cudgels, as if they were dogs or snakes.'  It was no small undertaking for Byzantium to confront hordes like these.

All the more so since another menace was threatening her at the same time—the Persians.[1]  The duel between the two empires, that of Constantinople and that of the Sassanids, had begun in 502, and was to be a very prolonged affair, lasting some one hundred and twenty-six years, various truces notwithstanding.  It was an ever-festering sore on the eastern frontiers.  Somehow or other, at the cost of heavy sacrifice, involving money, territory, and his own self-esteem, Justinian had succeeded in preventing this peril from becoming too pressing, in order that he could better devote himself to his 'grand design' in the West.  After his reign was over, in 572, a new alarm sounded: the Persians, clumsily provoked by Justin II, attacked Mesopotamia and Syria.  Then, threatened in their turn by the Turks, and counter-attacked by Maurice (the future emperor), the Sassanids, who were now in the grip of palace revolutions, fell back, and in 591 signed the disastrous peace which delivered almost the whole of Persian Armenia into the hands of the Byzantine Empire.  But the situation swiftly changed.  Whilst Maurice, who had now become emperor, was fast making himself unpopular on account of his harshness and his rigid authoritarianism, and whilst the dreadful Phocas, who had been raised to the throne by an army plot, was succeeding him, the man who was to be Byzantium's most dangerous enemy was establishing himself at Ctesiphon.  This was Chosroes II (590–628).

The last Persian 'King of Kings' is a fascinating figure indeed.  His glory rivalled that of his long-dead predecessors, Xerxes and Cyrus, and he aspired to revive the ambitions of the Achaemenids and to rebuild the unity of the Middle East to his own advantage.  'The heavens themselves are my desire, my treasures are boundless, and the whole world works for me and me alone!' he declared, at the zenith of his power.  He had the throne of Darius remade, decorated with the signs of the zodiac, and here he held court, sheltered in the winter by an awning of beaver and sable furs, warmed by golden bottles filled with boiling water.  His hunting expeditions afforded scenes of fantastic luxury: horsemen garbed in dazzling satins, countless falconers, menservants holding tamed cheetahs by their leashes. . . .  When he halted anywhere an immense carpet was spread upon the ground, on which all the parts of his empire were represented.  His army included nine hundred elephants and his harem twelve thousand women.

Byzantium blocked the path of his ambitions: conflict was thus inevitable.  As long as the Emperor Maurice lived, Chosroes maintained an attitude of grateful friendship towards him: was it not thanks

[1] The Persian danger is treated in Chapter III, at the end of the section: 'The Grand Design of Justinian: His Victories and His Weaknesses.'

to the emperor's support that he had been able to triumph, during the
bloody civil war at the beginning of his reign? But when Phocas
deposed and executed Maurice, the Sassanid attacked the Empire under
pretext of avenging his old friend (602). For twenty years, almost
without respite, Chosroes hurled his armies against the Byzantine
frontiers: one by one, Syria, then Anatolia, and then Egypt suffered
attack from the Persians and from the Mongol bands whom they
employed as auxiliaries. In 609 they almost reached Chalcedon, on
the Sea of Marmora, opposite Constantinople. The catastrophe of the
capture of Jerusalem in May 614 was one of the episodes—the most
tragic one—in this long and terrible ordeal.

But at this point a new leader was already occupying the throne of
Justinian—a leader who was about to alter the whole situation in
Byzantium's favour. The period of dissolution and general decline
was once again to be followed by an epoch of vigorous revival and
grandiose might. *Heraclius* (610–41) was the man responsible for
this revival. He attained the imperial crown after a popular and
military insurrection had put an end to the tyranny of Phocas. At
this time he was still quite young—thirty-six years of age—and an
outstanding man, pure and faithful in spirit, his character magnificently
resolute and equitable. Tall, strong, with red-gold hair and a bushy
beard, he was a man who could look his enemy straight in the eye
clearly and fearlessly. His personal courage was almost excessive.
He would allow no one else the honour of being in the centre of the
battle, going so far as to try his strength in single combat with various
of his enemies. Moreover, as a skilful strategist and a diplomat well
versed in taking his adversary by surprise, he had all the gifts of the
great leader. But above all, he was an ardent Christian,[1] enthusiastic
to serve Christ and the Gospel, the ancestor and indeed the prototype
of those knights who were later to brave a thousand dangers in order
to recover the Holy Sepulchre: it is not without justice that he had
often been called 'the first Crusader.'

The early years of his reign were terrible ones for the Empire.
Nothing seemed able to shatter the Persian momentum. Each year
the armies of Chosroes struck new blows in some unexpected quarter.
At the very moment when Jerusalem was falling, the enemy appeared
at Chalcedon for the second time. Four years later the Avar hordes

---

[1] His life was not so perfect however. As with most of the Byzantines carnal passions
played a large part in it. He could not curb his feelings for his own niece, and to the
patriarch who begged him to renounce this incestuous marriage he replied: 'All that you
have written me is perfectly true. You are but fulfilling your duty as my archbishop and
my friend. As for me, I mean to do just as I please. . . .' The chronicler adds that his
sin was justly punished, for of the nine children which the young Martina bore him one
was deaf and another deformed and paralysed. Here once again we see the law of
contrasts operating in Byzantine Christianity, the most energetic faith going hand in hand
with the most dubious morality.

* L

left their encampments in Hungary, invaded Thrace, and came on to besiege Constantinople. With Palestine and Syria captured, Alexandria occupied, and Byzantium hemmed in by the Mongols on the land and the Persians on the sea, Heraclius was on the verge of despair, and considered retiring to Carthage. Sergius, the patriarch, prevented him from doing so.

Thus occurred a complete reversal of the situation, which was of a quite miraculous nature, and which was to materialize into a true crusade. 'What we are witnessing here is indeed a crusade,' writes René Grousset, 'a crusade if ever there was one, for the Christian armies move on their way at the command of the Church's leader and have as their objective the deliverance of the Holy Sepulchre and the recapture of the True Cross.' 'No,' cried the patriarch. 'You have no right to allow the Persians to occupy the Holy City! You have no right to accept the fact that the Holy Cross of Christ is now in Ctesiphon, an object of derision!' All the treasures of the Church were put at the emperor's disposal. And since at the same time Chosroes, at the height of his conceit, had written Heraclius a letter in which he insulted both the emperor's honour and his faith, the whole Empire rose in a supreme effort. The Persian ruler's scurrilous missive was read from the pulpits, so that everyone should feel the injury of it. 'You claim to put your confidence in God; then why has He not saved Caesarea, Jerusalem, and Antioch from my hands? If I desire it, can I not destroy Constantinople in exactly the same fashion? As for your Christ, do not deceive yourself by reposing vain hopes in Him: He was not even capable of saving Himself from the hands of the Jews who crucified Him!'

The Holy War began on 6th April 622. It was to last no less than ten years and was to include bewildering and sudden seesaws of fortune. Having bought the Avars' retreat at a high price, Heraclius swooped on the Persian armies in Galatia and Cappadocia, threw them back to the Euphrates, cleared Armenia in a single bound, and did not halt at a simple reconquest of the occupied provinces. Instead he rushed into the heart of Persian territory, seized Erivan, and avenged the sack of Jerusalem by burning down the Mazdean temple at Tabriz: it seemed as if the Sassanid Empire was mortally wounded. But no, Chosroes counter-attacked; after the delirious ecstasy of these great imperial victories there followed one, two, three years of hard, exhausting defensive fighting. In June 626 the Avars returned to their former alliance and attacked the Empire once again. There followed a veritable onslaught against Byzantium, in which Mongols, Slavs, and Bulgars rubbed shoulders with 'Medes' and Persians. In this dire peril, the patriarch Sergius, the defender of the city, battled with a savage energy; the picture of the Mother of God, the supernatural protectress, was paraded continually on its walls, in front of the soldiers. The miraculous happened. For the enemy withdrew, while, from the Caucasian redoubt where he had been hiding, and where he had himself recruited various Mongol contingents, Heraclius, tireless as ever, took up the offensive again. In 627 victory favoured the other camp. The emperor swept down from the mountains, took Tiflis, crossed Armenia, invaded Assyria, and crushed the best of the Persian armies near Arbela, at the very spot where the great Alexander had defeated another King of Kings. The exhausted Persians begged for mercy. Lightning raids by the Byzantines struck at one corner of the Sassanid Empire after another. The holy cities of the Mazdeans were afire everywhere. Finally, on 25th February 628, the conclusive news broke upon the world. 'The impious, arrogant Chosroes is no more!' Heraclius told his people. 'The fiend who insulted Christ and the Virgin is dead: listen to the crash of his fall! He is burning in hell now, with all his like!' Deposed by his own son, the last King of Kings [1] had just been executed in the 'house of darkness.' Mazdean Persia was gone for ever.

When on 23rd March 630 Heraclius brought the Holy Cross back to Jerusalem, bearing it upon his own shoulders, the 'First Crusade' seemed crowned by the most striking of victories. But what realities did these splendid appearances in fact hide? Was the Byzantine Empire any less weakened than the empire which it had just defeated? In destroying the might of Persia, whom had the glorious soldier really benefited? Twelve years later Jerusalem was to see a new conqueror surging around her walls. For, at the very moment when the pious Heraclius was climbing the Hill of Calvary, barefooted, the champions of Allah were already poised to spring four hundred leagues to the south.

## RELIGIOUS DISSENSIONS, NATIONALIST AWAKENINGS

The peril on her frontiers was not the only one which threatened the Heraclian Empire; it was not even the most serious. There was something far more fundamental. This immense collection of countries and peoples, of varying traditions and convictions, was in permanent danger of falling to pieces. The religious disputes which had shaken it for centuries revealed the existence of violently conflicting tendencies within this mass of peoples, who were but roughly bound together by Byzantine despotism—tendencies which would

---

[1] The reader should remember that it was after this victory that Heraclius and his successors officially assumed the title of *Basileus*—equivalent to *King of Kings*—which previously had only been given them in popular usage, and which had never figured on official documents.

show themselves clearly at the earliest opportunity.   The astonishing speed of the Moslem conquest remains incomprehensible to anyone who does not fully grasp the picture of this torn and divided East, where the theological arguments on the nature of Christ only helped to lay bare submerged feelings of exasperated nationalism.

Wherever it was established, Byzantine domination proved despotic, meddlesome, and spoliatory; in Africa it needed but five years to elapse after the 'liberation' by Belisarius for the exactions of the Byzantine governor to make men regret the passing of the Vandals; in Italy people asked themselves which was preferable: Gothic terror, Lombard terror, or Byzantine taxation!   The two principal foundations of the Empire, Syria and Egypt, were being openly undermined; ever since the fifth century a phenomenon of capital importance had been taking shape there—the revival of nationalism, which was largely due to Christian influence.   The Syrian masses, the bloc of peoples who spoke Aramaic, stretching from the Mediterranean to the Persian borders, divided between the rival empires, subject to Hellenic civilization ever since the time of Alexander, had found a principle of unity and independence in the Christian faith.   The material centre for this principle was Edessa; the closing of the famous 'School of Edessa' in 489 by the Emperor Zeno had not prevented the development of an original Syriac-Christian literature, with increasingly Nestorian tendencies, which extended right into Persian territory, in the School of Nisibis.   In Egypt, Christianity, in effecting the fusion between the Greek element in the towns and the mass of the fellahin, tended, without so desiring, to disperse Hellenism amid the ancient indigenous traditions, a dispersal which was clearly shown in the growing use of *Coptic*, that is to say ancient Egyptian written in Greek characters. Thus nationalist claims grew up in both countries.

On the religious plane these nationalist tendencies were only too well marked.   They manifested themselves first of all in the hierarchy of the Church, where the organization of the *Patriarchates* was closely linked with them.   These ecclesiastical super-divisions had some diverse origins.   Some, like Antioch and Alexandria, were related to the most venerable glories of Christianity and drew their importance from all those great men who had filled their sees; that of Constantinople, on the other hand, was primarily the result of imperial policy, which was intent on giving the 'new Rome' all possible means of influence and power.   Fixed at the Council of Chalcedon, and officially recognized in Justinian's legislation as the basis of the Church's constitution, the hierarchy of the five patriarchates—Constantinople, Jerusalem, Antioch, Alexandria, and Rome—had contributed to giving the separatist tendencies of the various provinces of the Empire firmer foundations.   This was particularly marked in the

case of Egypt where the patriarch, who was long called the 'pope'—
the head of ten metropolitan sees and one hundred and one bishoprics,
proprietor of countless large estates, a naval commander who controlled the country's trade, a sumptuous donor of alms on whom
thousands of paupers depended—had literally taken the place of the
High Priest of Amen-Rah as the national leader: his official titles proclaimed him 'divine lord, thirteenth apostle, judge of the world,' and
he has been accurately described as a real 'episcopal pharaoh.'  His
great rival, the Patriarch of Antioch, although having one hundred
and fifty-three bishoprics under his thumb, was very far from exercising
a comparable authority over a territory which, though much more
extensive, was without cohesion, and which had been suborned by
countless heresies for centuries past; nevertheless, as the Syrians began
to realize their full stature, the religious leader at Antioch saw his
influence growing ever more vigorous.

Moreover the theological battles which had periodically shaken
Eastern Christianity ever since its very beginnings had their counterparts on the nationalist plane.  Already in Arian times, Alexandria,
the Alexandria of the great St Athanasius, had been the bastion of
orthodoxy as opposed to an Antioch which was in the grip of heresy.
In the fifth and sixth centuries the serious controversies concerning
Nestorianism and Monophysitism had helped to accentuate these
divergences still further; although both were opposed to the orthodoxy of Constantinople, which too often only manifested itself to them
in the guise of Byzantine police action, the Christian communities of
Egypt and Syria were at the same time opposed to each other.  Every
effort which the central power made to re-establish orthodoxy consequently came up against resistance which had its roots deep in the
people's souls; in an inverse sense, every effort at centralization proved
a source of strength to the various heresies.  Byzantium's fundamental
error, her claim to unite religious and political authority in one single
power, thus bore all these bitter fruits.

The Byzantine emperors were no more capable of discovering a
valid solution to this complex situation—whose difficulty would seem
to have been grasped by Theodora—than they were of finding one for
their political problems.  Perhaps no solution existed. . . .  Some,
like Justin II or Tiberius, treated the heresies with a moderation
which bordered on complaisance; others, like Maurice, swung between
tolerance and brutality, or like Phocas, who prided himself on his
extreme orthodoxy, applied the violent methods which were habitual
to him to the defence of the faith.  Furthermore the same ambiguity
was apparent in their relation with the popes, some grasping that only
one firmly founded authority could be capable of leading the many
very different groups of Christians, now torn asunder by heresy, back

to unity and harmony, and that consequently it was in their own interest to work hand in hand with the Roman pontiff; the rest clinging increasingly to the arrogant dream of Constantinople, the religious capital of the East, as the rival of Rome.   From this ambiguity stemmed sudden and violent changes in policy; under Maurice there was a bitter and continuous struggle between the imperial authority and that of the Pope—who was at this time St Gregory the Great—because the latter was intervening in the affairs of the Eastern patriarchate and setting himself up as the supreme guardian of Christian discipline; under Phocas, on the other hand, there was a cordial reconciliation with the Papacy, the Patriarch of Constantinople was forbidden to bear the title of 'Oecumenical,' and the see of St Peter was officially recognized as 'head of all the churches.'   One may well ask oneself what a loyal subject of the emperor could make of such a jumble of convictions, where loyalty to-day had every chance of being considered treason on the morrow, and where one need only change provinces to see everything else change too: principles of faith, administrative methods, even the moral climate.

In his great attempt to revive the Empire Heraclius could not neglect preoccupations of this kind; he could afford to neglect them the less because he could see that, during the war against the Persians, several Monophysite elements had come very near to treason, owing to their hatred of imperial orthodoxy.  Aided by the patriarch Sergius, who was as great a statesman as he was an ecclesiastic, he persuaded himself, as Justinian had done of old, on another theme, that by compiling new formulae he would be able to restore the wandering sheep to the fold. The presentation of Catholic orthodoxy in a milder form, and the heresies likewise in blurred terms—was not this the way to bring agreement to the whole world?   The result of this idea was the birth of a new doctrine, which, after some fumbling—at first a *Mono-energism* was considered—took concrete shape in what was called *Monothelitism*, the doctrine of the single will.   The Catholics wanted to distinguish two natures united in Christ, the Monophysites one. Therefore, if the single principle of the union of these two natures was discovered, would not all be in complete agreement?   It would suffice to say: 'One, and one only Son of God, our Lord Jesus Christ, effects both divine actions and human actions.'   This in itself is not wrong; but the commentary which was given to this prudent formula resulted in declaring that the divine will alone was in Jesus, that in so far as He was a man, He had no will, that, in short, He was but an incomplete man. . . .   And consequently one fell right into the middle of the Monophysite heresy once again.

At the start of the operation all seemed to go very well for Heraclius and Sergius.   Egypt and Armenia rallied to the new conciliatory doctrine. Pope *Honorius* (625–38), who was badly advised, and who was practically convinced that it was all simply a case of one of those quarrels on words to which the Greeks were so passionately addicted, approved the theses which were presented to him, in a somewhat attenuated form, however. The *Ecthesis*, or *Statement of Faith*, which was a real Monothelite manifesto, promulgated by Heraclius as an imperial law, appeared to be accepted everywhere. But, little by little, eyes and consciences were opened. Certain theologians, like St Sophronius and St Maximus the Confessor, began to denounce the error. In Africa some provincial councils condemned it. At Rome *Pope St Martin I* (649–55) organized resistance to the new heresy. Heraclius was now dead, carrying to the grave his ridiculous though well-intentioned scheme for conciliation. In the face of growing opposition, Constantius II replaced the *Ecthesis* in 648 by a new document, the *Model of the Faith*, which prohibited all discussion on the number of wills or energies contained in Christ's personality. This was sensible enough, but it was formulated in terms which were completely unacceptable to the orthodox. When Pope St Martin I united the *Model* with the *Ecthesis* in the same condemnation, a terrible crisis resulted. Mad with rage, the Byzantine tyrant had the old, sick Pope abducted by the army of Ravenna and taken to Constantinople, where he was kept in solitary confinement for three months. Then Constantius subjected Martin to a ghastly mockery of a trial, degraded him like the lowest criminal, and finally, not daring to kill him, sent him to die on the borders of the Crimea, in a loneliness and misery which made this end into a true martyrdom. Such was the result of an attempt at appeasement founded on ambiguity and error, and of course neither the Catholics nor the Monophysites were conciliated by it!

It took the Empire seventy years to emerge from the Monothelite crisis; the diplomacy of *Pope St Agatho* (678–81) succeeded in paving the way for reconciliation. A lengthy Council, the Third Council of Constantinople, the Sixth Oecumenical Council, which sat from November 680 until September 681, proclaimed the doctrine of the two natures according to the tenets of the Catholic faith and liquidated the heresy in all its forms. Thus was peace re-established in the Church at last, but another disturbing symptom manifested itself in this same Council. The Fathers castigated the memory of the patriarch Sergius, the principal author of the heresy; this was just enough, but at the same time they castigated that of Pope Honorius also, which was completely unjust, for the Pope, though he had been weak, had never professed the heresy. This was an Eastern manœuvre aimed at depreciating the authority of the Pope, and it was one that Pope St Agatho did not see through.

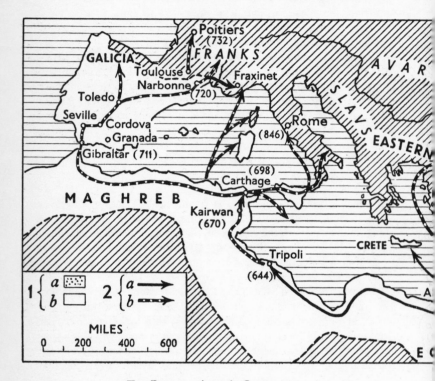

THE RAIDS OF ALLAH'S CHAMPIONS

1. *Extension of the Arabian Empire.*—(*a*) To the death of Mohammed (632).
   (*b*) To the fall of the Ommayads (750).
2. *Principal Expeditions.* (*a*) Under the first four caliphs (632–61).
   (*b*) Under the Ommayads (661–750).

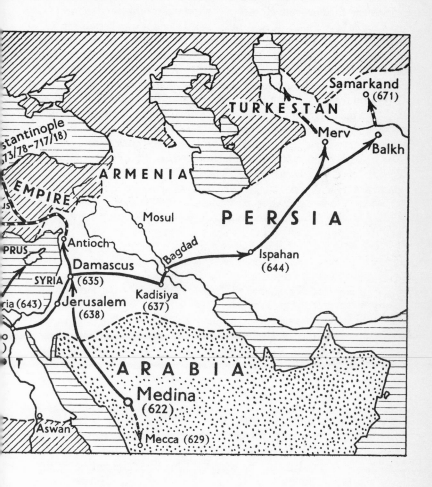

Thus the first theological drama of this period, as it drew to its close, marked one more step along the road which was to separate Byzantium further and further from Rome. Ten years after this the Council 'of the Cupola' (*in trullo*) in 691—also called *Quinisextus* because it was charged with completing the decisions of the Fifth and Sixth Councils by means of disciplinary canons—accentuated the tendency still further. It declared that the see of Constantinople had 'the same rights' as the see of Rome, a declaration which was to reopen the dispute on the famous twenty-eighth canon of the Council of Chalcedon. In making its inventory of the customs of the Byzantine Church it called the Roman customs sternly to task; in particular it allowed clerks who had married before their ordination to continue to live with their wives, with the exception of bishops, whereas the West compelled them to observe continence. It also forbade fasting on Saturdays, whereas in the Latin liturgy this day had no specially privileged position, there being no desire to diminish the number of fasts in the West. In short, for the first time this Council extended the dispute with Rome on to the disciplinary plane. Can we see in this the secret riposte of the Easterners to the resolution with which the popes had opposed their errors? It resulted in a conflict with Pope Sergius I (687–701), who refused to approve the Council's decisions; it was only quelled under Pope Constantine II (708–15), who succeeded in making Justinian II admit the reasons which had led his predecessor to adopt this attitude; the provisional agreement was concluded at Byzantium. Constantine was the last Roman pontiff to go there.

At the conclusion of the seventh century, which saw the most terrible menace that it had ever suffered weighing so heavily on the East, the position of Christianity there was indeed a heart-rending one. There was not a single one of those heresies which had swarmed on this favourable soil for six hundred years past, that had not left its traces and its surviving groups behind it. There were still Arians, Marcionites, Docetians, Sabellians, and even Gnostics, scattered throughout the various provinces. The two great heresies of the preceding epoch had deeply branded the Christian communities in the East. The different kinds of Monophysites were grouped into separate sects; the 'Jacobites,' the descendants of James Baradai, were the most vigorous of these; in Egypt, in the Coptic Church, as in Abyssinia, the doctrine of the single nature was everywhere emerging triumphant. On the other hand, in the great Aramaic zone which stretched from northern Syria to the Persian frontier, it was Nestorianism which was dominant, and it too was organized in a proper church of its own.

In all these provinces, which were now largely lost to *Mater Ecclesia*, those who remained faithful to the orthodox faith and to the emperor were called *Melkites*: *Melkite* comes from *melk*, the Syriac for king, and the word itself demonstrates how nationalist politics and religion overlapped.

One of the most curious episodes of the period, and one which admirably demonstrates the state of disintegration of Christianity at the time, is the foundation of the *Maronite* Church. At the very moment when the Sixth Oecumenical Council was liquidating Monothelitism, groups of the faithful in the Taurus area refused to accept its decisions. Did they have some secret sympathies with the condemned theses? This has been maintained, but there is no proof of it. More probably they were misinformed on the exact wording of the canons. It was an exceedingly noble feeling of absolute loyalty to the decisions of some of the Councils which prompted them to adopt an attitude of suspicious refusal in this case. On the banks of the Orontes, on the plains of Apamea and Cyr, a monastic community was founded around the tomb of a great fifth-century anchorite, *St Maro*. It was the monks of this community who, at the height of the theological conflicts, constituted the loftiest bastion of the faith. Fervent Chalcedonians, they refused to rally to positions which they considered heretical, and they formed themselves into an independent patriarchate, simultaneously hostile to the Monophysite Jacobites and suspicious of the official Church. They courageously resisted all the pressures brought to bear upon them. When the Moslem invasion forced them to leave the fertile plains they preferred to abandon all rather than submit or come to terms with the infidels. Taking refuge in the mountains of the Lebanon they became, under the leadership of their patriarch, the defenders of a Christian stronghold which neither the centuries nor the wave of force was to overcome: like Abraham of old, the Maronites had found the means of preserving their faith in a new land. Later on, at the time of the Greek schism, they refused to be associated with the errors of Cerularius and remained faithful to the great principle: '*Ubi Petrus, ibi Christus*.' In the eleventh century the passage of the Crusaders across their territory resulted in welding the bonds of loyalty which have bound them to Rome until the present day.

This was a happy conclusion, but it was a rare exception in this painful history, in which struggles continually began over and over again, and where quarrels broke out on the slightest pretext, but in fact revealed serious rifts. The Byzantine Empire offered the Islamic attack a wall which was already completely undermined from within, and half abandoned by its defenders: the consequences followed logically on such a situation.

## Mohammed and Islam

The great event of the seventh century, the one which was to weigh most heavily upon the destinies of the world, occurred neither in the West, which was in the act of absorbing its Barbarians as best it could, nor in the Byzantine East, which was paralysed by heresies and schisms. Its setting was a little town in Arabia. It was from there that a certain caravaneer was to preach his Monotheistic doctrine. From the religious revolution that he inspired a new power would arise which, in a single blow, would ruin the existing political equilibrium: there, where no one lived save camel drivers and petty princes, an impetuous force was to appear which would rapidly grow into a formidable menace. It would deal a mortal blow to the thousand-year pre-dominance of Graeco-Roman civilization. 'The Eastern response to the pretensions of Alexander was to be Mohammed.' [1]

Who could have foreseen that these grave events were to turn on the Arabian peninsula, and on the Hejaz? They were not in fact the concern either of the petty Arabian principalities in the north, which were directly under the influence of Byzantium or Persia, or of the Yemen in the south, which had an ancient culture and was in contact with Abyssinia. No, they occurred in this 'land of nomads, this rugged, mountainous land, with its alternation of sterile steppeland, which was green only after the rainy winter season' (Lammens), where, alongside a majority of Bedouin nomads, there lived some settled communities in a few oases and in three proper urban centres—Mecca, Yatreb, and Taif. Between the settled population and the wandering Bedouins, whose language and customs were relatively similar, there was complete opposition of interests and ideas. It was unthinkable that these forces in the Hejaz could one day organize themselves, unite, and threaten all their neighbours. [2]

The Arabs were Semites, closely related to the folk who had founded the glory of Akkad on the Tigris and the Euphrates three thousand years before, and cousins of the Jews, who bore them an age-old antagonism which, it was alleged, dated from the time when their ancestor, Ismail, the first-born son of Abraham, had been forced to flee into the desert with Agar, his mother. On the religious plane the majority of them remained attached to a rather crude fetishism and

---

[1] Christopher Dawson.
[2] The Arabian peninsula, an area of some 800,000 sq. m., as large as one-fifth of Europe, has never achieved political or religious unification, either before or since Islam. To-day, over half-way through the twentieth century, it remains divided into nine distinct political regions. On the religious plane too the inhabitants of the Arabian peninsula are divided between different Moslem sects: Sunnites, Wahabites of the Nejd-Hejaz, Zaidites in the Yemen, Kharijites in the Oman. . . . And there are still some pagan Arabs.

naturalism. Each region had its own gods; each tribe worshipped the formidable local spirits, the *jinns*. Mecca, a city which was both a trading centre and a place of pilgrimage, did, however, possess various idols grouped around a black stone, which was housed in a square-

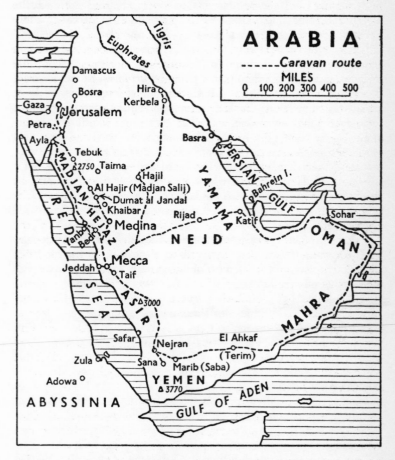

shaped building, *Al-Kaaba* in Arabic. There the great markets and the great pilgrimages were held during the annual truces which interrupted the otherwise incessant raids and vendettas, both being enlivened by what constituted one of the favourite Arabian pastimes: recitals by the national poets. However, new tendencies were coming to light amid this polytheism; the influence of the colonies of Jews, and of the heretical Christians from the Aramaic world in the north and from Abyssinia in the south, was calling the better minds to a

loftier type of religion.    Local divinities were still honoured, but one
of them began to prevail quite distinctly over the rest: Allah, recognized as 'the greatest,' *Allah akbar*; and there were already some
Monotheists—called *hanifs*—who were neither Jews nor Christians.

Mohammed—*Muhammad* in Arabic—was to be the most fortunate
and the most efficacious of the *hanifs*.    He was born at Mecca (probably
between 570 and 580), that is to say, in the 'republic of shopkeepers,'
which was the only place in this divided Arabia, and in the Hejaz in
particular, which could hope to play the role of a capital city.    Although his immediate family was poor, he belonged to the powerful
Kuraish tribe which controlled both the trading interests of the town
and its devotional ones, for skilful propaganda made countless pilgrims
converge on the Kaaba there.    Beneath his seemingly ordinary appearance—firstly, that of a handsome young man, with the eyes of a
gazelle, of noble bearing, with curly black hair, and later on a stout,
well-to-do merchant, with flowing beard and waxen skin—he hid a
quivering soul, readily excited to spiritual exaltation, but quite as
readily moved to doubting, a temperament that combined sensuality
with the desire to seek religious truth, and a mind frequently crossed
by visionary flashes.

He was orphaned very young and was brought up by an uncle who
was generous but without any great material means.    In order to make
his living he was forced, like most of the Kuraish, to turn to the caravan
trade.    He entered the service of a wealthy widow named Khadija and
quickly gained her closest confidence, becoming the leader of her
caravan drivers.    This life afforded him many long hours in which he
could think and day-dream, to the steady rhythm of his camels' feet.
At the caravan stages, the watering-places, and the distant towns—he
probably had to journey even beyond the northern frontiers of Arabia
—he liked to meet the 'men of the Book'—Jews, and Christians
belonging to various heretical sects—and a thousand ideas were set
jostling against one another in his still uncertain soul.    He was about
twenty-five years old when he married Khadija; although she was
fifteen years his senior, the union was a very happy one, rich in mutual
trust and devotion, and it freed him from all material anxieties.

During the years which followed, Mohammed outwardly appeared
to be nothing more than Khadija's husband, the manager of her comfortable fortune.    But religious doubts were wracking this serious
spirit, and towards the age of thirty he was tormented with the mystery
of the life beyond the grave.    The ridiculous folk-tales and the idols
satisfied him no longer.    The struggle within him manifested itself in
crises of profound dejection, which alternated with periods of violent
exaltation.    A spasm would take possession of him, and his head
would become so heavy that he was forced to hide his eyes and his head

beneath a veil.    Then strange sounds rang in his ears: the tinkling of bells, the whirr of wings, the murmur of blurred speech.    On other occasions he thought he could see a mysterious, celestial being standing before him.    And from these terrible and exalting visions he always emerged with the conviction of a single Monotheistic revelation, given him by God, a revelation which had already been granted to the Jewish nation and to the Christian 'nation,' and which it was his mission to impart to his own Arab nation, in Arabic.    Was all this merely a symptom of some nervous disease?    Auto-suggestion? The result of many complex influences, both Jewish and heretical Christian, and of his own lengthy meditations?    Was he 'possessed by a devil'? [1]    Who can decide where the exact truth lies between these undoubtedly intermingled facts?

Much troubled at first, but confirmed in his mission by the calm confidence of Khadija, he began to preach.    He spoke first to his nearest and dearest: his wife, his cousin Ali, his friends Abu-Bekr, Omar, and Othman, were his earliest disciples.    When he began to preach the doctrines of resurrection, Monotheism, and justice towards the poor in public at Mecca, the reception was less favourable.    Mocked by some, roughly handled by others, and soon reviled by all the influential folk in the town, Mohammed nevertheless continued to believe resolutely in his mission.    And when he came into contact with the Arabs from Yatreb, who were passing through Mecca, he found them much more receptive to his ideas than his fellow citizens had been. In consequence, in face of the sarcasm and hindrances set in his way by the materialistic and sceptical Kuraish, he decided to leave his native city and go to Yatreb.    This was the *Hegira*, or emigration, of 622—a vital date.    Islam was to date the start of its era from it.    Henceforth Yatreb would only be known by its new name of *Madinat an-Nabi*, or *Al-Madina*, in other words, Medina, 'the City of the Prophet' or 'The City'—and it was to become the centre for Islamic religious propaganda and government.    Thus established as the leader of the Moslem community, known as *al-Umma*, Mohammed succeeded in constituting his independent doctrine in spite of the intransigent attitude of the Christian heretics and, above all, of the Jews, who were more difficult to deal with, for they refused to accept the fact that a *Gentile* could have a prophetic mission.    From now on he was to follow a new plan of campaign.    Diplomacy and war took the place of the difficult, hazardous preaching.    Islam looked back, through Ismail, to Abraham—he 'who was neither Jew nor Christian,' according to the Koran—and even the Kaaba was said to have been founded by the Father of Believers and dedicated to the worship of Allah—the

[1] Mohammed had to defend himself constantly, even in the Koran, against contemporary accusations that he was possessed by a *jinn*.

Moslem was no longer to turn towards Jerusalem to pray, as he had originally done, but towards Mecca. Moreover war broke out. Successively victorious at Badr, defeated at Ohod, besieged in Mecca, but all to no avail, Mohammed never ceased spreading his propaganda, which found great favour among the poor owing to its bitterness against the wealthy Kuraish. And he made use of diplomacy too, for, having married the daughter of Abu-Sofian, the most influential of the well-to-do citizens of Mecca, and after lengthy negotiations, he entered his native city without a blow being struck in 629. Three years later he returned there at the head of the pilgrimage to the Kaaba. On returning to Medina he died there on 8th June 632.

While these events were taking place, and ever since the day when he had first told Khadija of the strange phenomena being played out within him, Mohammed had never stopped talking and preaching. He declared that he preached not on his own behalf but was simply acting as an agent in order to transmit what 'the supreme power' had taught him. And woe betide him who doubted the 'prophet's' divine inspiration! Mohammed's disciples believed that his instruction came from the 'Preserved Tablet,' the prototype of all the revealed Books, which was mysteriously preserved in heaven.

When Mohammed recited the Koran his supporters immediately noted down his words, no matter what they were: boards, stone barges, the bark of the palm-tree, the shoulders of the sheep: anything that could not be written down was preserved 'in the heart' and the rhythmical composition and 'oral style' helped this a great deal. Thirty years after the Hegira, twenty years after the death of Mohammed, an official version of this collection of sayings was compiled on the orders of the caliph Othman. It was divided into one hundred and fourteen chapters, each of these being subdivided into verses, the chapters arranged according to length, with the longest first. This was the Koran: the recitation.

Mohammed seems to have had a reflective mind and a deeply religious spirit, intent on the search for truth. He preached the necessity for the Arabs, his own people, to adhere to Monotheism, to believe in a single God—henceforth *Allah* in Arabic was to mean God —who, after sending mankind a series of prophets from 'Adam to Jesus,' had finally sent a prophet to the Arab nation—himself, Mohammed. To be a Moslem—*moslim* in Arabic—meant that one must submit oneself utterly to God, and abandon oneself to Him entirely. You must believe in Allah, repeated the Koran, and in the mission of his messenger, Mohammed. Then after you die you will go to the gardens of paradise where, reclining on couches of finest brocade, you will drink the living water from the spring of *as-Salsabil*, and take your pleasure of the houris, the beautiful daughters of Heaven, 'whom no one, neither angel nor man, has ever touched.' But if you do not believe, you will go straight to Hell, there to eat of the frightful fruit of the tree of Zakkum, among the everlasting flames.

To this strong, straightforward dogma, Islam added various rigid practices and a simplified moral code. There were five fundamental practices, the five pillars of the faith: the profession of faith ('there is no divinity save God, and Mohammed is the messenger of God'); ritual prayer; almsgiving; the fast of the month of Ramadan; and the pilgrimage to Mecca. The Moslem religion has always had these as its foundations. The moral code, which is buried amid the penal and ritual directions of the Koran, has nothing exceptional about it: it recognizes the principle of vengeance, does not condemn worldly wealth, insists on justice being given to the poor and the orphaned, e.g. through communal aid between members of the Moslem community, the al-Umma, and, as regards marriage, at the expense of non-Moslems, polygamy remained authorized, limited, it is true, to four wives, but with no limit set on the number of concubines a man might have.

This simplicity and accommodation partially explain the successes of Islam. The supreme condition, and almost the only condition, was the belief in God and in His 'messenger.' Without being faced by numerous dogmas which were beyond human understanding, without, if one had the taste for it, ceasing to be voluptuous, financially grasping, or swift to vengeance, the Moslem could feel himself truly religious, able to share in God and to possess life everlasting. Moreover the prophet himself had shown this by his own example: after the death of Khadija, her husband was divinely delivered to the passing joys of an enormous harem, which the first Moslems have described in detail and not without pride. . . . It is true that despite this simplicity and accommodation Islam was very soon to split up into various opposing sects. Some were Islamic only in name (Alouites, Druses, Behaists). To-day, although Kharijism dominates in Oman and Zanzibar, and Zaidism in the Yemen, the two most important sects are the Sunnites and the Shiites, the former being in the majority in Iraq and Persia, and the latter in the remaining Islamic countries. In total, the different sects springing from Islam number some three hundred million adherents at the present day.

To Catholics who ponder on the meaning of history, and who believe that no event occurs unless God allows it to so happen, the appearance and development of Islam raise a number of problems. It is quite obvious that Judaism and heretical Christianity profoundly influenced the religious philosophy of Mohammed, and that the books of the Bible, the canonical and the apocryphal books, and several more legendary accounts were superficially known and adopted by him.

Does not the 'apparent death' of Christ which is mentioned in the Koran recall Docetist influence? In other passages Mohammed speaks with respect of Mary and of her son 'the prophet *Issa*,' but he denies him any divinity. All this is bound up with the 'syncretist' view of Mohammed, who considered that Islam was a return to a *primitive* Monotheistic revelation which had been 'falsified' and 'polluted' by the Jews and the Christians, and which it was his mission to purify and communicate to the Arab nation. Islam did not become universalist until a good deal later on. The adherents of the various Moslem sects often talk of the 'heavenly religions,' understanding by this phrase not only Islam, but Judaism, Christianity—and even Zoroastrianism—and seeing in all of them, in short, nothing but 'a difference of prophets.' It is tragic indeed that Mohammed, with all his religious idealism and his sincerity—why not admit it?—was only acquainted, and that but slightly, with a distorted Christianity. For we must not forget the religious situation in the areas around Arabia at the beginning of the seventh century: the Church was no longer represented there except by a fine Catholic *élite*, which existed primarily in the Aramaic cities—the Melkites, faithful to the Church and to the Basileus (*melk* in Aramaic). For two hundred years more they were to give the Church popes and saints, but their numbers were declining continuously. There were heretics and schismatics everywhere, torn into fifty sects or so, divided up to the point of coming to blows with one another. If, instead of this veneer of heretical Christianity, Mohammed had known the Truth, and if he had accepted it, who knows what the future of the Church might have been in Arabia, and perhaps in the entire East and the entire world also? As for the suffering which God allowed as a consequence of Islam it is not impossible to believe that this terrible ordeal was in the nature of a supernatural judgment and an expiation: before our disloyalties, our schisms, and our heresies, the Lord does not scorn to deliver us to a false prophet, even to 'his servant Nebuchadnezzar.'

### THE CHAMPIONS OF ALLAH

In order to conquer his enemies, Mohammed had been obliged to make war, and he had presented this war, which was waged in the name of the religious ideal, as what it was indeed—a holy war, a supreme religious act, the greatest sacrifice that could be offered to Allah. For a Moslem to fall in the *jehad* was, according to the Prophet, 'to tread the road of God with certainty.' 'Paradise,' he has even said, 'is shaded with swords.' This doctrine of war, which proved a powerful lever of action upon men who put the most violent Arabian passions to the service of religious fanaticism, had, in

Mohammed's mind, been but a tool, intended for use in crushing local resistance. He had never thought of it as an instrument of imperialist expansion, still less, that it could be used to impose Islam by force. The Koran says explicitly: 'There should be no constraint in the matter of religion; the path of truth knows how to stand conspicuous from the path of error.' But in bestowing a unity upon the Arab world, which until then had been scattered into a myriad fragments, the Prophet had, albeit unintentionally, brought a new force, a formidable nationalism, into the world. 'His Islamism was, first and foremost, Pan-Arabism,' wrote Nau; the oriental world, which was vaguely awaiting its chance to shake off the yoke of Graeco-Roman civilization, was to find a leader in him. When, after Mohammed's death, the merchant class which he had swept aside reassumed the reins of government, it at once grasped the possibilities of fruitful expansion which the militant Puritanism of Islam offered; the *jehad* very swiftly became a war of conquest, and as the majority of the countries to be conquered were in Christian hands, it was the Christians who became Islam's principal enemies. The caliph Omar was to declare: 'It behoves us to devour the Christians and our sons to devour their descendants, so long as any of them remain on the earth.'

Another reason rendered the war of expansion even more necessary: the internal situation of the new state. Mohammed died at Medina on 8th June 632; he had done nothing to provide for the transmission of his authority, which was essentially a personal one, to anyone else. The problem of the succession was fairly and squarely posed to Islam for a period of thirty years. Mohammed's disciple, Abu-Bekr, and his friend, Omar, governed as *Caliphs*—successors—in turn, putting down an attempted tribal revolt against them. But on Omar's death conflict broke out between Ali, the Prophet's son-in-law and cousin, and Othman, his old friend; the latter was slain. Then Moawiah, Othman's grand-nephew, took up the struggle against Ali once again; it was a bitter struggle indeed, and in it Ali perished. Moawiah then settled the succession question by founding (662) the Ommayad or Ommiad dynasty, which was to last until 750, when it was overthrown by revolution. Consequently the situation of the young Islamic state was a precarious one, but all its leaders, all its caliphs, understood that the finest way of maintaining the cohesion of their people in this ordeal was by launching ceaseless military expeditions which would simultaneously satisfy its new fanaticism, its ancestral passions, and its economic interests. It was Omar, the astute politician, who indicated the directions in which the holy war should be waged, namely, at the areas on which the Arabian caravan trade depended: Mesopotamia, Syria, and Egypt. And in 634 the war of conquest began.

Its instrument was a first-class one: the Arab army; and it is not a little surprising to see how speedily the Bedouin hordes transformed themselves into well-organized troops, under the impulse of religious idealism. Composed primarily of a magnificent cavalry and of a light infantry of archers, knowing how to borrow the weapons of war from Byzantium and Persia, commanded by excellent leaders who insisted upon blind obedience, the Arab army rapidly emerged as the most terrible instrument of war that the world knew at that time. As it enlarged its field of action, it filled out with new elements coming from conquered regions, populations which had been won to Islam without losing their own especial character; soon the Arabs themselves were to be but a minority in the army of conquest. But the principles and the methods were to stay exactly the same. And for a hundred years the momentum of the Champions of Allah [1] remained as violent and impetuous as ever.

The Islamic conquest, which was unleashed upon Europe and Asia simultaneously, has no historical precedents. One can compare the fantastic rapidity of its successes with the speed with which the great chieftains from the steppes raised up their empires; but whereas the domains of Attila, or later on those of Genghiz Khan or Tamburlaine, were obliterated in the sands of Asia as quickly as they had risen from them, the conquest of Islam was a lasting one. The faith which its arms brought with it was to take root so firmly that it was to span the centuries. The decadent state of the empires facing the conquerors —Byzantium and Persia—and the partial complicity of certain populations explain the striking character of these victories up to a point: the lasting nature of this success remains an enigma, which goes down into the deepest recesses of the human soul.

In 634, two years after Mohammed's death, the Moslem troops moved off, crossing the frontiers of the neighbouring empires. One section made for Mesopotamia, where it occupied the kingdom of Hira, which was an Arabian vassal of Persia. The other invaded southern Palestine, where the patrician Sergius was killed to the west of the Dead Sea. When these two tests of strength went in their favour, they continued their advance. Gaza fell to them. Sixty Christian soldiers there suffered martyrdom rather than save their lives by abjuring their faith, as was offered them. One imperial army, which was commanded by the brother of Heraclius, was caught in a pincer movement by two Arab armies south-west of Jerusalem; henceforth the Moslem troops wandered about Syria and Palestine as if they owned them. On 20th August 635 Damascus capitulated.

[1] The expression has been used by J. and J. Tharaud as the title of the first volume of their romantic history on the beginnings of Islam. It is more appropriate to the period than phrases such as 'the Arab conquest,' for the really Arab character of the enterprise very quickly gave way to a Moslem empire, to a war waged by various heterogeneous peoples in the name of Allah.

Next the Moslems turned against the Persians, who were then in the grip of grievous internal dissensions.   After resisting for a few weeks, the young Sassanid king Sezdeged gave the Moslems a hard battle at Kadisyah, was beaten, lost his capital Ctesiphon, and was forced to stand by, powerless, and watch all the principal places in Susiana and Media fall to them, one by one.

Secure on this front, the Moslems brought their decisive effort to bear on Syria.   Heraclius pulled himself together; he was now an old, sick man, and in his dealings with the Arabs he never recaptured the vigour which he had once displayed against the Persians.   Nevertheless he collected a second army together and entrusted it to the strategist Trithyrios instead of commanding it personally.   This was another disaster.   On 20th August 636, on the Yarmuk, blinded by the sandstorms which a violent sirocco was hurling at it, tossed into the river from the height of its steep banks, the imperial army was smashed to pieces.   Moreover the enemy had been helped by treachery on the imperial side.   Heraclius was utterly discouraged.   He retired to Asia Minor, giving orders for the True Cross to be removed to Constantinople from Jerusalem.   It took the Moslems only a few years to seize all the strong-points in the land.   Jerusalem, well protected by her solid defences, and commanded by the patriarch Sophronius, held out for a long time, but being completely surrounded, and seeing that no aid was forthcoming from any quarter, she capitulated (February 638) in order to avoid the horrors of a direct attack; and Caliph Omar went to pray on the ancient terrace of the Temple of Solomon, in the place where his mosque stands to-day.

This was a terrible blow, and the whole of Christendom felt itself grievously wounded by it.   Even in Gaul men had the impression that they were witnessing a catastrophe without parallel, an apocalyptic cataclysm; the appallingly pessimistic tone of contemporary inscriptions (those on the hypogeum of Mellebaude, in Poitou, for instance) can hardly be explained in any other way, as Émile Mâle has pointed out.

At this point the Islamic momentum was so intense that no power in the world seemed capable of halting its advance.   The last Sassanid armies were destroyed one after another on the Persian plateau, and the Persian king was slain.   The tireless champions of Allah pushed northwards as far as the Caucasus, the Caspian, and the Oxus; they launched raids in the direction of the Indus basin in the East.   Caliph Omar, who prudently wanted to consolidate the territory already acquired before going on to make fresh conquests, was actually unable to restrain his warriors' enthusiasm.   Despite his orders, his general Amir took advantage of Egypt's chaotic state to hurl himself into the delta with four thousand of his men.   He established himself at Pelusium, on the coast, and then, in July 640, he put the imperial troops to flight near Heliopolis: first Cairo, then Alexandria, was forced to surrender. Amir was preparing to attack Byzantine Africa through Tripolitania when he was halted by Omar's express orders. By 643, only nine years after the beginning of the holy war, an area as big as half Europe, stretching from the Indus and the Caucasus to the edge of the Sudan, was Moslem.

The amazing speed of this conquest, and various incidents which took place during the campaign, lead one to think that the Arabs found some allies among the populations that they invaded. Moslem chroniclers laid a great deal of stress on this point. Undoubtedly the invaders could have had little difficulty in finding allies from among those whom Heraclius had recently persecuted. Thus the Jews, who had just been the victims of his odious and crushing anti-Semitism, hurried to assist the conquerors. Likewise the Monophysites in many areas held the opinion expressed by one of their Syrian spokesmen: 'The God of vengeance has sent the Arab to deliver us from the Roman!' At the battle of the Yarmuk the Moslems were able to bribe their opponents into treachery. In Egypt Benjamin, the Coptic patriarch, who had been persecuted by the emperor, entered into negotiations with the Arabs, and promised them the support of his flock in return for the restitution of the property of the Monophysite church, which the Byzantines had confiscated. It can safely be said that Islam found a resignation which bordered on connivance almost everywhere, even when there was no formal complicity. Why should the Egyptian people summon up any enthusiasm to defend itself? At the very moment of the Moslem attack it was in a state of semi-rebellion against the Basileus, who had just compelled it to accept the patriarch Cyros, a man who had been converted to the ideas of the *Ecthesis* and whom no one wanted! In Jerusalem the patriarch St Sophronius faced Omar's armies alone. How could he possibly feel deeply about saving the empire of a ruler whom he regarded as an enemy of the faith? And the troops who were recruited from provinces undermined by nationalism were hardly likely to be anxious to sacrifice themselves for the despot of Byzantium!

Whatever the attitude of these peoples may have been at the time of the invasions, one fact is clear: 'debyzantinization' proceeded with remarkable speed in both Egypt and Syria. The Hellenic civilization which had covered the whole of the Near East for a thousand years—ever since the time of Alexander—and which had given birth to scores of scholars and philosophers, was swept away; the swell surging up from the depths of the people's souls utterly submerged it. From the point of view of the history of civilization the fall of Alexandria to the Arabs in 643 is quite as important as the fall of Constantinople to the Turks eight hundred years later. In that moment an original cultural expression was snuffed out for ever. The fruitful influences of the Hellenistic East were no longer exerted on the West: the fine ivories and the sumptuous silks arrived there no more. As for Syria, it Arabianized itself enthusiastically. The emperor's Christian officials —even those who were Melkites, that is to say, generally loyal— agreed to enter the caliph's service. It should be noted, moreover, that the Arab occupation was a not unpleasant one on the whole; acts of pillage and violence were certainly far less extensive than those of which the Germanic tribes had been guilty in the West; the great acts of destruction of which they have been accused, such as that of the library at Alexandria, have no historical foundation. In certain quarters it seems proven that some Islamic chieftains actually helped rebuild the churches.

The Moslems were not cruel occupiers. In Syria, and above all in Egypt, they simply favoured the Monophysites against the Melkite Catholics, which was perfectly understandable, since the latter professed loyalty to Byzantium. But even at this difficult time the Melkite hierarchy was able to reconstitute itself into three Eastern patriarchates: regular elections took place at Jerusalem from 706, at Antioch from 740, and at Alexandria from 744, though not without occasional difficulties, for the patriarchs were obliged to gain support from the caliph's court, this being arranged primarily through the mediation of his Christian physicians; small synods could even be held. At all events the Church's vitality was not destroyed. Is it not at the height of Moslem domination that we find the orthodox Christianity of Damascus providing its supreme example of wisdom and lofty spirituality in the person of St John Damascene, who had actually been the caliph's vizier? And was it not from Moslem-occupied Persia also that the Nestorian missionaries—heretics, but nevertheless worthy of our admiration in so many respects—set out, taking the Gospel as far as India, China, Turkestan, and Tibet? Theirs was a remarkable apostolate indeed, and we shall deal with its episodes later on in this book. There was scarcely any genuine resistance to the Islamic occupiers save from the highlanders in the Lebanon and the Armenians, who were both aggressive, indomitable peoples: moreover they were to render assistance to the Byzantine emperors during the tenth-century imperial revival, and, a little later still, to the Crusaders, by attacking the Moslem lines of communications. Their feats were quite exceptional: in the main the Christian populations adopted an attitude of resigned submission.

All this leaves a disturbing impression. The historian has the feeling that Eastern Christianity, which was made incarnate at this period in the Emperor of Byzantium, showed itself unequal to its destiny when faced with the unforeseen Arab invasion. Spiritually speaking, it acknowledged itself everywhere incapable of giving battle on the very plane which should have been its own; it had been exhausted by too many centuries of theological argument and division. It is of course one of the most heart-rending sights of this period to see how easily Heraclius, 'the first Crusader,' the man who had won back the True Cross, let both the political masterpiece of Alexander and the edifice which the first generations of Christians had built up in all these lands at the price of their own blood, crumble to pieces.   The former hero of the war against the Persians was, it is true, now only a dropsical old man, beset by weird phobias.   For example, when he crossed the straits to return to Constantinople, he insisted on a bridge of boats, lined with leafy walls, being made for him, so great was his fear of water!   When he died, in 641, he left his successor with an overwhelming problem, an empire which appeared on the verge of collapse.

The situation during the next seventy years was indeed a terrible one.   Almost all Heraclius's successors, whether they were his direct heirs or usurpers, had to face rebellions, secessions, and palace *coup d'états*.   Some of them were not without merit: e.g. Constantius II (641–68), Constantine IV (668–85), and even Justinian II; but it would have needed supermen indeed to maintain the grandeur of the empire at this juncture!   One frequently witnessed a Basileus or a Basilissa suffering the supreme penalty in the Circus.   There were periods of almost Neronian madness, as under Justinian II, 'the noseless Emperor,' who was deposed after he had reigned ten years (685–95), and mutilated in this unaesthetic fashion, and who then seized power again (705–11) and proceeded to drown all resistance to him in a veritable blood-bath.

And whilst the ruling classes in Byzantium were thus indulging in the vilest political intrigues—and in debauchery too—the empire was receiving blow upon blow, and panting in its agony.   A new enemy was massing on the northern frontiers, the Bulgars, a people of Turkish origin who had entered into alliance with and strongly organized a whole host of Slavonic tribes: and they were extremely greedy!   The Arab raids never stopped.   Asia Minor became an open drill-ground and source of pillage for the champions of Allah.   They grew bolder and bolder, appearing in Phrygia, Cappadocia, and on the outskirts of Ancyra (Ankara).   After twenty years of semi-military and semi-diplomatic effort, they established their rule over Armenia. At the same time they built a fleet with the help of the shore-dwelling Lebanese, the descendants of the Phoenicians, and began to sack the Greek islands and harbours: Cyprus in 648–9, Rhodes in 653, then Crete and the Cyclades.   When Constantius II tried to resist them, they annihilated his squadrons in the twinkling of an eye.

It was a dire ordeal.   Yet the Eastern Empire was not to perish in it.

Byzantium still possessed much basic strength, and the promise of several centuries ahead of her.   But she underwent a decisive change. Up to the death of Heraclius all the emperors had striven to maintain the Roman tradition of a universal empire; they had tried, albeit in vain, to give a unity to this boundless power whose dream Justinian had bequeathed them.   From 641 there began what has sometimes been called 'the Byzantine Middle Ages'; the empire, assailed on all sides, was to resign herself to abandoning her excessive aims in order to consolidate herself as a more coherent, homogeneous Graeco-Oriental power.   This meant a loss of self-esteem, to be sure, but it was a salutary decision.

On two occasions it seemed that all would be lost.   Constantinople was directly attacked twice, by land and by sea.   In 673, first of all, and then for five years in succession, the Arab armies and fleets hurled themselves against the city; the defences held firm, and the 'Greek fire,' a mysterious substance invented at this time, whose secret is now lost, and which actually burned on the water, got the better of the Islamic warships.   The attack began again in 717; it was to last for a whole year, and the forces involved were enormous: did not men talk of one thousand eight hundred vessels?   This was the hour when the Arab's self-confidence was at its height, raised to exaltation point by the fantastic scope of his triumphs.   Had he not just seized Spain in one fell swoop?   Was he not ravaging the French Midi at this very moment?   He believed all Europe to be at his mercy.

But at this point a new *coup d'état* had just raised a real leader to the imperial throne, a rugged Asian highlander, Leo III the Isaurian (717–740).   He founded the dynasty which was to restore the Empire's glory.   The Moslems were so soundly beaten in front of Constantinople (718) that they long hesitated to return to the area: this victory raised a decisive obstacle in the path of the Islamic conquest of Europe from the East.   It was as important as that which was to be raised at Poitiers by Charles Martel and his Franks fourteen years later.   Once again Byzantium proved that she was still capable of saving herself by herself.

But she was incapable of saving the civilization of which she had claimed to be the guide.   For at the very moment when the Syrian Emperor of Constantinople was halting the Caliph of Damascus [1] in his tracks, the catastrophe which was to have the most grievous

---

[1] It is curious to note the important place held by Lebanese and Syrians, that is to say, by Easterners, at the beginning of the eighth century, when the ancient Mediterranean Greek civilization was coming to an end.   The Isaurian dynasty originated in northern Syria.   The Arab caliphs ruled from Damascus, surrounded by Syrian officials.   St John Damascene, the greatest philosopher of the period, was a Syrian.   There were actually five Syrian or Lebanese popes between 685 and 741: John V, Sergius I, Sisinnius, Constantine I, and Gregory III.   The mysterious influence of the East. . . .

political, economic, and religious consequences for centuries to come was nearing completion: the division of the Mediterranean—the ancient *mare nostrum* of the great Roman Empire—by the Moslem occupation of Africa and Spain.

## THE END OF CHRISTIAN AFRICA

The whole historical chapter which the Islamic invasion comprises is a tragic one for Christianity. But there is not a single page which is more heart-breaking than the one which deals with Christian Africa. When we remember all that Christian Africa had been, when we think of the wonderful witness it had given, of the age of St Cyprian and the humble faithful of Scili, of its martyrs, of the authority of its seven hundred bishops at the beginning of the fifth century, of the incomparable brilliance of St Augustine—we feel numbed and overwhelmingly grieved at the horror of the catastrophe in which this Church collapsed—and for how long! Various fundamental reasons explain this fall, here, even more than elsewhere. It is not enough to observe that the leaders of this Church in the seventh century were very far from possessing the virtues of their predecessors, that, in the main, they were mediocre men, even when they were neither simoniacal nor dishonest. This African Christianity had been stricken in its very vitals for a long time past. The feeble resistance which it offered the champions of Allah was the result of a series of long-standing failings, which can be largely accounted for by characteristics of local temperament.

African Christianity had never possessed the speculative character of its Egyptian and Syrian counterparts: nevertheless it had experienced several heretical crises; we can remember the campaigns which St Augustine had to lead against Manichaeism, Donatism, and other forms of error.[1] But in Africa, whether erroneous doctrines or even the most orthodox faith was concerned, all convictions were tinged with a particularism, with a kind of savage dignity which tended to enclose and isolate African Christianity a good deal. This characteristic had been specially noticeable in the case of the heretical schism of Donatus. In large measure this had been a phenomenon of African separatism, so violent and so firmly linked with popular sympathies that right in the middle of the seventh century, that is to say, after over three hundred years of strife, the Donatists revived their propaganda, which was intended, as usual, to harm the Catholics.

This African particularism had two sides to it: a political side and a religious one. As far as politics were concerned it must be remembered that, after being reconquered by the victorious armies of

[1] See Chapter I, section: 'The Champion of Truth.'

Justinian, the African provinces had not been slow to show their impatience with the Byzantine administration, which was oppressive and interfering there, as it was everywhere; the Berber populations, in particular, often caused the Byzantine officials a great deal of trouble. At the end of the sixth century Byzantium had officially recognized this separatist tendency up to a point, by establishing an *exarchate* in Africa: that is to say, an almost autonomous administrative entity, where the exarch, who was a veritable viceroy, might, although entrusted with the task of representing the central authority, also be sorely tempted to turn the separatist tendencies of his African subjects to his own advantage. We should remember that the military uprising which put an end to the reign of the wretched Phocas had begun in Africa, and that the new emperor, Heraclius, had shown his gratitude by enriching the province and showering favours upon it. On the eve of the Arab invasion the exarch Gregory was to take advantage of the general discontent to proclaim himself *Basileus*.

Overlapping this inclination to political separatism in Africa was a somewhat analogous feeling in the sphere of religion. Extremely proud of his traditions, very enthusiastic in his convictions and his moral principles, the African Christian possessed a marked tendency to remain somewhat aloof from the main body of the Church; this inclination is apparent even in some of her greatest saints, such as St Cyprian. It was not that the African churches had any systematic mistrust of Rome: on several occasions there were men among the higher African clergy who understood perfectly that only intimate union with the Papacy could maintain true religious life in their Church, men like Bishop Columbus of Numidia and Dominic, primate of Carthage, both of whom were friends of St Gregory the Great, and who worked in complete agreement with him. But there is no doubt at all that, despite the intensity of its spiritual life and despite the ceaseless labours undertaken by its provincial councils, the Church in Africa was not watered as it ought to have been by the main stream of Mother Church: this clearly explains the frailty it displayed when confronted by the enemy.

The very elements which made up this African Church were another source of its weakness. The ancient Roman populations, or those that had been Romanized long ago, were firm believers. But alongside these, there were a number of Barbarian tribes which had been baptized at different times, and whose convictions remained superficial and unstable. When the Byzantine victory had shown how strong the Christians were, the Berber chiefs had adopted their faith, though without abandoning their idolatrous practices; if this strength ceased to be obvious, the chances were that their Christian convictions would decline accordingly. During the years in which the fate of their country was being played out between the 'Romans' and the Arabs, the Berbers swung between conversion and abjuration quite unself-consciously. One Moslem historian writes, rather humorously: 'When the Berbers apostasize, they do it twelve times over!' In order to prevent this difficult part of the empire from cutting itself adrift at the first sign of trouble, it would have been necessary to treat its people with as much resolution as flexibility, to avoid coming into collision with them, and, above all, not to allow the motives of division that had caused such havoc in Egypt and Syria to be unleashed here too. The theologian-autocrats of Byzantium pursued a policy which was absolutely contrary to this. All the religious conflicts which shook the Empire had their repercussions in the African Church and all contributed to worsening its relations with Byzantium. Thus, when Justinian threw himself into the so-called affair of the *Three Chapters*[1] around 534, in the fallacious hope of bringing the Monophysites back to the fold, the African Church resisted him so vigorously that the enraged authoritarian emperor went so far as to arrest, deport, and depose its bishops, whilst a certain Firminus of Tipasa, primate of Numidia, converted to the imperial cause by self-interest, tried, all in vain, to compel his compatriots to accept the theological principles of the Basileus. A hundred years later, when Heraclius issued the doctrines of *Monothelitism* with the selfsame end in view, the African Church adopted the same suspicious attitude towards the official theses. After Egypt was occupied by the Arabs, in 640, large numbers of Egyptians sought refuge in Africa, bringing with them their eternal taste for theological wrangling. A violent crisis broke out in which the Africans, sustained by St Maximus the Confessor, the champion of orthodoxy, set themselves up as the declared adversaries of imperial theology. It goes without saying that the loyalty felt for the Empire by the Africans suffered terribly as a result of all these quarrels; the exarch Gregory knew how to turn these thousand grievances of theirs to his own account in order to proclaim himself independent of Byzantium.

Such was the situation in Christian Africa at the moment when the champions of Allah were about to swoop upon her; it was a singularly dangerous situation, analogous to that which had just explained the fall of Egypt and Syria into Moslem hands, and perhaps it was even worse. We have already seen how, immediately after the occupation of the Delta, Amir had pushed forward in the direction of Africa for the first time, occupying Cyrenaica in 642 and Tripolitania in 643; although momentarily halted by the orders of Caliph Omar, he took up his advance again in 647, in order to go and pillage the wealthy oases in the Tunisian south: the exarch Gregory, who had just created

[1] See Chapter III, section: 'The Religious Complexes of Justinian and Theodora.'

Sufetula (Sbeitla) as the capital of his 'empire,' was killed quite near it, at Akuba, while trying to stop the raiders' advance.    This was but the first signal of the danger: henceforth the champions of Allah knew which path to take.

Whilst Constantius II was exasperating the Africans once more by readopting a Monothelitist policy in his *Model* edict, the Moslems were returning to the attack at periodic intervals.    A new raid in 665 swept across the entire province of Byzacene (southern Tunisia) without encountering any real opposition; the Byzantines seemed resigned to sacrificing the south; the armies which the Basileus dispatched to help in its defence re-embarked without ever giving battle.    Before such obvious weakness the Islamic leaders decided on vigorous action; in 669 Caliph Moawiah hurled his troops on *Ifrikia*, seized Kafsa and the whole of Byzacene, and, to make it quite clear that he was resolved to stay there, built a fortress, a 'Kairwan.'    The present-day Tunisian town still preserves its name and its fame.

Now everything seemed bound to fall rapidly to pieces.    The empire was decidedly too far away, and too weak, and was incapable of defending Africa.    The final struggle, which the Byzantines could no longer lead, was the work of those Berber tribes who had resisted the Romans in olden times, and later the Byzantines, and who, in the nineteenth century, were to stand up to the might of France.    *Koceila*, one of their great chieftains, a rather lax Christian who apostasized two or three times, succeeded in driving back the champions of Allah for some time and even in snatching Kairwan from them.    The few surviving remnants of Christian Africa were able to live in peace in his 'kingdom.'    Another extremely weird episode was the savage struggle led by a woman, the *Kahena*—the 'Priestess'—who put herself at the head of a coalition of Berbers, Jews, and Christians, a struggle which was to last until this legendary queen met her death in battle.

In fact, these local resistance movements could not prevent the inevitable from taking place, any more than the few timid interventions on the part of the Byzantine fleet.    Carthage was taken in 698. Gradually the Moslems conquered town after town, district after district, throughout the whole of Africa and the Maghreb.    By about 704 *Africanus exercitus*, as the imperial nomenclature proudly called it, meant no more than the capeland around Ceuta and a few nearby mountains.    Julian, the last exarch, who was waging war against the Christian Visigothic kings of Spain, thought he was being extremely clever in using Tarik, the Islamized Berber, the lieutenant of Moussa, who was the caliph's legate and the commander of the Moslem forces, to play his game for him; he handed over to him the impregnable position of which he had charge; from there Tarik was to leap over into Spain, across the strait of Jebel.    His name is preserved in the modern 'Gibraltar' (Jebel-Tarik).   This act of treachery was the last blow ever struck in the name of Christian Africa.

The African Church was going to die.   Not immediately; some fairly large islets of the faith survived for quite a long time, but they became increasingly weaker, and their position grew more and more precarious.   The Berbers speedily adopted the conquerors' religion.   At first those Christians whose convictions were more resolute were permitted to retain their faith, on payment of a special levy consisting of one-fifth of their incomes, but this tolerance soon ceased and from the middle of the eighth century onwards they had only the choice of apostasy or exile.   Many of the churches were converted into mosques.   The bishops disappeared; little remained of them save their titles, which became purely honorary—similar to those borne to-day by our bishops *in partibus infidelium*—as bereft of any real jurisdiction as the political personage who continued to be ceremonially known at Byzantium as 'the most high and mighty prefect of Africa.'   By 1050 there were to be but five resident Catholic bishops remaining in *Ifrikia*.   Their flocks comprised only the Christian merchants who lived in the ports, the mercenaries in the sultan's service, and the prisoners and the child-slaves, for whom the religious belonging to the Orders of Mercy or the Trinitarians of St John de Matha, who devoted themselves to the redemption of captives, were to labour so selflessly.   This was a poor and wretched relic of the old glories of Christian Africa!   We must wait eight hundred years before we see the Gospel being sown anew on the ancient continent, and Cardinal Lavigerie laying the foundations of a new Christian community there.

### CHRISTIAN SPAIN IS OVERWHELMED FOR SEVEN HUNDRED YEARS

The fall of Spain was consequent upon the fall of Africa; it was also the logical result of the state of disunity which existed among the Christians.   Relations between the Byzantines, who still held Ceuta, and the Visigoth kings on the neighbouring peninsula were extremely bitter.   The exarch Julian gave willing asylum to Oppas, Bishop of Seville, brother of the deposed King Witizia, pretender to the throne of Toledo, and to a whole host of the present king's enemies and malcontents; as for *Roderigo*, the Spanish king (*Roderick the Goth*), he sought to put difficulties in the way of his neighbour, the imperial official, with all the means in his power.   Instead of banding together to fight the danger which was staring them in the face, the Christians could think of nothing save tearing each other to pieces.

One romantic anecdote has it that the powder was sparked off through the actions of a woman, the beautiful Florinda, Count Julian's daughter, nicknamed 'the Bad,' who, after several adventures, had herself abducted by Roderick; this suggests that the war in Spain began like that of Troy. In actual fact it was due far more to the result of a mass of intrigues. The Gothic and Jewish refugees who had been hounded from Spain importuned Julian and the Moslem leaders, telling them of the chaotic state of the Spanish kingdom, and encouraging them to intervene. Moussa, the caliph's representative at Tangiers, carefully appraised himself of the situation and even undertook a reconnaissance operation against Spain, which was a complete success. After referring the matter to Damascus, and, finally, negotiating the alliance with the Byzantines of Ceuta, he decided to attack Spain in July 711.

Accustomed as we are to the speed of Islam's successes, the rapidity of the Moslem conquest of Spain leaves us quite confounded. Tarik's seven thousand Berbers disembarked without hindrance at the foot of the 'Jebel-Tarik' and straightway marched on Algeciras. Roderick's troops were waiting for them on the banks of the *Guadalete*. The king commanded them in person, standing in his ivory-plated war-chariot, his golden crown on his head, wearing his purple cloak and his cloth-of-silver boots. The heat was terrible, and the tall, fair Germanic warriors suffered appallingly from it. Under a fiery sun, amid the howling and whirling of the Numidian horsemen, in the dazzling glare of the billowing burnouses and raised scimitars, the battle swiftly developed. It was like a tragic fantasia. The bewildered Goths collapsed completely. Roderick, mounting his own white charger, defended himself like a lion. When dusk fell nothing remained of the Visigoth army save a few fleeing remnants still pursued by the Arabian archers; the king himself had vanished; only his horse was found, trapped in the river mud, and, not very far from it, one of his silver boots. Julian's Byzantine contingents and Oppas's Gothic exiles had taken part in the battle—in the Moslem ranks (19th July 711)!

This single blow was enough. Visigoth Spain collapsed like a pack of cards. Having seized Seville, Tarik's Berbers flung themselves on Cordova, dislodged a small pocket of resistance at Ecija, and then marched on Toledo on Julian's advice. Here the treacherous Oppas planned to execute them all. At the same time Moussa landed in Spain in his turn. He stormed Medina and Carmona, suppressed a revolt in Seville, and, still guided by Christian traitors, hurried to Toledo to wrangle violently with Tarik, his lieutenant, over the latter's sumptuous booty. Nine-tenths of Spain was overwhelmed by Islam. Suddenly troubled by the results of their actions, Julian and Oppas began to discover that, for the Moslems, this was not simply a question of an ordinary pillaging raid, as they had believed.    Still less was it a Machiavellian enterprise in which they had naïvely thought they could make use of the Moslems to substitute one Gothic king for another.    Henceforth the green flag of the prophet floated over the Spanish coasts.    No less than seven centuries were to pass before it was torn down.

A collapse like this, analogous to that in the other Christian areas conquered by Islam, obviously reveals a deplorable situation.    Whilst Syria and Egypt had been undermined by religious and nationalist antagonisms, and whilst Africa largely owed her fate to her latent separatist tendencies, Spain, at the moment of the Moslem attack, was paralysed by a decadence which was eating her away in several different ways.    She was in a permanent state of violent feud: the Byzantines, whose territory had been reduced to a few coastal districts as a result of a treaty signed by Heraclius, looked back regretfully to the epoch when Justinian's armies had held the entire southern part of the peninsula; the Asturians and the Basques, who were a constant nuisance, had to be periodically suppressed; the loyalty of the Visigoth provinces in southern France was extremely doubtful, and from time to time the kings in Toledo were obliged to smash the revolt of one of their subordinates in Languedoc.    And there was an even greater menace than all these put together: the crown itself was unstable.    The reigning monarch was almost always threatened by conspiracies, and the succession was frequently disturbed by rebellion and assassination. In the hundred years since the death of Recared, one king had been executed, another forcibly tonsured and shut away in a monastery, another, the aged Wamba, inveigled into abdication under the influence of drugs, and another even hounded from his throne and forced to flee to Rome.    Faced with this appalling situation some of the kings had reacted by instituting a reign of terror; others had, in practice, allowed their subjects to do exactly as they pleased.

Another factor which caused the State serious harm was the Jewish question.    For reasons which are not at all clear, and which cannot be completely explained by their intransigent zeal for the purity of the faith, several Visigoth kings indulged in veritable anti-Semitic persecutions, going so far as to carry out forcible baptisms, abduct children, and compel the separation of married couples when one party was Jewish.    Several leaders of the Spanish Church, such as St Isidore of Seville, had protested against measures as odious as these; their protests fell on deaf ears, and in 698 a Council of Toledo actually ratified them. Driven to exasperation, the Jews were not to forget brutality such as this; they worked as hard as they could to throw off Visigoth rule, whether they were living among the Byzantines of Ceuta, and the Moslems, or in Spain itself, where they formed a kind of 'Fifth

Column'; during the invasion of 711 they were consistently on the side of the invaders.

It would appear that other causes—moral ones—must be added to these political reasons for Visigoth Spain's disintegration. Even if the recitals of the chroniclers, which represent this or that Visigoth king as being surrounded by a harem and encouraging all those around him to indulge in polygamy, are not taken too literally, it is all too clear that the balmy atmosphere and the long-standing habit of luxury—Toledo had become a sumptuous capital—had played havoc with Germanic morals; what had happened in the preceding century to the Vandals in Africa was now happening to the Visigoths in Spain. The lands of the sunny south never brought good fortune to the tall, fair Aryans.

Before the extremely rapid collapse of this splendid dream of Spanish Gothic Christianity, which had received its baptism in the blood of the martyr Hermenegild, and which had been integrated into the great reality of Catholicism by Recared, one question springs to mind: did the Church bear any responsibility for this catastrophe? To be quite honest, the answer must be an affirmative one. It should be remembered [1] that, following the conversion, agreement between the Visigoth monarchy and the Church had appeared so complete that the national Councils in Spain had acted like veritable Senates. They had legislated on the most important State matters. Various kings had asked them to make good defects in the laws. Forming themselves into Councils of State or into a High Court of Justice, they had condemned and dismissed the civil officers of state. The Church which had made the coronation into a sacramental ceremony from the time of the regal anointing of Wamba, was indeed closely linked with the crown.

However, this union did have some good results. Christian influence unquestionably made itself felt in the legislative sphere in a most beneficial fashion, and owing to it, the 'Visigothic Codes' were to be the least barbarous of all Germanic legislation. These Council-Parliaments used their official authority to effect an admirable organization of the clergy, to supervise it closely, and to maintain its moral standards. It seems too that a certain moral austerity which existed in Spanish Christianity was the result of a reaction by the Church against the lax tendencies of some of the kings.

But if the obverse is reasonably satisfactory the reverse is less so. As at Byzantium, though under different forms, as among the Merovingians, but in a worse degree, this too intimate alliance between Church and State had serious drawbacks. The Church was powerful in the State, but, in reality, did not the State control the Church? The king appeared to be the most humble son of *Mater Ecclesiae*; he

[1] See Chapter IV, section: 'The Arians Return to the Bosom of the Church.'

* M

prostrated himself when he entered the room where the Councils held their meetings; he withdrew to let the holy assemblies deliberate more freely. But it was he who convened them—or omitted to convene them. It was he who decided their agenda and ensured the execution of their decisions. It was he who added important members of the laity to the bishops and senior prelates who had been regularly elected. Finally, it was he who, on several occasions, forced the Councils to sanction his encroachments or usurpations of their authority. If it is added that here, as in Gaul, the royal intervention in episcopal nominations sometimes resulted in scandalous appointments, the danger of this too close alliance between the two powers can be understood all the more clearly.

It had yet another damaging result. Because it was so involved in political matters, the Church in Spain tended to judge purely religious affairs from a political standpoint. Its leaders considered themselves to be important temporal officials at least as much as shepherds of their spiritual flocks. They finished by thinking in Spanish, rather than Catholic, terms; this can be observed in their attitude towards Rome. They periodically sent emphatic witness of their respect and fidelity to Rome, but they also showed their surprise when a pope allowed himself to intervene in the affairs of the glorious Catholic kingdom of Toledo. This unduly close union with the State consequently limited the horizons of the Spanish Church, at the same time as it hindered its action. It was logical, therefore, that the Church should be involved in the fall of the Visigoth monarchy.

But though the Church as an institution suffered terribly from the catastrophe, Christianity was too strongly embedded in the Spanish soul for the invaders to be able to eradicate it. The Moslems were only a minority and they did not try to proselytize very much. They entrusted various vital posts to Jews in many cases; in others they employed Spaniards who were superficially Islamized, having been converted to the Koran by self-interest, and who were called 'Maulas.' In the main these showed themselves well disposed towards their former brethren. The position of the Christians in the Spanish Moslem state—of this Church which has retained the name 'Mozarabic'—although subject to variations from province to province and from century to century, was never so painful as that of the Christians in Moslem Africa. And then too they cherished in their hearts something which enabled them to bear the most terrible ordeals: the hope of a morrow of revenge and liberation.

For at the very moment when the Islamic onslaught occurred, a few Christian elements had overcome the distress and confusion of the great collapse, and had quickly turned to thoughts of resistance. They took refuge in the mountains where the enemy could not follow them. Gradually they collected themselves together again, they began to organize themselves, and then to arm. Less than five years after the catastrophe a real Christian 'Maquis' was operating against the occupiers, not hesitating to make foraging expeditions into the areas held by the Moslems. One of the earliest leaders of this Christian resistance movement was *Pelagius*. He took refuge in the *sierras* of Galicia, and in 718 he revived the royal title of the Visigoth dynasty to which he was, moreover, related. Although captured during a raid on the plains, this audacious leader escaped from prison and caused the Moslems so much trouble that they undertook an expedition against him. It went badly for them. Pelagius and his mountain guerrillas watched the column of their attackers enter a wild mountain pass—Berbers, Arabs, and Christian traitors, among whom was the wretched Oppas of Seville—and blocked it by rolling rocks down into it. Then they riddled the column with their arrows and rained stones down on to it, whilst a terrible storm, which made the mountain streams swell into torrents, completed the rout; this was the victory of *Covadonga*, which Spanish poets embroidered on a good deal but which really was, in fact, the first sound of the tocsin of liberation, the promise of a brighter future.

So, little by little, various pockets of resistance sprang up in the north of the peninsula. There were some in Navarre, in Aragon, and in Galicia. The tiny principality of Sobraiba, founded by Garcia Jimenez, gave promise of the kingdom of Aragon. *Alfonso I the Catholic*, Pelagius's son-in-law, made Oviedo the capital of the Asturias. In under twenty-five years a series of strongpoints arose behind the Douro: Leon, Zamora, Avila, Miranda, Segovia, and Salamanca. In front of them, stretching as far as the territories which were well and truly held by Islam, there was a kind of indeterminate area in which the combatants observed one another's actions. And, a very long time afterwards, this fragile bastion in northern Spain was to be the starting-point of the glorious counter-offensive known as the Reconquest.

Why did the Moslems fail to liquidate these feeble adversaries? Most probably because the internal position of their state made it impossible for them to do so. Their rule in Spain, which was to be a materially sumptuous one, was always somewhat uncertain and tenuous. Relations between the caliphs of Damascus and their Spanish representatives were far from good; one emir, who had married Roderick's widow, and who was therefore suspected of sympathy towards the vanquished, was assassinated on the caliph's orders. Moreover the Berbers were jealous of the Arabs, and this jealousy often reached the proportions of a revolt. Finally, a revolution within the Arab Empire was to have very important consequences for Spain.  In 750 the Ommayads of Damascus, whom the other Moslems accused of deviating from the principles of the Koran, were deposed and replaced by the Abbasids, who established their seat of government in Mesopotamia, where Abu Jaffa founded the new capital of Bagdad.  One member of the Ommayad dynasty, Abd-er-Rahman, who escaped the massacre to which the rest of his family were subjected, fled to Spain, and seized Cordova, which consequently became an independent caliphate, in revolt against the caliphate at Bagdad.  All these events gave the little Christian kingdoms the chance to take firm root.

And then, above all, the prodigious force which had pushed the Islamic world forward along the road of conquest for the past one hundred years was in decline; in the eighth century it could only progress in small stages, quite unlike the gigantic forward sweeps of its earlier days.  Islam had made two immense thrusts in the direction of Europe, the one in the East and the other in the West.  The first had been halted beneath the walls of Byzantium in 718, and the second was to be halted at Poitiers in 732 by the Franks.  The conquest of Spain was the last episode in the great Islamic attack on Europe.  Because it had failed to understand that it is better to instruct and to persuade than to fight, the Moslem world did not succeed in making its civilization into a global force really capable of rivalling Christian civilization.  The time would soon come when it would be forced to go on the defensive in order to resist the West, which had been organized by the Papacy.  The 'reconquest' of the Iberian peninsula would be one episode in this new phase of the struggle.  Providence still promised many future glories to the Christian communities of Spain.


## Byzantium, Her Morals and Her Faith

The destruction of some of the finest parts of Christendom was not the only result of this terrible and tragic seventh century in which the champions of Allah seemed to be indeed the instruments of an avenging God.  Epochs of great political upheaval are always periods of moral disruption as well.  The bitter struggles which ensured Byzantium's survival, the predominance of a military regime, the new invasions by the Bulgars and Slavs, the immigration of countless Armenian and Syrian elements throughout the Empire—all these resulted in a veritable barbarization of society, analogous to that to which the West had been subjected after the Great Invasions.  These characteristics of brutality and violence united with already existing tendencies of decadence, with results that were almost disastrous.

To obtain some idea of the state of Byzantine morality in this epoch it is enough to skim through the disciplinary canons of the famous Council 'of the Cupola,' also called *Quinisextus*. The reader is struck dumb with amazement by the prohibitions which this assemble had to make, and by the errors which it had to denounce: e.g. it was necessary to remind clerks that it was absolutely wrong for them to become proprietors of brothels, and to tell the faithful that sexual intercourse in the church itself profaned the House of God. . . . Immorality seems to have been universal: the Council had to excommunicate religious who had broken their vows, sellers of pornographic pictures, and doctors and midwives who specialized in abortion. . . .

Another characteristic of this diseased society is the cruelty of many of the punishments inflicted, not merely on those found guilty in common law, but on political enemies, even upon one's opponents in the theological disputes. Practices such as cutting off the nose, the ears, or the tongue, blinding, and mutilations of the vilest kind were commonplace. Capital punishment provided an oft-repeated popular diversion; during the reign of Justinian II, 'the noseless Emperor,' the idle mobs could take their pleasure of beheadings by the hundred. And the abominable way in which even saints, such as Pope St Martin or St Maximus the Confessor, were treated is well known.

When the reappearance of various ancient pagan practices is added to all this, particularly those which lent themselves most fully to licentious exuberances—the Saturnalia, the Brumalia in honour of Bacchus, the May-feast or festival of spring, together with the fact that magic, sorcery, and the exploitation of popular credulity were actually more widespread than in pagan times—it is easy to see how thin the veneer of Christianity, which six centuries of faith had impressed on this society, had become. In 717, when Pergamum was besieged by the Arabs, the population indulged in the ritual murder of a pregnant woman and smeared themselves with their victim's blood: strange aberrations for a world that called itself Christian.

But, because the law of contrasts continued to operate in this Byzantine society, the period which displayed this moral debasement also displayed, at the selfsame time, tendencies which were entirely opposite. It cannot be disputed that though the influence of Christianity was but feeble on its morals, it was much greater on its principles: this had already been very marked in the juridical achievement of Justinian; it was to be still clearer in the restatement of the law made by Leo III the Isaurian under the title of the *Ecloga*, in which jurisprudence is distinctly linked with Christian inspiration. Moreover, sinful though it was, Byzantine society was extremely devout; the very zeal with which it threw itself into theological disputes is proof of this. Fasts were strictly observed. In the main, services were well attended. The final canon of the Council in *trullo*, which is devoted to the guidance of souls or to the believer's struggle against sin, has an undoubted beauty, wholly inspired by the tradition of the Greek Fathers.   This Byzantine faith of the seventh and eighth centuries may appear rather formalist to us, and over-inclined to substitute genuflexions and the muttering of interminable prayers for true purity of heart; it cannot be denied that faith existed, and that, in certain people, it was faith of the highest order.

Moreover many of the aspects of this society have the power to move us deeply and to make us forget its darker side.   It was in this epoch that the cult of the Blessed Virgin sprang fully into being, to expand in a truly wonderful fashion.   As if in reaction against the blaspheming heresies of the Nestorians, the Byzantine soul turned towards Mary and recognized her unique powers.   In addition to the feast of the Nativity of Mary, which it had been customary to celebrate since the sixth century, the Emperor Maurice finally fixed the festival of the 'Dormition' of the Virgin upon 15th August; shortly after this he instituted the *panegyria*, in which a week was devoted to the singing of hymns and the presentation of sacred plays in which the Mother of Christ held the place of honour.   Finally, the feast of the Conception was established in the eighth century.   This was the epoch in which the Marian hymns of Romanos the Melodious were in use everywhere, just like our modern canticles; it was the epoch in which the mighty *acathistic hymn*—acathistic means 'something sung while standing'— developed both the mysteries of Mary, just as our Rosary was to express them (rather differently) later on, and the verses of a varied litany; it was the age in which St Sophronius of Jerusalem showed the position of Mary in the scheme of the Redemption with a depth of understanding which our modern exponents of the doctrine of Mary as the 'co-Redemptress' have scarcely surpassed.   It was also that in which St Andrew of Crete, the melodious *cantor* of 'the maid of God,' brought the first elements of a Marian theology of penetrating insight, expressed in often exquisite language, within the understanding of the ordinary people.

This Byzantine faith manifested itself in another glorious way: in the expansion of the liturgy; the seventh and eighth centuries are the great liturgical centuries of the Christian East.   The ancient liturgy of Antioch had been constituted in the fourth century.   As soon as its customs, which had long been too elastic, were fixed, it acquired, from the sixth century onwards, a beauty, a depth, a wealth of symbolism which the ceremonies of the Eastern Churches (Catholic, as well as the dissidents) have managed to preserve.   The majestic pomp of the services, their minutely ordered ritual, the use of vessels glittering with gold, and of liturgical vestments which were gradually accepted by the whole Church, the moving organ music—all this corresponded with something which was deeply ingrained in the Byzantine soul, and with which imperial etiquette was familiar. The so-called *Liturgy of St Basil*, which had been used for a long time, had been supplanted by one called the *Liturgy of St John Chrysostom*; in addition to this there was a special liturgy for Holy Week and for various days during Lent, which had been borrowed from the Jerusalem tradition and which was none other than our own *Liturgy of the Mass of the Presanctified*.

A mass in Constantinople, in the seventh or eighth centuries, was a fine and noble thing. It was very long—lasting more than two hours —and the development of its episodes had none of that hurried and sketchy character of which our modern low masses too often smack. It began with a 'preparation' which was rich in symbolism: the celebrants offered the leavened bread, the wine, and the water which were to be used in the Holy Sacrifice upon a credence placed apart from the main body of the church, in the treasure-house, or *prothesis*; these were arranged according to the most minutely ordered rites, and then, in order to make it quite clear that it was the whole community of the faithful which was making these offerings, the memorial of the living and the dead was read aloud at this point. Then a second stage in the mass began: the *Little Entry* took place in which, whilst the deacon, standing below the *iconostasis*,[1] recited the verses and prayers of the *Kyrie eleison* with the people, the celebrant took the Testament, and bore the holy book in procession to the strains of the *Trisagion*, the hymn to the Trinity; it was then that the readings from the Epistles, the Gospels, the homily took place, followed by the prayers for the conversion of sinners and catechumens. The most sacred part of the sacrifice now began. The *Great Entry* took place in all its glory. All the celebrants carried around the church the bread and the wine which were to be consecrated, whilst the magnificent responses of the cherub-ikon resounded, whilst the deacons waved the sacred fans 'like the wings of the angels,' and whilst the rhythmical acclamations of the people exalted the entry of Christ the King into His kingdom. When the bread and wine had been placed upon the altar the Creed was recited, according to the formula of Nicaea-Constantinople, then the doors of the iconostasis were closed, and the sacred Mystery was celebrated in an atmosphere of most profound recollection. It is undeniable: all this was very beautiful, it possessed a beauty which can only be attained by those divine rites which make it possible for man to participate in the ineffable realities. There were countless highly symbolic details: such as the custom of breaking a morsel of bread into

[1] A partition of wood or marble, sometimes very high, separating the sanctuary from the nave. It was richly decorated with ikons of the Virgin and the saints. The iconostasis contained three doors allowing passage from the sanctuary to the nave. (There is one in Paris, in the Catholic church of Saint-Julien-le-Pauvre, which follows the Greek rite.)

the wine in the chalice and adding a drop of warm water to it because the flesh of Christ is warm with life; and that of receiving the consecrated bread, at the Communion, with the arms folded to form a cross.

Consequently, although we have just enumerated several of the weaknesses and miseries that afflicted this unsettled, tortured Byzantium, we should neither underestimate nor treat lightly the reality of her Christian faith, which had so many magnificent sides to it. Another proof of the intensity of this faith must be found in the extension of *monasticism*. As has already been shown, the monastic institution had been extremely important in the East in the preceding epoch. It continued to develop throughout the sixth, seventh, and eighth centuries. Although new foundations were rare in Constantinople itself, owing to lack of building space there, they swarmed all over its suburbs and along the Asian coast, and around Chalcedon. In the lonely mountain regions veritable republics of monks were founded, foreshadowing the colony of Mount Athos. Some of these monasteries were certainly centres of Christian fervour which are most worthy of our admiration; the practice of 'perpetual prayer,' first conceived by the *Acimites*, who had been founded in the fifth century by the monk Alexander, had been adopted by several other communities. The monastery of Studium, founded by John Studios in 463, became a nursery of saints, scholars, and dignitaries, and from it, around 800, there was to emerge the glorious saint, Theodore Studites.

But though many of the elements of Eastern monasticism were sublime, various sins and dangers are clearly discernible in it also. The monasteries were extremely wealthy and exempt from all taxation, and their members were excused all public duties. Certain communities sometimes exerted a very unfortunate influence upon the common people, and hardly ever rose above this. At the end of the seventh century, the sight of this or that group of monks forming into bands of demagogic agitators was an unquestionable danger to public order. They were so numerous and so popular that the imperial authorities, as well as the ecclesiastical authorities, might well regard them with a mistrustful eye.

Moreover excesses had slipped into certain monastic customs. These had to be constantly attacked: e.g. the custom of putting young girls into convents by force, or without asking them if they did indeed want to be nuns; even worse, of dedicating little boys of six years of age to the cloister, and even children as yet unborn! The epidemic of reclusion had to be curbed, for some of these 'recluses' quickly tired of their grottoes and returned to the world in a manner which was not always very edifying. And it was even necessary to set the police on to the long-haired hermits who often ran abroad in the towns, claiming to be prophets and indulging in a thousand eccentricities: they were seized, shorn, and shut away in a monastery.

Excess: this was always Byzantine Christianity's most unfortunate characteristic, although it was so admirable in many other respects. We have seen its results in the theological sphere, where the slightest deviation turned to heresy.   It was also clearly marked in the excessive richness of the churches and the sacred vessels, and in the honours accorded to ecclesiastical dignitaries.

There was no field in which this excess was so marked as in the *cult of pictures*.   Christian art in Byzantium, which had known such a prodigious development under Justinian and Theodora, had narrowed in scope as a result of the Empire's misfortunes and had gradually abandoned its larger undertakings.[1]   But it had multiplied its efforts in other fields, in pictures, painted upon wood, in frescoes, mosaics, and *bas-reliefs* representing Christ, the Virgin, and the saints.   This art abandoned its former symbolism and strove increasingly to represent, relate, and evoke sacred truths and lofty examples in concrete terms: in the East, as in the West, the Church believed that a fine medium of instruction was contained herein and that, as Nicephorus said: 'Seeing leads to faith.'

But from the sixth century onwards there was a veritable epidemic of sacred pictures (*ikons* in Greek).   They were set up everywhere not merely in the churches and the monasteries, but in private houses, and on the most diverse objects: chests, furniture, shop-fronts, clothes, jewelled settings in rings, and earrings.   It was said of some that they had not been made by human hands but created miraculously by the will of God: thus were explained the cloth of Edessa and the veil of Veronica upon which, it was said, Our Lord's features were impressed.   The devotion to sacred pictures took such an excessive turn that it leaves us quite bewildered.   Was an oath to be sworn?   It must be done on an ikon.   Was one making one's Communion?   The sacred elements must have touched an ikon.   Was a child being baptized?   This must be done in the presence of an ikon, which was sumptuously draped and decorated with jewels and which sometimes took the place of a godparent.   Veritable aberrations occurred: sick folk took care to swallow the scrapings of paint from an ikon!   On the whole it seems quite certain that the common people distinguished less and less between the ikon before which they burned incense or lit candles and the saint whom it represented.   'Many people seemed to think that all they need do to honour their baptismal vows was to go into a church and rain kisses upon the cross and the sacred pictures.'

---

[1] However, it pursued various major undertakings indirectly, through its influence upon Moslem art.   Syrian architects, schooled in the Byzantine style, were to build the first mosques.

The lower clergy and almost all the monks encouraged this iconoclatry, whose commercial aspects, of course, were not to be despised.

It is this extremely strange characteristic of Byzantine piety—legitimate in principle of course, but distorted by excess—which, in the very moment when the Empire was being taken in hand by Leo III and the Isaurian dynasty, and was halting the momentum of the Islamic tide and effecting a really remarkable revival, was to provoke the crisis that lasted one hundred and twenty years and which was perhaps the most serious which had ever attacked Eastern Christianity. This crisis was to have the most tragic results for the future of the whole of Christendom.

## THE ICONOCLASTIC DISPUTE

Western historians have often considered the Iconoclastic Dispute as something particularly absurd, more absurd even than any of the other religious quarrels which had been a source of division to Eastern Christianity ever since its beginnings. It has been represented as a conflict in which priests and monks squabbled over unimportant details, as the very epitome of 'Byzantinism.' But those who follow this line of thinking convict themselves of complete ignorance of the gravity of what was at stake in this long-drawn-out drama, of understanding absolutely nothing of those forces which shook the very foundations of Byzantine society and of the State itself. *Iconoclasm*— 'the doctrine of image-breaking'—was in reality the occasion of a conflict in which the Eastern Empire was almost torn asunder, in which the opponents on the one side were the emperors, the army, and the Eastern lands; and on the other, the monks, and the West, sustained by the popes. Although, in a doctrinal sense, iconoclasm was probably not so serious as the great deviations of Arianism, Nestorianism, and Monophysitism, it crystallized within it so many inflammatory elements, and manifested itself in such circumstances, that it was to cause more damage than the gravest heresies.

Why did Leo III the Isaurian, the great emperor who had decisively halted Islam before the walls of Constantinople in 718, awaiting the day when, ten years later, he would harry it from Asia Minor—why did Leo the Restorer venture into this hornet's nest? The reasons behind his attitude are very complex. Religious motives were involved: everything in Christianity which was most violently opposed to Nestorianism preferred animal or plant symbolism and decorative tracery to pictures of Christ and the saints. When one represented Christ, was one not insisting overmuch on the human side of His being, and thus separating His two natures? This hostile attitude towards images was moreover reinforced by Moslem and Jewish influences. To this the orthodox faithful replied that the cult of images had always existed in the Church, that Christ Himself had been said by St Paul to be 'the image of God,' which seemed to them to authorize the representation of the features of God incarnate; that, moreover, in this hostility towards ikons, it was easy to pick out traces of the Monophysite heresy, which was against anything that might extol an incarnate spirituality. The dispute was being carried to great lengths, as can be seen. Leo III hailed from the Syrian borders, where the Monophysitism of the 'Jacobites' had many followers, and where there were frequent contacts with the Moslem world, which was hostile to images. He was therefore undoubtedly convinced of the danger of iconolatry, on conscientious grounds. It should be added also that as a representative of the Eastern provinces of the Empire, he would naturally be somewhat mistrustful of the Greeks of Greece and Byzantium, of these restless, turbulent masses who were fervent supporters of images. Finally, it is quite conceivable that the sovereign was desirous of restoring order among the unkempt army of monks and that he hoped to attain this end by waging a campaign against the iconolatry of which the monasteries were the principal bastions. Such a method would avoid the necessity of making a frontal attack on their harum-scarum but redoubtable power.

In 726 Leo III began the offensive against images: they were not officially prohibited, but those which were the object of excessive devotion had to be removed. Right at the beginning one bloody incident demonstrated that all was not to be plain sailing: the palace servants who removed the large Christ from over the gateway were attacked by a howling mob, and blood flowed. Excitement grew; the fleet of Greece and the islands rose in revolt and was only halted in front of Constantinople by Greek fire; there were disturbances at Venice, Ravenna, Rome, and in the Marches. Pope Gregory II condemned the iconoclastic measures. St Germanus, the Patriarch of Constantinople, an old man of ninety years of age, opposed the emperor so vigorously that the latter deposed him and replaced him by Anastasius, one of his creatures. Nevertheless, while Leo III lived, the affair was not driven to extremes; iconoclasm was proclaimed but fairly moderately applied. The movement might perhaps have died a natural death had there not been something more behind the doctrinaires than the ambition of the emperor and his desire for religious pre-eminence. This other underlying force consisted of the desire of the Church—especially the monks—to shake off the imperial yoke. Consequently the quarrel was just on the point of becoming even more acrimonious.

It reached its height under Leo III's son, Constantine V (740–55), whose people conferred on him the opprobrious nickname of *Copronymus*, which he has always retained.  Rejoicing in considerable theological scholarship, and perfectly clear as to what was at issue in this affair, the new emperor, an energetic leader who fought valiantly against the Moslems and the Bulgars, was only too inclined to impose his own religious views by force.  At the beginning of his reign he was infuriated by a rebellion led by his brother-in-law, who, in order to irritate him, declared himself a fervent supporter of images.  This revolt took place in the middle of a war against the Moslems, and almost brought about the Empire's downfall.  At once the religious struggle took on a critical character.  After ensuring himself of the support of an *Iconoclastic Council*, convened at Hieria in 754, Constantine launched a veritable campaign of persecution.  Pictures were forcibly torn down, mosaics painted out with whitewash, frescoes scraped from the walls, and the books written by supporters of images burned.  Arrests, depositions, and deportations multiplied. A second conspiracy had the result of exasperating the despot to the point of blind anger, and he set about striking out anywhere and everywhere.  When Copronymus died in 755 the Empire was in the grip of violent agitation, of a civil and religious war whose complications were prodigious, and in which it seemed likely that the Empire would be shattered into fragments.

It is difficult to imagine the violence of men's passions during this iconoclastic crisis.  Both sides indulged in similar excesses.  There were countless scuffles between women defending their ikons and the soldiers entrusted with the task of destroying them.  Woe betide the solitary soldier who was waylaid in the night by a handful of these shrews who were devoted to the sacred pictures!  He would be found torn to pieces next morning.  But then how exhilarating it was for the hardened troopers when an iconoclastic operation was begun on some quarter of the town, in which they could cut off arms and heads as they pleased with their long knives!  There were scenes of real martyrdom in the Hippodrome, which make one think of the darkest days of pagan persecution.  In 767 came the horrifying sight of the execution of the patriarch Constantine, there in the middle of the arena.  On days when the police were feeling less harsh they amused themselves by making hundreds of monks parade round and round it, to the jeers of the crowd, each holding a woman by the hand.  The most comic episode among all these horrors was the exhibition of the patriarch Anastasius, the bizarre creature of the iconoclasts, who let his side down and was consequently paraded through the streets and in the Circus mounted on a donkey, facing the animal's tail.  But to assess what insane madness this crisis was for the Empire it must be remembered that while all this was going on the Bulgars, who had established themselves at the gateways to the Greek world, were beginning the great attack which was soon to make them Byzantium's most menacing neighbours, and that the Moslem forces—the *Abbasid* caliphs of Bagdad had just taken them energetically in hand—were continuing to overwhelm Asia Minor, that they were established in Crete and Sicily, and that their pirates were spreading terror throughout the Mediterranean.    At such a time as this civil war seemed quite suicidal.

One woman grasped this fact: *Irene* (780–802).    This bewitching Athenian had a quite extraordinary personality.    The Emperor Leo IV (775–80) married her on account of her beauty, and when she was left a widow she governed as regent for her son, Constantine VI. She had such a passion for power that she had no wish ever to abandon it again.    Her official biographers have depicted her as a kind of saint, a superior type of woman, chaste, and shining with grandeur, a true heiress of Constantine and Justinian.    In actual fact she was arrogant and passionate as well as cunning and subtle.    She succeeded in liquidating all her enemies, she removed her own son, firstly by engaging in a strange story of bigamy in order to discredit him, and later by having him arrested and blinded, and she proclaimed herself 'emperor autocrator' and ruled through a regime of semi-terror, surrounded by her eunuchs.    This was the Irene who re-established the cult of images: the second Council of Nicaea, which met in 787, proclaimed that while it was unlawful to *worship* images, it was necessary to venerate them.    The monks were recalled.    The Pope gave his blessing to the 'Christophora.'    Looking still farther afield in her dream of restoring Byzantium's ancient glories, Irene was envisaging offering her hand in marriage to Charlemagne, in order to re-establish the bond between East and West, when a military uprising deposed her.    When she died, a recluse, at Lesbos shortly afterwards, the people brought her remains back to Constantinople where they were received like relics.

The question of images had been only provisionally settled; though apparently regulated on the religious plane, it left the question of the political opposition between the theocratic State and the Church still unsolved.    During the forty years following the death of Irene the opportunity to rekindle the conflict was not to be lacking.    In this period the imperial throne changed hands eight times and *coups d'état* and usurpations fundamentally shook its authority.    Whilst these transitory rulers were, with amazing courage, finding the means of containing Islam in its war of attrition, of halting the Bulgars, who actually got as far as Constantinople in 813, and of shattering a gigantic uprising by the Slavs who, for a time, dominated the whole of Asia Minor, they threw themselves anew into the iconoclastic struggle, without concealing their intention of destroying monasticism once and for all. Under Leo V the Armenian (820–9) and Michael II the Stammerer (820–9) there was fresh persecution of the defenders of the ikons, fresh beatings, blindings, and brandings. But this agony did not shake the resolution of the faithful: led by the energetic St Theodore Studites and the fervent monks of Studium, those defending the images held firm in their resistance.

When the Emperor Theophilus (829–42) died, his widow, *Theodora*, a woman of many charms, vigorous, yet gentle, pious, and artistic, confessed her loyalty to the images. As regent for her son Michael III (842–67)—the emperor whom history knows as Michael the Drunkard —she gathered around her all the supporters of the ikons. Supported by the monks and well beloved by the common people, she was able to rid herself of the iconoclastic patriarch and have a new Council convened which restored the cult of images to all its former glory. On 11th March 843, in a sumptuously decorated St Sophia, the whole Court and the people were present at a service in honour of this restitution; this date has remained that of one of the greatest feasts in the Eastern Church, the *feast of Orthodoxy*.

Thus, one hundred and twenty years after its beginnings, this unhappy quarrel came to an end, not before it had shaken the Empire to its very foundations. But it was to have some extremely grave consequences, some of which only made themselves felt a long time afterwards. The first was political in character. In appearance, the quarrel had ended in defeat for the secular power, in that so many emperors had tried in vain to impose their will by uprooting the ancient custom. But in fact the Church had been able to triumph only with the help of the sovereign; she had solicited the intervention, firstly of Irene, and later of Theodora; consequently she placed herself in the debt of those who had restored the images. Byzantine 'Caesaro-Papism' emerged from this drama considerably strengthened. Should not the patriarchs, the prelates, and the bishops now be more obedient than ever to these infallible emperors who had restored pure doctrine to its place of honour? As the allies of the power which had restored the cult of images, they increasingly became its agents. At the very moment when Theodora was restoring unity and peace to Christendom, the Eastern Empire's worst tendencies were being strengthened; the excessive concentration of authority in the emperor's person was never again to be checked; the influence of the Church would never compensate for the boundless power of the Basileus; the play between the spiritual and temporal powers which, even when it degenerated into serious crises, was to be a repeated opportunity for mutual enrichment in the West, was no longer possible in the East. Here (together with the Empire's withdrawal into its Graeco-Oriental framework which we have already observed) is one of the reasons why Byzantium was no longer able to maintain her leadership of European civilization, which she had possessed in Justinian's time.

Art also was to suffer severe repercussions from this crisis. Its development was violently arrested for more than a century. Before the quarrel it had showed tendencies towards a new and exciting realism, but it emerged from it fixed, immutable, contracted into a timid hieratism; pictures seemed so holy that no one dared paint them any differently than they had been painted in the past. Thus from century to century we shall see Byzantine ikons remaining absolutely identical with one another, stiff, stylized, glowing with gold and jewelled settings. But in these representations of Christ and the Madonna we shall never see the naïve spontaneity and fresh realism of the Italian or Flemish Primitives. In this sense iconoclasm has influenced the spiritual development of Eastern Christianity until modern times.

But it had an even worse influence in another way, for it prepared the way for the great division of Christendom in the next period: the rupture between Rome and Byzantium, the Greek schism. The attitude of the popes remained resolute throughout the dispute. Without accepting the excesses into which the Eastern cult of images had fallen, they refused to lend their support to a thesis which aimed at suppressing them entirely. Pope Gregory II laid down the doctrine of the golden mean at the very beginning of the affair: 'Images should neither be worshipped nor destroyed.' This wisdom brought down upon the popes the hostility of the iconoclastic emperors, who took advantage of this antagonism to remove Ilyricum, Sicily, and Calabria from Rome's ecclesiastical province, in an attempt to limit papal authority to Middle Italy. But at the same time, as defenders of images, the popes were more popular in Constantinople during this period than they had ever been before; the representatives of Pope Hadrian I were wildly acclaimed at the Council of Nicaea: the primacy of the Apostolic See was acknowledged. Naturally this popularity disturbed the leaders of the Byzantine Church, especially its patriarch; they took great exception to it and were not to forget it. The Photius affair [1] was to occur exactly four years after the end of the Iconoclastic Dispute: this was no mere coincidence.

For its part the West also learnt a good deal from this crisis. The loyalty of the Empire's Italian provinces was dashed to pieces by it: why should they remain faithful to this heretical Basileus, who persecuted the defenders of the faith, and who, moreover, was incapable of preventing the Moslems from scouring the seas and actually setting foot in southern Italy? The popes, who foresaw perfectly the future evolution of Byzantium, realized that a change of plan was essential;

---

[1] See further on in this book, Chapter IX, section: 'Photius.'

they therefore turned to the Carolingians.   In a certain sense, therefore, the coronation of Charlemagne in the year 800 was the result of
the iconoclastic madness.   Byzantium saw the implications of it and
her anger was extreme.   'Let Pope Leo III anoint Charles with oil
from top to toe—he will never be anything more than a Barbarian, a
rebel against the true Basileus!'   And it needed nine years of negotiations, and a small warning shot from Venice, before Constantinople
accepted the *fait accompli*.   Thus, from this crisis, which seemed
almost absurd in appearance, a new world was to arise: on the one
hand, Byzantium, 'Romania,' as she was still called, but a Byzantium
reduced to a Hellenic framework, forced to yield ground in order to
defend herself against Islam, the Bulgars, and the Slavs; on the other,
the Carolingian dynasty, closely linked with the Papacy, which was to
make the West aware of its unity.   By the middle of the ninth century the political rupture was an accomplished fact—the religious
schism would not be long delayed.

### The Last Greek Fathers

A sketch of the Church in the East during these times of trouble and
strife is incomplete and unfair unless two facts of considerable worth
are placed to these Christians' credit, to balance their somewhat
imposing debit sheet.   First of all there is the brilliance and the
wealth of their spiritual philosophy: as the final flame thrown up by
the great spiritual fire of the Greek Fathers, the Christian literature of
the period included, both within the Empire and even in the provinces
now occupied by Islam, masters whose work and influence were to be
extremely important.   It is very moving to see these blossoms of lofty
spirituality blooming in an epoch which might seem so unfavourable
to them.   In the darkest moments of the religious and civil wars,
certain souls raised the most worthy of declarations to God, in praying
to Him, invoking Him, and meditating on His mysteries.   'Believe
me, my children,' said one monk to John Moschus, who reproduces
his words in his *Spiritual Meadow*, 'the cause of schisms and heresies
in the Church is nothing other than the fact that we have not loved
God and our neighbour whole-heartedly.'

In one way or another all these great mystical figures are connected
with monasticism.   Many of them spent their lives going from one
monastery to another, spending five years here and twelve years there,
stopping to pass several long months in the solitude of some wild
retreat, enriching the soul with the lessons of poverty and unworldli-
ness, which they had learned as a result of their various experiences.
Prodigious feats of asceticism are told of all of them.   They thrived on
the most extreme austerities.   'The more the exterior man suffers the

more the inner man blooms'—such was the maxim of them all. They remained the descendants of the first Desert Fathers who had believed that they could find God only by renouncing everything. Thus freed of all the earthly cares which surround man and hold him fast amid the trials and troubles of life, these men went forward to meet the Holy Spirit with a sublime ease and simplicity, until death welcomed them as their supreme achievement.

For the most accurate and appealing picture of this spirituality which sprang up in the monastic life, we must turn to the *Spiritual Meadow* of John Moschus, which has been mentioned earlier in this section; this spontaneous and picturesque book can still touch the modern soul even more than the *Lausiac History* of Palladius, or the *History of Monasticism* by Rufinus.[1] John Moschus was probably born in Damascus about 550, and may have died at Rome about 619. Throughout his life he continually enriched his own spiritual experience by his meetings with countless holy people, and he noted down all the advice which they gave him. When, before his death, at the request of his friend St Sophronius, he assembled the 219 little chapters in which he summed up his knowledge, he was in no way trying to compile a dogmatic treatise, or a book of lofty speculation: no, by simply relating deeds and anecdotes, well interlarded with marvels, he made his reader feel exactly how the desire for God and the love of God surged up in these eremitical souls. People complained that one monk had become dropsical on account of his asceticism—'Brethren,' he replied, 'pray simply that the inner man within me shall not become dropsical also.' The whole of John Moschus is contained in short profound sentences like these.

Of all these spiritual figures who, from the end of the sixth century until the middle of the ninth, represented the last glorious phase of the Eastern Church, the most popular was *St John Climacus*, in other words 'John of the Ladder' (the Greek *climax* means ladder), thus named because of his great work, the *Ladder of Perfection*. This was the first of many ascetical and mystical treatises which were to appear under this title right into the Middle Ages. He eventually became abbot of a monastery at the bottom of one of Mount Sinai's rugged gorges, and here there was nothing to deflect him from meditating upon sacred subjects. Addressing himself first and foremost to the cenobites, he explained to them in thirty 'steps' how one could mount heavenwards, just as the angels climbed to paradise upon Jacob's ladder, by conquering vice and practising virtue, and how the superior mystical graces could flower in the peace and calm of a soul that had been released from all human passions. Because of its gifts of style,

---

[1] Father Rouët de Journel, S.J., has made a fine French translation of it, with an introduction and commentaries, in the 'Sources chrétiennes' in the Éditions du Cerf (1949).

its content, and its healthy realism, Climacus's *Ladder* enjoyed immense popularity: Guigues of Chartreux and St Bernard, and later on even St Ignatius Loyola, were to derive many lessons from it.

Solitary meditation was not alone in giving rise to these works of mysticism. Theological struggles in the East, it should be remembered, had always been occasions on which the philosophy of the great believers underwent considerable development; the desire to defend orthodoxy urged them on to self-expression. Thus, in a way, Arianism had created St Athanasius, Nestorianism St Cyril of Alexandria, and Monophysitism Leontius of Byzantium. The imperial initiative which manifested itself in the attempt at Monothelitism gave rise to several reactions on the philosophic plane which were expressed in various works. The glory of being the first to bring to light the cunningly concealed error of the patriarch Sergius belongs to *St Sophronius*, the contemporary, friend, and disciple of John Moschus. Sophronius was elected Patriarch of Jerusalem in 634, and shortly afterwards had to assume command of the defence of the Holy City against the Arabs. He was forced to negotiate its surrender with Omar and died in 638, broken by these tragic events. An intensely mystical soul, devoted to the Virgin Mary, St Sophronius knew how to set the orthodox doctrines on Christ firmly against the detailed theories of the Monothelites in his sermons, even in his poetry, which has a classical charm, and especially in his 'letter of enthronement,' which is a theological document of great distinction. The Sixth Oecumenical Council in 680 adopted the very terms which he had formulated.

However, another work surpassed that of St Sophronius, being richer, more extensive, and more sound in philosophy. This is the work of *St Maximus*, whose heroic conduct was to earn him the glorious title of *the Confessor*. He was a former imperial official, who had become disgusted by Court honours and who had withdrawn to a monastery. Maximus happened to be in Egypt in 633, at the time when St Sophronius, who was soon to be called to the see of Jerusalem, was living there and battling against the Monothelite doctrines. He was then fifty-three years old. His learning, his important connections, and his noble birth marked him out as an exceptional person. Within a few months he became the leader of the Catholic opposition to the imperial error, the inspiration of all those who felt the Caesaro-Papism of the Basileus to be intolerable. From then onwards his life was entirely occupied in this struggle. He arrived in Africa, with the Egyptian refugees fleeing before the Islamic invasion, and there he was invited to argue publicly with Pyrrhus, the former Patriarch of Constantinople, who professed the heresy of the single will; he accepted the challenge, and at Carthage so shattered his opponent by the force of his arguments that the latter announced his abjuration.

Did he go to Rome, to the Council of 649? He played a considerable part in it by insisting upon the philosophic arguments which were opposed to Monothelitism. His labours were so effective that he was seized by Constantius II's police and taken to Constantinople. On his refusal to accept the *Model of the Faith*, which the Pope had denounced as tainted by error, he was sent into exile. Then, because he would not yield he was again dragged before a mock court, condemned to be scourged, and to have his hand and his tongue cut off, and dispatched to an isolated Caucasian village, where he died in 662, a true martyr, as the result of the suffering he had endured. It was the very circumstances of this life of action which gave birth to a considerable literary work which, in many ways, serves as a bridge between the Greek Fathers and the scholastic Middle Ages. A spiritual disciple of St Gregory of Nazianzos, and an enthusiastic follower of the Pseudo Denys the Areopagite,[1] on whom he wrote several commentaries, Maximus was both an exegetist and an exponent of asceticism and mysticism. The more one studies his work the more one can assess the importance of his influence, especially upon the Eastern Church. Deeply involved as he was in the struggle against heresy, he gained therefrom a deep understanding of Christ's personality. He made one of the first attempts to write a life of Christ, and above all he demonstrated most admirably that its value lies, not only in the fact that His sacrifice brought salvation to mankind, but that it has an exemplary merit also, through the influence of His virtues and His personal union with God. St Maximus knew exactly how to speak of this Christ whom faith makes present in our souls, and who remains our everlasting hope; he contributed to bringing Him nearer to us.

When the great new crisis broke out in the next century, the tragedy of the images, the same phenomenon recurred. In order to resist the actions of the Basileus on the dogmatic plane, countless Christian philosophers applied themselves to finding just foundations for the veneration of the ikons, and at the same time they denounced the evil intentions and the doctrinal deviations which the meanness of iconoclasm concealed. Certain of the patriarchs, such as St Germanus of Constantinople, who was the first to rise against the policy of Leo III the Isaurian and who was deposed by him, or St Nicephorus the Confessor, who died of the sufferings he underwent for the faith, or St Methodius, the inventor of the *feast of Orthodoxy*, at the time of the re-establishment of images by Theodora, have all left us doctrinal works, though of unequal value. One man dominates them all, the last of the great Greek Fathers, whose defence of images was but a small part of his creative activity: *St John Damascene*.

Like St Maximus, he too began life as a high government official:

[1] See Chapter III, section: 'Byzantine Christianity.'

not in the service of the emperors, however, but in that of the masters
who had just occupied his native Syria: the Arabs.   His father had
been the 'logothetes,' entrusted with levying the tribute imposed upon
the Christians; he succeeded him in this office, but despite great
honours, like Maximus before him, he felt the overwhelming desire to
renounce everything and, in the words of the General Council, he
'preferred the shame of Christ to all the treasures of Arabia.'   He
became an apostle and monk in the 'laura' of St Sabas, in the fortress-
monastery which still dominates the gorge through which the Cedron
flows to the Dead Sea.   Then, although he himself had no love for
campaigning, his superiors ordered him to throw himself into the
theological battle.   He set himself up as the defender of images with
unflinching courage, founding their cult on theological bases and
defining its limits, and, though excommunicated by the Iconoclastic
Council, he was rehabilitated *post mortem* by the General Council.
There was not one of Christ's enemies that he failed to attack, not even
Islam, and this entailed considerable heroism, for his friend Theophanes,
a neophyte of Damascus, had his tongue well and truly cut out for
speaking against the Koran.   Ever humble and obedient, charitable in
the extreme, he led a life of such obvious sanctity that, when he died,
in advanced old age (749), the people had already almost canonized
him.   Aside from his controversial works written to stamp out
heresies, St John Damascene has left us some great theological treatises,
of which the most remarkable are the *Source of Knowledge*, some
exegetical essays, various manuals on asceticism such as the *Sacred
Comparisons*, countless sermons and religious poems, among them the
hymns which the Church of the Greek rite still sings.   The future was
to regard him primarily as the theologian of the Incarnation, an understanding commentator on the person of Christ, the theologian of
Providence and predestination, a subject upon which his doctrine is
rather different from that of St Augustine, and the theologian of the
Church, whose unity and oecumenical character he exalted so wonderfully.   At the moment when the tragic break between East and West
was about to occur, the saint of Damascus was the last Eastern figure
whose philosophy illumined all Christendom: Pope Leo VIII was
to recognize him, in proclaiming him a Doctor of the Church.

One single personality was to stand out after him, a man whom the
new iconoclastic battles were to place in the forefront of society: *St
Theodore Studites* (759–826).   In 790 he became abbot of the famous
abbey of Studium, a brilliant centre of cenobitic life whose immense
walls sheltered no fewer than a thousand monks, and he made it an
impregnable bastion of resistance to heresy.   Always ready to fight,
to go into exile, to suffer hardships and miseries for the truth, he
unflinchingly resisted all the Nicephoruses and Leos of the world.

Whether he was in his cell or in prison, he never ceased to exert a profound influence.   He was a monastic reformer, and he also founded a kind of academy of learning within his monastery, more or less inspired by the Carolingian models, which brought about a real intellectual renaissance.   Around this 'celestial man, this terrestrial angel,' as his earliest biographers called him, there gathered calligraphers, specially gifted in the transcription of books, painters, and miniaturists whose works were to be sought all over the Empire.   His written work—it fills a whole volume of Migne's *Patrology*—was rather improvised, but nevertheless it had great importance.   An impassioned supporter of the Church's liberty vis-à-vis the temporal powers, St Theodore was led thereby to understand and to say, with admirable clarity, that this independence was conditional upon the supreme and universal authority of one leader, the Pope.   In his letters to the Sovereign Pontiffs he collected a whole cluster of arguments in favour of the Apostolic See: the primacy of St Peter which was affirmed in the Gospels, Roman jurisdiction, the tradition of the Church, dogmatic authority, the necessity of a principle of communion.   He even affirmed papal infallibility in formal terms. Twenty years after the death of Studites, Photius was to set Eastern Christianity along the road which would lead her to schism; St Theodore was the last Eastern witness of a truly Catholic Church, in which the two halves of the world felt themselves bound by the same needs and the same loyalties; his claim to this title should never be forgotten.[1]

## The Christian Influence of the East

This wealth of Byzantine spirituality is not the only fact which must be set to the credit of Eastern Christianity.   Neither the rifts which it suffered on account of heresy, nor the political crises it passed through, nor the grievous damage which Islam inflicted upon it, prevented it from remaining faithful to the great commandment which Jesus gave His apostles: 'Preach the gospel to all nations!'   This uninterrupted missionary expansion remains one of the East's great titles to fame and honour.

The means used in this expansion varied a great deal.   Countless missionary endeavours remain unknown, particularly those of the individual monks and hermits who set out, all alone, into pagan territory.   Their endeavours would not have been very fruitful had they not been supported by the might of the empire itself.   For there was

---

[1] He even had the courage to compare the resolution and soundness of Rome in doctrinal matters with the uncertainty of Byzantium, which, he wrote, 'is a fief of heresy, used to living in frequently open rupture with the rest of Christianity.'

not one single Basileus, however cruel a tyrant he was, however much he might persecute the true Church, who did not have the sincere desire to spread his faith among peoples who had not yet received the light.   Naturally evangelization seemed to all of them an excellent means of extending Byzantine influence; but it would be unjust to see nothing but political motives in their goodwill.   Moreover Christian expansion was greatly favoured by the importance of the diplomatic and commercial traffic of which Byzantium was the centre; freed prisoners, foreign princes invited to the Court, auxiliary troops who had been billeted in Christian territory, merchants settled in far-away trading-posts, were often excellent instruments of evangelical propaganda.

The results were countless.   There were the uncivilized tribes in central Asia Minor who were evangelized by Justinian's immediate successors—often, alas! by force. . . .   There was an Avar chieftain whom Heraclius converted, during a visit which the Barbarian made to the imperial palace, and who departed to scatter some temporary evangelical seeds among his people.   There were the tribes settled along the Danube, among whom Christian elements are apparent from the seventh century onwards.   There is southern Arabia (before Mohammed).   There is the Caucasus.   There were the mountain Berbers who were fairly considerably influenced by the divine Word.   Quite a number of these seeds were destroyed by the Islamic catastrophe, but in different places many would remain which would never perish.

As has been said, the heretical crises did not halt the spread of Christian propaganda.   On the contrary it can be held that, in many cases, missionary activity became an area of agreement between the heretics and the orthodox, both of whom burned with the desire to spread their faith.   Threatened with repression as they were, the heretics needed to win new recruits in order to survive; moreover, as always happens, persecution stimulated characters, making men more ardent and more enterprising.   In this way, following the example of their greatest leader, the tireless James Baradai, the Monophysites conducted an enormous apostolate: the Monophysite Church exerted an unquestionable influence throughout the whole of the Near East right through the sixth century, and its missionaries spread the philosophy of its theologians and it scholars far and wide—scholars like Severus of Antioch, Julian of Halicarnassus, Philoxenes of Mabug, Sergius of Rechaina.   The last named was a former physician, who was a real bridge between Greek learning and the Eastern world, which was so soon afterwards to become Moslemized.

But the most astonishing page of this history of Christian expansion is that written by the *Nestorian missions*, in conditions worthy of an adventure story.  When these heretics began being persecuted by the Byzantine authorities in 457, and above all, when their famous school at Edessa was closed in 489, a fair number of them joined their brethren who were already settled in Persian territory.   Narses, the sect's great philosopher, whose followers named him 'the harp of the Holy Spirit,' removed to Nisibis, where, thanks to him and his disciples, the school became an important spiritual and intellectual centre.   In general, the last Sassanid kings, whilst themselves remaining perfectly faithful to their national religion of Mazdaism, were far from displeased to see these Christians bearing such an implacable hatred for Byzantium, and they showed them great kindness on many occasions.   In spite of certain grave crises, into which it was almost drawn by Maraba, its reforming patriarch, the Nestorian Church expanded continuously throughout the sixth century, going so far as to play its own part in the Persian state: already it had sent its missionaries beyond the Persian boundaries, and in this way it had converted the Kurds in the valley of the upper Tigris before the year 600.

In 633 the Moslems seized Mesopotamia.  The Nestorian Christians did not oppose them in any way.  Were not the new-comers their racial brethren, Semites like themselves; after all, the Arabs and the Aramaeans were blood-cousins!   Moreover the last great Sassanid king, Chosroes II, had viciously persecuted the Nestorians, partly out of political nationalism, and partly because he was under the influence of certain Monophysite Christians.   Consequently the Christians 'of the two persons' rallied to Islamic rule, and continued to develop under it.   When the caliphs chose Bagdad as their capital in 762 the Nestorian *Catholicos* also established himself there. These Christians lent their aid to these new masters of theirs: merchants, scribes, scholars, and doctors linked their work with that of their Moslem counterparts: Islam discovered Aristotle through the Nestorians.  The Moslems translated his works, and their translation, which they took to Spain, was to be used in the West in the Middle Ages, as the basis for the first Latin versions of the philosopher. However, this collaboration was not without its irritations: the Christians were forced to pay heavy taxes and to wear the Christian insignia on their clothing as a distinguishing mark (of opprobrium). No matter; by the eighth century the Nestorian Church stretched from northern Syria to Mesopotamia, from Armenia to Persia, and, although situated in the heart of Moslem territory, was full of life and vigour.

It was then that it threw itself into an apostolate whose scope is quite breath-taking.  What was the reason for this?  One thing must be made clear: although this Church was a branch which had been sawn off from the living trunk of Mother Church, its doctrine marred by an erroneous concept of the Incarnation, many of these Nestorians had souls afire with religious ardour, and were consumed with the desire to spread the Gospel far and wide.  Their monasteries were veritable seminaries which produced an incredible number of missionaries. Several texts of the *Eastern Patrology* give us an exact idea of their methods.  Their missionaries would set out with the caravans that scoured every corner of Asia, often actually going as merchants and caravan leaders.  They spoke the languages of the peoples among whom they were being sent: consequently, at each halting-point on the journey, they could mingle with the crowd, gathering a little audience around them to whom they would explain their beliefs.  If these first contacts looked promising, they would establish permanent mission posts, with hospices and schools, in which, it seemed, men sang Christian hymns excellently.  It makes us think of our own modern missionaries in Africa: the technique of apostleship has scarcely changed with the passing of the centuries.

What of the results?  They were prodigious.  The Nestorians penetrated India.  The Byzantine writer, Cosmas Indicopleustes, the author of a *Christian Topography*, says they were numerous in Ceylon, in the state of Cochin, and in Travancore.  There, mingling with the remnants of the ancient 'Christians of St Thomas,' they were to survive until the sixteenth century, when the Portuguese discovered some of them still in existence.  Following the silk route through Central Asia they reached China, where, from 635 onwards, under the Tang dynasty, they began a campaign of evangelization; an inscription has been found at Hsi-ngau-fow—the old capital of the Tang emperors—which can be dated to 781, which describes how the Christians, 'bearers of the books of truth,' established themselves in China, were obliged to struggle against the hostile Buddhist clergy, but were vigorously supported by the emperors; it is certain that the monks 'came with staff and scrip as their only possessions,' as one of their texts says, being completely faithful to the apostolic ideal, and that, thanks to them, some Chinese were made aware of Christianity, which was manifest in their example.  But, more important than India and China even, was the concentration of Nestorian missionary activity in Central Asia, that is to say, in the whole area which stretches from Turkestan to Mongolia and Tibet.  There the seeds of Christianity were sown by the Nestorians in great abundance, and there they took root.  Various tribes of Huns were converted, and the Gospel was translated into Hunnish.  During the eighth century, under the energetic impulse of Timothy, Patriarch of Bagdad, the Turks in Turkestan were so thoroughly converted to Christianity that, in 782, they demanded a metropolitan of their own, and this desire was granted them.  A little later on missionaries went to the Keraits on Lake Baikal and the Unguts on the great bend of the upper reaches of the Yellow River, and they were even found on the most inaccessible plateaus of Tibet, poor yet tireless, bearing witness to Christ despite the opposition of the lamas.

In the course of time the results of all this propaganda fell to pieces; except in Persia and Armenia, where its roots went very deep, Christianity gradually disappeared, or was replaced by new missionary forms. However, in the middle of the thirteenth century it was still so vigorous in Central Asia that the Christian Mongols united their efforts with those of the Crusaders and attacked Syria in 1258, dealing Islam a blow that was all but mortal. Even to-day, in Tibet, traces of Nestorianism can be picked out in various lamaic sects, where there is a secret ceremony which seems derived from the Eucharist. The mustard seed has a mysterious vigour. . . .

And whilst Christianity was undertaking this splendid Asian venture, albeit under heretical forms, other missionary propaganda was beginning to blaze a trail in another direction. When the Islamic invasion cut her off from the maritime routes upon which her wealth had been founded, Byzantium sought fresh commercial axes, and to do this she turned resolutely north, in other words, towards the Greek towns of the Crimea, southern Russia, and the Caspian. During the first decades of the ninth century, right in the middle of the second act of the Iconoclastic Dispute, the emperors never lost sight of these vast spaces to the north of their domains, where so many threats were piling up, but where expansion was still possible. At this epoch, what is now Russia was in that state of confused agitation which always precedes great historical crystallizations. The Khazar Turks were firmly settled on the Vosges and the Don; the Bulgars, half-way through their development, held the north of the Balkan peninsula; the Slavs, who were still in an extremely fluid state, were beginning to establish themselves permanently in various groups, in particular, the Moravians, who stretched from the Elbe and Bohemia as far as the shores of the Adriatic, where they were separated from the sea by the Croats; and the half-Slav, half-Scandinavian adventurers who were called Russians, though still wanderers, were in process of gaining control of the route from the Baltic to the Black Sea, and were soon to create the state of Kiev.

It is now certain that Eastern Christianity exerted its influence upon all these tribes from about the year 800 onwards. Byzantium sent missions among the Khazars, backed by diplomacy, and these obtained some results. Even before their king, Boris, became a Christian in 863, individual conversions were taking place among the Bulgars. And in Russia, while it is true that decisive action really began with the baptism of Prince Vladimir in 987, a sporadic evangelization preceded it, due either to the efforts of private individuals or to chance

N

trade relationships, or even to actual official missions; it was soon to collide, sometimes violently, with another missionary enterprise, stemming from the West and under the patronage of the Roman Church and the Carolingian emperors.    And it was in fact to be the defeat of the Western effort at penetration into Slav territory, under Louis the German in 835, which decided the Moravians to turn to Byzantium and ask Michael III to send them Eastern missionaries, who were to be Sts Cyril and Methodius.    Thus at the very moment when the Empire at Constantinople was withdrawing into itself politically, and containing itself within its Greek frontiers, new horizons were looming ahead for the Eastern Church as well as for Byzantine civilization, for both were to bloom again in the countries occupied by the Slavs.

# CHAPTER VII

# THE PAPACY AND THE NEW EMPIRE IN THE WEST

## The New Motivating Ideas

IN THE uninterrupted chain of events which constitutes the history of humanity, there are some moments in which it seems as if mankind makes a collective effort to found its future upon new bases in order to release, from the intellectual and moral data accumulated in the past, a few motivating ideas which, good or bad, are to push it towards its new destinies. The Renaissance epoch, with its professions of Humanism, later on, the era of nation-states, and to-day, the period which Ortega y Gasset calls that of 'the revolt of the masses' and which is taking place around us—all these are examples of crystallization of this kind. Even though the phrase has been cheapened by over-use, it is still true to say that these are 'turning-points in history,' after which the human caravan no longer goes in quite the same direction as before. The eighth century was one of these turning-points, and although the events which took place during it had not the same character of violent upheaval which they had possessed in the centuries preceding it, it is certainly the most important century in the whole of the period which we are studying; for the motivating ideas which it set free moulded the whole of the Middle Ages, conditioning their results and posing the most serious of their problems. Moreover the Church was deeply involved in this grasp of an entirely new situation.

The first of these motivating ideas was *that it was necessary to give new foundations to the political system* in the West. The Roman idea of the State, based on a thousand years of law and practical application, was in ruins; the right of force, the 'faustrecht,' which had compelled recognition at the time of the Invasions, no longer seemed sufficient justification for society. Where could these new bases be found? The answer was easy to find: in the Church; and the Christian idea to tend to absorb the notion of the State.

Why? Because, in practice, all the men who were capable of thinking deeply about the world, in this epoch, were clerics, men of the Church, and because all of them claimed the political doctrines of St Augustine as their authority. In reality they considerably distorted and systematized the theses of the *City of God*. It should be remembered [1] that the genius of Hippo had expressed his political philosophy in blurred and complex terms, particularly those aspects touching on the relations between Church and State, on the duty of obedience to the temporal power, on the protection which Christian rulers should afford their religion and on the use of the secular arm. Taken as a whole his political philosophy is clearly extremely sound and constructive. If errors of perspective mar this or that page they are invariably corrected by other sentences contained in this immense work.

But because they had inherited none of Augustine's flexible genius, his disciples were little bothered by shades of meaning; they retained those features of their master's work which appealed naturally to them as clerics. Because St Augustine had said that the Church had the right to judge the principles of the State according to whether they were faithful or not to the spirit of Christ, and that, moreover, she had the right to demand the State's protection and support, they concluded that the best way in which this supervision and this collaboration could be realized simultaneously was by uniting the institutions of Church and State.[2] One of the most rational supporters of this doctrine in the seventh century had been St Isidore of Seville, the great Spanish scholar and compiler, whose encyclopaedic labours made him the educator of his contemporaries and of the generations that followed them. From his pen came sentences like these: 'Secular princes sometimes occupy positions of supreme authority in the Church, in order that their might may protect ecclesiastical discipline. Moreover these powers would not be necessary in the Church, were it not necessary to impose by terror what the priests are unable to make prevail by words alone.' St Isidore found the mingling of spiritual authority and temporal power entirely natural; and he even thought it natural too that terror should be used to compel the acceptance of Christian principles! And straightway we see what potential crises such doctrines contained: the 'theocratic utopia' was expressly inherent in them, with all its consequences, with the conflicts between Church and State and the excesses of the 'secular arm.' Fruitful in the measure in which it declared the primacy of the spiritual, baneful in the measure in which it confused it with the temporal, this motivating idea bore within it both those things which brought glory to medieval Europe and those which caused her suffering.

A second motivating idea, which was less explicitly expressed but

---

[1] See Chapter I, section: 'Foundations for the Future.'

[2] By *political Augustinianism* is meant those theories deriving from St Augustine, though deviating from his expressed philosophy.

far more fruitful in its results, was one which can be defined thus: *it was time to build a Christian civilization*. It is certain that Christianity had already effected a renovation in men's moral values, and for a long time now the institutions of society, and the law, had been subject to Christian influence. But there had been nothing systematic about this. For example, the clergy had been trying to obtain privileges of jurisdiction rather than to build a Christian legal system. As far as pedagogy was concerned, the Church was primarily interested in promoting religious and moral growth, and it was only as a secondary consideration that, in creating her only schools, she gradually realized that a Christian culture was a possibility. Even where the Church's action had been most noticeable in promoting civilization, it had not been intentionally directed to this end: for instance, the monks had played an enormous part as pioneers of new territories, as civilizing agents who penetrated deep into the Barbarian countries: but it had never been their object simply to win land for the plough or to open up new economic channels. They had merely been obeying their Rule, which saw their labour as a means of attaining spiritual perfection. Henceforth things were to be very different. Partly as a result of these 'theocratic' ideas, the Church considered that she was tending to absorb the State, she felt herself invested with the responsibility for civilization; from this stemmed the development of the Christian school, the new role assumed by the monasteries, as bastions of Christianity in lands where the faith was not yet strong, and the effort to create a new, Christian art. This was a fact of prime importance which was demonstrated in striking fashion by the 'Carolingian Renaissance': the fusion between invaders and invaded was an accomplished fact; the intellectual and moral synthesis between the various elements of the future Europe was in process of taking place, and it was the Church who was to realize this.

Finally, a third motivating idea is apparent in men's minds in this epoch. It corresponds with a fundamental urge in the human soul, which has already been observed by Carlyle, Nietzsche, and Keyserling, and which has been emphasized very clearly by René Grousset. At the 'turning-points of history,' these moments when the new concepts on which the world is going to live make their appearances, it may be said that humanity feels the need to see these abstract ideas made incarnate in a few men who seem at the time to take upon their own shoulders the destinies of all their contemporaries. These are the 'leaders' of whom René Grousset speaks. In order to effect the synthesis of the State and the Christian idea, and to promote a truly Christian civilization, the men of the epoch all felt, more or less strongly, *that a heaven-sent man was needed*. Here we must admire the Church's historic prescience once again, for she understood this.

Augustinian political science underwent a slight change on this point. While the author of the *City of God*, and his disciples after him, such as St Gregory the Great and St Isidore of Seville, allowed that all authority came from God, for no one, as St Augustine said, following in the steps of St Paul, 'has the power to command, save that this power be given him by Providence,' the Church, going back beyond this doctrine to the lessons of the Bible, declared that certain men, certain families, were invested by God with the task of governing according to the law; thus had the aged Samuel anointed Saul, and later David, and thus had Solomon been 'the Lord's anointed.' The fundamental aspiration of the age towards the heaven-sent man consequently found Christian backing.

Such were the three great motivating ideas which, taken together, were to make the eighth century one of the most important epochs in the history of the West. The fifth century had been the century of the great collapses, of the liquidation of out-dated formulae; the sixth, the century of a grandiose attempt, albeit archaic and foredoomed to failure, to rebuild and revive the past: the attempt of Justinian; the seventh century, that in which Islam shattered the framework within which Rome and her genius had made the classical world live; and the eighth was to be the century in which, separated from the East, her axis no longer turning on the Mediterranean but on the Continent itself, Christian and medieval Europe was preparing to come into being. The fact that these three motivating ideas could become effective at this time is due to certain events and circumstances, which the Christian historian cannot regard as the result of chance alone. The fact that they could momentarily act together, even though at least two of them were mutually antagonistic, to result in a really astonishing flowering of civilization, was due to the efforts of one man, to his genius, his sense of proportion, and his wisdom. In these two senses we can indeed speak of a 'Carolingian miracle.'

## ITALY AND THE PAPACY

The situation in Italy must be placed in the forefront of the circumstances which were to determine the Carolingian success; it was to condition the attitude of the Papacy, without whose action the descendants of Pepin would never have been what they were. At the beginning of the eighth century the peninsula was divided into two parts, of quite unequal importance.[1] Since the Lombard invasion Byzantine domination, which had been re-established by Justinian's armies, had become very patchy; it was limited to southern Italy, the Duchy of Rome, and the bridgehead of Ravenna-Aquileia-Venice in

[1] See the map 'Italy in the Age of St Gregory' in Chapter IV, p. 222.

the north.   The exarch, the representative of the Basileus, resided at
Ravenna, where he was still completely obeyed; but at Rome, where
the people were irritated by the burdens of Byzantine taxation, he was
regarded only with impatience.   Against this there were the new
Germanic masters, the Lombards, right outside the framework of the
old imperial Italy.   They were an energetic, enterprising people, and
their territories, which were curiously entangled with those belonging
to the Empire, were thereby all the better starting-points for possible
future attacks: there was the kingdom of Pavia in the north, and the
duchies of Spoleto and Benevento in central Italy.   Ravenna and Rome
were particularly menaced by this strategic disposition.   Ravenna was
captured in 751-2 and Rome was threatened on several occasions.

To these two rival powers there was added a third, which, though
not apparent on any map, exercised considerable influence: *the Pope.*
We have already seen how the authority of the bishop of Rome had
been growing steadily.[1]   In the first place he possessed a moral and
spiritual authority: the successor of St Peter profited from all the
brilliance which was attached to the name of the Prince of Apostles;
the radiance of a personality as admirable as that of St Gregory the
Great (590–604) continued to halo the pontiff even a century later.
Through his charitable works, he was the only social leader in an
exhausted, ravaged, and tragic Italy; and he was much more than this.
In many cases he was called upon to play the role of arbitrator—in
Byzantine territory where he alone could defend the weak against
tyranny and the strong, and even in Lombard territory, where he was
greatly respected.   He alone still carried the light of hope in an age of
darkness.

Consequently his spiritual authority was enormous, but he also
possessed real temporal power.   Although the Pope was in no sense
the head of a state, he did possess vast territories all over Italy, territories where he was indeed the ruler for all practical purposes.   As we
already know,[2] since the *Pragmatic Sanction* of 554 various real
political rights had been recognized as pertaining to him; e.g.
he intervened in the nomination of senior officials; he could control
their accounts and summon them before his own tribunal in cases of
embezzlement.   He was a great administrator.   In Rome and its
duchy he concerned himself with a large number of completely
material affairs: food supplies, bridges, defensive walls, and even . . .
the public baths!   As a military leader he possessed a small army,
which grew in number as the Byzantine troops evacuated the town,
and which defended the ramparts successfully on several occasions.
He was a patient builder and restorer of churches, and his 'great works'

[1] Chapter IV, section: 'St Gregory the Great.'
[2] See the relevant note on p. 175 of Chapter III.

afforded a living for countless artisans.   It was entirely logical that, profiting from the antagonism between the Lombards and the Byzantines, the Papacy, as a lively and expanding force, should realize a mighty historic destiny.

In order to do this the Papacy needed to free itself of both Lombardy and Byzantium.   The attitude of the popes towards Byzantium underwent a complete change during the course of the seventh and eighth centuries.   The price of the privileges given to the pontiff by Justinian had been a veritable imperial protectorate over the Papacy. From 555 the popes had to seek ratification of their election from Byzantium, an occasion, of course, which the exchequer did not let pass without making them pay a tax!   So long as the decree of ratification did not reach Rome, they were forbidden to proceed with their consecration, a fact which, taking into consideration the (naturally) dilatory character of the Byzantine administration, could lead to the pontifical throne being vacant for long periods at a time.   When the Basileus delegated the right of ratification to the exarch at Ravenna in the seventh century, the inconveniences grew worse, for this important official was generally on rather icy terms with Rome, and, moreover, subject to the influence of the archbishops of Ravenna. These had been elevated to the rank of patriarch in 668 and were so jealous of the Pope that one of them even tried to make his see the rival of Rome.   The popes had accepted this imperial tutelage and it is rather surprising to see how even a man of Gregory the Great's stature was accustomed to write to the emperor almost as a suppliant. . . .

Things were not to remain like this.   It should be stated that the Papacy was greatly helped in its desire to free itself from this tutelage by the actual errors of the Basileus himself.   It seems as if the majority of the Byzantine emperors devoted themselves to irritating their Italian subjects.   The blunders of their officials passed the bounds of what the most long-suffering people could bear.   For instance, the exchequer contrived to limit the financial year to eight months, which enabled it to have two levies within the same calendar year!   When the motives of indignation inspired by the religious policy of Byzantium are added to these innumerable causes of discontent, the explosion was not slow to occur.

During the eighth century two facts showed that the East's tutelage over the Papacy was soon to cease.   In 710 Pope Constantine still journeyed to Constantinople, as his predecessors had been accustomed to do; but he was the last Roman pontiff to make the voyage.

Moreover, if we examine the list of popes who held office during this century, we observe a significant change.   The seven predecessors of the Roman Gregory II (715-31) had all been Easterners—Greeks, Lebanese, or Syrians; his two successors, Gregory III and Zacharias, were Easterners too, the first a Syrian and the second a Greek, but there were no more Easterners after this.   Zacharias is the last Hellenic name in the pontifical lists.   Since his death, in 752, there has never been another Greek pope, right up to the present day.

But above all, it was the doctrinal attitude of the emperors which was to provoke the estrangement between Rome and Byzantium. We have already seen the resolution with which the popes—with one partial exception, that of the wretched Honorius—opposed the heretical theses of the Basileus.   Even those pontiffs who have not left a great historical reputation behind them conducted themselves with magnificent courage; such as Severinus (638–40), who remained unconsecrated for almost the whole of his pontificate rather than accede to the emperors demands and accept Monothelitism.   We should recall too the noble figure of Pope St Martin [1] who was deported to Byzantium, and thence to the Crimea, and who died a martyr's death for having refused to comply with Constantine II's wishes on the same subject.   At the beginning of the eighth century affairs took a very bad turn; in 712–13 Italy, encouraged by Pope Constantine, refused to recognize the name, the edicts, or the coinage of Philippicus, an ephemeral heretic emperor, and took arms against the exarch.   Twelve years later, when Leo III the Isaurian embarked upon the destruction of images, Italy, which had just been justly exasperated by the doubling of the financial year, rebelled openly. All the Byzantine subjects in the peninsula, Venetians, Romans, Aquileians, and Campanians, made common cause: the *Liber pontificalis* declares that 'the whole of Italy, being enlightened on the wickedness of the Basileus, resolved to choose another ruler and to escort him to Constantinople.'   The rebels answered Byzantium's terror campaign with their own: the exarch of Ravenna was murdered; one Byzantine duke, who was taken prisoner, had his eyes put out. However, Pope Gregory II did not take advantage of the situation, for 'he prevented the Italians from carrying out their project, since he continued to hope that the emperor would be converted.'   His moderation was ill repaid, for four years later the emperor tried to have him assassinated and, between times, removed Illyricum and southern Italy from his ecclesiastical control.   But when the Iconoclastic Dispute went on and on, and especially when, after the brief gap in the gloom under Irene, it was obvious that the Byzantine emperors were continually falling into heresies again, the popes made their choice.   It can really be said that the popes had decided what their choice was to be from the middle of the eighth century; it was to be translated into practical actions at the beginning of the ninth.   Rome was then to opt decisively for the West.

[1] See the previous chapter, section: 'Religious Dissensions, Nationalist Awakenings.'

* N

All the more so, since the West alone would allow the popes to resolve two other problems with which they were faced.

The more serious of these was the Lombard problem.    Ever since the time of St Gregory the Great, Rome had lived in perpetual fear of the Lombards, a fear which was, moreover, kept alive by the refugees who were perpetually arriving in the Eternal City to seek asylum after being robbed and ill-treated by the Germans.    At the beginning of the eighth century Lombard power seemed increasingly formidable in proportion to the growing weakness of Byzantine rule in Italy.    One energetic and intelligent Lombard king, *Liutprand* (712–44), appeared determined to effect the unity of Italy to his own advantage, just as the Franks had united Gaul.    There was an obvious political danger here, for Rome was the principal obstacle to Italian unity—just as she was to be eleven hundred years later, in the age of Garibaldi.    This was a danger which Rome could hardly hope to avert by coming to an understanding with the Lombard dukes of Spoleto and Benevento, who were feudal lords in more or less open rebellion against the King of Pavia, but who were still clearly linked with him.

To this political danger another menace was added, more insidious in character, and which stemmed from the very demands which the Christian faith imposed upon the Pope.    As was its duty, the Papacy had done all in its power to convert the Lombards.    St Gregory the Great had cast the first great seeds of the faith; at the end of the seventh century, under Bertarid (671–88) and Cunibert (688–700), this Germanic people was finally received into the bosom of the Church, and, thanks to its efforts, Italy was covered with new Catholic basilicas. Many of these Lombards were worthy descendants of Theodelinda and were sincere believers: Liutprand's successor, Ratchis, was to abdicate in order to enter a monastery.    From the conversion onwards all showed the greatest respect for the Pope's person.    This was true even of the hard-bitten Liutprand who, in his official documents, made great play of his titles of 'Christian and Catholic prince,' calling himself the king of the 'most blessed and Catholic Lombard nation, beloved by God,' and who, before promulgating a marriage law, humbly sought the advice of 'the Pope of Rome, whom the whole world venerates as head of the Church.'    This excessive politeness smacks of insincerity! The Lombard kings' plan was obvious: in taking the place of the Basileus in Italy, they intended also to replace him as the Church's recognized protector.    Quite apart from the fact that the success of this plan would have subjected Rome to an intolerable tyranny, the Pope, in becoming a Lombard bishop, would very quickly have lost all his universal influence.    It was quite unthinkable that the successor of St Peter should submit to this.

Moreover Liutprand's impatience succeeded in making everyone well aware of these possible consequences; on two occasions, in 728 and 742, when his armies occupied a large part of Umbria and the Marches, he made as if to pounce on Rome itself, even advancing the first time along the right bank of the Tiber, into the 'fields of Nero,' in other words right up to the outskirts of St Peter's; at the last moment he dared not take the final step, but henceforth the Pope knew that he ought not to remain at the mercy of a new Lombard raid.

Finally, added to these two grave preoccupations—the disagreement with Byzantium and the Lombard menace—the Pope had a third cause for grave concern. At the beginning of the eighth century the situation in Rome itself was uneasy. Opposing the influence of the Papacy and the clergy was that of the *exercitus romanus*, that is to say, the local aristocracy, comprising the Duke of Rome, who was practically independent of the emperor, the town majors, the prefect of the city, and the important civil officials. After the fall of the exarchate of Ravenna at the hands of the Lombards in 751–2, it was this violent and authoritarian aristocracy who chose the Duke of Rome. Naturally it dreamed of appointing the pope too. In any case its intervention in pontifical elections was a constant danger. And in actual fact a tragedy which it provoked was to determine the decisive action of Charlemagne.

Consequently there were three reasons which impelled the Pope to appeal for support to a political power. Even if he played a skilful diplomatic hand, he himself, alone, could never hope to resist Byzantium, hold back the Lombards, and retain his position in Rome all at the same time. It was because of this that he sought for a sustaining power and turned to the Franks. Why to the Franks? Was it because there were historic precedents for this? Pope Vigilius had appealed for the protection of Childebert I against the Goths, 'for it is fitting for a Catholic king to defend the Church into which he has been baptized'; Pelagius II had asked for the help of Childebert II against the Lombards.[1] It was well known that Gregory the Great had already praised the Frankish royalty, born of the baptism of Clovis, as 'the most excellent example of royalty. . . .' Probably all these factors were not without influence . . . but the real reason for the choice is much more simple: by the middle of the eighth century Frankish power was the only one which really counted in Western Europe. The kingdom of the Franks had just been taken firmly in hand by the powerful Pepin.

[1] Moreover Pope Pelagius II had prophetic vision: in a letter addressed to Bishop Aunachar of Auxerre in 580, he declared that Divine Providence had destined the Catholic Frankish kings to be the saviours of Rome and of Italy, on account of their geographic position. How right he was!

PEPIN'S DESCENDANTS AND THE BIRTH OF THE PAPAL STATE

As we know, the history of the French monarchy down the centuries is divided into distinct sections by two ruptures, both of which occurred in almost identical circumstances. The Capetians were to replace the Carolingians in almost the same way as the latter had themselves supplanted the Merovingians; the Church played a decisive role in both these substitutions, manifesting, once again, her ever-keen awareness of the superior interests of Christian society and civilization, and that promptitude which she displayed in the moment when a choice became essential.

It took Clovis's [1] descendants less than two centuries to sink into decadence. At the very time when their realm was growing, to include, at its greatest extent, under Dagobert (629–39), almost the whole of Gaul, part of the Rhenish territories, Alemania, and Thuringia, even when their might was beginning to compel recognition in Friesland, Saxony, and Bavaria, and was attracting the attention of the popes, their monarchy was suffering from those incurable evils which were soon to kill it. This 'barbarian' royalty, which was founded upon conquest, had shown itself incapable of rising to the notion of the State. It regarded the conquered territories as the private property of the sovereign and had practised the custom of territorial division which had resulted in permanent civil wars and the impossibility of realizing a true political unity. After a marked revival during the two reigns of Clotaire II and Dagobert its downfall came quickly. The ruling dynasty in all these Merovingian realms seemed physiologically worn out. The traditional picture which depicts these *rois fainéants* travelling from town to town, lolling in their heavy bullock-drawn chariots, and whiling away their lives in idleness and debauchery, is a strictly accurate one; from the middle of the seventh century onwards the real authority was no longer in the hands of Clovis's descendants, although they were still quite capable of fighting one another most savagely. This abdication of authority by the kings naturally resulted in anarchy, anarchy which seriously threatened to destroy the 'kingdom of the Franks.' Five large states had been carved out of it: [2] *Austrasia*, stretching from the Somme to the borders of the Germanic dependencies, which was the real reserve of Frankish strength; 'New Austrasia,' or *Neustria*, an expansion of the Frankish state, extending from the Somme to the Loire; *Burgundy*, which retained the separate character of the subject Burgundian people; and *Aquitaine* and

---

[1] On Clovis's descendants see Chapter IV, end of the section: 'Your Faith is Our Victory!' and Chapter V, section: 'The Age of Darkness.'
[2] See the map on 'The Kingdom of Clovis and His Sons' in Chapter IV.

*Provence*, former Roman provinces, which the Merovingians controlled, though not without difficulty. A similar phenomenon, which followed naturally from the weakening of the central authority, occurred in all these five regions: anarchy developed, to the advantage of the great landowners who constituted the backbone of society in an epoch when the towns had either disappeared or shrunk in size and importance; of course, this growing aristocracy tried to keep the monarchy in the lamentable state into which it had been let slip by the Merovingians, for this was extremely advantageous to it.

But anarchy is not a situation which collective humanity can endure for very long; if the legitimate authority fails another takes its place. Beside the *rois fainéants* there appeared the man who exercised the real power in the realm, the former *major domo* who administered the royal domain in the king's name. Now, as the *Mayor of the Palace*, he became the king's 'prime minister.' This personage, who was usually a member of the aristocracy, acquired enormous influence during the seventh century; the sovereigns' deficiency turned him into a real dictator, a situation which was to be repeated in the Japan of pre-Meiji days, when the Shoguns exercised power instead and in place of the Mikados. And since there is a kind of superior finality of power which compels men's recognition, these mayors of the palace, motivated partly by ambition, and partly by a feeling of duty, were nearly always and nearly everywhere champions of order and unity against the party of the great landowners. In other words they appeared as the genuine trustees of authority and the genuine servants of the national interest, which was henceforth united with their own. Thus, in Neustria and Burgundy, the mayor of the palace of the two realms, Ebroin, shattered that coalition of landowning aristocrats and great ecclesiastics (among whom was Bishop St Leodegarius of Autun) who considered his authority excessive, in 678. Likewise, in Austrasia first of all and soon in the whole of 'France,' the interests of the monarchy were defended by a family of mayors of the palace, which had succeeded in making both its title and its power hereditary: to it the future belonged.

Although, like all famous dynasties, its origins are ringed with legends, the house of Pepin did not in fact have the glamorous beginnings which official genealogies were later to attribute to it. It sprang from the alliance of two wealthy landowners, whose vast properties stretched across Lorraine and Belgium, and whose children intermarried at the beginning of the seventh century. One of these was Arnulf, who was to be Archbishop of Metz, and the other was Pepin of Landen, who had led the resistance to Brunhilda and who was really a kind of vizier to Clovis II and Dagobert up to the year 639. Here it should be emphasized that these two ancestors of the future Carolingians

were both Austrasians, in other words, Germans who straddled what
to-day forms the frontier between Germany and France, men for
whom *Francia* and *Germania* were no more than geographic terms.
We must remember this if we are to understand why Charlemagne
placed the centre of his empire on the Rhine, and why it is useless to
argue whether the great emperor was a Frenchman or a German.    This
marriage between members of these two landowning families produced
a vigorous family, whose foundations were firmly based in the area: it
was to attain supreme power in three stages.

The first stage all but came to a bad end: Grimwald, the son of
Pepin of Landen, who became mayor of the palace in 639, wanted to
move too fast; in 656, judging his sovereigns to be quite decadent, he
ventured to make over the crown of Austrasia in favour of his own son
to whom he had given the Merovingian name of Childebert—deliberately no doubt.    But this usurpation was premature: Grimwald's
plan miscarried and he perished.    The situation was retrieved by
*Pepin of Heristal*, grandson of Arnulf through his father, of Pepin of
Landen through his mother, who skilfully succeeded in regaining
control of the mayoralty of Austrasia, with the title of duke.    He was
the real initiator of Carolingian greatness.

In a second stage Pepin aimed at adding the mayoralty of Neustria
to that of Austrasia; he was involved to the hilt—alongside Bishop St
Leodegarius, it should be noted—in other words, in the Church's camp
—against Ebroin, and though severely beaten by the latter in 680, he
continued the struggle nevertheless, and in 687 crushed Ebroin's
successor at the battle of *Testry*.    This victory ensured him control of
Neustria and Burgundy until his death in 714.    In fact he exercised
complete sovereignty over the whole Frankish kingdom.

The third stage was that accomplished by *Charles Martel*.    It began
badly.    The legitimate descendants of Pepin of Heristal were all
minors.    A vast and complex coalition of interests—Neustrians,
Saxons, and even pagan Frisians—rose against the house of Pepin.
Then Charles, a bastard, threw himself into the struggle, and within
the space of ten years he had made it end as he had vowed it would.
Charles was a tireless warrior, whose contemporaries had nicknamed
him 'Martel' (i.e. the Hammer) because of the enormous weight of
arms which he wielded so easily in battle, and he faced all his enemies
with such good fortune that it was said that God must be guiding him.
Neustrians, supporters of the legitimate branch of his own family,
Frisians and Saxons, who were chased right back into their own
territory, intractable Aquitanians—none of them escaped the wrath of
this terrifying man.    And his fame and glory knew no comparison
when, in 732, he conclusively shattered the champions of Allah's
attack on the West.

For, taking advantage of the disturbed situation and of the anarchy in the Frankish kingdom, the Moslems of Spain had advanced into Gaul. In 719 they cleared the Pyrenees in force and invaded Roussillon and lower Languedoc, reaching towards Nîmes and Toulouse; although checked by the Duke of Aquitaine on the Garonne, they dashed forward more freely along the length of the Rhône and the Saône. In 725 they actually ventured to pillage Autun, and no one could prevent them from carrying off their booty. It was a tragic situation: France was literally paralysed by the Islamic terror. It was now that Vaison-la-Romaine was almost deserted by its inhabitants, when the exploitation of the splendid marble quarries suddenly ceased; it was now, too, that at Guéret St Pardulf ordered his monks to leave and remained alone to defend his abbey against the infidel. One might have thought oneself back in the days of the Great Invasions: moreover, on the northern frontiers, the Bavarians, Alamans, Saxons, and Frisians were stirring dangerously. But Charles Martel had the energy to outwit them all. In 732, when he had thrown back the Bavarians, reduced the Alamans to obedience, and contained the Saxons and the Frisians, he turned to face Islam.

That year the emir Abd-er-Rahman had just thrown a new wave of his warriors into Gaul. From spring to autumn he had been able to pillage freely, and to hold Bordeaux and the whole of south-west France to ransom without any difficulty whatsoever. His covetous glances fell on Tours, the wealthiest city on the Loire: he advanced eagerly towards it at the beginning of October. Charles set out to meet him. The two armies came face to face with each other on the slopes of Poitou. They were very different; the one equipped in heavy armour, wearing coats of mail and metal helmets; the other mounted on high-spirited little ponies, accustomed to going into the attack like a whirlwind. For seven days the West and the East regarded one another carefully. The Moslems were unsure of themselves and scarcely dared approach this island of men which seemed screened by steel. Finally they hurled themselves at it. Their wild, mad charges, taken at full gallop, battered against the Franks' square formations. Shoulder to shoulder, like a solid sea, Charles's men stood stoically firm against the hail of enemy arrows. Any Moslem who came within reach of their pikes, their swords, or their massed weapons, was lost. When evening fell the battle broke up. Abd-er-Rahman was dead, slain in a battle charge. Islam's losses were very heavy, and the threshold to Poitou remained inviolate. At daybreak on the following morning the Frankish warriors noticed that the Moslem camp, with its rows of tents, was still standing there before them: they thought that the battle must be going to start again. But they were wrong. The Moslems had made off in great haste during the night.  *Poitiers, 732!*  It was a signal victory, which put a con-clusive stop to the Islamic advance in the West, just as the victory of Leo III the Isaurian beneath the walls of Constantinople, in 718, had halted it in the East.    It covered Charles Martel in a glory beyond compare.    Henceforth all Gaul rendered homage to him.    Thus it resulted in placing the house of Pepin in the position in which it could perform the historic task which awaited it.

The magnificent progress of this new dynasty had not gone un-noticed by the Church.    All the more so, since the descendants of Bishop Arnulf had never ceased to show her great respect and to lend her their support.    It is indisputable [1] that the missionaries had had constant need of Frankish protection throughout their evangelistic campaigns.    Only when Pepin of Heristal had defeated the Frisians could St Willibrord establish the first missions in the conquered land, and when the Franks had to evacuate part of the area in 716, following a defeat, the saint was expelled and obliged to take refuge in Austrasia. In 722 Pope Gregory II wrote to Charles Martel, 'knowing full well what a fine religious spirit animated the glorious duke of the Franks,' begging him to help and support St Boniface, who was then spreading the Gospel in Germanic territory; and the mayor of the palace replied with a comprehensive letter of protection which placed the missionary under his personal guarantee.    Seventeen years later Gregory paid a fine tribute to this protection in a letter to St Boniface: 'It is thanks to your efforts and to the support of Charles Martel that God has seen fit to bring one hundred thousand heathens within the bosom of the Church.'    Consequently relations between the house of Pepin and the Church were excellent.    Of course a number of incidents tended to endanger this relationship: in order to equip his troops Charles requisitioned a proportion of the Church's wealth, and—and this was even more serious—in order to pay his generals for their services, he arrogated to himself the right of giving them abbeys or bishoprics; this was an extremely deplorable procedure, which introduced some dangerous elements into the higher ranks of the French clergy.    But if the French clerics were little pleased with the situation, the Papacy took the greatest care to demonstrate its affection for the man who was the protector of the missionaries, and the conqueror of Islam—and who might be the enemy of the Lombards to-morrow.

For this was the plan which the Roman pontiffs had forged, and whose realization they were to work for patiently even at a time when the future Carolingians still did not understand the capital importance of this policy: the use of the Franks to raise the Lombard mortgage. In 739 Gregory III was much disturbed by Liutprand's raids in the direction of Rome, and he made an appeal to Charles Martel: 'In the

[1] See Chapter IV, section: 'St Boniface.'

name of God and His dreadful Judgment, do not reject my prayer, do not shut your ears to my plea, and the Prince of Apostles will surely not refuse you the Kingdom of Heaven.' But these words which the Pope had believed admirably suited to impress a Barbarian believer, left the conqueror of Poitiers completely unmoved. Relations between the Franks and the Lombards were extremely amicable at this period, all the more so, since in the task of unification which he was pursuing, the Lombards in Italy and the Franks in France, neither interfered with the other in the least. Liutprand's soldiers had just helped Charles to break up the bands of Arab corsairs in Provence. Consequently the Pope obtained nothing save some fine gifts and a thousand deferential gestures. Moreover Charles, who was just a simple warrior, was incapable of foreseeing the immense consequences of the Roman alliance: he certainly never envisaged the coronation of 800.

But his son was better informed. A well-known picture, which was already very popular in the Middle Ages, has impressed on our minds the features of this thickset, broad-shouldered little man, who, for a wager, amused himself by separating a lion and a bull who were in the middle of a fight in the circus arena. In actual fact Pepin the Short (741–67) did not simply possess exceptional physical vigour and keen practical intelligence, as his father had done; he had that instinctive understanding of men and events which is the mark of the true diplomat, an understanding which he was to hand on to his own son, Charles, and he was also possessed of extraordinary good luck, that mysterious privilege which Providence bestows on some men, for good or ill. Pepin had good luck right from the beginning of his reign: he shattered an attempted rebellion by one of his bastard half-brothers; his legitimate brother, Carloman, with whom he had been obliged to share the mayoralty, was drawn to the monastic life and became a monk at Monte Cassino, thus enabling Pepin to regain control of the whole kingdom. Although he was not so pious as this model of renunciation, Pepin was a good Christian, according to the accepted standard of the time, showing the Pope the deepest respect and interesting himself greatly in the Church's problems. Fustel de Coulanges has observed that there was a revival of religious feeling during the middle of the eighth century; moreover it was at this time that St Boniface reformed the French Church.[1] The Frankish mayor of the palace helped him with all the means at his disposal, calling Councils, enforcing the restoration of clerical discipline, and controlling the clergy's morals. From this firm alliance between Pepin and the Church was to spring an event of capital importance: the suppression of the Merovingian dynasty, and its replacement by the new family of palace mayors.

[1] See Chapter V, end of the section: 'The Church's Principle of Reform.'

During the final years of his life Charles Martel had already behaved exactly like a king, so much so that the throne beside him was left empty.   His son, compared with whom the last Merovingian, Childeric III, was no more than an empty shadow, dated his edicts from '*his* palace,' spoke of '*his* noblemen who surrounded *his* throne,' and declared that he exercised power by virtue of God's confidence.' This equivocal situation could not last.   In 751 Pepin risked a *coup d'état*: Childeric III was shut away in a monastery and Pepin assumed the title of king.   The operation of which Grimwald had thought about a hundred years earlier, but which he had failed to carry through, was successfully effected by Pepin.   This *coup d'état* was certainly the logical consequence of the existing situation, but nevertheless it ran completely counter to the Germanic tradition according to which only a race sprung from the gods could exercise royal power, by virtue of the *Geblütsrecht*, the blood privilege.   There was one way of legalizing the act: by appealing to an authority which was superior to pagan tradition, in other words, to Christianity, to the Church.   Envoys from the mayor had been dispatched to Rome to find out how the land lay and, according to the chronicles of the period, St Boniface himself agreed to ask the Pope this question: 'Is it fitting to call king him who has but the title of power, or he who really possesses it?'   The Pope was Zacharias, a subtle Greek: his reply conformed with Pepin's wishes.   The Papacy abandoned the Merovingians, not because it had any grievances against them, but because it could expect no help from them in the great task which it was pursuing.   During the summer of 751 St Boniface *anointed* Pepin at Soissons: regal anointing had been customary in Visigothic Spain since the accession of Wamba [1] and it was much more than a sign of agreement between the two powers, spiritual and temporal; regal unction (henceforth absolutely distinct from baptismal unction) was the mark which the Church impressed upon kingship.   Henceforth the royal institution was incorporated into the Christian organization of the world.   The Pope granted the Carolingians an investiture which no Merovingian had ever had; but at the same time did he not exact a recompense from them?

Zacharias died before he could exact this recompense.   His successor, *Stephen II* (752–7), was resolved to obtain it.   The Lombard peril was growing.   Aistulf, the new king of Pavia, had just seized Ravenna and was threatening Rome.   Byzantium had answered these encroachments with nothing more than a diplomatic note of protest! The Pope turned to Pepin.   Pontifical messengers came to Austrasia, and Frankish envoys went to Rome.   In the autumn of 753 Stephen II left the Lateran, crossed the Alps by the Great St Bernard pass, and made for Ponthieu, where the king was staying.   Forewarned of his

[1] See Chapter IV, end of section: 'The Arians Return to the Bosom of the Church.'

arrival, Pepin sent Fulred, abbot of Saint-Denis, to salute the pontiff when he reached Saint-Maurice-en-Valais, and his own son Charles (the future Charlemagne) went to greet him at Langres. Finally, when the pontifical procession was but one or two leagues' distant, the king himself went to meet it, dismounted in the presence of the Holy Father, prostrated himself before him humbly, and, taking the bridle of his horse as if he himself were a simple squire, led his respected guest to the palace.   This was a wonderful and touching greeting indeed, but it did not lack political competency!   Henceforth the Pope and the Carolingian king were firm allies: on 28th July 754, at Saint-Denis, Stephen II himself bestowed holy unction upon Pepin and his two sons, declaring 'anathema to whomsoever does not obey them or their descendants.'   A complete change in Frankish policy, and the intervention of Pepin's troops against the Lombards, were now certainties. Should anyone still doubt this, one title which the Pope awarded his friend ought to have enlightened them.   This was the title of *Patrician of the Romans*; it had been held by the exarchs of Ravenna, and had carried with it the obligation to defend the Holy City.

The affair was swiftly accomplished.   Aistulf accepted the conditions made by Pepin, whose soldiers were besieging Pavia, without offering a serious fight: he abandoned Ravenna and the exarchate to his vanquisher who immediately restored them to 'the Roman republic.'   But as soon as the Frankish warriors had gone back over the Alps, Aistulf breathed more easily and speedily forgot his undertakings: not only did he fail to deliver Ravenna to the Pope, but on 1st January 756 he even came to besiege Rome.   There were new complaints from Stephen II.   The Franks made a fresh attack.   Again the Lombards were speedily reduced to submission.   This time Pepin took various precautions.   So that the Pope might be shielded from hostile attacks of this kind, would it not be fitting to provide him with the material means for action, by making him into a real head of state?   Thus, out of Lombard pressure, the *Papal State* was to be born.

Here it is convenient to refer to a very singular story, whose historical role is unquestionable—the *false donation of Constantine*. Probably a legend had already long been current in Rome which, based on the authentic gift of the Lateran Palace to Pope Sylvester I by Constantine, claimed that the first Christian emperor had given the successor of St Peter immense territories, primarily over all the patriarchal sees and even ... the imperial authority and dignity, actually including therein the imperial purple mantle and sceptre!   As if by mere chance a deed had been discovered at the very moment when Stephen II was leaving to beg the Frankish king to save Rome, in 753, a fine deed, consisting of ten pages, which referred to the famous donation and which was full of the sort of details which the folk of the time loved; e.g. describing Constantine as a leper who had been miraculously cured on the day of his conversion. Did Pepin believe that this document was genuine? After all, the men of the Middle Ages were to think so, including Dante. At all events it was politic for him to believe in it, in order to shatter the power of the Lombards in Italy and to assure himself of the permanent alliance of the Pope; in other words, he harked back to the promises of 'Constantine' when he handed these lands over to the Papacy.

Consequently Rome, Perugia, and Ravenna, together with Commachio, were assigned to Stephen II, no longer simply as an estate but in order to constitute a state. Fulred, abbot of Saint-Denis, ceremonially laid the documents confirming the donation and the keys of the ceded cities upon the tomb of St Peter. Constantine V, Emperor of Byzantium, tried to object, but all in vain. The Papal State had been born, and it was to endure for eleven hundred years (756–1870); from now onwards the Pope was independent of the Basileus [1] . . . even though he was not entirely independent of the king of the Franks. The Papal State had a curious shape, like a dumb-bell, the two territorial masses of Ravenna and Rome linked by the slender stalk of Perugia, and it still appeared exceedingly fragile. The Lombards would be sorely tempted to call the whole matter in question again as soon as they had the strength. But, fragile as it was, its foundation had considerable consequences; it involved the Papacy in new destinies; it sealed its alliance with the Carolingian dynasty; it conclusively determined Frankish policy towards the Lombards. And to the son of the man who had just taken this fruitful option on the future it was soon to bring a corollary of exceptional value.

## CHARLEMAGNE

For the hour of the heaven-sent man, for whom Europe was waiting, was about to sound. Four generations of his own family had worked for him, and countless events had combined to favour his emergence. His reign of forty-five years was to be one of the most glorious that mankind has ever witnessed. He was to give Europe new foundations, to bring to a conclusive end the crisis caused by the Invasions, to restore forgotten opportunities to civilization, and to impress history with a seal which we still bear to-day. Charlemagne! This

---

[1] Until then the popes had dated their official documents according to the reigns of the Byzantine emperors. From 757 the imperial dates were omitted, and in 775 Pope Hadrian was to date a document both according to the reign of the Eastern emperor and according to that of Charlemagne's 'Patriciate.'

word, hallowed by long-standing custom [1] in which the honorary
qualifying adjective of 'great' is joined to the ancient Christian name
possessed by many members of the house of Pepin, has important
symbolic value in its very consonance: greatness clings to this personality like bark to a tree; one cannot describe this 'leader of men' without reminding oneself first of all that he was of a stature which few
others can even approach.

When Pepin died, in 768, Charles, his eldest son, was twenty-six
years old.  What had he done, this boy who was promised to such a
lofty destiny, between that day in 742 when Bertha, the daughter of the
Count of Laon—the 'Bertha of the big feet' of the *chansons de gestes*—
brought him into the world in some royal villa or other in Austrasia,
and the premature hour of his accession?  No one really knows, and
Einhard of all people, who faithfully chronicled his reign, is strangely
discreet about his hero's early years.  Can we see in this reserve
evidence of a certain shame which Charles felt at being born outside
holy wedlock, his father not having judged it necessary to marry
Bertha until 749?  His position as a bastard—a legitimized bastard,
but a bastard all the same—would straightway account for a certain
embarrassment, a kind of jealous animosity, which he scarcely concealed towards Carloman, his younger brother, who had been born
after the marriage ceremony.  It is quite possible that this antagonism
was based on an inferiority complex.  Moreover it was not merely
from the psychological view-point that Charlemagne found his brother
embarrassing: the division of the State between the two young men,
which had been ordered by Pepin, according to the same principle
which had proved so damaging to the Merovingians, entangled the
brothers' territories in a most bizarre fashion, making any great work
of unification impossible, separating the elder from the Italian field of
action, since only the younger's domains bordered the Alps, and quite
clearly paved the way for the rivalry between the two capitals—
Charles's at Noyon and later at Laon, and Carloman's at Soissons.
But scarcely three years had elapsed when an unexpected death
completely broke these shackles: leaping at the first chance which
fortune offered him—and sweeping aside the two young sons of his
dead brother, who were minors—Charles claimed his brother's
heritage and thus rebuilt the unity of the paternal realm under his
leadership.

In this promptitude to turn an event to his own advantage, this
exact understanding of the decision that had to be taken, and of the

---

[1] In French, the other Romance languages, and in English at all events.  The phrase
*Carolus Magnus*, probably already common during Charles's lifetime, seems to have
appeared in writing for the first time in 841, when it was used by Nithard, his grandson,
in his *History of the Sons of Louis the Pious*.

means whereby it could be accomplished we can see one of the first proofs of his greatness—even though, in this case, strict morality was little considered.   Charles was like this throughout his life—quick, far-sighted, and energetic.   In these instinctive qualities lies the secret of his incomparably fruitful labour, and, to their service, a never-failing vigour lent an activity which was truly prodigious.   Usually the failing of this type of man is that he relies overmuch on the strength which he knows he possesses, that he acts for action's sake, and goes beyond his limits.   But this was certainly not so in the case of the son of the wise Pepin: never—not even when one thinks of his Spanish policy—did he allow himself to be carried beyond his immediate possibilities; never did he yield to what the Greeks called *hubris*, that opiate offered by the jealous gods.   And he had other complementary qualities, which decisively defined his grandeur: prudence, moderation, a realistic appreciation of the possible, a mistrust of unconsidered actions.   It is the Emperor Augustus whom Charlemagne recalls, rather than Caesar or Alexander.

These psychological characteristics are easily discernible throughout Einhard's text, as well as in the political deeds of the reign.   But can we read them in the actual physical features of the man?   People like to think that greatness shines from the faces of those who have the rare privilege to possess it.   Was it so in the case of the greatest of the Carolingians?   Truth to tell, nothing very detailed can be put forward on this point.   What is certain is that Charlemagne was not in fact the giant 'with the flowing beard' whom the *Chanson de Roland* has immortalized; the mighty build is a poetic exaggeration, and the beard is an anachronism which owes its origin to the Byzantino-Arab fashion which, in the tenth century, considered that all distinguished Western Europeans should be excessively hairy.   The famous equestrian statue, which is now in the Louvre, and which very probably represents Charles, certainly dating from the ninth century, and the Lateran mosaic in which the emperor and the Pope are shown kneeling before St Peter, both depict a thickset, rather squat man, with a round face and long, heavy moustache.   Moreover this is the impression which the reader obtains from a reading of Einhard.   With his co-ordinated body, assured bearing, virile appearance, and energetic voice, Charles's physical appearance suited his every action.   He had a magnificent constitution, which only failed him in the last four years of his life—and then the quacks of the period and their ridiculous diets were to be partially responsible for this.   Then, too, he had a lively taste for physical exercise—swimming, hunting, and violent games; now and then, as a kind of jest, Charles would seize one of his nobles in one hand, carry him at arm's length, and throw him up in the air like a baby.   His appetite was of the kind which was nicely satisfied by a whole hare accompanied by four or five other courses. And he was possessed of a temperament which the fifth and sixth commandments were quite incapable of holding in leading-reins!

Was he intelligent? Most certainly; and when we think of his profound knowledge of men, of his ease at grasping situations, of the immensity of the tasks which he conceived and of the undertakings which he imagined, we realize that his intelligence was far above the average. Of course he was no 'intellectual.' Ordinarily he spoke the Germanic tongue, but he learned to be almost word perfect in Latin, and he could even stumble through a little Greek. He liked to read or to have books read to him, though it is hard to refrain from feeling that if, as Einhard assures us, the *City of God* was his bedside book, he must have found it difficult reading. But over and above a truly personal culture, what he really possessed—together with a thirst for knowledge—was an exact understanding of the hierarchies of scholarship, a respect for education and for those who distributed it, and the desire to make use of political achievements for the good of men's minds. He unquestionably had a supreme appreciation of the overriding need of the moment—the foundation of a new culture— and this is one of the aspects of his character in which his genius shines forth most brilliantly.

In so far as the renaissance of a civilization necessitates a moral effort, was Charles really qualified to accomplish it? The answer to this question is not at all simple. Nothing is more absurd than to judge a man of the eighth century according to twentieth-century standards—things are quite different nowadays, and there is less candour and simplicity. To a large extent his moral outlook remained that of a Barbarian, and when political issues were involved the results were certainly highly questionable so far as the laws of God were concerned. Must we condemn or justify the eviction of his nephews from the throne of Soissons, or the systematic massacre of some five thousand Saxon prisoners, carried out on his personal orders? In both cases the stakes were so high that strict obedience to the Decalogue might have had sorry results for Charles. As for his personal morals, they too remained typical of his epoch: this virile man, who married four times, and who probably had at least ten or twelve mistresses, certainly followed Old rather than New Testament practices in his private life. And the court at Aix-la-Chapelle, where the public scandals of the emperor's daughters mingled with their father's licentiousness, was definitely not an edifying place.

But for a sovereign, the moral principles which he tries to put into practice in his official capacity are far more important than his personal morality (at least, when the latter does not affect public policy, and Charles never allowed his womenfolk to encroach upon this in any way).   On this point the great emperor was quite clear-sighted.   In one way he was very humble, as a Christian ought to be.   He never yielded to the temptation of display, of excessive wealth, and of vain-glory; as for the Roman purple, 'he only wore it again on one occa-sion,' according to his biographer (although this is probably a slight exaggeration), and he detested all ceremonial; Louis XIV was no descendant of his.   And he possessed another Christian virtue, a great sense of equity.   One anecdote, which is probably tinged with legend, but which is none the less both pleasing and significant, tells how he had a bell placed by the palace gates, which anyone seeking to have justice done by him could ring, and how, when an old abandoned horse pulled the rope one day, Charlemagne had the man who could treat an old and faithful servant so badly well and truly punished. Finally, though he himself was violent and terrible in anger, he yet fought violence with all the means in his power, quelling disturbances and preventing private wars: order was essential to him in order that he could undertake his great work.   Thus the indiscretions of his private life have no connection with the strict rules he applied to public morality.

Does all this add up to make the portrait of a Christian?   Not entirely, perhaps, according to our criteria—even taking the pharisaism and hypocrisy of a more 'advanced' civilization into account—but against the background of his own time, it certainly does.   Charles was personally devout, rigorously observant in his prayers and his fasting (and the latter cut into his fine appetite), and he was indeed the man as portrayed by the chroniclers, the man who attended inter-minable religious services entirely of his own free will, his own strong voice mingling with those of the choir.   The clerks who surrounded him told him again and again of the necessity of living according to Christian principles; in an oft-quoted letter, one of these, named Cathulf, instructed him, in sublime terms, to tell God everything, to love above all else Him who had drawn him from naught, who had entrusted him with the task of governing men, and who would require him to render an account of his actions, on the Day of Judgment.   It was from this excellent teacher that Charles learned the habit of always having a Bible within arm's reach and of reading a passage from it each day.   Charles declared that this loyalty to Christian principles was the axis of his entire policy, and one of his most famous Capitu-laries, the *General Admonition* of 789, is a perfect exposition of those foundations upon which a Christian society ought to rest.   To make his subjects live in perfect harmony, to establish the *concordia pacis* between men, above all to fight against all the evils which ravaged the world: famine, cruelty, and injustice—such was the ideal of this mighty and awe-inspiring monarch, scarcely a year of whose reign went by without some war or other: and this ideal completely corresponded with a Christian vocation.  And the certainty which this man held at the bottom of his heart, of 'taking the place of God on earth, of having, as his task, the exaltation of His Law,' made this ideal into a supremely pressing necessity.  Personally but a mediocre Christian, rough-hewn from gnarled Germanic wood, Charles is, on the historical plane, a witness of God, after the style of Solomon, Constantine, and Justinian, and, despite all his faults, it was towards a truly Christian policy that he was to aim.

## The Iron Crown and the Papal State

The first problem which Charlemagne faced on assuming the crown was that concerning Italy, Rome, and the Lombards.  At the time of his accession this question had just been considerably confused owing to the political mistakes of Queen Bertha, his mother.  This outstanding woman, rightly but overmuch preoccupied by the situation created in Neustria [1]—we would say France—by the indifferent understanding which existed between her two sons, had personally practised a diplomatic policy of 'peace at any price' towards the Lombards, in which, of course, she was encouraged by the extremely astute *Desiderius*, King of Pavia.  At the time when he succeeded Aistulf (in 756), with the support of Abbot Fulred and the blessing of Pope Stephen II, the former Duke of Tuscany had made much of the extreme purity of his intentions, even while he was manœuvring to encircle Rome and to establish a network of family alliances in all the neighbouring countries which, he hoped, would make him the leader of the Germanic world.  One of his daughters was Duchess of Bavaria, and another, Duchess of Benevento; his son, Edelgise, had married Gisela, the sister of the two Frankish kings; the crowning touch had been set to these manœuvres when Queen Bertha had married her elder son, Charles, to Desiderius's daughter, Desideria. Pope Stephen III, who was more clear-sighted on the matter than his predecessors, Stephen II or Paul I, had protested about it—but all in vain—on the grounds of the state of public concubinage in which the young prince was living, which, in this epoch, was considered to amount to a 'contractual marriage'—in reality, because he was well aware that this union hallowed the abandonment of the Frankish policy towards Italy which had been devoted to the protection and preservation of Rome.  Despite his twenty-five years Charles had

[1] Probably it was Bertha's influence too which decided her sons' choice of the two capitals of Laon and Soissons, which were in Neustria, not Austrasia: this was a veering westwards, which clearly betrayed the abandonment of the Germano-Roman policy of Pepin, to which Charlemagne was to return.

appeared to defer to his energetic mother's wishes. But he fretted under the restraint.

Consequently, when the unexpected death of his brother in 771 gave him a free hand, Charlemagne envisaged a change of policy. His young sister-in-law, with her two fatherless boys, took refuge at Pavia and then at Verona, where she protested vehemently against the spoliation of which her children had been the victims: proof, if proof was needed, of the existence of Italian intrigues against the King of the Franks. Moreover the Lombard attitude towards Rome and the young Papal State became more pressing. An extremely painful incident had just shown to what extent the Pope's authority was threatened, in 768, on the death of Paul I. Duke Toto of Nepi had set his own brother, Constantine, a layman, on the papal throne by force; Desiderius had intervened to annihilate this intruder. But the Lombard party had then immediately attempted to impose its candidate, a certain deacon named Philip, and it had needed all the resources of Roman diplomacy to ensure the final regular election of Stephen III to the pontificate.[1] At almost the same time, at Ravenna, a patriarch by the name of Leo was trying to found a kind of papal state of his own in the former exarchate. Here again Lombard diplomacy was clearly at work. When, in 772, an energetic, wealthy, and well-educated Roman patrician, thoroughly conscious of the rights and duties of his see, succeeded Stephen III and assumed the name of Hadrian I, the distrust of both Pope and Frankish king towards the Lombards joined hands. Two significant things happened: the Pope refused to support the complaints of Carloman's widow regarding the fate of the throne of Soissons, and Charlemagne repudiated Desideria, his Lombard wife, and sent her back to Pavia post-haste. Bertha's policy was abruptly abandoned, and Charlemagne was returning to that pursued by Pepin.

Desiderius saw his intentions clearly. He retorted by declaring the donation 'null and void'; in the spring of 773 he occupied Commachio and Faenza, then Gubbio and Urbino, and following the course of the Tiber, proceeded to march on Rome. Because all land communications were cut, Hadrian sent an ambassador to Charles by sea to implore him to act. In July 773 the Frankish army, which had been concentrated at Geneva, crossed the Alps by the Mont-Cenis and St Bernard passes, fell on Desiderius's flanks, seized Verona, where Carloman's children were taken prisoner, and besieged Pavia, where

---

[1] As a result of these serious incidents the Lateran Council of 796 forbade any layman to put himself forward as a candidate for the papal throne, a decision which was, however, a theoretical one which was difficult to realize in practice at the time. Constantine's usurpation ended in a frightful fashion: the deposed Pope had his eyes put out, and several of his supporters had their tongues cut off or were blinded. Then, some time later, those responsible for these horrors suffered likewise, in their turn. . . .

the king held out for six months. At Easter 774, in a grandiose ceremony, the victorious Frank was to be received at St Peter's like a hero; the three doors of the basilica were opened in his honour. As he ascended the steps he kissed them piously, one by one, and prostrated himself upon the apostle's 'confession,' whilst the choir sang: 'Blessed is he who comes in the name of the Lord!' Then Hadrian confirmed Charles's title as Patrician of the Romans, and the king confirmed Pepin's donation to the Pope, and extended it still further. The alliance between the Papacy and the house of Pepin was sealed anew; the policy which had led the father to the royal crown was taken up once more, and it was to lead the son to the crown of an Empire.

Two months later Lombard resistance collapsed. Charles entered an exhausted Pavia in June 774, his young bride Hildegarde riding by his side, whilst Desiderius went into exile at Corbie. And it was then that Charlemagne carried out the first great political act of his career: instead of leaving a king at Pavia *he himself assumed the iron crown*,[1] supported, so it seems, by certain Lombard tribes and by the clergy; thus he placed in position the first stone of the great edifice that was to be a united Germanic world. Henceforth Charles was to bear the title—it appears on a document dated at Pavia, 16th July 774 —of 'by the grace of God, King of France and of the Lombards and Patrician of the Romans.'

The ease with which Charles could impose his rule on Italy in this way remains astonishing. It is true of course that two years later he was forced to return to the peninsula to crush the rebellion of the Lombard dukes of Benevento—Desiderius's son-in-law—and Spoleto. These two had allied with Edelgise, the son of the dethroned ruler, who, although he was now living at the Byzantine Court, was trying to regain control of his former realm; but only two short campaigns were needed to settle them for good. Northern Italy was henceforth firmly held by Charlemagne; the duchy of Benevento was allowed to remain independent under a moderate measure of Frankish control, for Charles, with his profound political understanding, had straightway realized the usefulness of this buffer state which prevented him from being in direct contact with the Byzantine possessions in the south. In 780 he made his son, Pepin, king of Italy. Surrounded by sound advisers chosen by his father, this young sovereign was little more than a senior official: thus the first step towards the system of federal empire of which Charlemagne was to dream, was put into practice.

In fact the conqueror of Desiderius was the real master of Italy.

[1] This, it should be remembered, was made of gold, like all royal crowns, but was mounted upon an iron circlet in which, it was claimed, a nail from the True Cross had been welded.

What did the Pope think of this situation? On the practical plane
he had seen his powers confirmed. The donation of Pepin had been
enlarged, and lines of demarcation had been drawn between the papal
and the Frankish zones of expansion. According to the *Liber
pontificalis*, the frontier of the 'promised' territories was as follows:
starting from Spezia, it cleared the Apennines, and included Parma and
Mantua, the whole of the exarchate of Ravenna, 'considered in terms
of its former boundaries' (in other words, before Liutprand's annex-
ations), Venetia, and Istria. Corsica, on the one hand, and the duchies
of Benevento and Spoleto on the other, were also promised to the
Holy See, in a somewhat vaguer fashion; the frontier in the direction
of southern Italy remained undefined. This recognition of the Papal
State by the man who, from now on, dominated Europe, was a fact of
capital importance. But could a far-reaching Pope like Hadrian I
accept this result as final, pleased with it though he might be?

The Pope's position was certainly extremely delicate. He was in
open conflict with the Eastern Empire on account of the Iconoclastic
Dispute. Moreover he was well aware that he was dependent upon
the Frankish armies and that, without their protection, his tiny state
would not count for much before the reawakened appetites of the
Lombards, who were being secretly aided by Byzantium. But, in
addition, he did not want this protection to turn into subjection and,
being an astute politician, he could see the danger of this only too well.
When Charlemagne swooped on Italy again in 786 in order to bring
the Duke of Benevento to reason, and when he went to celebrate
Christmas in Florence and then came on to visit Rome, all Italy had
the strong feeling that the Pope was less important than this rugged
soldier who walked around the peninsula exactly as if he owned it.
Furthermore, certain of the territories which had been promised the
Pope in 774 were not handed over to the Papal State: Modena,
Mantua, Vicenza, and Verona were never added to it, and even in
Sabina the Lateran officials were not obeyed so readily as those of the
Franks. There is a clearly discernible disappointment, bitterness, and
irritation in Hadrian's correspondence, which the writer makes little
attempt to conceal.

Hadrian I died in 795 and Charlemagne never failed to pay tribute
to his memory. But circumstances were soon to show how much,
whether it liked it or not, the Papacy depended on the Frankish king.
*Leo III*, the new Pope, was also a Roman, but not of illustrious
descent like his predecessor. He was a man of the people, and an
upright and God-fearing priest. Against him was the *camarilla* of
the *exercitus romanus*, actually directed by the nephews of the deceased
Pope. As soon as he was elected, Leo III hastened to announce his
accession to Charles, promising him his loyalty, and sending him the

keys of St Peter's 'confession' and a flag bearing the arms of the city of
Rome. The Frankish king replied with a serious and haughty letter,
in which he exhorted the Pope to conduct himself uprightly, to observe
the canons, and to govern the Church piously! The precautions
which the Pope had taken did not prevent a *coup d'état* against him.
Perhaps they even hastened it. On the day of the Great Litanies, in
799,[1] while Leo was riding at the head of the religious procession,
according to an ancient custom, he was attacked, brutally beaten,
thrown from his horse, and stripped of his pontifical vestments: it was
a miracle that his tongue was not cut off and his eyes were not gouged
out, in the Byzantine fashion. He was accused of all kinds of vices
and crimes, and was shut up in a monastery to await his 'trial.' Luckily
for him he managed to escape from his prison down a rope, reached
Spoleto, where he was restored to health, and then hurried to Paderborn, where Charles was residing, to beg him to restore him to power.
The king embraced him, weeping, and gave him an escort of soldiers
and important officials so that he could return to Rome and re-establish
himself there.

It was then that an episode of capital importance occurred, which
puts in its true light the much more famous fact of the coronation
which was soon to follow. In what conditions would the Pope re-
establish himself in the Papal See? Since he had been the victim of
an odious plot, it ought to have been enough to restore his powers to
him and to punish the criminals who had made the attempt upon his
life. But this was not what happened. Leo III re-entered the Holy
City in the autumn of 799, to be followed, a year later, by Charlemagne
himself. The Frankish king was welcomed by the Pope and by a
gigantic procession when he was 7 miles from Rome, and was received
in great pomp on the steps of St Peter's on 24th November. He
seemed to be celebrating his triumph. What was he going to do in
Rome? One chronicler tells us quite unequivocally: 'He was going
to carry out an investigation into the crimes of which the pontiff was
accused.' In other words, the temporal sovereign was setting himself
up, if not as the judge, at least as the appraiser of the conduct of the
Sovereign Pontiff. Nothing better shows how dependent on Frankish power the successor of the proud Hadrian I had now become! It
was true of course that no one really dared *judge* the Pope, and this
process was undertaken with the declared intention of clearing his

[1] As has already been stated, the Great Litanies were a festival celebrated in Rome on
25th April. On this date the pagan rites of the Rubaglia had formerly taken place: a
procession would leave the city and go far into the countryside in order to sacrifice a lamb
in honour of the old Italian goddess, Robigo. At the end of the seventh century Pope
St Gregory the Great 'baptized' this pagan festival and commanded that a great procession should be held each year to ask God to prevent public calamities from affecting
the land. See Chapter V, section: 'Faith in the Midst of the Darkness.'

name; Alcuin had reminded his master of the famous maxim which went back to the differences between Pope Symmachus and Laurence, the antipope: 'No one can sit in judgment upon the Holy See.' Nevertheless an assembly of prelates, of ordinary clerics, and of secular dignitaries was called at St Peter's on the 1st December under the presidency of Charles himself, and on the 23rd Leo III submitted to the arduous obligation, forced upon him by his protector, and had to swear solemnly that he had 'neither perpetrated nor ordered the wicked and scandalous deeds of which he was accused.' This was what was known as a 'purgatorial oath' according to the custom of the period. By a painful irony the formula contained these words: '... being neither judged nor constrained by any man, and as an act of my own free will, I swear ...'

Such was the situation, then. As Alcuin wrote in a poem written for the occasion, the Frankish king appeared as the guide of the leader of the Church, he himself being 'guided by the strong hand of the Lord.' It was a topsyturvy state of affairs! In order to enhance the master's glory still further, two monks arrived in Rome from Jerusalem, on the very day of the purgatorial oath, as if by chance. They came to give Charles the keys of the Holy Sepulchre and of the city itself! Meanwhile Leo III was proclaiming that 'conscious of the favours he had received, nothing, save death, could separate him from the love which he bore Charles.'

### Christmas 800 and the New Empire in the West

This 'love' was soon to be demonstrated in striking fashion. Two days later, on 25th December, Charlemagne returned to St Peter's to be present at the Christmas mass there. In the midst of an immense gathering of both Franks and Romans he entered the basilica amid shouts of triumphant acclamation. He knelt on the apostle's 'confession' and prayed. As he made to rise the Pope approached him and placed a crown upon his head, whilst the crowd acclaimed him thrice: 'Long life and victory to the most pious Charles, Augustus, crowned by God, mighty and peace-loving emperor of the Romans!' Next the pontiff anointed the forehead of the 'new David' with sacred oil and, uniting the ceremonial imposed, since Diocletian's time, by the protocol of the Roman emperors, with the ancient biblical rite, he prostrated himself before him and 'adored him.' Henceforth the West had a new emperor, in the descendant of the palace mayors of Austrasia.

It goes without saying that this theatrical gesture had been most carefully prepared in advance. The crowd would not have shouted the triple and ritual acclamation unless some team of applauders had taught it to them. To tell the truth, an enormous movement of feeling, in which various and numerous complex currents of opinion were mingled, had for some time been pushing forward in the direction of the step which had just been taken. In 800, after thirty-two years of his reign, Charlemagne appeared to embody a glory which no man had equalled for several centuries. He had forced Islam back beyond the Alps and had imposed his rule upon almost the entire Germanic world, at all events upon the whole of the civilized West; he had been the great converter as well as the great conqueror. His domain, which spread to the Elbe, to the middle Danube, to Brussels, and even as far as the outskirts of Rome, seemed now too large for the ordinary word 'realm' to fit it any longer. The realistic argument used by Zacharias in favour of Pepin could find a new application in Charles's favour: who should bear the emperor's title, if not this man, who possessed the imperial power? All the more so since, at the same time, the imperial throne at Byzantium was occupied by a woman, Irene, who had just ridded herself of her own son and proclaimed herself *Basileus*! And then it was necessary to take popular feeling into consideration, to remember this expectant belief—which has been referred to at the beginning of this chapter—in the heaven-sent man, ever-ready, at the turning-points of history, to assume control of the destinies of the world. Who in the world fitted this role more perfectly than this glamorous personage, who set every man's imagination afire and who seemed so much larger than life? The unfettered fanaticism of the mobs, from which Augustus, Constantine, and Napoleon (and, need we add, Hitler?) have all benefited, worked completely in Charles's favour. Ever since the disappearance of the Western Empire, in the disastrous days of Romulus Augustulus, the imperial idea had survived as an undercurrent, deep in the popular mind, as a kind of nostalgia, as a picture of unity and concord, of strength and peace. Among the Germans—or so certain German historians have maintained—this idea also mingled with Pan-German aspirations. And the clerks, for whom the true emperor had always been Constantine, the founder of the Christian Empire, and not Augustus, saw in the Papacy's protector 'the new, reborn Constantine,' to quote the words actually used of Charlemagne by Hadrian I. The unanimity which ensured the Frankish king's astonishing promotion in status was not hard to find.

How were these as yet confused desires in the popular mind crystallized? How was this idea of the past which the Empire had been projected into the present? It seems that the gesture of Christmas 800 had in fact a triple origin. Surely it was born from the philosophy of the scholars whom Charles attracted to his Court at Aix-la-Chapelle. Because they spoke Latin, they revived the concepts of the classical philosophers, of Claudian and even of Virgil, and this was especially so in the case of *Alcuin*, Charles's great prelate, adviser, and friend: had not the abbot of St Martin of Tours explained to the king in a letter that, since the apostolic dignity had been humiliated in Leo III, and the imperial dignity was vacant, it was necessary for the royal dignity, made so completely incarnate in him, Charles, to be exalted in order to replace the one and to control the other?

Not merely did the Pope raise no objection to these plans, he actually associated himself with them. He did even more than this. He became the leader of the movement which was striving for the resurrection of the Empire. At first sight this seems somewhat surprising, since the movement hallowed an only too real subjection of the Papacy to the Frankish power; to us it is quite clear that all the seeds of the medieval tragedy of the relationship between Pope and Empire are already here. But the dreadful conflicts of ideas which preoccupied the eleventh century should not be transposed to the ninth. At that time neither Pope nor emperor had the slightest thought of those intentions of autonomy and supremacy which Innocent III or Henry IV of Germany were to possess. Both rather had the feeling—a very Augustinian one—of being agents of the divine Will: the formula of acclamation, 'crowned by God,' says this quite explicitly. Consequently it is just as false to imagine Leo III reviving the Empire in order to promote the interests of the Papacy as it is to see him as nothing more than the dependant of the great Charles, obliged to obey him in all things. The truth is, that even though it was guided by a pontiff whose hands were tied, the Church had a much wider horizon. For her the revival of the Empire in the West ensured her freedom in respect of Byzantium; it meant that her temporal realm, the Papal State, the pledge of her independence, was confirmed and guaranteed; it signified the foundation of a new juridical status, according to which the Barbarian king, until then foreign to the Roman tradition, henceforth entered into a definite relationship with the Pope. Finally—and it is absolutely certain that the clerks, both those of Rome and those at Charles's court, understood this—the revival meant that Christian civilization and Roman universalism were given a new chance. Leo III was not the only person who wished for the Empire's resurrection; but there is not the slightest doubt that he did wish it.

There only remains the third element which was responsible for the great event of Christmas 800: Charles's own will. This is the point upon which we know the least. Was the imperial coronation the result of a well-matured plan on the part of the Frankish leader, a ladder which he had long ago resolved to climb? It is quite impossible to give an answer. In human life it often happens that something occurs in which one eventually rejoices and glories, but which one had not really wanted, and which one had even regarded with suspicion at the time. Of course the coronation was in no way contrary to Charles's intentions. The plans of his clerical entourage were not unknown to him; for years his Court flatterers had applauded his actions with the word *imperialis*; had he been too obtuse to understand their meaning? Einhard claimed that whereas joy overflowed the hearts of all those gathered in the brightly lit basilica of St Peter's, it was completely absent from the soul of the man principally concerned in the event, 'so much so that he declared that he would not have gone to church that day, even though it was a solemn festival, had he guessed the pontiff's plan.' But can anyone believe for a moment that the wretched, feeble Leo III, who had submitted himself to the humiliation of the 'purgatorial oath' but forty-eight hours before, could have treated the conqueror of the world like a small boy, in this way?

It is therefore beyond any doubt whatsoever that Charlemagne wanted to be emperor. Why, then, did he show the ill-humour which his faithful biographer echoes so aptly? There is no lack of hypotheses to explain this mystery. It has been suggested that, being fundamentally German at heart, he would have preferred to hold the Empire of his lords, of his companions in arms, which would explain why he always appeared to detest wearing the purple; but in this case why had he waited so long to have himself proclaimed emperor by his own followers? It has also been claimed that, although he was thoroughly pleased about the coronation itself, he was annoyed by the manner in which the ceremony took place: the crowning by the Pope [1] and the acclamation by the crowd; that he saw in it the declaration of a universal power which was superior to his own; but to admit this hypothesis is to turn Charlemagne from the Augustinian which we know he was into a Gallican of the first order. . . . Einhard himself gives the impression that his master's displeasure was solely diplomatic; it was aimed at presenting the coronation as something carried out on the Pope's personal initiative in order to calm Byzantine susceptibilities. This hypothesis, which is held by many modern historians, seems a little unreal: it implies that Charles was quite surprisingly naïve, for who could hope to dupe the most skilful diplomats in the world so clumsily?

At all events, if this really was the object of the manœuvre, it did not succeed very well. For the Byzantines were furious. At the palace on the Golden Horn no one could be too sarcastic about this Barbarian

---

[1] This was certainly why Napoleon, who had studied the history of Charlemagne closely, crowned himself and then crowned Josephine, without giving the Pope time to intervene.

who had made himself emperor, and the Pope who had anointed him
with oil!    Until then the Eastern Empire had been able to maintain
the fiction that the Barbarians were occupying Roman territories, *her*
territories, by fraud and violence, and that one day they would be
restored her by the victories of a new Justinian or a second Heraclius:
to such an extent that important officials continued to bear, as we have
seen, the titles of the ancient functions that their predecessors had performed, *in partibus*, in those provinces that were now lost.    But
Charlemagne's usurpation was even more serious than this; it was a
kind of sacrilege which neither Theodoric nor Clovis would have
dared to commit, it was a juridical monstrosity.    Consequently the
Court at Byzantium refused to recognize the new Empire.    The
empress, Irene, who had conceived the rather mad plan of marrying
Charles, a widower at the time, in order to reunite the two halves of
the *Imperium romanum* in this romantic fashion, was dissuaded from it
by her *entourage*.    After her fall Byzantine diplomacy engaged the
Frankish king in a war of nerves, of offensive silences, and of intrigues
in liaison with the exiled Lombard leaders.    Charlemagne suffered all
this patiently for quite a long time.    He did not, moreover, consider
settling the matter forcibly: the Eastern Empire, which was paralysed
by a new Iconoclastic Dispute, and which was occupied with both the
Arab raiders and the Bulgar threat, would probably have been easy to
beat, and Haroun-al-Raschid, the Caliph of Bagdad, who was the
Franks' ally, would have asked nothing better than to move against
Byzantium.    But either because he respected the ancient Empire, or
because, as a Christian, he refused to engage in a fratricidal war between
believers or, finally, because, with his outstanding realization of his
own capabilities, he distrusted a venture which would have committed
him to an expedition eastwards, Charlemagne preferred to wait nine
years.    After that a limited demonstration against Venice, which was
well within Byzantine territory, taught the Eastern diplomats that his
patience had its limits.    Three years later—two years before Charlemagne's death—the desired result was attained; in the spring of 812
the *Basileus Michael* sent his ambassador to Aix-la-Chapelle to salute
his *brother*, the *Basileus Charles*.    Henceforth, legally, there were two
empires: the one in the east, the other in the west.

One question remains: what did Charles himself and the West
Europeans of his epoch understand by this imperial title?    It is clear
to us that the action of Christmas 800 contained, institutionally, the
seeds of the Western Europe which was striving to be born.    Did the
man of genius who received the title foresee this future?    The answer
is probably no.    The main argument supporting this negative view is
that, in 806, when making provision for his inheritance, he divided up
his territories according to ancient Barbarian custom, cutting the Empire

into three pieces. Regarding it as an institution, the notion of *Imperium romanum* can therefore have meant nothing to him. How did he see the imperial title? Perhaps as little more than a kind of striking reward, as a worldly 'citation' or 'decoration'; likewise, in the same way, Clovis had been overjoyed to bear the honorary title of consul. And this would explain why he so disliked wearing the purple, just as nowadays a born leader refrains from sporting his decorations all the time. He held this reward from the Pope, and this meant a great deal to him; as a convinced Christian he was certainly happy to be thus linked to the work of the Church; though the tutelage he imposed upon her was sometimes rather onerous, his intentions always remained good, in the true tradition of the *City of God*. Around him were the protagonists of the imperial idea, who were incapable of understanding that the true resurrection of the imperial notion presupposed a remodelling of the State, a return to the governmental methods of Constantine or Augustus. These scholarly and idealistic groups saw the Empire as much more than a regime. To them it represented a moral aspiration, a wonderful picture—a picture of a West united under a strong, peace-loving leader, exercising the fullness of his power for solely Christian objectives. This ideal appears extremely clearly in the famous *Capitularies of 802*, in which Charlemagne was to inaugurate his imperial legislation, after his return from Rome. Moreover was it not an ideal which had ruled both his external and internal policy ever since the beginning of his reign? In every sense of the word the great act of Christmas 800 was indeed a *crowning*.

### Christian Europe Protected and Extended

'It is my duty, with the help of the divine Mercy, to defend the holy Church of God with my arms, everywhere.' All his life Charlemagne was magnificently faithful to the mission which he expressed in these words. Mounted on his horse, sword in hand, the tireless leader pursued this ideal of the Christian warrior as long as he lived. In the forty-five years of his reign he made no less than fifty-five expeditions; he was still fighting six months before his death. Generally his wars were short, begun in springtime after the *May-Field*, the solemn review of the troops, and ending with the first frosts. His wars were aimed in many directions: towards Italy, as we have seen, but towards Germany, too, at the Rhine and the Danube, towards Friesland in the north and Islamic Spain in the south. Did they all follow from this primarily Christian intention on which Charles prided himself? Are not some much more ascribable to a grandiose plan of expansion, to a genuine imperialism? There is no sense in posing the question in these terms; Charles identified the interests of Christianity and those of his own personal power in entirely good faith.

At all events this justification is never more apt than when Charles tackled the Saxon problem. In the middle of the eighth century two Germanies stood side by side: the one Rhenish, Alemanian, Thuringian, and Bavarian, resting on the ancient Roman substratum of the former imperial provinces, and already civilized and converted to Christianity by the efforts of the missionaries a century before; [1] the other, Saxony, which was still pagan, a savage guardian of barbarian customs, and a reservoir of heathen strength and violence.[2] Why did Charles want to crush the Saxon bastion? Undoubtedly because, as a Christian, he could not tolerate the existence, on his frontier, of a people who massacred the missionaries and refused the gospel message, and also because, as a far-sighted politician, he had no intention of making the mistake which had killed the Roman Empire. He knew that there could be no compromise with Barbarism, and that if he did not destroy Saxony, Saxony would one day destroy all his work. The great Saxon war lasted for thirty-one years, and was fought with equal energy by both sides. The gripping episodes of these campaigns in the heart of the dense forests are well known. There was the destruction of the heathen sanctuary at Irminsul, the continuous revolt against Frankish domination directed by the Saxon Vercingetorix, *Witikind*, the terrifying episodes of the double 'disaster of Varus' suffered by the Frankish armies on the slopes of Süntel in 782, and at the Weser ford in 793, and Charles's bloodthirsty reply—the massacre at Verden, of over four thousand five hundred Saxon prisoners who were beheaded by the axe. Finally, crushed, ravaged, and exhausted, her population partially deported to France and replaced by docile elements, Saxony capitulated. Led by Witikind, she accepted Christian baptism. A third of a century of bloodshed had imposed the double graft of Western civilization and of Christianity on this Germanic trunk. The dubious consequences of this remained to be seen.

The Christian ideal could justify Charlemagne's enterprise against Saxony; as far as Bavaria is concerned the argument appears invalid at first sight. There the country concerned was a Catholic one. The Archbishop of Salzburg was deeply respected. It was the home of an

---

[1] See Chapter IV, section: 'St Boniface, the Father of German Christianity.'

[2] The word is not synonymous with present-day Saxony. The Saxons in this period occupied the whole of north-west Germany, from the Elbe to the Rhine, from the North Sea to the Ruhr, the upper Weser and the Main. They formed a confederation of four peoples: the Ostphalians between the Elbe and the Weser, the Westphalians between the Weser and the Rhine, the Angrians on the lower Weser, and the Nordalbingians in the territory from which the whole race were said to have originated, Holstein. Periodically they held a federal assembly at Marklo on the Weser. Their religion was the old Germanic paganism and attempts at Christian penetration had been unsuccessful.

ancient civilization, full of Roman memories. Duke Tassilo, Charles Martel's grandson, and Charlemagne's cousin, who had been established there by Pepin the Short in 748 as a Frankish vassal, was certainly no Witikind. But he was Desiderius's son-in-law, and in a fairly natural desire to acquire his independence he intrigued with the Lombards, flirted with Byzantium, and even came to an understanding with the Avars, the Asiatic bandits on the Danube; Ratisbon was a centre of plots against Charles, or rather against his Italian policy, in other words against the Papacy. Consequently when, exasperated by finding himself continually frustrated by the petty Bavarian duke, the Frankish king decided to liquidate him, the Church gave him her full support, and in 788 Bavaria was linked to the Frankish state once more.

This unification of Germany under Charlemagne [1] resulted in a series of measures and campaigns, all of which, it must be confessed, were to be singularly useful to the future of Christianity. There was Friesland, that redoubtable bastion of paganism, where St Willibrord had almost wasted his time, and where St Boniface had been martyred. This was forced into unconditional surrender, and was transformed into a Frankish province, where Bishop Liudger could take up his preaching again. There were the Danish lands, still totally heathen, whence the terrible Norse pirates were to come, soon after Charlemagne's death. It was the great leader's genius that he foresaw this threat and transformed the region into a Frankish 'march,' despite ten years of Danish resistance and the heroic struggle of King Godfrey. There were the Avars, Mongol bandits who, by the eighth century, had replaced the Huns on the middle Danube and whose raiders were continually attacking the Frankish forward posts. Charlemagne brought them to their senses in some extremely hard-fought campaigns, fought far from the Rhine, beyond the dense forests, in country where communications were so difficult that, in order to ensure them, he undertook the building of a canal from the Main to the Danube, the remains of which have been discovered. In 796 the Avar camp, their strange, ring-shaped fortress, with its ten concentric defensive walls, capitulated, and their 'khan' had to surrender all the fabulous treasures which he had stolen from all over the east. What the most lucid of the emperors, Trajan, had deemed necessary, but which he had only been able to accomplish in part, Charlemagne realized in full; the annexation of this 'Mongolia in Europe,' which was indispensable to

---

[1] René Grousset has quite rightly emphasized the fact that Charlemagne's policy had the double result of preparing for the division of Italy into petty principalities, and, on the other hand, of working towards German unity. When Napoleon called Charlemagne 'our illustrious predecessor' he little knew how right he was; on this point the ninth-century emperor was the predecessor of the nineteenth-century one, and he also anticipated the latter's mistakes.

Western safety, was the prelude to the conversion of Hungary which was later to be carried out by St Stephen.

Consequently in the north, the north-east, and the east, Christian Europe owed a very great deal indeed to Charlemagne's armies. One problem remained. A sore had been left open in the south ever since Poitiers; it would have been inconceivable for the leader of the West to be disinterested in the question of Islam. Here again political and religious reasons combined to spur him on to action. Ought he not to ensure the security of the young kingdom of Aquitaine, which he had created for his son Louis in 780? Could he remain deaf to the appeals of the Spanish Christians, both those living under Moslem rule and those who, crouching amid the mountains of Asturia, continued to resist the invader? Certainly Charles must have been sorely tempted to embark on a holy war, to open the era of the Crusades two hundred years before its time. In 777 it looked as if he would yield to the temptation: answering the appeal of the *wali* of Barcelona, who had rebelled against the Emir of Cordova, Frankish troops had dashed across Aragon, Navarre, and Catalonia; but, left in the lurch by their Moslem allies, they had been obliged to return to France. It was then that the famous ambush of *Roncevalles* took place, the bloody rear-guard action fought by the Franks against the Basque highlanders, the defeat from which the genius of the poets was to make an epic (778). From then onwards Charlemagne recovered his prudence and his usual understanding of his own limits. In order to prevent the champions of Allah from clearing the Pyrenees, as they did in 793, when they ravaged the country as far north as Narbonne, the emperor undertook ten years of campaigning (801–11) with limited objectives in view, namely, to establish himself firmly along a line of strong-points: Lerida, Barcelona, Pamplona, Tarragona, and Tortosa; the Spanish marches were created, a French area south of the mountains, the first step towards what was subsequently to be the *Reconquista*, the bastion from which the Cross would launch the offensives against Islam. Here again Charles had laboured usefully for the future of Christendom.

Thus the work accomplished by the sword of the Frankish leader was great indeed. Thanks to him Western Christianity was extended and strengthened. It found a unity the like of which it had not known since the Invasions, for in addition to the lands which he actually administered, Charlemagne had considerable influence in many others, in Scotland and Ireland, where the petty kings felt a certain loyalty to him, in England where he was able to impose his choice on the throne of Northumbria, and even in the Slav principalities on the fringes of the Germanic world. And he possessed much more than temporal glory. He possessed exceptional moral prestige:

no sovereign since Constantine had assembled so many territories beneath his sceptre; like Constantine he appeared to mankind as the witness, as the herald, of Christ.

However, shadows did exist in this magnificent picture, and they

The Empire of Charlemagne

were to deepen once the great emperor was dead. The methods by which he built this monumental empire seem scarcely Christian to us, and massacres and deportations like those which ensured the conquest of Saxony leave us horrified. Of course we must beware of anachronism, and it is highly probable that Charles could have employed no other methods; in his epoch they were the only effective ones, and moreover they were the selfsame methods which the converted Saxons were to use later on, in order to 'civilize' the Wends, Balts, Finns, and Slavs farther east.    The thing that hurts is that such means were used to establish Christianity; Charlemagne's soldiers saddled Saxony and Hungary with the Gospel exactly as the champions of Allah had saddled Spain with the Koran—exactly too as the margraves of Brandenburg and the Teutonic Knights were to do in Prussia.

There is worse to come.    Charlemagne actually practised a policy of conversion by terror which, once past the moment of inescapable violence, established a system of coercion in religious matters which is almost unbelievable.    We need but read the capitulary, promulgated on the morrow of the first conquest of Saxony, to assess the justification for the use of the word 'terror' in this connection.    In practice only one penalty existed, capital punishment: those who were considered to deserve it included not only the murderers of a priest, or members of heathen 'resistance groups,' or thieves of sacred objects, but even anyone who refused to fast during Lent, anyone who ate meat on Friday, anyone cremating a body according to the old Germanic rite, even anyone who refused baptism!    Never, perhaps, has a more complete system been applied in order to make a people adopt a new faith and a new 'civilization.'    It remained to be seen whether, in forcing the pace so fast, Charlemagne was not in fact paving the way for formidable counterstrokes of savagery; and whether, in integrating these Barbarian masses into a West which was as yet unsure of its own principles, he was not working for a future barbarization.    The very near future was to give the answer.

It must, however, be stated that the Church, speaking through her most clear-sighted leaders, gave warning of this.    In Alcuin's correspondence there are pieces of advice which have a genuinely Christian ring.    Preach before baptizing! he declared again and again. Heathens who are ignorant of the whole Gospel ought not to be brought to the baptismal trough at sword-point: first of all they should be made to feel 'the light yoke of Christ.'    Persuasion, gentleness, charity—these are the real weapons for winning souls. The vanquished should not be driven to exasperation by material obligations or by excessive tithes.    An excellent programme!    It reappears under the pen of several other bishops, as wise and as Christian as Alcuin was.

Moreover the Church did not confine herself to reminding Charlemagne on points of principle.    She acted practically too.    Obviously Charlemagne's triumphs simplified the work of the missionaries; her propaganda retained little of the heroic character it had possessed in the times of St Columbanus, St Amandus, St Willibrord, even St Boniface.    But a profound, silent labour, whose detail is little known, even though its results are still visible, was carried out by hundreds of missionaries and monks in all the areas where the 'sweeping Christianization' of Charlemagne had left many open sores. It is wonderful to see how Saxony, which had suffered so from the Christians, became a Christian bastion, with its bishoprics of Bremen, Verden, Minden, Paderborn, and Münster; however, the fight against paganism, the loftiest symbol of a secret nationalist resistance, was to be a hard one. Friesland, the lands around the Main, the Eastern Alps, where the metropolitans of Salzburg and Arn multiplied their missions, the Avar regions, worked by the missionaries of Paulinus of Aquileia, even the Slav tribes, where the Catholic missionaries from the West competed with those whom Byzantium was beginning to send forth: an immense task was carried out, which firmly planted the seed of Christianity in the lands where Charles's sword had parted the furrow.

### TOWARDS JERUSALEM BY WAY OF BAGDAD

Another aspect of Charlemagne's 'Christian policy' struck his contemporaries very strongly; it is almost unbelievable, and brings into this career, which is almost devoid of poetic quality, a note of exotic charm similar to that which the visit of the Queen of Sheba casts upon the reign of Solomon: in other words, his relations with *Haroun-al-Raschid*, the Caliph of Bagdad.

Ever since the revolution of 750, which had raised the Abbasids to the caliphate and shifted the heart of Islam towards the direction of Mesopotamia, the Moslem Empire had acquired the characteristics of a centralized authoritarian state, in which religion served to support an absolute monarchy. As 'commander of the faithful' the Caliph of Bagdad's intention was to force all his peoples—i.e. in Irak, Persia, Syria, and Egypt—to accept the doctrine of the Koran and to submit to him absolutely. Though the secession of North Africa, Morocco, and Spain might irritate him, it affected him very little. He was an awe-inspiring, sumptuous sovereign, who, through his viziers and the various sections of the *divan*—an administration copied from the Persian King of Kings—exercised authority over everything. His capital, Bagdad, was the commercial emporium of the East, a leading financial centre, and a city where literature and the arts flourished. The time had long since gone by when the successor of the prophet of Arabia had lived like one of the ordinary faithful, in a small house on the outskirts of Medina!

In Charlemagne's epoch, *Haroun-al-Raschid* (766–809) was reigning in Bagdad. He was an intelligent, well-educated, and relatively sympathetic man, in the sense that the executioner was not yet his chief minister, nor the leathern carpet on which men walked to execution the principal sign of his authority, as was to be the case under his successors.    Probably no Eastern ruler ever equalled the glory of this great caliph: he lived in the palace of the 'Golden Gate,' whose famous green dome dominated the Mesopotamian plain, amongst his priceless carpets and tapestries, in the midst of a gigantic court of servants, concubines, and eunuchs, and he was worthy indeed to become the hero of the *Arabian Nights*.    But he was also a skilful diplomat and a soldier.

At first relations between the caliph and Charlemagne were close for political reasons.    As the enemy of the Ommayad Emir of Cordova, whom he saw as 'a wretched rebel just ripe for beheading,' the Caliph of Bagdad was bound to look with a sympathetic eye upon the Frankish warrior who was fighting him.    Moreover, since both were on extremely bad terms with Byzantium, the Carolingian and the Abbasid had but to look at the map to invent an excellent encircling manœuvre against the Basileus.    To these two practical motives Charlemagne added a third: here, too, politics and religion were both spurs to his action.    Jerusalem and the holy places, towards which pilgrimages were becoming increasingly numerous, were under the domination of the caliph.    A few Christian communities administered them, and these communities were praying ardently for the Frankish king's protection—as was proved by the solemn sending of the keys of the Holy Sepulchre and of the city on the eve of his coronation. Could Charlemagne remain deaf to supplications such as these?

These harmonious relations between the two sovereigns were marked by exchanges of gifts, which the Carolingian chroniclers enlarge upon charmingly and freely.    Everyone at Aix-la-Chapelle was enraptured by the arrival of a chess set with the figures finely carved in ivory, of spices with unknown scents, of a clock which moved by means of a cunning hydraulic mechanism, and even of elephants and other strange animals!    It is quite possible that offerings such as these influenced the development of Carolingian art.    But the ambassadors who came to present these marvels were also engaged in much more serious matters; one suspects that the caliph had some influence on Charles's Spanish policy, on the tenacity which he showed in gaining a foothold there; and the recognition of the emperor of the West by the Basileus in 813 was perhaps due in large measure to certain stirrings of arms in Bagdad, which made themselves heard in Constantinople at the opportune moment.

It was in this atmosphere of friendship that Charles obtained from his Eastern colleague the placing under Frankish protection of all the Christian communities in Palestine and of the pilgrims who journeyed to the holy places.    Of course there was no question of a 'protectorate' in the political sense of the word; the rights conceded to

Charlemagne's representatives resembled those nowadays accorded to
consuls under international law. But, limited as it was, this action was
of immense importance. It indicated the future direction of the Crusades. The French West gained a foothold in the East, so much so
that, until modern times, the word 'Frank' in the East was to be used
in reference to all Westerners, synonymous with 'Roumi' (Christian),
meaning strictly an adherent of Rome. On this subject, as on so
many others, Christian civilization owed a very great deal to the son
of Pepin for many generations to come.

### 'The Pious Overseer of the Bishops'

Is there another side to the admiration which we cannot withhold
from such a great achievement? At the same time that Charlemagne
was working so wonderfully for the Christian future, was he not continually helping to undermine his own achievements?

All the criticisms which can be directed at the great emperor from
the standpoint of his relations with Christianity, are summed up in the
phrase which the monk of Saint-Gall, who was one of his finest
chroniclers, applied to him, quite unmaliciously: 'The pious overseer
of the bishops.' It is a dubious compliment. The root of the matter
is to know whether it is fitting that a sovereign should set himself up
and be accepted as the 'overseer' of the Church.

We must look for the origin of this attitude in the religious psychology of Charles himself, in the most secret depths of his personality.
He was the descendant of the first Pepin and of Bishop Arnulf, in
whom the two fundamental elements in the West at that time were
united, the blood of the Germanic warriors and that of the saintly
Gallo-Roman prelates; he had read his St Augustine, and, as a Christian who was profoundly aware of his duties, he could scarcely conceive
his task as any other than 'to govern the Churches of God and to
protect them against all wickedness.' Did he not read in Chapter V
of the *City of God* that the reigns which deserved to be called happy
ones were not those of the kings who had conquered their enemies and
maintained order among their subjects, but 'those which put their
might to the service of the propagation of Christianity, who thus
feared and worshipped God . . .'? Charlemagne's whole ambition
was undoubtedly to translate these principles into actions, even if he
had only an approximate success. Consequently, just as we have
seen him preoccupied in his external policy in protecting and extending
the Church, so, as he himself said, he was anxious 'to fortify the
Church from within in the knowledge of the Catholic faith,' 'to
ensure that everyone applies himself to God's holy service, according
to his faculties, his energies, and his circumstances.' In the state of

dependence in which the Church was, in fact placed, such intentions could only result in the complete confusion of the spiritual and the temporal.    And this is indeed what happened.

*The confusion of the spiritual and the temporal.*    It is necessary to return to this notion again and again when studying Charlemagne's religious policy.    Moreover it makes itself apparent in a most artless fashion.    Thus the formula for the notification of the imperial edicts opens with these words: 'Be it known to the minds of the faithful of the Holy Church of God and of ourselves that . . .'    By *faithful* is meant, simultaneously, a Christian and a subject of the emperor!    A kind of ministry existed to translate this confusion into deeds, the *Imperial Chapel*, controlled by the *Archichaplain*, and composed of a whole pleiade of clerics, who had among their tasks the celebration of the divine office in the imperial oratory, but who were at the same time entrusted with the Great Chancellery, that is to say, that in reality they controlled everything—nominations of bishops as well as judicial decisions, diplomatic relations, and education.

The entire hierarchy of the Church was supervised by the sovereign. In practice it was he who appointed the bishops and the abbots of the important abbeys, with a freedom which no Merovingian, and perhaps no Basileus either, had ever enjoyed.    The bishops were literally civil servants, under the prince's 'Mainbourg,' and they swore him the following oath: 'I swear to be faithful to you and to obey you, as a liege man obeys his lord.'    One bishop might receive the command to leave his diocese and come to Court, where he was needed.    An abbot might have to carry out a regular mobilization order and to repair to a certain spot with a fixed number of men.    The *missi dominici*, the master's envoys, who went everywhere to control everything, actually included bishops among their number—generally a bishop accompanied a senior civil servant—and these political inspectors could administer criminal justice.    It must be confessed that we to-day do not take kindly to the idea of the Church being employed in this way, like a kind of superior police force. . . .

The same confusion between the spiritual and the temporal existed in all the great imperial assemblies.    At the 'May-Field' Germanic tenants, bishops, and fighting lords stood side by side.    Both military and religious matters were discussed.    Moreover the national Councils of the Church frequently met at the same time, and in the same place.    During Charlemagne's reign there were sixteen capitulary assemblies and sixteen national Councils; the sovereign presided over all of them.    Furthermore the capitularies, which were civil laws as a rule, completed and amended the decisions of the ecclesiastical Councils.    The kind of questions on which the imperial government felt the need to legislate are really astounding: Sunday rest from labour, attendance at religious services, the method of administering baptism, the obligation of alms-giving, monastic discipline, the daily recitation of the Lord's Prayer, and even the necessity of believing in the Holy Spirit. And all these on pain of dire penalties! The confusion was complete in the penal field too; infringements of the commandments of God and the Church were punished by imprisonment and other restrictive penalties; moreover the law even added actual 'penances' to the punishment of a civil crime and to the suppression of civil misdemeanours.

Thus the Carolingian Empire gives the impression of being an enormous clerical administrative machine, in which everything is ordered to the glory of the monarch and the exaltation of religion, both of which were synonymous in Charles's mind. The Pope played a rather minor role in all this. Values were certainly subverted here, in practice, not in theory, and in her present position the Church could do nothing about it.

Does this mean that she derived no benefits from this situation? Certainly not. From many points of view the forty-five years of Charles's reign were a glorious epoch for the Christian Church. Pagan survivals and superstitions, heterodox or dubious practices, incantations and the wearing of lucky charms were all rigorously put down: the Sovereign Pontiffs and the Councils frequently congratulated the emperor for suppressing them so thoroughly. The firm foundation of the Christian faith throughout all the old Gallo-Roman areas was certainly completed during this period.

Another advantage which the Church derived from this royal protection was the enormous development of the monasteries; the Carolingian epoch saw the rise of a large number of new foundations which were favoured by immunities, gifts, and privileges, and the old foundations expanded considerably. The great abbeys ceased to be primarily colonies of ascetics, who engaged in work for spiritual reasons alone, and increasingly turned into intensely lively centres of both a spiritual and an economic kind. Certain enormous monasteries like Saint-Gall, Fulda, Reichenau, Saint-Wandrille, Ferrières, and Corbie exercised a dominant influence over immense areas of territory. Fulda worked fifteen thousand estates. We still possess the plans of Corbie and Saint-Gall, and here it is obvious that there was a veritable lay city around the abbey, with its own churches, schools, workshops, hospitals, mills, and farms. Such a splendid development as this would not have been possible had the imperial administration not desired it. Was not each monastery a pillar upon which the Empire could lean? There was of course a somewhat irritating corollary to all this for the monks: this included the obligation to give 'presents' to the sovereign on far too many occasions, while the right to monastic hospitality was claimed not merely by the ruler and his Court, but by the hosts of messengers, officials, and so on who had received the king's authority to do so; there were royal nominations to political or diplomatic posts which the monks could not decline, or calls to arms. Being fully aware of the services which the government was rendering them the abbots protested against all this only in most guarded terms.

Moreover what member of the clergy wanted to protest very strongly against the actions of such an excellent, pious, and well-intentioned sovereign? Against a sovereign who had just assured the churches' prosperity by making *tithes* a State institution? The gradually established custom of giving the parish an annual payment of about one-tenth of one's income, a custom which had been applied in a fairly haphazard fashion until now, was codified by the capitularies of 779 and 794, which also made it obligatory. The 'sacred custom' became a tax. The clergy received a tenth share of every harvest and of all manufacturing and trading profits; the receipts were divided into four, one part being allotted to the parish priest, the second to the maintenance of the church, the third to the bishop, and the last to the poor and to charitable works. When, after doing all this, Charlemagne sometimes confused the Church's property with that of the State, in cases of need, and requisitioned the resources of a bishopric or a monastery's stable, one could well forgive him.

Even another kind of intervention, which seems still more surprising to us, was not held against him: this was his interference in the very life of the Church, in its discipline and its dogmas, as well as in the conscience of the faithful. It was even an accepted fact that he controlled the ecclesiastical administrative organization, confirming the existence of ancient metropolitan sees, having the archbishoprics of Mainz and Salzburg created for political reasons, yet refusing to allow the strictly hierarchic system, which many of the clerks desired, to be established in return! [1] It was actually considered natural that he should choose the archbishops, name the bishops, and insist that everything should be referred to him before being referred to the Pope! Since the episcopate had allowed itself to be transformed into a body of senior civil

---

[1] We have seen (Chapter V, end of section: 'The Church's Principle of Reform') how some reformers, and St Boniface in particular, had dreamed of having a network of archiepiscopal sees, over and above the ordinary bishoprics, in order to systematize the hierarchy. Charlemagne does not seem to have encouraged any move in this direction, probably because such centralization would have threatened his own authority. Consequently the metropolitan sees remained exactly as they had been before, with one exception, Narbonne, which was created in 813, bringing the number of archiepiscopal sees in the Empire to twenty-two: these included Rome, Ravenna, Milan, Friuli, Grado, Cologne, Mainz, Salzburg, Trèves, Sens, Besançon, Lyons, Rouen, Arles, Vienne, Tarentaise, Embrun, Bordeaux, Tours, and Bourges. The occupants of all these sees received the *pallium* from the Pope.

servants, since the pontiff himself had accepted the fact that he no longer really retained the right of conferring the *pallium*, the sacred band of white woollen cloth, symbolic of their powers, upon the arch-bishops, all this could easily pass as normal; it was simply a political and administrative matter.

But was it any more irregular than the sight of the emperor involving himself in clerical reform? His predecessors, and his father in particular, had helped the reformers in their work: Charlemagne actually controlled it. The results of this imperial action were far from harmful. The 'pious overseer' was very conscious of express-ing the divine Will, which of course coincided with his own, and he worked hard to choose as bishops men who were qualified for the position—devout, wise men, most of whom he had already seen at work in the 'Chapel.' There was a complete reaction against the scandalous procedures of Charles Martel's time, and Charlemagne's episcopate presented a noble sight, including men like Arnulf of Salzburg, St Lullus of Mainz, Theodulf of Orleans, and Hincmar of Rheims: they were vigorous characters in whom gentleness and moderation were not perhaps the most obvious virtues, but they were right-minded men, doctrinally and morally sound, zealous to conquer for the faith.

Charlemagne applied these same principles of reform to all the other elements in the Church. The secular clergy was the object of atten-tion, the like of which it had scarcely had until this time: the parish priest was required to possess not simply pure morals but a modicum of learning besides. Periodically the bishop or his delegate was to hold oral examinations in order to ensure that the priests knew suffi-cient Latin, and enough about dogma and the liturgy. One law made it compulsory for every parish priest to preach in the vulgar tongue each Sunday. Likewise Charlemagne wanted to impose order and unity on the monasteries. Strict rules were promulgated for the recruitment of monks; the 'perpetual wanderers,' who were always changing monasteries, were prohibited. The emperor had the genuine text of the Rule of St Benedict, which seemed to him the best one, sent from Monte Cassino; and since, at the same time, a great monk named St Benedict of Aniane was striving with might and main to realize a unity of monastic observance, Charles and his son Louis of Aquitaine (the future Louis the Pious) gave him fundamental support. Great abbots like Smaragdus of St Mihiel followed in his footsteps. The conclusive triumph of the Benedictine rule dates from this period.

Even ordinary laymen were the object of the master's detailed and authoritarian attention. 'Everyone should know how to recite the Creed and the Lord's Prayer,' states one capitulary: 'and, when necessary, they should be compelled to learn them through fasting and penance.' Thus piety was considered a social duty; he who was a poor practising Christian was a rebel and an anarchist. Such were the principles which a vigilant police force put into practice. It was all seasoned with the kind of minutely detailed regulations in which authoritarian minds delight; men were ordered to be present at the *Rogation* ceremonies under pain of a fine, and to take part in the thanks-giving prayers that followed a royal victory (and there were plenty of these) or go to prison. It ill behoved those with children to choose a godfather and godmother for them who did not possess a minimum knowledge of Christian doctrine!

Though morality was the object of most detailed attention, the liturgy was not neglected either, for it so happened that the emperor had a great taste for it. And he applied his desire for unity in this field also. In Gaul the liturgies, sacramentaries, and missals were still particular, following old Byzantine models. On his visit to Rome, in 781, Charlemagne had been much impressed by the beauty and simplicity of the liturgy he had witnessed there; he asked Pope Hadrian to let him have the Roman sacramentaries and missal and he decided to enforce this manner of celebrating the services throughout his empire. Thus the Gregorian liturgy and plain-song spread across the Frankish domains, complete with elements borrowed from the Gallican usages (dioceses like Lyons and Milan which resisted this were rare). And the liturgical works of Amalarius of Metz, one of Alcuin's disciples, were to be regarded as authoritative throughout the Middle Ages.

Thus little by little we see the indefatigable emperor interfering in everything that concerns the Church, even in the most fundamental matters, the very bases of faith. In this field there is nothing more pungent than the story of the *Filioque*. In 589 a canon of the Council of Toledo, in opposition to the theses held by the Arians, had expressly stated that the Holy Spirit proceeded from the Father and from the Son at the same time; *Filioque procedit*. Charlemagne was extremely enthusiastic about this formula, and he had it embodied in the Creed which was sung in his chapel. When this innovation was heard of in the East there was much shrugging of shoulders: the Holy Spirit, it was declared, proceeded from the Father *through* the Son, but not from the Father and Son together. This was a subtle distinction which the theologian in Charles probably did not understand at all. At all events he kept to his innovation, even against the wishes of Pope Hadrian, who doubted whether the time was opportune for this definition. In 808 the Latin monks on the Mount of Olives at Jerusalem, whose Greek neighbours accused them of being heretics, because they sang *Filioque procedit*, asked Pope Leo III to settle the dispute. And the Pope, who was anxious to avoid a conflict, suggested that Charlemagne should renounce the formula; but the emperor clung to it stubbornly, calling excellent theologians like Smaragdus, abbot of Saint-Mihiel, and Bishop Theodulf to his rescue, managing matters so well that the Aix custom prevailed, even at Rome, and to-day, as the result of the emperor's determination, we still sing the Creed with his addition in it!

Other incidents also show the sovereign interfering in the most difficult dogmatic questions, always with the same determined vigour. Thus when the *cult of Images* was made lawful in 787 by the second Council of Nicaea, Charlemagne and his Frankish clerks entered the lists against both Byzantium and Rome. The Latin translation of the conciliar decisions seemed ambiguous to them; besides, the Germans had always been somewhat suspicious about the representation of the human face and body, and this attitude was accentuated by the profound influence of the Old Testament upon them. Charlemagne invited his theologians to compile some treatises against the Council, and these were published under his name: *the Caroline Books*; he even sent an ambassador to the Pope, charged with communicating eighty-five *reprehensions* to the Holy Father, and in 794 he convened an anti-Nicaean Council at Frankfurt. Not until the end of the ninth century —and after various iconoclastic excesses, notably in Thuringia—did the orthodox doctrine on this question triumph completely in Frankish territory. By contrast, the same Council of Frankfurt in 794 gave the Pope its total support in the affair of *Adoptianism*, a heresy originating in Spain, where two bishops, in the belief that they were settling the difficulties on the nature of Christ, had maintained that He was the 'adoptive son' of God. As one of these bishops resided in Moorish territory it was impossible to bring him to submission, and his tiny heretical church was to survive miserably; but in all the regions controlled by the Franks the heresy was persecuted mercilessly.[1]

It must be admitted that, taken as a whole, this permanent intervention by the temporal power in religious affairs is highly disconcerting to the modern observer. In a way the confusion was even worse than at Byzantium, where religion constituted a part of the State's services, whereas in the Frankish Empire it was intermingled

---

[1] This was almost the last of the great theological conflicts in the West for a long time to come. There was still to be the dispute over *Predestinationism*, after Charlemagne's death. This was raised by a certain *Gottschalk*, a Saxon monk belonging to the abbey of Orbais in Bire, who was a Calvinist before his time. He stated that there were two predestinations—that the good were predestined to life, and the wicked to death. Bishop Hincmar of Rheims had him condemned. At the same time men were also arguing about the eucharistic theses of *Paschasius Radbert*, a monk of Corbie. He maintained that Christ's presence in the eucharist was spiritual, not properly real. The interest of these two arguments lies in the fact that they give forewarning of the great problems of the period of the Protestant Reformation: but they were very muddled, and contributed little to the progress of theological knowledge.

with all its services. However, this one reservation should be made—and the future was to show that it was of fundamental importance—in principle, because of the very fact of the emperor's anointing by the Pope, the Church retained the upper hand; so long as the sovereign was a man of the stature of the great Charles this supremacy remained quite theoretic; but the situation would change under his weaker successors. Whereas at Byzantium the coronation did not take place until long after the actual installation of the new Basileus, and then more as a ceremonial than as a decisive action, in the West it was the essential core of the accession; the fact that the Church preserved the privilege of creating the emperor was therefore a fact of immense importance there.

In another respect this same confusion between the spiritual and the temporal was not without its happy results. It led the Church to intervene in everything that constituted the foundations of civilization, far more systematically than she had done in the preceding epochs. Long before Charlemagne's time, of course, she and she alone had occupied herself with social problems; she, and she alone, had concerned herself with education. But henceforth officially her work had State backing, and an intimate alliance existed between her and it. It was upon the Church that the imperial government placed the Christian obligation—and this was something that Charlemagne did not treat lightly—of succouring the poor, the sick, the infirm, and the abandoned children; thus, as we have seen, one-quarter of the income derived from tithes was allocated to such causes, and the enriching of various religious foundations by generous financial gifts did in fact constitute a veritable social budget.

Likewise education was completely entrusted to the Church. Charlemagne was led to realize a scholastic reform which was to be of decisive importance because he did not want his clergy to remain ignoramuses; and he looked to the priests and monks themselves to carry it out. Henceforth the clerk automatically became a pedagogue. The ordinary parish priests were ordered to provide instruction for the local children. The great abbeys and cathedrals all controlled schools providing either what we should call 'secondary' or 'higher' education; in the first type, the three primary subjects were taught, grammar, rhetoric, and dialectic—a syllabus which was beginning to be known as the *trivium*; in the latter the pupils were instructed in the *quadrivium* of advanced learning—arithmetic, geometry, music, and astrology. Some of these schools were famous all over Europe, those of Corbie, Saint-Wandrille, Aniane, and Fulda, for example, and above all, the school attached to St Martin's, at Tours, and that at Aix itself. The last-named, the *Palatine school*, was a nursery of important prelates and great officials. Charlemagne and his sons liked to attend its lectures, and all the best minds of the age were educated there. Naturally, in this field as in all the rest, the confusion between the political and the ecclesiastical was complete; the bishops and abbots whom Charlemagne sent out as *missi dominici* were also to play the role of inspectors of education; in an inverse sense the sovereign's officials made the priests take examinations in order to check their knowledge. A famous anecdote, told by the monk of Saint-Gall, describes Charlemagne inspecting the Palatine school in person, questioning the pupils there, congratulating the best ones, chiding the others, and above all giving the lazy young noblemen a lecture in which he threatened to bestow all the important posts, abbeys, and bishoprics on their fellow pupils of humble birth, unless they worked harder. Consequently the Church owed the privilege of being the most important source of education to this scholastic reform of Charlemagne's. It was a privilege which she was to preserve into modern times and which was to have a decisive effect upon the development of Western civilization. When the University of Paris made 'St Charlemagne' its patron some time about the seventeenth century, it may have been mistaken in canonizing this great man, but the gratitude that it thereby demonstrated to him was not in the least undeserved.[1]

## THE CAROLINGIAN RENAISSANCE

The intermingling of Christianity and imperial power never bloomed to happier effect than in this great event in the intellectual order, which is known as 'the Carolingian Renaissance.' It is difficult to describe how low cultural standards were at the time when Charlemagne came to power. The political decadence of the Merovingians had gone hand in hand with a veritable intellectual collapse; written Latin had become atrocious; poetry and theology itself were almost abandoned, and art, which had been cut off from its sources of inspiration by the Arab invasions, and made sterile by anarchy at home, was mortally stricken. From this point of view Gaul was not merely lagging behind Byzantium and the caliphates of Bagdad and Spain, but even behind Anglo-Saxon Britain and Lombard Italy.

[1] In our secular age the French award of 'palmes académiques' preserves the memory of this intimate alliance between Education and the Church: its sash is episcopal purple in colour. Regarding Charlemagne's 'canonization,' it should be added that Frederick Barbarossa, the German emperor, while in violent conflict with Pope Alexander III, had Charles well and truly canonized by his creature, the antipope Paschal III. This canonization, which was celebrated with great pomp on 29th December 1165, was nothing more than a political gesture destined to enhance the imperial authority. The Church did not recognize it. But several authors have noted that a certain degree of tolerance was exercised in this matter, and the Holy See never called to order those churches who were accustomed to celebrating St Charlemagne's cult. Pope Benedict XIV himself inclined to this tolerance. The scholars' 'St Charlemagne' also derives from it. His cult survives at Aix-la-Chapelle; it is also celebrated in Poitou.

Little building was done any more, and no one had the means with which to continue the sumptuous decoration which had been the glory of the Merovingian basilicas.    It was a true collapse. . . .

The half-century of the great emperor's reign marked a break in this mortal sickness.    Contemporaries clearly had the feeling of discovering a new hope.    Einhard saw Charles as a new Augustus, and Bishop Modoin of Auxerre presented his age as an age of resurrection; both were right.    It is probably here that we can best grasp the man's genius and the greatness of his character; in the fact that this almost unschooled warrior understood the importance of such a task of rejuvenation and devoted himself to it whole-heartedly.    Even though it might be ephemeral—and ephemeral it was in reality—the Carolingian Renaissance was to mark a distinctive stage in time, to establish a kind of bastion for the future on which the intellect could lean in order to wage its fight against the Barbarism of the mind.    In a sense it may have been more important than the infinitely more brilliant Renaissance of the fifteenth century.    By the master's will, and by the very conditions in which it was achieved, this Renaissance, permeated as it was by Christianity, was to make Christianity and the entire intellectual activity of the West inseparable for centuries to come.

The vital centre of this Renaissance was *Aix-la-Chapelle*, the ancient 'villa' of Pepin the Short's time, which was situated some distance off the great Roman roads.    From 794 onwards Charlemagne made it into a Carolingian Versailles, judging from its intellectual atmosphere and the splendour of its appearance.    The geographical position of this new capital has given rise to much discussion: why was this Rhineland area chosen, rather than some town in Gaul, or even Rome itself?    Because it was a central point in the empire, as Charlemagne conceived it?    Because it was near to threatening Saxony?    Because the descendant of Pepin of Lauden wanted to remain faithful to the Austrasian tradition, by contrast with the Merovingians, who had become more and more Neustrian?    Because, since the Mediterranean axis had been shattered by the Islamic invasions, it was better to face the continent proper, and not the sea any more?    All these reasons must have played their part in the choice.    What is certain is that during the last decade of the reign, a magnificent city sprang up on this spot, around the imperial palace, which was the master's residence and the centre of the State's official machinery—a city probably containing forty or fifty thousand people, and whose buildings, unhappily destroyed by fire in the thirteenth century, aroused the admiration of all contemporaries.

Aix was the centre of the intellectual Renaissance; and the centre of Aix, and especially the Palatine school, was a kind of general headquarters of the mind, which influenced the entire Empire through the medium of the abbeys and the bishoprics.   There, acting like a true European, Charlemagne summoned around him all those who counted for anything in the cultural field—thinkers, scholars, and theologians: there was Agobard from southern Gaul, and Theodulf, a Gothic refugee from Spain; Alcuin came from Anglo-Saxon England; Paul the Deacon, Peter of Pisa, and Paulinus of Aquileia from Italy; Clement and Dougal from Ireland, and Angilbert and Einhard from old Frankish territories.   He sought out intellectual civilization wherever it had survived, among the Lombards, the distantly connected disciples of Boethius and Cassiodorus, and among the Spaniards the spiritual sons of the encyclopaedist, St Isidore of Seville, and above all, in the British Isles where, half a century earlier, mighty figures like the Venerable Bede [1] had brought a veritable Anglo-Saxon *pre*-Renaissance into being.   The proofs of confidence and friendship which the emperor bestowed upon these scholars are too many to enumerate: did he not make one of them, Angilbert, his son-in-law?   And on others, like Alcuin and Theodulf, he showered fine gifts of bishoprics or abbeys.

Several of these men were undoubtedly outstanding people. *Alcuin* (735–804) was a former pupil of the English Benedictine monasteries, and head master of the episcopal school at York.   Charles enlisted him in his service after meeting him in Italy and made him his 'minister of education'—to quote Guizot's expression—director of the Palatine School, his assistant and his inspiration in the scholastic task he had set himself.   Alcuin was an academically minded man, who had little contact with the world outside his studies, and who was inclined to be pedantic, but he had a benevolent mind and was full of intellectual curiosity.   He exerted an enormous influence, not simply through his theological treatises, his pamphlets against Adoptianism, his manuals of piety, even his catechism, but even more through his teaching: disciples such as Rabanus Maurus are witness of his value as a master.   Then there was Warnefrid, the Lombard, known as *Paul the Deacon*, the historian of the Lombard people, whom Charlemagne met in most moving circumstances.   Paul had come to beg him to have mercy on his brother, who had been condemned for rebelling against the emperor.   He was a cultured man, with some knowledge of Greek, a poet, and a tireless historian.   The emperor asked him to teach him the topography of Rome as well as the rudiments of Latin grammar and epigraphy.   Besides all this, he was a saintly minded man who commented lovingly on the Rule of St Benedict, and wanted to end his days at Monte Cassino.   Finally, there was *Einhard*, one of the few educated laymen at the Court, an artist as well as a scholar, who was simultaneously architect-in-chief of the royal buildings and

[1] See Chapter IV, end of section: 'The First Pontifical Missions: the Conversion of England,' and Chapter V, section: 'Chinks of Light.'

Alcuin's successor as director of the Palatine school, and to whom we owe the most complete and best-documented biography of the emperor, an intensely vivid work, despite its over-frequent echoes of Suetonius.

The leaders of this pleiade of scholars and cultured men formed a sort of club, a small, self-contained group. Historians are accustomed to calling this group the Palatine Academy. Each of its members bore a pseudonym borrowed from antiquity. Charlemagne himself, who was not a whit averse to presiding over this learned assembly, was known as David, which overestimated the power of the *cantor* of the Psalms and overrated even more outrageously the poetic talents of the son of Pepin! In the same way *Alcuin* was Horace, and Angilbert, Homer. Although no one yet hoped to make an encyclopaedia at the meetings of this academy, many important literary and theological subjects were discussed there, and its members argued over all the great questions concerning public education.

What were the results of these worthy efforts? They should not be sought on the creative plane; the authors of this period were almost all impersonal in style, limiting their ambitions to be faithful echoes of the past. Compilation was their great method of work, and almost their only one, whether the humanities alone, exegesis, theology, or ascetic writings were concerned; collections of *Flores*, of *Sententiae*, and of *Excerpta* abounded, and were to be prolific for a long time to come. Perhaps the most original work was that of Smaragdus of St Mihiel, who was no mean mystical author, and who dedicated his *Royal Road* to the emperor. Still, in a modest way, the Carolingian Renaissance was fruitful in restoring the tools of labour to intellectual culture. *Handwriting* was transformed; in place of the illegible Merovingian script there appeared the extremely beautiful and distinct 'Caroline minuscule'—probably stemming from Corbie at first—which Alcuin and the monks of Tours perfected and spread far and wide. Latin, which had suffered considerable debasement in France and Italy, where, although remaining a living language, it had been contaminated by its Barbarian speakers, was considerably improved by the Anglo-Saxon monks—of whom Alcuin was one—for whom it had remained a learned tongue. The long-neglected classical *literary works* were given a place of honour once more, even by those who were solely interested in 'the divine Wisdom'; Virgil and the great Latin authors were studied; the works of Boethius, Cassiodorus, and the Venerable Bede were used, although, admittedly, in a very narrow schoolroom sense; the book in which Martianus Capella had collected the *Dream of Scipio* and Ovid's *Metamorphoses* played the part of a real teaching manual. And Latin culture was not the only one which benefited from these efforts; Charlemagne was devoted to his maternal tongue and he laboured personally towards the development of what was later to become the *German* language, eliminating words of foreign origin, giving the months the Germanic names which they have retained, editing a kind of grammar, having the epics collected, in which the great deeds of the heroes of old were sung at the time. Much of the fundamental material of the Middle Ages was contained herein.

The work achieved by the Carolingian Renaissance in the artistic field was equally important and decisive to future development. Even here the influence of the Church predominated. Because in this epoch liturgy underwent the development to which we have already referred, *music* was the object of much attention; every cathedral and great religious house had its *cantors* and its schools of young choristers. And because the building, decoration, and beautifying of the House of God was one of the major preoccupations of the master, *architecture* and the plastic arts developed so much that Dawson has been able to write: 'Charlemagne founded a Holy Roman architecture as well as a Holy Roman Empire.' In fact, it was not only Roman, but followed tendencies which we have already noticed in the Merovingian epoch, mingling Eastern and remote Asiatic influences with the revival of classical features. As in the case of the writers, Charlemagne summoned to him architects and artists from every land: thus Odo, one of the builders of the Palatine chapel at Aix, was an Armenian. The artists of the Carolingian Renaissance drew their inspiration from everywhere: from the Latin ruins of Trèves and from Theodoric's Ravenna, from Justinian's St Sophia, from the famous buildings in Jerusalem, from the early monuments of Armenian Christianity, and even from the Islamic art of the caliphs of Bagdad and the emirs of Cordova, capping it all with the composite art of the Angles and the Celts, those lovers of geometric ornament, of stylized animal motifs, and of splendid tracery. As in the literary field, the most important result of these efforts lay in the restoration of a technique to the West: instead of the solid masses of the Merovingian walls there was a return to a more delicate style of building; instead of the clumsy squaring of capitals a return to true sculpture. However, in stressing the 'classical' elements and sweeping aside the 'barbarian' traditions, in other words in abandoning many of the things which had created the savage beauty of the Merovingian basilicas, it is possible that this Renaissance lost much that was vivid and valuable.

We no longer possess many examples of the architecture of this great reign. The church of St Gereon at Cologne was destroyed in 1940, and in 1945 air-raids seriously damaged the charming chapel of St Michael at Fulda. Now but two Carolingian masterpieces remain. One is the famous Palatine chapel at Aix, which is to-day the choir of the modern cathedral, a mighty octagonal mass, surmounted by a cupola, in which the diffused light plays so splendidly on the heavy stalls and the strong, regular arches.   The other is Germigny-des-Prés, this tiny masterpiece, whose perfect proportions, so accurately balanced, take the thrust of the apsidals, the chapels, and the half-domes.   Its splendid central tower rears its oddly exotic silhouette against the sky of Orléannais.   It seems that all the finest architectural creations of the age were planned in the shape of a Greek cross; however, larger buildings comprised a long nave, side aisles, and two transepts, one at the entry to the nave and the other in front of the choir, on the model of the minster built at Steinach by Einhard, which was to be copied by all the Rhineland churches.   The Romanesque style is foreshadowed in the architecture of this important reign.   It had been hinted at in the Merovingian epoch, but henceforth it made swift progress towards its realization.   And if its simple outlines were still heavy, although moving, the daring architectural feats of the future were already taking shape; it was in Charlemagne's time that the idea of substituting vaulting for the former flat wooden roofing became accepted.   This was an idea which the Merovingian architects had already seized from Rome, but which was now to become an architectural principle, despite all the technical difficulties, opening up infinite horizons to the art of building.

To this architecture, whose new-found nobility so impressed contemporaries, mosaic art added its own wonderful brilliance.   As in the preceding epoch, this too was borrowed from Byzantium and Ravenna, and 'borrowed' in the most literal sense of the word, for it has been proved that, with Pope Hadrian I's permission, Charlemagne removed marble, smalts, and tessera from the capital of the former exarchate in order to decorate his own buildings.   With its rigid technique, its fixity, and its love of colour, mosaic art delighted the eye and uplifted the soul.   We are lucky enough to know what this Carolingian mosaic art was like, whereas that of the Merovingians is almost unknown.   In the choir at Germigny, under the gilded light rising from the small bay-windows where an experienced hand has restored the alabaster glass, this art glitters with a thousand bursts of brilliance, in which azure, sinople, and purple predominate, strewn with darts of gold and silver; angels, whose figures follow the curve of the apse, rest on the Ark of the Covenant in the traditional biblical pattern, whilst their gigantic wings cross one another in the middle of the sky.   Only the mausoleum of Galla Placidia at Ravenna gives a parallel impression of sustained splendour and religious brilliance.

However, this flowering of mosaic art was to be a brief one.   But at the same time sculpture made its beginnings, particularly in splendid ivory-work; it was to grow and develop along the same lines as those which it was then travelling; the Romanesque hieratism of the eleventh century was a legacy from the Carolingian age.

There was one other medieval art which was to owe a very great deal to the Renaissance at Aix: that of illumination and miniature. Imported in large measure at any rate from the Anglo-Saxon monasteries where it had flourished for one hundred and fifty years, it was to incorporate several new decorative elements, borrowed from Antiquity or from the East. The famous Gospel Books of Vienne show the degree of perfection attained by the painters of this epoch and there are few more charming pages in the whole of religious art than the miniature in Charlemagne's Breviary, in which the Church is depicted in the guise of a fountain, welcoming all the people who have come to ask for her 'living water.' These Carolingian miniaturists and illuminators were the direct ancestors of the extremely remarkable schools of painting which the Rhineland was to possess from the tenth century onwards; through them Carolingian influence upon the artistic style of the Middle Ages was of capital importance. In this field, as in so many others, the great emperor moulded the future in a most fundamental way.

## LEGEND AND TRUTH

On 28th January 814, at nine o'clock in the morning, Charles departed this life, carried off by a lightning attack of pleurisy: at dawn on that same day he had tried to make the sign of the cross with an arm already grown heavy with death. 'And when Charles died the world lost its father,' wrote Einhard. This was certainly the opinion held by all his contemporaries.

Consequently, no sooner had the body of the master of the Western world been placed in an ancient marble sarcophagus, beneath the cupola of the Palatine chapel, than the glory which had shone round about him so brilliantly during his lifetime, haloed him with darts of fire. A double conspiracy gathered around his name quite spontaneously, turning him into something completely legendary: that of all those tens of thousands of humble, unknown men, who owed him a half-century of stability, order, and progress, the anonymous masses in whose eyes the heaven-sent man is always larger than life; and that of the intellectuals, the writers and the artists, who owed him their finest opportunities and who were ready to magnify the popular new legend in works that would be lasting. So even before the *Chanson de Roland* and the other medieval verse-chronicles came three centuries later, to hallow the mighty emperor conclusively as an epic character, the materials for this poetic transfiguration were already welling up from the depths of the collective Western soul.

*'Aureus Carolus!'* Bishop Jonas of Orléans was to say. 'He shone like gold!' Everything he had done, everything that he touched, was wonderfully illuminated. Every feature of his life was linked with miracles, copied from those read in *Lives* of the saints. Soon he would become 'the emperor with the flowing beard,' and this is how he would be remembered; men would tell of his voice, mighty as thunder, of the sixty thousand buglers that had walked before his charger, of the thousands of corpses cut to pieces by his sword, Joyous; his spirit of equity, his just rages, his witticisms, and his good deeds would all be held up as examples. All this assembled itself into a collection of complex material, from which some marvellously talented poet was later to extract the immortal *chanson de geste*.

Straightforward history quite obviously suffered from this transposition into legend. The real person was blotted out by the poetic picture. The chaste, wise, reasonable hero of the *chanson de geste* has little in common with the Frankish leader as he actually was. A rearguard defeat like Roncevalles became a wonderful example of sacrifice; an unknown leader, Roland, was proclaimed as the king's 'handsome nephew,' and regarded as a kind of saint. However, one truth survived amid this fairy-tale: the Christian witness provided by this great reign so struck contemporaries that it was to be the very axis of the legend. And there is more to it than this: it is clear that a certain Christian way of life was born from this poetic transposition of Carolingian reality, a way of life which was to be acknowledged by the Crusaders, and which was to make Godfrey de Bouillon the direct heir of the great emperor's knights.

This is a miracle of poetry, and its fundamental need lives on in man's heart, despite the lessons of the facts, despite all disillusions! The Emperor Charles seemed even greater still, and even more wonderful to those who considered him in the perspectives of later centuries, and who raised his statue on the unhappy pedestal of his unworthy successors. The Christian Europe of the Middle Ages was to venerate as a kind of model this ideal society which, it believed, the mighty leader had led towards the light for half a century. And yet the reality had been less brilliant and more modest; the immediate future was to show the extent to which this attempt to establish one Western Christendom would prove ephemeral, and how much secret fragility was hidden beneath the brilliant emperor's grandiose structure.

# CHAPTER VIII

# THE CHURCH IS FACED WITH NEW DANGERS

## Unhappy Aftermaths of Glory

CHARLEMAGNE's death ushered in an extremely tragic period for the West—a period of violence, disorder, and degradation. The half-century of light which the great emperor's genius had managed to give to Europe was succeeded by a period of two hundred years of decline into darkness. This immediate collapse of an enterprise which had been hallowed by intelligence, courage, and faith, and which had seemed bound to endure, is perhaps the most arresting spectacle which the epoch of the Dark Ages has to offer us. Four centuries earlier, when the Roman Empire had crumbled beneath the blows of the Barbarian hordes, this collapse had seemed logical enough, a just punishment for failings that were all too obvious; at first sight the *débacle* in the ninth century is disconcerting. However, the reasons for it are easy to discern through the *aura* of glory in which the glamorous reign is bathed.

The problem which was to present itself to Charles's descendants in the most tragic way might seem already solved; in fact it was not, although it appeared so; it was the problem of the Barbarian menace, the resumption of the Invasions. The blows struck to the north, the east, and the south had obviously resulted in keeping all possible aggressors at a respectful distance. But they were there nevertheless, and their greed was there too. 'A kind of halo enveloped the actual trunk of the imperial territories,' writes one historian.[1] 'A girdle of dependent lands surrounded its frontiers, and, according to the date concerned, the imperial boundary exposed or covered all or part of these areas to a depth that was essentially fluid in character.' Was not the flood, which the leader's strong arm had been able to push back beyond the 'halo' and immobilize, now about to break over it again? The *Slavs* or *Wends*, another enormous wave from the endless Aryan sea, who had just settled as far West as the Elbe and the Moravia-Danube confluent, were contained and even used by Witikind. In other words, Charlemagne could not or would not shatter their avid power conclusively: to-morrow would not their state of *Great*

---

[1] Calmette.

*Moravia*, which stretched from the Baltic to the Adriatic, dominate the isthmus of Europe, and would not Saxony, Thuringia, and the Rhineland itself be their alluring objectives?

In the Mediterranean the folk who were now known as *Saracens*, from a word which roughly means Moslem—a pack of pirates, in whom the Arab strain was mingled with the remnants of the ancient Mediterranean sea-faring peoples—were the masters of the *mare nostrum*, whose economic life they had dislocated for some centuries past; the defensive watch-towers—the famous 'Saracen towers' of Corsica and Liguria—might seem effective against the danger of their raids, but this was only because a fleet based on the Balearic Islands was ready to reply to any of their attacks, and because the Moslems were not very inclined to attack the Empire, owing to its obvious might; however, nothing had been done to suppress their bases, especially in Africa, and it would need but a little falling off in the defence for the coasts of Europe to find themselves the object of large-scale plundering raids.   The situation was exactly the same on the Atlantic coasts, where the danger was even worse.   The Norsemen, Aryans from Denmark and Scandinavia, who had remained immobile within the boundaries of their territories for a long time, were now displaying an aggressive energy and a feverish lust for conquest whose causes have never been satisfactorily explained, and were starting on that period of epic expansion which was to take them from North America to the Caspian, from the Polar North to Sicily and Byzantium.   Charlemagne dealt with them by sea by launching his fleets against them, and on land by making Saxony press hard upon them, a policy which threatened their original settlements; but here again he could go no farther, in other words, he was unable to wipe out their points of departure in Denmark and Norway themselves.   In one famous page the chronicles of Saint-Gall describes how the emperor made a journey along the Atlantic coast, and how he saw the Viking sails slipping by against the horizon like black birds.   He suddenly began to weep, clearly aware of the danger threatening his successors; and this insight into the future expressed a fundamental truth.

The Barbarian peril, as visibly inscribed upon the political map, was made doubly dangerous in a far more insidious way.   Charlemagne had grouped together and unified as much of the Germanic race as he could; moreover he had tried to achieve a fusion between 'Germania' and 'Romania'; he had apparently succeeded and the synthesis which he had realized had many semblances of an advanced civilization.   In fact, this introduction of masses who were still virtual savages into the imperial framework, and this effort to impose a common standard upon elements who were at entirely different stages of civilization, carried with it most formidable dangers.   Certain fundamental laws of history can never be averted. When a relatively primitive people conquers another which is more civilized than itself, the vanquished teaches the victor the essential elements of civilization; this had occurred when Rome conquered Greece and was consequently intellectually 'conquered' by her in turn. But when an already civilized mass attempts to integrate another mass which is still in a primitive state, the influence of the vanquished upon the victor can only be disastrous. The Carolingian synthesis was premature; the savage forces in Europe were still too full of life for the humanism of the scholars and the clerks to be able to absorb them, even with the aid of the grace of baptism. Thus the policy of the great protagonist of the Barbarians carried within it the decisive causes of a new barbarization of the West.

In order to deal with dangers as great as these, the Empire would have had to remain the powerful reality, the spontaneous force of unity and discipline that it had been in the time of the great Charles. Instead, the raiders attacked; men returned to a savagery from which they had barely ever emerged; the different nationalities, who had been placed side by side rather than welded harmoniously into one, pulled in all directions, and everything fell to pieces. Indeed his work scarcely survived his death at all; this was partly his own fault, but it was partly due to factors beyond his control. His mistake lay in failing to settle the problem of the succession in the way in which his entire policy demanded. He had to choose between the universalist Romano-Christian principle and the ancient particularism of the Germanic tribes, and he chose the latter. In 806 he actually divided his domain between his three sons, giving the eldest *Francia* and Saxony, the second southern Gaul, and the third Italy and Germany, with the obvious intention of placing them all on an equal footing according to Frankish law. As for the imperial title, this act made no mention of it, save in an allusive fashion, and then without fixing its attribution to anyone in particular. Circumstances might make this act remain a dead letter, and chance might assure a revival of the old unity. No matter; the principle of land-sharing had been laid down, the principle which Charlemagne's descendants were to continue to practise and which was to result in the inevitable division of the West. This is clearly the weak spot, the prime failing, of this man of genius, and it proves that he never really rose to the Roman concept of the State. The great emperor cannot, however, be held responsible for the fact that none of his successors valued this concept either, or that a rather indifferent line of rulers sprang from him, at a time when men of his own great stature were needed.

On the other hand, he bears a responsibility for certain decisions whose result was nothing less than the future expansion of the *feudal system*. Feudalism, which was to form the basis of the medieval world, had been evolving for a long time past, owing to force of circumstances. The continuous disorder of the Great Invasions had encouraged the weak to gather around a few strong men, who were better able to protect them than the representatives of official authority; this was the principle of commendation. When the central authority defaulted, the local chieftains tended to make themselves autonomous: we have seen this happening nearly everywhere, in Byzantine and Lombard Italy as well as in Merovingian Gaul. The collapse of urban civilization, by giving agriculture an enormous importance, had made the farming unit, the *villa*, into an independent economic centre, and the great landowner into a kind of petty ruler. To these factors, stemming naturally from historical evolution, were added two others: *immunity* and *vassalage*, which were willed into existence by the central governments themselves. The weak monarchs, who were unsure of their subordinates, authorized the great landowners to free themselves from the control of the royal officials, and to take the latters' place in the dispensing of justice, collecting of taxes, and raising of warriors on their own estates. A direct link between the local lord and the ruler permitted the latter to exercise his authority over the former, without ever going through the medium of the government officials. It is easy to see the advantage which the sovereign hoped to derive from this alliance, in theory. He would be the controller of a whole network of loyalties which depended upon him alone and which would be more reliable than those of the dukes and counts, his over-powerful subordinates; the king believed that his personal authority would increase thereby, and that his orders would be better applied. And, in fact, this was true wherever a powerful, energetic sovereign was concerned; on the other hand, if he was weak, would not the bond of vassalage become distended and anarchy become a major threat? And this was exactly what happened.

Now all the evidence shows that Charlemagne was involved in this process. Not only had he accepted commendation, but he had amplified immunity and vassalage in several capitularies. He had wanted every free man to have his lord, whom he obeyed, and who in turn was subject to someone more important, and so on, until the line reached the emperor himself, who would then hold this whole prodigious skein of loyalties in his own strong hands. Fustel de Coulanges, who has demonstrated the mechanism of this growing system in a remarkable way, says explicitly: 'Charlemagne's Empire was already a feudal State.' Was this an aberration? An illusion based on his own very real strength? Have not many other states provided us with analogous spectacles? [1]

[1] 'Before our very eyes we see the heirs of the former Napoleonic state coming to terms with the new social forces, or, to phrase it better, thinking along the latters' lines

Threatened with Barbarism within and without, threatened by the break-up of Europe, by general anarchy ... these perils weighed heavily on Charlemagne's heritage, and were to weigh more and more heavily as time went by. The decline began at the accession of his son Louis, and it was to continue at an accelerated speed and to result in more and more tragic consequences as time went by. A West swept by new Barbarian hordes, disturbed by social troubles, torn by dynastic dissensions—authority dissolving in a kind of atomization, brute force regaining the upper hand over the principles of civilization: such was the sight which the world was to look upon for more than two hundred years. It is a distressing sight, and it would be even more so, were it not for the fact that some promises of salvation, some hopes of revival, are discernible even in the midst of this bloody chaos. Thus, though men seemed crushed by despair, the epoch appears to us as an important period of gestation. It appears thus in the following century also, and even more clearly.

In circumstances such as these what part was to be played by the Church, whose destiny was henceforth intimately linked with that of society at large? It was no different from that which she had always played ever since the time of Constantine, when she had begun to undertake responsibility for the whole world. Patiently, heroically, simultaneously leading the fight against the hostile forces which threatened humanity and against the most cunningly concealed dangers of internal contamination, she was to pursue her age-old effort, her eyes fixed on Him who guided her, knowing, and repeating continuously, that nothing was done without Him willing it so. To the men held fast in the bondage of anguish she repeated the words contained in the *City of God*, which mankind had read in the hour of the Great Invasions, namely that the real causes of this suffering were but the sins of men and the just wrath of God. Thanks to her this time of confusion retained an ultimate goal and an ultimate meaning. And because of this, and also because she represented the only element of stability in a West that was fast falling into ruins, she was even to see her own authority increase—at least momentarily—and, in an astonishing reversal of roles, her *de facto* submission to the imperial authority was transformed into an energetic declaration of superiority. Seen against this background, the century which followed

---

in order to govern more smoothly. They thus derive simultaneous advantage (at least temporarily) from the traditional authority of the old bourgeois state and from the facilities which their colleague accords them from what they believe to be the world of the future. They are all the more certain of the approbation of the fundamental forces through which they are working. They seem to direct the movement in proportion to their own obedience to it. Now, proportionately speaking, this was almost Charlemagne's attitude in respect of the social movement in his time.' (René Grousset, *Figures de proue*, p. 115.)

Charlemagne's death, this ninth century which is so little known, is of capital importance. During this period also the great Augustinian debate was played out.

## The Church Regains the Upper Hand over the Emperor

During the half-century which followed Charlemagne's death, a 'prodigious transfer of authority' took place, to use the apt expression of Mgr Arquillière; when the ninth century dawned the direction of the Christian West was entirely in the hands of the emperor, and less than fifty years after Charlemagne's death (814) it had passed into those of Pope Nicholas I (858–67). To what was this evolution due? To the very conditions in which Charlemagne had conceived and realized the Empire.

What was in fact the common bond which he had wanted to give all the peoples whom his arms had made into his subjects? Baptism. Was it not logical that the Church, who dispensed baptismal grace, should exert the principal authority over these same peoples? The emperor, who had assumed the role of leader, was essentially only a kind of substitute for the Church, a provisional trustee of authority, who presided over the mystical unity of Europe until such time as the Church could take over command. The absorption of the Roman notion of the State in the emperor's religious functions carried this reversal of rules within it; while the Church was weak and the emperor strong the latter could dominate the former, in the actual interest of Christianity, as this interest was understood at the time; when the balance of powers changed the situation was reversed.

All the more so since, as we have also noticed, the emperor himself had considered that 'provision for the service of God' ought to be the first of his duties, and that the Christian ideal constituted the be-all and end-all of his policy. In his own eyes, his power rested on moral, religious, and ecclesiastical bases, far more than on juridical ones, as had been the case with the former Roman emperors and the Byzantine Basileus. In short, the Empire was founded on the Church. The Christian writers, who were almost all clerks, did not fail to repeat this —writers like Smaragdus of Saint-Mihiel, Sedulius Scottus, Hincmar, Agobard, and Jonas of Orléans. The last-named writes: 'The king's principal role is that of defender of the Churches and the servants of God. His office consists of zealously supervising the safety of the priests and the exercise of their ministry, as well as in protecting the Church of God with his arms.' Here we see the sliding towards error, the confusion of the two authorities, contrary to true principles. St Augustine never wrote that the 'principal role' of the State was the defence of the Church. According to these theorists, it was the authority of the Church, the sacerdotal authority which founded those of the State, and kingship was really nothing more than an office. This is the origin of theocracy.

However, at first events did not seem to be leading in this direction. *Louis*, the man whom history knows under the appellatives of *the Pious* or *the Debonair*, had the unexpected good fortune to see unity being rebuilt to his own advantage. When his brothers Pepin and Charles died in 810 and 811 his father had, after consulting his advisers, proceeded to crown him himself, in 813. The Church, as an authority, had been swept aside from this important action; it was the aged emperor who had transmitted the crown to his son. 'Louis succeeded his father by consent of the Franks,' wrote Einhard. Was the Empire about to detach itself from ecclesiastic tutelage? It seemed quite possible. While visiting Rheims in 816, Pope Stephen IV did indeed assign the crown to Louis, in a proper anointing ceremony, declaring as he did so: 'Peter glories in making you this gift in order that you may guarantee his just rights'; but it was an almost super-fluous ceremony. The following year, repeating his father's action, Louis himself crowned the eldest of his sons, *Lothaire*, at a great assembly held at Aix.[1] At the same time, as if to mark quite clearly the proud pre-eminence of his throne, Louis was signing his official edicts with the single title of *Emperor Augustus*, abandoning the royal titles of France and Lombardy which the more modest Charlemagne had borne on an equal footing with the imperial one. There was no doubt at all: the conflict was latent.

This conflict should not be reduced to the rather sordid status of a competition for the domination of the world: the loftiest values, the fundamental ideals of society, were at stake. Around the Emperor Louis there was quite a gathering of enlightened, intelligent, and dis-interested men, heirs of that *élite* which had laboured beside Charle-magne. This was like a real political party, extremely united, a general staff of prelates, diplomats, and senior civil servants, which regarded itself as the depository of the Augustinian doctrine according to which the emperor, God's chosen, the mandatory of Christ, must ensure peace to all Christendom within the unity of faith. The principal leaders of this party were Abbot Wala of Corbie and Arch-bishop Agobard of Lyons. These men burned with the ideal of a unified Christian empire, such as the most outstanding of Charle-magne's friends had conceived it, such as the great emperor had more or less made incarnate. Consequently the historical importance of these advocates of unity would seem to be enormous; they defended the rights of the State against the counts and the nobles who

---

[1] When Lothaire went to Rome in 823, Pope Paschal I hastened to anoint him: but it was a repetitive action, without any great significance.

P

represented local interests, and who tended towards feudal anarchy; they raised justifiable protests against the abuses of secular intervention in the nominations of bishops and in other Church matters, and demanded reform; they upheld the thesis of single inheritance against the Frankish tradition of division.    When Louis's reign began they were the dominant force: various happy decisions were taken regarding choices of dignitaries and secularizations; the crowning of Lothaire, in 817, was their work, and his coronation was accompanied by testamentary clauses giving the imperial heritage to the eldest of the three sons, and leaving the others only small apanages.    And Louis was so attached to the idea of absolute centralization that when one of his nephews, Bernard, the viceroy of Italy and a mere boy of twenty, was made the tool of a party of malcontents and demonstrated an over-insolent desire for independence, he crushed him mercilessly.

Suddenly everything changed.    Beneath his attractive outward appearance, enhanced by undeniable qualities of courage, charity, and equity, Louis was a weak, nervous man.    Although capable of taking a firm stand on occasion, he was usually extremely easily influenced. His rages were terrible; the wretched Bernard knew something of these.    But they left him humbled and prostrate, ready to repent of all and to pardon all.    *Louis the Debonair*.    In repeating this title, one immediately thinks of Napoleon's scathing remark: 'When people say the king is good, the reign is lost.'    *Louis the Pious*.    It is certainly very fine that a man so highly placed should be conscious of his personal wretchedness, and that he should devote himself to meditation, religious reading, and prayer, but only on condition that, as in the case of St Louis, subsequently, these Christian virtues sustain and exalt the virtues necessary to his state; it is not the task of a man who should have been a monk to govern the world.    In 822 Louis was grief-stricken at having treated his nephew so frightfully, for Bernard had died as the result of having his eyes put out.    The emperor decided to submit to a public penance, and before his entire Court he proclaimed that he considered himself guilty 'in innumerable circumstances, touching on his faith, his life, and his duties.'    But was it not a fact that this humiliating demonstration of repentance, though laudable in the case of an ordinary individual, degraded, by degrading him personally, the dignity of the leader of the State also?

But the piquancy of the story rests in the fact that this crowned monk possessed an extremely amorous nature.    At the age of forty he remarried, his bride being an attractive Bavarian named Judith— whom he had chosen from a gathering of beauties—and, having fallen wildly in love with her, he wanted to ensure for Charles (the future Charles the Bald), the child he had had by her, a domain equivalent to those which the division of 817 had ensured for his three eldest sons.

This measure unleashed a storm.   Against the emperor arose both the partisans of unity, led by Wala and Agobard, and also the three princes' tenants, whose shares were cut down.   A campaign of claims and calumnies, in which the virtue of the Empress Judith was thoroughly vilified, was the prelude to an open rebellion.   For ten years there was a succession of palace revolutions and civil wars.   At first the emperor was beaten and was forced to return to the decisions of 817, but he then fell under Judith's influence again and resumed his policy of new divisions.   After being attacked by a coalition consisting of his elder sons, and totally deserted by everyone on the plain of Alsace, at Rothfeld, his collapse was so complete that only one solution remained open to him—abdication.   He bowed to this course at Compiègne, in 833, with the utmost Christian humility.   A few months later he was restored to the throne, thanks to the mistakes of his adversaries, who were scrambling for the spoils of the kingdom in a most scandalous fashion, and he took advantage of the death of his son Pepin to add to the share of his beloved little Charles, thus causing a fresh war to break out.   He died in 840, just as his son Louis was marching against him.

What was the Church's attitude throughout this painful period? At this moment, when the imperial authority began to decline, it is interesting to see how the ecclesiastical authority succeeded in regaining the upper hand.   It is quite certain that the role of the Frankish bishops was a decisive one, the bishops actually playing a greater part than the popes, who maintained an attitude of reserve.   It was obviously men like Agobard and Wala, Paschasius Radbert, Bernard of Vienne, and Ebbo of Rheims who controlled the threads of these complicated intrigues, acting with unquestionable disinterestedness and sincerity, making use of the ambitions and greed of the laity for the greater glory of God.   A man like Agobard of Lyons, who was probably the most cultured man of his time, an authority on Tertullian and St Augustine, certainly pursued quite consciously the ideal of a Christian empire dominated by the spiritual authority.   When Lothaire, a son in revolt against his father, inveigled Gregory IV into going with him into Alsace-Lorraine, in his war against Louis, and when the Pope hesitated to set himself up as an adversary of the imperial authority in this way, it was the abbots Wala and Radbert who, with the help of a great array of texts, proved to him that he was the custodian of supreme authority and that 'not being judged by any man himself' he ought 'to judge all the faithful,' including the emperors; and it was they too who whispered the response he should make to Louis's supporters who reproached him for committing a political act.   And when the miserable emperor was obliged to recognize his faults at Compiègne, on the eve of abdication, it was the princes of the

Frankish Church who drew up the record of this penance, after which, it was written, 'there would be no more worldly fighting.'

Why was this attitude adopted? The bishops gave their reasons quite categorically. 'Because they are the vicars of Christ and have the keys of the Kingdom of Heaven.' Their thesis was clear enough: it was the Augustinian thesis once again, as it appeared in the *City of God*. The emperor's reign was justified in so far as he assured *peace* and *justice* to all Christendom, and the Church's authority supported his in the proportion in which he did so. But since her authority, being a spiritual one, was superior to his, the Church reserved the right to judge his attitude. If he neglected his duties she abandoned and condemned him. Pope Gregory IV spoke in similar terms: 'I am discharging a mission of peace and justice; it is a gift of Christ and His own ministry.' As the official judge of sins the Church claimed the right to judge even the sins of princes.

What a change from the still so recent past, when the popes had counted for very little beside Charlemagne! Obviously the time was not yet ripe when the Church would 'depose' an emperor because of his sins, as Gregory VII was to depose Henry IV of Germany in the eleventh century. The assembly at Compiègne, although packed with clerics, was not considered to be a Council, and it was not the Church who deposed Louis; Lothaire undertook that task, and the Pope and the bishops merely encouraged him. Nevertheless a new perspective was opened to history, a perspective wherein the Church's future glory and her dangers were clearly apparent.


## The Hollow Fraternity

On Louis's death, in 840, there was a fresh attempt to re-establish the principle of unity. Lothaire, to whom the dying emperor had sent his sword and his crown, demanded his brothers' absolute obedience. The Church, represented by her important dignitaries, lent him her support, and the palace of Ingelheim was crowded with a throng of prelates, archbishops, and abbots, among whom were the real leaders of the Western Church, men like Drogo of Metz, Rabanus Maurus of Fulda, and many others. In fact, the noble idea of a united Christian Empire was tending to fade from men's minds. Although still supported by a few idealists, but rather more by self-interested parties, it was now attacked by contrary interests which upheld the separatist tendencies embodied in Louis and Charles, the younger brothers of the new emperor. Allying against him, these two began the fight for the independence of their realm in autumn 840, and in the following year they defeated him at Fontanet-en-Puisaye, not far from Auxerre.

This defeat was interpreted as a judgment of God.   On the battle-field, while the armies were burying their dead, the bishops proclaimed that the war being waged against Lothaire was a just one.   The idea of unity was collapsing, and the Church, as realistic as ever, was taking note of this fact.

But she did not despair.   Something else must be substituted for the discredited principle of unity.   All the more so, since the situation of Western Europe was growing worse and worse with every month that passed by; the Norsemen, taking advantage of the fratricidal wars, had just landed in the mouth of the Seine and pillaged Rouen; the Slavs on the Elbe were becoming threatening, and the Saracen pirates were not the only threat that existed in the Mediterranean.   It was now that the Church's leaders arrived at a new concept, that of a kind of *entente cordiale* between the three sovereigns—a fraternity of kings, a 'Holy Alliance,' as a similar notion was to be named a thousand years later.   'United in Christ's Charity,' the three Masters of the West would jointly safeguard the spiritual unity of Christendom.

On the morrow of Fontanet, the two victors strengthened their ties in the famous *Declarations of Strasbourg*, wherein it was stated that 'since equity demanded that one should defend one's brother,' each would undertake to aid the other, 'provided that his brother did the same on his part.' [1]   Still, it was a very singular kind of fraternity, since it aimed at nothing less than the defeat of the eldest brother, who stood in the way of the younger two!   However, after some months of hesitation, negotiation, and bargaining, a solution was agreed upon. This was the famous *Treaty of Verdun* of 843.   The Empire was cut into three sections. [2]   Charles the Bald received Western Francia as his kingdom, which was to become the future France, Louis the German obtained Eastern Francia, the future Germany, and between these two was Lothaire's realm, an incongruous strip of territory, stretching from Holland to Rome, which was flattered by the inclusion of both the Western capitals but which was incapable of pursuing any important policy and which constituted the most fragile basis for the extremely vague imperial authority which his brothers recognized as his.   Henceforth France and Germany, two entities whose languages were already different and whose customs and traditions were soon to be different too, were to pursue their separate destinies, and 'Lothar-ingia' was to become the battle-ground and the object of their rival

---

[1] The documents embodying the Declarations of Strasbourg are fundamental to the history of the languages of Western Europe.   Since Louis took the oath in the Germanic tongue, and Charles in a Romanic one, the written texts are the earliest documents which we possess which show the beginnings of modern French and German.   Here is the beginning of Charles's oath: 'Pro Deo amor et pro christian poblo et nostre commun salvament. . . .'

[2] See map in the preceding chapter, p. 409.

ambitions. This ill-starred decision contained the seeds of European dissensions which a thousand years of history have not yet healed.

But at least the idea of fraternity was applicable to such a situation as this. The Church stubbornly reminded the interested parties of this fact. In 844 the synod of Yutz told them: 'Take care to preserve charity amongst you. . . . Help each other by rendering good advice and prompt aid. Instead of serving the discord which the Devil spreads among your peoples, serve peace, that peace which the Christ, when He ascended into heaven, left His disciples as the most precious of all gifts.' The Church did far more than merely remind the brothers of these excellent principles: she encouraged the kings to hold fraternal assemblies like those at Thionville (844), Meersen (847 and 851), Valenciennes (853), Liége and Attigny (854). It was an admirable effort, and for some time it even seemed to be bearing fruit. Laws were published which were applicable to all these realms, to the 'common subjects' of them all, capitularies were promulgated 'under the common reign.' The institution of the *missi dominici* acquired new lustre; the Church contributed to this by entrusting these posts to first-class men.

There is no question at all that the Church had strengthened her authority during this troubled period, by strictly obeying the gospel spirit. As Hincmar was to write: 'Although the Empire, which our fathers had built into a mighty unity, was divided, one thing remained intact despite these domestic divisions: the Church.' The effective agents of this action were, once again, the bishops; the popes still appeared to be holding themselves somewhat aloof from events. It is true that circumstances did not make it easy for them to act: they succeeded one another too quickly on St Peter's throne (there were ten popes within fifty years); their own territories were under considerable pressure from the African Arabs, who had been masters of Palermo since 831, from the Serbs of Dalmatia, established in Aquileia, and from the Spanish Moslems, who prowled continually around the Tyrrhenian coasts; moreover they were embarrassed by various Roman intrigues, which went to the lengths of setting up antipopes; and lastly, the experience of 833 had taught Gregory IV that the Papacy's influence gained nothing by interfering in these complicated brawls between warring fathers, sons, and brothers. However, they knew how to link themselves discreetly but firmly with the policy of brotherly concord, and their voice rang clear on several occasions. Thus, after the Partition of Verdun, Sergius II (844-7) wrote to the three brothers, telling them that 'if they did not remain united in the Catholic peace' he would intervene against them; the energetic Leo IV was to repeat the same idea in almost identical words, claiming as his own the task of being the preserver of peace and the guarantor of justice.

Possibly the popes did not talk more loudly because they were aware that this policy of fraternity, splendid though it was in theory, was a delusion. At all events certain clear-thinking people had no illusions about it, and saw the warning of the Empire's future collapse in its partitioning; this was so in the case of Florus, the famous teacher from Lyons, whose indictments are most moving, and also in the case of Walafrid, abbot of Reichenau who, with admirable foresight, told Lothaire exactly what was going to happen: the inevitable decomposition of the Carolingian heritage.

What this system of fraternity lacked, was lacked too by our twentieth-century League of Nations: an authority capable of rising above the conflicts of interests and of compelling the application of certain principles. The emperor, although recognized by the kings, was nothing but a phantom. It was all in vain that he tried to increase his authority beyond his own realm, partially helped by the Holy See, nominating men like Drogo as 'vicars for the Gauls and for Germany,' a system which would have given him a measure of control over his brothers; but the situation was already so crystallized that manœuvres of this kind were doomed to failure. As the years went by the brothers' distrust of one another grew. Louis the German and his greedy sons scarcely concealed their intention of rebuilding imperial unity to their own advantage, and Lothaire and Charles were obliged to strengthen their alliance against them. But they themselves were on bad terms with each other, and the slightest incident, such as the nomination of a bishop, was enough to make them 'fly at each other like dogs,' as one chronicler expresses it. The fraternity of 844 had long since perished when Lothaire died in 855, completely discredited.

The treaty of Verdun was clearly nothing but a humiliating make-shift for the three signatories. Each dreamed of rebuilding the imperial heritage to his own advantage. The balance of power, which had been precariously preserved while there were three competitors involved, collapsed when the middle zone fell to pieces on Lothaire's death, leaving the future France and the future Germany face to face. Faithful to the custom of territorial division, the dead emperor had divided his realm into three parts: Louis II, Lothaire's eldest son, received Italy and the imperial crown, which he had, however, already been given in advance; Lothaire II the northern territories, stretching from the sea to the Langres Plateau and Alsace ('the Lotharingian kingdom' = Lotharingia = Lorraine); and Charles obtained what was left, namely the Jura, the Alps, and Provence. Taking advantage of the internal disorders in Charles the Bald's kingdom, which was beset by civil wars and by the Norse invasions, the Germans marched into France. For a moment it looked as if the operation was going to succeed, as if the important figures in Charles's kingdom would rally to Louis, and as if the two Francias were about to be welded together beneath the German sceptre.    It was the Gallic clergy who saved the French monarchy at this juncture.    Angered by these fratricidal wars the bishops protested against Louis's conduct in language of magnificent resolution.    They went so far as to remind him that, since he held his crown from the Church, the Church could take it from him, just as Samuel had abandoned Saul in order to anoint David!    Consequently this dramatic crisis signified a new increase in the Church's authority. She no longer considered herself only the overseer of kings.    She now began to assert that it was she who made them, by the bestowal of Divine Unction.

The Frankish clergy's resistance to Louis's encroachments gave Charles the Bald the opportunity to reform his army, to march against his brother and to defeat him.    The real conqueror was Hincmar, the great bishop of Rheims, who had been the inspiration of the resistance to the Germans; he was one of the very first to foresee the reality of what the Middle Ages were to call 'Christendom,' namely, the solidarity of the society comprising all the baptized; it was he who took the initiative of bringing about a general reconciliation.    An assembly which took place under his guidance, at Metz, was inclined to regard Louis extremely severely, as one who was guilty of having 'divided the Church, which is one body.'    Two years of negotiations were needed to arrive at the foundations of a peace which seemed sound enough (860); the Church had saved Western unity, somehow or other.

It was high time!    For the situation was an appalling one.    Anarchy was around the corner.    Desolated by civil wars and invasions, every country in Europe, but France more so than the rest, was being paralysed by outbreaks of unbelievably violent pillaging. Under pretext of aiding this or that king, various bands of ruffians ravaged the countryside, attacking the monasteries, abducting entire religious communities.    Even in the period of the Great Invasions, nothing so frightful as this had been seen.    These bandits were spoken of as 'living like Norsemen,' for they did not hesitate to come to terms with and even to join in the actual raids [1] carried out by these pirates from the north, whose own attacks were becoming more threatening and terrible with every day that went by, and against whom the forces of law and order were almost powerless.

---

[1] Thus for a long time it was believed that Hasting, the famous 'Norse' chieftain who was such a formidable figure in the Mediterranean, was a peasant from Champagne, completely French in origin, born near Troyes, and 'Norse' by adoption.    This is now considered legendary by historians, but the allegation is understandable enough, because similar cases to this one did occur.

## THE MEN FROM THE NORTH

The Norsemen! It is hard for us to understand what these two guttural Germanic syllables meant for the whole of ninth-century Europe in terms of terrifying power. As soon as the watch-posts spied the terrible sea-raiders arriving in the river mouths the warning would be sounded; the towns bolted their gates; the ramparts bristled with anxious defenders; long, miserable processions fled from the farms and monasteries which could not hope to sustain a serious battle, processions whose chances of massacre were far greater than their hopes of safety. Wreathed in a mystery spun from the mists from which they sprang, and bearing with them a well-deserved reputation for extreme savagery, the men from the north haunted Europe, like living symbols of a punishment brought down upon it by its own sins. And soon the liturgy would include the words: *A furore normannorum libera nos, Domine!*

The term *Norsemen* covers them all. In fact, they were divided into three large groups: the Danes, who had settled in Scandinavia first of all, then in the Baltic archipelago, and finally in the peninsula which still retains their name; the Norwegians, who were perhaps the most daring of all these bold robbers, who clung to the Scandinavian fjords and, from the seventh century onwards, scattered throughout the North Sea, in the Shetlands, Orkneys, and Faroes; and finally the Swedes, at first massed in the region around Uppsala and then attracted southwards, like the Danes, to ruin the Gothic principalities of Gothland, and simultaneously drawn towards Finland and the Lithuanian coastlands, in the direction of the Dnieper. They all possessed roughly the same characteristics: they were a type of handsome, fair-haired Aryan, which survives in its purest form in Norway, well built, energetic, vigorous, and brave. Among all these people society seemed to be divided into two main groups: there was the settled element, comprising the peasants, shepherds, wood-cutters, and wood-sculptors; and there were the wanderers, for whom war was not simply a source of wealth, power, and prestige, but a kind of moral principle, glorified by their religion, their literature, and their art. The kings, whose authority was based solely on strength and success, were essentially the leaders of a *hird* of warriors, dominating a group of tribes. Their tumuli still proclaim that they were powerful and highly respected. There are several of these throughout Scandinavia and they are among the most imposing historical monuments that Europe possesses.

Although they had remained aloof from the rest of the continent for

\* P

a long time, these tribes of Dano-Scandinavians had had various contacts with the other Germanic peoples nevertheless: their art proves this.   Here we see the same buckles, the same heavy bracelets, the same jewellery settings, the same enamel-work, the same patterns of plants and stylized heads which we can admire on Germanic tombs. They knew all too well that beyond the vast expanses of empty sea there lay fine, sunny countries—gentle, rich lands, whose rulers' weakness and disunity made them an easy prey for their own greedy appetites.   There, in their hands, lay the most effective means of conquest: a fleet, beyond compare elsewhere at this time.

From the chieftains' tumuli modern science has recovered these Norse 'cruisers,' these *drakkars* in which the mighty pirates hoped to spend their eternity.   Their long ships can still be seen to-day in the museums of Denmark and Scandinavia.   They were about twenty-seven feet long, open, tapering constructions, perfectly proportioned, and they give the impression of masterpieces right down to the decorations that stretched from prow to poop.   Using oars or sails, they could easily travel at ten knots; they had a keel depth of little more than three feet, which enabled them to cross all the shallows and to sail up all the rivers; and their radius of activity can be judged from the journey made by an exact copy of one of them some twenty years ago, from Norway to New York, by the same boat which sank in the North Sea in 1950.   Groups of about fifty warriors sailed in these wonderful ships, led by picked expeditionary leaders, the *Vikings*, whose fame shines out from the verses of the sagas.   The Norsemen sought out adventure with a dauntless courage and audacity.   'The storm lends aid to our oarsmen,' cried their battle-song, 'the hurricane works for us, and takes us wherever we want to go!'

This great strategical weapon of the maritime raid was completed by land tactics which were equally skilful.   The Norsemen had an inborn knowledge of rivers, and they excelled at sailing up any course, however unknown, towing their ships when oars or sail were not sufficient, even carrying them on their backs when it was necessary to avoid a fortified strongpoint or a stretch where ambushes were likely.   When they left the water they did not hesitate to undertake long marches in pursuit of those they sought, and when they changed from sailors into horsemen they knew how to make good use of the horses which they either stole from the lands they conquered or even brought over with them in their boats.   Finally, unlike the Huns, or the Hungarians later on, both of whom were useless without their horses, the Norsemen, who were specialists in every kind of warfare, were perfectly capable of constructing fortifications, either to defend themselves or to attack places which were better fortified.   Their war-machine was really perfect.

Consequently their sphere of activity grew ever wider and wider. For about thirty years—to be exact from 793, the date when they first pillaged a monastery, that of Lindisfarne in Northumbria, until about 830—they confined their desires to a few fruitful but disorganized raids. Next they acquired bases in the islands (the Shetlands, Orkneys, and Hebrides), and in Ireland and Scotland also, and then they perfected their methods of warfare by establishing permanent, fortified posts at the mouths of the major rivers, which were used as military depots and as storehouses for their plunder, and from which they could more easily set sail for the fine lands they wanted to attack. In this way the Scheldt, the Seine, and the Loire came under their control, and the incredible weakness of the Carolingian administration did scarcely nothing to get rid of them. The Norwegians chose England and Ireland for their main targets, and fell on them in swarms like flies in August. 'There is not a single place that does not possess its fleet,' writes one chronicler, meaning its fleet of pirates, and about 840 the Viking Turgeis actually set up a Norse kingdom in St Patrick's island, a pagan kingdom, which was to exist until the twelfth century. On the Continent the attack was principally waged by the Danes. Practically every important city in the Empire received one of their troublesome visits at this time. They were everywhere: at the mouths of the Rhine and the Scheldt, and in Saintonge; then suddenly they would appear before Hamburg, only to arrive in the Gironde in no time at all. Next it was the turn of Lisbon and Seville to suffer their depredations, and soon Ligurian Italy would know a similar fate. In France it is impossible to list all the places they attacked: Beauvais, Chartres, which was surprised at dead of night, Noyon, Melun, Orléans, Blois . . . the list of calamities grew larger, week by week. Paris was besieged four times in forty years, pillaged three times and burned twice. . . .

What could the Empire do against attacks such as these? It was paralysed by internal discord, and its rulers no longer controlled it properly. Here and there there were courageous demonstrations of resistance, on the Seine, for example, and in Friesland; certain kings, like Charles the Bald in his better days, or local lords like Robert the Strong in Paris, refused to yield to the general panic. All too often the sovereigns 'bought themselves off,' in other words they agreed to pay the raiders a ransom to persuade them to depart: Charles the Bald, Lothaire II, and several others adopted this practice, which was of course a perfect way of inviting the Norsemen to return. In many quarters the Western authorities did nothing. They neither fought nor attempted to negotiate. Around 850 the ravages of the Norsemen in the area between the Seine and the Loire were appalling: the peasants no longer dared to go about their work. Flight! It seemed to be the only solution left. Were it not so calamitous and so shocking it would be almost comic to follow on the map the movements of the relics—or rather, of the precious reliquaries, which were greatly coveted by the plunderers—which the monastic communities carried off with them; thus St Martin was swept from Marmoutier to Corméru, then to Orléans, next, after a brief return to the original foundation, to Leré in Berry, to Marsat in the Auvergne, and finally to Chablis in Burgundy; likewise too the remains of St Philibert, which were hounded from Noirmoutier, stayed for a short while at Déas (which became Saint-Philibert-de-Grandlieu), and then went deeper and deeper into the heart of Gaul: to Curnault on the Loire, Messac in Poitou, and Saint-Porcien in the Auvergne, until they finally reached Tournus, in Burgundy, following a zigzag course all the while, according to the danger which pursued them. (And these migrations of relics were to have a curious result: they gave rise to some cults of saints far from their land of origin, e.g. that of St Philibert at Tournus, St Lauto (Lô) at Angers, etc.)

Understandably enough the Church had little difficulty in seeing proof of the wrath of God in calamities such as these. On many occasions the synods followed the purest Augustinian doctrine and proclaimed that the sins of the Christians were the real cause of these terrible happenings. Everyone was agreed on this, but no one wanted to agree to reform his own behaviour! For example, King Carloman told an assembly: 'We ourselves are predatory men. How can we possibly struggle confidently against the enemies of the Church and ourselves when we leave for battle with our bellies full of our own stolen spoils? How dare we claim the right to victory when our mouths are full of our brothers' blood and our arms heavy with injustice? There is the explanation for our defeats!' In a way this was some consolation!

What had been the Church's attitude to this new invader? In general, historians deal rather severely with the clergy and the faithful of the period. Leaders, real leaders, were rare: there was no St Geneviève to rise before the new Attila; no bishop set himself up as *defensor Civitatis*; the priests could only groan: 'God is punishing us for your sins,' they told the faithful and they preached resignation and surrender. There is no doubt about this failure on the part of the episcopate and the clergy. But the comparison between the attitude of the Church at the time of the Norse invasions and its attitude towards the Barbarians in the fifth century is in danger of distorting the fundamentals of the problem, unless one takes into account certain circumstances which had changed in the intervening period. Let us return to the original question and rephrase it: What was the Norsemen's attitude to the Church? As we read in the *Histoire de*

*France* of Lavisse: 'The Norsemen's main target was the monasteries, the real centres of Carolingian civilization, where they found plenty of rich treasures (the shrines of the saints), full granaries, and flourishing workshops.  Besides, the majority of the monasteries were unfortified.'  This has nothing in common with the fifth century: the Barbarians of that period do not seem to have 'singled out' the Church and the clerks as the Norsemen were to do four hundred years later. Obviously the Church's position had changed a great deal during these four centuries: the clergy had become a great landowning class. Countless monasteries had been founded whose wealth excited the pirates' lust for treasure.  Moreover the Norsemen's cruelty left that of the Germans' far behind it.  The latter were a people on the march, semi-invaders, semi-immigrants.  The Norsemen, on the other hand, came in far smaller parties, but they were parties composed solely of warriors: their raids were made by a kind of 'commando' force. Only much later on did they have the idea of making permanent settlements.  The Church was the particular target of pirates who *operated by surprise*, and this explains why she found it impossible, in the ninth century, to play the magnificent role which had been played by the episcopate in the fifth century.  It was far easier for a prelate in the time of St Lupus and St Anianus to parley with the leader of a people on the march, than for a ninth-century prelate to make himself understood by the captain of a pirate band resolved on a surprise attack on the episcopal town.  What conversation could Bishop Gunhard have with the Norse robbers who swept down on Nantes on 24th June 843?  They murdered him before the altar of St Ferreolus, in the church of Sts Peter and Paul.  The patron saints of the churches and the monasteries, so far from acting as 'lightning conductors,' attracted the thunderbolts, not on their own account, but because of the precious shrines in which their bodies were housed.

However, there were some courageous exceptions.  For example, in the north, the monks of Saint-Bertin, who had gathered within their walls all the refugees from the surrounding countryside, defended themselves so fiercely that the plunderers passed them by; the monks of Saint-Vaast at Arras, of Saint-Quentin, and of Tournus on the Saône, did the same.  Langres was to be defended by Bishop Geilo, and Chartres by Bishop Ganteaume, whilst Rheims was hastily fortified by Bishop Fulk, who, it was said, actually slept close by the city gates.  The most famous episode of this clerical resistance to the new dangers was the Norse siege of Paris in 885.  The little town of the Cité and its two suburbs on the river-banks held out against all attacks for a whole year, braving famine as well as the enemy scaling ladders; the Parisians saw their bishop, Goscelinus, and Ebles, his nephew, abbot of Saint-Germain-des-Prés, fighting alongside Count Eudes, the son of Robert the Strong, and the ancestor of the Capetians; and when Sigfrid, the Norse chieftain, came to parley, it was the bishop who received him in the episcopal palace, refused any compromise with him, and spoke to the pirate in the severe tones of a biblical prophet. Compared with the attitude of the imperial authorities this was to make a great impression, for, at the time when his army was camping on the hill of Montmartre, Charles the Fat, Charlemagne's descendant, could, instead of fighting, find nothing better to do than to hand Burgundy over to the Norsemen in order to make them raise the siege. Upon learning of this the Parisians were so indignant that they refused to allow the *drakkars* to sail under their bridges, and the Norsemen had to handle them over dry land in order to skirt the town!

To this kind of resistance the Church added another, equally typical of the line of conduct which she had always pursued. So far from despairing of these terrifying bandits who did her so much harm she continued her great efforts to convert them. The men from the north were pagans: they remained loyal to the old Germanic cults, to their warrior-gods, Odin, Thor the soldier, the violent Assir, and such nature gods as Frey, Frejya, and Niordr. Circumstances were quite favourable for those real Christians who were anxious to try to lead these handsome flesh-eating animals to the faith. When, thanks to the palace revolutions in Denmark, Louis the Pious established fairly friendly contacts with the refugee king, Harold III, the Bishop of Mainz took advantage of the Barbarian's stay in his city to persuade him to be baptized. This first conquest made the dispatch of missionaries into the heart of Norse country much easier. Ebbo, Bishop of Rheims, threw himself into this task, and then, when kept in France by the duties of his office, he saw to it that he was replaced by one of the leading monks from the abbey of Corvey, in Saxony, a daughter-house of Corbie. This man devoted himself to the herculean task with wonderful tenacity. His name was *St Anschgar*, meaning 'God's javelin.' He was even bolder than St Boniface, who had worked only under the protection of Frankish arms, for he plunged deep into the heart of heathen territory, just as the missionaries to the Red Indians were to do, in the seventeenth century. Although repulsed on several occasions, he always returned to his task; taking Hamburg as his apostolic centre and starting-point, he threw the seeds of Christianity far into Denmark and Sweden. In 845 he saw his work suddenly destroyed by the ferocious assault of the Norwegian Vikings on his see, but he immediately started his evangelical endeavour all over again, now tolerated and now rejected by the Norse kings. He ended by creating two Christian centres, Birka and Riba. These results seem paltry enough, but his work was to be of immense importance for the future, for it was the prelude to the evangelization of Scandinavia about 1000.[1]

## WAITING FOR A STRONG PAPACY

Under the most hostile conditions, amid all the tragedies which crowded this mournful ninth century, the Church extended her influence.   The Western clergy's membership had been purified, and its education improved, ever since the efforts made by Charlemagne and his devout heir.   Now it prepared to take the leading place in the Christian community.   Even though, until this time, enlightenment had come from the East and it had been the theologians of the Greek Church who had seemed to dominate, the dogmatic importance of the West was now beginning to increase: there was already promise of the blooming that would take place in the Middle Ages.   Once the Iconoclastic Dispute was settled, in 843, the light in the Eastern Church began to grow gradually dimmer; but her sister in the West was just awakening.   Theological controversies began to excite her. We have already noted the dispute concerning the *Filioque* under Charlemagne; during the time of Louis the Pious, Florus, the deacon of Lyons, did battle with Amalarius, and Rabanus Maurus, abbot of Fulda, crossed swords with Paschasius Radbert, abbot of Corbie, on the question of Christ's presence in the Eucharist.   Later on the mystery of predestination, which St Augustine had already considered a great deal, provoked an extremely violent crisis in which the great and terrifying Hincmar tore the Saxon monk, Gottschalk, verbally to shreds and was himself accused of heresy by Prudentius of Troyes and Lupus of Ferrières, a crisis which three Councils were unable to settle and which was finally denounced by the Pope.   The fact that these men were able to become so impassioned by disputes of this kind, at a time when the West was tearing itself to pieces, when its cities and monasteries were burning under Norse attacks, when famine and distress were prowling about its deserted countrysides, is surely proof of the Church's exceptional vitality, rich in promise for the future.

The Church's political development continued.   This supremacy of spiritual power, which she had begun to state in a modest way, was soon loudly proclaimed by the more energetic of her leaders.   They took the kings to task, boldly and resolutely.   In the chaos into which

---

[1] These first contacts between Christianity and the Norsemen, prior to the Great Invasions or their attendant circumstances, account for the famous anecdote, told us by the monk of Saint-Gall, about the old Dane who, out of ignorance or guile, was a tireless participant in baptismal ceremonies.   When he was presented with a slightly used baptismal garment on leaving the fonts, he declared: 'Keep your old cloak for a cowherd.   This is the twentieth time that I have been baptized, and no one has ever offered me rags like these before.'

Iona
563
Lindisfarne
634
397
Whithorn
Bangor
630
Jarrow
674
Whitby
658
IRELAND
York
625
WALES
ENGLAND
Menevia
Worcester
Ely 673
c. 676
Barking
Utrecht
695
FRIESLAND
Bremen
804
N. Co
Canterbury
597
Winchester
Loo
London
Gand
FLANDERS
Aix la
Chapelle
Pade
SAX
Wimborne
c. 660
St.
932
Fecamp
Fecamp
Riquier 640
657
Liège
Cologne
Fu
St. Wandrille
648
655
Corbie
650
Stavelot
Mainz
Lorsch
764
Bayeux
Jumièges
LORRAINE
Trèves
NORMANDY
Caen
Rouen
St. Denis
626
Rheims
Worms
Mt.
St. Michel 709
Paris
Metz
Gorze
730
Marmoutier
Chartres
Toul
Strasbourg
BRITANNY
Orleans
Troyes
727
Tours
373
Fleury 640
590 Luxeuil
Murbach
Noirmoutier
675
FRANCE
Dijon
Reichenau
724
St. Gal
Ligugé
360
910 Cluny
BURGUNDY
Lausanne
720
HOLY ROMA
Clermont
Lyons
Mila
Bordeaux
AQUITAINE
le Puy
Pavia
LOMBA
782
Aniane
PROVENCE
Bob
612
Toulouse
Arles
Lucca
NAVARRE
Carcassonne
Narbonne
Marseilles
406
Lérins
410
Saragossa
Gerona

MONASTIC
EUROPE*

4th to 10th Centuries

*This map attempts to indicate
only some of the principal
monastic houses

rg 831

aim

Magdeburg
968

POLAND

urt 741

NGIA
rg        ● Prague 976

BOHEMIA

tisbon 716              ● Velchrad 863

MORAVIA

● Passau 716
ng

ARIA   ● Salzburg
716

TRANSYLVANIA

CARINTHIA

HUNGARY

Aquileia

ice

d Ravenna

SLAVONIA

ssa
RIMONY
OF
PETER

to o    705
● Farfa

o Rome   ● Monte 529
Cassino

o Benevento

540 ●
Vivarium

partitioned Europe was slipping the act of royal anointing seemed the only firm reality, the one immovable rock. Consequently its importance grew and the Church gained an advantage thereby. 'Receive the sceptre, insignia of royal authority,' declared the coronation formula, 'in order that you may rule well over Holy Church and the Christian people in your charge!' In other words, the king was only king in order to serve the Church and her cause. And better still, the kings themselves accepted this doctrine; when he was threatened with deposition in 859, Charles the Bald invoked the following astonishing argument: 'Since my anointing, no man on earth can depose me, at least not until I have been judged by the bishops who anointed me,' a statement which implicitly recognizes that the leaders of the Church have the right to depose kings. . . . Once the doctrinal point of view is admitted, it is logical enough, since 'pontiffs can anoint kings, but kings cannot consecrate pontiffs!'

The last word on the subject was Hincmar's. This is the mighty bishop whom we have already seen playing a decisive role in political conflicts as well as in doctrinal battles. He was the great theorist of this primacy of the spiritual power, that is to say, in reality, of the confusion of the temporal and the spiritual to the latter's advantage. His ideal was a glorious and powerful empire, perfectly organized according to the principles of justice, but an empire controlled by the Church, directed by an oligarchy of mighty metropolitans, in which the religious leaders reminded humanity of its duties, and guided it resolutely towards the City of God. It was Charlemagne's ideal, with the parts completely reversed: in this tragic age, when civilization felt itself once again upon the brink of the abyss, it was probably the only cogent programme, but it raised a number of problems.

The first difficulty related to the general situation itself: if the Church was to serve as the bastion of resistance in the midst of the tempest, it was essential that the actual stone of which she was made should not crumble nor be cracked by enemy blows. Now it was perfectly obvious that some lines of resistance to this theory were already visible, and they were to grow all too fast. Feudalism, which was becoming established far and wide, aimed at incorporating the Church. The operation took place in three ways at the same time, and it is hard to assess which was the most damaging. First of all, just as in the worst decades of the Merovingians, or in the early days of the Carolingians, the sovereigns—who were for ever at war and for ever impecunious—were in the habit of secularizing Church lands, handing them over to their supporters, or confiscating them to provide for their own needs; this was simply a material loss and could have been much worse. But later on—and this was far more serious—the appalling state of society at the time induced a number of priests,

abbots, and even bishops, to 'commend themselves' to a lord; thus the
political bond took the place of the canonical one.   'It is not simply
ecclesiastical wealth, but the churches themselves which have become
the property of laymen,' writes Agobard indignantly.   Finally, and
this was the crowning evil, the sovereigns considered that they had the
right to distribute ecclesiastical titles exactly as they distributed secular
offices; they would name some worthy royal servant as abbot of a
wealthy monastery in exactly the same way as they appointed the count
of a province, and quite often the two titles were held by the same
individual.   Moreover circumstances helped this to happen: for
instance, in monasteries and bishoprics it was customary to make a
distinction between the income of the abbot or the bishops and that of
the community.   Naturally this made the attribution of the first-
named of these to some lord or other a simple matter: bishoprics and
abbeys became royal benefices.

And the results of all this?   They are easy to guess.   The parish
priest deserted his flock to become the lord's chaplain and sometimes
his bailiff too.   The abbot went to war with a troop of men-at-arms,
thus carrying out his oath of feudal loyalty.   The parish, and the
wealth of the parish, were treated as capital to be exploited, tithes were
usurped, gifts presented by Christians were shamefully stolen.   In
the abbeys and bishoprics which were in lay hands the real clerks were
humbled, put on 'short allowance,' and forced to beg their living,
according to statements made by the Councils on the subject.   And
above all, there was the scandalous designation of hitherto venerated
titles to nominees who were completely unworthy of them: the reader
can get some idea of the scandal involved here by remembering that
Waldrada, Lothaire II's concubine, received from him a monastery!

Faced with evils like these, the healthy elements of the Church
clearly reacted very strongly.   For instance, here is the sermon which
Wala, abbot of Corbie, preached to Louis the Pious: 'How dare you
come to this pass of distributing dignities, or, to be more accurate,
ecclesiastical charges?   Know, first of all, that all the wealth justly
assigned to the Church in the form of alms belongs to the churches
alone.   And if you want to transmit, by royal decree, the blessings
and the gifts of the Holy Spirit which His chosen hold from the Lord,
through the medium of consecrated bishops, know also that you are
greatly exceeding the office which is yours.'   Similar protests occurred
elsewhere: here against Pepin of Aquitaine, there against Charles the
Bald.   At the synod of Yutz, in 836, in the presence of three assembled
kings, the bishops vehemently demanded an end to these abuses.   At
Vers, three months later, they even dared to talk of 'sacrilegious
attitudes.'   At Paris, in 846, their complaints and demands for reform
were so pressing that Charles the Bald yielded to them, and promised

not to nominate any more laymen as abbots, not to secularize Church property, even to make restitution for goods improperly acquired. . . .

These were vain promises. Twenty weeks later, when he held the yearly 'pleas' at Épernay for his followers, he was abruptly made to see reason. The lords did not mean to renounce so many fruitful prebends at any price, and the fine Parisian programme was never put into effect. 'Never before have the bishops been treated with such shameless lack of respect!' declared the indignant Bishop Prudentius of Troyes. The danger promised to be extremely great in the future. In the following century the Church, contaminated by the feudal system, was to be brought to the verge of ruin. But one lesson had already emerged: in order to resist these destructive forces it was no use counting on the local hierarchies, who were too close to the kings and too dependent upon them. The true reform movement to counter the perils of feudalism was to be a much later undertaking, and it would be led by a superior authority, namely, by the Pope. From the middle of the ninth century onwards the world was awaiting Gregory VII.

Another problem also beset this courageous Church in the age of Carolingian decadence—this Church, which was attempting to impose its authority upon man's society in order to protect it against fate and itself. On what level should this authority be situated, or, to phrase the question in another way, who should exercise it? In the political conflicts it was the archbishops, the metropolitans, who played the leading role. They were personages of considerable importance, connected with everyone who counted in the State; they had free access to Court, were often ambassadors and ministers, and constituted the episcopate's aristocracy; many of them cherished Hincmar's ideal, the idea of a control exercised over Church and State—intermingled, thanks to them—by a handful of ecclesiastical leaders, with the ordinary bishops as their subordinates and the king as their executant. We should remember that St Boniface [1] had wanted to develop this machinery of metropolitans, but his purpose in doing so had had nothing in common with these later ideas; perhaps because he suspected the danger, Charlemagne had shown no desire whatsoever to adopt the views of the English reformer; [2] but as the imperial authority collapsed the metropolitans established their position. There was thus a double conflict in prospect: between the metropolitans and the bishops who would see their power diminishing in an intolerable fashion, and between the metropolitans and the Papacy, which would not be able to tolerate indefinitely something which amounted to a usurpation of its powers.

[1] See Chapter V, end of section: 'The Church's Principle of Reform.'
[2] See Chapter VII, note on p. 416.

Moreover this episcopate, which was plundered by the nobles, and stripped of its authority by the great, was simultaneously attacked from below.  Here the enemy was the *pastoral bishop*, who in theory helped the diocesan bishop to administer the sacraments; the institution had come from the East,[1] and had been adopted nearly everywhere in Christendom around the fourth and fifth centuries.  Then it was reabsorbed into the regular episcopate in many quarters, especially in Italy, where the multiplication of bishoprics had conclusively put an end to it, but it continued to exist in Gaul.  Being very close to the peasantry, the pastoral bishop had an enormous influence.  In practice he became its leader and was able to flout the often far-distant bishop whom he represented: this was particularly easy for him to do in times of universal disorder, when the authority on the spot was the only one which could hope to be obeyed.  The solution was obvious: these unruly subordinates ought to be replaced by a more modest structure, and this was to be the origin of the archdeacons; but to carry these ideas into practice a superior authority needed to be involved.  Here again the need for a strong Papacy made itself felt.

Consequently a very distinct trend became apparent, springing from several different sources, which tended to enhance the prestige of the Papacy.  It combined a touching expectancy and feelings of hope blended with love; men looked to this see where the successor of St Peter was still perhaps not sufficiently active or assertive, but where, it was felt, indestructible authority resided none the less.  This trend is particularly noticeable in some curious documents which were published at this time and which are known to history as the *False Decretals*.  By this title is understood a collection of apocryphal writings, undoubtedly fabricated by a spokesman of the reforming episcopate, which claimed to represent the ancient traditions of the Church with a very definite object in view.  This skilful forger is known by the pseudonym of Isidore Mercator; nothing is known about him.  We should not be over-hasty in damning his memory, for the folk of his own time had none of our modern respect for historical truth, and did not even see the necessity for it.  The lay-out is straightforward; there are two collections of papal decretals and conciliar decisions, the one compiled in Italy in the sixth century, by the well-known Denys the Little, and the other in seventh-century

---

[1] The institution of pastoral bishops had been made use of by the Anglo-Saxon missionaries during their apostolate.  It has even been said that they invented it.  In the ninth century the reformers within the Church waged a campaign against the pastoral bishops, and they gradually disappeared.  They survived longest in Germany and Ireland (until the twelfth century in Ireland).  The institution was unknown in Italy (owing to the large number of dioceses, each very small in area).  It was unknown in Spain.  There is only one known example in Anglo-Saxon England.  (Cf. Theodore Gottlob, *Der abendländische Chorepiskopat*, Bonn, 1928.)

Spain.   Isidore took these as the basis of his work.   He interpolated, faked, and mutilated the texts.   Because no documents of this kind existed prior to the fourth century he made up sixty covering the period between the death of St Peter and that of St Miltiades!   Then he later slipped thirty-five of his own crude productions in amongst the authentic texts.   And his contemporaries walked blindly into the trap.   It was eight hundred years before the hoax was discovered!

What were the exact intentions of this brilliant forger?   They were excellent.   He sought the reform of the Church.   He furbished arms for her defence against every danger that threatened her.   For instance, his texts demonstrated that the powers of the pastoral bishops were extremely restricted, in particular, that they could not administer the sacraments, and his influence in this direction was so great that from this time onwards the pastoral bishops vanished completely from the French scene.   To counter the metropolitans he declared that in olden days the primate, the Pope's direct representative, had possessed all the powers.   He fulminated threat upon threat against the feudal nobility and the secularizers of church property, threats that were all the more effective because they were represented as originating many centuries earlier.   And, above all, he reiterated the idea of recourse to Rome, of appeal to the Holy See.   He asserted the incontestable primacy of the successors of St Peter.   The tendency which had been so admirably manifested in the English Church,[1] the tendency to recognize the Pope not merely as a highly distinguished personage but as an authority embracing the whole Church in practical terms, was impressed upon men's minds by the enigmatic Isidore as an established, definite fact, which allowed no further argument.

Of course the Papacy did not need this falsehood to establish its authority, but it could no longer remain insensible of this trend towards it, a trend which this famous collection expressed so clearly.   In various documents emanating from the Roman Curia, it is even possible to trace some influence of the Isidorian texts.   Moreover did these forgeries not follow the direction of the doctrine which had been expanding logically ever since the Church's beginnings—the doctrine of the primacy of Rome?   These Isidorian writings are an interesting commentary on the fundamental psychology of Western Christendom, which, taken as a whole, longed for a strong Papacy.   Now it only needed a man of vigour to be raised to the Holy See for many things to change radically.

[1] On the Church in England and its close relations with Rome see Chapter IV, sections: 'The First Pontifical Missions: the Conversion of England' and 'St Boniface.'

## St Nicholas I (858–67): the First Great Medieval Pope

The Papacy's hour was about to sound. This might have happened ten years earlier, while St Leo IV (847–55) occupied the throne of St Peter; the *Liber pontificalis*, edited by Mgr Duchesne, says of him that 'he possessed in his heart both the wisdom of the serpent and the simplicity of the dove,' and Voltaire paid him this fine tribute in his *Essay on Morals*: 'He was a born Roman. The courage of the early days of the republic lived again in him, in a time of cowardice and corruption, like one of those splendid monuments of ancient Rome which we sometimes find rising above the ruins of the new.' But circumstances did not allow this remarkable man to show his full capacity. Because he was preoccupied in defending Rome against Saracen threats,[1] he could not impose his authority on the princes as he desired, for he had too much need of their help; at all events he anointed the young heir to Italy, Louis II, Lothaire's son, at Rome in 850. However, on many occasions he showed that he knew how to speak his mind fearlessly. After him,[2] unfortunately, the Church underwent a period of violent crisis: Anastasius, the antipope, all but supplanted Benedict III, the rightful Pope, a saintly but weak man, who was reviled even in his own apartments and who was only reinstated thanks to the wrath of the Roman people, who were hostile to the usurper. This violence so impressed him that he proved to be a timorous pope, and the three years of his pontificate marked a set-back for the Holy See's authority; the Gallic metropolitans took advantage of the opportunity to increase their autonomy. But at least he had the merit of picking out one young deacon of outstanding calibre from the Papal Curia. This was Nicholas, who became the Pope's secretary and who tried to instil some spirit of decision into him. In 858, on Benedict's death, Nicholas succeeded him.

He succeeded him, thanks to the support of the Carolingian authorities—to be precise, thanks to the support of Louis II of Italy, who imposed him upon the Roman clergy. At the very beginning people consequently imagined that this retiring clerk, whom they had seen making a few modest appearances at the windows of the Lateran,

---

[1] See section further on: 'Rome and the Saracen Danger.'

[2] It is between the reigns of Leo IV and Benedict III that a certain legend, which was current in the Middle Ages, and which later on was to be proclaimed by some Protestants and by the followers of Voltaire, claimed to place the two years of 'Pope Joan's' pontificate. There is now proof that there was an interval of only a few weeks between these two pontificates. As proof of this, some Roman coins bear the effigies of Benedict III and the Emperor Lothaire (who died 17th September 855); Leo IV only died on 17th July. There is an excellent restatement of this question by the Abbé Vacandard in his *Études de critique et d'histoire religieuse* (4th series, p. 15) which throws much light on various controversial subjects.

would be a creature of the imperial authority.    And when they saw the emperor according him the very same honours that the temporal leaders of old had accorded the spiritual leader, and which had not been seen since the time of Hadrian I—prostration, the pontiff's horse being led by the prince himself, on foot—they were convinced that this was all a kind of comedy and that the real suzerain here was the man who walked humbly at the horse's head.

They were wrong.    This priest, 'handsome of face, strict in his morals, and generous in his habits,' was true to that line of Romans who had occupied the papal throne in former times and who had known how to transpose the ancient Latin virtues on to the framework of the Christian ideal.    A worthy successor of St Leo the Great and St Gregory the Great, he hid a personality of extreme vigour beneath his rather modest appearance; he was a blade of steel which took care not to glitter unnecessarily, but which never bent.    He had the most exalted idea of this pontifical dignity with which God had willed that he should be invested; he looked beyond personal ambition, and was desirous of asserting a grandeur for which he felt himself responsible. He combined a marvellous wisdom with qualities of energy and courage; we have only to read the letter which he wrote to Boris, the king of the Bulgars, who had become a Christian, and who was seeking priests and advice from him, to see the extent to which this man surpassed his age, in this epoch of violence.[1]

Was he going to innovate as regards the functions of the Holy See, and inaugurate a new policy?   Of course not.   He had no need to do so.   His programme was to be that which the most clear-sighted of his predecessors had conceived, but he was about to breathe new vigour into it.   During the nine years of his pontificate every single formula stemmed directly from the tradition of St Peter, but his energy rendered these traditional formulae more effective and enlarged the scope of their application.   His aim was obvious: to place the pontifical authority above that of all the temporal powers, to insist that all recognized that it was his right to lead the world to a state of Christian order.

The situation favoured the Papacy's entry on to the political scene at this juncture.   During his pontificate the conclusive failure of the famous 'fraternity' which, illusory though it had been, had maintained the appearances of concord among Charlemagne's descendants, began to be recognized as an accomplished fact: its collapse inaugurated an era of crises, sordid intrigues, fratricidal treachery, and wars in which

---

[1] Here is a passage from this splendid document: 'Regarding those who reject the precious gift of the Christian faith, who sacrifice to idols and prostrate themselves before them, we can only advise you to lead them to the truth by exhortation, encouragement. and reasonable argument, rather than by force, which they will not understand.'

the various interests became inextricably tangled with one another, but whose only clear result was the conclusive decline of what had once been the glorious empire of the West. Lotharingia, the famous intermediate zone created by the Partition of Verdun, was yielding to the forces of division inherent in it, and was falling apart more and more day by day, thus throwing open the lists to every greedy power in the area. One of the kings had but to die, like Charles of Provence and Burgundy in 863, and one of his close relations would try to filch his heritage; in this particular case the operation was attempted by Charles the Bald. There was a perpetual play of alliances which knit together and fell apart again; of one power intervening in the territory of another; of combinations with the internal enemies of one's adversary. The imperial title, borne since the death of Lothaire I by his son, Louis II of Italy—who, as we shall see, was a vigorous and intelligent person, but who could only depend on Lombardy for support, in practice—had lost much of its importance. It goes without saying that all these factors greatly favoured the Pope, provided he was an energetic individual. There was one black spot: the Saracen threat, which, in forcing the Pope to appeal for the aid of Carolingian forces, left him with his hands not entirely free; but after the terrible raid of 846, when the Moslems had pillaged St Peter's, during the pontificate of Sergius II, their pressure slackened and the danger was no longer immediate. The Pope could now act.

And act he did, on every occasion that presented itself. The most characteristic of these actions, the one which shows most clearly how the straightforward affirmation of Christian principles could lead the Papacy to intervene on strictly political ground, was the affair concerning Lothaire II's divorce. On the religious plane this was a simple matter. Lothaire, sovereign of the territories between the Meuse and the Rhine, was a violent but quite intelligent young prince who had lived in a state of concubinage with a Lorraine noblewoman for some years, and had had children by her. For political reasons he married Theutburga, sister of the Burgundian Count Hubert, who as lay abbot of Saint-Maurice-en-Valais had made his monastery a place of unspeakably evil repute. After a few months Waldrada, who was jealous of the rightful queen, persuaded her lover to repudiate his wife and—this is a sorry sign of the relaxation in morals—Lothaire found his bishops quite prepared to acquiesce in this mournful operation. For reasons which remain just as obscure as those which, in certain twentieth-century countries, decide certain of the accused to acknowledge themselves utterly guilty, Theutburga confessed to countless sins which she swore she had committed with her rascal of a brother, and the marriage was annulled. But the rightful queen soon recovered herself and appealed to the Pope, supported by Hincmar of

Rheims.   Nicholas I unhesitatingly upheld the dethroned queen: he faced the king, affirmed the indissolubility of marriage, and ordered Lothaire to take back his wife.

But at the same time this affair was of vital importance to Western politics, for if Lothaire, who had no children by Theutburga, died without a legitimate heir, his heritage would probably be divided among his neighbours.   From this followed a hotchpotch of events and intrigues in which the uncles of the King of Lorraine played the role of good apostles, in which the Pope himself, while upholding the inviolability of Christian principles, never lost sight of the supreme interest of peace within Christendom.   In the midst of this imbroglio Nicholas I showed exactly of what stuff he was made; the most dreadful acts of violence did not succeed in intimidating this man of God, who one night crossed the Tiber alone in a boat in order to escape his enemies and take refuge in St Peter's.   Although threatened and reviled, he held firm.   Even defeat did not discourage him.   In the end Lothaire was obliged to take back his wife and, despite his wily attempts to twist the judgment, he never dared bring Waldrada back to Court; at the same time the Pope succeeded in preventing an implacable war from breaking out between the brothers, nephews, and uncles who were at enmity with one another.   At the Council of Rome in 865, at a time when the Norse invasions were playing havoc with the kings' authority, the head of the Church, who possessed no arms of his own, really appeared as the arbiter of Europe, whose judgments and reprimands the temporal rulers had to accept, whether they liked them or not: Nicholas I had triumphed by virtue of the spiritual power which he embodied, and nothing else.

The great Pope displayed the same unfaltering energy wherever he considered that the paramount interests of the Church were at stake. Even whilst he was struggling against the attacks of the Western princes, he resisted the Byzantine Court throughout his entire pontificate, as we shall see,[1] refusing to ratify the deposition of the patriarch Ignatius and his replacement by Photius, because he could not tolerate the imperial power's insolent interference in one of the Church's strictly internal affairs.

Within the very heart of this Church he worked with all his might and main to make men respect the pontifical authority, that pledge of order and of unity.   Hincmar himself was made to understand it; Hincmar, the powerful archbishop who was so proud of the prerogatives of his see; Hincmar, the great upholder of the metropolitans' semi-independence.   On every possible occasion Nicholas I made him feel that he too must understand that if the spiritual authority was to dominate, this authority sprang only from the Pope: he was to submit

[1] See the beginning of the next chapter.

to the Church or expect the worse.    The most important episode concerned the deposition of Bishop Rothad of Soissons, which Hincmar
had had pronounced by a provincial Council—and not without a
number of good reasons besides—but which the Pope judged to be
irregular.    Hincmar was ordered to release the bishop, and on being
threatened with suspension *a divinis*, was forced to execute the order.
Rothad had his episcopal insignia restored to him in Rome.    Against
the—prematurely Gallican—thesis of the authority of the provincial
Council and of the metropolitans, Nicholas I enforced the thesis of the
primacy of the Apostolic See.    This example was to be followed.

An analogous affair occurred in Italy, although there it was more
intermingled with political elements.    Archbishop John of Ravenna,
aided and abetted by his brother Gregory, proclaimed his see autonomous, confiscating all the surrounding dioceses, and, in addition,
oppressed and exploited the subjects of the Papal States.    When summoned to Rome John of Ravenna attempted to shirk the order;
Nicholas I had him condemned.    Louis II tried to make the inflexible
Pope give way on this matter, but all to no avail.    'Do you dare to
pride yourself on defending an excommunicate?' cried Nicholas I to
the emperor's envoys.    He then went to Ravenna in person, had John
expelled, and did restitution for the latter's injustices with such
courage that the archbishop yielded.

Thus, in nine short years singularly packed with incident, the great
Pope had placed the see of St Peter in a position such as it had never
before attained.    With the mortgage of Byzantine domination, which
had hung over it so long, removed completely, and the threat of vassal-
ization, with which the Carolingian Empire had threatened it, utterly
dissipated, the Papacy really emerged as the crowning-point of the
Christian world.    The principle which Nicholas loved to repeat prevailed: 'The things of the spirit triumph over the things of the world
inasmuch as the spirit is superior to the flesh.'    Contemporaries were
perfectly aware of the importance of this fact, and the wrath of his
enemies proves it: thus two archbishops belonging to Lothaire's party
dubbed Nicholas 'the man who calls himself Pope, who claims to be an
apostle among the apostles, and who sets himself up as the emperor of
the world.'    These protests were all in vain.    The logic of history,
helped by the circumstances in which the Carolingian Empire was
collapsing, demanded that in the midst of the danger the leader of
Christianity should assume such responsibilities.    Consequently
Nicholas I was the first Pope whom Western civilization completely
recognized as its guide; he was the first medieval Pope, the direct
spiritual ancestor of Gregory VII and Innocent III.    His pontificate
presaged the future conquests of the Papacy.    Undoubtedly this
success was exceptional in character and was principally due to the

vigour of his personality.    After his death anarchy soon gained the upper hand, and even the Church was to let herself be led astray by it. But the fact that the example had been set was of considerable importance, even though it was not to be followed.    'No pope since the blessed Gregory can be compared with Nicholas,' wrote Regino, the chronicler; 'he ruled over kings and tyrants, and he made them subject to his authority as if he were the master of the world.'

## REMAINS OF FORMER GLORY AND PROMISES FOR THE FUTURE

We have just seen the Church assuming the leadership of the West on the political plane.    There is another sphere in which this leadership is also apparent: in the field of scholarship.    Two equally serious questions confronted Europe at this period.    Fear that the general collapse would bring about the rapid destruction of all the brilliant results achieved by the 'Carolingian Renaissance' was a very real one; the fear that the break-up of the Empire into rival states might shatter the cultural unity of the West for ever was equally real.    These two dangers were both overcome.    Even amid the worst episodes of this age of increasing darkness, enough elements of light survived to enable the flame to leap up again later on from the embers which had been preserved.    And, despite the development of national antagonisms, the fundamental ideals survived, upon which medieval universalism would subsequently be built.

The Church's role was decisive in both these cases, and it is even true to say that the outcome was due to her alone.    It was she who assessed and proclaimed the importance of the things of the mind, in an epoch when outbreaks of violence made the laity's sole preoccupation with physical force pardonable; nothing is more moving than the plea addressed to Louis the Pious by the prelates meeting at Worms in 829, which begged him to maintain his interest in the schools and in intellectual pursuits 'so that the efforts of his father should not have been in vain.'    It was the Church also, who, in compelling not only adhesion to the same dogmas and the same moral laws everywhere but in using Latin as the liturgical and scholarly language, safeguarded unity at a time when the specialization of languages from area to area, going hand in hand as it did with the vague birth of a national consciousness, was in danger of destroying a truly European culture; if the difference between the autonomous nations, despite the sufferings for which it was responsible, ended in the development of a civilization beyond compare, this was primarily because the common foundations had been safeguarded, thanks to the work of the Church.

Moreover it is interesting to see that the clerical character of culture became even more pronounced at this period.    Very soon laymen, who, like Einhard, had belonged to the court of splendid minds at Aix-la-Chapelle, disappeared.   The only lay writer of any importance in this period was *Nithard* (grandson of Charlemagne through his mother, Bertha), who was the historian of the fratricidal wars and to whom we owe the actual text of the famous Declarations of Strasbourg.   This is easily understandable: absorbed in the administration and defence of their estates and in war and politics, the laity increasingly abandoned the pursuits of the mind.   The art of writing seemed the art of monks and priests: the word clerk, 'a member of the clergy,' came eventually to mean also 'an educated man.'   Amalarius, the deacon, went so far as to state that 'the only man who can be free to study, and who has the ability to do so, is he who neither marries nor possesses land and animals.'   Even the schools tended to specialize in producing young clerks.   These were the monastic schools for future novices, and the cathedral schools for future canons.   This trend did indeed encounter some resistance: certain reformers, St Benedict of Aniane in particular, showed a certain distrust of intellectual pursuits which they suspected of encouraging false pride; but this resistance was far from being decisive, and throughout the West the monastery became increasingly what it had been in a more modest sense after the Great Invasions: the haven of the mind, the citadel where the hopes of the future might find shelter.

The picture which has impressed historians the most, and which is engraven on all our minds, is that of these copyist-monks, who spent their lives covering their parchments with beautiful lines of Caroline script, decorating their capitals with tracery and pictures, sometimes inserting glorious inset-plates.   This patient and monotonous effort was really the basis of all intellectual development.   The standard which had been regained in Charlemagne's time was maintained. Thanks to the reproductions made by these ninth-century monasteries a goodly number of classical authors have come down to modern times; copies before this date are very rare.   Devoted attention was lavished on this work.   From Italy—that is to say, generally from Ravenna, Monte Cassino, or Bobbio, the Columbanian abbey, whose libraries were very rich in books—a precious manuscript, bought or borrowed, would arrive at Fleury, Tours, Saint-Gall, or Fulda; sometimes it was even one of those priceless works which had emerged from the copying-rooms of Antioch or Alexandria in bygone days, or one of the astonishing masterpieces whose secret only the Irish knew. This arrival was a great event.   It was more than this, it was a title to fame for the religious house concerned, and the teams of calligraphers would immediately set to work making copies which these famous workshops would later distribute far and wide.

Consequently the great intellectual names of this age are almost exclusively linked with the large abbeys.   Many bishops were indeed writers, but nearly every one of them was a former monk (Hincmar, for instance, came from Saint-Denis), and besides, their books were primarily works written for specific occasions, treatises on political morality or pastoral letters; Hincmar, who was a historian and who wrote the *Annales* of the Empire, was an exceptional case. On the other hand there was scarcely a single abbey of note that did not produce at least one or two men who, taking all the circumstances into consideration, can be considered important.

In the Germanic territories, both east and west of the Rhine, the great abbeys were fortresses of the mind: Fulda, custodian of St Boniface's tomb, influenced Hesse and Franconia; Corvey, the new Corbie, morally dominated Saxony; near Lake Constance, Saint-Gall, the Columbanian foundation, and Reichenau were such sound bastions that the last elements of Carolingian culture were to survive within their walls until the disasters of the tenth century. The great name at Fulda was that of *Rabanus* (c. 776–856), whose master, Alcuin, had nicknamed him *Maurus*, in memory of St Benedict's favourite disciple; a scholar of the monastery, then its librarian, and finally its abbot, he took part in all the great events of the age, and in all the theological disputes. Yet this did not prevent him from leaving us an enormous mass of original work, particularly commentaries on the Bible and monastic pedagogy, such as the *Education of Clerks*. At Reichenau the leading scholar was *Walafrid Strabo*, a fascinating and mystical mind whose *Visio Wettini* somewhat anticipates Dante's *Inferno*; his *Ordinary Commentary* was to be the Bible of scholasticism. At Saint-Gall, monastery of the famous chronicler of Charlemagne's pomp, glory, and legends, intellectual activity never ceased its growth, flowering right down the centuries, and producing *Notker*, a man who was certainly one of the masters of the chronicle and who has been declared by some to be the greatest of the German medieval poets.

Saint-Gall and Reichenau were in Lothaire's territory; their principal intellectual competitor was Lyons, which was extremely important. Three names glittered there: Bishop Agobard, whose enthusiasm, although inclined to be tendentious, was very infectious; following in his footsteps was Amalarius, an impassioned commentator on the Scriptures and the liturgy, whose symbolism reaches heights of ecstasy; but the deacon Florus, on the other hand, was an extremely learned man, with a very precise type of mind, who was a formidable dialectician.

In western France there were numerous illustrious abbeys: Saint-Denis, Ferrières in Gâtinais, Saint-Martin of Tours, and Saint-Benoît-sur-Loire; Jumièges and Saint-Wandrille in Normandy, Saint-Riquier, Saint-Bertin, and above all Corbie, were all famous, and all possessed their outstanding intellectual figures. At Ferrières there was Servatus Lupus. The more one studies his personality, the more obvious it is that he was one of the great ninth-century humanists. At Corbie there was Paschasius Radbert, whose studies on the *Body and Blood of Christ* were a fundamental element in the theological disputes concerning the Eucharist. One of the greatest scholars, and certainly the most penetrating and controlled mind of the epoch, was *John the Scot, surnamed Erigena*, apparently because he had been born in Ireland. He probably lived from about 815 to about 877. His written work was immense. He studied the Eucharist as well as pre-destination, he translated the Pseudo-Denys the Areopagite, he set forth a system of the universe: his *De divisione naturae* took up the old Neo-Platonic ideas again and was tinged with a kind of pantheism which, in the thirteenth century, was to cause John the Scot's condemnation in the works of his successors. But this should not make us forget that he was unquestionably one of the intellectual animators of his time.

Paradoxical though this seems, it can consequently be said that not only did the intellectual 'renaissance' of Charlemagne's time continue for some seventy years after his death, but that it bloomed even more brilliantly—before being blotted out at the end of the century. On considering this intellectual activity as a whole, one is impressed by the universal curiosity contained therein, by the variety of aptitudes and talents. Obviously wholly religious studies dominated it. Theology was still not properly distinguishable from philosophy, but men like Paschasius Radbert had already a nice understanding of the direction which should be taken. Moral science was important, and especially political morality, and its principles were judiciously set forth to their sovereigns by various saintly scholars in their *Princes' Mirrors*: the *Royal Road*, written by Smaragdus, abbot of Saint-Mihiel, is an example of these. Exegesis was studied too, and here, far in advance of his own time, *Christian of Stavelot* put forward the remarkable idea that the allegorical explanation of the Scriptures was not sufficient, and that it was necessary to rest them upon as accurate an historical explanation as possible. Of course hagiography flourished: the lives of the saints were re-edited (and often altered, to suit the taste of the day). What they lost in fidelity to the truth they gained in elegance of style. But alongside these religious branches of learning, all the others were studied too. There was poetry, particularly poetry written in the Germanic tongue. Three major works, the *Heliand*, the *Muspilli* or *End of the World*, and the *Book of the Gospels*, are considered to be the beginnings of German literature. In mathematics the computation of the ecclesiastical calendar was the principal preoccupation, but men also translated and commented on Euclid's geometry and Nicomachus's arithmetic. Regarding natural sciences, whilst zoology was full of poetic fantasy—the unicorn being taken as seriously as the lion or the horse—botany, on the other hand, was quite advanced, particularly as regards the study of vegetables, for the monks, being vegetarians, were well acquainted with these.[1] In geography attempts were made to enlarge the field of knowledge, and there is one treatise which talks authoritatively of the Faroes and Thule (Iceland?). Was there any subject in which these men were not interested? A monk named Hubald even composed a poem on baldness, whose fundamental theme was that all geniuses are bald; his enthusiasm on this matter was so great that every noun in his poem was made to begin with the letter C, the initial of *calvus*!

Was this the sport of a few scholars? A literature of clerks and superior beings? Not at all. All these great monasteries possessed, in a high degree, an appreciation of their responsibility as civilizing agents, and they strove valiantly to make the dogma and morality contained in the Gospels penetrate the souls of the masses. Before the catastrophe of the Norse invasions, the influence of abbeys like Corbie or Jumièges or Saint-Benoît-sur-Loire was immense. In the Germanic territories the monks' habit of translating the baptismal formula, the principal prayers, and the blessings, into the vulgar tongue greatly contributed to developing and fixing the *lingua theodisca*, the 'thiot,' the future 'deutsch.' [2]

And if literary activity resisted the progressive collapse of Carolingian society in this way, the arts were not abandoned either. They even made fresh progress. *Music*, which had made great strides following the development of the Gregorian chant, was enriched by new formulae. Notker, the monk-poet of Saint-Gall, who was also an excellent musician, developed the *sequence*, a series of notes which expressed the gladness of the alleluia, and which were set to words. Some of these sequences—such as the Easter sequence, where the springtime gives thanks for the resurrected Lord—possess an exquisite charm: the liturgy of the Middle Ages was to cherish this kind of music very dearly. A little later on, in the same monastery, Tutilo had the

---

[1] It has been noticed that the majority of the German names of flowers and fruits come from the Latin: *Frucht* (fructus), *Pflange* (plante), *Rübe* (rapa), *Kohl* (carilis), *Lattich* (lactuca), *kürbis* (cucurbita), etc. This is due to the influence of the monks.

[2] It should be noticed that in ninth-century Italy the intellectual movement retained a rather special character. The bishops, who were very numerous and very powerful, controlled the country beyond the Alps; being deeply involved in political affairs they did not devote themselves much to cultural matters. The great intellectual centres were either monasteries like Bobbio or Monte Cassino, or the Papal Court, where the librarian *Anastasius* exercised considerable (but always good) influence under several popes, and Ravenna which, being extremely proud of its past, was anxious to remain a place of scholarship. On the whole, the peninsula does not display the enthusiastic intellectual vigour that is found in Germany, Lotharingia, and France. Aside from the *Liber pontificalis*, a collection of papal biographies, which ceased in 891, it appears to have produced no work of real merit.

idea of introducing to the West the Byzantine *motets* which are inter-spersed amid the liturgy: the Introit, the Kyrie, and the Offertory of the Mass thus had their words developed, repeated, multiplied, borne aloft on the powerful wings of melody.    The new style was built upon the ancient traditions and several of its elements have survived into modern times.

In architecture, the ninth century displays the same characteristics which we have already noted in Charlemagne's glorious reign—the same straining towards the future, the same feeling of questing and groping for perfection.    The plan based on the Greek church—used in the Palatine chapel at Aix and at Germigny-des-Prés—was tending to disappear; except when it attained the ambitious boldness of St Sophia, this style was unsuitable for housing the enormous monastic communities which were the principal builders.    Consequently the ancient basilical plan was now to predominate, henceforth including the transept, so that the whole plan inscribed the shape of a cross upon the ground; sometimes, as at Aniane, Saint-Riquier, and Saint-Gall, there were so many monks that one choir was not enough.    Here that at the east end was given a counterpart at the west end, and in order to satisfy the taste for perfect symmetry this led the monks to build a second transept: this type of double transept, which originated in the East, made a brief appearance in the West around the sixth cen-tury and then disappeared, to reappear in the age of Carolingian de-cline.    The choirs were raised in order to shield the monks from the distractions of the public.    In front of the city churches that were not monastic an atrium separated the nave from the noises in the street outside.    As regards roofs, the cupola continued to be used in churches built on the Greek plan, but there were still flat wooden roofs too, and the vault, which had returned to the West three centuries earlier, began to undergo a great development; the splendid tower above the cross of the transept appeared almost everywhere, and often, though still not part of the main building, watch-towers too, dedicated to St Michael and St Gabriel, the archangels of battle.

All these churches were decorated, no longer with mosaics but with mural paintings, and with painted panels and stained glass.    The tragedies of this epoch and of those that followed it have prevented these delicate productions from surviving into our own day.    But we can obtain some idea of their artistry by looking at the miniatures which enrich the manuscripts of the period.    Here this wonderful art which had attained such splendid results during the great reign produced some veritable masterpieces.    Its themes expanded, its techniques multiplied, and each monastery produced a different style. At Saint-Martin the inspiration was either classical or derived from the first centuries of Christianity; at Saint-Gall Lombard and Anglo-Saxon influences intermingled; at Saint-Denis, where the teachers were Irish, there was a loyalty to delicate tracery motifs and to abstract design.   Certain productions of this period, such as Charles the Bald's Bible in Paris, the Saint-Gall Psalter, or the 'manuscript of Ada' at Trèves are really most wonderful things.   What is so astonishing, and what often gives these miniatures their own strange charm, is that the artists cut themselves quite free from nature, that they used colour according to their liking and not in accordance with the truth —violet, scarlet, or green horses, faces or hair of purple and emerald; all this, most certainly, with some symbolic intention.   As for sculpture, it continued to be confined to ivory-work, and is particularly marked in the bindings for liturgical books.   But in this field its beauty, although moving, was still rather clumsy.

It is quite clear that all this activity constitutes a bright ray of hope in the picture of an age where pessimism seems to be the ruling spirit.   Naturally the intellectual life of the ninth century cannot be judged by our modern standards; it is the philosophy and art of an adolescent and still naïve society, fumbling between a slavish imitation of the past and excessively bold experiment, but it contains creations which foreshadow the greatness of the future.   The great historian Gustav Schnürer, who understood the interest of these little-known times so well, writes: 'The ninth century left behind it one of the foundations of the future development of intellectual and artistic civilization.'   But he immediately adds, with equal justice, that, unhappily, 'progress in these two fields does not necessarily mean an equal progress in other fields, particularly in that concerning morals, and a moral decline can easily lead to a decline in scholarship and the arts.'   The immediate future was to prove this only too well.

## ROME AND THE SARACEN DANGER

When the great Pope Nicholas I closed his eyes for the last time, in 867, the symptoms of a change in the Church's position, and the premonitory signs of the approaching collapse, soon became obvious. Truth to tell, the extremely majestic picture portrayed by Christianity during his pontificate had had its darker side.   Without mentioning either the disturbing situation which was created to the north and west of the Alps by the virtual antagonism of the two 'Francias,' each of which was equally tempted by the Lotharingian territories, or the Norse threat which showed no signs of diminishing, the Papacy had many serious anxieties much nearer home.   Italy, which Charlemagne and then Louis the Pious had had to supervise very closely, was sliding into anarchy.   Torn between the south, which depended on Byzantium, and the north, which was subject to the Franks (except for

Venice, which was still Byzantine), governed in the central provinces by a papal administration whose powers were far from being undisputed, and by the Lombard Duke of Benevento who dreamed of recovering his former authority, she, too, was, like the rest of the continent, much troubled by the fever of feudalism; the local nobles, the towns, and even, sometimes, the politician bishops, were all trying to go their own separate ways.    This anarchy might verge upon treason: we shall see the Neapolitans inviting the Arabs into the peninsula, on being attacked by the Lombards.

Moreover in Rome itself the internal situation remained extremely delicate.    The various factions which had been muzzled by Charlemagne's heavy hand were engaged in complex intrigues.    To them the papal election was of vital importance; if a slightly weak pope should succeed Nicholas I troubles would become possible again. Besides, the very status of the Papal States contained an inherent ambiguity; did the Pope exercise absolute sovereignty there, in other words, could be himself order the arrest of any troublesome nobles, or must he refer them to the Carolingian kings, especially the one who reigned from Pavia?    Various treaties and constitutions, in 816 and 824, had tried very hard to settle this delicate question, but had been unable to do so completely: on this point again everything depended on the personal authority, or rather, the vigour, of the Pope.

Finally, and above all, there was the Saracen danger.    At this period the Moslem Empire was in a state of decay, but its different fragments remained formidable, nevertheless.    Whilst the Ommayad emirs of Cordova were terrorizing the western Mediterranean with their corsairs, a new dynasty was reigning in Tunisia, in the holy city of Kairwan, the Aghlabite dynasty, sprung from the Ibrahim-ben-Aghlab who had successfully revolted against Haroun-al-Raschid.    Its followers very soon came to consider Sicily and southern Italy as their hunting-ground.    From 826 their raids ravaged the island.    They were halted in front of Syracuse, but caused much damage; in 831 they took Palermo; in 839, Messina; then, in 859, they occupied the centre of the island, including the Byzantine strongpoint of Castrogiovanni; aside from Taormina, which did not fall until the beginning of the tenth century, the whole of Sicily was now to pass under the yoke of Islam, and this would leave a profound mark upon her.

The straits of Messina were clearly not enough to halt the conquerors' impetus.    All the more so since the disunity of the Christians on the mainland made their task far easier.    The Neapolitans called the Moslems into the country in 836, to help them against the Lombards.    Although the newcomers did indeed 'liberate' the splendid port, they took advantage of the opportunity to establish themselves at Taranto, and when the Byzantines from Venice tried to succour the place the Moslems retorted by a lightning raid along the whole length of the Adriatic which, after the destruction of Ancona, brought them as far as the mouth of the Po.    In 840 another act of Christian treachery delivered Bari into their hands and henceforth, going up the Apennine valleys, the Saracens undertook a series of plundering raids which reached right into the heart of central Italy, whilst their corsairs, who were established in the Ponza archipelago, made pirate attacks all round the coasts.    In 846 the tragedy acquired a character so striking that men felt quite overwhelmed by it.    The infidels disembarked at the mouth of the Tiber, seized Porto and Ostia, travelled up the right bank of the river and pillaged the basilica of St Peter's, which was then outside the city walls.    A counter-attack by the Romans failed: King Louis II was also beaten; only the thickness of the ancient walls of the city made the attackers decide to withdraw, taking their sacrilegious plunder with them.    The de-fenders' sole consolation was the subsequent news that, like the army of Pharaoh in bygone days, the enemy expedition had been swallowed up by the stormy sea, a sure sign of heaven's intent.

The tragedy of 846 had terrified all who were alive at the time; its memory was to survive in the *chanson de geste* entitled *The Destruction of Rome*.    It was looked upon as a divine warning.    The emperor had ordered the levying of special taxes to pay for the restoration of the apostolic basilica, and from 848 onwards Leo IV had undertaken the construction of enormous defensive walls which were planned to protect St Peter's and which, when extended as far as the castle of St Angelo, joined the whole of this outlying district to the city proper: this was the *Leonine City*, whose magnificent remains can still be seen to-day, especially the well-known *Leonine tower* which dominates the Vatican gardens.    No matter: despite all these precautions the thought of a possible Saracen return hung heavy on Rome.    A pope like Nicholas I was not the kind of man to allow his policy to be mort-gaged by this threat; but a weaker successor had only to be impressed by it, and many things would quickly change.

*Hadrian II* (867–72) was certainly not the equal of his great pre-decessor.    It is not quite true to say that he put himself 'at the emperor's beck and call,' as has been suggested,[1] but he was certainly very far from possessing Nicholas the Great's inflexible intransigence. Lame and one-eyed, with absolutely no physical or social graces, this self-effacing, charitable, and kindly man wanted to 'complete with sweetness what Nicholas had begun with severity.'    But this was hardly the attitude to take when one was faced with the ravening beasts who occupied the thrones of Europe at this time.    Moreover, although personally beyond reproach, Hadrian was bespattered by a

[1] Halphen.

scandal concerning his private life; although he had been a priest for twenty-five years when he was elected pope, Hadrian had nevertheless been married before being ordained and, somewhat unexpectedly, he allowed his wife and daughter to live in the papal palace; when the latter was abducted by a young nobleman named Eleutherius, the Pope was forced to ask Louis II to intervene against the seducer, an extremely painful situation for a pope! To crown this misfortune, the scandal ended in a very tragic way: Eleutherius murdered his mistress and his quasi-mother-in-law, the daughter and the wife of the Pope! It goes without saying that Hadrian's prestige was not enhanced by this tragedy.

Understandably enough, all the men in the Church who had hoped to continue Nicholas I's work and policy were greatly troubled. 'Now,' wrote Anastasius the librarian, on the morrow of Nicholas's death, 'all those whom he punished for adultery or other sins, are working enthusiastically to destroy everything he did, and to suppress everything he ordered.' This Anastasius, who was an otherwise rather troublesome character, a kind of Talleyrand of the Vatican, had at least the ability to see things clearly. In actual fact Hadrian's attitude cannot be criticized in any way, in the sense that he never disowned his predecessor's work. Lothaire II was even made to swear that he would have no more illicit relations with his concubine; after which the Pope showed him, prettily enough, but without excessive demonstration, that he was forgiven. But it was quite obvious that the mighty authority which Nicholas I had managed to give the Apostolic See was fast slipping away.

This was shown all too obviously after Lothaire II's death in 869, when his uncles, Charles the Bald and Louis the German, wanted to gather in his heritage. The Carolingian in France acted quickest. He had himself crowned king at Metz four weeks later. There was great danger that he would also try to seize the imperial throne from Louis II, the King of Italy, who alone was capable of defending the peninsula against the Saracens. At all events, in 870, the two brothers, the German and the Frenchman, came to an understanding at Meersen whereby they agreed on the literal dismemberment of the dead sovereign's lands, without any regard for equity, nor for the general interest. When the Pope courageously raised his voice on behalf of Louis II's territorial rights, Charles gave the violent Hincmar the task of replying to him. He did this in words of almost unbelievable insolence. Among other things he told the Pope that policy was made by sword-blows and not excommunications, and that 'if ecclesiastical matters are the Pope's province, political affairs are the king's!' Ideas had certainly changed a great deal in the space of three years!

Consequently, the pontificate of Hadrian II marks a return to the temporal power's offensive against the spiritual authority. The situation made anything else impossible. A military force was indispensable to resist the Saracen danger which was growing ever greater in central and southern Italy, and the gentle Hadrian knew this better than anyone. This indispensable force was made incarnate in the person of *Louis II*.

This little-known Carolingian is a splendid and attractive figure. For thirty years he faced every danger with unfaltering vigour, and we can see and admire in him much of the spirit of the Crusaders of a later age. He was born in 822, the eldest son of Lothaire I, who gave him, at the age of twenty-two, the actual viceroyalty of Italy, with the title of 'king of the Lombards,' and this he completed in 850 by associating his son with him upon the imperial throne. Louis was passionately attached to the ancient peninsula, which well deserved his love, and he scarcely ever left it until his death (in 875). When the demands of strategy were not summoning him to the coast of Benevento, he resided at Pavia, the magnificent Lombard capital, and whenever he was forced to depart to the wars, his wife, the energetic and beautiful Engelberga, took over the reins of government, suppressing trouble-makers, or negotiating with his troublesome Carolingian relatives. The man whom Hincmar disdainfully dubbed 'the Emperor of Italy' was in fact the last great king in the peninsula, and it was to take history a thousand years to replace him.

The thirty years of his reign were one long battle against countless enemies, and the most formidable of these were not always those who fought him openly. He must needs be continually on horseback, crushing rebellions, punishing traitors, driving the invaders out of the peninsula. All the time he was in danger of being stabbed in the back by some Lombard duke of Benevento, or even by a bishop or by one of his uncles or brothers. His very title, the imperial title which Pope Leo IV had conferred upon him in 850—in other words, four years after the pillaging of Rome—because he alone was capable of fighting Islam, was hotly contested. The other imperial throne, at Byzantium, now occupied by a man of some stature, Basil I, the founder of the Macedonian dynasty, refused to consider the throne of Pavia as its equal. Louis II was obliged to remonstrate with an energy worthy of Charlemagne that, consecrated by the Rome of St Peter, heir to the old Rome, he was a more lawful emperor than the Basileus of the 'new Rome'—this questionable Easterner who did not even know how to talk correct Latin!

Deeply religious and acutely sensible of his responsibilities towards Christendom, Louis II, unlike his grandfather, was absolutely con-vinced of the necessity for a crusade. He was quite sure that Islam must be driven right out of Europe. In 847 he halted the Arabs decisively near Benevento, and in 852 he crushed their offensive in southern Italy. From 866 until 871 he never left southern Italy, directing many difficult operations in person, now victorious, now in danger, striving everywhere with all his might and main to strike at the Moslems. His principal aim was the recapture of the great Saracen base of Bari. For four years he fought for this, going so far as to negotiate the support of the Byzantine fleet, neutralizing the Duke of Benevento, and finally taking the stronghold by direct assault at the head of his troops. In this often distressing ninth-century world few men were as conscious of their royal duties as he was.

What was the Pope's attitude to an outstanding man like this? Ever since he became king, Louis had always exercised those prerogatives at Rome which were his according to a treaty of 824; on Leo IV's death in 855 he had exercised an extremely vigorous right of control over the papal election, even demanding that the ballot which had elected Benedict III be taken again, because his prior agreement had not been sought. Three years later the deacon Nicholas had quite openly been his candidate, and relations between the emperor and the new Pope had at first been extremely affectionate; the personal affection remained, but we know that Nicholas I resisted many imperial undertakings and that there were numerous disagreements between these two strong characters. This was no longer so in the case of Hadrian. Although elected during Louis II's absence and without imperial pressure, the worthy Pope was filled with such anguish at the thought of the Saracen danger, that any ruler capable of warding it off had his every confidence and favour. On all possible occasions he sang the praises of him who 'so far from wasting his forces in fratricidal wars against fellow Christians, fights for the defence of the Church, for the safety and security of the Apostolic See, and for the deliverance of the faithful.' Thus, during the third quarter of the ninth century the situation seemed to be reverting to something of what it had been in the time of Charlemagne; was the effective direction of Christendom about to return to the emperors? The balance between the two powers remained uncertain; everything depended on the personalities of the men occupying the thrones of St Peter and Charlemagne.

In reality all these recent achievements were extremely fragile. Nicholas I's attempt to build a spiritual hegemony had been successfu only because he was an exceptional man: although it provided a fine example for the future, it could have no immediate future and Hadrian II's pontificate had proved this. As for the emperor, despite his steadfastness, and despite his claims to suzerainty over his uncles' realms, how could he ignore the fact that his power was confined to Italy and did not extend a foot beyond it? When, on the death of his brother, Lothaire II, Charles the Bald and Louis the German dismembered the dead man's lands between them, Louis could not raise the most meaningless protest. Worse followed. In August 871 Louis had the misfortune to be taken prisoner during a riot in Benevento. On being freed, the luckless king saw that, believing him to be dead, his uncles had immediately positioned themselves ready to attack his territories. His brave wife, Engelberga, had no resources left, save the hope of setting one of these possible aggressors against the other. Hadrian died while all this was taking place; Louis followed him to the grave in 875, right in the prime of life, but sick of a world which no longer seemed to contain anything save hate, sordid greed, and treachery. The forces of disintegration which had been attacking the Empire ever since the great Charles's death, were now very near to triumph.

## THE FINAL EFFORT OF AN AGED POPE

It was now that the Pope tried to face the situation once more. The new Pope was a very old man, *John VIII* (872–82). He had held important offices in the Roman Curia for at least forty years past; he had been Nicholas I's private adviser and had been sorely distressed by Hadrian II's weakness. From the moment that he was elected, he displayed outstanding vigour, despite his advanced years—he was about seventy years old when he became pope, which was considered a great age in those days. When the Saracens landed at Terracina, that is to say, a good twenty-five miles from Rome, the Pope led the charge against them in person, captured eighteen of their ships, and took six hundred prisoners, drowning their insolent attack in a bath of blood.

An exploit like this could not be repeated very often. Italy needed a protector, for the death of Louis II now robbed her of the man who had defended her so well. The succession question had particularly serious implications: the safety of the whole peninsula might depend upon the choice of emperor, and on the general policy which he adopted. It must be emphasized that this choice belonged to the Pope alone. Various precedents, especially that of the coronation of Louis II, had conclusively settled this tradition. Since the Empire did not possess any succession law, and since Charles the Bald and Louis the German might lay equal claim to the crown of Charlemagne, the entire West accepted the fact that the final decision lay with the Pope.

John VIII chose the sovereign of France, Charles the Bald. Why? Was it because this educated individual, who was a devout and right-thinking Christian and one well versed in the theological matters of the day, knew exactly how to win a priest over to his party? This was not the only reason. Charles had also demonstrated that he could be energetic and courageous; he had given clear evidence of his fortitude and initiative in several almost hopeless situations. The Pope invited him to come to Rome at once. Charles in fact had not bothered to wait for the invitation before starting on his journey. At Christmas 875 Charles was consecrated emperor there, seventy-five years to the very day after his grandfather's coronation.

The first step in a long considered policy had been taken. Immediately afterwards the Pope took another. By using all the resources of diplomacy, manœuvring against the Italian nobility, against the courageous Engelberga, Louis II's widow, and against Carloman, the son of Louis the German, he managed to gain for Charles the crown of Pavia. This indicated a new notion of the Empire. It now comprised both Italy and France, on an equal footing; consequently the emperor had an immediate personal interest in defending the peninsula; and it followed that the Empire would become more and more Roman in character.

It was a remarkable plan. Unhappily events were not to permit this splendid scheme to become a reality. How could Charles the Bald's kingdom possibly be controlled with the firmness that circumstances demanded, straddling the Alps as it did? In France, the new emperor was at grips with numerous difficulties. The Norsemen were increasing their attacks there, and Charles, in his turn, was giving up the idea of fighting them, preferring instead to buy their withdrawal with gold, the gold of the *tributum normannicum*, which was deservedly unpopular. The nobles, who were annoyed at being forced to participate in the Italian expeditions, were agitating violently, despite all the pains to which the emperor had gone, at the assembly at Quierzy (877), to explain the new concept of the Empire to them, and their agitation soon turned into a rebellion headed by the most important men in the kingdom. Finally, since this notion of the Empire naturally displeased Louis the German and his sons, various wars broke out of which the most important ended in Charles's defeat before Coblenz. His authority was contested in Italy itself. The great feudal lords, such as the Duke of Spoleto, behaved exactly as they pleased, and those in the south, like the dukes of Naples and Amalfi, were solely interested in making money either through trade or through piracy and took not the slightest notice of the Frankish king.

The support which John VIII had believed he was acquiring was poor indeed!

However, he did not despair. He strove most doggedly to form a united front against the Saracens, and he pathetically begged Charles to hasten to Italy, where their raids had again been on the increase since 877. Treachery multiplied all around him. The Duke of Spoleto, who was theoretically the 'protector' of Rome, was pursuing an entirely personal policy which aimed at his own domination of the

* Q

city. Formosus, the Bishop of Porto, a mixture of fervent ascetic and cunning intriguer, made famous by the mission to the king of the Bulgars, with which Nicholas I had entrusted him, but also furious at not having been made patriarch of the Bulgars, nor even ... pope, fabricated plot after plot in alliance with Engelberga, the widowed empress; the southern despots indulged in treason to their hearts' content, defying excommunication, continually linking arms with the Saracens until matters reached such a pass that Naples was currently known as 'a second Palermo, a second Africa.' In the end John VIII had almost succeeded in forming some kind of coalition against the Saracens, by dint of every kind of guile, negotiation, and promise, when everything collapsed: in the autumn of 877 Charles the Bald had barely crossed the Alps when sickness laid him low; he died miserably in a tiny hamlet whose site is now lost.

Providence seemed to be against John. However, the aged Pope never allowed himself to be disheartened. An emperor! An emperor was urgently needed! In other words, a protector. But who could it be? The situation was a shocking one. In Rome, the Duke of Spoleto, aided and abetted by the Marquis of Tuscany, was exercising a reign of terror; John VIII, who was shut up in St Peter's, was practically cut off from Christendom. He managed to escape, and, taking the sea route—the land route was impossible—made for France, determined to seek a king there. Alas! Disappointment after disappointment awaited him. Two of the four Carolingians upon whom he was counting were sick men: Carloman, the son of Louis the German, and the Frenchman, Louis the Stammerer. On being restored to health, the latter was forewarned of the Pope's intention and made his escape: this son of Charles the Bald, this greatgrandson of Charlemagne, was 'simple and gentle and loved only peace.' Count Boso, who was related to the royal family by marriage, also declined the dubious honour of wielding the sceptre of the West, and took himself off to occupy Burgundy and Provence, where he carved himself a comfortable little kingdom which was virtually independent.[1] In short, there was only one possible candidate: Charles the Fat, the son of Louis the German, who was a feeble-minded epileptic. John VIII resigned himself to anointing him as emperor, for want of any better candidate (881).

For a brief moment it looked as if the mere presence of this one tiny girder of strength might enable the union that was so vital to be re-created around the imperial idea. By a curious freak of chance this nonentity was to rebuild the unity of the Empire to his own advantage, for his own two brothers were dead, and in France, where two of

[1] Boso, who did not lack a certain sense of humour, prefaced his acts with this unexpected phrase: 'I, Boso, who am what I am by the grace of God!'

Louis the Stammerer's sons had vanished likewise, the great nobles who were disposing of the crown preferred the far-off Germanic king to a French sovereign, even though the latter might be only a young posthumous child. What an irony of history: just as it was on the point of collapse Charlemagne's Empire seemed to be reviving.

Let the imperialists take courage! and the aged Pope forthwith redoubled his efforts. The Saracen raids were beginning again. This time, acts of treachery were patently obvious: the duke-bishop of Amalfi, a bizarre character who foreshadows the subtle and savage adventurers of the Renaissance period, had established the Arabs at the foot of Vesuvius. The city of Gaeta went even further: it, too, called in the Saracens and hurled them into papal territory. Charles the Fat, as might have been expected, proved a disappointment. He took no action against anyone, neither against the Duke of Spoleto, who was a permanent menace, nor against the Saracens. The only enemy that he deigned to fight at all was Boso, the King of Provence, who, however, resisted the Carolingian enemies very strongly indeed. All in vain the aged Hincmar of Rheims increased his pleas for a revival of the former imperial ideal. The well-informed Norsemen were making raid after raid; all over the West feudal anarchy grew greater year by year. Charles the Fat behaved deplorably as regards the Norsemen, being afraid to do battle with them in front of Paris, which was heroically defended by its inhabitants. He was in process of abandoning all idea of aiding Italy, when he was taken mortally sick.

In circumstances like these, the Pope's surrender to distress is well understandable. 'We have sought the light,' he wrote, 'and have found nothing but darkness! We are in desperate need of help, for we dare not even go beyond the walls of the city, so frightful are the ravages there! And no help is forthcoming, either from the emperor, our spiritual son, or from anyone else, anywhere.'

Then, faced with this appalling situation, John VIII thought of a solution. He found it in the very core of his faith, inspired by nothing less than the Holy Spirit Himself. It was an idea which proved that this elderly Pope, who has been so often vilified, carried a spark of genius within his soul. He decided to appeal to the conscience of all *Christendom*. Until now this word had simply been synonymous with Christianity, i.e. the doctrine of the Christians. John, however, understood and used it as signifying 'the Christian community,' the temporal society of the Christians which is quickened by the spiritual Christian society. He discovered and formulated this demand for a collective responsibility of baptized folk, an idea which was to be one of the foundations of medieval society. *Christendom!* It was a rallying cry, a call to alliance; and alliances are always made against something and someone. John VIII was at least one hundred and fifty years in advance of his time in sensing the idea of Christendom rather as we sense it to-day. And 'in defence of Christendom,' he decided to appeal to the one state which still counted for something: Byzantium. It was an immensely serious decision for the Church to make: for at this moment, controlled by the ambitious Photius, whom the Papacy had been resisting ever since the time of Nicholas I, the Eastern Church had just proclaimed (13th March 880) the principle of Byzantium's sovereignty over Rome. The threat of schism was contained therein.[1] Despite this fact, John VIII was convinced that Byzantine might alone, now so soundly restored by the Macedonians and so firmly established in Bari, could halt the Saracen advance. The diplomatic manœuvre succeeded—and, had its success been prolonged, who knows whether it might not have prevented the rupture between the two churches? Led by the eminent strategist, Nicephorus Phocas, the Byzantine fleets dealt the Saracens some deadly blows. The small disloyal southern principalities were made subject to the Basileus. By his vigour, by the extraordinary inventiveness of his diplomatic tactics, and by his remarkable insight into the requirements of the future, the aged Pope had saved Italy from the Saracen threat.

But the results of this policy were not achieved until after his death. During the last days of his life he believed that all was lost: in a letter to the Empress Richarda he foresaw that the infidels would soon bear him into captivity, and perhaps murder him . . . Hincmar, the tireless herald of Carolingian glory, died on Christmas Eve 882, at Épernay, having been forced to flee there when Rheims was seized by the Norsemen. Although southern Italy was to be delivered from the Saracen peril by Byzantium, the West was in a state of festering decay and the old Pope knew this intuitively. In the early weeks of 883 a ghastly report spread across Europe. A plot had been formed against John VIII at the end of the previous year, fomented by those whom the pontiff was seeking to purge. The conspirators had succeeded in making him take poison, but seeing that the effects of this were too long delayed, they had finished the old man off by battering him to death with hammer blows. Thus ended the tragic and heroic life of the last ninth-century pope who possessed any understanding of the need for a united West, and who had also been the first pope in history to grasp the meaning of Christendom. Is it not fitting to render some tribute to this almost unknown figure?

## DARKNESS FALLS OVER THE WEST

The last fifteen years of the ninth century marked the final downfall of the great Carolingian dream and the triumph of darkness. It

---

[1] See the first section of the next chapter.

seemed as if all the forces of death were joining hands to destroy the still extremely fragile structure of Western civilization, and, in particular, the two foundation-stones upon which it had sought to rise: the Papacy and the Empire. Society was falling apart: morals disintegrated still further. This decline was quite unlike the slow-moving process of decay which had taken place during the last days of the Roman Empire. It was a bloody and brutal death-agony, full of violent shudders, although this in itself afforded some hope of a subsequent resurrection.

All the dangers which had hung heavy upon the world ever since the great emperor's death were now set loose. Moreover others were added to them. Barbarism threatened everywhere. The Norsemen, who were encountering resistance on all sides, seemed to be redoubling their efforts. In 881 they earned themselves a title to fame by occupying Aix, destroying the palace, and using the famous chapel as a stable. Certain Western leaders covered themselves with glory simply by daring to resist these plunderers. One of these was the twenty-year-old French ruler, Louis III, the son of Louis the Stammerer, who halted them for a time on the Somme. Another was Eudes of Paris, who saved the capital with the help of Bishop Goscelinus. But these partial defeats did not stop the bands of raiders permanently. Their boldness was boundless. The Saracens, who were contained in southern Italy, multiplied their attacks elsewhere: in 890 they established themselves in the mountain chain which still preserves their name, built themselves a number of fortresses, and from these raided the Alpine valleys within a radius of many miles; they have left their mark on many of them. For instance, in the Maurian valley inscriptions from the Koran can still be found. The Wends or Slavs from Great Moravia, who had pillaged Saxony and Thuringia on several occasions, were quieter, but this was only because they were at grips with new enemies who had just appeared on the scene, the *Hungarians* —who called themselves Magyars—a new wave of yellow-skinned peoples, who were related to the Huns and who had come from the steppes beyond the Urals. Under the leadership of the mighty Arpad, they were now beginning their great assault upon the West.

This tragic situation contributed enormously to the growth of the feudal system, which was born from the very difficulties of the age. In this panic-stricken epoch the only authority that was recognized was the one which was capable of ensuring society's safety. Every great family whose sons knew how to fight thus imposed its supremacy over one region or another: in this way local dynasties appeared, like that of Robert the Strong, the ancestor of the Capetians, who resisted the Vikings with great courage along the Loire and the Seine, or that of Bruno, Duke of Saxony, who held his own against both the Danes and the Wends; the astonishing success of Boso in Burgundy and Provence can only be accounted for by similar circumstances. As the king's authority declined the system of vassalage gained ground proportionately. The officials and government agents increasingly came to consider themselves as rulers of the regions they administrated; honours and public trusts were more and more confused with 'benefices,' in other words, with the property which the king granted his servants in return for their services. The disintegration of royal authority reached such a stage that when the counts were dismissed by their master they resisted him by using armed force, and thus preserved their position. In this way, although it had not yet acquired the systematic form it was to possess in the eleventh century, feudalism was in process of establishing itself conclusively upon the decaying remains of the Carolingian world, delivering the West into the hands of a myriad of petty authorities.

It goes without saying that the Church suffered tragically from the consequences of this process. Secularizations multiplied to an unbelievable degree: we can quote the case of the German abbey of Tegernsee, whose lay 'protectors' stole 11,746 of the 11,860 messuages that it possessed. In Bavaria, Arnulf secularized nearly all the Church's property. In France, the feudal nobility seized large numbers of monasteries which had been destroyed or merely threatened by the Norsemen. At the same time there was an enormous increase in the 'laicization' of ecclesiastical titles: warrior bishops and abbots were to multiply rapidly. Later on in this book [1] we shall have occasion to see to what point of moral decadence this would-be clergy could sink, but the end of the ninth century was only a prelude to the gloom of the tenth. And the most serious fact of all was that the Church could no longer find either support or moral direction in the two authorities which had guided her so carefully in the past: both the imperial crown and the papal tiara had been flung into the dust.

In 885 a cerebral haemorrhage had brought Charles the Fat's insignificant life to an end. Who should succeed him? One of those local kings who were all fairly closely related to the same great ancestor? Berengar, the Marquis of Friuli, descended from Charlemagne through his mother, Gisela, and a grandson of Louis the Pious, or Louis, King of Provence, a grandson of Louis III through his mother, Irmengard? In Germany Carloman, the eldest son of Louis the German, had left a bastard, Arnulf, Duke of Carinthia, who also claimed the title. And even though he had no blood connections at all with the Carolingian dynasty, the all too notorious Guy of Spoleto, who based his support on a band of Saracen mercenaries, actually meant to take his final revenge and make himself emperor!

[1] See Chapter X, section: 'Christians of the Year 1000: the Slough.'

What was the Pope to do amid this imbroglio—or, rather, the popes? For, unfortunately, pontificate succeeded pontificate with a speed which put any lasting action out of the question: Marinus I reigned less than three years, Hadrian III seventeen months; later on there was to be a pontificate lasting four months, then one of one month, and another of only seventeen days. In addition, various strange combinations of interest were behind these elections to the Apostolic See: Formosus, the Bishop of Porto, busier and more formidable than ever, worked in the midst of a network of countless intrigues, actively paving the way for a reform of the Church. But he was perhaps ill-qualified for the undertaking, for his name was sullied by so many compromising actions.

For twelve years this tangle of interests remained unravelled. So far as the imperial crown was concerned, it passed in turn to Guy of Spoleto, whom Pope Stephen IV was obliged to recognize for fear of the Saracens—and then to Arnulf, whose aid had been secretly sought by the same Pope and in whom *Formosus*, who finally became pope (891–6), believed he saw the saviour of the world, and whom he crowned; then, on the premature death of Arnulf, it passed to puppet rulers, Lambert of Spoleto, Louis of Provence, and Berengar of Friuli, who considered the imperial title so unimportant that they were not even crowned at Rome; and all this took place amid a holocaust of violent incidents of which the most frightful was the capture of the wretched Louis of Provence by his cousin, Berengar, who had the captive's eyes gouged out in his presence.

But even these tragedies were nothing as compared with that which dishonoured the Papacy. When Pope Formosus died, all his enemies —Lambert of Spoleto, his mother, the aged empress, and all the clerks in whom this gruff ascetic had tried to instil a proper respect for their station, all those whom this despotic man had exasperated—combined to take a horrible revenge. The corpse of the aged Pope was snatched from its grave, seated on a chair, and judged by an assembly presided over by the new Pope, Stephen VI, who had hated him. His entire past was resurrected, all his adventures and intrigues were recalled, and his every infringement of canon law was denounced. A terrorized clerk replied to the charges on the dead man's behalf, acknowledging his 'crimes.' An abominable ceremony followed, in which the dead man was degraded, stripped of the pontifical vestments, to which the putrefying flesh was still clinging, even to the hair shirt which Formosus had been accustomed to wear; the fingers of his right hand, those unworthy fingers which had blessed the people, were cut off. Finally, the corpse was handed over to the rabble, which threw it into the river. Moreover this ignoble carnival was to have an inevitable conclusion: divine wrath caused the collapse of the Lateran basilica; Stephen VI himself was overthrown by popular indignation, imprisoned, and strangled. Formosus's memory was rehabilitated, and the acts of the 'cadaveric council' pronounced null and void, and, when a flooding of the Tiber deposited the Pope's remains on the river-bank, men swore that the very statues of the saints themselves saluted his memory all along the route of the expiatory procession which bore him back to St Peter's.

The twofold result of these disturbances and ignominious occurrences can be described in one sentence: after the death of Berengar the imperial throne was to be vacant for fifty years; and for sixty years the Apostolic See was to be literally in the hands of a faction of women, who disposed of it exactly as they pleased. The West had had two leaders: it no longer had any.

Was everything lost, however? No. In the midst of this chaos various little islands of resistance can be picked out nearly everywhere, and around these, civilization would be able to crystallize later on. The means for this crystallization were there: the resistance of those local leaders, who, like the French Capetians, stood firm against the Norse hordes; the resistance of Alfred the Great, the scholar- and soldier-king who saved England from destruction between 871 and 899 and preserved there the great heritage of the monks of former times; the resistance of Germany, where the structure of the great nobility remained sounder than anywhere else and decisively prevented the slide to anarchy; even the resistance of the Italian towns, which organized themselves into virtually autonomous units when faced with the universal threat of chaos, and thus preserved the traditions of culture. The great outlines of the medieval West were already emerging from these elements. And though decadence also affected political doctrines, two encouraging facts were obvious nevertheless: the survival of the imperial idea, which was never to disappear, which a worthy monk of Montier-en-Der, in Champagne, was to describe in 950 as *apparently*, but not *potentially*, abolished and which was to be revived in 962 by Otto, the founder of the Holy Roman and Germanic Empire; and, secondly, the appearance of a number of elective monarchies, which seemed at first to be mere docile emanations of the feudal lordships, but which soon shook off their tutelage, as in the case of the splendid Capetian adventure, and, finally, were to make feudalism subject to them.

Nevertheless, it remains true that the ninth century drew to a close amid an appalling decline in moral standards and in civilization itself, and amid disaster which almost defies description. Materially, the uninterrupted sequence of invasions over the past seventy-five years had resulted in unbelievable devastation; villages comprising three hundred homes had become hamlets of only five houses, and some of

the fortified towns had been abandoned: the two principal ports of the
period—Durstedt, in the Rhine delta, and Quentovice, at the mouth of
the Canche—were nothing but wretched fishing villages.    Countless
monasteries had been destroyed—and here intellectual ruin was added
to the material destruction, for the treasures of the libraries went up in
flames with the monasteries which contained them.    What trade
could there be in an epoch when plunder along the roads was so
commonplace that contracts of sale and hire guarded against it expressly?    It is easy to imagine what became of men's morals in a
social climate of this kind.    We need only quote a decision of the
synod of Trosly, held in 909, to obtain some idea of the despair into
which Christian Europe had sunk: 'The towns are depopulated, the
monasteries ruined and burned; the good land turned into desert.
Just as primitive man lived without law, and without the fear of God,
giving himself up wholly to his passions, so to-day everyone does
what seems good in his own sight, in defiance of human and divine
laws and the commandments of the Church; the strong oppress the
weak; the world is filled with violence towards the young and the
unprotected; and men steal the goods which belong to the Church.
Men devour one another like the fishes of the sea.'

What hopes did the West still possess, amid this maelstrom?    Its
best hopes resided in the Church.    Although terribly weakened by
the disasters of the age, and decapitated by the temporary collapse of
the Papacy, the Church remained a last light in this period of darkness.
She alone embodied certain spiritual and intellectual values; she alone
still spoke with a voice of love and charity.    One of the most touching
facts of this epoch is the evidence of the appeals made by some of the
priests on behalf of the most outcast and wretched elements of the
community: we read of the supplications made to kings and princes
for the abolition of serfdom, on the grounds that the sons of God are
all equal; is it not a comforting sign that, in this age of violence and
injustice, some men existed who were willing to undertake a campaign
in this direction, far in advance of their own epoch?    The problem
which faced the world, on the threshold of the tenth century, was a
simple but tragically serious one: could pacific society, made incarnate
in the Church and concentrated in the monasteries and the episcopal
cities, survive this outburst of Barbarism, and could it also impose its
authority on this society based on brute force, which the feudal system
was necessarily establishing in Europe?    For more than one hundred
and fifty years we shall watch this frail dike standing alone against the
raging seas; but, though swamped several times, the dike will hold
fast in the last resort.

# CHAPTER IX

# THE BYZANTINE REVIVAL AND SEPARATION FROM ROME

## The Glory of the Macedonians

No greater contrast could be imagined than that afforded by the Empires of the East and of the West in the last third of the ninth century. One, a prey to irresistible forces of destruction, wallowed in a sea of decadence from which there appeared to be no escape, while the other enjoyed one of those epochs of fulfilment and splendid recovery, of which her history could show several examples. It was as if the uncertainties and torments of the preceding age had prepared the soil for fresh harvests; and this revival of Byzantium was the work of a new dynasty founded by Basil I in 867, and known as 'Macedonian.'

Basil was an adventurer, a member of one of those Armenian houses which had struck root in almost every part of the Empire; his own family worked on the land in Macedonia. He and his successors remained in power for two centuries, *coups d'état* and palace revolutions notwithstanding, each emperor taking care to have his son crowned in his presence so that the ties of kinship might not be subject to the hazards of succession. For two centuries then, the *porphyrogenetoi*,[1] descended from the Macedonian peasant, asserted themselves with such authority and prestige that when a usurper seized the throne —which happened three times—so far from wishing to get rid of the reigning family his one anxiety was to unite their blood with his own.

The good fortune of this dynasty, like that of the Capetians and Hohenzollerns, lay in their producing, almost uninterruptedly, remarkable personalities whose talents, however various, were devoted by each of them to the glory of the crown and the interests of the State. Very few of the Macedonians were mediocrities, and some were of exceptional calibre. The founder, for example, Basil I (867–87), was an illiterate rustic, a rough and ready athlete. He joined the Court as a groom and ended by thrusting himself upon the last Isaurian emperor, Michael III, a good-for-nothing drunkard, and also,

---

[1] Legitimate members of the royal family, capable of inheriting the throne, were known as *porphyrogenetoi*, 'born in the purple,' and so indeed they were. For when a child of the reigning house was born its mother brought it into the world in a special room adorned with porphyry and red marble. This sufficed to guarantee its legitimacy and, incidentally, goes far to suggest the reasons which could often be alleged to dispute it.

though more gently, upon Michael's sister. He then proceeded to eliminate all those who stood in his way, the emperor included; but once having obtained the mastery, he proved himself an emperor of outstanding ability, upright of purpose, just in his policies, and a hero in battle against the Moslems. He was an assassin turned crusader. Constantine VII (913–57), a subtle thinker, a good writer, and an artist of unfailing good taste, was not prevented by his inclination towards intellectual pursuits from acting with the utmost harshness when it was a question of upholding his authority, and his reign is one of the high-water marks of Byzantine civilization. The chroniclers represent Nicephorus Phocas (963–9) as 'a pigmy with an enormous head,' black-haired, black-skinned, and black of character, a graceless soldier. Yet he came to the throne by the caprice of a beautiful woman, and no sooner was the diadem set upon his brow than he was seen to be the most imperial of imperial rulers, the most resolved to have his rights respected, the most determined to resist his enemies. Again, Basil II, known as 'Slayer of the Bulgarians,' became emperor at the age of eighteen. He showed immediately and throughout his long reign a sense of responsibility, energy in the execution of his duty, and an understanding of men and events worthy of Louis XIV. It was owing to him that the influence of Byzantium was felt throughout the East and even in distant Russia. No doubt we respect rather than love these characters; they are far too deeply dyed in blood for our liking. But to do them justice we must surely take account of the terrible situation in which they were placed.

For the proven greatness of the Macedonian dynasty cannot be attributed to any circumstance that might be said to have facilitated their task. The age-long perils which had for centuries confronted the Byzantine emperors were still present; they were no less grave, and their number had been increased. We can recall those that loomed in and near the capital: popular rebellion and the constant threat of conspiracy. If the latter were successful yesterday's monarch became a bleeding corpse whose head was offered to the derision of the mob; at best he was mutilated or his eyes put out. Nor was this all: the provinces always tended to separatism, which might at any moment become active; and new heresies, such as the Paulician, worked like leaven in the State. There were encroachments by the great landowners and civil servants, who planned—more slowly indeed, but no less certainly, than did their opposite numbers in the West—to substitute feudal anarchy for the centralizing authoritarianism of their masters. True the advance of the Moslems through Anatolia had been halted in 863, and they were torn by internal strife; but they remained as formidable as ever, dominated the Mediterranean, controlled the islands, and had already struck a terrible blow at Byzantine trade. To the north there were new enemies, the Bulgars, a slavonicized Asiatic people who had taken advantage of the humiliation of Byzantium at the beginning of the ninth century to spread themselves over the region of the lower Danube. In the time of Boris I (c. 865) they had invented the idea of pan-Slavism; they attempted to give it effect under Tsar Simeon (893–927), bringing Constantinople within an ace of surrender; and their final collapse was due only to the drastic and continuous methods of extermination employed by Basil II.

The wonder is that the necessity of unending struggle against these dangers never deterred the Macedonian emperors from a home policy so firm and enlightened as to make them the equals of Justinian. After an interval of one hundred and fifty years they resumed the great and supreme Byzantine task, concentrating upon law, revising the statutes, and improving the codes. The organization of government at this period attained a perfection hitherto unknown. Finance was so skilfully managed that it is said they were able to dispose of a revenue amounting to the equivalent of 600 million gold francs with a reserve of 250 million; the empire of Bagdad alone enjoyed such wealth. Economic regimentation of the masses by the clergy and civil service rendered the system not unlike that prevailing in modern totalitarian states. This rigid and orderly control is impressive when compared with the spectacle of anarchy and dissolution presented by the West.

Byzantium under the Macedonians had regained her glory. Her commerce, now barred from Syria, Egypt, Ethiopia, and maritime Asia, looked towards the north. She held undisputed sway over the Aegean and the Black Sea; through Trebizond she linked Central Asia and India; timber, furs, and slaves reached her via the rivers of Russia; the Adriatic seaboard, which she also controlled, was at the height of its prosperity, and Venice stood on the threshold of a magnificent career. The Byzantine armies were reliable, and the system of recruiting *themes* provided soldier-agriculturists stationed on the frontiers, thereby guaranteeing a high rate of enrolment. The navy, lately reorganized, was soon to make possible a counter-offensive which would roll back the Arabs from southern Italy, from parts of Sicily, and above all from Crete. This phase of Byzantine pre-eminence, which was felt both materially and politically from the shores of Italy to the Armenian plateaus, and from the Danube to the confines of Syria, was contemporary with a moral, intellectual, and spiritual radiance worthy of the greatest periods. During the two 'Macedonian' centuries there took place a veritable renaissance which was to the advantage of both art and literature.

Under this dynasty, more than ever before, Constantinople felt herself to be not only the capital of the world and the head of civilization, but also the bastion of the Christian faith. For she laboured on behalf of Christianity in the firm conviction that all her glory rested thereupon; or rather, she thought of her own interests as identical with those of Christ. Was it not the cause of the Gospel that her soldiers served when face to face with the pagans or the Moslems? Did not the works of her scholars, architects, and artists contribute to the glory of Almighty God? Christianity was part and parcel of the popular conscience as well as of the imperial policies—at least it was easy to imagine so.

But Christianity in the Byzantine Empire was still of that disconcerting type whose characteristics we have noticed in former periods, characteristics which had become even more pronounced. It was a closely knit web of living piety and formalism, of very high moral standards and passionate outbursts that always tended to excess whether for good or ill; a religion of sublime ascetics, of howling mobs, and of prelate-politicians. Theological debate, so violent in earlier centuries, no longer stirred men's minds to the same degree, for the imperial authority enforced submission to the articles of faith; but since the revival of the cult of pictures the devotion paid to them had become so ardent and pervasive that there was danger of a relapse into those extravagances which had brought about the crisis.

The emperors regarded themselves as the best witnesses to Christianity, or rather as its incarnation. But Christianity as they practised it is certainly calculated to make us wonder. It would be impossible to imagine a more complete admixture of contradictory elements. Basil I, for instance, reached the throne by a succession of crimes and reigned with implacable harshness; yet towards the poor and humble he showed inexhaustible tenderness and charity in the true spirit of the Gospel. Nicephorus Phocas hesitated between the cloister and the throne, leading for years the life of a soldier-monk; then he suddenly became enamoured of a woman who enabled him to seize the crown, and gave himself up to fleshly delights with all the fervour of youth, although he was well past fifty. Some of these imperial figures lived on the borders of mystical neurosis. The beautiful Theophano, for example, wife of Leo VI, practised such a crazy form of asceticism that, apart from official ceremonies, when she was obliged to wear robes, she never appeared before her husband dressed in anything but rags, offered him no better bed than a mat spread on the floor, or better meals than vegetables and water. It goes without saying that Christianity of this sort, so full of contrasts, was marked by outbreaks of licentiousness and cruelty for which Byzantium had always been conspicuous. One of the emperors, four times married and thrice divorced, openly paraded his mistresses in the palace; and he the representative of Christ! The terrible conqueror, Basil II, took prisoner fifteen thousand Bulgarians and had them all blinded, all except a privileged hundred whom he left with one eye apiece so that they could lead home their hapless countrymen.

However, these Macedonian emperors, against whom much might be said from the Christian viewpoint, were true defenders of the faith and heralds of the Gospel, whose action proved decisive. Iconoclasm, suppressed under the Empress Theodora in 843, never again raised its head, although it continued to exist in clandestine circles, especially in the distant provinces where it merged with the more or less clearly defined opposition to imperial authoritarianism. There appeared in Asia Minor a new heresy, or rather a recrudescence of the ancient Iranian dualism which had long ago found embodiment in Manichaeism. This was the Paulician heresy, which was stamped out by the Macedonian emperors, particularly by Basil I, to such good effect that it never reappeared.[1] At the same time these emperors aided the missionaries and opposed the Moslems, thus lending powerful assistance to the Church, that vigorous and enterprising Church which they served even while making use of her.

## CONVERSION OF THE SLAVS

One of the most important events which must be credited to Byzantine influence is the conversion of the Slavs and kindred peoples. It is all the more remarkable because it coincided with the emergence of these races from the nebulous home of Barbarism into the full light of civilization. The Slavonic hordes, which in the third century had overrun the great plain known to-day as Russia, had planned, on a gigantic scale and within a space of five hundred years, a twofold movement of invasion. Westward it reached the Elbe, the Saal, and swept over Bohemia; southward it had permeated and almost absorbed the Asiatic element in Bulgaria, and was pursuing its course into the Balkans; while to the rear the compact nucleus of Slavism was moving from the Valdai Hills to the Dnieper and from the Volga to the Dvina. In the last third of the ninth century there were three important Slavonic states: Bulgaria, the rival of Byzantium; Moravia, which the Hungarian invasion was beginning to split into two groups, Bohemia and Yugoslavia; and above all Russia, which was to expand considerably. This last state, it was said, originated in the conquest of the great market-towns of the plain by a band of Scandinavian

---

[1] At any rate in Asia Minor. Introduced by Armenian colonists it spread among the Bulgarians, thence among the Russians, and also in Serbia where its adherents were known as Bogomils. About the year 1000 it threatened Christianity in Russia and the Balkans. Historians are not agreed as to whether Paulician and Bogomil influence gave rise to the Albigensian heresy in the West. Bogomil art, especially sculpture, with its curious symbolism, reveals very clearly the immemorial influences of Asia.

warriors and their establishment in the two capitals: Novgorod in the north and Kiev in the south.

It is not surprising that the Church became interested in these still barbarian peoples. Long ago, as we have seen,[1] the sporadic work of evangelization had begun, for which the ground had been prepared by commercial intercourse as well as by returning mercenaries and prisoners of war. But it was mainly under Charlemagne and his successors that the penetration of Slavonic territory became a real part of the Church's programme, in which both East and West were concerned. Charlemagne brought missionaries to Pannonia and Croatia which he had recently conquered, and encouraged the dispatch of evangelists to the borders of what was afterwards Poland. Byzantium likewise sent priests and monks into the Slavonic lands, where her military, diplomatic, and commercial contacts were steadily increasing. In certain areas this rivalry of Christian East and West produced unfortunate consequences which are still with us: among the southern Slavs, for example, the Croato-Dalmatian element adhered to Rome while the Serbo-Montenegrin entered the Byzantine sphere. But that same rivalry, though its results were occasionally harmful, was the well-spring of some holy emulation.

The first Slavonic land won for Christ was Moravia (modern Bohemia and Slovakia), which at the beginning of the ninth century was in full bloom, and where Greek and Venetian traders, with the help of Frankish missionaries from Passau and Ratisbon, had sown the Gospel seed. In 845 fourteen Czech princes had themselves baptized by Western priests. In 852 the Council of Mainz referred to 'the still half-savage Christians of Moravia,' although Greek monks were still at work in those parts. In 846 Ratislav ascended the throne of Bohemia under the auspices of Louis the German, who hoped thereby to control his dangerous neighbour. From the moment of his accession, however, the young prince had but one ambition: to throw off the yoke of the Germanic Empire. He himself had already been baptized, and he foresaw clearly that the manner in which he brought about the conversion of his people would have great political significance. He applied first to Rome, asking for Italian missionaries who could speak the Slavonic language of his subjects. But Rome was unable to oblige, and Ratislav turned to Byzantium. In 862 a Moravian ambassador arrived at the imperial palace. At that date the Basileus was Michael III, a sorry specimen, but at whose side, fortunately, stood the brilliant patriarch Photius. The latter at once perceived the chance thus offered him of outwitting the Apostolic See of Rome, relations with which were beginning to become strained. Accordingly he sent a favourable reply to the Bohemian prince's request.

[1] End of Chapter VI.

Two men were appointed to carry the Gospel into Moravia, two brothers: *Constantine* (who afterwards took the name *Cyril*) and *Methodius*, the first of whom was particularly shrewd. Born at Thessalonica, where there was a large Slav population, both of them spoke that language fluently. Constantine, still a young man, had already shown extraordinary gifts in accomplishing a delicate mission, half diplomatic and half religious, to the Khazars of the lower Volga and Dnieper. Obviously blessed by God, he had also had the good fortune, while passing through Cherson, to discover the remains of the great Pope St Clement who had died there in exile. His outstanding qualities were revealed in the care he devoted to the preparation for this new campaign of evangelization. The Moravians had no alphabet capable of expressing their language; Cyril invented one by combining the Greek with Hebrew and Coptic elements; this was the *glagolitic* alphabet, ancestor of the Russian. And in this new script he translated the principal parts of the liturgy, so as to be understood by those among whom he was going.

Reaching Moravia in 863, the two brothers had no easy task. The Latin (i.e. Germanic) missionaries were not much inclined to smooth their way; and since the German Carolingians constantly intervened by force in the country's affairs, the repercussions they provoked threatened the work of Cyril and Methodius. But in spite of all, and thanks to their knowledge of the language, they made rapid progress: the rank and file of the people began to ask for baptism. The Western clergy, however, suddenly became anxious; the use of Slavonic in the liturgy, too, seemed to them blasphemous, and they denounced their rivals to the Pope as dangerous heretics. In 868, while the two brothers were at Venice waiting for a boat to take them to Constantinople with some of their disciples who were to be ordained,[1] they received from Pope Nicholas I an invitation to come and explain their conduct. But when they reached the Eternal City their luggage included the finest present that could be offered to a pope, the relics of St Clement; so all was well. Hadrian II authorized them to say mass in Slavonic. Cyril died in Rome, and when Methodius departed alone he did so with the title of archbishop and authority over an enormous diocese that covered the whole of modern Czechoslovakia, together with most of what is now Yugoslavia.

But for all that the last years of Methodius were no more tranquil. However, the heroic missionary stood firm, though repeatedly and strongly criticized by German prelates, though actually arrested and scourged, though denounced to Rome time after time as a heretic, and though partially disavowed by Pope John VIII, who, being badly informed, directed him to use Slavonic for sermons only and not in the

---

[1] Cyril and Methodius were not bishops.

liturgy. When Methodius died, in 884, the whole of Moravia was Christian. But once he had gone the Germanic influence regained the upper hand; his disciples were expelled and took refuge in Bulgaria. The new Christian centres founded by the two apostles turned towards the West and attached themselves to Rome. We must, however, do justice to their blessed memory by recognizing that it was owing to the two Byzantine saints, Cyril and Methodius, that Bohemia one day became the bastion of Christendom in Central Europe.

Arriving in Bulgaria, the disciples of the two apostles of Moravia found Christianity flourishing. About twenty years earlier King Boris, observing the progress made by the Gospel in his dominions, and the gradual penetration of his subjects by Byzantine influences, had realized that his kingdom, surrounded as it was by Christian countries, could not remain an island of paganism. In 863 or 864 he had had himself baptized, and in his ardour as a Barbarian neophyte he had, by dint of capital punishment, induced the nobility to follow his example. Being, however, a clever politician, and fearing that the conversion to Christianity might subject his kingdom to Byzantium, he had asked the patriarch, Photius, to place an independent patriarch at the head of the Bulgarian Church. The wary Photius had replied evasively, substituting for the expected promise some fine pages of metaphysical speculation. Boris thereupon had turned to Pope Nicholas I, begging of him the same favour and asking questions on many points that troubled him. Did baptism, for example, forbid him to wear trousers, which were the national dress? Might he continue to display his horse-tail standard? Was he allowed to have several wives? Nicholas I had answered so skilfully, promising an archbishop and sending a number of good Latin books, that Boris straightway drove the Byzantine missionaries from the kingdom.

Unfortunately, this policy, which might have linked Bulgaria with Rome, was not continued: Hadrian II refused to create the patriarchate. Boris, enraged, sent an embassy offering to attach Bulgaria to the Byzantine see. This was accomplished in 870; and even when, nine years later, Photius proposed abandoning the Bulgars in order to secure his recognition by Pope John VIII,[1] King Boris resisted: the Latin priests were driven out and replaced by Greeks. Bulgaria, then, was Byzantine in both religion and culture, but the language of the liturgy was a problem. When the disciples of Cyril and Methodius arrived in this new country they did as their teachers had done, preaching in Slavonic and celebrating the offices in that language. They also invented a new alphabet, the Cyrillic, forerunner of the Bulgarian alphabet. Boris, realizing that herein lay his opportunity to reconcile his spiritual dependence upon Byzantium with his desire

[1] See the paragraph on Photius, p. 503.

for independence, embarked upon an enterprise which was to cul-
minate in the slavonicization of the original Asiatic element.  His
younger son and heir, Simeon, continued this policy.  Having
succeeded as 'tsar' (emperor), he set out to secure the recognition as
autocephalous of his own Church, the head of which was the Archbishop of Ochrida; and even at the beginning of the eleventh century,
when the terrible victories of Basil II annexed Bulgaria to the Empire,
this religious independence survived at least nominally.  Impregnated with Byzantine culture, but Slavic in its liturgy and rites,
Christian Bulgaria served thenceforward as a link between Byzantium
and other Slavonic peoples: the Serbs, who were converted between
870 and 890, and the Russians, among whom the Gospel triumphed
about the year 1000.

The earliest relations between Byzantium and Russia had been anything but happy.  In 861 a Russian fleet, imitating Norse strategy,
attacked the capital, and only the energy of Photius, together with a
miracle obtained by the Virgin of Blachernae, had prevented the fall of
Constantinople.  But this first contact, however disagreeable, had
made possible the establishment of some intercourse, and a mission
actually started for Kiev where there was already a small Christian
community.  At the beginning of the tenth century relations between
the Eastern Empire and Russia were as numerous as they were complex.  On the one hand there was a busy and continual trade via the
great Russian rivers; on the other there were such warlike incidents as
Prince Igor's abortive attack on Constantinople in 941.  Nothing,
however, could prevent the flow of Christian influences to the various
Russian cities through the twofold channel of Latin and Greek
missionaries.

In 945 Princess Olga, widow of Igor, openly embraced Christianity.
It is not known for certain whether she was baptized according to the
Greek or the Latin rite; but having more or less the same purpose as
had once inspired King Boris of Bulgaria, it is likely that she played a
double role, receiving baptism at Constantinople and asking the
German emperor, Otto I, for missionaries.  In this vast country,
where paganism was still a living force, the progress of the Gospel
was not easy, and for at least half a century it met with strong resistance: the practice of human sacrifice continued and missionaries were
often obliged to pack their baggage.  Only about the year 1000
was conversion able to proceed systematically, thanks to the formidable efforts of Olga's grandson, Vladimir, a strange figure of
apostolic zeal.

This bawdy giant, this ferocious warrior, who was to die in penitential fustian and become celebrated for his charity and gentleness,
was the representative *par excellence* of Russian Christianity, of its

endless contradictions wherein extremes of lively faith and readiness to sin would be constant bed-fellows. While yet a pagan, pre-occupied with warfare [1] and women rather than with prayer, Vladimir had learned one great lesson from his grandmother, St Olga. She had taught him the necessity of becoming a Christian in order to establish relations with 'the city protected by God.' According to a famous legend he summoned to his Court representatives of every faith, including the Moslem, and then sent ambassadors to inspect the various kinds of churches. The most persuasive of his visitors were the Greeks, and as for the envoys sent to Byzantium, they proved by far the most enthusiastic: 'We thought we were in paradise.' A mere legend, it is true, but one that reveals the state of mind that gave it birth. Converted in 987 Vladimir knew no rest until he had obtained in marriage a princess 'born in the purple,' Anne, sister of the Basileus. Her coming marked the decisive establishment of Byzantine influence in Russia. Churches with gilded cupolas imitated from the Greek Orient, arose in cities whose walls were mere earthen ramparts. Byzantine clergy provided the initial framework of ecclesiastical organization. Almost all the religious books introduced into the country were by Greeks, notably the works of St John Damascene. This spiritual attachment of Russia to the 'orthodox' and dissenting Eastern Church, which took place when Byzantium was on the way to a final break with Rome, was to have far-reaching consequences, involving the whole history of Christendom.

It must be observed, on the other hand, that 'attachment' did not amount to enfeoffment. The Christians of Russia, in regular contact with those of Moravia and Bulgaria, perceived the advantages they would derive from the Slavonic liturgy, variations of which had been introduced by the numerous Moravian and Bulgarian refugees who settled in Russia after their countries had been overwhelmed by the Hungarians and Basil II respectively. The great prince Yaroslav encouraged this tendency when he consolidated Russian territory between 1019 and 1054. At that time Russian Christianity took on its final form, which it has ever since retained: Byzantine by spiritual affiliation, Slavonic in its external characteristics.

On the whole, it was owing to the efforts of Byzantium that these enormous numbers of people were won for Christ, and historians of the Church must recognize as much with gratitude. Gratitude, how-ever, should be tempered with reserve. In a celebrated work,[2] Vladi-mir Soloviev, the most oecumenical of Russian authors, gives a vivid

---

[1] He waged terrible wars against the Poles at the very time when Boleslas the Valiant was forming the Christian state of Poland. See Chapter X, section: 'New Conquests for the Cross.'

[2] *Russia and the Universal Church.*

account of the Byzantine origins of Christianity in Russia. He rightly points out that Russia's adherence to the Greek Church placed her, from the very beginning of her national life, outside the historical framework of Europe, within which the Catholic Church forged the civilization of the West. Moreover, as indicated by the legend of St Vladimir, Russian Christianity took over the worst defects of Byzantium, appealing mainly to the aesthetic sense, to outward pomp and those superficial characteristics which could not penetrate far into the ancient pagan soul. Neither the Byzantine bishops, who were civil servants rather than pastors, nor the Byzantine monks, who lived completely isolated from the world and were hostile to the grand conception of culture, could take the parts which we have seen played by the hierarchy and religious orders in the West. All the special qualities of Slavonic Christianity may be traced to this fact. About 1054, when Yaroslav was dying and the whole of Europe was entering upon the Middle Ages, Russian Christianity presented two salient features: 'A Church attracting the faithful by the mystic splendours of her worship, but giving no other teaching than that afforded by the ritual formulae in the magnificent Slavonic version, and a monastic ideal far removed from everyday life'; in other words, an ineffective Church. But with these reservations it remains true that Byzantium accomplished a work of the first importance by her conversion of the Slavs. We should not forget that during the three centuries since the Moslem invasion enormous areas had been lost to Christendom; that while Greek missionaries were at work Christian Spain lay gasping under the rule of Abd-er-Rahman and then of the vizier Almansur, freedom being confined to a few poor little mountain kingdoms; that the glorious and ancient Churches of North Africa were in the throes of extinction; and that in Syria the survivors of the Christian hierarchy were to all intents and purposes at the mercy of Islamic officials, while those Christians who remained free were forced into hiding. The conquest of new lands, therefore, was a providential compensation for Christianity; it is not without significance that so much ruin and destruction was offset by the increasing glory of the princes of Kiev, with whom all the kings of Europe dreamed of uniting their own blood. Thanks to Byzantium, the Christian East, torn and diminished in the previous era, was restored through this expansion of her territory.

## THE BYZANTINE CRUSADES

The great Macedonian emperors were not satisfied with the amount of compensation afforded Christianity by the conversion of the Slavs. They would not recognize the Moslem annexation of Christian countries, and in a spirit of faith which foreshadowed that of the Western crusaders they attacked the Mohammedan world with extraordinary courage and tenacity. The tenth century was the age of the Byzantine epic with its many illustrious names.

During the last twenty years of the Isaurian dynasty the Moslem drive towards Constantinople had been checked. The last serious incursion had taken place in 845, when Ancyra had fallen, and when the siege of Amorium had witnessed an act of sublimest heroism in the sacrifice of forty Greek officers. Taken prisoner and offered their lives if they would abjure Christ, they chose death as the soldiers of Gaza had done two hundred years before; and in return for the blood of these martyrs God had sustained His champions. In 858 the Byzantine fleet, which the Moslems believed to be laid up, had ravaged the city of Damietta in Egypt. In 863 an Islamic army, having ventured too far on the Paphlagonian plateau, was surprised by one of Michael III's generals and cut to pieces; its emir was among the slain.

But these successes gave Byzantium no cause to rest upon her laurels. The Moslem peril, halted at one point, was found to be as formidable as ever elsewhere. It was at this period that the Saracens established themselves in southern Italy, in Dalmatia, and then (870) in Malta, so that the Mediterranean became virtually a Moslem lake. It was also at this period that the German emperor Louis II was fighting stubbornly against the infidel, and that the aged Pope John VIII offered Byzantium an alliance against Islam. It is to the credit of the Macedonian emperors that, in this matter, they understood and accepted their responsibilities as Christians.

Their task, however, was made easier by the internal state of the Moslem world, which was in process of disintegration. The authority of the Abbasid caliphs, in decline since 861, extended only to Bagdad and Iraq; provincial dynasties were in process of formation, nominally subject to them but in fact autonomous. In Africa the Fatimites, direct descendants of Mohammed's daughter, secured their complete independence at the beginning of the tenth century, captured Sicily, and advanced upon Egypt, which they occupied in 969. In Spain, where Fatimites and Abbasids were opposed to one another, a third dynasty advanced its claims; this was the ancient house of the Ommayads whose members asserted that they alone were legitimate. Thus in the peninsula three sovereigns called themselves successors of the Prophet and leaders of the faithful. Before long anarchy had spread throughout the vast and mighty empire of Islam; its possessions fell apart, Algeria and Morocco forming themselves into small Berber principalities, while Syria threw off the yoke of Cairo. Among the Abbasids there was constant civil war, family rivalry, and rebellion of subject peoples. By about the year 1000, the Mohammedan empire would be no more than an emaciated body, a shadow of its former self, swarming with foreigners (Berbers, Negroes, Asiatics, and even Slavs) and ripe for the mortal blow that new aggressors, the Turks, were about to strike.

The Byzantine crusade did not begin in earnest until 924, under the Emperor Romanus Lecapenus (919–44), a usurper whom Constantine VII had wisely associated with himself in the Empire. Before him Basil I had been too preoccupied to do more than fortify the roads against possible Arab incursions and destroy the Paulician heretics who often welcomed the Moslems. The danger from Islam remained formidable, as became only too clear on that unhappy day in July 924, when a squadron from Africa took Thessalonica, massacred almost the entire population, and sold the survivors (22,000 young men and girls) in the slave-markets of Crete and Tripoli. Immediate retaliation was impossible, owing to the more urgent need of meeting the Bulgarian menace. But after the signing of peace in 927 the death of Tsar Simeon greatly weakened the strength of his kingdom, and Romanus Lecapenus turned against the Moslems, and the great offensive began.

Henceforward there was scarcely a year in which the Byzantine sword did not strike at the vast body of Islam, either by land or sea. Romanus, assisted by such experienced officers as the Armenian Kurkuas, who was known as the 'second Trajan,' was able to combine the diplomatic and strategic resources of the Empire. In alliance with Armenia and Iberia he created serious difficulties for the caliphs in their own territories, while a series of bold operations across the frontiers brought the Greek army to the upper Tigris and Euphrates, by a wide sweep from the north-east which encircled the Arab-occupied regions in Asia Minor. The burning of the Tripolitanian fleet in the roadstead at Lemnos, the capture of Erzerum, and the brief siege and destruction of Melitene, were the most brilliant feats of arms at this period. Byzantine hopes revived.

This was only a beginning of which Romanus could not take full advantage, hindered as he was by palace intrigues that were too much for him. The situation remained obscure for almost twenty years throughout the reign of Constantine VII [1] and that of his young son, Romanus II. The latter did well in delegating his power to a man of outstanding quality, Joseph Bringas, a eunuch in whom, strangely enough, there shone the light of a crusader. On the Moslem frontiers the well-trained armies of Byzantium desired nothing better than to fight. Their leader was *Nicephorus Phocas*, a great soldier, keen, able, and untiring. To him the eunuch entrusted the struggle against Islam.

---

[1] Constantine, a good scholar but a useless soldier, was more interested in writing his manual of etiquette, *The Book of Ceremonies*, than in fighting.

The succeeding years were indeed phenomenal, comparable with the greatest in Roman history. The first objective was Crete, which had to be taken at all costs in order to deprive the Saracens of their bases and to clear the Aegean. It was reoccupied in 961, Candia falling after a terrible siege that lasted for eight months. Then, crossing at once to the mainland, Nicephorus took Tarsus, crossed the passes of the Taurus, swept down upon Cilicia with his mobile columns that spread terror throughout the Moslem empire, and brought back what was believed to be a portrait of Christ, a precious relic supposedly miraculous. Temporarily interrupted in this victorious career by the political situation at home, he hurried to Constantinople, returned as emperor and husband of Romanus's lovely widow Theophano,[1] and renewed his offensive. Cyprus, which had been lost to Europe in the seventh century, was reconquered for the faith. Syria, scoured by Byzantine raids, began to shake off the Islamic yoke. In the autumn of 969, avenging centuries of shame, Nicephorus restored to Christendom Antioch, one of the cities nearest to his heart. The greatness of this man may be judged by the fact that, in pursuance of a policy inaugurated by Pope John VIII, he intervened at the same time in southern Italy with a view to expelling the Moslems from Calabria, which was also threatened by the complicated intrigues of the German emperor and the Lombard princes. How far would his crusade have carried him had not the heroïc soldier fallen victim to female treachery a few days after the capture of Antioch? He was assassinated by John Tzimisces, another illustrious general, whom the fickle Theophano had taken as her lover.

Master of the Empire as well as of the heart of this beautiful and alarming woman, and guardian of two young princes, the new Basileus had only one purpose: to follow in the footsteps of his brilliant predecessor. The situation, however, had become more difficult. The Tunisian dynasty of the Fatimites had just overrun Egypt; their troops, far more reliable than those of the unfortunate Abbasids, were in process of occupying Palestine and the Lebanese seaboard; and in 974 Beirut was retaken from the Byzantines. But these events served only to strengthen the determination of Tzimisces; ignoring the vain threats of the caliphs of Bagdad, he made straight for the holy places. Tidings of new victories reached Byzantium and roused the spirit of crusade: prayers were offered, money poured in, and volunteers were recruited for the deliverance of the Holy Sepulchre. When Damascus fell the Turkish governor, Aftekin, who had rebelled against the Caliph of Cairo, was so anxious to surrender that there was rumour of his conversion. The Greek army entered Palestine through Banyas and its celebrated defile; the soldiers of Christ once more trod that sacred

---

[1] She must not be confused with the half-demented mystic referred to above.

ground for the first time since the disaster of Heraclius 335 years earlier. 'At Nazareth, where the Virgin Mary heard the glad tidings from the lips of the angel,' says an Armenian chronicler, 'on Mount Tabor, where Christ, our God, was transfigured,' John's troops mingled their prayers with shouts of victory. Jerusalem seemed within his grasp, but the Basileus called a halt. Doubtless he considered it necessary to obtain a firm hold on the coast, and he spent several months, not without difficulty, in securing the Lebanese ports; but there can be no doubt that the Holy City was his ultimate goal, for he warned the Doge of Venice to carry on no further trade with the Moslems. This grandiose scheme, however, was not to be fulfilled. During the winter of 975 John Tzimisces fell sick, probably of typhus; he had to be carried back to Constantinople, where he died in January 976.

Would it have been possible to conquer the holy places? Was the undertaking premature? The Macedonian dynasty, which so nearly achieved this glorious ambition three hundred years before the Western crusade, renounced the enterprise. Basil II, a great soldier, a man of iron determination, an excellent statesman and diplomatist, who for fifty years (976–1025) guided the affairs of Byzantium, preferred to extend and consolidate Christendom towards the north by conquering Bulgaria and Armenia. He confined himself to punishing the more outrageous excesses of the Moslems by a few spectacular raids. He abandoned Palestine and did not retaliate even in 1009–10, when the caliph Al-Hakim proceeded to persecute the Christians, obliging them to wear a badge of infamy, burning churches, and actually destroying the Holy Sepulchre. But one result at least had been achieved. The frontier which about 920 followed the line of the Taurus, whence Moslem guerrillas swept across the Anatolian plateaus, was now firmly established 180 miles farther south, to the borders of Syria; and the eastern Mediterranean was once more Greek. The Macedonian emperors had thus prepared bases for the crusaders under Godfrey de Bouillon. At the end of this period, from about the year 1000, relations between Greeks and Arabs became more cordial in an atmosphere of mutual respect.

To Byzantium, therefore, belongs the credit of having paved the way for a future holy war. The memory of these events would survive in the most beautiful of her epic poems, *The Song of Digenis the Akrite*, which deserves to be compared with the *Chanson de Roland*. Long after the Mohammedan Turks had reduced the Christian towns and villages of the East to servitude, men would recite the doughty deeds of the young leader, the Akrite, the baron *sans peur et sans reproche* who, throughout his life, waged war against the infidel with superhuman courage. They would recall his beauty, his generosity, and his modesty. Ballads which are still sung in Greek lands, and even in Russia, would keep alive the tender memory of his loves, expressing in their spirited verses all the glamour of Byzantium, all the splendour of the Greek rite. Here again legend would bear witness to reality.

## 'Caesaro-Papism' and the Oriental Clergy

It is not surprising that the renaissance of Byzantine power under the Macedonian dynasty considerably strengthened that cult of which the Basileus had always been the object. At the period in question Court etiquette attained its zenith, investing every aspect of the sovereign's life with a quasi-sacramental character. The *Book of Ceremonies*, written under the personal direction of Constantine VII, set out precise details of the ceremonial to be followed at baptisms, marriages, coronations, and funerals of the *porphyrogenetoi*, at the reception of ambassadors, and indeed at the most ordinary functions in the emperor's day-to-day existence. Never had there been so many prostrations, so many genuflexions, so many kissings of the foot, or so many laudatory titles. Few, very few indeed, were the emperors who dared shake off this golden yoke: Basil II was almost the only one.

The religious character of this ceremonial likewise attained its highest pitch. Etiquette became a form of liturgy. The 'Sacred Palace' was declared 'holy as a church,' and even at times when it was the scene of events altogether unchristian, the bedrooms and banqueting halls were unfailingly blessed each month to the accompaniment of spectacular processions, display of ikons, and singing of hymns. The imperial robes, henceforward regulated by tradition, were not unlike liturgical vestments, with the long *chlamys*, white as an alb, and the chasuble stiff with golden embroidery and precious stones.

All this may shock our sensibilities; but what would a Christian of to-day have said in presence of the Easter ceremony enacted beneath the domes of St Sophia? In a kind of stage play, a cross between mass and mime, the Basileus acted the part of Christ risen from the dead. He stood facing the people, his torso bound with narrow bands of gold, his thighs wrapped in a shroud, golden sandals on his feet, holding in one hand the sceptre tipped with a cross, and in the other the *akakia*, a satchel of purple stuff containing dust from the Holy Sepulchre. Twelve dignitaries stood around him, representing the Twelve Apostles. . . .

Mere theatricals? No, an expression of the truth. The Basileus, a spiritual head in the fullest sense, assumed a sacred duty as from the time of his coronation. He was in some way a priest. 'The patriarch,' wrote Simeon of Thessalonica, 'makes the sign of the Cross

R

with holy oil upon the emperor's brow, in memory of Him who is king of the universe and who, by virtue of His own anointing, establishes him in power on earth.' His authority was thus supernatural. When he appointed a high official he did so in the name of the Blessed Trinity and by 'the majesty which I hold from God.' Was this hieratic sovereign in fact the symbol and representative of God on earth, or was the Almighty a reflection in heaven, so to speak, of this glittering individual? It is hard to say.

In practice, throughout the two Macedonian centuries, this quasi-deification of the Basileus resulted in a more complete subjection of Church to Throne than ever before. 'Caesaro-Papism,' which had always been the curse of Byzantium, had reached its zenith. The victory of the true faith over iconoclasm had been won by the emperors, and the Church at once found herself more thoroughly under their control than at any time in the past. There was no distinction between the religious and the politician. Prelates and eunuchs rubbed shoulders at Court, and masterful monks of dubious reputation, like Rasputin long afterwards, often had a hand in the worst disorders. The most influential office was that of the Master of Cults, the *Syncellus*, intermediate between the emperor and the patriarch, who was generally the latter's successor-designate. Everything passed through his hands. Hence total and intentional confusion. The situation was very different from that prevailing in the West, where the emperors, even when they exercised strict control over the Church and meddled indiscreetly in her affairs, recognized her as an authority quite distinct from themselves and one to which they must sometimes yield. At Byzantium the Church and the Crown were literally one. Coronation did not make the emperor; it merely recognized a fact, established by right of birth or by force, the assent of the people and nobility.

What could serve as a counterpoise to Caesaro-Papism? The authority of the patriarch? It certainly existed and was by no means inconsiderable. We must speak henceforth of *the* patriarch, for since those of Antioch, Alexandria, and Jerusalem resided *in partibus infidelium*, at the mercy of any vicious emir, there was only one patriarch—he of Constantinople, who acted as though he were pope in the East. It was the patriarch who crowned the emperor and received from him on that occasion the prescribed ritual oath to abide by the dogmas of the Church and protect the true faith. He disposed of enormous wealth in almost every part of the Empire, which assured him unlimited goodwill; and an army of monks, anxious to defend themselves against episcopal authority, considered themselves directly subject to the patriarch. In the capital his prestige was unbounded; he was recognized as enjoying political rights, such as that of intervening in all affairs where orthodoxy might be imperilled (and God knows how easily, at that period, it was declared to be in danger), of judging or appointing judges in all capital cases, and of acting as a member of the council of regency whenever the Basileus was under age. Immediately after his appointment he took an oath of loyalty to the emperor, and promised not to intrigue against him; but at Byzantium hell was paved with good intentions of that kind.

Theoretically, then, the patriarch might have represented the independence of the Church as against the Throne; in practice he did no such thing. The Macedonian emperors were not children, and they took care to have so dangerous a personage under their control. The first of them, Basil I, abolished the right of election. Hitherto the patriarch had been chosen by a sort of conclave in which the clergy, the people, and the palace were all represented. Henceforward things were differently arranged: the metropolitans, gathered in St Sophia in presence of the *Syncellus* as the emperor's representative, submitted three candidates. If one of them was acceptable to the master he was consecrated; if not the Basileus chose another. The patriarch was thus inevitably a dependant of the prince, sometimes a member of his family—his younger brother, as happened three times— and nearly always officials of high rank, as was the case with Theodore Cassiteras, Tarasius, Photius, and Nicholas the Mystic, who had been secretaries of state before their elevation to the patriarchate. Once invested with a spiritual charge, could they forget their secular antecedents? Did they, in the archiepiscopal chair, remain 'prime ministers' of the emperor? Under the Macedonian dynasty many of them were able administrators, intelligent and energetic leaders, but always politicians rather than churchmen. Their private schemes and the interests they served were those of the Byzantine state rather than of Mother Church. They lacked something which has always been the glory of the Western episcopate and of its head, the Roman pontiff: that is to say, that high sense of a duty to something far above the claims of politics, a duty to the needs of Christendom. The error which confuses the City of God with the City of Man, an error long ago recognized by St Augustine, reached its climax in Byzantine Caesaro-Papism of the tenth century. Its disastrous consequences would very soon appear.

All things considered, we may well be astonished to discover that the Byzantine clergy were not more subservient than we have found them. Several of the patriarchs resisted the emperor, not, however— and this is characteristically Byzantine—in questions of morality and faith, but in matters of ecclesiastical discipline to which the Eastern Church attached the greatest importance, especially when they were peculiar to herself. For example, she forbade a widow to marry a widower, and this was the occasion of a violent dispute between the patriarch and Nicephorus Phocas.   She also prohibited fourth (and even third) espousals, a fact which the Emperor Leo VI learned to his cost, for he was opposed by two successive patriarchs.   At Rome, where the marriage laws followed the principles laid down by St Paul and placed no obstacle to remarriage of widowed persons, controversy on such formal questions would have been unthinkable.   On the other hand one is astounded by the ease with which the high Byzantine clergy agreed to bless unions that were manifestly based upon murder and adultery, and to crown emperors who had obtained the throne by no other means than poison or the dagger.   The prostrations of the patriarch before John Tzimisces after the butchery of Nicephorus, to cite but one example, were no more edifying than their flattery of Theophano, who exchanged husbands with such graceful facility, or of the Empress Zoë, one of the last great Basilissae of the dynasty, whose matrimonial career was one long train of scandal and who, at the age of fifty, obtained the blessing of the Church upon her union with an effeminate youth of twenty years. . . .   That is evidence enough of submission to the secular power; yet there is on record an even more terrible example of the clergy's willingness to supply the needs of statecraft.   An archbishop, in order to rid the emperor of a trouble-some enemy, administered poisoned bread in Holy Communion.

Here we must notice one very important fact.   The Western Church was certainly not free from defect, but she possessed within herself a spiritual deposit which served her as a means of reform. This was the monastic order, a decisive influence, as we have often seen, in preventing the Church from yielding to the tendencies of fallen nature.   But in the East monasticism was unable to resist the mortal dangers of Caesaro-Papism.   As a result of the iconoclastic dispute the oriental religious were enclosed more strictly than ever in their convents, preoccupied solely with their prayers and mystical speculations.   Greek monks of the ninth and tenth centuries, unlike those of the sixth or seventh, took no part in public life, were seldom seen, and were virtually dead to the world.   St Theodore even forbade his monks to hold any conversation at all with laymen!   To flee society in order to 'save oneself' had become the formula of the monastic vocation, imposed by the Studium.   Hence the lack of any desire to make contact with the rest of mankind, to organize studies, or even to preserve the elements of culture, all of which the Benedictines did so well.   This attitude certainly contributed to the atrophy of the Eastern Church and left nothing to outweigh the curse of Caesaro-Papism.

It was indeed the excessive interference with the Church by the imperial power that gave rise to an unhappy conflict in the course of which Christians ceased to be one 'as the Father and the Son are one.'

The apogee of the Macedonian dynasty and of Caesaro-Papism was contemporary with the collapse of the Carolingian Empire and the consequent strengthening of papal authority and Roman prerogatives, of which the pontificate of Nicholas I and the fame of the 'False Decretals' are indications. Even in the East, where the defeat of iconoclasm was an imperial victory, the Pope's prestige had been greatly enhanced, thanks to his firm stand throughout that affair. Was conflict then inevitable between Rome and Byzantium? The formalities were still observed and the authority of the Roman See was not disowned: it was invoked by monastic cliques in their disputes, as well as by the emperor Leo VI in the question of his fourth marriage. The patriarch continued to notify the Pope of his appointment before he was consecrated, and Councils were generally held under the presidency of a papal legate. But in fact the opposition was so fundamental that there was bound one day to be trouble, and in that light we must view the several episodes of a complicated struggle which ended in the Greek schism.

## PHOTIUS

The story begins late in the Isaurian dynasty with one of those disputes as to the validity of a patriarchal election that were so common a feature of Byzantine history. The patriarch Ignatius, a creature of the pious empress Theodora—she who had restored the cult of images—was a man whose outward humility concealed a will of iron: neither meekness nor diplomatic tact, nor even discretion, were his ruling virtues. Disquieting rumours were current as to the behaviour of the young Basileus, Michael III, who, it was said, referred to his companions in debauch as 'my bishops and patriarchs.' There was also criticism of Bardas, the emperor's rich and all-powerful minister, who was openly engaged in a disgraceful love-affair with his own daughter-in-law. Ignatius, a holy man but without much experience, had lent a ready ear to these rumours and had not hesitated to protest. He had actually gone so far as to offer Bardas a public insult by refusing him Holy Communion on the feast of the Epiphany in 858. Retaliation took the form of involving the patriarch in an imaginary plot, and in the following November Ignatius had found himself blamed for some trouble stirred up in the city partly through his fault. He had been persuaded to resign and found himself in a monastery of the Archipelago of Princes, imprisoned and deposed. It was not the first time that a Basileus had contributed to the personal sanctification of a patriarch by restoring him to a life of cloistered contemplation; but this time the fall of Ignatius was the beginning of an extraordinary crisis.

The one appointed to succeed him was named *Photius*.  It is not easy to form an opinion of this man upon whom some historians have lavished undue praise while others have vilified him unjustly.  Son of a noble family, one of whose maternal uncles had married a sister of Theodora and whose uncle on his father's side had been patriarch, Photius had entered the government service at an early age and had been highly successful.  Ambassador to the caliph of Bagdad, and then Palatine Secretary, he was one of the most powerful figures at Court.  He had, moreover, an encyclopaedic mind, thoroughly acquainted with literature, grammar, philosophy, and theology: 'a true heir of classical Greece,' as Mgr Amann describes him, 'the spiritual son of Demosthenes, Aristotle, Lysias, and Plato.'  His character was a blend of ability and astuteness combined with the firmness of a leader that sometimes bordered on the authoritarianism of a schoolmaster.  From the religious point of view he was un-doubtedly a sincere believer, as were most Byzantines.  Photius was the man dreamed of by the huge party that upheld the Caesaro-Papist pretensions of the Basileus and of all those who desired a more pliant form of Christianity, more adapted to the age than was the rigid puritanism of Ignatius and the monks.

Did Photius willingly accept the holy but heavy charge thus laid upon him?  He himself declared that he had been most reluctant thus to disturb the even tenor of his way.  But he was made to understand his suitability for the role of peacemaker between the Church and the Throne, and the realization of his own worth easily convinced him that he would fulfil the public expectations.  There was one obstacle to his selection as patriarch: he was only a layman; but the elevation of a layman to the episcopate was not without precedent, as witness the case of St Ambrose, and besides, mere trifles of that sort did not matter at Byzantium.  Tonsured on 20th December 858, he received on the four succeeding days the seven degrees of Holy Order, which enabled him to be consecrated patriarch on Christmas Day—by an archbishop, incidentally, who had been suspended and excommunicated by Igna-tius.  These irregularities were nothing; the continued existence of Ignatius was more troublesome.  It was all very well to make him fine promises, to grant him a kind of pension, and finally, when he resisted, to secure his denunciation by a hastily summoned and compliant Council; but matters did not end there.  Anti-Photian disturbances broke out in several places, notably at Smyrna and Neocaesarea, the archbishops of which declared for Ignatius, and at the Studium, whose abbot was banished to the Chersonese.  That did not exactly make for a peaceful settlement. . . .  The aged patriarch was removed to the island of Mitylene.  He had formally resigned, he recognized the authority of Photius, he had appealed to neither Pope nor Council, and yet he was a living symbol of opposition to the emperor. Some enemies of the Basileus, conspiring to bring back Theodora to power and Ignatius to the patriarchate, had been arrested; after which the old man himself had been worried by the police and ultimately deposed.

It was at this point that the Holy See intervened. Every patriarch, on his election, used to address a letter to the occupants of the other four patriarchal sees. Known as the 'synodical letter,' it explained how he had been chosen and consecrated, and made a profession of faith. This proceeding was, of course, a mere formality so far as concerned the patriarchs of Antioch, Alexandria, and Jerusalem, who were prisoners of Islam; but at Rome it was of supreme importance. The answer of the Curia amounted to official recognition. Now when Photius's synodical letter reached the Eternal City, the Pope was none other than Nicholas I (858–67), one of the strongest characters to occupy the throne of Peter at that time. He was the very last person to admit that, as patriarch of patriarchs, he had simply to confirm the decision of Constantinople; he meant to exercise the right of control derived from the Roman primacy. Skilfully drafted though it was, the letter from Photius was not altogether satisfactory. Nicholas I replied briefly, but sent to the Basileus Michael two legates whose duty it was to investigate the circumstances of the patriarchal election. They also brought a letter drawing attention to the irregularities involved, and took occasion to suggest that the emperor would do well to restore to the Western Church those territories which had long ago been snatched from her jurisdiction by Leo III the Isaurian. The situation was beginning to deteriorate. In due course the legates reached Byzantium. Here, either because they had been circumvented by Photius, or because, being on the spot, they understood the position more clearly and believed, as good canonists, that the Eastern Church's recognition of Rome's right to sit in judgment on the patriarch was worth a few concessions, the two papal ambassadors held a council which not only recognized Photius but renewed the condemnation of Ignatius. This, however, was not recognized by Nicholas I, who at that very moment was stoutly resisting the master of the West, Lothaire II. When he heard the report of his legates he immediately deposed them for having exceeded their powers. Soon afterwards there arrived in Rome a delegation of Ignatius's supporters, though not sent by him. A Council met there in 863; Byzantium was notified of its decisions, and the other three patriarchs were informed that the Pope refused to recognize Photius. A more formal condemnation of Photius was transmitted to the emperor, but its tone revealed no wish for a decisive break.

Affairs had reached this stage when the conflict suddenly became more acute because of the Bulgarian question. The date of the

Photian quarrel, in fact, coincides exactly (863–4) with the baptism of
Boris and his having to choose between the Latin and the Greek rite,
between obedience to a far-distant but more liberal pope and submission to a nearer and alarming neighbour, the Caesaro-Pope of the
East. There was nothing extraordinary in Bulgaria's decision in
favour of the Apostolic See. As for the Papacy itself, what should be
its policy in this affair? In the West the popes had succeeded in
bringing together Barbarians of every sort—Germans, Franks, and
Saxons; in the East they had been obstructed in this work by the claims
of Byzantium, and more particularly by the usurpation of Illyricum
(i.e. the northern Balkans) accomplished by the Byzantine clergy
under Leo III. The restitution of these lands had been sought in vain;
and to receive the Bulgars was to throw a bridgehead into eastern
Illyricum, to combat oriental influence on its own ground. Nicholas
I was careful not to miss an opportunity. We should recall that,
profiting by a blunder on the part of Photius, he had shown towards
King Boris a high degree of friendly understanding. The expulsion
of Greek missionaries from Bulgaria had infuriated Byzantine opinion,
and the patriarch hastened to exploit the incident. A papal mission,
sent to Constantinople to inform the Basileus in no uncertain terms
that Bulgaria was henceforward Roman, was molested, detained for a
while, and then expelled, to the accompaniment of bitter words.

Photius was not ignorant of the considerable difficulties confronting
Nicholas I at this time, when the Pope had just deposed those archbishops who had approved Lothaire's divorce; [1] it might be possible to
launch a concerted attack upon the Holy See. In a written memorial,
and in an actual Council which was attended by all the great Pope's
enemies, Photius charged Nicholas with harbouring 'unjustifiable pre-
tentions,' and of holding some dangerous novelties in the field of
dogma. Byzantium then took the unprecedented step of declaring
the Pope deposed! Thus was inaugurated a system of manœuvre
which would prove so harmful to the Church, the principle of empha-
sizing the least points of difference, of intentionally poisoning the
small wounds of vanity, of purposely inflaming jealousy and rivalry.

In the month of November 867, when tension between Rome and
Byzantium was at its height, the two adversaries disappeared from the
scene within ten days of one another. Nicholas I died on the thirteenth; Photius was dismissed on the twenty-third. The dead Pope
was succeeded in the normal way by Hadrian II; what had happened
to remove Photius? Nothing less than the revolution which brought
the Isaurian dynasty to an end. Basil I, the Macedonian, had just
obtained the throne by the twofold assassination of Bardas and Michael
III, and it was to be expected that he would not be slow to liquidate the

[1] See Chapter VIII, section on 'St Nicholas I.'

creature of Bardas. (He did so, perhaps, rather too hurriedly, and the Council of Constantinople, 869–70, was long omitted by the Eastern Church from the list of oecumenical assemblies.) Moreover, the attitude of Photius, who treated the emperor as a murderer, helped to bring about his own fall. By forthwith restoring peace to the Church by associating himself with Rome and including in his suite all the partisans of the 'martyr' Ignatius, Basil wiped out the stains of blood which he had shed; the soldier was not devoid of shrewdness.

The Papacy, then, had been successful, but Hadrian II looked for a too decisive victory: it is not a good thing to be too much in the right. The Byzantines would gladly welcome the Roman legates in procession, with candles and torches; they were not prepared to accept the papal decisions without a word in reply. It was even necessary to summon a Council at Constantinople to pass a true judgment on Photius, who maintained complete silence, 'like Jesus before his judges,' waiting for the future. It was not long before Basil I found himself too closely tied to Rome. He was jealous of the Western emperor, Lothaire, whom Hadrian II greatly admired, and he considered that too humble a submission had been required of Photius's adherents. Then once again the situation was aggravated by the Bulgarian question: King Boris, furious at having asked Rome in vain for an independent patriarch as head of his Church, turned to Basil, who understood the importance of the gesture and hurried to negotiate with the Bulgarians. This step revealed how far the Byzantine prelates could be trusted: Ignatius agreed to consecrate an archbishop and ten suffragans for service in Bulgaria, thus linking hands with the very see that had rejected him. Hadrian II attempted to counteract Byzantine influence in the Balkans by consecrating St Methodius as Archbishop of Sirmium, but the game was lost. Antagonism between East and West, brought to light by the proceedings of Photius, led to serious results at a future date.

For the final rupture was long deferred. There were still too many links, too many traditions between the two branches of the Church. The popes, moreover, who in the days of Charlemagne had looked to the West, were once again to turn eastward when the disintegration of Carolingian Europe left them alone and unarmed against innumerable enemies, particularly the Saracens. As we have remarked,[1] it was the policy of John VIII (872–82) to appeal to the Greeks to resist the Moslem invasion. A diplomat rather than a fighter, the successor of Hadrian II favoured conciliation. Meanwhile Photius had played a waiting game, and had even employed certain individuals at Rome in order to establish contact with the aged Pope. Ignatius, being out of favour with the Holy See for his near-felony in the Bulgarian affair, made overtures to Photius; while Basil himself, needing a tutor for his

---

[1] See Chapter VIII, section: 'The Final Effort of an Aged Pope.'

sons, appointed this highly cultured man. The result was that, when Ignatius died, Photius was again raised to the patriarchal throne. At Rome a more peaceful wind was blowing. In November 879 the so-called Photian Council recognized the new patriarch, annulling his earlier condemnation; and Photius, in true Christian spirit, welcomed the admonitions addressed to him by the Pope. Everything, then, seemed for the best in the most saintly of worlds; except for the fact that Bulgaria continued to refuse entry to Latin missionaries, while the Eastern Church, as if to provide herself with grounds for dispute, began to rebuke the West for certain innovations which were declared suspect, especially for the use of the *filioque* in the Creed.[1]

In the closing years of the ninth century the situation appeared not altogether unsatisfactory. The Eastern and Western Churches were reconciled, and Byzantine troops were in southern Italy helping Rome to drive out the Saracens. In fact, however, a wound had been opened which might again become poisoned. Photius had disappeared: the circumstances of his removal are obscure, but he had been dismissed in 886 by Basil's successor, Leo VI, who hated him.[2] His books, on the other hand, became increasingly popular, especially the pamphlet *Against Those who Say that Rome is the Premier See*, and, above all, his great *Treatise on the Holy Ghost* in which he criticized Roman 'innovations.' These documents flattered the worst sentiments of the Byzantines. Henceforward antagonism between East and West assumed a new asperity: whereas erstwhile the primacy of Rome had never been seriously disputed, now it was called in question; whereas it was the Papacy that had hitherto condemned heresy in the East, now the Byzantine Church presumed to criticize the Apostolic See upon doctrinal grounds. The career of Photius, an episode in the struggle of Caesaro-Papism against the primacy of St Peter, opened the way to schism; the patriarch becomes ever more clearly the herald or precursor of the Byzantine Church separated from Rome, as happened one hundred and fifty years later.[3]

[1] See Chapter VII, section: 'The Pious Overseer of the Bishops,' and further on in the present chapter, 'The Religious Spirit of Byzantium.'

[2] Leo VI was legally the son of his predecessor; actually he was a bastard son of Michael III who had married his mistress to his favourite, Basil. His putative father was thus the murderer of his real father—a truly Byzantine situation, which explains the hatred of the young emperor for those who had served Basil I.

[3] In 996–8 Photius took his place, together with his former enemy Ignatius, among the canonized patriarchs of Constantinople. From this period onwards his name became more and more of a stumbling block between East and West. The Westerns abhorred his memory; the Orientals cherished above all his opposition to the 'tyrannical claims' of the Papacy. A right assessment of the man would take a middle road between exaltation and denigration. After having long been severely handled by Western historians of the Church, he has been so fairly treated since 1930 that it is possible to speak of his 'rehabilitation' (Père de Moreau, 'La Rehabilitation de Photius' in *Nouvelle Revue théologique*, February 1950).

## MICHAEL CERULARIUS AND THE GREEK SCHISM

Why was the rupture so long postponed? The Byzantine historians were concerned mainly to exalt the anti-Moslem and anti-Bulgarian 'epic'; but in the half-light which they throw upon the religious aspects of the tenth century, the underlying reasons for this delay are fairly clear. They will be found both in the West and in the East. This century, as we shall see, witnessed an eclipse of the Papacy, torn by faction and befouled by scandal; it was the darkest period in Church history. How could the Apostolic See follow a rigid policy in these circumstances? Again, the successive ruin of the several branches of the Carolingian dynasty removed one cause of antagonism: the Basileus had never forgiven Rome for the *coup d'état* of Christmas 800, the 'surreptitious coronation of a Barbarian,' which the Eastern Church had regarded as a kind of sacrilegious schism tending to place the whole of Christendom under the tutelage of a Frankish Church— Frankish and therefore contemptible. But as soon as Charlemagne's descendants had ceased to exist, Byzantium felt reassured.

From the oriental point of view also several considerations favoured an understanding with Rome. Some of them were only spasmodic, but were none the less important. For example, when the Emperor Leo VI, desirous of contracting a fourth marriage, found himself opposed by the patriarch, he sought to overcome the resistance of his own Church by appealing to the Pope, who gave him satisfaction—a service which was not forgotten. There were also political motives. Romano-Byzantine collaboration, inaugurated by Pope John VIII against the Moslems, became absolutely essential as a new and no less formidable danger arose in the shape of Norse threats to papal territory. The Papacy, then, found itself, throughout the tenth and at the beginning of the eleventh century, playing a considerable part in Byzantine diplomacy. What, however, was the use of an alliance which no longer rested upon a deep sense of universalism, on the spiritual need of unity in Christ, and which lay at the mercy of interest or ambition?

Far more decisive than these motives for agreement were the ever-present causes of antagonism, the former plain for all to see, the latter hidden but controlling. The magnificent revival of Byzantium under the Macedonian dynasty led the Eastern Church to claim a higher and higher degree of independence (autocephalism), especially as the virtual disappearance of the three other patriarchs, who were subject to the Moslems, brought the ecclesiastical rulers of ancient and new Rome face to face. Photius's successors in the patriarchate of Constantinople might from time to time show the Pope some mark of diplomatic respect, but their spirit of detachment from the Holy See continued to increase; thus the practice of sending to Rome the synodical letter after their appointment was very seldom observed. There no longer appeared to be doctrinal differences between the two Churches, which was in one sense a pity, because during the great theological disputes there had always existed at Byzantium a party which relied upon the Pope, and the Papacy now no longer served thus as a bulwark of orthodoxy.    The question of the *filioque* clause, raised by Photius, and which concerned the essence of the Holy Ghost, did not trouble men's minds until later.    On the other hand, there were innumerable difficulties in the field of rites, which in the East were rigid and uniform for the whole Church, whereas in the West they were more varied.    Details of little or no importance could appear as abominable scandals in the eyes of a Byzantine.

Many other causes too made for schism.    There was a notable divergence between the intellectual culture of the East and that of the West; the new Hellenic patriotism, fostered by the Macedonian revival, led the governing classes of Byzantium to despise the Barbarian West, a prey to bloody strife.    The Christian *élite*, that is to say, the better elements of monachism, which was in a flourishing condition at this time, shrank from Rome through disappointment at having seen the popes accept Photius, authorize the fourth marriage of a Basileus, and help unworthy men to the patriarchal throne.    We can understand the wrath of those holy monks when they beheld the miserable Pope John XI, aiding and abetting the choice as patriarch of Romanus Lecapenus's youngest son Theophylact, who had been ordained at the age of ten and consecrated bishop at fifteen.[1]    In practice, the cause of loyalty to Rome found no support in the Byzantine conscience; a mere political accident was enough to effect the transition from detachment to open rupture.    Two historical facts went to prepare the climate. One, in the last third of the tenth century, was the emergence of the Holy Roman Empire, an alliance between the Ottos and the Papacy, which proved to Byzantium that the Apostolic See remained true to its Western policy, true to its 'barbarians.'    This infuriated the Orientals: 'What! confer the imperial title on a Barbarian, on a man of straw, the same title as was conferred upon Augustus?'    The other historical fact was a period of forty years after the year 1000, under Cluniac influence and with the direct support of the Germanic emperors, particularly of Henry III.    For those years witnessed a reform of the Papacy, with a succession of excellent Cluniac popes, which resulted in a toughening of papal policy towards Byzantium.    The

---

[1] A strange patriarch, this horse-lover, who, one Maundy Thursday, left the divine office on receiving news that his favourite mare had dropped a foal, went to see what the foal was like, and eventually died from a fall while riding in a race!

conditions for rupture were now present, and only the will of one man was needed to bring it about.

The man who premeditated and determined upon this rupture was *Michael Cerularius*, Patriarch of Constantinople from 1043 to 1058. A strange personality, unattractive but remarkable, was this patrician whose youth had been so entirely occupied in politics that he had taken part in a serious conspiracy and had even dreamed of seizing the throne, and yet who, after he had been converted and become a monk, revealed himself only as the sternest of ascetics and a keen theologian.

The ambition he had been unable to assuage in the antechambers of the Sacred Palace he now concentrated upon the patriarchate, declaring at his election that he viewed his function as 'not one whit inferior to that of the purple or the diadem.' Both forthright and subtle, knowing how to assume the rigidity of stone, 'as if,' says the historian Psellos, 'he possessed the tablets of Jupiter,' but capable also of infinite patience, infinite cunning, and infinite perfidy, he was resolved to make himself undisputed Pope of the East. There can be no doubt that his plan to precipitate the crisis had been long matured.

Why was it that Cerularius launched his offensive about 1050? The Normans were in process of establishing a kingdom in southern Italy, and an alliance of all Christian forces was in the air. The Byzantine high commissioner in Italy, the 'Catapan' Argyros, a Lombard, favoured this policy and won over the emperor Constantine X during a stay in Byzantium. Pope Leo IX was informed, and in 1052 visited the German emperor Henry III to invite his support. There was widespread talk of a prophecy, according to which 'the lion and the lion cub would destroy the wild ass,' meaning that the old and the young emperor would combine against the Saracen. But the Patriarch of Constantinople had reason to fear that such a move might give the Pope greater authority in southern Italy than his own. That, however, was a minor disadvantage; above all it was clear that such a triumvirate, by placing the Pope and the two emperors on an equal footing, would relegate himself to second place. By temperament, as well as by virtue of his political background and monastic profession, he detested Rome. His ambition was threatened. During the year 1052 something occurred to show him that the primacy of his see, upon which he had set his heart, was gravely imperilled. The newly appointed Syrian patriarch, the wise and saintly Peter of Antioch, who would so bitterly deplore the schism, had revived the ancient custom of addressing a synodical letter to the Pope. Cerularius of course had not done so; he resolved to act at once and force the emperor to abandon all thought of an alliance with the West by restoring him to his former role of 'Caesaro-Papist' and posing as more royalist even than the monarch. To this end the patriarch set on foot a scheme which was enabled to succeed only too well by the clumsiness of the West.

Michael Cerularius opened his offensive upon grounds where he knew the Byzantines would follow him, that of the sacrosanct rites, and in order not to show his hand too soon he acted in the first place through subordinates. Archbishop Leo of Ochrida, in Bulgaria, which was at that time completely subject to Byzantium, wrote a letter to the Bishop of Trani, in southern Italy. Now Trani belonged to Rome, although situated in Byzantine territory, so that the archbishop's letter was equivalent to a communication from Cerularius to the Pope. Soon afterwards a monk of the Studium, Nicholas Stotathos, published a kind of pamphlet. Both these documents had a single purpose: to denounce the errors of the Western Church. And what monstrous errors! The Occidentals communicated with unleavened instead of leavened bread; they used dead bread, matter without life, in imitation of the horrid ways of Israel! They ate meat that had not been drained of blood, a grave breach of scriptural law! They sometimes fasted on Saturday, which clearly meant that they observed the Sabbath. They omitted the *Alleluia* in Lent, a dreadful lapse from tradition! Finally, their priests were clean-shaven, which was manifestly indecent! Such were the trifling matters of food and ritual that were to be the subject of so terrible a conflict. Photius had at least raised dogmatic questions.

Rome met this assault, of whose significance she was well aware, with the utmost determination, having regard particularly to the fact that Cerularius had ordered the Latin churches at Constantinople to be closed, and that during the disturbances occasioned by this measure some consecrated hosts had been trodden underfoot. The chief adviser and confidant of Leo IX was Cardinal Humbert of Moyenmoutier, a man of high intelligence and strong character, though somewhat lacking in tact and affability, and one of those who at that time advocated a much needed reform of the Church.[1] He translated the above-mentioned documents into Latin and was entrusted with the Pope's reply. He fulfilled this task with suitable firmness, not scorning to discuss the pettifogging details alleged by the Byzantines, but affirming the rights of the Holy See, which, according to the Council of Nicaea, 'may not be judged by anyone,' and contrasting the age-long vacillations of the patriarchs with the consistency of the popes in doctrinal matters. In a word, he set the affair on its true basis, the primacy of Rome and her oecumenical character. Michael Cerularius at the same time came into the open with a letter to the Holy Father: 'If you will have my name venerated in a single church in Rome, I undertake to have yours venerated likewise throughout the

[1] See Chapter X, section: 'The Spirit of Reform Enters the Church.'

world.' This was a subtle way of placing himself on a level with the Pope, and he too received a firm answer: the Eastern Church must remain in communion with Peter or agree to become 'a cabal of heretics, a conventicle of schismatics, a synagogue of Satan.' The temperature was beginning to rise.

It was not, perhaps, altogether adroit of Leo IX to send as his ambassadors to Constantinople the impetuous Cardinal Humbert along with the Chancellor of the Church, Frederick of Lorraine (afterwards Clement IX), who was equally unyielding and equally inexperienced in the complexities of Byzantine diplomacy. These two allowed themselves to be caught in a network of quibbles, agreeing to discuss leavened and unleavened bread, criticizing the oriental custom of married clergy, and generally, in fact, playing into the hands of Cerularius, who desired nothing so much as to prolong and inflame the dispute. The people of Byzantium, duly instructed, told one another that all masses said by the Occidentals, from the very beginning, were null and void. The patriarch kept silence, taking little part, waiting till his hour should strike.

It was none other than the papal legates who tolled the bell. On 16th July 1054 Cardinal Humbert and his suite attended a solemn service in St Sophia. After fulminating violent denunciations of the patriarch, who was described particularly as a rebel against the Pope's authority, they laid upon the high altar a document announcing his excommunication. Then, leaving the basilica, they shook the dust from their shoes, crying: 'May God behold and judge us!' This spectacular performance, so they thought, would prove decisive and persuade the emperor to get rid of Cerularius. Canonically, however, it was meaningless, for two reasons: (1) the legates had not been authorized to take such a step; and (2) since Leo IX died on 19th April, the powers of his representatives had lapsed *de facto*, though the event was as yet unknown. Their gesture was certainly decisive, but in a sense very different from that hoped for by the legates.

Michael Cerularius was on top of the world. Instead of being, as it were, a prisoner at the bar, accused of having sought by his pride to rend the seamless garment, he now appeared as defender of the Eastern Church against the mockery of the West. The people were solidly behind him. Constantine IX, more than ever anxious to maintain his alliance with Rome against the Normans, attempted to interfere; but a first-class riot, stirred to the intensity required by the patriarch, showed the feeble Basileus more clearly the limit of his power. He was satisfied with the one lesson and returned for consolation to the arms of his mistress. An attempt at mediation by the holy patriarch Peter of Antioch was repulsed with disdain. Undisputed master of the East, Cerularius completed his work: the bull of excommunication was publicly burned,[1] and on 24th July 1054 the synod of the Eastern Church—a dozen metropolitans and archbishops —met in St Sophia and promulgated a synodal edict which declared the Latins guilty of seeking to pervert the true faith.   Some weeks later Cerularius supplemented this edict with an indictment in which, under the pretext of establishing the rights of his see as against Rome, he put himself forward as sole representative of the true religion of Christ.

So Michael Cerularius had won the day.   At Constantinople he was supreme; too much so, in fact; for he wished to take part in the political crises which, after 1054, succeeded one another with increasing rapidity during the collapse of the Macedonian dynasty.   Annoyed at finding that Michael VI resented his domination, he organized a conspiracy which overthrew the young emperor in 1057 and set up in his place *Isaac Comnenus*, the founder of a new dynasty.   Comnenus, however, pleased though he was to have the crown, was not content to stand like a little boy at the side of the terrible patriarch.   At Christmas 1058 he took advantage of a retreat which Cerularius was making in a convent far from Constantinople to have him arrested, and was about to bring him to trial when the patriarch died.   Public opinion was so inflamed that the emperor himself had to bring back the 'martyr's' body with great pomp and allow the Church to confer on him a regular apotheosis.   Later, under Isaac's successor, Constantine X, who had married a niece of Cerularius, the patriarch was canonized and an annual feast instituted in his honour.

Thus was achieved this unhappy stage in the history of the Church, one of the most grievous (with the Reformation) since the beginning until now.   In 1054 the Greek schism was consummated; it has never, to our great misfortune, been resolved.   We need hardly say that both sides were to blame: on one side there was pride and perfidy, on the other clumsy mishandling and intransigence.

Was the gravity of what had happened understood at the time? Rome and Constantinople each claimed to have been victorious: the Latins boasted of having broken the patriarch's pride, while the Byzantines congratulated themselves on having saved their faith from the impious errors of the West.   In a long report Cardinal Humbert awarded himself a handsome testimonial.   On the shores of the Bosphorus men read with satisfaction a small pamphlet entitled *Treatise on the Franks*, which informed them, to their horror, that in the West women frolicked with the priest during mass, and even sat on the episcopal throne!   Such idle talk eventually imbued men's minds with stupid antagonism.   Only a few rare and truly Christian

---

[1] It was characteristic of Byzantine cunning that Cerularius had only a copy burned; the original was kept as 'proof of the eternal disgrace' of the Westerns.

souls were deeply pained by this wound inflicted on the Church. 'If the queens of the earth are at enmity,' exclaimed Peter of Antioch, 'all the world will be in tears'; and in 1064 a monk, George the Hagiorite, went so far as to declare: 'There is no difference between Greeks and Latins.' Christendom indeed took a long time to recognize the fact of schism;[1] pilgrims to the Holy Land continued to pass through Byzantine territory; the popes were still in official relations with the Basileus, and some of the Byzantine emperors, e.g. Michael VII, even made gifts to Western monasteries, above all to Monte Cassino. Nevertheless the cleavage was incapable of repair and steadily widened; it was rendered final by the loss of the Byzantine possessions in Italy to the Normans and, later, by the incidents of the Crusades.

## The Religious Spirit of Byzantium

As Byzantium separates from Rome and the two branches of the Church of Christ set out to follow their separate paths, we should stop to consider not only those distressing events, those proud patriarchs and aggressive theologians. For that is not the whole of the Greek Church, heir to so many generations of good Christians, depositary of patristic teaching, and towards whom even to-day many Christians in the West turn as to a vast but unknown well-spring. Surely the faith of the great Cappadocians, of the heroic defenders of images, must not be forgotten because of those evil shepherds who led their flocks into the way of schism. However cruelly a Christian heart may feel the break of 1054, this cannot impair our admiration of everything wherewith the Greek Church, in communion with Rome, has endowed Christian faith and practice.

In the ninth and tenth centuries we can no longer admire the Byzantines on the doctrinal plane, where formerly they reigned supreme. We may recall that the conclusion of the great theological disputes also marked the end of oriental theology's most flourishing period; the torch had been passed on to the West. After the death of St John Damascene in 749, and of St Theodore Studites in 826, it was no longer possible to name anyone in the Greek Orient who could

---

[1] This is clear from the history of Christianity in Russia. The schism of 1054 provoked no reaction in Kiev and caused no change in her relations with the West. For example, the three daughters of Prince Yaroslav (died 1054), who were married to the kings of France, Hungary, and Norway, were never confronted with any religious difficulty. Again, those Western princesses who were married to princes of Kiev did not feel themselves to be living in a schismatic country. It is well known too that the Rheims Gospel, used at the coronation of the kings of France, was a Slavonic book, brought by Queen Anne, daughter of Yaroslav, at the time of her marriage to King Henry I. A century later we have the case of a Russian princess who went with a group of young ladies to found a convent in Jerusalem and who was canonized by the Latin Church as St Euphrosyne. The Christian conscience was not quickly resigned to the gaping wound of schism.

be compared with them. The only theologian of consequence was Photius, and his influence was by no means beneficial. Greek polemists from this day to our own have relied for evidence against the Latins upon his *Treatise on the Holy Ghost*, a skilful but perfidious work. Taking the celebrated formula *Filioque procedit* in its narrowest sense, and interpreting it to mean that the Holy Ghost 'proceeds from a principle without principle,' Photius endeavoured to show that the Western Church, by applying it to the Holy Ghost in relation to the Son, was erroneous to the point of heresy in its doctrine of the Trinity, and he brought together a whole scriptural and patristic arsenal against this imaginary error. The subsequent influence of this disastrous work was to be considerable.

The soul of Byzantium must be sought elsewhere. It resided in a people fascinated by ritual, with a mania for small observances and quasi-superstitious practices, but whose faith was from many points of view so moving. We find it in those priests for whom the liturgy was the framework of the spiritual life and who devoted themselves so joyfully to their ceremonies. We find it in the monks, hidden away in far-off mountains and in whom there seems to have lived the spirit of the early Fathers, anchorites who retired into the desert that they might give themselves more perfectly to God.

The steady growth of ritualism among the Byzantines is quite astonishing. We have seen striking examples of it in the dispute with the Latin Church, and many others can be cited in other connections, such, for instance, as the clash between Byzantium and the Armenian Church because the latter forbade eggs and cheese on fast days which the Greeks denounced as 'loathsome heresy.' On the other hand we may ask whether strict rites were not absolutely necessary to an excitable, vacillating, and inconsistent people; whether its submission to stern discipline did not save it from being overwhelmed by those heresies whereby it was so often threatened. Love of ritual did not prevent the flowering of a deep faith, of which there are many proofs. Devotion to Mary, which we have seen rise and develop in an earlier age, continued to increase, and when the schism of 1054 was complete, so far was that devotion from being extinguished that it is safe to say that the Marian homilies of the Byzantine Middle Ages are worthy of former times. The ardent faith, so full of contrast, which we have seen in those emperors and nobles, who passed from sin to repentance with astonishing ease, had its counterpart in the more serene faith observable in many families, incarnate in the holy figures of wives, mothers, and religious.

Among the most impressive evidences of the vitality of oriental Christianity in the ninth and tenth centuries was the monastic institution. One might have thought that its development in preceding eras could never be surpassed, and yet the Macedonians gave it so powerful an impulse that many houses founded at that time have survived into our own day. The Iconoclastic Dispute had almost led to the suppression of convents within the Empire, and some stern laws went so far as to forbid the reception of novices, and even, for a time, to secularize both monks and monasteries. The defeat of the iconoclasts was therefore looked upon as the victory of monachism, which had glorious results. Such ancient conventual sites as Olympus, whence had come resistance to the destroyers of images, welcomed armies of postulants. New ones were also established.[1] Emperors, empresses, princes of the blood, and noblemen multiplied their foundations, over which they enjoyed a right of control that was not always considerate. The attraction of religious life became so widespread that the government was several times obliged to limit the age of entry (attempting to raise it from ten to sixteen years) or to forbid certain officials and soldiers to leave their posts without permission in order to become monks. For the most part enormously rich, these communities of the ninth and tenth centuries were veritable nurseries of good Christians, and they had, in practice, a virtual monopoly of the episcopate.

It is impossible to speak of Byzantine monasticism without great respect. The *hegoumenoi* (superiors) of these convents were in many ways comparable with the great Western abbots; and if, being farther removed from the world, they had not the same influence upon society, the faith, austerity, and sanctity which are evident in so many of them demand our admiration. At this period the anchoretic life, the ancient form of oriental monachism, originating with St Anthony, St Pachomius, and St Sabas, was out of fashion; most monasteries followed the Rule of St Basil, the strict observance of which had been revived by the Studite reform and the influence of St Theodore. Community life, obedience, abstinence, and obligatory manual labour were practised almost as at Cluny; perpetual prayer, the *laus perennis*, was in general use. Monasticism in the East was subject to lay influence, but to a far less degree than in the West, which was subject to the system of commendation. The great oriental monasteries produced few works of art, literary or otherwise, but who can fail to recognize their merit in the eyes of God?

Among the outstanding events of this epoch, associated with one of the noblest examples of an *hegoumenos*, was the founding of *Mount Athos*. Situated in northern Greece, and forming one arm (about thirty miles long) of the peninsula of Chalcidice, Athos had long been peopled by ascetics, living alone as hermits, but federated under a

---

[1] The spread of Byzantine monachism at this period was so great that Greek convents were founded even in Italy, e.g. at Grotta Ferrata near Rome.

*protos*.  About 962 there landed at Athos a remarkable character in the person of *St Athanasius of the Laura*, who was to give the 'holy mountain' the appearance it has to-day.  Born at Trebizond and educated at Constantinople, he had become a monk and acted as spiritual director of the future Basileus Nicephorus Phocas.  In order to escape being elected superior of his monastery, for he was a man of extraordinary humility, Athanasius had once, in 958, stayed at Athos as a hermit.  Nicephorus had torn him from his retreat and appointed him chaplain-general of the fleet which captured Crete from the Saracens in 961.  But the memory of the dear, silent peninsula had remained in his saintly heart.  He returned as soon as he was able, this time to found a real monastery, a *Laura*, to which Nicephorus gave all the booty taken from Islam.  After some initial difficulty with the hermits, the whole of Mount Athos quickly recognized this monastery as its head and heart.  The great Laura was the centre of a monastic republic, which has ever since remained a living force, respected by history, spared by war, and even by the Turks.  Other convents soon arose—Vatopedi, Zographon, Philotheou, and many more; the passing centuries have only added to their number.

It is to Athos that we must still go, if we would conjure up all that is most impressive in the spirituality of Byzantium.  There, on that wild landscape, where the memory of paradise seems to live on, amid singing waters, friendly beasts, and the voice of gentle winds among the olive branches, a continual prayer mounts to God from those thousands of souls who, coming from all parts of 'orthodox' Christendom and speaking five or six different languages, unite in a single flight of devotion.  As the ship follows the rugged, foam-fringed coast, the traveller sees everywhere the many signs of this age-long faith.  In the walls of rock, sometimes inaccessible, there are the caves of anchorites, who, as in the days of St Anthony, live all alone in God, all alone till death.  Clearings in the woods reveal small rustic convents of cenobites, and little hamlets where sarabites dwell in twos or threes.  And there, in the far distance, enormous, like fortified cities, brilliant with ochre, red, and gold, with stage upon stage of rickety balconies looking out to sea, rise the great monasteries, regular citadels of faith.  Has the religious life of Athos changed much since the days when Macedonian emperors, between one campaign and the next, went there on spiritual retreat?  The *Catholicon*, or church in the shape of a Greek cross, always stands at the centre of a square court, with its family of attendant chapels scattered round about.  In the refectories marble tables, with shallow holes at regular intervals to serve as plates, have been polished by the hands of generations.  The walls, adorned with complicated and amazing frescoes, recall the pomp of the Byzantine Church in forms that have not altered during a thousand years.

This place, devoted to prayer, impresses one deeply with a sense of peaceful and joyous contemplation. Beneath the bright Greek sun colours and tones blend in a symphony of light: the blood-red of façades, the pale ochre of old marble, the emerald and sapphire of frescoed galleries, and everywhere the orange stain of bignonia, the violet clusters of bougainvillea. The surge of the nearby sea serves only to emphasize the silence. In the fountain basins gently falling waters sing a litany of divine love. Black-clad monks in their long habits walk to and fro, silent, recollected. Suddenly there is a loud noise, at once dry and heavy, the sound of wood on wood: a young brother passes holding under one arm a long lath of cypress which he strikes with a hammer. It is a signal, the equivalent of our Western bells: the dark silhouettes of the monks hurry from all directions to the *Catholicon*, and we hear through an open door the start of their slow psalmody. . . .

There we have an ever-living image of the Greek Church, which, despite nine hundred years of separation, no Christian can but feel to be fraternal, the concrete witness of all that her spirituality has given to Christendom. How can we withhold grateful acknowledgment? How too when we remember all that the Byzantine epoch contributed to the Christian world in other ways: the conversion of the Slavs, the check and repulse of the Moslems, the revival of civilization at a moment when, in the West, it seemed condemned to death?

## THE MACEDONIAN RENAISSANCE

The last, but not least important, benefit conferred by Macedonian Byzantium upon mankind was the marvellous recovery of civilization, which marked the two centuries of that dynasty. No age, not even that of Justinian, has surpassed in glory, wealth, or fruitfulness that during which the great Basil's descendants held the imperial sceptre. It was a golden age the memory of which still gleams in the splendour of Venice, daughter of Byzantium, and which served as a counterpoise to the miseries of that iron age through which the West was passing.

The formidable economic development of Constantinople, the New York, so to speak of the Bosphorus, to which foreign trade and many forms of industry drew the riches of the world; the prestige of this capital city whence, by the twofold command of Church and State, there came forth those influences which hellenized many anomalous peoples and thus forged them into a living unity; the will of the victorious Basileus—all these things helped to further the Macedonian 'renaissance,' which redounded in turn to the glory of the dynasty.

Constantinople at this period was a city of more than one million

souls, of every race and every type.   Having sufficient space within
her walls to allow for large tracts of open ground where dogs, children,
asses, and pigs might wander, she presented, as to-day, some remarkable contrasts between the sumptuous decoration of magnificent
avenues and fine arcaded streets and a stinking network of slums where
thick mud alternated with suffocating dust according to the season.
The city was crossed from east to west by the *Mesa*, leading, via
several large squares, to a point where the imperial and Christian power
burst upon the sight.   This was the Augusteon, a stupendous group
of buildings consisting of St Sophia, the Senate House, the Hippodrome, and the Sacred Palace.   Everywhere in the gigantic city there
were churches, porticoes, and columns—everywhere an impression of
wealth and magnificence.   And it was here, in this medley of teeming
life, that there blossomed the new flower of civilization, the flower of
art and thought, which derived many currents of fertility from the deep
strata of the past, and thereby took on a new and splendid appearance.

The most striking manifestation of this rebirth was the new impulse
given to architecture.   Little had been done under the Isaurians,
during the iconoclastic disputes; but there was enormous building
activity under the Macedonians—mostly, of course, in the shape of
residences for the Master of the World.   The *Kenourgion* arose with
its columns of red marble, its mosaic floors inlaid with green Thessalian
marble, its walls covered with slabs of iridescent crystal and topped
with a band of gold.   The old fortified castle of Boucoleon was transformed, enlarged, and splendidly decorated.   Indeed, so many works
were undertaken in these two centuries that the Sacred Palace eventually covered nearly seventy acres with its labyrinthine porticoes, its
courts, galleries, peristyles, and terraces.

Architects, however, devoted as much, if not more, attention to God
as to the all-powerful emperor.   Churches began to arise in incredible
numbers, and many of those to be found in Greece and Asia Minor date
from this period.   The primitive basilican plan of nave and triple apse
continued to be followed here and there, e.g. in the great Laura at
Mount Athos (1004).   But the so-called 'Greek cross' plan, consisting
of two naves of equal length intersecting at right angles, prevailed;
and a famous example may be seen in the nearby convent of Vatopedi
which served as a model for all churches of the Antonian community.
The cupola, already favoured because of the glorious success of St
Sophia, was more and more frequently adopted; it tended to become
less heavy, and also more lofty, as a result of springing from a windowed
drum, which not only improved the lighting, but also gave a more
soaring effect to the exterior.

The masterpiece of 'Macedonian' architecture was the *Nea*, the
'New Church' begun 876 by Basil I within the palace area, together

with which it has unfortunately disappeared. We know its magnificence through the description by Constantine VII, who, writing under the name of Constantine Porphyrogenetos, tells us that in size, beauty, and splendour it rivalled Justinian's St Sophia. It included two intersecting naves and had five cupolas; one of these was built over the intersection, but it is impossible to say whether the others terminated the arms of the cross or were in the angles. As for the decoration, so Constantine told Photius, who refers to it in a sermon, 'to describe it was to cry out in admiration.' One was astonished by its beauty from the very forecourt, where two fountains flung their liquid pearls high into the air, one of white stone ornamented with bronze rings, the other of Egyptian syenite supported by dragons. Within, all was brocade, mosaic, enamel, metal picked out in pearls and precious stones. Aloft, in the cupola, an enormous Christ Pantocrator, surrounded by angels, seemed to preside over a reproduction of the Last Judgment. On the vast walls and on the drums of the cupolas the Blessed Virgin, the saints, and heroes of the Old Testament formed an uninterrupted gallery of more than life-size figures. And on the floor plants and buds in oriental style were represented in mosaic and polychrome marbles with such subtle colouring that 'one thought he walked not upon stone but upon carpets.' How did this art differ from that of former ages, particularly the age of Justinian? In the fact that being less dominated by clerical exigencies—the Iconoclastic Dispute had at least served to lessen the cloying hold of the clergy upon the artists—it enjoyed more liberty. New methods were sought and found. To the subjects suggested directly by religion were added many others, e.g. of historical inspiration. The hieratic spirit of early times gave place to a far more expressive realism, which borrowed elements from classical Greece, from the most charming masterpieces of the Hellenistic age, and from the decorative fantasies of Islam; the vegetable and animal worlds also provided an almost unlimited number of exquisite motifs. 'The result was a blend of dignity and grace, of control and order, and a serene refinement, which became the chief characteristics of Byzantine art in the period of its maturity.' [1]

One of the strange things about decoration in the ninth and tenth centuries was that it no longer confined itself to the inside of a church, but spread all over the exterior. Mosaic and designs in coloured marbles reached the façade, and buildings thus became like enormous reliquaries, rich and colourful as never before. A modern traveller who emerges from the narrow streets that lead into the Piazza of St Mark at Venice can still have a very exact idea of Byzantine magnificence in its greatest period. There, on tympana and lunettes as well as on the interior of semicircular arches, covering every surface,

[1] O. M. Dalton, *East Christian Art*.

brilliant at every level, the mosaics shine with gold and vivid colouring, with the richness of a coronation robe. Everything delights the eye: variegated columns, the play of shadow, the brief flash of white marble, the warm glow of breccia and porphyry flooring. Even the great French Gothic cathedrals, with their wealth of statues, fail to give this impression of wellnigh excessive richness, more suited to exalt the triumph of Him who is the plenitude of all riches than to magnify the humility of the Conquest of Calvary. Byzantine Christianity ever preferred the theology of Glory to the theology of the Cross.

St Mark's, at Venice, was begun in 828 and rebuilt after the fire of 976; it is therefore a typical 'Macedonian' edifice. Its existence shows us an important factor in the history of art, the spread of oriental Christian art during the two centuries of the dynasty. Its influence was considerable. We find it from the Black Sea to Kiev and in the heart of Russia, as well as in southern Italy from Sicily to Rome, and in northern Italy of which Venice and Ravenna are the jewels. Bulgaria, Rumania, and Armenia would never have had the architects we know they must have had, but for this profound and radiant impulse. How often, on some chance journey in Italy, at Amalfi, for instance, at Grotta Ferrata, or in certain churches and chapels in Rome, we feel the hand of Byzantium! Think, too, of Orvieto Cathedral, that wonderful masterpiece of the Italian Grand Renaissance, that casket of white marble covered with luminous mosaics: would it have been such if the decorators of Constantinople had not made their influence felt among the distant hills of Etruria?

All the other arts reveal, at this period, similar characteristics: love of fine materials, a return to the naturalistic and concrete ideal of the Hellenists, which produced rare and precious masterpieces. We possess hardly any Byzantine stuffs, but those which we still have— for instance, the famous brocades in the Musée de la Soierie at Lyons —are evidence of creative power no less convincing than a church or a mosaic. Manuscripts, with their numerous miniatures, were produced in great quantity, aristocratic manuscripts with full-page illustrations rich in gold and purple; simpler and more popular manuscripts, the work of a supple and lively art. In many cases, as if from mischievousness, the artist has introduced into the decoration of some pious book, some good patristic treatise perhaps, subjects from pagan mythology —Artemis and Actaeon, fabulous events in the life of Zeus, or the dance of the Curetes. The masterpiece of this bookmaker's art is undoubtedly the famous Paris Psalter, preserved in the Bibliothèque Nationale. It has existed for a thousand years without sign of wear and tear or age, a marvel of grace and light that seems to have been born but yesterday.

Thus, from Macedonian Byzantium, there came forth a form of art which both gathered up the elements of the past and formulated them anew. Exactly the same thing happened in the intellectual sphere. From the middle of the ninth century Constantinople began to take her place at the hearth of that high culture from which she had previously tended to withdraw. Her university, reorganized by Bardas in 863, brought back a crowd of students, and professors from all over the Greek world came there to teach. From the ninth to the eleventh century a long line of scholars eagerly devoted themselves to classical studies, to the rediscovery of ancient learning, playing in fact the same part as did the Palace school under Charlemagne and the masters of the Carolingian period in the West. The great humanists of the Renaissance were foreshadowed by Photius and Aretas in the ninth century, by the encyclopaedists who used the pseudonym 'Suidas,' and by Constantine Cephalas who published the *Greek Anthology* in the tenth; then at the beginning of the eleventh, by *Michael Psellos*, the most celebrated writer of his time, who was followed by John Mauropos, John the Italiot, and Christopher of Mytilene. They all had the same passion for antiquity, the same devotion to Plato and Homer, the same habit of imitating ancient authors, the same vanity, and the same ardour in the combat of ideas.

It was thus a period of intense intellectual life: theses were disputed and endless subjects put forward for discussion. Nevertheless it was not a creative age. The characteristic type of work, as at Rome under the late Empire, was the compilation, the lexicon, the encyclopaedia. It was believed that nothing could be more useful than the assembling of texts, information, and documents to form an imposing collection. The literary Basileus, Constantine VII Porphyrogenetos, for example, devoted to that end every free moment allowed him by the cares of state. The Church did likewise, availing herself of the opportunity to recover and reassemble the texts upon which she relied, especially the writings of the Fathers and lives of the saints. In the tenth century work of this kind was methodically pursued by Simeon Metaphrastes, the Abbé Migne of the period, whose *Martyria* forms an extremely valuable miscellany, drawing as he did upon many sources that are no longer available, Coptic and Syriac, Arabic and Armenian. The encyclopaedia 'Suidas,' of about the same period, is no less useful for its notes on a crowd of otherwise unknown saints and martyrs.

Literature also, in the Macedonian epoch, was less concerned with creating new forms than with preparing an inventory of resources at the disposal of Byzantium, a particularly useful work of preservation. Had the men of that age a presentiment of the fragility of their civilization? Did they guess that this glorious epoch would be succeeded by another period of decadence which would bring Byzantium to a tragic end?

## The Eve of the Middle Ages

Basil II, destroyer of the Bulgarians, died in 1025, and the decline immediately began.  We know that the outward glory of Byzantium concealed deep-rooted misery and fatal weaknesses: anarchy was always on the point of breaking loose in an overwhelming flood. Upon what did power actually rest? Heredity? No; even when the principle was observed it had not the force of law.  Coronation? No; experience proved that the Church, far too submissive, would consecrate with holy unction the victory of no matter whom.  Popular consent?  No; the mob was fickle and it too understood nothing but force.  Everything depended, therefore, in the last resort, upon the qualities of the ruler: all-powerful if admired and feared, weak and despised if he could not employ the terrors of despotism.  If the idol in golden dalmatics showed himself undecided, slack, or faint-hearted, the ground opened beneath his feet.

Thus matters stood in the second quarter of the eleventh century. Providence, which had for long bestowed upon the Macedonian dynasty the good fortune to produce none but strong men, now turned away her face.  Delivered into the hands of a woman, *Zoë*, niece of Basil II, who had been forcibly married to Romanus Argyros, a high official, the diadem at once began to totter.  There followed a terrible drama in the palace, in which the Basilissa, tired of her husband, first attempted to poison him and then had him drowned in his bath so that she could marry her lover at the victim's funeral ceremony and with the blessing of the patriarch Alexis.  The succeeding acts followed in quick succession.  The new master of the queen and of the Empire, appalled at his crime, abandoned his blood-stained wife and gory crown to enter a monastery and win God's forgiveness by a life of expiation.  The lascivious Zoë then took another husband, an artisan, a young caulker, whom she raised up as Michael V; but he too most ungratefully attempted to get rid of her by shaving her head and shutting her up in the cloister.  The indignant populace of Constantinople forthwith seized the caulker, gouged out his eyes, and demanded the return of the aged Basilissa, who, at the age of sixty-four, straightway married her fourth husband, Constantine Monomachus!  Finally, there emerged from the convent, where she had lived since girlhood, Zoë's sister Theodora, demanding a finger in the imperial pie.  In 1050 the greatest of all Christian thrones was shared by the following persons: Zoë, a faded beauty of seventy years whose only concern was 'to repair the irreparable ravages of time'; her sister Theodora, almost as old, torn between the devotions of a nun and an avarice which made her count her fortune every day; Constantine

IX Monomachus, a gouty old beau, intelligent but indolent, a rake who viewed the world with a sceptical eye; and finally, to shed a little light upon the picture if not to appease the moralists, Constantine's youthful and delightful mistress, Sklerene, whom he had installed in the palace on the same footing as his wife, and who took her seat in the Council, where her opinion more than once prevailed. How were such puppets able to hold fast the helm at a time when the enormous vessel was exposed to one storm after another and shipping water at every point?

For danger once again threatened on all sides, first from beyond the frontiers. The Petchnegs, a new Asiatic horde, had settled on the Danube; they were far more terrible than the Hungarians, who were now in process of conversion to the Christian faith. The situation was not unlike the worst days of the Bulgarian menace; the Balkans were in peril once again. Attempts were made to hold the Petchneg assault by enrolling one of their clans as mercenaries; but this only made it easier for them to raid across the Danube. All the middle years of the century were troubled by their repeated aggression: they occupied the plain of Sofia; Adrianople was overwhelmed by their assault; and the imperial armies, though reinforced by European and Russian auxiliaries, by no means always had the upper hand.

In southern Italy the principal menace was the Normans. They had long since passed the stage of troublesome vagabonds, possessing such fortified places as Melfi, on the upper reaches of the Ofanto, where they stored their arms and booty. Holding these bases, they set out all the more confidently to attack the mercantile cities and maritime convoys. Unfortunately too the Lombards, in revolt against Byzantium, lent them a helping hand, and from 1042 onwards the offensive was maintained by a regular Lombardo-Norman condominium. Robert Guiscard's great adventure was soon to begin, and the imperial troops continued to hold only a few strong points: Brindisi, Otranto, and Taranto.

The gravest peril, however, lay in Asia, although it did not then appear immediate and the Eastern Empire could consider itself undisturbed on that side. Since about the year 1000 the Fatimite caliphs had shown themselves so well disposed, and relations with them were so cordial, that Byzantium supplied Moslem Syria with corn during a famine and helped to rebuild the Holy Sepulchre. In Armenia the age-long efforts of the Greeks had achieved their purpose, and almost the entire country was subject to them. However, another enemy had just appeared, against whom the Greeks, the caliphs of Bagdad, and the Armenians could do very little. By their domination of the Moslem world the Seljuk Turks, with their youthful and warlike ardour, would supplant the Arabs and Persians who had

been enervated by civilization.   Issuing from the steppes around the
Aral Sea, where they lived as nomads, they had (*c.* 1040) subjected the
other Turkish peoples to their own ruler, Togrul-Beg, and then taken
Iraq from the Iranians.   They captured Ispahan in 1051 and Bagdad
in 1055, and the Abbasid caliph appointed Togrul-Beg his 'temporal
vicar.'   Henceforward the Seljuk sultan was responsible for the Holy
War, which had more or less lapsed.   At the turn of the century the
peril had still not revealed itself except on the confines of the Empire,
notably in Armenia, where the Turkish companies were spreading
desolation; but they were soon to appear, ferocious and implacable, in
the provinces.   It was the end of those courteous relations which had,
on the whole, existed between Byzantium and the Moslems for a
hundred years.   The Moslem world, once more in the grip of fanaticism, and prey, moreover, to a frightful regression towards Barbarism,
was about to resume a policy of intolerance.   Byzantine Christendom
would be seriously affected thereby, but would make scarcely an
effort to retaliate.   Western Christendom was to have the honour of
providing an answer—the *Crusades.*

It was at this juncture, when perils from without were gathering on
the frontiers, that the masters of Byzantium deliberately created
another and interior threat that was to paralyse the defence and at the
same time give rise to the worst possible confusion in the State.
Since the death of Basil II the direction of affairs had been monopolized by the eunuchs of the palace,[1] and this fact had produced increasing antagonism between the civil government and the military leaders.
Alarmed, and to some extent justly, by the increasing power of the
generals (who behaved more and more like feudal lords, often considering themselves virtually independent of the central authority), but
feeling unable to subdue them, the high officials devised underhand
measures that were to have disastrous consequences.   The navy was
neglected and very soon became useless.   The army was systematically weakened and a tax was substituted for military service.   The
generals were repeatedly humiliated.

The result was not long delayed: the military revolted.   Two great
risings of the army occurred, one after another, the first in Sicily,
where the troops proclaimed their commanding officer Basileus and
crossed the Adriatic, and again at Adrianople, where the rebels proceeded on the same pattern, but this time reached the walls of the

---

[1] The custom of castrating young boys had become very common in Byzantium.   A
majority of the higher civil servants were eunuchs.   Liutprand, in his account of an
embassy, says that he had even come across emasculated bishops; but Liutprand's word
is not necessarily gospel truth!   On the Church's attitude to castration see particularly
Père Riquet's pamphlet, *La Castration*, Paris, 1948, which contains an excellent historical
account of the subject.   It is worth noting that medieval doctors castrated their clients
on the slightest pretext.   Hernia was a valid reason!

capital. Grave symptoms indeed, because they brought to light not only a cleavage within the State, but also the advent of feudal power, which would dominate society in the East as in the West.

Such was the condition of the Eastern Empire in the middle of the eleventh century. Outwardly strong, wealthy, and powerful, it was undermined by hidden and incurable ills, menaced by awful dangers that steadily increased. Could it hope to preserve on the moral and intellectual plane what it risked losing in the political sphere? Here again appearances were good. Everything seemed to indicate that the conversion of Russia had given birth to a new Byzanto-Slavic Christian culture, no less alive, and perhaps even more fruitful, than the Romano-Germanic Christian culture of the West. But in this domain also appearances were to prove deceptive. Obliged before very long to meet fresh attacks, Byzantium no longer had sufficient strength to follow up a grand policy of cultural expansion. Kiev, a splendid nucleus of civilization, would soon be virtually annihilated by the Tartars. And then, it must be said, the closing years of the Macedonian dynasty witnessed an intellectual recession. Basil II had closed the university; he had found it too expensive to maintain and thought, like most tyrants, that intellectuals are a danger to the State. Half a century later, Constantine IX Monomachus, alarmed by the decadence which followed in public administration, re-established schools of law and philosophy with the help of Psellos, 'consul of philosophy'; but the urge was gone and these reforms did not last. Byzantine intellectualism, which had always been the monopoly of a select few, in close liaison with Church and Government and unable to inspire the masses, became gradually more sterile and withdrew into the narrow framework of 'Byzantinism.'

Early in the second half of the eleventh century when many events —e.g. the Turkish invasion and the growth of feudalism—heralded the Middle Ages, when the last great Byzantine dynasty crumbled into dust, we note one striking coincidence. Between the tragic event of the *Greek schism* (1054) and what I have called an intellectual recession, there set in a kind of hardening process which was to become characteristic of Byzantium. Despite increasing difficulties, the Greeks managed, for another four hundred years, to preserve the outward forms of their civilization. The new way of life, however, the new social, moral, and ethical standards upon which the glory of the Middle Ages rested, would not be discovered by them but by the Western Barbarians who possessed an irresistible dynamism.

Here we see the precise weaknesses of the Greek Church. They may be summarized in what may seem a paradox: she was too closely linked with the State, and at the same time too remote from the world, to assume the task of protector and of guide. She was so closely

associated with the Empire through those of her elements most external
to the faith, through that side of her in fact which corresponded to the
ever-present tendency of every Church to identify the communion of
saints with an administrative organism, that she could not but share
its fate both in prosperity and in disaster.    Her most truly admirable
characteristic, her deep spirituality, urged her to flee the world instead
of trying to reform it.    How far we are from those monastic reformers of the same period, who directed the Western Church according to the highest standards, and from those great popes whom we shall
find so brave and independent in face of the powers!    The truth of
Christ, truth in action, which is the leaven of history, was not entrusted to the patriarchal civil servant of the Sacred Palace, nor to the
*hegoumenos* of *hegoumenoi*, remote in the pious solitudes of Athos;
for the Benedictines of Cluny and for the Roman pontiffs, predecessors
of Gregory VII, a very different future lay in store.

# CHAPTER X

# THE TRAGIC DAWN OF THE YEAR 1000

## FEUDAL ANARCHY AND THE CHURCH

THE YEAR 1000! The very utterance of these syllables evokes the picture of a dismal age, haunted by intolerable anguish, abandoned to the forces of destruction. A legend of doubtful meaning would set the period against an apocalyptic background, and associate the end of the first millennium with some vague terror of judgment day. The truth is sufficiently dramatic without recourse to fable. The historical truth is that not only the year 1000, but the whole century which preceded and part of that which followed it was a period of obscurity during which men, blinded with blood, groped their way fearfully through a quagmire of filth. All that we have seen in the ninth century at the time of the Carolingian collapse—unbridled cruelty, immorality, the decadence of institutions—now reached its culminating point. The fifth century, prey to Barbarian invasion, was as nothing beside its distant successor.

It would none the less be a mistake to confine ourselves to such appearances. One world was dead, another was seeking to be born: was not all the discord and suffering a sign of impending parturition? Yes; therein lies the enormous interest of the age, a period unfamiliar and summarily judged, but one from which there ultimately proceeded that human masterpiece which we know as the medieval Christian civilization of the West. The night of the tenth century is an indubitable fact, but we should not forget the dawn that followed, a dawn unconsciously awaited and made possible by the men of that unhappy time.

It is nevertheless true that first impressions last longest; they are overwhelming. The Barbarian inroads were not yet finished; Europe was still a place besieged, against whose walls horde after horde continued to fling themselves. There were moments of respite, there were points at which the breaches were stopped; but more often and at many more points the danger was imminent.

The Normans were ever present, 'panting with desire for booty,' as the chronicler William of Jumièges expresses it. At the beginning of the tenth century Charles the Simple decided he would come to terms with them and settle them in France; and thus, in 911, the Viking chief Rollo became 'Duke Rollo of Normandy.'    Ten years later another friendly settlement was made on the lower Loire.   It would be wrong, however, to suppose that peaceable arrangements of this kind sufficed to ward off the danger.    Individual chieftains continued to indulge their taste for plunder, and newcomers arrived by sea with appetites as yet unsatisfied.

The raids continued: Burgundy was bled white in 924; in 1013, a hundred years after Rollo's installation, almost the entire plain of France had been overrun by Olaf, the selfsame who was later baptized and became the patron saint of Norway.   Few countries of the West escaped: Spain was attacked in 970, when the shrine of St James at Compostella was sacked; the Rhine delta at Utrecht in 980; and the Waal in 1006.   Byzantine Italy, where the first Normans appeared as pilgrims, soon witnessed the arrival of others invited by (though less piously disposed than) their forerunners.   This marked the beginning (c. 1037) of the great adventure of Tancred d'Hauteville's twelve sons, led by Robert Guiscard, who by a mixture of guile and force, carved themselves out a new domain, the kingdom of Naples and Sicily, and then, oddly enough, became a stabilizing factor.

In the Mediterranean the Moslem threat appeared somehow less grave than of old.   It no longer represented the systematic effort of a great power; for the Arab empire had been weakened by disunion and anarchy.   Even so, independent companies of 'Saracens' committed dreadful atrocities over a wide area.   The Moorish units, in particular, wrought havoc.   Hardy mountaineers—'like real goats,' says the chronicler of Saint-Gall—they fell unexpectedly upon the high valleys of the Alps, pillaging market towns, kidnapping wealthy merchants and powerful abbots on the high roads; and no state could so much as lift a finger against them until the eleventh century, when the Italian cities of Pisa, Genoa, and Amalfi, furious at the sight of corsairs ruining their trade, proceeded to attack their bases in Spain and the Maghreb.

Normans and Saracens: these names evoked nothing like the horror caused by that of a third Barbarian group, the Hungarians.   It was possible to buy off a Viking or a Moor, but the Magyars did things more thoroughly.   In 924, for instance, they massacred the entire population of Pavia without exception, from bishop to new-born babe. At the beginning of the tenth century, under the leadership of Arpad, who died in 907, they dismembered Moravia, and thereafter they directed their murderous offensive principally against the Germanic lands of Bavaria, Thuringia, and Saxony.   Alsace and Lorraine suffered likewise; Flanders, Champagne, and the kingdom of Arles were scoured by their hosts, and even the remote vale of Orléans was visited by the yellow horsemen.   During most of the eleventh century every inhabitant of Western Europe could foresee the possibility of his being killed or sold into slavery by the terrible successors of the Huns. Two heavy defeats, on the Unstrut in 933 and, twenty-two years later, on the Lech, checked their drive; but the Hungarian peril lasted until the year 1000 when the conversion of their king, Stephen, transformed these nomads into a sedentary agricultural nation, saving both Europe and themselves.

This first historical datum (persistence of the Barbarian menace, together with its corollary, the continuation of banditry, which increased the unhappiness of the age) gave rise to a second—the final establishment and propagation throughout Western Europe of what is commonly known as the *feudal system*.   Several causes, which have been recognized in the long process of historical evolution, combined during the tenth century to beget new institutions: economic causes, which, since the Invasions, had restored landed property to its original importance and thereby created the rural lordship; political causes, which had tended, even under the powerful Charlemagne and with still greater reason under his feeble successors, to free the great landowners from central control through the system of immunity; lastly and above all, social causes, which at a time of unremitting danger, based the human hierarchy upon force, allowing first place to those who could fight and protect others.

The system to which these various elements conduced was that which we shall see in operation from the end of the eleventh century. It was, so to speak, a pyramidal arrangement in which one allegiance was subject to another, one tenure to another, from the humblest knight to the highest suzerain.   That stage had not been reached in the tenth century; society was as yet in a fluid state which was emerging more or less haphazardly into one of order.   The central authority had completely disintegrated; it was re-established, after a fashion, on the local and regional plane, where the great lords had seized power as it was about to be submerged.   They were able to do so either because of the numerous 'commendations' which had come into their hands, or because they were the descendants of royal officials who had usurped the territory which they administered.   Feudal society, as it existed during the twelfth and thirteenth centuries, was begotten in this way, spontaneously, without a preconceived plan, merely by virtue of stern necessity.   This 'first feudal age,' as Marc Bloch has so aptly called it, was a period of painful gestation.

It is hard to imagine the complexity and instability of that which took the place of organization.   In theory the vassal was dependent on the man to whom he had done homage and from whom he had received

S

the only benefit which then counted—land, the fief. But many other factors interfered with this basic consideration: rivalry between kinsmen, conflict of interests, personal feelings, the activity of kings and of the Church. After the disappearance of ancient law, which foundered together with the State, new legal systems were improvised, which bore no relation to justice. The multitude of independent principalities, each based on a very vague hierarchical order, was in perpetual agitation, dispute, or open war. Such was the world in which the Church of Christ had to embark upon her mission.

At first it seemed she must prove unequal to the task. On the morrow of the Invasions, she had constituted a solid dike; but now she appeared to have been undermined by the waves of Barbarism and about to sink beneath them. It was not only, as we have seen,[1] because the disturbances of the age, and particularly the destructive raids of new invaders, had opened terrible breaches, but also and above all because an inevitable process of evolution tended to include her in the system of this embryo feudal world. Holding land, how could she escape the current law, which required the 'commendation' of all land, i.e. that it should owe obedience to him who protected it? A religious superior (bishop or abbot) was led by force of circumstances to play a part analogous to that of a layman. Is it then surprising that the two functions were confused? No land without a lord!

The secularization of ecclesiastical goods, that evil of the ninth century, continued and surpassed in gravity that which we have observed under the Merovingians. Appointment by the civil power to ecclesiastical offices, a practice too highly favoured by Charlemagne, became the general rule.

At this period, then, Christian society was endangered, as never before in five hundred years, by distraint of the civil power and the systematic identification of the two. Episcopal elections, which might in theory be either canonical or royal, depended in practice exclusively upon the sovereign, a principle so well established that in 921 we find Pope John X rebuking the Archbishop of Cologne for having been reluctant to allow the King of Lorraine, Charles the Simple, to appoint the Bishop of Liége. Whether his name were Otto of Germany or Hugh Capet, civil rulers claimed to control the episcopate.

Secular domination of the monasteries was even more complete. The custom of giving or of taking a monastery as if it were a mere chattel was everywhere admitted. Hugh Capet, for example, was secular abbot of nearly all the rich abbeys in his dominions, and it was from this abbatial charge that the surname Capet (wearer of the cope) was derived. It was easier to obtain control of a monastery than of a

[1] See the final section of Chapter VIII.

bishopric, for canon law required at least that the titular of every see should receive episcopal consecration.   There was no such rule for the monasteries; any scoundrel could be an abbot, governing a community of monks and regulating even their spiritual life and the divine office.

That was not all: there were still lower depths of degradation. These sacred titles and functions were commonly recognized as articles of trade.   *Simony,* which the Church never wholly eradicated, was rampant.   The great lords demanded money for the appointment of a bishop, of an abbot, and even of a simple parish priest.   Conversely, priests who had paid for a dignity demanded payment for the exercise of their duties.   Abbo of Fleury puts into the mouth of a simoniac these piquant but distressing words: 'I was consecrated by the archbishop, and in order to win his good graces I paid him a hundred sous; if I had not done so I would not now be a bishop.   I obtained a bishopric in return for money.   But if I do not die I shall soon recover my sous; for I ordain priests and deacons and thereby replenish my coffers. . . .'   In order to allay subsequent scruples it was of course argued that what a man bought was not the spiritual function but the material benefice—land and the revenues accruing to the charge; but this was a mere sophism which deceived nobody. From the greatest princes, via the bishops, to the humblest parish priest, there was one infernal chain of complicity in abuse.   It is possible to cite glorious exceptions in the form of kings and prelates who did not yield to the temptation.   But one is entitled to ask whether even they were completely free of guilt.   Without being simoniacs in the strict sense of the word, i.e. without handling 'thirty pieces of silver,' how many were there who compromised with simony in the wider sense, by granting or obtaining holy things and sacred functions on the ground of interest, family, politics, or connections?

The fact is that, in one way or another, everything clerical was linked with the feudal system.   Ecclesiastical lands were traded or granted like other lands; priests, bishops, and monks were bound to fight or provide troops for the incessant wars of that period; and it seemed as though the Church were on the point of being absorbed by the very society whom it was her duty to evangelize.   Antagonism between the warrior caste (mistress of force, power, and money) and the religious caste (guardian of the supreme values of civilization) seemed on the point of being resolved in the most deplorable of fusions.   Would the feudal world contaminate Christianity as the Barbarian world had almost done?   If that happened it was not difficult to see what mankind would lose.

That it did not happen is the most surprising aspect of this obscure age.   The crisis of the tenth century was to be extremely grave for

Christianity in the West, but it would not be mortal. Whereas feudal anarchy would result in the virtual destruction of the State, its effect upon the Church would remain superficial. There we see the fundamental difference between East and West: the Byzantine Church was part and parcel of the regime, an integral part of political society; but the Western Church managed to preserve its independent life. The effort of the bishops after the death of Charlemagne was not in vain, nor was that of such saints and monks as Benedict of Aniane, who strove for the freedom of the mind. An ideal of spiritual independence lived on in certain souls, and it was that spirit which, in a word, enabled the Church to right herself and at the same time to prepare a second spring.

### St Peter and the Tyrants of Rome

The Church deserves our admiration for having protected her spiritual life, especially in view of the fact that throughout the whole period she could not rely upon the see of St Peter, which had so often in days of trial played the part of an unshakable rock assigned to her by Christ. No previous age had shown the Papacy so weak, so unequal to its task. 'It was,' says Moehler, 'one of the most lamentable periods, perhaps the most tragic, recorded in the annals of ecclesiastical history.' One would prefer to cast the mantle of Noah's sons over the spectacle of these disorders, but in considering them one notes also the existence of untainted forces ready to act. We discover, beneath the corruption on the surface of events, a deep and purer current.

At Rome the ninth century drew towards its close, in 897, with the vile business of Formosus.[1] The tenth was no less ignominious. The Holy See, made the plaything of feudal ambitions, was dragged hither and thither, torn between two powers that stuck at nothing. The Nordic brutality of the Lombards and the Franks combined with the subtle cruelty of Byzantium in an incessant renewal of horror. The tragedy was continual; it is remarkable how obligingly an unwanted man, pope or prince, died at the right moment if he fell into the hands of his enemies. It was one long story of tortured prisoners, women viciously flogged, corpses thrown on to refuse heaps or left to rot, hanging from some statue in a public place. Orgy went hand in hand with cruelty in circumstances that will scarcely bear recital and which may be compared with, but were not surpassed by, the notorious scandals of the Borgias. And, as in the days of the Quattrocento, women stood in the forefront of the scene, beautiful, ambitious,

[1] See the final section of Chapter VIII.

dissolute, skilful alike in the use of their charms and in the administration of poison.   Such were the two Theodoras, the two Marozias, whose authority in Rome was so apparent that the common people used to whisper as a kind of proverb: 'We have female popes!' [1]

It is useless to follow in detail the painful events of this period, although it must be admitted they are as picturesque and diverting as a novel by Alexandre Dumas.   It is useless to catalogue the popes, many of whom were no more important than a castle or a bishop on a chessboard.   The most notorious of this monstrous tribe was John XII (955–64), a young rascal of twenty who was invested with the tiara by the will of his father, Alberic, 'Prince of all the Romans.'   He was a feudal pope if ever there was one, mixed up in all kinds of intrigue in which the fate of the Eternal City was at stake; and stories were told—with some exaggeration, perhaps, but with some element of truth—of banquets attended by the Pope, at which the guests toasted Lucifer!

Reduced to essentials, the facts of this period, which covers the years 896 to 1045, fall into two main groups.   Until about 960 the Papacy was dominated by the *Theophylacts*, a wealthy and ambitious Tuscan family descended from a former duke of the militia, who, at the end of the ninth century, administered Ravenna and made himself virtually an independent prince.   His wife Theodora, his daughters Theodora the younger and Marozia, interfered for years in the affairs of Rome.   Among their creatures were such popes as Sergius III, who is charged with having been the lover of his protectress; John XI, who was undoubtedly Marozia's own son; and John XII, who, through his father, Alberic, was grandson of the same woman.   Mostly too young and often incapable, these popes, made and unmade by conflicting ambitions, had no effect upon the destinies either of the Church or of the world.

Then, in 962, the picture changed.   John XII, abandoned by the Roman aristocracy and threatened by the plots of a self-styled 'King of Italy,' Berengar the younger, Marquis of Ivrée and grandson of that other Berengar whom Benedict IV had crowned as emperor in 901, turned to Germany and sought the help of Otto I of Saxony.   Instead of being mainly a stake in the squabbles of Italian feudatories, the papal throne became also an object of strife between the Roman nobility and the German emperor.   There were more bloody conflicts during which popes mysteriously disappeared, when antipopes arose (at one time there were actually three popes elected together!), when the rival clans of Crescenzi and Tusculum (both families

---

[1] Hence, probably, the legend of Pope Joan; popular gossip imagined that a woman had once occupied the throne of St Peter.   (On this ridiculous legend see note 2, page 457.)

descended from the Theophylacts and Alberic) fought one another savagely for the privilege of setting one of their own number on the papal throne, and when simony was practised with utter cynicism. . . . The last pope of the wretched series was Benedict IX (1033–45), who, consecrated at the age of twelve and already leading an immoral life, gathered to himself so many scandals that the Roman mob was shocked into getting rid of him.

Such is the picture of this grievous period, in which the Papacy was subject to the worst of tyrannies and seemed on the point of ultimate disaster. Should we confine ourselves to appearances alone in order to judge it fairly? Without wishing to play the advocate, we must point to certain facts which are not without weight. First, the majority of scandalous details that have come down to us concerning the papal court are furnished by Liutprand, Bishop of Cremona, whom we have seen as the German emperor's ambassador to Nicephorus Phocas.[1] Now Liutprand was an indifferent character, choleric, sycophantic, prostrate before his master Otto the Great, and detesting the Holy See. Is not his work entitled *Antapodosis*, i.e. *Revenge*? He had an axe to grind: it is highly probable that he emphasized the horrors of Rome, 'that tavern, that brothel,' to exalt, by comparison, the glory of his lay patron. Recent scholarship has proved that one must be cautious in listening to the tittle-tattle of this venomous backbiter.

However, there is considerable significance attached to Liutprand's indignation in so far as it is sincere and reflects (as conciliar decrees show that it did) that of many of his contemporaries. That the Christian conscience was shocked at not finding on the throne of Peter those high standards which the past had taught it to expect, is proof that respect for the Holy See was unimpaired and also that a lofty moral ideal continued to exist. The situation of Rome must not blind us to that of other parts of Christendom. 'Our neighbours, Belgium and Germany,' wrote Arnulf, Bishop of Orléans in 991, 'contain many eminent bishops of outstanding piety.' Even in Italy Atto of Vercelli and Rathier of Liége, Bishop of Verona, were preparing to launch the grand ideas for reform which would triumph in the eleventh century. The success and glory of Cluny would be sufficient to demonstrate that the corruption of Rome was local and transient.

Furthermore the scandal and violence which disgraced the papal throne at this time were by no means attributable to the divine institution, but to the oppression which it suffered. The real culprits were not the ephemeral, incapable, and sometimes unworthy popes who mounted St Peter's chair, but the secular lords who placed them there —Tuscan princes, Roman nobles, or German emperors. In the 'first

[1] For Liutprand's embassy see the third section of Chapter IX.

feudal age' all was still too violent, too confused for the Church to be able to undertake, immediately and with determination, the task of freeing herself from nascent feudalism; but she retained sufficient vigour to achieve that goal at a later date.

In order to be just it is not enough to render to Caesar the things that are Caesar's; we must also fix the blame where it belongs.   And here is another point: even among those 'feudal popes,' raised to the papal chair by conspiracy or violence, we find holy souls and characters who, in terrible circumstances, tried to do their duty.   For instance, the first five popes appointed by the tyrant Alberic were of sound morals and perfect doctrine, and even the sixth, his son, John XII, though morally base, cannot be criticized upon dogmatic grounds. Among the bulls issued by these mediocre pontiffs, we can discover nothing that compromised the purity of faith or the stability of principle.

Many of the popes deserve more than contempt and silence.   John X (914–28), a brave man who revived the policy of his namesake John VIII, fought valiantly against the Saracens, charging their ranks in person, and finally dying by assassination on the instructions of Marozia, who found him too independent.   John XIII (965–72), a creature of the emperor Otto I, to whom he was recommended by his piety and care for the welfare of the Church, did all he could to support those who in France, Germany, and England were preparing to reform the Church; after the scandal of John XII's pontificate, this was at least encouraging.   Benedict VII (974–83) presided over no fewer than fourteen Councils, most of them concerned with reform.   He wrote to the abbot of Cluny these prophetic words: 'Your community has no more devoted protectress than this Roman Church, which would like to spread it throughout the world and undertakes to defend it against all its enemies.'   Gregory V (996–7) was a young German prince of twenty-three years, a grandson of Otto the Great.   His nobility and generosity were combined with great energy; it was he who dared to excommunicate Robert the Pious, King of France, and who perceived the extraordinary merits of Gerbert.   The epitaph of Sergius IV (1009–12) describes him as 'bread of the poor, robe of the naked, teacher of the people, shepherd revered by all. . . .'

One figure at this time stands head and shoulders above other popes—that of *Sylvester II* (999–1003), pope of the year 1000 and the first French pope, whose short reign did not allow him to reveal his full stature, but who at least had time to bear testimony that would not be in vain.   In 998 the monk Gerbert, from Aurillac in Auvergne, was appointed Archbishop of Ravenna.   When he was elected pope in the following year and with the support of Otto III, his former pupil, all Christendom knew that Peter now had as successor a man of outstanding quality. His erudition was celebrated;[1] he had studied mathematics, astronomy, Latin literature, music, and, above all, the religious sciences of philosophy and theology, in which he took St Augustine as his master. 'The just man lives by faith,' he used to say, 'but it is good that he should combine science with his faith.' Formed on the principles of Cluny, he remained, even on the papal throne, an austere monk, exacting towards himself and others, according to the pattern established by the Benedictine reform, which would impose itself on the whole Church. Not only did he set an example, but he encouraged in many ways those who advocated reform. Imbued with the idea of a Church to be proclaimed, enlarged, and defended, he it was who freed Poland from German tutelage and who crowned St Stephen, King of Hungary; he was also the first person in Western history to foresee how important was the problem of the holy places, and who, one hundred years before the first Crusade, issued a call to arms for the deliverance of Jerusalem. He was a man humble but brave, a soul both of tenderness in God and of unwavering intrepidity. Circumstances betrayed him in the end: another Roman riot sent him to die in exile. But he had pointed the way for his successors, Gregory VII and Innocent III. Though somewhat exaggerated, his epitaph is not altogether false: *Gaudet omne saeclum, frangitur omne reum*. He had not 'crushed every crime,' but he had certainly adorned his period.

There is then a contrast, upon which it is not a bad thing to dwell, between the painful, scandalous appearances, which are usually considered, and the spiritual reality of the Papacy in that age of iron. When all is said and done, this contrast is noticeable even among those who bear the heaviest responsibility in the matter. Christians in the year 1000 were men of temperamental extremes, tending to excess but still capable of deeds inspired by a touching faith. In this respect they were not so very different from the Christians of Byzantium, whom we have often seen veering between mysticism and the most terrible sins. Alberic, for example, who seems to be the incarnation of feudal violence, who held the Papacy in his grip for thirty years, shared a childlike devotion to St Odo, the great abbot of Cluny,

[1] He was so learned that some curious legends grew up around his name. He had brought the Arabic numerals from Spain and endeavoured to propagate their use. People were alarmed, and told one another that he had made a pact with the Devil in order to obtain knowledge and honours. The pact, it was said, provided that he would leave his soul to the Evil One when he went to 'Jerusalem,' and one day, after he had become pope, he was celebrating mass in the church of Santa Croce de Gerusalemme, when Satan appeared at his side. Sylvester broke out into a cold sweat and died the same day, ordering that his body be cut up into small pieces so that the Evil One should not carry it off! Afterwards, the legend stated, a cold sweat spread over his tomb and his bones rattled every time a pope entered the agony of death. We may add that the tomb, opened in 1648, revealed the body of Sylvester intact, hands crossed on the breast, and mitre on head.

whom he treated with the greatest respect and even assisted in his efforts for reform; one chronicler calls him 'protector of monasteries.' Another example is the German emperor Otto III who remained throughout his life a disciple of Gerbert as he had been in his youth, and when the interests of their respective thrones were at variance he submitted to the Pope.

All these were favourable signs.  The crisis through which the Church was passing was grave but not mortal, as the future would prove.  It remains true, however, that at the time the consequences were very harmful.  We have already seen to what extent the bankruptcy of the Holy See helped the Eastern Church to take a road at the end of which lay Michael Cerularius and separation from Rome. Did not the same tendency towards rupture threaten the Western Church also?  Do we not observe in France, for instance, a movement that may be described as a forerunner of *Gallicanism*, and of which Arnulf, Bishop of Orléans, was the leading exponent towards the end of the tenth century.  At the Council of Saint-Basle de Verzy, in 991, these phrases might have been heard: 'Where are the Leos and the Gregorys?'  'Is it our fault that the head of all the Churches, that stood so high, crowned with honour and glory, have fallen so low, covered with infamy and shame?'  'We are witnesses, it seems, of the coming of Antichrist, for behold the ruin of which the apostle speaks, not the ruin of nations, but of the Church.'  Or again, the following, which is almost a call to rebellion: 'Is it to such monsters (men such as John XII or Boniface VII), blown up with ignorance and utterly devoid of knowledge, human or divine, that the innumerable priests of God, scattered about the world and remarkable for their learning and their virtue, must be subject?'

These cries of indignation must of course be understood as a protest of the Christian soul, driven by her very respect for the Holy See to pass severe judgment on its unworthy occupants.  Later such protests took effect, and the Papacy, coming to its senses, headed the movement towards reform.  All the same, in a space of one hundred and fifty years, Rome set such a bad example that the trouble afflicting men's souls became even more severe in an age that was already and grievously afflicted. . . .

CHRISTIANS OF THE YEAR 1000: THE SLOUGH

The men of that age had good reason to be disturbed.  Material conditions were a source of anguish, and collective suffering is rarely a school of virtue.  Imagine what life was like when every day might bring the Normans, the Saracens, or the leathern jackets of the Hungarian squadrons.  This constant fear of impending catastrophe, so

*s

familiar to the twentieth century through the aerial bombardment of cities, that anxiety which blends with every sentiment, with all re-actions of the conscience, and ends by obliterating everything else, was the psychological keynote of those generations, though as yet, perhaps, slower to act upon boorish, elemental souls in an age when no real pro-tection was conceivable.

Violence, however, was not the only source of fear; there was not only danger of being slain by Barbarian raiders.   The result of the new invasions (as well as of feudal wars) was a terrible decline of agriculture since the days of Charlemagne.   The work of breaking up the land for tillage was interrupted.   In the most fertile plains, forest, heath, and marsh resumed the offensive.   Moreover famine was rife on that badly cultivated land, the produce of which was continually threatened. In certain years it became general, as happened at least five or six times between 900 and 1050; it wandered ceaselessly from one region to another, thanks now to a bad harvest, now to an invasion, and now to war.   The Burgundian chronicler Raoul Glaber, in a celebrated pas-sage, describes the horrors of the great dearth in 1033, which seems to have affected the whole of Western Europe, where, 'the supply of birds and beasts being exhausted, hunger could be appeased only by devouring corpses, or rooting up trees and the grass in the valleys. . . .' It is not in vain that he adds: 'The memory of man recoils from remind-ing itself of all the horrors of that abominable time'; some scenes of cannibalism described by him are scarcely credible.   And since, of course, these frightful forms of nourishment, together with a lament-able system of hygiene, could not but give rise to epidemics, dysentery, the plague, and innumerable diseases which are no longer easy to identify sent living men by thousands to the charnel-houses.

Yet despite these nameless miseries, life irresistibly continued on its way.   The enormous mortality was offset by a vigorous and never-failing birth-rate.   The West was then in the full flower of its youth, nor could the gravest crises halt the fermentation of her vital force. But what affected men psychologically and morally at that time was unhappiness, a crushing pessimism, universal terror; bowed down under a black sky, towards what light could they lift their eyes?

To that of religion.   Certainly; the very horror of the times drove them to do so.   'All is vain,' cries Raoul Glaber, 'for who can screen us from the wrath of God, except God Himself?'   Faith was thus universal: the brazen-faced unbeliever was non-existent.   But what was that faith?   What exactly did it represent for the average man?   It was still, as we have seen it to be during a period of four or five hundred years, a body of precepts and customs without sure foundation.   The great majority had absolutely no philosophical or theological training, nor, except in a very few cases, was there any spiritual impetus.   Tied to the goods of this world by the dreadful bond of fear, men gave no thought to the doctrine of renunciation and love of one's neighbour. Religion became once more what it had been in pagan Rome, an almost mercenary relationship with God and the saints, to whom certain acknowledgments were due in return for their favour. The truly Christian spirit was absent from the services of the Church which people too often attended without understanding much of the liturgy, and from almsgiving, which was practised without charity in the heart. Relics were venerated, but there was no following the example of those saints! Let us repeat, there *were* exceptions which it is proper to recognize; but on the whole the above description applied to nearly all men, including the ruling class, the nobility, unrefined and brutal souls in whom Grace could not build secure bulwarks against the wild storms of passion. . . .

Nor, of course, did morals reflect the gentle influence of the Gospel. Violence, which had been endemic since the Barbarian Invasions, attained its zenith. Had nascent feudalism any basis other than brute force? The fact of its being a necessary evil in a period of perpetual menace and bankruptcy of the State did not render its prestige less formidable: *faustrecht*, the law of the fist. The organization it helped to establish hallowed the custom of private vengeance, of the old Germanic vendetta which the twofold influence of Roman tradition and the Church had tried to stamp out in the sixth and seventh centuries, which the strength of Charlemagne had virtually abolished, but which had again reared its head after his death. Jealousy, envy, the unbridled wish to enlarge one's estate at the neighbours' expense were rampant; perfidy joined hands with violence, and political assassination was as common throughout Western Europe in the tenth century as in Italy during the fifteenth. Brigandage, destructiveness, and looting were so commonplace that such risks were provided for in commercial contracts.

Would you care to take a look at one of those 'Christians' of the year 1000, one of those terrible fellows who were at that time masters of the world? Here is one. His name was *Fulk Nerra* (987–1040) and he was related to the counts of Anjou. He is credited with the idea of replacing the old wooden palace forts with the enormous stone buildings that would become familiar later on. He was filled with unbridled passion, a temper directed to extremes. Whenever he had the slightest difference with a neighbour he rushed upon his lands, ravaging, pillaging, raping, and killing; nothing could stop him, least of all the commandments of God! He cared nothing for the respect due to the priests of the Lord: we find him attacking the convent of St Martin of Tours, plundering the house of a canon, setting fire to the monastery of St Florentine. . . . This appalling man had countless crimes upon his conscience, but when seized with a fit of remorse he abandoned himself to wellnigh incredible penances. Thus the very tomb of St Martin, whose monks he had ill treated, saw him prostrate, with bare feet and in penitent's dress; and four times during his life he went to Jerusalem as a devout pilgrim, treading half naked the sorrowful road of the Passion while two of his servants flogged him till the blood came, crying: 'Lord, receive thy perjured Fulk!' He was typical of his age.

One need hardly say that the same indifference shown towards the precept 'Thou shalt not kill' appears likewise in respect of the sixth and ninth commandments. Sexual immorality was found everywhere: among the lower classes, where the material conditions of life were such as to excuse the more bestial practices, and among the feudal lords also, whose luxury was allied with violence, as female prisoners too often experienced. Some of these noblemen had morals—the morals of the Moslems. Fulk Nerra's son, Geoffrey Martel, kept a regular harem; and a certain Duke of Burgundy, Robert the Elder, put away his wife, proclaiming quite frankly that he wished to live more freely, and killing his father-in-law who had the audacity to rebuke him!

The most serious feature of the whole set-up was that this demoralization did not spare the clergy, which was not infrequently caught up in the whirlwind of unbridled passion. Himself a feudal lord, a bishop or abbot of a great monastery could hardly avoid meeting force with force. True we sometimes meet touching examples of non-resistance, as when the chapter of St Martin, attacked by Nerra, barricaded itself in the cloister, praying and singing hymns. But there are many examples of the opposite kind, of veritable wars waged between bishops and secular landlords; Geoffrey Martel, for example, was at loggerheads for twenty years with the Bishop of Mans. There we have the disastrous result of the Church's absorption by feudalism.

It is unnecessary to add that the crisis of sexual immorality which we have seen rampant among laymen ravaged the clergy likewise. It is a picture upon which many anti-Christian historians have been pleased to dwell, and unfortunately it is quite authentic. One need only read the conciliar decrees to be convinced of the extent of the evil (and of course the existence of such decrees indicates that there were still many healthy elements in the Church). In 909 the Council of Trosly fulminated against the concubines of priests; that of Augsburg, in 952, ordered such women to be seized, whipped, and shaven. The Councils of Anze (994) and Poitiers (1000) repeated those decisions, and in that of Pavia (1023) Pope Benedict VIII himself publicly denounced the morals of the clergy and decreed that all children of priests and monks should be reduced to the status of serfs. It seems that clerical incontinence—known as *Nicolaism* after the Nicolaites mentioned in the Apocalypse—was a universal evil.    Those who had most respect for morality, instead of keeping a mistress, entered officially into the state of wedlock; when rebuked they quoted the famous words of St Paul: 'It is better to marry than to burn'!    The situation was the same in Germany, Italy, and France.    Bishops and other prelates set the standard.    St Peter Damian speaks without equivocation of one Raimbaud of Fiesole who lived 'surrounded by a swarm of lovelies,' and of another, Denis of Piacenza, who was 'more of an expert on feminine charms than on ecclesiastical science.'    At Bremen we find good bishops having to call in the police to get rid of concubines kept by their canons.    As regards France, chroniclers such as Raoul Glaber and Guibert de Nogent refer to the same weakness, and various Councils condemned some bishops who had no fewer than three or four sons.    Even though chroniclers and preachers may have painted too black a picture, the peril was still great.    The Council of Trosly had quite rightly said that 'wicked priests who rot on the dunghill of luxury infect by their conduct all those who live chastely, for the faithful are all too prone to think, "Such are the priests of the Church."'

This was a normal reaction, and its effects were very soon revealed. *Heresy*, which had almost disappeared in the East two centuries ago, once again emerged and adopted a distinctly anti-clerical attitude. Towards the end of the tenth century, at Vertus in Champagne, a man of the people named Leutard, having dreamed that a swarm of bees 'entered his body by the secret natural opening' and came out of his mouth in the form of inspired words, set himself up as a reformer and declared himself a prophet of God.    He repudiated his wife 'according to scriptural principles,' rushed into the church and tore down the crucifix, claiming that it was defiled in such a place, and began to preach a doctrine of revolt against the clergy and lords and also against tithes, which assured him a large audience.    Summoned before the episcopal court at Châlons, he was released as a harmless idiot, but he put an end to his revolt by throwing himself head first into a well.

That episode was not particularly serious; far more so was the reappearance of Manichaeism, which took place at first insidiously and timidly, then with a good deal more noise.    The ancient dualist doctrine, which St Augustine had fought and which was long since believed buried for ever, was seen once again, dressed up to suit contemporary taste, at Mainz, Orléans, and Arras, then at Limoges and Toulouse as well as in northern Italy.    The most alarming event occurred in 1022 at Orléans, where a regular sect was formed and joined by priests, canons of the chapter, professors, and even by the queen's confessor.    It taught a form of doctrine that foreshadowed the tenets of the Cathari: rebellion against the established Church, rejection of certain Christian dogmas (notably the Incarnation, Passion, and Resurrection), abandonment of worship, of the hierarchy, and of images. Moreover they declared their loathing of earthly life, of the flesh, even under the form of cooked meats and of the marital act. . . . As in the case of the Albigensians, too stern a moral teaching amounting to utter contempt of life went along with great profligacy: if all flesh is sinful what matter a little more or a little less? The most terrible rumours about these heretics passed from mouth to mouth.[1] They were accused of magic, sorcery, and infamous morals until at last King Robert the Pious had their four principal leaders arrested. They were tried, refuted, and condemned, without flinching from their curious faith.[2] Amid a storm of fury, such that Queen Constance put out one of her former confessor's eyes, they perished in the flames, though not before declaring that they had looked for nothing better than this martyrdom. The king derived much glory from this great act of faith; the Church, through Bishop Wazo of Liége, made a vigorous and charitable protest. For the first time in Christian history the stake had been lighted for heresy; it would burn, alas! for a long, long time. . . .

These sudden reappearances of error and the frightful eddies they provoked in the popular conscience are characteristic of the intellectual weakness of that dark age. Religion as these practised was completely riddled with superstitions so absurd that one can hardly allow that they ever existed. Between God, the terrible Master, upon whom depended all the evils that range the world, and miserable man who hardly dared look upward, there swarmed a host of intermediate beings, good and evil, angels and demons, among whom one could not always clearly recognize himself. The cult of saints was universal and assumed all the worst forms of worship. There was no town, no parish, which had not its protector, its intercessor, who was so greatly admired that the Almighty was eventually forgotten. Relics were more and more sought after: they were bought and sold, cut up, exchanged, and even if needs be stolen. . . . All were genuine, all

---

[1] Here is Raoul Glaber's account: 'They met on certain nights in an appointed house, each one carrying a light, and chanted, in the form of a litany, the Devil's names, until suddenly they saw the Demon come down among them in the guise of a beast. All lights were immediately extinguished, and they gave themselves up to a nameless debauch. Each man seized the nearest woman and abused her, not inquiring whether she were his mother, his sister, or a religious. The child born of this impure union was brought in on the eighth day after its birth; a great fire was lit and the baby passed through the flames in the pagan manner. The ashes of the poor little creature were gathered up and preserved with the same veneration wherewith Christians preserve the body of Christ. They were possessed, in fact, by so strong a diabolical power, that no one who had experienced it could abandon the heresy and return to the way of truth.'

It is of course not known how much of this account is accurate and how much was the fruit of popular fancy.

[2] Only one of the fourteen abjured—an early proof of the uselessness of capital punishment in religious matters, a lesson which was never really understood.

efficacious! The rod of Moses, discovered at Sens about the year 1000, was no less authentic than the tibia of St Stephen. Everything was a sign or symbol or threat from heaven. If Vesuvius rumbled, if there were many fires among mud houses with thatched roofs, if an eclipse made men's faces ghastly, or an enormous whale appeared in the Channel, there in each case you had a warning, and the smallest thunderbolt traced on the walls of the universal Babylon the *Mane, Tekel, Phares* of the Book of Daniel. What prodigious events, worthy of heedful faith, happened in those days! At Orléans a wolf took the sacristan's place and rang the alarm bell to call the people to a fire. Elsewhere the Blessed Virgin groaned or stretched out kindly arms. Elsewhere again there were weeping crucifixes, or tombstones that sweated cold tears. As for the Devil, he was everywhere, multiform, restless, always at work to lure souls to his domain. Do you see him there on top of that tower, a grinning gnome? Or in the cell where Raoul Glaber is working at his book, that demon with flattened nose, enormous mouth, goat's beard, dog's teeth, and humped back? Or standing with a crowd of other demons by the death-bed of a wicked monk? He was laughed at and scorned in popular writings, and before long in the sculpture of churches, but one did not feel too comfortable at nights, thinking of his power.

The psychology of Christians in the year 1000 is summed up in the person of one man and in one book that provides us, if not with true facts, at least with a contemporary view.

The man was *Raoul*, author of *Tales* and known by the nickname of 'Bald-Pate' or *Glaber*. He was very much of his time, that restless, insufferable monk whom no abbot could keep within the rule and who all his life long rolled from one monastery to another; that semi-visionary, ever haunted by superstitious fears, who saw the Devil at every turn of the road; that credulous chatterbox who collected with no discrimination every piece of tittle-tattle, all the most ridiculous legends, which he forthwith committed to parchment. Born about 980, he died about 1050, and was therefore at the height of his career at the fatal date, A.D. 1000. Notwithstanding his own pretensions he was by no means an historian, but his work is a most useful miscellany —and wonderfully picturesque—of all that went on at that time in the minds of poor Christians in the West. We may perhaps say with Gebhardt that 'he seems to have lived in the crypt of a romanesque cathedral by the light of a sepulchral lamp, hearing only sobs and cries of distress, seeing nothing but a procession of melancholy or terrifying figures.' But that is not all. Undoubtedly he compiled a huge account of war, violence, fires, invasions, famine, pestilence, and all sorts of prodigies in order to reinforce his naïve apologetic with striking proofs. But we find also in his work passages with a different ring, the ring of Christian hope; he is the chronicler who tells us of the 'white mantle of churches' wherewith Christendom was robed, who paints a smiling picture of the joy in heaven on the completion of the first millennium after our Lord's death, who recalls the part played by our Blessed Lady and other saints in victories over the infidel, and who so rightly pointed out how significant was the conversion of the Normans and Hungarians. Raoul Glaber is not the unqualified pessimist he has been made out to be; in that respect also he is of his age, a dark age, bowed down beneath the most awful perils but which foretold the dawn.

It is to this psychological panorama which I have just attempted to outline, and to Raoul Glaber in particular, that we must trace the celebrated and indeed notorious historical problem, the *terrors of the year 1000*. I do not for a moment deny that there is such a problem; but how many people to-day are aware that it has been solved and put in its right perspective once and for all? As soon as one mentions that famous date the average person thinks of 'the end of the world.' Here is the legend. During the tenth century men were convinced that the thousandth year of the Christian era would be the last and that 'the day of the Lord' would come to the sound of apocalyptic trumpets. Did all the undeniable misfortunes of the period proclaim the final catastrophe? Was not the human race— unhappy, troubled, and tormented as we have seen it—in the state foretold by Holy Scripture? Visionary imaginations have given free rein to the subject. 'The captive waited in his dark dungeon, the serf in his furrow, the monk in his cloistered abstinence,' exclaims Michelet with tremendous gusto. 'In their dreadful affliction they could look forward to nothing but the appalling prospect of the Last Judgment.' This romantic picture was inspired by other than literary intentions. Modern anticlericalism has ground its axe by pretending that the Church exploited the 'terrors of the year 1000' for purposes of gain, and a publication of about 1880, entitled *L'Enseignement patriotique par l'image*, even contained a wonderful picture to illustrate this point of view.

Is there any truth in the story? Not much. Study of the most reliable texts [1] has shown that the only documents that refer expressly to the 'terrors of the year 1000' date from several centuries later; the chronicle of Tritheim of Hirschau, for example, published in 1559, only the second edition of which, one hundred and thirty years later, contains an explicit passage on the question. All the most ancient texts, especially those contemporary with the fatidic date, often allude to the apocalyptic character of the misfortunes of that age, but none links those misfortunes with any belief in the approaching end of the

[1] See E. Pognon, *L'An mille*.

world in A.D. 1000. Raoul Glaber, whose testimony is often alleged without examining his words too closely, says that the seventh epoch of history, in which he lived, would be the last, but he never suggested that it would close with the year 1000; it was rather to 1033 (the millennium of the Passion) that he perhaps attributed an apocalyptic significance.

Well, did the men of that age really believe in the end of the world? Some undoubtedly did: in Lorraine, for example, in 970, a year in which Good Friday and the Annunciation fell on the same day, some simple-minded folk thought that since our Lord's conception and death could not have been simultaneous, the coincidence foreshadowed the worst calamity. Some exegetes and theologians, e.g. St Odo of Cluny, who died in 942, professed this belief, interpreting Apocalypse xx. 1–7 (which says that an angel will chain the ancient serpent for a thousand years) in such a way as more or less to revive the old millenniarism. But others would have none of the idea. One such was Abbo of Fleury who, hearing it preached in 960 in a Paris church, opposed the preacher then and there with quotations from the Gospels, the Apocalypse, and the Book of Daniel. This idea that the world is about to end has attracted a certain type of mind ever since the coming of Christ. An historian writing in about 2100 and describing the events of our own day will most probably find numerous books and articles, some of them quite serious, written to show that people in the twentieth century expected the end of the world to occur in the year 2000. Étienne Gilson has written of *the terrors of the year 2000*. . . . That does not mean to say that the majority of men now living are haunted by this fear.

It was not otherwise in the tenth century. Prophets of the end of the world were answered categorically by facts. We possess many deeds of gift and wills, made shortly before A.D. 1000, the provisions of which look many years ahead. In 998 the Council of Rome imposed on the French king, Robert, a penance of seven years. In 999 Pope Sylvester II granted the Archbishop of Rheims the privilege of crowning future kings of France, a proof of his assumption that others *would* be crowned. In the year 1000 itself Otto III announced his intention of governing the world from Rome. And one has only to look at the solid piers of a basilica such as that of St Philibert at Tournus, which in A.D. 1000 was in course of construction, to agree that its builders were prepared to defy time.

There were no new terrors on the eve of the year 1000. There was only too much reason to fear the evils of the age, which some interpreted in prophetic vein and won over many of the common people. More true than the famous legend is the statement of another contemporary chronicler, Thietmar of Mersebourg: 'There had come the

best year since the immaculate Virgin brought forth our Salvation, and
a radiant dawn was seen to shine upon the world'; for in spite of all the
darkness, the light awaited its chance; amid the slough of that epoch
water still flowed, water that would revive all things.

## CHRISTIANS OF THE YEAR 1000: LIVING WATER

There is obviously a great gulf between a society such as that of a
large part of Western Europe in the twentieth century, which has
almost wholly forgotten God, and claims to be rid of faith, and a
society such as that of the same Western world in the tenth century,
whose faith, though it may appear far too external and conventional,
was no less the basis of all civilization.    Even if it was reduced in many
cases to a body of customs and unable to repel the combined flood of
violence and superstition, it was no less the immediate and most undeniable factor of the collective conscience, one upon which nobody
dreamed of turning his back.    We can understand nothing of the
way in which the radiant success of the Middle Ages was slowly and
painfully prepared unless we recognize that, despite its baseness
and its bloody dissensions, the world that preceded it was a Christian
world.

We may smile at the sudden reversals of conscience as, for example,
in the case of Fulk Nerra, at one moment a bloodthirsty brute and at
the next an edifying pilgrim; irony here is simply failure to understand.    God vomits up the lukewarm!    The case of the celebrated
Count of Anjou is not unique; there were hundreds like him.    Robert
the Elder, Duke of Burgundy, did the same kind of humiliating penance
after indulging to the full in similar atrocities.    Barons of the second
grade acted in like manner: crime and repentance alternated with
astonishing rapidity; those terrible feudal lords, who persecuted
bishops and plundered monasteries, still respected the clergy whose
members they had ill-treated, summoning them to their death-beds and
bequeathing them handsome legacies.    When one of them came face
to face with a genuine saint his cruelty often ceased.    Eudes I of
Burgundy, for instance, a descendant of Robert the Elder and his equal
in conduct, arrested St Anselm of Canterbury, but was so impressed
by him that he treated him with every courtesy, 'believing that he
beheld an angel of the Lord.'

Naturally the faith of these wild men is not the only kind we can
admire; there are in feudalism many examples worthy of respect, and
even of veneration, so many that it would be unfair to enumerate them.
Despite the weaknesses into which he allowed himself to be drawn,
despite the unfortunate matrimonial affair which brought him into
conflict with the Church, despite even the somewhat too 'clerical'

character of his religion, Robert the Pious, King of France, deserved his surname; he was truly a man of faith, 'gentle and humble of heart,' says his biographer Helgaud. His ancestor Eudes was scarcely his inferior in this respect. We find him, after the victory which had just given him the monastery of St Vaast in Artois, falling on his knees at the tomb of the saint, giving thanks to God, and weeping over the fratricidal war which had opposed him to another Christian, Count Baldwin. Some of these princes of the tenth and early eleventh centuries are noble figures, in whom already there appeared the ideal of knighthood. Such was Count Gerard of Toulouse, whose biographer, the Benedictine abbot Odo, praises unreservedly his modesty, moderation, purity, self-denial almost to the verge of poverty, and gentleness. William the Great, Duke of Aquitaine, was also, at a later date, a model of piety and equity. What was true of the French nobility was just as true elsewhere: in Germany, for example, where Otto III, amid pomp and glory, practised asceticism and mortification, where Henry II made himself so popular by his goodness, his charity, his love of peace, and moreover so greatly respected for his quasi-monastic life on the throne, that he was canonized by the Church less than a hundred years after his death. Similar examples are to be found in Poland, Bohemia, and Hungary—the Hungary of St Stephen. Need we add all those members of noble families who renounced everything to enter the cloister, where many of them reached great heights of sanctity? They include Gerard of Brogne in Lotharingia, one of the first protagonists of monastic reform; a son of the Duke of Ravenna, who was to become St Romuald; and Pier Orsolo I, Doge of Venice, who, after an interview with St Romuald, left all he had and became a monk.

During the tenth century, and even more at the beginning of the eleventh, the number of those Christian princes increased, and we discover in them something new. Not content with proclaiming their faith, they conformed their life thereto and sought to propagate its ideal. And, be it noted, these virtues won the respect of their subjects. This is particularly striking in the case say of St Henry or St Stephen; if we recall the insults earned for Louis the Debonair by his piety, we can allow that, appearances notwithstanding, a change had taken place between the ninth century and the beginning of the eleventh.

The current of living water found among the ruling classes is not so easy to trace in the souls of the common people, but one can see reflections. Their faith, riddled though it was with superstitious fears, was none the less a solid faith; it was as a Christian that disinherited man could feel himself truly a man; he knew it obscurely and clung to the Church. One of the most touching signs of this link is the generosity shown towards her. The medieval Christian is often represented as exploited by the clergy and cheated of his labour by ecclesiastical taxation.    The truth is quite different, and many instances can be cited in which a man's voluntary donations far exceeded the sum total of his feudal dues and tithes.

Another and equally touching aspect of this faith is the cult of the saints, for it reveals a sense of community with them and ancestral fidelity to the land.    We may be amused by the strange devotions of which relics were the object, and we may take with a pinch of salt the fantastic stories which pretend to trace the origins of a parish to some particularly glamorous saint; but even so this cult of the saints, which has been profoundly characteristic of the old European countries, represents an effort to establish contact between man and God. Henri Pirenne, the great Belgian historian, has said of these local saints: 'They are like God's tenants in chief, under whose protection men place themselves.'    The miracles worked at their tombs were a leaven of faith.    There was no mistake about these miracles; even chroniclers like Glaber, who reflect all that was most naïve in the popular conscience, knew that God alone is the author of a miracle, the relic being only an occasion.    How the holy intercessors were loved! It was to them personally that gifts were made and not to the church or monastery which preserved their blessed remains.    Patronal feasts held in their honour were of primordial importance in every parish, and the procession in which was carried the reliquary of a holy patron was a great event.    It was a time when the Parisians cherished St Geneviève, St Marcellus, and St Severinus, a period when many French villages adopted the name of their patron saint, a period when devotion to the Blessed Virgin, without finding expression in any important document, was written in the soil of innumerable French place-names beginning 'Notre-Dame'; we should be hopelessly in error if we reduced its religion to a body of superstitions and formalities.

If further evidence is required of the vitality of that Christian faith, which was then stirring the West and would snatch it from the bloody slough of the Dark Ages, look at the institution of *pilgrimage*.    We have seen it originate in the fourth century and develop amid the crisis of the Barbarian Invasions.    Thenceforward it grew to incredible proportions.    Every year thousands of pious travellers took to the roads, the most celebrated of which led to the Holy Land.    The conversion of the Hungarians, by enabling them to follow the overland route, avoided a dangerous sea crossing.    Who were the pilgrims? They belonged to every class of society, including such lords as Fulk Nerra and Guy of Limoges, such prelates as Audouin, bishop of the latter place, Canon Peter of Dorat, Bishop Raoul of Périgueux, Gauzlin, natural brother of King Robert and later Archbishop of Bruges.    Very many pilgrims, however, were poor and unrenowned folk who set out at the instigation of divine love.   What cries of fury and distress arose throughout the Christian world when news was received, in 1010, that the caliph Hakim had destroyed the basilica of the Holy Sepulchre!   Lacking the means of instant retaliation against Islam, the masses gave way to a ridiculous outburst of passion and hurled themselves upon the Jews whom they accused of being in alliance with the Moslems!   For a time pilgrimages to Jerusalem were rare; only a few bold individuals, e.g. Fulk Nerra, dared go back there. But as soon as conditions improved the flow of pilgrims recommenced. Pilgrimages started in large groups; in 1026 one such included thousands of people from Lorraine.   Once again these visitors to the holy places were welcomed in the parishes as messengers of God: what emotion when one of them—Ulric, Bishop of Orléans, for example—described how he had been present at the miracle of fire on the stone of the Sepulchre.

Palestine was not the only place of pilgrimage.   The pious columns wound their way also to Rome, visiting not only the basilica of St Peter, but also Santa Croce, St Paul-outside-the-Walls, St Sebastian, where the bodies of Sts Peter and Paul had once lain, the Pantheon, and the Colosseum rich in the memory of martyrs.   There were also pilgrimages to shrines rendered famous by the memory (sometimes more or less legendary) of great saints.   In Spain the relics of St James the Greater, it was said, were discovered in Galicia and authenticated by miracles.   Compostella thus became the famous centre of devotion which it remained throughout the Middle Ages, when the 'Christian Baron' Sant' Iago welcomed enormous crowds, a messenger of hope whom Dante (*Paradiso*, xxxv) would one day question on this beautiful virtue.   In France, at Tours, St Martin continued to attract many visitors, but there were other centres quite as popular: Sainte-Baume, the high place of Provence, where St Maximinus was supposed to have hidden the Magdalen's remains in an alabaster tomb, at which kings and popes loved to pray.   Then there was Vézelay, where part of the same saint's relics were deposited, in 1037, in an abbey which soon became a centre of Christian attraction. Less important than the above were innumerable shrines called after local saints.   Many were called after our Lady, among the most famous of which was Notre-Dame of the underworld at Chartres with its ancient statue of gleaming grey ebony; Notre-Dame de Puy, rich in miracles; Notre-Dame de Fourvière above Lyon, venerated since 840; and the Virgin of Rumengol in Brittany, associated with the legendary catastrophe of Ys.   It is hard to imagine Christendom thus marching in God's service as identical with the amorphous, stagnant, suppurating masses of whom an altogether exaggerated picture has been drawn.

It was dominated by lofty and saintly individuals; the tenth century and beginning of the eleventh produced no fewer than preceding ages, and the process of canonization, carried out with more prudence than before, was probably a better guarantee of the virtues of its Carolingian ancestors.     Reference has already been made to the Holy Roman emperor *St Henry*, and many others can be named.     *St Adalbert* of Bohemia, driven by persecution from Prague, took refuge in Rome and, at a time when the Papacy set a bad example of attachment to this world's goods, lived in absolute poverty, a precursor of St Francis of Assisi; he returned to his diocese to bear the supreme witness, suffering martyrdom as a missionary in Prussia.     *St Nilus*, a Greek of southern Italy, driven from home by the Saracens, settled near Capua, where his community followed the oriental Rule of St Basil and served as a link between East and West.     *John of Fécamp*, one of the very first great French mystics, was nicknamed 'Little Johnny' because of his small stature.     As abbot of the Trinity he wrote so sublimely, that the Middle Ages attributed his *Meditations* to St Augustine.     Later, when we come to study the reform of the Church at this period, we shall meet many noblemen who were faithful to Christ—a series of great abbots at Cluny as well as the moving and ardent personalities of St Romuald, St John Gualbert, and St Peter Damian.[1]

The truth about Christianity at this date must not be sought exclusively in the unedifying spectacle of corrupt prelates, priests with concubines, incapable or unworthy popes.     There is a striking contrast between these distressing externals and the profound reality of the Christian spirit which lay behind them.

In the abbeys subject to lay jurisdiction and used as so much capital, there were many souls who had the sense of a living, authentic faith, and who would soon impose their ideal upon society.     Far better, it was common to hear a prince, even while he cynically exploited religious estates, disposing of abbatial or episcopal titles, declare that the Church must be reformed and brought back to her ancient purity. But the purpose was more evident than its fulfilment.     Most of his contemporaries agreed at rock bottom with a passage in the *Satirical*

[1] One of the most curious forms of piety, which began to flourish at this period, was that of the *recluse*.     Found in the West as early as the fourth and fifth centuries (there were recluses on the isle of Lérins in the time of St Eucherius), it was to become important owing to the attention it received from many Councils.     Men, and sometimes women, had themselves enclosed in small cabins measuring only ten by ten feet, the door of which was sealed or bricked up, but having a little window through which the occupant received his food, material and spiritual.     St Romuald's Rule provides for this singular vocation. The ceremony of making a recluse was accompanied by a joyful procession, to the sound of bells and hymns, which escorted the recluse wearing a hood (or veil in the case of a woman) to the place of his voluntary imprisonment, and which then returned in silence, praying.     In theory a recluse never went out again until death, or at any rate until he was dying.

*Poem* of Adalbero, Archbishop of Rheims; 'The Church, in the persons of her clergy, has the sole duty of remaining pure in body and soul, to have exemplary morals, and to protect those of others. It is the eternal law of God that obliges her ministers to preserve themselves free from stain.' The Christian soul continued to have trust even in Rome, about which there were so many painful and disquieting rumours. It took care not to confuse the unworthiness of certain pastors with the supernatural dignity of their office. Let us hear the cry of love springing from a little guide written for the use of pilgrims about A.D. 1000. 'O noble Rome, mistress of the world, red with the blood of martyrs, white with the spotless lilies of virginity, we bless thee! Mayest thou live through the ages! While the Colosseum stands Rome will live; if the Colosseum should fall, Rome will also fall, and with Rome the world!' How better express the bond of loyalty towards those who founded Christianity in the blood and love of sacrifice? A society capable of such thoughts was ready for a splendid springtime.

## New Conquests for the Cross

We can point to other features of Christianity at this period which heralded the approaching dawn. One of the most important was the expansion of the Church through her wonderful missionary effort which had continued unbroken for six hundred years. The disintegration of the Carolingian Empire had not halted the impulse given by Charlemagne to the work of evangelization. At a time when the Byzantine East was sowing the Gospel seed among the Bulgarians, in Greater Moravia, and then in Russia—and it was also the time, we may recall, when the Nestorian missions were winning many peoples for Christ from Malabar to Tibet, from Turkestan to the Yellow Sea—the Western Church also was hard at work achieving new conquests. Her missionary labour was remarkable not only because of the results obtained but also because of a somewhat altered outlook. Whereas, in the past, baptism had almost always signified that the converts submitted, as it were, to a conqueror and abandoned their national traditions, now, in the tenth and eleventh centuries, the Church sought rather to help in the formation of 'national' Christians; baptism would hallow the personality of a converted people without trying to reduce it to a power, which was far more in keeping with the spirit of the Gospel and would facilitate its expansion.

That this was the right method may be judged by the mediocre results obtained by using force among the Slavs of Germany. Neither Charlemagne nor his successors had thought of making headway among the compact mass of Slavonic tribes who dwelt within a quadrilateral formed by the Baltic, the Oder, the Elbe, and the mountains of Bohemia.   When the Saxon princes took in hand the fortunes of the Empire, they intended to shatter this bulwark of resistance.   Under Henry the Fowler and Otto the Great the Church shared in their enterprises in a manner akin to that used by Charlemagne towards the Saxons themselves, but even more brutally.   Priests and monks followed the army; ecclesiastical organization buttressed the military administration; and the racial struggle was envenomed by the religious. The consequence could easily be foreseen: bitter hatred of the conquered pagans for these German missionaries with their blood-stained hands, and for the religion of love which they so poorly represented. It was easy enough to install, by force, archbishops at Magdeburg and Hamburg.   But the Wends took the first opportunity to revolt (980–983), strangling one of their bishops, capturing and torturing the clergy, plundering the cathedrals and monasteries.   New campaigns and new missionaries were required before Christianity could strike a few slender roots in these lands.   Even St Adalbert, a man truly faithful to the spirit of Christ, was able to achieve very little, as a fresh revolt in 1066 proved only too well.

Very different was the method employed in Hungary, where one of the great pages of Christian history was written at that time.   There emerged in Hungary the glorious figure of *St Stephen*, and all the sovereigns who afterwards reigned at Budapest considered it a point of honour to claim the spiritual heritage whose name, until recently, the crown of Hungary bore.   In 997 the young prince Vajk became 'Duke of Hungary,' of whom Raoul Glaber says that 'he counted it the greatest honour to be a good Christian.'   At that time nearly half a century had passed since the tenacious and repeated efforts of the Church had tamed the rough conscience of the Magyars.   After a phase of expansion by brute force at the beginning of the tenth century, during which Greater Moravia had been dismembered, the Hungarians, checked at the battle of Lech in 955, had settled behind the Leitha in the great Danubian plain, where they gradually became a sedentary peasant folk and mingled with the native population.   Soon they had obtained some idea of Christianity.   Magyar prisoners in Germany had interested the clergy, and numerous missionaries burned with desire to win for Christ this people who were said to be so formidable. Purely apostolic considerations were not, however, the sole driving force.   A certain bishop of Passau, named Pilgrin, cherished a secret plan to erect Hungary into an archbishopric with his own see as metropolitan, a plan for which he won support in the Roman Curia with the help of some resounding lies, and which quickly turned to his own shame.   But God makes use of everything to accomplish His work, and the ambitious Pilgrin at least had the credit of sending many preachers to the banks of the Danube.

The goal was ultimately reached.    In 970 Duke Gesa saw that the one hope of his nation's survival was its conversion to Christianity. His wife, St Adelaide, a Slav princess, was another Clotilde, while St Adalbert of Prague, her relation, strove valiantly to enlarge the field of faith.    In 997 Gesa's son, who at baptism had received the name Stephen, came to power; he splendidly fulfilled his mother's task and at the same time revealed himself to the Christian world as the model of a prince faithful to Christ.    Husband of a German princess, Giselle, he made intelligent use of Otto III's ideas on a Christian 'federalism' to have his state recognized as an independent kingdom, and in 1001 Pope Sylvester II crowned him 'Apostolic King.'    The national Church of Hungary had its administrative organization, its archbishops and bishops. Numerous monastic communities were settled in its territories, baptizing the countryside, building villages, and spreading civilization. Years of effort would still be required before the Gospel reached these remote districts and the mountains of Transylvania, an effort glorified by the names of such great missionaries as *St Bruno of Querfurt*, former chaplain to Otto III, a young nobleman won to the apostolate by St Adalbert of Prague, and who ended his life as a martyr.    But the decisive stage had been passed.    St Stephen had proved himself, to a more splendid and more saintly degree, the Clovis of Hungary.

The Church had, in this case, sanctified a nation, but she would not, for all that, take part in the contest of nationalistic rivalry.    Labouring to bring forth Christian lands, she remained more than ever faithful to the great Augustinian ideal of a union of Christians under her aegis, to the theories of Paul Orosius and the intuitions of Pope John VIII as to the real meaning of Christendom.    Even while she was baptizing the Magyars she was converting other peoples who would regard them as their worst enemies—the heirs and the debris of Greater Moravia, which the terrible Hungarian cavalry had recently overwhelmed. Bohemia, whose mountains had resisted the invaders, had also been affected by the teaching of Byzantine missionaries—of Sts Cyril and Methodius; but paganism still flourished there, mainly because it appeared as the exemplar of national independence in face of Germanic influence.    The introduction of Christianity was thus accompanied by some appalling crises.    *St Ludmilla* suffered martyrdom, about 920, for having propagated the Christian faith, strangled by her pagan daughter-in-law.    Her grandson, *St Wenceslaus*, having invited missionaries to his diocese and built the cathedral of Prague, likewise suffered martyrdom, in 935, at the hands of his younger brother Boleslas, leader of the pagan party.    The blood of these victims, however, was not shed in vain.    Boleslas I repented of his crime and adopted his brother's policy. His daughters were Christian and founded the first nunneries in Bohemia. His son, Boleslas II, had Prague made a bishopric with the future *St Adalbert* at its head. Here again, about the year 1000, much remained to be done, as St Adalbert himself had understood; for he left his see in disgust and retired to an Italian monastery before laying down his life as a martyr in Prussia. But the decisive step had been taken.

The same had happened, and at about the same time, in Poland, another Slavic group which, like Bohemia, was destined to become a great Christian kingdom. The evangelization of Poland was less dramatic. In this case also the efficient cause was a woman, the Bohemian princess, *St Dombrowska*, in whom dwelt the spirit of those Christian queens whom we have seen, century after century, bear witness to Christ before the throne. Her husband, Duke Miecislav, on her advice, adopted a policy that favoured both Christianity and agreement with the German emperors. A bishopric was established at Poznan, and soon, in concert with the Germans, Christian Poland reached the Baltic. Wisely, however, in order to escape subjection to the Empire, Poland became a vassal of the Holy See, thus inaugurating a close union with Rome that was to be an outstanding feature of the Polish kingdom. The royal and Christian house of Poland was created by the son of Miecislav and Dombrowska, *Boleslas the Valiant* (992–1025). While conducting a brilliant series of campaigns against the still savage Slavs of the north and east, which won him his surname, he showed himself as able a diplomat as his contemporary, Stephen of Hungary. He took advantage of the idealistic and generous theories of Otto III to free his country from German tutelage. After the translation of St Adalbert's relics to Gniezno, Boleslas's capital, Otto III went to pray at the tomb of one he had admired in life; and the Polish prince availed himself of this occasion to have himself recognized as sovereign. The Polish Church was constituted at the same time, with Gniezno as the archiepiscopal see, and Kolberg, Breslau, and Cracow as its suffragans. Once more, as in the case of Hungary and Bohemia, the work was not complete; pagan reaction was still possible, as happened in 1033 when convents were burnt and many of the clergy massacred, a crisis that was prudently ended by the 'Restorer of Poland,' *Casimir I*. But the Gospel seed had taken root and nothing would ever eradicate it.

This work of evangelization produced wonderful results, tangible proof of the Church's vitality. This was all the more remarkable because her efforts were not confined to the one area of Central Europe; but were directed also towards the ungrateful north and the Islamic south. In the north there occurred a thrilling series of events, which we cannot follow in detail, because of gaps in the record, but which are full of adventure and of curious and attractive personalities. Within a period of three hundred years—from the ninth to the eleventh century—Scandinavia emerged from the misty paganism of her great maritime and warlike dreams into the Gospel faith. Those corsairs, whom we have so often seen plundering Christian countries, sought baptism, sometimes on the very site of their rapine; and their change of heart even led them to steal relics—a sure proof, in that age, of their great faith. At the same time heroic missionaries descended upon those savage countries, sent mainly by the Archbishop of Hamburg, to whom St Anschar had bequeathed his lesson. Closely linked with the invasions of France and England by the Norsemen, this story of the conversion of Scandinavia has the quality of an epic; here are its principal figures.

Harold Bluetooth was the first Nordic prince known to have received baptism, about 950. Aided by his wife Gunhild, he strove to convert his Danes. *St Olaf*, King of Norway, once a sea-rover, worked successfully to stamp out paganism with the help of numerous priests and monks whom he had brought over from England. In Sweden St Eric wavered all his life between the two beliefs; his son Olaf was a militant Christian, but it was during his reign that there occurred the martyrdom of the English-born *Archbishop Wulfred* who, wishing to repeat the exploits of St Boniface, smashed the national idol at Uppsala and was cut down on the spot. The most fascinating of these personalities, of whom there were so many, was undoubtedly *King Knut the Great*, who in 1001 carved himself out a magnificent kingdom consisting of the British Isles and the whole of Scandinavia, and who laboured hard to make his dominions a Christian empire. His great political achievement did not survive him, but his efforts to abolish paganism were successful.

After Knut's death, in the states resulting from the disintegration of his empire, Magnus of Norway, a worthy son of St Olaf, and Emund Gamul of Sweden remained true to his principles. About 1050, then, with the intelligent support of Archbishop Adalbert of Hamburg, some Nordic national Churches were created, having their own hierarchies and directly linked with Rome. Christianity was now firmly established in Scandinavia and sent out missionaries to conquer far distant lands. Some of them went to Iceland, where they found memories of the ancient Celtic monks, disciples of St Columba and St Brendan the Navigator, and founded Christian colonies, traces of which, in the form of crude inscriptions on stone crosses, may still be seen.

Greenland became Christian soon after its discovery in the tenth century. Eric the Red, a Viking nicknamed 'the Gangster'—and he was one!—has the credit of that discovery. He recruited Christian colonies from Iceland; churches and converts arose in that inhospitable land (less so, however, than to-day), and ruins of twelve churches have been found.   There has also been found the grave of a bishop—there had been bishops since 1126—who had been buried without a coffin but with a superb cross made from the tusk of a walrus.   These tusks played an important part in the economy of the country, and were used by the Greenlanders to pay their dues to Rome.   Christianity disappeared from Greenland when its population died out in the fifteenth century, as a result, it is believed, of a fall in the temperature, which ruined the vegetation essential for the rearing of flocks and herds.[1]

We may admire the same enterprising spirit elsewhere and at the same period.   Most of Spain had been subject to the Ommayad caliphs for three centuries, but in the north the visible sign of Christian indestructibility was the Castilian state, heir of 'King' Pelagius (718) and including Leon and Galicia where St James of Compostella was the torch of the faith.   The Christian sovereigns of the mountains were already fairly powerful, thanks to the increasing Moslem decadence. Farther to the north-east, the tiny kingdoms of Aragon and Navarre, and, on the Mediterranean, the former 'Carolingian March,' which had become the county of Barcelona, lay in the Pyrenees.   Their inhabitants, though splendid fighters, were too weak to prevail over their adversaries, and the caliph Al-Mansur taught them a terrible lesson by ravaging Barcelona.   The Moslem peril existed in Spain throughout the tenth century, as even France learned to her cost when attacks were made on her cities in the south.

It was, in fact, the Christians of France who, about the year 1000, initiated the 'Reconquista.'   Was not St James of Compostella dear to the hearts of believers?   In 987 Count Borel of Barcelona appealed to Hugh Capet for help against Al-Mansur, but unsuccessfully: the little French king had other preoccupations.   But this appeal—a call to the crusade—stirred the barons of France.   Adventure!   Adventure! Christendom!   Christendom!   Even love took a hand, when the beautiful Countess Ermessinda of Barcelona called upon Roger of Normandy for help and he flew gallantly to her assistance, spreading terror among the Saracens.   Shortly afterwards Duke William of Gascony crossed the Pyrenees with his merry men and proceeded to ravage the Moslem cities of the Ebro.   Burgundy, at the invitation of Odilon, the saintly abbot of Cluny, sent an expedition to attack the east coast of Spain, and the famous abbey received a large part of the spoils.   Thus, in the first half of the eleventh century the battle for Christ had been joined in the peninsula of St Hermenegild.   The medieval history of the Reconquista was beginning.

[1] See the article 'Groenland au moyen âge,' by Paul Norland, in the *Revue historique*, 1933, tome 172, p. 409, with photographs of Christian remains in wood and ivory.

## The Structure of the Church

It is not only to her expansion beyond her ancient frontiers that we must look for proof of the Church's vitality in that tragic dawn of the Middle Ages.   Her constitution, her structure, damaged as they were by the feudal system, not only remained unaffected in its essence, but acquired new strength in several ways.   From top to bottom of the institutional ladder the same fact is observed: the Church of the Middle Ages was in progress of formation.

At the bottom, at ground level so to speak, the principal factor was the extension of the *parochial system*, the beginnings of which we have noticed in the Merovingian epoch,[1] and its development under the Carolingians.   In the countries of ancient faith, Italy and Gaul, where a close network of churches spread over the countryside, new ones were built on freshly cleared land.   In Germany, though few in the middle of the ninth century, country churches were springing up everywhere a century and a half later.   Bohemia, Poland, and Hungary underwent a similar transformation.   Around the church spread the parish: it was at this time that the world finally came to signify the elementary district which we call by the same name to-day.[2]   Each parish had its head, who was still known as the *presbyter* or, sometimes, as *rector ecclesiae*; although, admittedly, he had the *cura animarum* (cure of souls) he was not yet called *curatus* (parish priest).   He was the true and only immediate shepherd of the flock, bound to it so closely that he was forbidden to allow members of other parishes to attend his mass, unless they were travellers.   He was strictly subordinate to the bishop, in theory at any rate, although the episcopal authority was often enough in conflict with that of the lay overlord within whose territory the parish lay.   The parish church, whether a humble building of clay and thatch or an edifice of stone, was the symbol of community, not only a sacred place where the divine offices were celebrated but a true community centre where the Lord's 'pleas' were held and in the forecourt of which there took place transactions, sales, and other public business.   It was loved and revered.   It received generous offerings; tithes, which had been imposed by the Council of Trosly in 909, and taxes of one-tenth levied on all incomes (not only on agricultural revenues) did not seem too heavy.   The church, where a man was baptized, where he attended the offices throughout the seasons, in the shadow of which he dreamed of being buried, was truly the living cell of the Christian organism.   The faults of certain priests, the avarice of landlords, none of these things could undo the great fact of Western Christendom.

[1] See Chapter V, section: 'A Long and Patient Endeavour.'
[2] See Chapter V, note on p. 260, on the meaning of the word 'parish.'

On a higher level, corresponding to the parish on the bottom rung, was the organization of *bishoprics*. Over against the *seigneurial* institutions, which tended to absorb everything, stood the network of great ecclesiastical districts. They had of course been penetrated by feudalism which, in too many instances, had confiscated episcopal dignities and goods, but the structure was still there and would never be broken. The old Roman *civitas*, which no longer had any administrative or political significance, survived in the *episcopatum*, but in current language the word 'city' was coming more and more to denote what it now does for us—an enclosed town. At this period the term was limited to enclosed towns where a bishop resided, even though they had never been the capitals of Roman *civitates*. There, behind the shelter of walls, the bishop had his church seat, his 'cathedral' church, mother of all churches in the region. The Christians were proud of it and spent a great deal to make it lofty and large. It was placed under the protection of some illustrious saint—very often of the Blessed Virgin, of St Stephen the Protomartyr, or perhaps of an apostle or other character from the Gospels—who was claimed, on the basis of much legendary evidence, to have established the faith in that particular neighbourhood. Around the bishop there grew up an administration, a kind of general staff; the canons, united in chapter, were first of all entrusted with the collective prayer of the episcopal city, and their life, somewhat like that of the monks, was subject to a rule. This body of men, chosen from the *élite* of the clergy and often very numerous,[1] also assumed administrative duties, helping to manage the goods of the bishopric, supervising the schools and works of charity. At their head was an important individual who was at first the archdeacon and subsequently the provost; other members of the chapter were the cantor, the master of schools, the chancellor or protonotary, and the custodians of the treasury. The episcopal jurisdiction extended far beyond the city; it included the *suburbium* which was beginning to be called by the old imperial name of 'diocese.' In theory this jurisdiction was derived from that of the 'metropolitan bishop' or 'archbishop.' Proprietor and manager of vast estates, having the disposal of a budget fed by parochial tithes and pious offerings, the bishop remained, though in a very different way, the leading figure, the mainspring of Christian society, which we have seen him to be for seven or eight centuries. *Ecclesia in episcopo!*

In this connection it must be understood how solid was the structure of the Church. All that has been said about the unfortunate results of feudal encroachments on the bishoprics is true; the laicization of the episcopate, the moral degradation of some of its members, were only

---

[1] In France the smallest body of canons was that of Maguelone (twelve), and the greatest that of Chartres (seventy-two, in memory of the seventy-two disciples).

too real. But there was some distinction in these feudal bishops between the man as such and the titular of the see; and the second often proved infinitely superior to the first. How many of them were indefatigable builders! About 900 the Bishop of Noyon rebuilt his cathedral which had been ruined by the Normans; the Bishop of Metz completely transformed his; the Bishop of Beauvais completed his after seventy years of effort (924–96), and at Chartres, in 1020, immediately after a serious fire, Bishop Fulbert set to work on reconstruction. The list might be prolonged: many examples from Germany could be cited. How many of those feudal bishops were also generous Christians, charitable, kind to humble folk, and around whom the tenants, the people of the *familia*, were certainly happier than before. 'It is good to live under the crozier,' said a proverb dating from this time. Far from debasing the episcopal institution, the 'first feudal age' handed it on in good condition to the following epoch.

Another essential element in the structure of the Church was the *monastery*. We have seen the growing importance assumed by the monastic institution since the triumph of the Benedictine rule; convents had been bulwarks of Christianity as well as of civilization, and they continued to be so. Each of them was the religious and cultural centre of a more or less extensive region; groups of people settled in its immediate neighbourhood, giving rise to communities that often developed into towns. The whole of Western Europe was covered with a network of monasteries which steadily increased.[1]

Now monasticism was perhaps the institution which resisted better than any other the disintegrating activity of feudalism. Obviously this resistance was not victorious everywhere and at the same time. We have seen how dangerous was the intrusion of lay abbots; but the fact remains that the regular clergy was better armed than the secular when confronted with the baronage. It commanded, in fact, a three-fold means of defence: the protection of the king, that of the attorneys, and, above all, pontifical exemption. The two enemies of an abbey were almost always the count and the bishop, both of them equally (though for different reasons) jealous of the power, wealth, and independence of the regulars. The count thought mainly of converting monastic property to his own use; the bishops, to whom such considerations were by no means alien, looked with a distrustful eye upon Father Abbot who, in his community, was master under God and with whom the prerogatives of 'visitor' allowed to the bishop, meant very little indeed. In the tenth and at the beginning of the eleventh century the feudal episcopate often represented the twofold menace, and the monks fought back with their triple arms. A fair number of abbeys 'gave themselves' to the king, a step which prevented the count

[1] See the map of monastic Europe in Chapter VIII.

and the bishop from going too far.    The Capetians, from the very
beginning, adopted this policy of protecting the abbeys, which became
independent centres, bulwarks of unity and loyalty in face of the
increasing anarchy of the feudal lords, and seminaries which trained
the statesmen and writers who would aggrandize France.    The
Capetian monarchy would owe much to such great abbeys as Fleury,
Cluny, St Denis, St Martin at Tours, St Benignus at Dijon, and
St Riquier.

If the king was too far distant or preoccupied, he appointed a
neighbouring lord as 'attorney' to protect the abbey, if necessary by
force.    That these attorneys were themselves too often like crows in
a wheat-field, is attested by innumerable documents; but it was a
necessary evil, and one less serious than would have been the abandonment of an abbey to the covetousness of anyone and everyone; and
many an attorney proved himself a faithful servant of the communities
entrusted to his care.

Finally, and most important, there appeared in the eighth century
and developed during the next hundred and fifty years, the custom of
pontifical exemption which was monasticism's principal defence.    In
751 Pope Zacharias had placed the abbey of Fulda 'under the immediate jurisdiction of Rome so that it be not subject to any Church,'
and this example had continued to be followed ever since.    To owe
obedience to none but the Pope became the dream of every community.
Vézelay obtained exemption in 865, Fleury in 878, and there were
many others. . . .    The results were so happy that we shall henceforward find that princes themselves, when founding a monastery,
often placed it 'under the protection of the Blessed Apostles.'    No one,
under pain of the most terrible sanctions, might injure these 'exempt'
abbeys, which therefore naturally became devoted instruments of the
Holy See's grand policy when the latter was inaugurated.

The Apostolic See itself, which we have seen exposed to the worst
forces of destruction, began at the same time to develop its own
institutions and to prepare, almost unconsciously for a better future.
It was not only on the sentimental level that Rome remained Rome,
where the piety of thousands surrounded the tomb of the apostle; it
was also on the level of historical loyalties, where something stronger
than human appetite and passion was a guarantee of permanence.

Around these popes, however weak or unworthy, attendant on this
Court that was so frequently corrupt, was a whole society of clerics who
laboured for the glory of the Church.    There were the ordinary or
Palatine judges who assisted the Pope in his governmental duties, just
as the officials of the palace assisted the Byzantine emperor.    They
were the provost, pro-provost, protosecretary, *arcarius* or guardian of
the chest, *sacellarius* or minister of expenses, *nomenclator* (forerunner

of the chamberlain), and advocate who pleaded causes before the Holy Father. The functions of these seven tended to decline during the tenth century, because the popes often found them insubordinate. The first three belonged to the *Chancellery*, a body of officials which drew up and issued the pontifical Acts, and which had existed for at least four centuries. This organism was the depository of a tradition which cannot be exactly defined: popes might come and go, but the Chancellery remained, and the Chancellery it was that held the rudder of Peter's barque through storm and stress, as is shown by the fact that even to-day the Acts are drafted more or less according to rules laid down in the time of St Gregory the Great. In addressing the most powerful sovereigns it preserved the tone adopted by the greatest popes towards princes, and the Holy See was much indebted to these obscure scribes. The Pope also had in his service a number of *apostolic legates*; and here again it is worth drawing attention to the fact that even the most disreputable popes never failed to make their authority felt wherever they could, and the intervention of their legates very often achieved its purpose. The weapon employed so success-fully by Gregory VII and his successors was already to hand.

The most important factor, however, during these one hundred and fifty years, was the increasing prominence of certain individuals known as *cardinals*. Originally the term signified, somewhat vaguely, clerics who were, so to speak, the hinge (*cardo*) of the Church; to 'incardi-nate' a cleric was to attach him to a church as a hinge to a door. At the beginning of the tenth century the word cardinal took on a more general meaning; it signified 'principal' or 'chief.' Moreover it was employed at first as a mere qualificative term, one of respect, which was used not only at Rome but also at Constantinople, Milan, Ravenna, Padua, Laon, Sens, Cologne, Compostella, and elsewhere. But at Rome, during the same century, the 'cardinal clergy' acquired con-siderable prestige, partly because so many of the popes were nonenti-ties, and strict rules were drawn up to define its character. It com-prised the three famous categories which still exist: cardinal bishops, cardinal priests, and cardinal deacons. The first were the seven bishops of towns in the immediate vicinity of Rome, e.g. Ostia, Albano, Porto; the most distant, Palestrina, was only about twenty-five miles from the Eternal City. Little occupied with their minute dioceses, they were, in practice, at the disposal of the Holy See, attending the Pope on state occasions. The cardinal priests were the pastors of the chief parishes of Rome. They had for long numbered twenty-five; a twenty-sixth title—that of San Stefano on the Coelian —was created in the tenth century. While the cardinal bishops served the church of St Saviour in the Lateran, the cardinal priests officiated in the three great basilicas of St Peter, St-Paul-outside-the-

T

Walls, and St Lawrence-outside-the-Walls. Lastly, the cardinal deacons were so named after the original deacons and those seven regional deacons who administered the seven sections of the city; actually, from this time onward, they were not much concerned with their regions and worked at the Lateran. These three categories did not as yet form a single college, nor were they as yet entrusted with papal elections. But, owing to the fact that members of the three groups were brought into the limelight, it was natural that they should become an organized body. When the Holy See wished to remove the election of the pope from the influence of the German emperor, it was to this body that they had recourse, and the most outstanding innovation of Nicholas II, in 1059, was to confer the responsibility of choosing the Sovereign Pontiff upon the College of Cardinals, a decisive step to which the medieval Papacy owed its special character.

### 'A WHITE MANTLE OF CHURCHES'

The dawn of the Middle Ages could be detected at many points in the sky of the year 1000; was it perceptible in the quarters of art and culture? Baronius, in a celebrated passage of his *Ecclesiastical Annals*, declares that 'because of its crudeness, its sterility, and the bankruptcy of its writers, this [tenth] century deserves to be called, as it is generally called, the Dark Ages.' But is that quite true? Certainly in the last years of the ninth century, and particularly after the death of Charles the Bald, there had been a progressive obscurity. The impulse given by Charlemagne had gradually ceased and mental inertia became the rule. Amid the terrible chaos of invasion and fratricidal strife the very means of culture were gravely imperilled: doomed to pillage and incendiarism, many monastic libraries had disappeared; the exchange of manuscripts, so frequent and so fruitful in Carolingian days, had virtually ceased, and this limited students to local sources. Again, the evolution of manners and customs, which tended to make culture the appanage, or speciality, of the clergy, and therefore contemptible in the eyes of the barons and mercenary soldiers, did not encourage the young to study. The surprising thing is, not that, in such conditions, the tenth century was an age of obscurity, but that it was not even more so, that islands of true culture, art, and disinterested thought continued to exist. The impression made upon the West by the Carolingian Renaissance had been so profound that two hundred and fifty years of return to barbarism could not efface it completely.

The centres of intellectual formation did not disappear altogether. It was still in the monastic schools that young people rubbed shoulders in an atmosphere of Christian equality; but the cathedral schools tended to supplant them, about the year 1000, as urban civilization grew in importance. In them the theory and practice of Latin were held in great respect, not only for liturgical purposes, but also, as an English archbishop wrote, 'because that language is indispensible to anyone who desires to perfect his education, to anyone who seeks to attain a high position.' The Latin in question was often of poor quality and badly taught in schools where the several branches of the *quadrivium* were seriously neglected, but which nevertheless produced highly cultured men and true scholars such as Gerbert, the future Pope Sylvester II. Fleury-sur-Loire, Auxerre, Saint-Gall, Liège, Pavia, and Ravenna were the Oxfords and Sorbonnes of this period; nor did the misery of the time ever extinguish the cares of the spirit.

Thus, although few in number, and often threatened, the intellectual centres of the Dark Age continued to prepare the future. Those convents which we found, in the ninth century, devoting themselves with such fervour to the copying of manuscripts, to translation of the great Latin works, carried on, in even more hostile times, the work to which we owe so much. In France the abbey of Saint-Germain-des-Prés, so often attacked by the Normans, preserved the taste for classical scholarship and poetry. The workshop at Corbie turned out manuscripts in endless succession. In Lorraine, a border territory, where many influences met, Prüm, Toul, and Gorze combined Germanic elements with those of eastern France; it was there that was composed the Latin ancestor of the famous *Roman de Renart*. Germany and Lotharingia, less ravaged than the rest of Europe, possessed two centres before which all others fade into insignificance: Corvey (New Corbie) and, above all, Saint-Gall, whose library and scriptorium were world famous, and which invited Greek monks to come and copy manuscripts written in their language. At Corvey history and poetry were cultivated; there Witikind wrote his *Saxon Chronicle*, and there the poetess Hroswitha of Gandersheim related in verse the acts of the martyrs and the life of the Emperor Otto, and even wrote lively comedies modelled upon Terence.

A real activity then existed, and would continue to exist, throughout the tenth century; it would increase soon after the year 1000, when circumstances began to improve, and would thus make ready the approaching spring. Was this epoch, therefore, as sterile as Baronius says? True, its theological fruit was poor. Even the most famous theologians of the age, Odo of Cluny and Rathier of Liège, do not appear to us more than mere commentators and compilers, inferior to such men as Alcuin or Rabanus Maurus. Only one appears to have been in advance of his time, and that was Berengar of Tours, who insisted upon the part played by reason in faith but quickly lapsed into heresy. Juridical works were no more original at the turn of the year 1000.

Burchard of Worms, too, was only a compiler. It is perhaps in historians and chroniclers, despite all their faults, that the age was richest —the scurrilous Liutprand, the naïve and racy Raoul Glaber, Guibert de Nogent, Adémard de Chabannes, Adalbero, Helgaud, and Witikind the Saxon. But in such circumstances the works left by men count for less than their testimony; it is good that, in spite of all, we have evidence of permanence and fidelity.[1]

The same kind of evidence is provided, and in a more impressive manner, by contemporary art. There was no longer question of simply keeping alive a few elements from the past, but of looking forward, of discovering, of beginning to realize the future. Here we have an historical paradox of which something must be said. In the darkest days of the tenth and early eleventh centuries, when civilization was most gravely threatened, unknown artists were at work, creating and inventing; exalted by faith, they represent a greater marvel of the human soul than is found in any other sphere.

This creative fever is admirably described in a famous passage of Raoul Glaber, where the Burgundian chronicler states that, shortly after the year 1000, the Christian West multiplied its religious buildings: 'One might have said that the whole world was shaking off the robes of age and pulling on a white mantle of churches.' It would not be right to infer from this passage that the year 1000 marked a break in history of religious art; it is only a figure of speech, and as much building was done in the last years of the ninth century as in the first of the eleventh. The chronicler's charming phrase, however, conveys exactly the impressions one receives when considering the art of this period: gestation, presentiment of the dawn, groping but fervent longing; all these terms would apply to an effort so pregnant with the future.

How delightful to the eye were these churches of the year 1000! Many examples have survived, generally in remote districts of the French countryside, where, at a later date, there was insufficient money to pull down and rebuild. From Saint-Martin d'Aime, from Saorge or Vallouise in the French Alps, from San Giovanni dei Campi or Santa Maria de Sasso in Piedmont, to those strange Catalan naves where there are clear indications of Mozarabic influence, or to those amazing structures at Bernay, Saint-Vorles near Châtillon, and the original Saint-Remy at Rheims, there are many of these forward-looking churches, all of which plainly represent a deliberate effort, an

---

[1] A more popular form of literature was also beginning to appear. It is certain that 'minstrels' already existed, who went about reciting their poems in castle and market town. From the beginning of the tenth century there is proof of the existence of true 'mysteries' played in churches, especially at Easter, Christmas, the Epiphany, and Holy Innocents; these mysteries were made up of miming scenes and more or less rhyming dialogue.

attempt full of boldness and sagacity.   Early Romanesque art was emerging from the Carolingian chrysalis.   At the turn of the year 1000 Saint-Philibert at Tournus received its powerful, almost perfect forms; it was followed in turn by Saint-Gilles on the Rhône, Saint-Étienne at Caen, Saint-Sernin at Toulouse, and Notre-Dame la Grande at Poitiers.

Monuments of the Roman imperial age, more or less destroyed, more or less carefully restored, still served as models.   But the transformation of the ancient basilica, which took place during the ninth century, posed a number of problems: the lengthening of the building, the addition of the transept, the erection of towers and belfries (which now, as in the East, formed a framework for the central doorway), and the enlargement of the ambulatory so as to give easy access to the relics.   All these problems had, at all costs, to be solved.   From one church to another we can trace the attempts of architects to find those solutions.   Consider, for example, the column, a survival from the ancient temple.   It had retained its original form for centuries, but no longer appeared solid enough for the much larger edifices intended to hold enormous congregations.   What was to be done?   Instead of arranging the stones to form a cylinder, they were built up as pillars. The innovation was considered so audacious that the two forms were long made to alternate; then the composite pier was invented, resembling a bundle of columns, which was the solution adopted by architects.

The Latin cruciform plan, with which we are familiar, became the general rule.   However, the swarms of pilgrims returning from Jerusalem brought back from the Holy Sepulchre memories of the rotunda crowned with a cupola, invented in Merovingian times, much favoured under Charlemagne, and again fashionable for small churches such as Charroux, Neuvy Saint-Sépulcre, Saint-Michel at Entraygnes, Quimperlé, and above all (except that the building was much larger) Saint-Bénigne at Dijon.   As it was lengthened, the normal plan became more complicated, for the central nave was flanked by lateral aisles and the choir surrounded with an ambulatory; on each arm of the transept there began to appear small apses arranged like the main apse.   When the monks of Cluny came to build their great churches, this was the form they imposed on the whole of western Europe.

But as structures were enlarged a new problem arose—that of the roof.   An exciting period in this history of architecture began and was to continue step by step throughout the Middle Ages.   I refer to the struggle waged by architects to free themselves from the tyranny of weight and thrust, so as to widen the nave to the utmost possible extent, and to raise it higher.   So long as the church was relatively narrow, beams very often sufficed, and open woodwork, decorated or otherwise, was very commonly employed; vaulting, though used since Merovingian times, was uncommon, except for the brick-vaulted apse, which was the beginning of the art.   But the nave was widened; so skilful were the journeymen carpenters that it was covered with a mass of slender spires and rafters, but these forests of beams would burn like tow. . . .   So the problem of vaulting had somehow to be solved—vaulting which had been known four centuries earlier, imported from Rome and the East.   Then, however, it was applied only to quite small churches as at Jouarre or Saint-Laurent at Grenoble. Henceforward gigantic naves would be roofed with dressed stone. But what labour, what experiments, what calculations, in order not only to ensure the correct dressing and assembling of the stones, but also to avoid the thrust of their weight forcing the walls outwards, as often at first happened.   Such were the inquiries made by men in the so-called Dark Ages with wonderful faith and intelligence.   In these first pre-Romanesque churches, heavy, awkward, with rustic vaulting and walls too thick, how can one help admiring those precursors of the great masters of Gothic, who would never have been what they were but for the obscure efforts of their predecessors?

Tenth-century churches, naturally, have nothing like the sumptuous ornamentation of later Romanesque and *a fortiori* of Gothic.   Their beauty resides in naked simplicity.   Nevertheless, timid experiments were made as, for example, about 1020, at Saint-Genis-des-Fontaines, a little church in Roussillon, the door of which is ornamented with a Christ in Majesty surrounded by angels and saints, all within a charming border of foliage.   As a rule the only points at which some play of fancy was allowed were the capitals, but fancy here was extremely hesitant, taking the form of stylistic plants and animals, or geometrical patterns copied from Byzantium.   Sometimes, particularly in Germany, a cubic shape was adopted, which made for easier carving. We are still a long way from those splendid biblical scenes which adorn the capitals at Saint-Benoît and Vézelay.   Bold, though more archaic than the architecture, sculpture remained true to its traditions enshrined in ivory carvings.   There was one important exception: the bronze doors at Hildesheim, which an enterprising bishop brought from Constantinople.   Its panels recall those of Trajan's column, but foreshadow those found on all similar doors of the Romanesque period, for which it served as a pattern.

If sculpture was as yet mean and mosaic had been abandoned, painting certainly made enormous strides.   There was painting on glass, stained-glass windows, and Adalbero says that in Rheims Cathedral, which was rebuilt about 980, 'the windows told all kinds of stories.'   There was painting in fresco, specimens of which are now and then discovered by some lucky chance under the whitewash of a later date, and which herald the magnificence of Saint-Savin, of Saint-Chef, of old Pouzauges, and of Rocamadour. . . . Already regular Bibles in paint were instructing the faithful in sacred history.    In the celebrated abbey of Reichenau there has been discovered the most enchanting of these pictures; it is the twin brother, though immeasurably larger, of other pieces which the monastic copyists were creating, in miniature, in their manuscripts.

For the art of manuscript was very much alive, despite the misfortunes of that age.    Reichenau itself was famed for its miniatures; so were Saint-Gall, Fleury, and other houses.    In Ireland the marvellous interlacing of capital letters was still carried on.    Popes, bishops, and kings placed their orders, and books of this kind are extremely valuable.    At Saint-Maximin, at Trèves, Bishop Egbert even founded a school of miniaturists, and their masterpiece, a book of Gospels, the *Codex Egberti*, bears his name.    More sober, less 'Byzantine' than those of the Carolingian period, the miniatures of the 'Dark Ages' were already almost as perfect as those of the thirteenth century.

## PEACE FOR CHRIST

In the year 1000 there was yet another quarter of the sky where dawn appeared, faintly, dimly, but full of promise; a quarter in which the night had seemed darkest, that of morals.    Here we can best study the determination of the Church and her fidelity to the message of Christ. In the savage world of nascent feudalism, where, as one preacher said, 'men have claws and live with the wild beasts,' she alone was prepared to recall the existence of certain higher principles.    Despite the evils to which she was herself a prey, she applied herself to this task and, small results notwithstanding, would not be discouraged.

About the year 1000 it became certain that the grave problem which had faced Europe since the disintegration of the Carolingian Empire [1] would be solved.    In spite of appearances, the Church would never allow the bases of civilization, with which she was entrusted, to dissolve in a sea of barbarism.

She began by continually insisting upon the evangelical principles. Look at any of the canons of any Council held between 900 and 1050, and you will find that they contain excellent provisions with a truly Christian ring.    Were they voices crying in the desert?    Certainly not.    When a bishop or a monk told a prince that his sole duty was 'not to allow the continued existence in his realm of any iniquity,' the person addressed fully admitted that he was right, even though in practice he behaved himself otherwise.    A profound observation of

[1] See the end of Chapter VIII.

Hugh Capet deserves to be quoted: 'The sublimity of our devotions is of no avail unless we render justice by all means and to all men.' Vast numbers of the great feudal lords said and thought likewise; it was highly significant that, even when violated in fact, the principles of charity and justice were admitted by all as superior.

The Church did not limit herself to this Platonic reminder. By every means at her disposal she tried to act. Homicide, that plague of the 'Dark Ages,' in which human life counted for so little, she denounced unmercifully; no Council ignored it or failed to chastise those guilty of a crime that had at all costs to be prevented. The Church was well aware that she possessed a weapon capable of subduing those souls which, however gross, were still subject to the dictates of religion. She was the guardian of oaths; she gave a solemn character to those which the warriors swore to their suzerain, and she had more than once to remind a vassal that such undertakings must be treated as sacred. Could she not use the same method to enforce obedience to her principles?

It was in answer to this question that there were born, during the tenth century, those magnificent ideals in which were founded the grandeur of the Middle Ages—*the Peace and Truce of God*.[1] It is a splendid thought that the primary purpose of the Church was to protect from unbridled force those humble, weak, and insignificant folk who could not defend themselves. Never perhaps in the history of this age did Mother Church reveal herself as so truly a mother. The crusade for peace dates chiefly from the Council of Charroux, on 1st June 989, and from that of Puy-en-Velay in the following year. Those Councils inveighed, in noble language, against the excesses of violence and denounced as sacrilegious any scoundrel who destroyed or stole the goods of the poor. Very soon, and almost everywhere, the Church introduced treaties of peace to which the feudal lords swore obedience by solemn oath. This oath was first exacted at Verdun-sur-Saône in 1016. Resistance was inevitable: noblemen fought shy, even such bishops as Gerard of Cambrai (1013–51), a too faithful servitor of princes, would not take it, rejecting, as they said, the necessity of excommunicating too many barons! This striving after peace, in a society that loved war, was

---

[1] The next volume [*Cathedral and Crusade*] deals with the origins of chivalry, an institution that illustrates particularly well the Church's effort to christianize force. The most ancient documents referring to it date from about A.D. 1000; e.g. this prayer of the young German noble girding on the sword: 'Hear our prayers, O Lord, and with Thy majestic hand bless this sword wherewith Thy servant desireth to be girt in order to protect churches . . . widows, orphans, and all God's servants against the cruelty of the pagans, and in order to strike fear into all criminals.' After 1050 chivalry became more and more widespread, but, as Henri Pirenne says: 'The manners of chivalry, that code of courtesy and loyalty which distinguished the gentleman after the Crusades, did not as yet exist. More refinement was needed to produce it.'

a splendid dream, perhaps an example of midsummer madness, and certainly a paradox; but at least it expressed a justifiable Christian hope that would spread gradually throughout the world.

It is necessary to distinguish within this great movement two separate institutions: the *Peace of God* and the *Truce of God*. The express purpose of the first was to protect the clergy, the poor, and their property, in fact to limit the havoc that might be caused by outbreaks of violence. The text of the oath of Verdun-sur-Saône, very precise and amusing in its details, states the matter clearly. The influence of the assembled bishops had to be such that the secular lords would be ready to take the oath of peace, and indeed many of them took it. Sanctions were provided against those who violated their oath, even going so far as to impose an interdict on the whole region within which the breach had occurred: no public masses, no baptisms, marriages, burials, or sounding of bells. . . . This movement towards peace, starting from Auvergne and Poitou, gradually extended to the whole of France. We may guess it was welcomed by the people, and Raoul Glaber says: 'Those present at the Council shouted with joy: Peace! Peace! Peace! symbol of the everlasting alliance that had been made with God!' And as marvels were readily believed in that age, one good bishop declared that a mysterious letter had fallen from heaven, enjoining men to observe the pact of peace. Towards the middle of the eleventh century the movement extended beyond the Rhine, the Alps, and the Pyrenees; it was favoured almost everywhere by kings, who realized that this invention of the bishops would help to control the anarchical tendencies of feudalism. Thus Robert the Pious, in France, wished the conciliar decrees to have the force of law. Was he not dreaming of a universal peace? Did he not speak of it seriously to the German emperor Henry II when they met at the Council of Ivois in 1021? In 1023 the Emperor Henry III promulgated a 'day of indulgence' (an amnesty), undertook not to seek vengeance for wrongs suffered by him, and invited all rulers to do likewise. Such trends of thought indicated well enough that all was by no means lost in that age of darkness. On the one hand there was perpetual war, shedding of blood on the slightest pretext or none, and the horrors of invasion and famine. On the other there were generous attempts to secure a more happy state of affairs. Hope remained of better things to come.

A second step towards the realization of this ideal was the *Truce of God*, the *treuga Dei*, which had a different end in view. The 'Peace of God' was intended only to protect the helpless from the sufferings of war; the Truce forbade war itself within certain periods of time. It was first suggested in 990 by Pope *John XV* (988–96), during the conflict between the Duke of Normandy and the King of England, but

*T

without success.   In 1017, at Elne, the episcopal city near Perpignan, a synod ruled that all military operations should cease 'from the ninth hour of Saturday until the first hour of Monday.'   Twenty-four years later, when the great famine of 1041 had terrified the hearts of men, the Council of Nice went further and ordained an absolute truce from Wednesday evening to Monday morning.   The good bishops who made this wise decision explained why those four days should be days of peace: Thursday because of our Lord's Ascension, Friday because of His Passion, Saturday because of His burial, and Sunday because of His Resurrection.   With a little care it might have been possible to celebrate every day of the week in this manner!   Their example was followed.   In some dioceses the Truce was extended to two great parts of the liturgical cycle, Advent and Lent; elsewhere it ran from the Rogations to the octave of Pentecost.   Certain feasts of our Lady and the vigils of ember days were also to be observed in peace.   In 1054 the Council of Narbonne would codify all these regulations. While the Truce of God spread in northern France, then to Liège, Rhenish Germany, England, Italy, and Spain, the Papacy took up this initiative by associating it with a new purpose.

In practice what were the results of this fine teaching?   Not many, to judge by appearances.   The threat of excommunication did not suffice to prevent brutal excesses.   The eleventh century still wallowed in blood and violence.   The chronicler Lambert of Waterloo, for example, states that his father's ten brothers were killed on one day in a private war against a neighbouring lord!   Nor was this case unique. To strive for peace and brotherhood had never been an easy task.   It sometimes happened that such attempts had consequences exactly opposite to those intended.   For example, Aimo, Archbishop of Bourges, had, in 1038, instituted a 'militia of peace,' composed of volunteers who would punish those lords who violated the Truce of God and who in fact, so it seems, did chastise quite a number of them; but after some time this pious militia began to imitate those whom it pretended to attack, and committed innumerable depradations for which, according to the *Miracles of St Benedict*, God punished it by causing their utter defeat at the hands of a better armed force.   But, however slight the results may now appear, the creation of these pacific institutions was important: what progress may not such good intentions have effected in the human soul?

The most clear-sighted rulers of the Church began to understand the virtual impossibility of exterminating feudal violence and that they would do better by directing it towards some other object.   In the Council of Narbonne (1054) it was stated that 'a Christian who kills another Christian sheds the blood of Christ.'   Another Christian . . . but what about an unbeliever?   The conclusion was obvious.   Had not John VIII already suggested that Christendom should combine against the infidel? And so, when adopting the Peace and Truce of God, the Papacy joined thereto a new intention: she would turn the feudal bandit into a crusader. The famous discourse of Urban II at Clermont, calling for the crusade, is a formal indication of this fact.

There is another point of view from which we can observe the Church's influence upon morals. She offered men of humble conditions a means of rising to the top. Adalbero, Archbishop of Rheims, says in his famous *Satirical Poem*: 'The divine law recognizes no distinction in nature among ministers of the Church. She grants them all an equal status, however unequal they may be by rank and birth; in her eyes the son of an artisan is not inferior to the heir of a monarch.' Nor was this assertion merely theoretical: on episcopal and abbatial thrones, even on the very throne of Peter, we find both princes and men of the common people. St Peter Damian, as a boy, had herded swine, and in his youth Gerbert, the great Pope Sylvester II, had been a shepherd. The Church thus helped, in feudal society, to preserve for those who could not attain to nobility by force of arms the indispensable opportunity of personal success; and this made possible a constant renewal of the upper ranks.

The same conception of Christian equality before God induced her also to fight for that most oppressed of all classes, the *serfs*. True, serfdom was not slavery as known to the ancient world; beginning in the fifth century, its evolution was now complete. The slave was treated as a chattel; the serf was a man possessing family, hearth, and property. He was 'tied to the land,' of which, however, he could not be deprived. But certain limitations restricting his freedom appeared more grievous, notably the law which forbade him to marry a woman belonging to a different lord, i.e. outside his own master's fief. The Church fought vigorously against this rule which affected family freedom; numerous councils and synods concerned themselves therewith, and during the tenth century a custom arose of allowing a serf to marry outside the fief on his paying a fine for having, by marriage in another fief, 'lessened' his master's estate. The Church went much further in this matter of equality. She demanded for serfs the same liberty as that enjoyed by other peasants. Already in the ninth century, as we have seen, some religious leaders had urged lay proprietors to free their serfs; during the tenth century serfdom decreased, and the movement for their liberation, which was to take final effect in the twelfth, became increasingly popular.[1] Preaching by

---

[1] The Church's effort to liberate the serfs was probably assisted by certain technical discoveries made in the tenth century. Commandant Lefébvre des Noëttes, in his work *L'Attelage, le cheval de selle à travers les âges* (Paris, 1931), has shown that it was about

example, a number of monasteries freed their serfs *en masse* about the year 1000, notably the great Norman abbeys of Saint-Wandrille and Jumièges.    A profound social transformation was on the way.


## CLUNY AND THE MONASTIC REFORM

In many ways then, in the so-called night of the tenth century, the Church proved herself faithful to the task she had undertaken at the time of the Invasions.   Such an effort would scarcely have been possible if she had allowed herself to become hopelessly entangled by worldly influences, if all that was best in the Christian soul had not withstood the process of decline which revealed itself in so many deplorable symptoms.   The same problem arose as we have seen [1] arise in the sixth and seventh centuries.   Just as the Church had had to protect herself against contamination by the Barbarian world she sought to evangelize, so she had now to withstand the pressure of feudal anarchy.   In the sixth century the instrument of resistance had been the *Council*, an assembly of bishops rising above passion and self-interest to make straight the way of the Lord.   In the tenth century this instrument was the *monastery*, where there survived all that was spiritually most fertile and most vigorous.   It was the mysticism of the monks that would deliver the Church from the dangers to which she was exposed and at the same time preserve two essential factors of civilization: the idea of the universal, which was gradually fading from the political framework with its innumerable subdivisions, and the idea of the human person, which the social organization tended to efface.

For this purpose, however, monasticism had to cast its own slough. It bore too many signs of grave deterioration.   Many communities

---

this time that the old method of horse traction, by means of a soft collar tied round the animal's neck, was replaced by the present method of a hard collar resting on the shoulder bones.   By the first method no more than 1,000 lb. could be drawn, whereas the second raised this figure to 5,000 lb.   The modern form of traction appears first in a tenth-century Latin manuscript (8085) preserved in the Bibliothèque Nationale at Paris, and again in a slightly later manuscript of Saint-Gall.   Other inventions belong to the same period: the general use of the horse-shoe and the discovery of the stern-post rudder which took the place of steering oars.   All these inventions helped to put man in possession of far more energy than hitherto, and the use of human strength in the form of serfs became less necessary.   One should not exaggerate the argument of historical determinism, that the liberation of the serfs was the *consequence* of technical inventions, but it is certain that they played a part therein.   We have here an example of spiritual effort on the Church's part to render the organization of society more humane, combining with new opportunities offered by technical progress.   It is remarkable that the first great liberations of serfs took place on monastic lands; the Church was in the vanguard of progress.   (See Daniel-Rops, *Par delà notre nuit*, 1943.)

[1] See Chapter V, section: 'The Church's Principle of Reform.'

no longer embodied the ideal of sanctity, prey as they were to most pernicious secular influences, exposed to the violence of the warrior caste, and more or less infected by the two contemporary evils of nicolaïsm and simony.   The restoration of discipline under St Benedict of Aniane had not survived the disintegration of the Carolingian Empire.   Once again there was manifest the great law which governs the Christian conscience as regards both institutions and individuals: spiritual progress is never set on foot once and for all; there must needs be a constant struggle with the powers of darkness, against the weakness of the human heart so prone to compromise; reform is a continual necessity, and the Church understood as much in the tenth century as she had done in the days of St Columbanus and St Boniface.

Monastic reform started in Lotharingia, where in 914 one *Gerard*, a young noble hungry for God, built on his lands at Brogne, near Namur, an abbey subject to the Rule of St Benedict.   His undertaking, supported by the counts of Lorraine and Flanders, had repercussions throughout Belgium, and even in Normandy where one of his disciples reformed Saint-Wandrille, Mont-Saint-Michel, and Saint-Ouen at Rouen.   A rival of Gerard now appeared in the person of John of Gorze, who, after visiting Monte Cassino, resolved upon a literal interpretation of the Holy Rule; many monasteries followed suit and reformed themselves in the dioceses of Metz, Toul, Liége, and Trèves. The initial impulse had been given.   A desire for monastic life in all its perfection uplifted the souls of men, who lived for, strove for, and devoted themselves to this ideal.   Indeed they were ready even to lay down their lives for it.   Erluin, abbot of Gembloux, for example, was one night carried off from his monastery by some anti-reformist monks who beat him, put out his eyes, and cut off half his tongue! Supported by many bishops, notably by Bruno of Cologne, brother of Otto I, the movement increased throughout the frontier territory between France and Germany.   About A.D. 1000 a new urge was given by Richard, abbot of Saint-Vanne, at Verdun; then by his disciple Poppo, abbot of Stavelot.   Magnificent efforts though these were in themselves, and evidence of outstanding holiness, in order to be truly effective they still needed bringing together, to become a single sheaf. This concentration and organization of the will to reform was the work of *Cluny*.

The traveller who to-day turns aside a little from the national highway between Paris and Lyons to visit the small Burgundian market town which bears this name cannot but feel grieved if he is moved by certain loyalties.   True there are still reminders of a splendid past: the palace of Pope Gelasius, the church of Saint-Marcel, Notre-Dame, the abbatial residence, and many Romanesque houses of antique charm.   But the substance is lacking: gone is the enormous church which for centuries soared to heaven with its seven towers, the glory of Cluny.   The most appalling act of vandalism ever perpetrated in France resulted in the demolition, between 1798 and 1812, of that masterpiece of Romanesque art.   The monastery is no more; of its gardens and buildings, which covered a rectangle of 450 by 350 sq. yds., only a few subsidiary edifices remain.   Of the seven towers, only one now stands (that of the northern arm of the great transept and called the Tower of Holy Water), standing side by side with the square clock-tower, but so noble and so impressive that it alone almost suffices to recall the ancient grandeur.

That grandeur was the fruit of so much labour, of so much good fortune, and of such enduring fidelity that we are undoubtedly entitled to see in the history of Cluny a divine purpose.   When in 910 William the Pious, Duke of Aquitaine, gave land belonging to his fief of Mâcon to St Berno, abbot of Baume, who was to settle there with twelve companions, he cannot have thought he was doing more than many other feudal lords of his time, who made similar foundations for the love of God and the salvation of their souls.   But the new house was governed almost continually for two centuries by a succession of saintly abbots, each of whom enjoyed a long reign.   They were *St Odilo* (926–42), *St Maieul* (954–94), and *St Hugh* (1049–1109), all of them, in different ways but in the same spirit, devoted to the great scheme of monastic reform.   In other words they were monks entirely faithful to their vows.

Profiting by circumstances—not feeling itself tied to the wavering fortunes of a political power, but at the same time drawing upon the enormous number of vocations prompted by the insecurity of the times—Cluny would lead the way towards monastic reform, so much so that she would eventually absorb every independent effort.   Berno, the founder, had long since recalled his brethren to the principles of monasticism: prayer, poverty, and silence.   Odo, a young Aquitanian noble eager for reform, definitely imposed the laws of poverty, chastity, and obedience as laid down by St Benedict, and Cluny began to live accordingly.   This great monk—the perfect model of an abbot according to the Holy Rule, as described by St Benedict's disciple St Gregory the Great—at once marvellously good and supernaturally firm, went back to the true tradition by centring the whole monastic life upon the *opus Dei*, the glory of God.   Maïeul had only to follow in his footsteps, which he did perhaps with more charm, tempering Odo's austerity with a gentleness to which his own commanding appearance and eloquence made irresistible.   And then, for fifty-five years, the mighty ship was guided by Odilo, another young noble, a vigorous and excitable little man, hard on himself but gentle towards others. 'If I am to be blamed,' he used to say, 'I would rather it be on account of kindness than of severity.'

Life at Cluny was the full Benedictine life, the Rule observed to the letter, but also in its sensible and humane simplicity. The use of time was most carefully regulated; the hours of prayer and work were strictly laid down, and manual labour tended to lose its importance in favour of the liturgical office. The diet consisted of vegetables, a dish made with flour, a little cheese, and fish; meat was excluded altogether, but the monks drank wine each day. Silence was absolute; the brethren learned to communicate with one another by signs. The rule of chastity was observed with unprecedented rigour. One detail in particular showed the Benedictines of Cluny to be in advance of their time: the extraordinary cleanliness required of all who joined them, for which purpose St Odo had installed wash-basins and towels. Lastly, charity also was held in veneration: every day hundreds of poor folk and travellers were fed by the community, and eighteen old men were constantly supported by the monks who were obliged to wash their feet each day.

There was thus established a regular Christian militia of an entirely new kind. Recruited mainly from the young sons of the neighbouring peasantry who attended the abbey school, where they were trained to humility and obedience and taught to despise the world, these monks of the high Cluniac tradition have been likened to 'an immense army of soldiers of the Lord, with its several ranks and possessing in the abbot of Cluny a unique and all-powerful commander,' an army in which fellow-feeling, under the influence of faith, attained an extraordinary degree of intensity. Individually the Cluniac monk was nothing, but collectively he was conscious of being the herald of God. 'Cluny,' says E. Pognon in his *L'An mille*, 'is the new force, pure and relentless, that was to smash the decaying framework of Christian society and, despite simoniacal and immoral bishops, to introduce everywhere the reign of virtue and the fear of God.'

Very soon the prestige of Cluny became enormous. Raoul Glaber pays it homage: 'In this monastery, which has no equal in the Roman world for the salvation of souls,' he tells us, 'mass is celebrated continuously from first light to the midday meal, thanks to the great number of monks,' and there were so many communions that every day hundreds of souls were rescued from the Evil One. The example was infectious. The Cluniacs were very often invited by the monks themselves to reform a monastery; in other cases the lay proprietors of abbeys, won over to the idea of reform, sent for the famous Burgundian envoys. Without actually absorbing the whole monastic, or even the whole Benedictine, world, Cluny gradually included in its orbit a growing number of religious houses. The most accurate

figures are those for the year 1100 or thereabouts, and they are sympto-
matic of the movement as it existed at an earlier date.    Fourteen
hundred and fifty houses, inhabited by ten thousand monks, were then
dependent upon Cluny; 15 of these were in France, 109 in Germany,
23 in Spain, 52 in Italy, and 43 in the British Isles.    About the year
1100, also, Rome was asking whether it would not be a good thing to
unite the whole monastic institutions under the banner of Cluny.

This achievement, largely the work of the saintly abbots of the first
monastery, enabled the Cluniacs to form a *centralized organization* of
an absolutely new type.    Whereas reform had been hitherto a sporadic
affair subject to personal influences, they applied themselves to

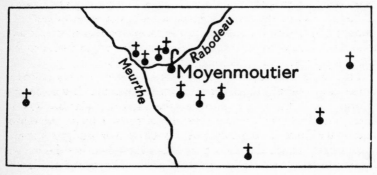

A monastic 'nebula'

strengthening their links.    The principle of this organization was
simple.    The whole Cluniac congregation was treated as if it were a
single monastery; the abbot of Cluny was abbot of all.    In practice
this theory was modified in detail by a certain variety of statutes.
Priors were appointed by the abbot; and new foundations were called
priories, even though the community was very large.    There was a
tendency to reduce newly annexed abbeys, the abbot was sometimes
appointed by Cluny and sometimes elected by the monks under the
presidency of the Abbot-General.    Further, as the Cluniac movement
increased, 'daughter' abbeys established other priories, whose superiors
they themselves appointed.    Each good abbey was the centre of a
veritable monastic 'nebula'; Charité-sur-Loire, for instance, had no
fewer than fifty-five dependent priories.    The fact, however, remains
that the theory was absolute: all abbots and all priors were obliged to
come and take an oath at Cluny, and, at any rate until the twelfth
century, it was at Cluny that every monk of every house had to take
his vows.    The Abbot-General controlled and supervised the entire
organization, assisted by the Grand Prior, the Claustral Prior, the

Chamberlain, and the Cellarer, and advised by the daily conventual chapter which foreshadowed what was to be, in the twelfth and especially in the thirteenth century, the Chapter-General. The Cluniac organization was indeed a state within the Church.

It is not surprising that the tremendous expansion of Cluny [1] and the emergence of its strength provoked resistance. Assuredly Cluny found powerful support both in the Church and in the world.

Such popes as Benedict VII, observing the dangers that threatened Christendom, encouraged the reformers, and we find John XI writing to congratulate St Odo upon his achievement 'at a time when most abbeys are unfaithful to their rule.' The Emperor Henry II and King Robert the Pious of France were also great friends of the Cluniacs. Success engendering success, the authorities almost everywhere began to respect these monks who enjoyed a high reputation of holiness. Besides, was God not with them, as was proved by the report of many miracles—multiplication of fishes, crossing of rivers on foot, and the changing of water into wine, attributed to St Odilo?

This view, however, was not universal. Cluny had her enemies. Some abbeys, proud of their ancient titles, declared that they needed no reform. At Fleury, for example, the modern Saint-Benoît-sur-Loire, the monks withstood a three-day siege by Cluniac inspectors sent by the Duke of Burgundy. At Lobbes in Normandy an attempt was made to secure the election of a Cluniac abbot, but the monks insisted upon voting for one of themselves and appealed to Rome. Incidents of this sort were not uncommon. In some cases—e.g. at the

---

[1] The radiance of Cluny and of the Cluniac monasteries is apparent also in the economic field; the influence of reformed communities made itself felt in the same way as that of older houses, but was especially beneficial at a time when Norman and Saracen depredations, together with civil wars, had increased the suffering of Europe. The foundations of numerous monasteries gave rise to peasant colonies, and to small market towns which would develop quickly. On the intellectual plane, Cluny in the tenth century, and even at the beginning of the eleventh, was not particularly remarkable; among so many monks there were (excepting Odo) very few writers. But at Saint-Bénigne at Dijon, at Fleury, at Bec in Normandy, and elsewhere more literary work was done; Raoul Glaber, d'Albo, Lanfranc, and somewhat later Anselm, were Cluniac monks. The Cluniac reform favoured literary production by bringing back order to the monasteries. Finally, in the artistic sphere, it is usual to speak of the link between Romanesque art and the great Burgundian abbey; yet here again we must pay attention to dates. Undoubtedly the very principles of Cluny, by giving pride of place to the divine office, would eventually lend a powerful impulse to architecture: nothing was too beautiful for God. But it was not the monks of Cluny themselves who directed this impulse, not at any rate before 1050. At Cluny, in 981, St Maieul had replaced the small primitive church with a more imposing structure, which St Odilo transformed. It was already Romanesque, with its barrel vaulting, its central tower, its two western towers, its wide and lofty porch; the choir was square, a plan imitated at Romainmoûtier, Payerne, and Hirschau. But it was not until later that the Cluniac style of Romanesque emerged, a style to which we owe so many masterpieces. The enormous church at Cluny was built between 1088 and 1130. At that period was the spirit of Cluny, the spirit of her founders, still alive? While the monastic architects were building their mighty works, the spiritual movement which had produced them was already in decline; the Cistercian reform was on its way.

abbey of Saint-Gilles, which was immediately subject to the Holy See
—nothing less than the personal intervention of the Pope was needed
to restore calm.

Relations with the bishop were often more tense.   The first concern of the Cluniac abbeys was of course to obtain 'exemption.'
Shortly before the year 1000 Gregory V had laid down that 'no bishop
or priest should dare to enter the venerable monastery of Cluny for the
ordination of priests or deacons, for the consecration of a church, or
for the celebration of mass, unless invited by the abbot,' and he specified that the abbot, elected by the unanimous consent of the religious,
should be blessed by a prelate chosen by himself.   In 1016 Benedict
VIII declared that Cluny 'is absolutely free from the authority of kings,
bishops, and counts, being subject only to God, St Peter, and the
Pope.'   It was only natural that some bishops should resent this kind
of thing, and there were frequent quarrels.   The abbots of Cluny
themselves waged epic struggles against the counts of Mâcon, which
even involved physical violence and excommunication.   At Clermont
the canons of the cathedral went out in bands to attack the Cluniac
priory of Saint-Loup.   At Orléans the bishops did battle with Fleury,
which was also a reformed house.   One of them seized a vineyard
belonging to the abbey, but the religious won it back by the use of a
most curious instrument of warfare in the shape of two caskets full of
sacred relics, before which the episcopal troops fell back in disorder!
The question of spiritual and canonical independence was not un-
mixed with motives of self-interest, for 'exempt' monks were not
obliged to pay tithes to the bishops.   At Limoges, for example, the
Cluniac monks of Saint-Martial claimed that, since their patron was
one of the seventy-two disciples of Christ, they need pay nothing;
whereupon the bishop, having recourse to arguments which modern
criticism would not disavow, pointed out that this high-sounding title
had been usurped and that therefore the monks should pay like everyone else!

But in spite of resistance the movement was under way.   It would
become enormously important, because for the first time—and this
was the ingenious idea of the abbots of Cluny—an attack was made
upon the real danger threatening the Church, her contamination by the
feudal system.   Certain lords, and even certain kings, might order the
reform of a religious house, as Philip I of France did with the nuns of
Faremoutiers; but however well intentioned they may have been,
they were interfering in the spiritual domain and thereby promoting
the decadence of the Church.   Besides, they sometimes interfered in
the opposite way, as did Philip I by appointing unworthy abbots to the
monasteries of Saint-Médard and Saint-Denis.   True reform had to
come from the Church herself, through a break between her and feudal

society.    The monks of Cluny understood this fact, and what they did was nothing short of revolutionary.[1]

## The Spirit of Reform Enters the Church

The secular clergy were subject to the same peril as were the monks. The threat of moral decadence was equally serious; for nicolaïsm and simony were just as rife, if not more so.    Wallowing in landed wealth, integrated into the framework of feudalism, the whole Church seemed in danger of being absorbed by the regime.    Reform of the bishoprics and parishes was no less indispensable than that of the religious houses.

To this idea of a general reform the Church gradually turned her attention.    What part would Cluny play in this effort?    The question has been much debated.    From a practical and immediate point of view, reform—that which would be known at the end of the eleventh century as the Gregorian reform—was the work not of the monks but of the Papacy.    The very spirit of Cluny tended to withhold the order from activity in the world, but this fact does not detract from the considerable influence of the Benedictines.    To begin with they preached by their example, and by denouncing the vices of the age through such powerful voices as St Odo and Abbo of Fleury, they set before the eyes of the world a vision of pure Christianity.    The Cluniac monasteries were true oases where the soul could recollect herself and take on a new life; around them the moral climate changed. They were also nurseries from which, before long, the Church began to derive leaders according to the mind of Christ, bishops, and even popes.    As soon as the heads of the secular clergy were inspired with the Cluniac spirit the battle for reform would be as good as won. The manifest conclusion from the experience of Cluny was that she could never have become what she did except by effecting a revolution against the age-long established order, by escaping from lay investiture, which was the cause of simony.    The free election of abbots had been her salvation.    *Mutatis mutandis*, the free election of bishops, the liberation of the secular clergy from lay interference, was likewise the salvation of the Church.    The action of Cluny, then, was not external, combative, and violent, but intensive, silent, and profound.    To underestimate its importance would be quite unjust.

It was fortunate that so many souls were already disposed to hear

[1] During the eleventh century there emerged a curious institution which assured close relationship between the various monasteries.    This was the 'Roll of the Dead,' discovered by the learned palaeographer Leopold Delisle about 1860. . . .    Imagine a long roll (as much as 9 yards in some cases) which was carried by an official known as the 'roll-bearer' from house to house, and on which were written notices of death and other notable events.    The coming and going of these priceless documents foreshadowed the postal service.    (See E. Vaille, *Histoire générale des postes françaises*, Paris, 1947, vol. i, p. 210.)

Cluny's appeal.   How many were enlightened by God's flame that burned in the hearts of Odo, Maieul, and Odilo!

In Italy *St Romuald*, a young prince of Ravenna, entered a monastery to expiate a murder committed by his father, and was thrust by the love of Christ into a terrible and sublime experience.   To a society whose defects he knew so well, he decided to oppose the example of Christian heroism, the heroism of early times.   What matter if he passed the bounds of moderation?   He cared little for the counsels of prudence enjoined by the sage of Monte Cassino.   His ideal was the ideal of St Anthony and the Fathers of the desert, those ascetics whose exploits had passed into legend.   He paid for his example, delighting in the most extraordinary mortifications.   His hair shirt bristled with steel; his lenten diet consisted of dough and wild herbs; and when he emerged after a retreat, brown as a berry and with long matted hair, one might have wondered whether one was face to face with a madman or a saint.   He was a fool of God.   He would go one better than St Benedict by reviving the eremitical life.   His disciples would live in cells, not, however, too far from a monastery in which they would pass their novitiate and where they would from time to time seek spiritual recreation.   It was reminiscent of the oriental 'Laura'; indeed the Greek St Nilus was then living in Italy.   Thus in 982, in the Tuscan Apennines, was born the conventual hermitage of *Camaldoli*, mother of the *Camaldolese* congregation.

The same protest against contemporary decadence was made some years later, though in a different fashion, by *St John Gualbert*.   At *Vallombrosa*, a beautiful site in the Apennines, amid holm-oaks and ferns, his community lived a life no less austere than that of the neighbouring Camaldolese, but they lived it in community.   Absolute enclosure, which the religious formally undertook never to leave, refusal of all contact with the outside world, and rejection of all gifts were the careful precautions taken to guarantee poverty, discipline, and chastity.   What an example to simoniacal prelates and fornicating priests were these Camaldolese and Vallombrosians!   Christians began to recognize the contrast.   The movement would become irresistible if only a great voice would openly proclaim what so many thought in secret.

That voice arose from the people as the *pataria*.   The *pataria*?   A term of contempt, used in Italy to designate old-clothes dealers and pedlars, a class known to-day in some provinces of France as *pattiers* and who give their name to the *Via de' pattari* at Milan.   It was by this name that the nobles described shopkeepers, traders, and the urban bourgeoisie whom they saw mount the ladder of wealth but whom they heartily despised.   Now since the nobility, closely linked by ties of family and of interest to the higher clergy, was likewise hostile to reform, the *pataria* made that cause its own.  It acclaimed St Ariald, the simple parish priest of a village near Milan, who flayed the bishops as too wealthy and too fond of hunting, married prelates, and those who bought and sold their functions.  It marched behind St Landulf, a nobleman made hostile to his own class through love of Christ, who foreshadowed Savonarola, and who did not hesitate to lead punitive expeditions against simoniacal priests or lewd canons.  This popular movement became so violent that Rome herself was forced to take notice and answer its imperious demands.  Nor was Italy the only scene of its activity; there was a *pataria* in France also, notably at Rouen, where the cathedral witnessed some incredible rioting.  Such reactions, though regrettable, were significant; the Christian conscience demanded that the Church should be worthy of Christ.

There now appeared a man to give some definite aim to a movement that had previously been confused.  This was *St Peter Damian* (1007–1072).  Born of humble parentage at Ravenna and brought up the hard way by one of his brothers, and still a youth when he entered the hermitage founded by St Romuald at Fonte Avellana, Peter was a giant of asceticism, a record-breaker in the field of penance, who reminds one of the heroes of the *Lausiac History*.  He thought nothing of fasting five days out of seven!  The monk should find satisfaction in a daily taste of the discipline—a daily scourging till the red blood ran, for as long as it took to recite forty psalms, and even sixty in Lent!  He wrote a book in praise of this holy torture; and as he preached by example in the communities now under his direction, he had many followers.  One of them, Dominic, went so far as to chant twelve psalms every night, scourging himself non-stop, a practice which so tanned his skin that he was nicknamed 'the man in the cuirass.'  Such behaviour of course was not above criticism, but one can imagine the feelings of such a man when he considered the iniquities of certain prelates.  Nicolaïsm, the sin of priestly fornicators, was denounced by St Peter Damian with a frankness compared with which the tirades of Tertullian and Hilary of Arles are mere child's play.  No decent person could undertake a translation of Peter's *Liber Gomorrhianus*.  Wives of the clergy were dragged through the mud by this terrible preacher: 'prostitutes, impious tigresses, creatures of the charnel-house . . .'  Such expressions were among the most restrained to issue from his saintly mouth.  He was equally severe on simony, particular cases of which he denounced without mincing names or words.  One can guess with what avidity sermons of this kind were heard by the *patari*, the protagonists of reform, as they listened to the condemnation of their worst enemies.  The tireless herald of God continually spread his influence through his letters and treatises.  Monastic communities arose on the pattern of Fonte Avellana, and became nurseries of so many ascetics that they attracted the attention of the Papacy. At first the popes used Peter Damian as a legate to arbitrate upon several matters connected with reform. In 1057 Stephen IX went still further, investing him almost by force and quite unexpectedly with the ring and pastoral staff. As Cardinal Bishop of Ostia, St Peter Damian was to be among the authors of the reform accomplished by Gregory VII.

Thus in the middle of the tenth century reform seemed to be well under way. But it met with a good deal of fierce resistance. Married and simoniacal priests and pampered prelates hit back with all their might. At Rouen the chapter instigated a riot in the cathedral and expelled the bishop because he favoured reform. At Milan, on the contrary, Archbishop Guido, an enemy of the cause, was attacked by the mob and his palace sacked. At Florence there were incessant and fanatical upheavals. The most deplorable episode in this struggle, reminiscent of Italy under the Guelphs and Ghibellines, was the martyrdom of St Ariald. Made prisoner by a niece of Archbishop Guido and two married clerics, he was tortured with horrible refinement on the shores of Lago di Maggiore, where he was found without nose, ears, lips, right hand, or tongue, and of course with his eyes gouged out. . . . In those days one paid for the privilege of bearing witness to the truth of Christ.

But could all this agitation, however symbolic of the new spirit, attain its end? St Peter Damian dreamed of a reform brought about by the bishops and supported by the Empire. But that was a contradiction in terms. Would the bishops sincerely, readily, and unanimously agree to measures that deprived them of many advantages? A reforming bishop might be succeeded by an unworthy one, and the whole matter would be back where it started. Again, would the civil powers, whether kingly or imperial, encourage a policy that was equivalent to their own suicide? There had to be an absolute rupture between the Church and the feudal world: men would have to learn the stern lesson of Cluny. Chief of those who deserve credit for perceiving this truth was *Cardinal Humbert*. Before him there had been bishops who saw as much, notably Rathier of Liége in the middle of the tenth century, who had learnt from his unhappy quarrels with the civil power, during two periods as Bishop of Verona, to mistrust the secular authority. One hundred years later the idea had made progress. In an assembly held at Aix-la-Chapelle in 1044, Wazo, another Bishop of Liége, formally declared that the emperor had no right to a voice in the appointment or deposition of bishops. Simultaneously, at the abbey of Moyenmoutier in Lorraine, the monk Humbert was pondering these questions and writing an enormous treatise, in three volumes, *Against Simoniacs*, which was to appear in

1057. While on a chance visit to Italy, Humbert was appointed Bishop of Silva Candida, then cardinal, by Pope Leo IX; he was destined to play a leading part in the history of ecclesiastical reform, a part no less prominent, though more fortunate, than that which he would play in the miserable affair of the Greek schism.[1]   St Peter Damian, a mystical ascetic, had devoted himself mainly to preaching moral reform, a struggle against the most serious errors of the clergy. Cardinal Humbert, a realistic Frenchman, saw clearly that the axe must be laid to the root.   He said, for example, in his rather droll way: 'We, the hounds of God, so far from barking freely and biting the robbers, go about yapping and wagging our tails, blind flatterers that we are, and thus encourage every act of robbery.'   One conclusion was inescapable: lay investiture must be suppressed, but it required no less a person than Gregory VII to say so openly and to take the necessary steps.

For indeed the whole of this reforming movement could never bear fruit unless taken in hand and directed by an authority superior to all secular authorities.   Only one such authority was conceivable: the Papacy.   So long as the throne of Peter was occupied by unworthy men the Papacy could not undertake this task, but at the beginning of the eleventh century the situation changed.   To begin with, the monk Gerbert became Pope Sylvester II and thereby united the spirit of reform with the tiara.   Then there was a succession of Cluniac popes: Clement II (1046), Damasus II (1048), Leo IX (1049), Victor II (1055); after them both Stephen IX and Nicholas II were also partisans of reform.   These pre-Gregorian popes who prefigured the glory yet to come deserve our respect for having discerned the way, amid surroundings even more obscure than that in which Gregory VII found himself.

In 1050 the Holy See was occupied by one of the most active and most remarkable of these pontiffs: *St Leo IX* (1049–54), a fiery Alsatian, a sound theologian, and a strong military leader, but at the same time a man of great holiness and humility.   Chaplain to Conrad II, then Bishop of Toul, and closely connected with the events that forced Gregory VI to leave Rome (1046), he was summoned to the papal throne by the unanimous voice of the German bishops.   He hesitated for a moment, but his friend Hildebrand (afterwards Pope Gregory VII) persuaded him, and they set out together for the Eternal City, dressed as pilgrims.   The election at Worms being ratified, Leo set to work with amazing energy.   What did he not do in a space of five years?   A Council summoned by him began the struggle against simony and clerical adultery.   Berengar, the heresiarch who denied the real presence, was condemned.   The Emperor

---

[1] See Chapter IX, section: 'Michael Cerularius and the Greek Schism.'

Henry III, King Edward the Confessor of England, and King Ferdinand of Castile were invited to promote the reform. The 'collection of seventy-four titles,' made on his instructions, brought together those elements of canon law that would be useful to the reformer. Meanwhile the indefatigable pontiff travelled throughout Europe, campaigned against the Normans, opposed the Byzantines, and suggested a plan, realized by Nicholas II ten years later, to have the Pope elected by the cardinals. . . . During the five years of Leo's pontificate Rome became once more the heart of the world. And who is this coming from so far off to kneel before the Pope? Why, none other than our old friend Macbeth!

Here is another fact of capital importance. Thanks to these pre-Gregorian popes, reform was carried out not *in spite of* Rome, as was to happen in the sixteenth century, but *through* her. From a century and a half of crisis there emerged the medieval Papacy, the pontificates of Gregory VII and Innocent III, with all their towering stature and prestige.

## The Church and the New Forces

It was now certain that the Church would not, as had once seemed likely, succumb to the fatal powers of anarchy, but would resume the part of a great governing principle which we have so often seen her play. But at the same time, about the year 1000, another controlling force began to emerge from the first feudal age: hereditary and national monarchy. The relations between the Church and this new political power afford a fresh example of that sense of historical exigency which she has revealed in so many different circumstances, a fresh example of that inspired intuition which enables her to see into the future.

There were many grounds for an understanding between the monarchy and the Church. First they had the same enemies in the feudal lords. The Church had learned only too well that they prospered as she herself declined. The kings, who represented a unifying and civilizing influence, had nothing so much to fear as the anarchical consequences of disintegration (brought about by the feudal system), which were of advantage to the barons. In another field also the Church had cause to protect and uphold royalty; for by virtue of the coronation rites, which were now in general use, kings possessed a quasi-sacerdotal character. They formed, in one sense, part of the religious hierarchy such as it was then conceived to be. In every country, therefore, though in different ways according to circumstance, we find the Church supporting the emergence of royalty, favouring one dynasty rather than another, endeavouring also to make use of this new force for the purpose of reforming the Christian world. There we have the final aspect under which the dawn of a new world was made manifest.

In France the principal event, one that gave promise of the future, took place on *3rd July 987*. This was the coronation at Rheims by Archbishop Adalbero of *Hugh, surnamed Capet*. As in 751, when the future Carolingian ousted the last slothful Merovingian, so now the Church played a decisive part in the replacement of one dynasty by another. However, there had been nothing sluggish about the last of the Carolingians, those energetic and brave 'kings of Laon': Charles the Simple, better called the Loyal; Louis IV Outremer, whose youthful valour would one day be immortalized in the *chansons de geste*; Lothaire; and Louis V. But these descendants of Charlemagne, caught between the marches of Lorraine, which they sought to retake from the Germans, and the country of western France, had not been able to control the nobility, nor to prove themselves capable of maintaining order and peace under stress of invasion. There was one family to supplant them. Firmly established on the Loire and the Seine, definitely French, and ardent in their defence of the land, were the descendants of Duke Robert the Strong who, in 886, had lost his life at the battle of Brissarthe, resisting the Normans, and whose son, Eudes, defended Paris at the time of the great siege in 885. A conflict was inevitable between these two families, one of which was in the ascendant while the other declined. It broke out several times, the nobility always playing its trump card by supporting the family which appeared for the moment to be the weaker. It was thus that the crown was long at stake between the descendants of Robert and the Carolingians. Election by the nobles prevailed four times (888, 922, 925, and 987) in favour of Eudes, Robert, Raoul of Burgundy, and Hugh Capet; the dynastic principle was also four times observed (898, 936, 954, and 986) to the advantage of Charles the Simple, Louis IV Outremer, Lothaire, and Louis V. This complex struggle was finally decided by the Church.

At the beginning of the century she was attached to the Carolingians. Again, in 936, she recognized Louis IV against Hugh the Great, Duke of France (although the latter was by far the most outstanding figure in the land), whom she even excommunicated for treason against the king. Fifty years later the situation had altered. Why? Because the Church now saw that only a family with its roots deep in the soil of France could control this nobility, and also because, being faithful to the idea of Christian universality, she mistrusted the 'Austrasian' policy of the last Carolingians, which could only provoke conflict with the reconstituted Roman and Germanic Empire, another force indispensable to European and Christian order. The futile war which, in 978, had been carried by the French to the gates of Aix-la-Chapelle, and then by the Germans to the hill of Montmartre, had served as an example of this danger. The monk Gerbert, for instance, wrote: 'King Lothaire is only the nominal ruler of France—the real leader is Hugh.' Can we not hear in those emphatic words an echo of the celebrated answer made by Pope Zacharias to Pepin the Short? Likewise, when Louis V, last of the western Carolingians, accused Adalberon of high treason in having assisted both the German and the Robertian, the Church of France stood firm behind the archbishop, the friend and agent of Hugh Capet.

The advent of the third French dynasty, then, was undoubtedly in large part the work of the Church. She soon received from her ally a new proof of friendship. What was the use of raising a man to the throne if, after his death, the crown passed elsewhere through the process of election? In order that the step taken in 987 should make sense it had to be made lasting; only the Church could do that, and she did so. By anointing and crowning Hugh's son Robert king while his father was still alive, the Archbishop of Rheims re-established the rule of heredity in favour of the Capetian family, and the same practice was long followed throughout successive reigns.

Church and Throne, the twin poles of medieval France, had been fixed. From 987 onwards the three elements of the coronation rite were firmly established, with an unmistakably ecclesiastical character. These were the *royal oath*, wherein the prince swore to protect the Church and to administer justice; the *election*, proclaimed by the archbishop, ratified by the attendant prelates, and only then submitted to popular acclamation; and finally the *anointing*, performed with oil from the sacred ampulla, which was supposed to have been brought from heaven by an angel at the baptism of Clovis. One family was thus set by the Church above all others. It mattered little that from a material point of view it was not as yet very powerful; what really counted was its sacred character. Were not these kings, who would be recognized as thaumaturges and healers of scrofula, successors of the biblical kings? In a thoroughly Christian society the sacred unction carried enormous weight.

Does this mean to say that in fact relations between the house of Capet and the Church were always friendly? Theoretically, the Church had the upper hand. For example, when Robert the Pious married his mistress, Bertha, in defiance of canonical impediments which were then considered to invalidate the union, he was brought to heel by excommunication and the threat of an interdict. In practical matters, however, it was not quite so straightforward. The Papacy managed to prevent Hugh Capet from deposing Arnulf, Adalbero's successor at Rheims, but no power on earth could prevent him laying hands on all the principal abbeys in his dominions. Robert the Pious did exactly the same kind of thing and established bishops in certain dioceses contrary to the will both of the clergy and of the people. His son, Henry I, openly trafficked in ecclesiastical functions and goods, which caused him to be described by Cardinal Humbert as 'tyrant of God' and Antichrist. It was an ambiguous situation, in which the truly Christian tenets of the kings, many of whom supported the reform, often clashed with their material interests.

In England, too, the activity of the Church is clearly distinguishable. If we judge by appearances, that activity may seem surprising and even scandalous; for in England there was question not merely of one dynasty supplanting another, but of foreign conquest. Here again the Church had a presentiment of new forces at work and took steps to encourage them. The Saxon monarchy of Wessex, at the end of the ninth century, in the days of Alfred the Great, had most certainly been Christian, and in the tenth century the fusion of Church and State had become so complete that little or no distinction was recognized between ecclesiastical councils and lay assemblies. However, at the turn of the year 1000, the Church broke with the Saxons in favour of the Norsemen, in whose hands their future lay. The Norsemen had first been established in the British Isles in 878 by Alfred the Great, who made them a gift of certain lands, taking care at the same time, with the help of a powerful army, to keep them within 'the king's peace.' But the history of Alfred's descendants, throughout the tenth century, was one of decadence, such as affected the Continent. While the coasts were once more at the mercy of pirates, while morality declined, and while culture disintegrated, the process of feudalization went ahead with the same consequences as in France.

On 13th November 1002, the feast of St Brice, the Saxons, in an outburst of vain fury, turned upon and massacred the Norsemen, whose kinsmen from Denmark, led by their king, Sweyn, overran the whole of England. In 1017 Sweyn's son *Knut* was recognized as 'king of all the English' in an assembly dominated by the bishops. Here again the clergy played an important part, as is proved by their influence over the great king during his reign. By helping and serving Knut they fostered the re-establishment of order in England, and at the same time obtained from him the dispatch of missionaries to Scandinavia. Though recently converted, Knut was a firm Christian, founding numerous monasteries, supporting the first movements towards reform, and endeavouring to base his laws upon the Gospel. Before his death he had made a pilgrimage to Rome 'for the salvation of his soul and the welfare of his people'; and whilst in the Eternal City he proved himself faithful to the traditions of the English Church, which had always been closely attached to the Holy See, by placing his kingdom under direct obedience to the Pope. His successors continued the same policy, and the Saxon Edward the Confessor (1035–66) was a saint. England too received the essential characteristics of medieval Christian monarchy.

Much more was this true of Germany. In the ninth century, under its first elected kings, that country also had passed through a grave crisis, ravaged by Magyar incursions, harried on the north-east by the Slavs. The eastern Carolingians, like those of the west, had witnessed the decline of their power and the rapid advance of feudalism. But feudalism in Germany was different from the kind we have seen in France; it was not simply a result of anarchy, but a return to the old tribal framework, which reappeared in the shape of the grand duchies of Saxony, Franconia, Bavaria, and Swabia. The kings were no more than phantom kings. As for the imperial diadem, which had once adorned the brow of a German prince, it had passed to some crazy Italian heads and then vanished altogether; there was no emperor for thirty-seven years. Germany, however, was less troubled than other European countries by invasion; she had seldom been attacked by the Norsemen, never by the Saracens, and so enjoyed greater stability. There was opposition between the higher clergy, under the powerful archbishops of Mainz, Trier, and Cologne, and ambitious dukes. This opened a door to superior strength, and longing for the Empire remained so strong in the hearts of countless Germans that its restoration seemed always possible. To reconcile the Germanic decentralization of the great fiefs with Roman and imperial centralization was a design encouraged by the Church and accomplished by a new dynasty, that of the *Ottos*.

After the death of the last Carolingian, Louis IV the Infant (895–911), the nobles had elected the Duke of Franconia, Conrad I (912–18), because he was related to the imperial family and, above all, because they considered him none too powerful. Outwitted by the nobles, betrayed by his brother, attacked by the Hungarians, and faced with an Italian competitor in the person of Berengar of Friuli, this poor man advised the princes to give him as successor Duke Henry of Saxony. Thus in 919 was founded the Saxon dynasty which endured for more than a hundred years. *Henry I* (919–36), surnamed *the Fowler* because a subsequent legend told how he was preparing bird traps when he received news of his election, at once revealed himself as wonderfully energetic, assured the crown to his son, cut to pieces the Hungarians and Slavs, and, with the ready support of the Rhenish archbishops, obliged the dukes to acknowledge him. Clearly he was as yet no more than head of a confederation of states, 'king of the Saxons and Franks,' and not the king of Germany; but he had taken the first step towards that goal.

The decisive stage was reached by his son *Otto I the Great* (936–

973). This prince, aged twenty-four, handsome and brave, with heavy beard and broad shoulders, may have lacked the genius of Charlemagne, but he was the embodiment of true greatness. Extremely pious after the fashion of his age (which meant that piety never stood in the way of his sexual whims), he posed from the beginning of his reign as a friend of the clergy. At his coronation the Archbishop of Mainz foretold that he would be the 'slayer of wicked Christians'; helped by the priests, he made his kingdom the one truly organized state of that time. The dukes revolted; he broke them, reduced them to their original status as civil servants who might be dismissed at the sovereign's pleasure, and virtually supplanted the authority of the barons with that of the bishops, who became in fact temporal administrators. After exterminating the Hungarians on the Lech, he undertook that campaign against the Slavs which was intended to impose Christianity by force, and from that point of view, as we have seen, turned out to be something of a fiasco. The Church, however, could not but feel grateful to him. She thanked him by crowning his son, during his (the father's) lifetime, in order to establish the principle of heredity in his family. But that was not enough: one crown alone could satisfy so great a man—that of the Empire. Summoned to Italy in 951 by the charming but unfortunate Queen Adelaide, Otto delivered the fair lady, married her, and, by way of avenging her, brought the Italian nobility to reason. In answer to an urgent appeal from Pope John XII, he recrossed the Alps in 962, marched on Rome, and on 2nd February was crowned emperor with a solemnity not unworthy of Charlemagne. Thus was founded what would soon come to be known as the *Holy Roman and Germanic Empire*.

Outwardly, then, the Church rode a high tide of success. In fact, here as everywhere, things were not so simple. Otto the Great was indeed a friend of the clergy, but upon condition that he kept them well in hand. It seemed to him quite natural that he should appoint, translate, and if needs be dismiss bishops, and also that he should usurp the spiritual authority by giving them investiture. Charlemagne had never enslaved the episcopate to this extent. It was the first cause of conflict with the Holy See, which, however unworthy the reigning pope, objected to such interference. Again, by meddling in the affairs of Italy, Otto was treading on a hornets' nest. He claimed to revive the Carolingian act of 824 by placing papal administration under the control of imperial officials. This was another cause of conflict, which broke out eighteen months after the magnificent coronation, when the emperor captured the city, which was defended by the Pope. There followed a regular orgy of pontiffs: the Antipope Leo VIII, Pope Benedict V, who was quickly deposed, and Pope John XIII. The Roman families, even those normally at daggers drawn with one another, forgot their differences and combined to resist Otto. In the end peace was restored by terror. The *Ottonian Declaration*, considered as a law of the imperial State, decided that in future the Sovereign Pontiff might not be consecrated until he had sworn fealty to the emperor. The refounding of the Empire, then, as the Holy Roman and Germanic Empire seemed to have this twofold consequence: in Germany an episcopate of vassals reduced to the status of government officials; in Rome a Papacy in strict subjection to the secular power.

Actually, however, things worked out differently, and the Church took advantage of her circumstances to escape from this twofold and alarming restraint. The enormous and glorious achievement of Otto the Great was not sufficiently well shored up, and his successors were not equal to its weight. In Germany the bishops enjoyed both power and wealth, which had made them indispensable in all political, diplomatic, and even military business; they seized every opportunity to emancipate themselves, and the emperors, entangled in the affairs of Italy, could not but afford them many such opportunities. As for the Papacy, the emperors themselves endeavoured to reorganize it.

At least two of Otto's descendants were true mystics, who were deeply affected by religious influences and who served the Christian cause zealously by sanctioning reform. The first was *Otto III* (983–1002), a most attractive and complex character in whom was mingled the German blood of Otto I and that of his mother, Theophano, daughter of the Basileus Nicephorus Phocas. A deep and generous soul, who dreamed splendid dreams, Otto III thought of the Empire in a new light. No more of that rugged bastion, held together by force, which his father had created to dominate the West; no more even of Charlemagne's empire; but an ideal Empire after the pattern envisaged by Constantine, a universal empire in the shadow of the Cross, where pope and emperor would work, each in his own sphere, for the happiness and welfare of mankind. The idea was derived from St Augustine; it represented the fulfilment of those great plans elaborated by his disciple Orosius. A new outlook was in process of formation: Christendom was to be a fraternal community.[1] This attitude might be merely Utopian; but at all events the Papacy would not run the risk of subservience.

It was in fact no more than a dream, which was almost completely abandoned by *Henry II* (1002–24), grand-nephew of Otto the Great, who had inherited his realism. The astonishing thing is that Henry

[1] It must be emphasized how favourable this conception would have been to the constitution of the independent Christian states of Hungary and Poland. The liberal Otto III, in refusing to keep these neighbouring countries under the tutelage of the German clergy, was certainly a fine architect of Christian expansion. On the 'Augustinianism' of these ideas see footnote 1, p. 45.

II was a genuine saint, canonized by the Church in the twelfth century, together with his faithful wife and collaborator, Cunegund, but a saint with both feet on the ground.   Re-establishing order everywhere, smashing the Roman baronage and setting up Pope Benedict VIII, and controlling the German bishops as they had never been controlled since the death of Otto the Great, the emperor sincerely believed that Christ's glory and his own were identical.   The famous Ottonian Declaration was once again enforced, and it seemed that the old perils were returning.

But Henry II was a saint.   He was therefore a strong advocate of reform.   His one idea was to see the popes worthy of the papal throne. It was for this purpose that he and his successors used their rights, to such good effect that when a pope such as Benedict IX proved himself unworthy he was turned out, and even such unscrupulous emperors as Conrad II—another 'tyrant of God,' according to Cardinal Humbert —could not do otherwise.   The Cluniac popes, from 1050, were all creatures of the Germanic emperors, but they were none the less excellent popes, pre-Gregorian reformers.

Here then was a paradoxical situation: the Germanic emperors exercised strict control over the Papacy and the episcopate, which seemed to perpetuate the danger of laicization which threatened the Church; but through her influence upon them the Church won them over to the cause of reform, that is to say, in effect, to the cause of her own liberation.   At a moment when the imperial crown was weakened through falling, for instance, into the hands of a child, and when simultaneously Rome had a pope who was conscious of her greatness, the Holy See in the person of Gregory VII shook off the tutelage of her Germanic protectors.   The future then was brighter than it may have seemed; but it was already possible to foresee that most serious crisis of the Middle Ages, which is variously known as the Quarrel of Investitures and the Struggle of the Priesthood with the Empire.

## After Six Centuries of Effort

Nothing, surely, is more difficult or more arbitrary than to draw a line of demarcation between two periods of history.   Life, which cares nothing for classifications, links up inextricably the past, the present, and the future.   At the very moments that seem to us, as we look backwards across the ages, to have been the most decisive for civilization, men usually lived almost completely unaware of their importance. Human life is not a continuous series like the chapters of a book; it is not a systematic whole, but is subject to a law of perpetual surprise.

It is clear, however, that the eleventh century was characterized by so astonishing a combination of outstanding events that their very enumeration marks the closure of one period and the beginning of another.   Take the history of the East: the collapse of the Macedonian dynasty was the death-knell of Byzantium; the schism condemned 'Orthodox' Christendom to an evermore isolated existence; and the appearance of the Turks on the frontier of Palestine was to be the proximate cause of the rise of Western chivalry.   The combination was even more striking in relation to those countries where, after six hundred years of tragic groping, there began to emerge that civilization from which our own is derived.

What was happening in the West about the year 1050?   First, there ended the era of invasions, which had opened in A.D. 405. After the settlement of the Norsemen [1] and Hungarians, Europe was no longer victim to those waves of Barbarian invasion which had until then formed a large part of their history.   Byzantium and Russia would continue subject to that trial for centuries, while the Turks and Mongols hardly appeared on the frontiers of the West.   'It is permissible to think,' says Marc Bloch, 'that this extraordinary immunity . . . was one of the fundamental factors of European civilization.'

At the same time the feudal system, produced by the disintegration of the Roman Empire, which for about three centuries had been a more hazardous compromise between anarchy and brute force, became an organic hierarchy, which tended to embrace the whole Western world. At the same time, however, there arose centralizing monarchies and the

---

[1] It is interesting to observe that the establishment of the Norsemen and their conversion to Christianity were parallel events.   The settlement of the Norsemen occurred, as we know, at the end of the ninth or beginning of the tenth century, in the British Isles by the treaty of Wedmore (878) and in France on the lower Loire by the treaty of Saint-Clair-sur-Epte.   The chief who negotiated the French treaty was Rollo.   According to the great Norman historian, Henri Prentout, conversion was one of the conditions of peace; besides, had not Rollo been checked before Chartres, where the miraculous tunic of our Lady had served the besieged as a palladium?   The chronicler Dudo of Saint-Quentin states that in 'the year of the Incarnation, 912, Franco, Archbishop of Rouen, baptized Rollo.'   In fact, the archbishop at that date was Guitto.   This prelate played an important part during the negotiations; he interposed between the two parties, swayed the counsels of Pope John X, and worked patiently for the conversion of the Norsemen, who were thus led to what they called 'the mass of lances,' i.e. to the mass.   Few in numbers, they soon mixed with the native population, especially as they had come without wives and therefore married French women.   The chronicler Dudo is responsible for a legend according to which Normandy became, as it were, overnight, an ideal Christian territory with so high a moral sense that theft became virtually unknown and it was possible to leave a golden bracelet hanging from a tree.   M. Prentout has disposed of this legend, but it is certain that the dukes of Normandy governed wisely.   The twofold influence of Christianity and a fertile soil overcame piratical instincts.   'The Normans,' says Larisse, 'showed the zeal of neophytes in the cause of their new religion.'   Normandy became one of the most Christian provinces of France; its dukes, such as Richard I at Mont Saint-Michel, laboured for the reform of the Church.   Normandy also sent out numerous missionaries.   The Church therefore looked with a favourable eye upon this ducal dynasty, and it was with the Pope's approval that William conquered England.

urban bourgeoisie, those two powerful forces whose struggle with the feudal regime coloured the whole of medieval politics.[1]

The year 1050 was also a turning-point in the moral sphere. The violence of the descendants of the Barbarians started to abate; they found pleasure not in destruction alone, but also in creative activity; the warrior chief and guerrilla leader was slowly transformed into an administrator; the intellectual field tended to regain its importance, and it was at this period that there took shape the ideal glorified in the *chansons de geste*.

The year 1050, again, marks a decisive stage in the history of Western culture, the end of the 'Dark Ages,' the starting-point of a material progress that has lasted into modern times. Whereas the revivals initiated by Justinian and Charlemagne were swallowed up in barbarism, that which originated in the eleventh century would prove far more solid and enduring, though more modest and harder to define. It was the age in which the intellect foresaw future syntheses, the age in which the Romanesque style began to emerge from the still awkward heaviness of its vaulting and its columns. . . .

The Church was closely associated with these fundamental elements of the new world then in process of being born. It was she who did more than any other institution to settle the new Barbarians; baptism was both the symbol and the means whereby the Hungarians and Norsemen entered the community of civilized peoples. It was she who, in extremely difficult circumstances and despite the terrible problems she had to face, strove to humanize the feudal world, to balance the powers of the baronage against those who opposed them. It was she, above all, who fought unremittingly for the triumph of a higher moral ideal, to give back man to himself. And it was she who, as the unique depositary of superior intellectual values during the Dark Ages, prepared in her own bosom their full flowering.

The 1050's were also a turning-point in the history of the Church herself. In these western lands, shaken in every direction by six hundred years of storm and stress, the best of her sons, Cluniac monks and saintly popes, were sowing the seed of life, endeavouring to infuse the life of Christ into that body which for ten centuries had worn His Cross upon its brow. It was not so much that she was confronted with such grave problems as her relations with the civil powers or her contacts with the feudal world in which her roots struck deep; for good or ill these problems were ultimately solved. What really mattered was the new impulse wherewith she was inspired

---

[1] M. Olivier-Martin, in his *Histoire du droit français*, rightly protests against the traditional phrase 'feudal anarchy.' For feudalism was a thoroughly hierarchic system, highly organized, and authoritarian. But before reaching that stage it had dismembered the kingly regime and set up a reign of anarchy. The phrase, though valid when applied to the beginnings of feudalism, ultimately ceased to be so.

and which would enable her to carry the West to the goal of its fulfilment.

That impulse is noticeable everywhere and at every level. It was found not only in the holy monks who, in the cloister, accomplished an heroic task of self-conquest, but also in their many brethren who carried the Good News beyond the monastery walls. Missionaries were, more than ever before, eager to spread the Gospel. Instead of turning inwards upon itself, the Christian civilization of the West prepared for fresh expansion: northward, eastward, to Scandinavia, in all directions. Later the impulse of faith would turn ancestral instincts to good use by launching the Church's sons upon those grand adventures which we know as the Reconquista and Crusade.

The conquering fervour, which would characterize the new humanity of the West, was as yet in the embryo stage, deriving nourishment from the most life-giving of sources. The spirituality of the Middle Ages, as represented in turn by such men as St Bernard, St Francis of Assisi, and St Louis, was not essentially different from that, for instance, of John of Fécamp, St Romuald, and St Henry about the year 1000. The ideal of chivalry which was to fuse, in a single human type, two antagonistic factors—the warrior and the Christian —was in process of welling up in the souls of the better type of baron. The form which our modern type of piety would assume—that of the *Imitation*, for example, or that of the Marian cult—clearly has its roots in the much maligned High Middle Ages. Overlaid with superstition, vaguely defined, and subject to violent temptation, the faith which animated souls about the middle of the eleventh century was a living faith, upon which it would be possible to build as on a rock.

Briefly then the principal fact at this decisive moment of history was the emergence of a new Christian consciousness. Believers understood more widely and more profoundly the role of faith in life—not only in private life but also in society. On the historical plane this meant that a new idea was born, an idea expressed by a word then coming into general use, the idea of Christendom. The Empire, the grand memory of whose unity and harmony had floated nostalgically down the ages, would be revived only in part, in its Germanic shape; the reality of the future was a community whose supernatural essence informed human society and directed it towards its true goal. That which Pope John VIII had foreseen was now becoming the driving force of the West, an ideal of which Otto III dreamed, upon which Gregory VII and Innocent III would base the whole of their work, and for which the crusaders of Godfrey de Bouillon gladly laid down their lives. The synthesis made necessary by the Invasions was now brought about: the faithful became conscious of belonging to a unique collective reality, at once supernatural and human, world wide, and reaching into heaven; the earthly city foreshadowed the City of God. The idea of Christendom, thus emerging, prepared the foundations of Western union. Unless one recognizes this fact it is impossible to understand the Middle Ages. There then is the stage to which the Church had come after six hundred years of patient effort.

Patient effort. . . . These words occur immediately to our minds as we look back over this long period of confusion and disorder. They may appear too modest, but there is no better means of describing the work accomplished in six centuries, the final result of which was nothing less than the salvation of mankind and of civilization.

Just at the moment when the Barbarian Invasions destroyed the ancient world, Mother Church was first to conceive the plan of resisting the awful tempest, of preserving, together with the deposit of faith entrusted to her, the fundamentals of society. Alone in the midst of men who despaired of themselves, she refused to despair. It was she and she alone who reached out to men across the darkness and kept alight the lamp of hope. Thanks to her, all was not lost.

The storm had not yet subsided when, going beyond her first duty as protectress, she devoted herself entirely to what seemed the almost impossible task of harnessing the terrible forces that had been released, of making them serve the glory of God. She had come to love these Barbarians who had just overthrown a world, to love their violent souls for whom Christ called, and she managed, by long and heroic endeavour, to win them. At the same time, profiting by a kind of law of alternation, whereby the East ascended as the West declined and vice versa, she employed the ambitions of the Byzantine emperors for her own deep purposes.

In the seventh century, when Islam dismembered the Christian world, when she lost a great part of the huge territory won by her sacrifices, the Church redoubled her efforts to make good these losses by new conquests. She understood clearly that the temporal destiny of her children lay no longer in the Mediterranean, but in the European continent. She likewise foresaw that Byzantium could no longer, in the very nature of things, act as the guide of Europe, and she accordingly threw in her lot with those who could.

The middle of this period was one of high hope. The grandiose design of a man of genius to bring order from chaos, to enlarge the Christian world, and to lay firm foundations for culture, was supported by the Church with all her strength, perhaps with too much confidence and generosity. Charlemagne, thanks to her and with her help, thought he could once for all effect the necessary synthesis of the surviving elements of the old world and all that was best in what the Barbarians had introduced. After half a century this appeared to have been accomplished, and the consequences, it seemed, would prove fortunate.

But the attempt was premature.    There was a relapse into darkness; a new tide of Barbarism rose.    The Christian barque was once more in danger of sinking; the peril was in a sense even greater than that of the fifth century, for the Church herself was to some extent affected by this ascendancy of evil.    The vessel appeared to be shipping water. Nevertheless in these dire circumstances the Church no more despaired than she had done in the days of Attila and Alaric.    While her cloistered religious were busy saving not only their own souls but the very bases of human culture, she kept watch for anything that might enable mankind to regain his balance and resist the enemy.    Feudalism, kingship, empire, and even deceptive Byzantium, were all used by her for one single end—the cause of Jesus Christ.

And it was at that time, during two centuries of increasing night, that there appeared innumerable indications, however small, of a splendid dawn to come.    New hordes of Barbarians might overrun Christian lands; the children of light might compromise with the sons of darkness; even the very successors of St Peter might prove themselves unequal to the crisis—but the soul of the Church continued to declare itself, so youthfully and so vigorously that she ultimately triumphed.    Just when the strange conjunction of events seemed to mark the end of the period, those six centuries of effort, whose results appeared so meagre, were in reality preparing the foundations upon which there would arise one of the masterpieces of the human race. Mother Church was responsible, but her work was not done for human ends, nor even exclusively by human means.    Her one and only purpose was to bring man a message of salvation, to raise the earthly city towards the City of God, to bring about the daily petition in the Lord's Prayer: 'Thy Kingdom come!'    Her patient endeavours are not to be explained by human criteria: their causes were supernatural—the virtues of faith and hope.

'No human institution,' wrote Joseph de Maistre, 'has endured for eighteen hundred years.'    And in no other epoch does the very survival of the Church appear so wonderful as in these six centuries when everything seemed leagued against the Gospel.    But she was *not* simply a 'human institution,' except in a secondary sense.    If she managed to resist the forces of destruction, and, while saving herself, to save civilization, it was not merely because of her 'political' aptitude, but because she had received a promise that 'the gates of hell shall not prevail against her'; it was not merely because he had men of courage and intelligence, but because so many of her children were saints.

Such, in fine, is the great lesson to be learned from that period of tragic confusion.    The guides who led mankind towards the light, who were they but those determined bishops who withstood the Barbarian hordes; those missionaries who carried on, at no matter what cost to themselves, the work begun in the early ages of the Church by the apostles and martyrs; those monks who, in another sort of combat, the combat of self against self, resolutely recalled the Christian soul to its duty; those great popes, whose work was so often and so manifestly inspired by the Holy Spirit—all those, in fact, for whom Christ was verily 'the Way, the Truth, and the Life.'

The true Church is the Church of those saints, of those who gave testimony upon earth, and of all those who, according to their humble means as men, strove for the one ideal—to be with Jesus Christ. The history of the Church is none other than the history of her sanctity; and never has this fact been so apparent as in the days of misery and dereliction, when mankind, as though called by the abyss, was about to fall.

# CHRONOLOGICAL TABLE

## FIFTH CENTURY

| DATE | WEST | EAST | THE CHURCH |
|---|---|---|---|
| | Reign of Honorius (395–423). | Reign of Arcadius (395–408). | St Augustine, Bishop of Hippo in 396. |
| 405 | Invasion of Italy by Radagase. | | Pope St Innocent I (401–17). |
| 406–9 | Vandals, Alans, Suevi, and Burgundians invade Gaul. | Reign of Theodosius II (408–50). | |
| 410 | Alaric sacks Rome. | | |
| 413–26 | | | St Augustine writes the *City of God* (413–426). |
| 416 | The Visigoths in Aquitania. | | Pope St Zosimus (417–418). |
| | | | Pope St Boniface I (418–22). |
| c. 410– c. 429 | Rome evacuates Britain; invasions by Angles, Saxons, and Jutes over the next hundred years or so, resulting in permanent conquests and settlements. | | Pope St Celestine I (422–32). |
| 423 | Death of Honorius, accession of Valentinian III. | | Monastic development of Lérins: St Honoratus and St Hilary. |
| 430 | Capture of Hippo by the Vandals. | | Death of St Augustine, 28th August 430. |
| 431 | The Vandals masters of Africa. | | Council of Ephesus (3rd oecumenical, against Nestorius, 431). |
| | | | St Patrick in Ireland (432). |
| | | | Pope St Sixtus III (432–40). |
| c. 350–450 | Number of Britons emigrate to Armorica. | | Pope St Leo I the Great (440–61). |
| 451 | Defeat of Attila at the Catalaunian Fields. | Reign of Marcian (450–457), first emperor crowned by the Church. | Council of Chalcedon (4th oecumenical, against Monophysitism, 451). |
| 455 | Genseric and the Vandals sack Rome. Assassination of Valentinian III. | | |
| | | | Pope St Hilary (461–468). |
| | | Reign of Leo I (457–474). | Pope St Simplicius (468–83). |
| 472 | Death of Ricimer. | | |

| DATE | WEST | EAST | THE CHURCH |
|---|---|---|---|
| 476 | Deposition of Romulus Augustulus. | Reign of Zeno (474–491). | |
| 476–93 | Reign of Odoacer in Italy. | | |
| 480 | | | Birth of St Benedict. |
| 481 | Clovis, king of the Franks. Conquest of Gaul. | Schism of Acatius (483–518). | Pope St Felix III (483–492). |
| 493 | Death of Odoacer. Accession of Theodoric. | Reign of Anastasius (491–518). | Pope St Gelasius I (492–6). |
| 496 | Victory of Clovis over the Alamans. | | Pope St Anastasius II (496–8). |
| 498 or 499 | Baptism of Clovis. | | Pope St Symmachus (498–514). |

## SIXTH CENTURY

| | | | |
|---|---|---|---|
| | | | Conversion of the Burgundians (c. 500). |
| 507 | Battle of Vouillé. | | |
| 511 | Death of Clovis. | | Pope St Hormisdas (514–23). |
| | | Reign of Justin (518–527). | Pope St John I (523–526). |
| 526 | Death of Theodoric. | | Pope St Felix IV (526–530). |
| | | Reign of Justinian the Great (527–65). Nika Riot (532). | St Benedict founds Monte Cassino (529). Pope Boniface II (530–532). |
| | | Africa recovered from the Vandals (533). | Pope John II (532–5). |
| 534 | Disappearance of the Burgundian kingdom. | Building of St Sophia (consecrated 537). | Pope St Agapitus I (535–5). Pope St Silverius (536–537). |
| | | Silk industry brought to Europe (552). | Death of St Benedict (c. 547). |
| 553 | Victory of the Byzantines over the Ostrogoths at Vesuvius. | | Pope Vigilius (537–55). Second Council of Constantinople (5th oecumenical). Pope Pelagius I (555–560). |
| 558–61 | Reign of Clotaire I in France. | | St Columba founds Iona (c. 565). |
| 568 | Lombards invade Italy | | |
| 571? | | Birth of Mohammed (between 570 and 580). | Conversion of the Suevi (c. 570). |
| 582 | Agilulf marries Theodelinda. | Reign of Maurice (582–602). | |

| DATE | WEST | EAST | THE CHURCH |
|---|---|---|---|
| 585 | | | Martyrdom of St Hermenegild in Spain. |
| 586 | Recared, king of the Visigoths in Spain. | | Conversion of the Visigoths (589). St Columbanus in Gaul (Luxeuil founded in 590). |
| 590 | | | Election of Pope St Gregory I the Great. St Augustine lands in England (597). Conversion of Ethelbert, King of Kent (597). Foundation of Canterbury. |
| 600 | Death of Fredegunda. | | |

## SEVENTH CENTURY

| DATE | WEST | EAST | THE CHURCH |
|---|---|---|---|
| 603–10 | The Roman Senate ceases to meet (603). | | Death of St Gregory the Great (604). Pope St Boniface IV (608–15). Westminster Abbey founded (610). |
| 610–41 | Death of Brunhilda. Re-establishment of Frankish unity by Clotaire II (613). | Reign of Heraclius. | Beginning of the Monothelite crisis. |
| 622 | | Jerusalem taken by the Persians (614). The Hegira (beginning of the Moslem era). | Pope Honorius (621–638). |
| 628–38 | Dagobert. | Collapse of the Persian Empire. Death of Chosroes II (628). The first four caliphs (632–67). Moslem conquest of Syria, Palestine, Persia, and Egypt (633–643). Constantius II (641–68) | Jerusalem taken by the Arabs (638). |
| 653 | | | Pope St Martin I (649–658). Conversion of the Lombards (653) Pope St Eugenius I (654–7). Synod of Whitby (663). St Theodore of Canterbury, second papal mission to England (669). |

\* U

| DATE | WEST | EAST | THE CHURCH |
|------|------|------|------------|
| 653 | | The Ommayads (661–750). Constantine IV (668–685). Conquest of North Africa by the Arabs (669–708). First check of Islam before Constantinople (673–8). | Pope St Agatho (678–681). Third Council of Constantinople (6th oecumenical); end of Monothelitism (680–681). |
| 687 | Victory of Pepin of Heristal at Testry. | Justinian II (685–95, 705–11) Capture of Carthage (698). | Pope St Sergius I (687–701). Trullan Council (691). |

## EIGHTH CENTURY

| DATE | WEST | EAST | THE CHURCH |
|------|------|------|------------|
| | | | Pope Constantine (708–15). |
| 711 | | The Arabs overrrun Spain. | |
| 714–41 | Charles Martel. | Beginning of the Isaurian dynasty. Leo III (717). The Moslems defeated before Constantinople (717–18). The Iconoclastic Dispute (from 726). | Pope St Gregory II (715–32). |
| 716–54 | | | St Boniface evangelizes Germans. |
| 732 | Christian victory at Poitiers. Moslems halted in the West. | | Pope St Gregory III (732–41). |
| 741–68 | Pepin the Short. | Constantine V Copronymus (740–75). Dismemberment of the Moslem Empire. Beginning of the Abassid caliphs at Bagdad (750). | Pope St Zacharias (741–752). |
| 751 | Pepin the Short, King of France. Beginning of the Carolingians. | | St Boniface crowns Pepin the Short (751). |
| | | | Pope Stephen II (752–757). |
| 756 | Pepin defeats the Lombards. | | Birth of the Papal States (756). Pope St Paul I (757–767). |
| 768 | Accession of Charlemagne. | | Pope Stephen III (768–772). |
| 771 | Charlemagne, sole king of the Franks (death of Carloman). | | |
| | | | Pope Hadrian I (772–795). |
| 774 | Destruction of the Lombard kingdom. | The Empress Irene (780–802) re-establishes images. | Second Council of Nicaea (787). Re-establishment of images. |

| DATE | WEST | EAST | THE CHURCH |
|------|------|------|------------|
| 778 | Roland at Roncesvalles. | | |
| 788 | Bavaria included in the Frankish state. | | |
| 793–800 | Subjugation of Saxony. | | Pope St Leo III (795–816). |
| 796 | Victory over the Avars. | | |
| 800 | Coronation of Charlemagne. Re-establishment of the Empire. | | |

## NINTH CENTURY

| DATE | WEST | EAST | THE CHURCH |
|------|------|------|------------|
| | | Haroun-al-Raschid (785–809) | |
| 803 | Charlemagne completes conquest of and baptizes the Saxons. | | |
| 814 | Death of Charlemagne. | Iconoclastic Dispute resumed. | |
| 814–40 | Reign of Louis the Pious. | | Pope Stephen IV (816–817). Pope St Paschal I (817–824). |
| c. 820 and onwards | | | Pope Eugenius II (824–827). Pope Valentine I (827). Pope Gregory IV (828–844) |
| | Norse and Arab invasions. | | |
| | Lothaire I, emperor (840–55). Charles the Bald, King of France (840–77). | Theodora, regent for Michael III (842). | |
| 843 | Treaty of Verdun. | End of the Iconoclastic Dispute. | |
| | | | The Antipope John (844). |
| 846 | Sack of St Peter's by the Arabs. | | Pope Sergius II (844–847). Pope St Leo IV (847–855). |
| 850 | Louis II of Italy associated with the imperial throne. | The affair of Photius (beginning in 858). Boris of Bulgaria baptized (863). | Anastasius, Antipope (855); Pope Benedict III (855–8). Pope St Nicholas I the Great (858–67). Sts Cyril and Methodius evangelize Moravia (862–84). |
| 866 | Duke Robert the Strong killed at Brissarthe while opposing the Norsemen. | | |
| 867 | | End of the Isaurian and beginning of the Macedonian dynasty (867). Basil I (867–86). | Pope Hadrian II (867–872). |
| 869 | Death of Lothaire II. | | |
| 871–99 | Alfred the Great in England. | | Pope John VIII (872–882). |
| 885–6 | Siege of Paris by the Norsemen. | | Pope Stephen V (885–891). |

| DATE | WEST | EAST | THE CHURCH |
|---|---|---|---|
| c. 890–900 | Many Norse invasions. | | Pope Formosus (891–896). |
| | | Simeon, Tsar of Bulgaria (893–927). | |
| | | | 896–900: five popes in four years. |

## TENTH CENTURY

| | | | |
|---|---|---|---|
| | | | Pope Sergius III (904–911). |
| 910–55 | Hungarian invasion. | | |
| 911 | The Norsemen settle in Normandy. Extinction of the Carolingians in Germany. | Constantine VII (913–957) and Romanus Lecapenus (919–44). | Foundation of Cluny. Pope John X (914–28). |
| 919 | Accession of the House of Saxony: Henry the Fowler (919–36). | | St Odo reforms Cluny (926–42). |
| 936–73 | Kingdom of Arles founded (933). Otto I, King of Germany. Many Saracen and Norman invasions. | | |
| | | Baptism of the Russian princess Olga (945). | |
| 955 | Otto I checks the Hungarians on the Lech. | Crete recovered from the Moslems (961). | St Maieul, abbot of Cluny (952–94). Pope John XII (955–964). |
| 962 | Foundation of the Holy Roman and Germanic Empire. | Nicephorus II Phocas (963–9). Antioch recovered from the Arabs (969). John Tzimisces (969–976). | Pope John XIII (965–972). |
| 973–83 | Otto II. | Basil II (976–1025). | |
| 983–1002 | Otto III. | | St Romuald founds Camaldoli (982). |
| 987 | Accession of the Capetians in France: Hugh Capet, king. | Conversion of Prince Vladimir. | |
| | | | The Councils of Charroux (989) and Puy-en-Velay (990) call for the Peace of God. |
| 992–1025 | | Boleslas the Valiant, founder of Poland. | Pope John XV (985–996) suggests the Truce of God (990). |
| 997–1038 | | St Stephen I, Duke then King of Hungary. | St Odilo, abbot of Cluny. |
| 999 | | | Gerbert becomes Pope Sylvester II. |

| DATE | WEST | EAST | THE CHURCH |
|---|---|---|---|

## ELEVENTH CENTURY

| DATE | WEST | EAST | THE CHURCH |
|---|---|---|---|
| 1002–24 | Henry II (St Henry), emperor. | | Death of Sylvester II (1003). Pope Sergius IV (1009–1012). Destruction of the basilica of the Holy Sepulchre (1010). Synod of Verdun-sur-Saône institutes the oath of peace (1016). |
| 1017–35 | Knut the Great in England. | | |
| 1019–54 | Henry III, German emperor (1039–1056). | Yaroslav, prince of Kiev Advance of Seljuk Turks begins (1040). Zoë, Empress of Byzantium, and her four husbands (1042–55). Michael Cerularius, Patriarch of Constantinople (1043–1058). | Council of Nice institutes the Truce of God (1041). Reforming activity of St Peter Damian (cardinal bishop in 1057). Pope St Leo IX (1049–1054). |
| c. 1050 | | The Greek schism (1054). End of the Macedonian dynasty (1056). The Turks in the Near East. | Cardinal Humbert publishes *Against Simoniacs* (1057). |
| 1059 | | | Nicholas II entrusts papal elections to the College of Cardinals. |

# SELECT BIBLIOGRAPHY

It is hoped that the following selective list, which has been taken from M. Daniel-Rops's much more extensive bibliography in the French edition of this work, will be of value to French-speaking readers who wish to study aspects of the period described in greater detail from some of the author's own sources.

## GENERAL WORKS

### A. Primarily Secular

Louis Halphen: *Les Barbares, des grandes invasions aux conquêtes turques du XIᵉ siècle*, 1926.

R. Latouche: *Les Grandes Invasions et la Crise de l'Occident au Vᵉ siècle*, 1946.

Pierre Courcelle: *L'Histoire littéraire des grandes invasions germaniques*, 1948.

J. Calmette: *Le Moyen Âge*, 1948 (beginning only).

Henri Pirenne: *Histoire de l'Europe, des invasions au XVIᵉ siècle*, 1936 (beginning only).

Christopher Dawson: *The Making of Europe*, London, 1932.

Jacques Pirenne: *Les Grands Courants de l'histoire universelle*, vols. i and ii, 1945, 1946.

### B. Primarily Religious

*L'Histoire de l'église*, ed. A. Fliche and V. Martin: vol. iv, *De la mort de Théodose à l'élection de Grégoire le Grand*, by G. Bardy, P. de Labriolle, Louis Bréhier, and G. de Plinval, 1937; vol. v, *Grégoire le Grand, les états barbares et la conquête arabe*, by Louis Bréhier and René Aigrain, 1938; vol. vi, *L'Époque carolingienne*, by Émile Amann, 1937; vol. vii, *L'Église au pouvoir des laïcs*, by Émile Amann and A. Dumas, 1942.

René Draguet: *Histoire du dogme catholique*, 1946.

*Specifically on religion in France:*

Georges Goyau: *Histoire religieuse de la France*, 1922.

Ferdinand Lot: *La Naissance de la France*, 1948.

Émile Mâle: *La Fin du paganisme en Gaule et les plus anciennes basiliques chrétiennes*, 1950.

## Chapter I. THE SAINT OF THE NEW AGE

There are *Lives* of St Augustine in French by Louis Bertrand, 1919, and G. Bardy, 1940, and in Italian by Giovanni Papini, 1930.

For Augustine's thought and influence see:

Paul Monceaux: *Histoire littéraire de l'Afrique chrétienne*, vols. vi and vii, 1922.

ÉTIENNE GILSON: *Introduction à l'étude de saint Augustin*, 1929.

H. A. MARROU: *Saint Augustin et la fin de la culture antique*, 1938.

F. CAYRÉ: *La Contemplation augustinienne*, 1927.

P. BATIFFOL: *Le Catholicisme de saint Augustin*, 1920.

(There are various English translations of St Augustine's major works, and the reader is recommended to the *Everyman's Library* editions of the *Confessions* and the *City of God*.)

## CHAPTER II.  THE BARBARIAN HOLOCAUST AND THE PILLARS OF THE CHURCH

ERNEST STEIN: *Histoire du Bas-Empire*, 1949.

FERDINAND LOT: *La Fin du monde antique et les débuts du moyen âge*, 1927, and *Les Invasions germaniques*, 1930.

G. BARDY: *L'Église et les derniers Romains*, 1948.

J.-R. PALANQUE (ed.): *Le Christianisme et la fin du monde antique*, 1943, and *Le Christianisme et l'Occident barbare*, 1945.

## CHAPTER III.  BYZANTIUM, EMPIRE OF THE AUTOCRATS AND THE THEOLOGIANS

LOUIS BRÉHIER: *Le Monde byzantin* (3 vols., 1947, 1949, 1950) and *L'Art byzantin*, 1934.

See also Stein's *Histoire du Bas-Empire* and *L'Histoire de l'église*, ed. Fliche and Martin, vol. iv, previously listed.

## CHAPTER IV.  THE CHURCH CONVERTS THE BARBARIANS

MGR DUCHESNE: *L'Église au VIᵉ siècle*, 1925.

ÉDOUARD SALIN: *La Civilisation mérovingienne*, 1950.

DOM L. GOUGAUD: *Les Chrétientés celtiques*, 1911.

See also *Life* of St Boniface by G. Kurth, 1913, and *Life* of St Gregory the Great by Mgr Batiffol, 1928.

## CHAPTER V.  CHRISTIANS OF THE TWILIGHT

P. IMBART DE LA TOUR: *Les Paroisses rurales du IVᵉ au IXᵉ siècle*, 1900.

C. DE CLERCQ: *La Législation religieuse franque de Clovis à Charlemagne*, 1936.

DOM G. MORIN, *Les Véritables origines du chant grégorien*, 1890.

L. BRÉHIER, *L'Art chrétien, son développement iconographique jusqu'à nos jours*, 1928.

There are studies of St Benedict and Benedictinism by Dom Cabrol, 1933, Cardinal Schuster, 1950, and Dom C. Butler (in English), 1924.

## CHAPTER VI.  TRAGEDIES AND DIVISIONS IN THE CHRISTIAN EAST

J. PARGOIRE, *L'Église byzantine de 527 à 847*, 1905.

L. BRÉHIER, *La Querelle des images*, 1904.

G. Marcais and C. Diehl (ed.): *Le Monde oriental de 395 à 1081*, 1936.

See also *L'Histoire de l'église*, ed. Fliche and Martin, and *The Making of Europe*, by Christopher Dawson, already listed.

Chapter VII. THE PAPACY AND THE NEW EMPIRE IN THE WEST

L. Halphen: *Charlemagne et l'empire carolingien*, 1947
J. Calmette: *Charlemagne, sa vie, son œuvre*, 1945.
René Grousset: *Figures de proue*, 1949.
Mgr Duchesne: *Les Premiers Temps de l'état pontifical*, 1911.
L. Levillain: *La Dynastie carolingienne et les origines de l'état pontifical*, 1935.
H.-X. Arquillière: *L'Augustinisme politique*, 1934.
R. Bonnaud-Delamare: *L'Idée de paix à l'époque carolingienne*, 1939.

See also *L'Histoire de l'église*, ed. Fliche and Martin, already listed.

Chapter VIII. THE CHURCH IS FACED WITH NEW DANGERS

J. Calmette: *L'Effondrement d'un empire et la naissance d'une Europe*, 1941.
Marc Bloch: *La Société féodale: la formation de liens de fidelité*, 1939.
F. Lot: *Les Invasions barbares et le peuplement de l'Europe*, 1939.
T. D. Kendrick: *A History of the Vikings*, London, 1933.
Henri Pirenne: *Mahomet et Charlemagne*, 1937.

Chapter IX. THE BYZANTINE REVIVAL AND SEPARATION FROM ROME

See the books listed for Chapters III and VI. Also:
F. Dvornik: *Les Slaves, Byzance et Rome au IX^e siècle*, 1926.
R. P. Jugie: *Le Schisme byzantin*, 1941.
Père de Moreau, *La Réhabilitation de Photius* (*Nouvelle Revue théologique*), 1950 (February).
E. Pognon, *L'An mille*, 1947.

Chapter X. THE TRAGIC DAWN OF THE YEAR 1000

See E. Pognon, *L'An mille*, listed in Chapter IX. Also:
E. Gay: *Les Papes du XI^e siècle et la chrétienté*, 1926.
A. Fliche: *La Réforme grégorienne*, 1924.
A. Chagny: *Cluny et son empire*, 1949.
J. Leflon: *Gerbert, humanisme et chrétienté au X^e siècle*, 1946.
L. Bréhier: *L'Art en France, des invasions barbares à l'époque romaine*, 1930.
J. Rupp: *L'Idée de chrétienté*, 1939.

# INDEX OF PRINCIPAL NAMES

# INDEX OF PRINCIPAL NAMES

Main references are shown in heavy numerals